The Hundred Day Winter War

The Hundred Day Winter War

Finland's Gallant Stand against the Soviet Army

Gordon F. Sander

 University Press of Kansas

Published by the University Press of Kansas (Lawrence,
Kansas 66045), which was organized by the Kansas
Board of Regents and is operated and funded by Emporia
State University, Fort Hays State University, Kansas State
University, Pittsburg State University, the University of
Kansas, and Wichita State University

Library of Congress Cataloging-in-Publication Data

Sander, Gordon F., author.
   The Hundred Day Winter War : Finland's gallant stand
against the Soviet Army / Gordon F. Sander.
      pages ; cm. — (Modern war studies)
   Includes bibliographical references and index.
   ISBN 978-0-7006-1910-8
 1. Russo-Finnish War, 1939–1940. I. Title. II. Series:
Modern war studies.
   DL1097.S26 2013
   948.9703′2—dc23
                                         2013016109

British Library Cataloguing-in-Publication Data is
available.

Printed in the United States of America

10 9 8 7 6 5 4 3 2 1

The paper used in this publication is recycled and contains
30 percent postconsumer waste. It is acid free and meets
the minimum requirements of the American National
Standard for Permanence of Paper for Printed Library
Materials Z39.48–1992.

THIS BOOK IS DEDICATED TO THE MEMORY OF THE ESTIMATED 150,000 *Finnish and Russian soldiers and civilians, as well as volunteers from various nations, who perished during the Winter War,*
    and to
My father, the late Lt. Col. Kurt Sander, United States Army, decorated veteran of Normandy, the Bulge, and the conquest of Germany, who bequeathed to me his love of history.

Contents

Acknowledgments

The number of people on both sides of the Atlantic I have to thank for making this tome happen is a long one.

At the top of my honor roll is my good friend Ami Hasan, of hasan & partners, who has been behind this project in every way since its inception. Sharing high honors with him is my friend and collaborator Michael Franck, of Franck Media, who has also been extremely supportive in every way, along with his wife and partner, Nina Pulkis. Laurels, too, to Ilkka Ranta-aho of *Apu Magazine*, who not only encouraged me to go forward with the book, but also conducted four of the interviews with veterans of the *Talvisota* that play such a crucial part in it. Thanks, guys!

I am deeply grateful to Petri Tuomi-Nikula, the former director general of the Department of Press and Culture of the Finnish Foreign Ministry, and his colleagues, who have been a bulwark of support. I would also like to thank my friend Christian Moustgaard, whose father was amongst the brave Danish contingent who sailed to Finland to volunteer in the *Talvisota*, and who helped trigger my original interest in the subject.

My friend and mentor, the great Max Jakobson, also has my profound thanks.

I would particularly like to thank the score of Finns and Russians who either fought during the war or lived through it and who took the time to share their sometimes painful memories with me or my designated interviewers. They are, in Finland, Harry Berner, Colonel Olavi Eronen, Eino Heikala, Lilja Juntunen, Antos Kela, Irja Kela, Dr. Eric Malm, Reino Oksanen, Mai-Lis Paavola, and Eevi; and in Russia, Nikolai Bavin and Edward Hynninen.

My friend and Helsinki assistant, the lovely Mau Vuori, deserves a special plaque of her own. For tracking down, copying, and translating myriad Finnish documents, including everything from the first page of every issue of the *Helsingin Sanomat* from the *Talvisota* to an old TV interview with Mannerheim's adjutant, Aksel Airo; for conducting and transcribing numerous interviews; for winnowing and condensing hundreds of pages of material; for helping to keep both my morale up when I was down and my eye on the ball during my three extended Finnish sorties, she has my eternal thanks. There is a big part of her in this book. *Kiitos,* Mau!

Kiitos, too, to the chief of my "Suomussalmi bureau," Marketta Raihala, who was my host, driver, guide, and translator during my two visits to the site of the best-known battle of the war, who translated numerous valuable books and documents for me, and otherwise anchored the northern front of the battle. Before leaving that sector, I also would like to thank Markko Seppanen, the director of the Raatteen Portti, for a personal tour of his splendid museum and for providing numerous various valuable contacts.

This book would not be what it is without the help and assistance of some of Finland's leading military historians, most notably Carl-Fredrik Geust and Martti Turtola. I am also grateful to Carl for helping me track down the extraordinary photos, many of which have never been published before, at the Finnish Army Archives, in addition to other favors too numerous to name. Carl's and Martti's historiographical colleagues Ohto Manninen and Lasse Laaskonen were also extremely helpful and supportive. I am also indebted to Lt. Col. Ari Raunio for reading the manuscript in its entirety. I am especially grateful to Jussi Kamarainen for helping to illumine the sensitive subject of the residents of the town of Suomussalmi, the site of Finland's most celebrated victory, who were taken hostage during the war. Thanks, too, to Professor Turtola's assistant, Jukka Salli. And gratis to Sam Svard for the superb maps that accompany this volume.

The fantastic Hotel Klaus K has been my principal base of operations during my numerous sorties to Helsinki. I am grateful to its general manager, Marc Skvorc, and his amazing staff for helping to provide a home away from home for me in Helsinki. Speaking of logistics, where would I be without my friend Erkki Kallunki, the proprietor of Tori, and his partner Fredrik, who greeted me every morning with a steaming cappuccino and allowed me to turn his window seat into my field headquarters? Thanks, guys!

The estimable historian-cum-guide extraordinaire Bair Irincheev created and accompanied me on a customized tour of Vyborg (or Viipuri, as the Finns used to call it) and the former Mannerheim Line, including the great castle there that is featured in this book; then on to St. Petersburg and Petrozavodsk, where he tracked down and served as translator for me with several Russian veterans of the war, and otherwise helped me to understand the Russian side of the conflict. *Kiitos,* Bair—or, should I say, *spasibo!*

I am thankful to Sergey Verigin, the chairman of the Department of History at Petrozavodsk State University and one of Russia's top experts on the Winter War, who, along with the late Pavel Razinov, not only was my host during a visit to his splendid campus but who also hosted a conclave about the war on my behalf. Gratis, too, to Yuri Kilin, who vetted the manuscript and added several key insights.

Jumping across the ocean to my beloved alma mater and historiographical headquarters, Cornell University, I would like to express my heartfelt thanks to my assistants—and now passionate Fennophiles—Michael Gluck Cornell '12 and J. J. Manford '06, for their respective contributions to this project. For reading my indecipherable handwriting, for running down hundreds of hard-to-find facts, for putting in numerous all-nighters, and for their consistent support and good cheer, I am forever grateful. I literally could not have finished this book without them.

I wish to thank my formidable former assistant Fiona Kirkpatrick '10, who graciously put in a second tour of duty with Sander Media, for her painstaking care in revising and preparing the international edition of the book. Ditto her formidable successor and my new aide-de-camp, the eagle-eyed Courtney Stevenson '13, who arrived on the quarterdeck just in time to play a crucial role in the final editing and trimming of the American edition, along with her comrade, the stalwart Scott Reu '13, and his redoubtable successor, my current assistant, Phoebe Hering '16. Thanks, too, to the extremely helpful staff of the Cornell Fine Arts Library, under whose dome I wrote a good deal of this book.

I also am very grateful to my friend Zuzanna Obajtek, who came all the way from Warsaw to Ithaca to help me sort through and scissor the 3,000-odd articles about the Winter War from the *New York Times*. I am sure she never wants to see another index card in her life!

I am indebted to John Ackerman, the director of Cornell University Press and a distinguished Sovietologist in his own right, for encouraging me to go forward with this tome, as well as helping me to shape it.

Thankful I am as well to Sari Forrstrom, the former head of non-fiction at WSOY, my Finnish publisher, for taking a chance on having an American write a major book about her country's finest hour, as well as to my talented and hard-working editor, Joni Strandberg, who acted as simultaneous editor, fact-checker, and coach during the intense final run of the original Finnish edition.

These acknowledgments would not be complete if I did not also mention my friend and mentor, the late great Sir John Keegan, the greatest military historian of his generation, who encouraged me to write this book in the first place and continued to support me in every way, as did his wife and fellow writer, Lady Susanne, and their daughter Rose and son Matthew.

Finally, a thirteen-gun salute to the staff of the University Press of Kansas, particularly editor-in-chief Mike Briggs, for his patience and grace (and patience!), and his heroic production editor, Kelly Chrisman Jacques. Also, Eric Schramm, my eagle-eyed copy editor, deserves a special mention in my dispatches for his extraordinary work.

Other friends on both sides of the Atlantic to whom I am indebted for tips, information, and other forms of support include Ian Bourgeot, Jesse Braverman, Veli-Pekka Elonen, Eric Goldstein, Anatoly Gordienko, Satu Grunthal, Christer Haglund, Eddy Hawkins, Tony Ilmoni, Mika Karttunen, Erkki Lahti, Antero Lahtinen, Nick Lambrou, John Liebkind, Dr. Ronald Liebkind, Christian Moustgaard, Jouni Molsa, Ilpo Murtovaara, Kimmo Oksanen, Pekka Parikka, Markus Selin, Petri Tuomi-Nikula, and the irrepressible John Zissovici. I am also deeply indebted to my cousin Roger Widmann for his unflagging support, as well as that of my brother, Elliot Sander.

And last but not least, I would like to award my own White Rose to my beloved mother, Dorrit, who, at the age of eighty-eight, visited Finland herself in 2010, and for otherwise keeping the home fires burning.

Introduction

The whole story of the Finnish defence is like a page from an epic poem, except that their [the Finns'] victory has been won not merely by bravery, but also by intense study of the art of war as applied to a country like their own.
—*The Times* (London), December 26, 1939

No other episode of the Second World War has been as enshrouded in myth as the 1939–40 Russo-Finnish "Winter War." How could it not be? At first blush, it may seem as if the 105-day war-within-a-war that began with the Soviet surprise attack on its northwestern neighbor and former Russian grand duchy was something out of Greco-Roman mythology. A nation of 3.7 million is attacked by another fifty times its size—and fights the towering, flat-footed invader to a standstill amidst the swirling snows of the Finnish fells, even besting him for the first six weeks, armed with little more than Suomi submachine guns, homemade Molotov cocktails, and a large supply of *sisu,* the Finnish equivalent of grit. The Finns were led into battle by their aristocratic septuagenarian commander-in-chief, Gustaf Mannerheim, also known as "The Last Knight of Europe," a onetime chevalier in the court of Tsar Nicholas who had returned to his native land during the Russian Revolution to lead the White Forces against the Reds during the fratricidal Finnish Civil War whence modern Finland was born. It was a nation hoping against hope that her sister democracies, particularly the Allies, as well as Sweden and the United States (prior to its formal entry into the war), would hasten to her aid, not with rhetoric and "ice shows," as the sympathetic but still steadfastly neutral Americans did, but with planes, tanks, and ammunition. These the Finns ultimately received from the Swedes and the Allies to varying degrees, before the infuriated Soviets mounted their final, overwhelming drive on the Mannerheim Line and time ran out on the nation whose cause was so compelling as to inspire thousands of young men from around the world to sail, fly, ski, or walk to *Suomi* (Finland) to fight for her.

Mannerheim bolstered the *legenda* of the *Talvisota,* as the Finns call it, by declaring that Finnish forces were fighting "a Thermopylae every day" and by issuing similarly mythic pronouncements from his headquarters in Mikkeli in eastern Finland before returning to his map tables to ponder his next move against "the hereditary enemy."[1] Given such powerful rhetoric, along with the corresponding flood of dispatches from the northern front about the Finns' spectacular—if deceptive—early successes against the stumbling Red Goliath, one can understand why the Manichean drama taking place above the 60th parallel inspired writers around the free world to write their own allegories.

Robert Sherwood, author of such celebrated entertainments as *Petrified Forest* and *Abe Lincoln in Illinois,* and probably America's best-known contemporaneous playwright, was so moved by the Winter War—as well as frustrated that his own country was not doing more to help "Brave Little Finland," as *Suomi* was then known—that he decided to write a play about it that revolved around the family of a peace-loving Finnish doctor who reluctantly but firmly decides to take up arms against the invader. Sherwood feared that the Winter War would not last long enough for *There Shall Be No Night* to see the light of day. He was nearly right: the play debuted on March 28, 1940, sixteen days after the overwhelmed Finns were forced to put down their arms following the final overwhelming Soviet assault. Still, *There Shall Be No Night* continued on stage for another two years, until Finland's confusing and unpopular decision in the West to join forces with Germany after the latter's invasion of Russia fifteen months later forced the play's producers to close it. Thus the myth engendered by the war, in works such as Sherwood's play, far outlived the actual war.[2]

And so the myth continues today, particularly in Finland, where the *legenda* of the Winter War has become one of that country's origin stories alongside that of the *Kalevala,* the nineteenth-century epic poem that was instrumental in the development of Finnish identity, while its publishing industry continues to churn out monographs about "the last glorious war." Thus the mythic aura surrounding this anomalous conflict persists, posing a major challenge for any historian who essays to write about it. What is true? What is not?

Playwrights weren't the only ones who were caught up in the fervor surrounding the Winter War or who contributed to the myth surrounding it. So were a number of prominent British and French politicians, including the ardently pro-Finnish British Lord of the Admiralty, Winston Churchill. "Only Finland, superb, nay, sublime in the jaws of peril," Churchill declared in a speech over the BBC on January 19, shortly after the stunning Finnish victories at Suomussalmi and Raate Road. "Finland shows what free men can do."[3]

Churchill was also one of the principal instigators of the daft Allied plan, also known as the "Finnish wild goose enterprise," to relieve the Finns by dispatching an Allied expeditionary force across Norway and Sweden, over the protest of both of those avowedly neutral countries—an operation that, in the unlikely event it had come off, would have seen British and French forces fight their future Russian allies on Finnish soil and changed the complexion of the rest of the war.

Adolf Hitler, for one, was certainly paying attention. As Albert Speer and other intimates of the Führer have attested, Moscow's initial, flat-footed performance during the war was a factor in Hitler's decision to invade the Soviet

Union in June 1941. If the once-vaunted Red Army had such difficulty in putting down the vastly outnumbered Finns, Hitler evidently concluded, then the vast land and air armada he had assembled for the invasion and conquest of his erstwhile ally ought not to have too much trouble putting down the befuddled Red Army, either.[4]

The German dictator was so impressed by the instant legend of the Finnish superman that he didn't apprehend how rapidly and effectively the Russians had strengthened and revamped their forces. Hitler was wrong, of course, but not by much: the *Wehrmacht* was indeed stopped, but not before it had reached the gates of Moscow; Stalingrad could have gone either way. One of the reasons why the Red Army ultimately gained the upper hand and defeated Hitler, many historians believe, was because of the changes and reforms it enacted following the April 1940 postmortem that Stalin ordered. These included dispensing with the clumsy dual politico-military command structure by which unit commanders had to vet their orders with their *politruks*, the tactically obtuse political commissars assigned them, and which had proven so disastrous during the *Talvisota*. Conversely, noted historian Roger Reese, author of *Stalin's Reluctant Soldiers: A Social History of the Red Army, 1925–1941,* contends that the Red Army became overly preoccupied with the lessons of the Winter War and was actually handicapped as a result.[5] In any event, it should be clear that, contrary to a sometimes-heard notion, the Winter War was far more than a mere sideshow.

The Western media was also swept up in the origin myth of the Winter War and played a pivotal role in both creating and propagating it, as evidenced by the absolutely massive volume of newsprint that exists from the war.

A small press contingent, mostly from Scandinavia, was already installed in late November 1939 at the Hotel Kamp, the storied hotel located in the center of the Finnish capital, to cover the mounting tensions between the USSR and Finland, after the on-and-off negotiations between the two neighbors over Soviet demands for Finnish territory broke down.

Nevertheless, it is safe to say, all the pressmen on hand that day were as shocked to see Russian bombers appear in the leaden skies over Helsinki as were the local populace. One of those astonished reporters was Herbert Elliston, the British-born correspondent for the *Christian Science Monitor.*

"It was a perfect winter morning, with the sun coming out of a blue sky, unflecked save for one cotton wooly ball cloud," the awestruck reporter wrote. "Inside that cloud were Russian planes. Through the trailing steamer of the cloud a couple of planes could be seen in nebulous outline. With its destructive weight, the solitary cloud moved across the heavens like a Spanish galleon in full sail."[6]

Nary six months later, after the so-called "phony war" had come to an end, and the German blitzkrieg had overrun Norway, the Low Countries, and France, bringing such atrocities as the terror bombing of Rotterdam in its wake, such naïve, even romantic language would seem as dated as it does today. But this, after all, was November 1939, when the press was still referring to the new war as the European war.

"Storm over Europe!" Elliston exclaimed in quaint fashion. "What on earth had Stalin started in this part of the world? It was the beginning of a wild day."[7]

In any case, it certainly was one of the wildest thus far. As it happened, Elliston missed most of the action, departing Finland after a week via the western port of Turku, where he and his fellow reporter, Curt Bloch of the *New York Times*, saw how the spirit of Finnish resistance and solidarity had galvanized Finland's third largest city. Nevertheless, he was able to weave a book (of sorts) from his breathless dispatches. The overripe tome, which bore the title *Finland Fights!*, was rushed into print in a single breathless month in order to satisfy the American public's intense interest in the Arctic war. And an interesting, even valuable book it is, particularly for its vignettes of the Finnish home front—although there technically wasn't such a thing as a home front in the war since the Red Air Force ranged virtually over the entire country. Elliston's description of the uncannily disciplined behavior of his fellow passengers on the machine-gun-riddled train from Helsinki to Turku provides an excellent snapshot of the Finnish character. If one wishes to understand *sisu,* the Finnish word that roughly translates as "grit" but means so much more, there it is, even if it has to be extracted from a mass of purple prose.

There was no shortage of journalists to take Elliston's place in Finland, especially after it became clear that the outgunned and outnumbered Finns were indeed fighting and fighting very well, and that the Soviet aggressor was stumbling over himself. Ultimately several hundred journalists from around the world covered the Winter War, making it in proportionate terms one of the most intensively and extensively covered campaigns of World War II, at least from the Finnish side. (Unsurprisingly, the Kremlin didn't allow any of the few Western correspondents accredited to Moscow to get near the battlefront—although Russian officials were so confident of easy victory that, at least initially, they didn't even censor their dispatches.)[8]

There were a number of reasons why the foreign press descended on Helsinki in such droves in December 1939. For one, of course, there was the remarkable nature of the conflict itself, which saw some of the most spectacular fighting in modern military history. For another, at that early juncture of the European war, the Soviet's blatant aggression reminded many of the German invasion and "rape" of Belgium that had outraged the world at the onset of the previous world war. Here, it seemed, was the story of Belgium violated again—except that this time the innocent being violated, Finland, was fighting back and, to all appearances, fighting extremely well.

Or, as Richard Collier puts it in *Warcos,* his excellent if forgotten book about the correspondents—"warcos"—of World War II: "Here for the first time since World War One was a David and Goliath situation with Finland standing in for 'Brave Little Belgium'; the Finns, fighting against odds fifty to one, were battling with a determination that the Poles never mustered. Before the war was a week old 100 correspondents had flooded in to cover it."[9]

Put another way, here was a conflict custom-made for headlines. And for illustrations, who could beat those photos of the Finnish "ghost soldiers" skiing off single-file to do battle with the unseen barbarian invader? Or the bathetic images of the miserable Russian prisoners of war the Finns captured? Or, yet more horrifying, the pictures of the frozen Soviet carcasses after being cut down by the sharp-eyed Finnish riflemen, or who had simply frozen to death? Recall, too, that the press now had access to the radiophone, allowing reporters to send photos along with their copy to their eager readers in London, Paris, New York, and Salt Lake City. Newsreel camera crews were also there in force, including a prescient newsreel man who filmed the initial Soviet terror attack and provided several images that became fixed in the public's imagination; among them was an especially gruesome one of the incinerated remains of a Helsinki passenger bus.

Another reason for the intensity of the press coverage of the *Talvisota* was that it took place in a virtual news vacuum, when the Western front (as such) was quiet. Situated in time between the invasion of Poland the previous September and the German blitzkrieg of the following spring, the conflict had not yet achieved its capitalized status as the "Second World War."

The only story that competed for attention with the Winter War during that somewhat anti-climactic six-month span was the Royal Navy's pursuit of the *Graf Spee,* the German raider that was chased down by Her Majesty's South Atlantic fleet in late December and bottled up in Montevideo Harbor, before dramatically scuttling herself.

Of course, earlier that month there had also been the emergency session of the League of Nations that had been convened at Finland's request over the aggression of its fellow member state, the USSR. That, too, was good for copy, albeit of the harder-to-chew kind.

Still, there was little suspense about how that diplomatic minuet would turn out, any more than there had been after the moribund body had met to "debate" Germany's invasion of the Rhineland in 1936 or Italy's invasion of Abyssinia the year after that. Still, as Geoffrey Roberts points out in *Stalin's Wars,* the Soviets, who (it is well to remember) had striven to enlist Britain and France in a system of collective security before resorting to *Realpolitik* mode, were more unhappy about the League's ultimate decision to expel them than they let on.[10]

In any case, who cared about the League of Nations when a drama of such spectacular dimensions was taking place amidst the snowdrifts above the 60th parallel? Here, at last, after all the walkovers the world had witnessed over the course of the past decade, was a "little nation" that was actually standing up to the authoritarian powers, no less in extreme conditions, including double-digit subzero temperatures, with no precedent in modern military history.

Or, as Martha Gellhorn, the noted war correspondent, who had covered the Spanish Civil War as well as the *Anschluss* and the Czech crisis and who arrived in Helsinki just in time to catch the Soviet surprise attack, put it, "I like those who fight." And the Finns, unquestionably, were fighting.[11]

How could anyone—or at least any non-Communist—*not* sympathize if not outright identify with the stalwart Finns, while admiring their remarkable military prowess?

As it happened, both Elliston and Gellhorn were assigned the Finnish story, without having any notion as to just how big that story would become. Yet other members of the international journalist brigade came on their own, drawn by the urge to bear witness to this extraordinary match-up for their readers back home in London, Manchester, Paris, and Buenos Aires, as well.

One of these impassioned journalistic volunteers, who along with Gellhorn belonged to the small, growing band of distaff war correspondents, and who also happened to be Gellhorn's best friend, was Virginia Cowles, the London-based correspondent for the *Sunday Times* and the North American Press Alliance. Cowles, who had also covered the Spanish Civil War, as had many members of the Kamp Corps, describes how she came to her somewhat impulsive decision at a London New Year's Eve fete to fly to Helsinki in her superb, recently reissued memoir, *Looking for Trouble.* Like virtually everyone else, Cowles expected the Soviet invasion to be a snap. "When the headlines announced that Helsinki had been bombed I thought it would be another Poland—that the country would be obliterated so quickly that there would be little chance of getting there before it was over," she recalls.[12]

That was before the aroused Finns started fighting back, and the Arctic mythmaking began: "Then the papers began recording the amazing feats of the Finns; incredible though it seemed, the Russian 'steam-roller' was being held in check."[13]

And off Cowles went by biplane—first to Amsterdam, then to Copenhagen, Stockholm, and finally Helsinki, which is how one traveled from London to Finland in those days—to join the press scrum. Unlike her friend Gellhorn, who famously had no truck with that "objectivity shit," as she put it, Cowles prided herself on covering both sides of a conflict and had risked her life doing so in Spain, where she managed to file reports from both the Republican and Loyalist flanks. Getting the actual story of what transpired on the thousand-mile-long battlefront past the intense Finnish press censorship proved difficult enough. Nevertheless, Cowles's sympathy for the hapless Russian men and women who were initially thrown with little or no preparation into the fight and who had little or no idea what they were fighting for, is evident in her poignant dispatches, which compose a major source for this book.[14]

No such empathy for the Soviets appears in the passionately pro-Finnish reports of another American, Leland Stowe, the noted correspondent of the *Chicago Daily News,* who also rushed to Finland at about the same time as Virginia Cowles. Like most of his colleagues, Stowe made no bones about whom *he* was rooting for—or against. Witness the following dispatch he filed in mid-January from the Lappish front, where the white-hooded Finnish "ghost soldiers" were still raising havoc with the woebegone elements of the Russian 9th Army, which had been assigned the task of severing Finland and instead had been severed itself by the vengeful "white death."

"It is breathlessly silent, and we still hear no sound, when suddenly a dozen white figures sweep across the crest of the hill to our left," Stowe's pulse-pounding report from the front line begins:

> They dig their sticks into the tight hard snow and slide into formation, Indian file. Each wears a pair of Turkish-like white overpants, a white cape, and a white hood. Each carries a rifle slung across his back and a Finnish *puukko* at his belt. They wait for a moment. Then, with a low word of command they glide like ghosts down the slope and across the bridge. They slide swiftly, noiselessly past us and down, and as they pass I notice with amusement the last soldier in the line holds a half-smoked cigar clenched in his teeth. There is something marvelously Finnish about that. . . . They may be trapped by a Red army patrol. Some of them may not come back. But as you watch them fade like phantoms and disappear into the crystalline forest you feel a warm, deep pride, as if these were our people. You know that no people on earth could be braver or stronger or more gallant than they are.[15]

Stowe, who went on to become one of the most famous correspondents of the Second World War, was a diehard Fennophile. So was the whole Western world—outside of orthodox Communists, who continued to tout the official Moscow line about the war being a "liberation action" requested by the notional Finnish proletariat—it seems, at least for those remarkable 105 days.

Obviously, Stowe's dispatches, like those of most of his fellow scribes, must be taken with a sizable piece of salt, particularly in light of the considerable obstacles put in their way by the increasingly restrictive Finnish press censors, who were anxious to put the best possible light on Finnish operations for foreign consumption without compromising security (as press censors are wont), including a ban on photographs of Finnish casualties.

Nevertheless, as I pored over the hundreds of articles and dispatches filed by the American and British press from the war as well as the numerous memoirs that came out of the now obscure conflict, I was consistently surprised by how much new information I found.

One example was the Soviet Union's use of paratroopers. Neither Allen Chew nor William Trotter, the authors of the two better-regarded—if considerably dated—previous histories of the war, *The White Death* (1973) and *A Frozen Hell: The Russo-Finnish War of 1939–1940* (1991), respectively, has anything to say on the subject of Russian airborne troops during the war. Nor did any of the Finnish military historians I consulted know anything about it. Perhaps one or two individual Russian troops had been dropped behind Finnish lines, but certainly not more.

And yet the *New York Times* and the *Times* of London carried numerous reports of such drops during the initial stage of the war. Evidently these airborne operations were a disaster for the Soviet Union, as the easily spotted Red paratroopers were quickly hunted down by Finnish troops—which also helps to explain why Moscow abandoned the use of airborne troops until much later in the war. The reports, often based on second-hand information, may well have exaggerated the number of such assaults, as well as the number of troops who participated in them.

However, there is little doubt that Moscow dropped several groups of paratroopers on Finland. And there is no denying the fear these inspired in the Finnish populace, along with the related fear about the use of poison gas, a hangover from the First World War that fortunately proved unfounded.[16]

This was news to me, as it was to the surprised Finnish military historians to whom I showed copies of those dispatches. I also was surprised to read about at least one dramatic battle, the battle of Pelkosenniemi—or the battle of Kemijärvi River, as British correspondent Geoffrey Cox calls it in his gripping memoir of the war, *The Red Army Moves*—which I had not heard of before. That crucial engagement, where an adroit Finnish battalion stopped and destroyed an armored Soviet regiment that had previously been rapidly advancing across northern Finland at the tiny riverside village of Pelkosenniemi, clearly presaged the larger and much better known battle of Suomussalmi that occurred later in December, including the use of *motti*—cordwood— tactics, the technique by which Finnish ski troops blocked off the front and rear of a Soviet column and proceeded to methodically "cut it up" that made the latter battle so famous.[17]

In addition to being one of the first outright Finnish victories in the north, the battle of Pelkosenniemi was as much of a strategic reverse for the Soviets as was Suomussalmi, if not more so, effectively halting the Soviet 9th Army's advance across southern Lapland. Cox, rightly, gives this now all but forgotten battle a whole chapter in his book. I don't go quite that far, but I try to give this pivotal engagement its rightful place in the larger story of the war. If I hadn't read Cox's memoir, I doubt I would have mentioned it.

A lot of information about the war, it is clear, is hiding in plain sight—right there in the old microfilm reels of the *New York Times* and the *Times* of London, as well as the numerous memoirs of the many journalists who wrote about the war, which together form a valuable trove on their own.

Nor was all the information I discovered in these secondary sources flattering to the Finns. It was in Cowles's and Cox's memoirs that I learned just how repressive the Finnish military press censors were. That hidebound attitude toward the press also helps explain why both the Finnish Army and the Finnish populace had little or no idea of what was actually happening during the climactic phase of the war, in late February and March 1940, when the beleaguered Army of the Isthmus was losing up to 1,000 men a day.

This helps explain why both the nation and many if not most of the troops in the field were genuinely shocked when the war suddenly came to an end. It seems that the Finns, too, had come to believe their own press. And how could they not, when the Western press was continuing to shower them with laurels while casting their struggle in such Manichean terms? Moreover, as the late Max Jakobson, the great Finnish diplomat and historian and one of those who encouraged me to write this book, pointed out, it was helpful if not necessary for Finns to believe in their myth, along with the corresponding notion that the Western powers were coming to Finland's aid, which, to the Finns' everlasting bitterness, proved false.[18]

Fortunately, the Finnish Army was too busy fighting to pay much attention to the mythological ballyhoo the media was whipping up. From a secondary source of a different kind—in this case, a Suomussalmi tourist brochure—I learned to my considerable astonishment about the 269 Finnish civilians who were seized by elements of the Soviet 163rd Division when it overran that central eastern Finnish district at the start of the war, another revelation that considerably altered the picture I had of the war (as well as the competence of Finnish civil authorities).

Too, a great deal of information can be found in the memories of the rapidly thinning ranks of the few thousand surviving veterans of the war—or those who were young enough at the time to remember anything about it. One of the reasons I was impelled to write this book was that I knew that this was my last chance to mine the memories of the relatively few extant survivors, either Finnish or Russian, of the *Talvisota*. And so it was: about half of the two dozen or so Finns, Russians, and Swedes whom I or my researchers spoke to have since passed on.

But what valuable testimony they were able to provide into such varied aspects of the war: the nature of combat on the Mannerheim Line; or what it was like to be in Helsinki on the first day of the war, as well as its sister city of Viipuri, bombed at the same time; or what it was like to be a young member of the *Lotta Svard*, the Finnish women's auxiliary organization that played a wide range of roles during the war, manning the Russian bomber watch atop an icy forest platform.

I also found out what it was like to be a Soviet marine assigned the thankless duty of guarding a motorboat base on frozen Lake Ladoga. And from one bemused veteran of the Finnish People's Army whom I interviewed in St. Petersburg, with the aid of Russian-born Winter War historian Bair Irincheev, I learned of the surreal-comic nature of that ersatz army, which was designated to raise the Red star over the Finnish presidential mansion before it was abruptly disbanded and made to vanish at the war's end.

From the one Finnish internee I was able to track down from the original unfortunate group from the Suomussalmi area, I learned what it was like to experience the shock of the initial invasion, as well as the dreadful conditions in the converted logging camp where she and her fellow hostages were held for the remainder of the war. I will forever be indebted to these survivors who shared their still vivid, sometimes sad, often haunting memories of the war, and occasionally provided me new information.

That said, there is general agreement among historians about the basic contours of this most unusual war. The essence of the Winter War can be summed up fairly quickly, as Roger Reese does in *Stalin's Reluctant Soldiers*: "Before the [Red] army could do anything to correct the deficiencies that had been exposed during its engagements in Spain and Poland," Reese writes, referring to the army's previous involvement in the Spanish Civil War and the invasion of Poland, which had exposed systemic problems of coordination and efficiency in the supposedly invincible Red Army machine, "Stalin ordered it to attack Finland in November, 1939."[19]

"The RKKA [Red Army] expected a quick and easy victory," Reese continues. "With an unsound strategy and poor coordination of units, the Red Army blundered into the Finnish defensive line on the Karelian Isthmus only to be decimated by the outnumbered Finns. Only when the RKKA assembled a huge infantry and artillery 'steamroller' did the Army manage to overwhelm the Finnish defenses by sheer weight of men and materiel."[20]

To be sure, it is hard to find fault with Reese's summary of the war, but perhaps we should expand on that, as well as add a few words about the path that led to it.

Technically speaking, the path that led to the Winter War began on October 5, 1939, when the Soviet Union "invited" the center-right Finnish government to send a delegation to Moscow in order to discuss a mooted Finnish-Soviet mutual assistance pact. The Kremlin had sent similar signals before via the Soviet embassy in Helsinki; however, the center-right government of Aimo Cajander, confident that the USSR did not wish to provoke Nazi Germany, with which Finland had enjoyed a fraternal relationship dating back to the Finnish Civil War, felt sufficiently secure not to respond to the "invitation."

The shocking Nazi-Soviet non-aggression pact of August 1939, by which Berlin ceded Moscow freedom of action in the Baltic in return for allowing Hitler the same privilege in western Europe; the subsequent German invasion of Poland, which actually triggered the new European war; and the fairly rapid way with which the Germans and their odd new bedfellows, the Soviets, disposed of the Poles—all these convinced the Finns that perhaps they had better deal with Stalin after all.

Stalin and his new aggressive-minded foreign minister, Vyacheslav Molotov, quickly taking advantage of their new freedom of action, had already sent similar subpoenas to the governments of the three smaller, neighboring former tsarist provinces of Estonia, Latvia, and Lithuania. The three obliged the Kremlin by dispatching their foreign ministers to Moscow, whereupon all readily acquiesced to the new Soviet demands, which, in addition to the obligatory treaties of mutual assistance, also called for the stationing of Soviet troops and naval forces on the Balts' territory. Of course the three, with their negligible, respective armed forces, had little choice in the matter.

By contrast, the Finns felt secure enough not to accede to the Kremlin's demands. Finland possessed significantly longer and less penetrable defenses, including the much vaunted (though overrated, as it turned out) Mannerheim Line of fortifications and gun ports that stretched across the Karelian peninsula, as well as an intricate mass of forest and lakeland extending from the Karelian Isthmus to Lapland, plus a well-trained standing army of a third of a million. The demands included moving the Fenno-Soviet border eastward to a point only fifty-one kilometers west of Viipuri, then Finland's second largest city, which the Soviets felt was necessary in order to protect Leningrad in case of a future invasion from the west—a not unreasonable concern in light of the attack on that city that Nazi Germany would launch via Karelia with the aid of their Finnish co-belligerents two years hence.

Additionally, Stalin and Molotov wanted a thirty-year lease on Hanko, the strategic Finnish fortress overlooking the approaches to the Baltic, as well as the obligatory assistance pact. In return the USSR was willing to cede Helsinki two municipalities with twice the amount of territory it was demanding from Finland.

In addition to the harshness of these demands, which it knew the Finnish public would never approve, the Finnish government feared that granting these would only lead to more demands and the loss of Finnish sovereignty. Which of course is exactly what happened to Estonia, Latvia, and Lithuania the following year, when the three short-lived Baltic nations were formally annexed by Moscow. Nevertheless, although prepared for war, the Finnish cabinet was still prepared to negotiate on November 30, 1939, the day of the Soviet surprise attack.

Significantly, one of those who urged the government to reach some sort of territorial accommodation with Moscow before the outbreak of the war was Carl Gustaf Emil Mannerheim, the uncompromisingly anti-Bolshevik top Finnish general. Amongst Mannerheim's well-founded concerns was the army's alarmingly low stockpile of ammunition and fuel, which could only sustain the army for several weeks at most. "The Army cannot fight!" insisted the one-time imperial Russian general, who had resigned several times over the Finnish cabinet's refusal to allocate more funds for defense. Of course if necessary, it would. And so would Mannerheim, who would be commander-in-chief in case of such a war, though he certainly wasn't angling for the job.[21]

For his part, Stalin may have been initially sincere about negotiating with the Finns. At the same time, it is clear, he certainly had a Plan B for invading and occupying his recalcitrant neighbor. Indeed, his ambassador and other agents in Helsinki had assured him, the downtrodden Finns would welcome such an eventuality. The Soviet general staff was prepared for it, having drawn up not one but two operational plans for the conquest and absorption of *Suomi*. The first, developed by Boris Shaposhnikov, the Red Army chief of staff, called for a concentrated attack by a large Russian force on the main Finnish defense line in Karelia. Even then, the clear-eyed Shaposhnikov envisaged a difficult war lasting several months at a minimum. As a two-time former head of the Leningrad Military District (1925–27, 1935–37), the Soviet general knew whereof he spoke.[22]

Nevertheless Stalin, who obviously did not share Shaposhnikov's opinion of Finnish capabilities, discarded that plan. "You are asking for such immense strength and resources to defeat a country like Finland," Stalin maintained. "Such strength is not needed." Instead the Soviet dictator ordered Kirill Meretskov, Shaposhnikov's successor as head of the Leningrad Military District, to devise a new plan for a multi-prong attack that would accomplish the same objective in a matter of weeks. The working deadline for the "liberation of Finland" was December 21, Stalin's sixtieth birthday, when Kliment Voroshilov, the incompetent Russian defense minister, intended to make a present of Finland.[23]

Meretskov duly obliged, ultimately coming up with a plan for a nine-point attack. The main thrust of the Red assault would still be in Karelia, with other units crossing the border at the eight other points along the Fenno-Soviet border, up to and including the Petsamo peninsula overlooking the Arctic Sea—a mechanized blitzkrieg bearing a strong resemblance to the one Hitler successfully employed against Poland. Also similar was the *casus belli* Stalin used to start the war: a putative Finnish artillery attack that supposedly had caused the deaths of four Russian border guards, for which an apology was demanded, along with a demand that the Finns move their forces twenty to twenty-five kilometers from the border. Unsurprisingly, Helsinki denied responsibility for the mythical attack, rejected the Kremlin's new demands, and called for a joint Finnish-Soviet commission to investigate the incident.

Moscow, in turn, denounced the Finnish response as hostile and renounced the seven-year-old Fenno-Soviet non-aggression pact. In the meantime, the Finnish Army completed the mobilization it had begun earlier that summer.

Nevertheless, being prepared for war was not quite the same as being totally ready for it. Government officials continued to exist in a state of partial denial, as evidenced by the scandalous failure to properly evacuate the civilian population living close to the border, as well as the corresponding failure to devise a plan to evacuate the capital. Although a number of light anti-aircraft artillery guns had been installed around the city, the notion of anyone actually bombing Helsinki from the air, something that had never happened before, was still unthinkable. The general sense was that some sort of solution to the crisis would be found. Certainly most Finns hoped so.

That illusion was roughly dispelled on the morning of November 30, 1939, when the first flight of Russian SB-2 bombers appeared in the skies over the city and began dropping incendiaries and high explosives. Mixed with these were leaflets written by an anonymous Finnish-speaking Red pamphleteer urging the supposedly repressed Finnish proletariat to rise up against the "Cajander-Mannerheim" clique, as Moscow still harbored hopes of changing hearts and minds. The surprise attack interrupted a meeting of the Finnish cabinet, which had been deliberating how to respond to the Kremlin's latest sally.

Any notion that Moscow was amenable to negotiation was further retired the following day when Radio Moscow announced that it had come to terms with the government of the People's Republic of Finland, a puppet regime it had installed for that very purpose. Additionally, this new government had, not surprisingly, readily agreed to all of the Kremlin's territorial conditions, while also agreeing to a treaty of mutual assistance. This act of political flummery was confirmed the next day when *Pravda* carried a photo of Molotov signing the USSR's new pact with the Democratic People's Republic of Finland, as Stalin, appearing very much like the cat who had swallowed the canary, looked benignly on, along with a blank-faced Otto Ville Kuusinen, the so-called president of the DPRF. In one fell swoop, the legitimate Finnish government had been made to vanish, or so it seemed, and replaced with a more cooperative understudy.[24]

The rest, Stalin was confident, would be a formality. Stalin was so sure of himself that he didn't even take a meeting, according to Nikita Khrushchev, then the top Ukrainian *apparatchik* and later Stalin's successor as premier. "He thought that all he had to do was to fire a few shots and the Finns would surrender," he wrote in his autobiography. So did the rest of the world.[25]

But the world didn't know the Finns, and neither did Stalin. Soon came reports that the Red colossus had become bogged down in the Finnish fells, that the Finns were skiing rings around the Reds, even decimating them. Thus, on December 18, the nineteenth day of the war, *Time* breathlessly reported:

A blinding blizzard, which grounded aviation, smashed tanks against half-concealed boulders and granite tank barriers, gave the Finns an almost even break. The Russians, who had thought they were starting a *Blitzkrieg,* were still hammering desperately at the [Finnish] defenses. . . . Finally there was the snowstorm. Out of the swirling blizzard poured the Finns themselves, almost invisible with white capes covering their grey-green uniforms and white fur caps on their heads. Their machine guns barked and their knives were loose in their sheaths and they did not take many prisoners.[26]

Actually, that was not true. The Finns wound up taking quite a sizable number of prisoners—5,600 in all.

And what prisoners! The Western correspondents who were allowed, even encouraged, to interview and photograph them were uniformly astounded at the woefully inadequate clothing and general abysmal state of the Russian POWs. Typically, and not inaccurately, Leland Stowe wrote: "The Russian troops the Kremlin has thrown against the Karelian bottleneck are probably the most miserable-looking creatures to be seen in uniform in this part of Europe since

Napoleon's half-starved soldiers straggled back from Moscow. None of the men had high boots, and several of them, as a result, had feet so frozen they could hardly walk." One unnamed Finnish colonel told Stowe, "Such infantry we have never seen. They are not soldiers."[27]

The public's image of the war, which was mirrored in the dispatches of other Western correspondents who were allowed near the front line, was set: Finnish ski soldiers pouring out of the snow, machine guns barking, the wretched Russian soldiers being cut down and, if they were lucky, being taken as prisoners.

The truth, of course, was a little more complicated. On the main front in Karelia, the Russian monolith had indeed bogged down as the Seventh Army's initial thrust petered out before the withering Finnish fire. The farthest initial westward penetration was made by the Soviet 19th Regiment, which secured a slim bridgehead on the west bank of the River Vuoksi before it was beaten off.

However, in the far north, the 14th Army had already captured its main objective, the port of Petsamo, after overcoming light Finnish resistance, and was rapidly advancing down the Arctic Highway for its intended link-up with the 9th Army, the westward-moving Russian force that was about to attack the strategically located eastern central town of Suomussalmi, site of its future Golgotha. North of Lake Ladoga, the 8th Army had similarly overwhelmed the meek Finnish defenses, capturing the town of Suojarvi along with a large number of civilian hostages, and also seemed to be making progress toward its ultimate objectives in the heart of the Finnish lake country.

Still, on the whole, the image of the Soviet Goliath stumbling over itself while the fleet, white-hooded Finns harried him on the ground and the tiny Finnish Air Force badgered him from the air, was accurate enough to cause mounting distress in Moscow. Already by December 9, operational control of the four armies assigned to the initial assault, as well as the Baltic and Northern fleets, was moved from the Leningrad Military District to the direct control of *Stavka,* the Red Army High Command. At the same time, Meretskov, the author of the misconceived Russian invasion plan and top Soviet field commander, was relieved and reassigned to command the 7th Army, while commissars Lev Mekhlis and G. I. Kulik were dispatched to the 9th and 8th Armies, respectively, in order to help those units intensify their attacks.[28]

Not that any of this did the mostly second-rate Russian forces assigned to the invasion much good. The Finns' superior fighting skills and leadership, coupled with both their knowledge of their home terrain and their indomitable will to resist, came into full play in the second and third weeks of the war, causing the 7th, 8th, and 9th Armies to suffer a remarkable and well-publicized series of humiliating defeats. The relatively forgotten battle of Tolvajarvi, where an augmented Finnish regiment engaged in a running fight with two Soviet divisions before nearly destroying one of them, was the first outright Finnish victory and a major morale booster for the Finns.

December 19, the twentieth day of the war, when the Soviets experienced setbacks on various fronts—and the date that serves as the climax of the first part of the book—was a major watershed. Thus, in the course of twenty-four hours, in Lapland, the 9th Army was simultaneously stopped at Pelkosenniemi, while to the south, the 7th Army was thwarted again in Karelia in close fighting in which the Russians lost nearly seventy tanks. That same day the Bristol Bulldogs of the Finnish Air Force blunted the latest Russian aerial offensive, shooting down over a dozen Soviet bombers, while at sea—the Winter War also included a limited naval war, even a submarine war of sorts—the battleship *October Revolution* mounted an unsuccessful attack on the Finnish island fortress of Sarenpaa before being driven away by its artillery. The Finnish military star was now clearly on the ascent. Or as *Time* mordantly (and not inaccurately) put it, "After three weeks of war, Russia's planned *Blitzkrieg* had definitely failed to blitz. All in all, Joe Stalin did not have a happy birthday."[29]

And the Finnish star continued to rise for the remainder of December and into early January, through the back-to-back "annihilation victories" at Suomussalmi and Raate Road, where Colonel Hjalmar Siilasvuo, using the same *motti* tactics displayed at Pelkosenniemi, methodically eliminated the Russian 163rd and 44th Divisions in that legendary battle, the high point of Finnish arms. Meanwhile, in Karelia, on December 23, the Finns were sufficiently emboldened to launch their one and only counteroffensive against the surprised Russians in front of the Mannerheim Line with a two-sided encirclement. The Finnish attack ran out of steam, but it came close enough to the headquarters of the 50th Corps, which Meretskov was visiting at the time, to give the Russian commander a bad scare—as well as to help persuade Stalin and his cronies that maybe they needed a Plan B, after all.[30]

Impressed by the Finnish show of force, the British and French now committed themselves to the notion of dispatching a combined relief force to succor the Finns. This was the same harebrained operation that would come to be called Operation Avon Head, or the "Finnish wild goose enterprise," as British general Alan Brooke—then head of British Southern Command, later chief of staff—accurately dismissed it. At the same time, the Allies continued to send the Finns a considerable amount of guns, ammunition, and planes, just enough to encourage Helsinki to think that they would eventually, somehow, come in with both feet, which in fact had been the ultimate aim of Finnish strategy: to force the rest of the world to come to their aid before they were annihilated. As a result Finnish morale couldn't have been higher. It was further bolstered by the famed fighting speech from Winston Churchill, then Lord of the Admiralty, on January 19, 1940, in which he exhorted, "Finland, superb, nay sublime in the jaws of peril, Finland shows what free men can do." The generally pessimistic Mannerheim was in such buoyant spirits that he told a British military envoy, General Christopher George Ling, that he could hold off the Russians until May.[31]

This, of course, was fantasy. Mannerheim, it seems, had begun to believe his own myth, which all those reporters squeezed into the Hotel Kamp had helped create for him. However, neither he nor they had seen the real Red Army—at least yet. They would shortly. Mannerheim also seems to have misjudged the American political situation, and particularly President Franklin Roosevelt's latitude for action; he sent the president a "very urgent," if somewhat unhinged, telegram asking the United States to dispatch 150 pursuit planes and thirty-six two-engine bombers to Finland, not fully appreciating that Americans, though ardently supportive of the Finns, just as ardently wished to remain neutral.[32]

Meanwhile, also during the January interregnum, the Finnish government, which was still anxious to find a way to make peace with Moscow even though the latter no longer recognized it, managed to establish an unusual back channel with the Russians via the Fennophile Soviet ambassador to Stockholm, Madame Alexandra Kollontai, and her friend, the left-wing Estonian playwright Hella Wuolijoki. The results of this conduit, which involved a series of *sub rosa* meetings at Stockholm's Grand Hotel, ultimately became serious enough to merit the attention of both governments. Molotov, who was also keeping an eye on the battlefield, where the Finns were still besting the Russians, signaled on January 19 (the same day that Churchill made his pro-Finnish speech) that the Kremlin was willing to do business with the Finnish government—not the Finnish People's Democratic Republic, which was promptly made to vanish, but the same "White Guardist regime" it was supposed to depose. By now, Stalin, realizing his folly (as well as how badly served he had been by his advisors), had given up any notion of "liberating" Finland. As Geoffrey Roberts writes, "Stalin was blinkered by his ideology, not blinded by it."[33]

Indeed, if anything, whatever fissures that existed in the Finnish commonweal between left and right had been soldered shut by the Soviet invasion. There were a number of cases of espionage and sabotage committed by Finnish soldiers to the Communist cause at the start of the war, but no more than a handful, and even that number dropped as the war progressed and the inhumane character of the Soviet regime became clear, as spectacularly manifested by the pathetic state of its own captive, frostbitten troops. There was no fifth column in Finland to speak of; even Stalin could see that now. So negotiations there would be.

But first, Stalin decreed, the battered prestige of the Red Army had to be restored. The prevailing image of the clumsy, ill-clad Soviet Goliath stumbling about in the Finnish snowdrifts, underscored by the back-to-back Russian disasters at Suomussalmi and Raate Road, which the press eagerly peddled as well as exaggerated, could not be allowed to stand.

Geoffrey Roberts drily summarizes what happened next: "In January 1940, the Soviets regrouped, reinforced their armies and Stalin appointed Semyon K. Timoshenko to overall command of the Soviet assault. In mid-February Timoshenko launched a well-prepared offensive, again concentrated on the Mannerheim Line. This time the Soviets succeeded in breaching Finnish defenses and in driving back Mannerheim's men along a broad front."[34]

Western observers, used to tales of Finnish military prowess, as well as of Soviet military incompetence, were surprised and disappointed by how quickly the revamped Russian juggernaut was able to break through the main Finnish defense line. They ought not to have been. The massive initial artillery barrage on February 11, in which the Russians threw over 300,000 shells in a twenty-four-hour period, was the heaviest such barrage since the Second Battle of the Somme. More important, the crack, expertly led, well-motivated echelons who now charged the pulverized Finnish defenses were of a different order altogether than their woebegone predecessors. So were their tactics and equipment, which included tank-drawn snow sledges and other innovations.[35]

Finnish military historian Otto Manninen, who advised the author on this book, accurately describes the dramatically changed tenor of the fighting on the Karelian front:

> Fighting was fierce from the start. The attackers had to cross a zone full of granite posts and anti-tank ditches, fields of barbed wire, minefields, obstacles, and entanglements. The infantry attack took place under the protection of the artillery's avalanche of fire. The distance of impact for the infantry was to be 200 meters at most, and the tanks were to advance to holes cleared in the obstacle zone on a level with the first echelon of infantry, and then cover the infantry and make way for it while fighting alongside it. The assault troops attacked behind the first echelon of the infantry. After the artillery preparations, the strike detachments set off to capture bunkers and firing nests.[36]

This was the real Red Army. Put another way, the Red Army had learned from its mistakes, and quickly. In the end, the Soviet High Command proved more adaptable than anyone gave it credit for, especially Hitler, who wound up taking the wrong lesson from the Winter War. In this, Geoffrey Cox, perhaps the best military analyst amongst the Kamp corps, compared the Red Army's performance to that of the British Army in the Boer War:

> The Soviet High Command showed a willingness to learn from its errors so that in the end it emulated the habit ascribed to us [the British] of losing every battle but the last. Just as in the Boer War we recovered ourselves and worked out tactics suitable for the country after we had suffered disaster upon disaster by sending troops in scarlet coats in close formation, the Russian commanders worked out their way of bringing the great ponderous weight of the Red Army machine against the elusive [Finns].[37]

Moreover, those "elusive" Finns were a spent force. Desperate for replacements, the army once again lowered its requirements. Convicts serving light sentences, men up to age forty-six, and those once rejected for physical infirmity, were now rushed into uniform. Meanwhile, the shell-shocked veterans who peered over the parapets of their trenches or through the embrasures of their battered bunkers, awaiting the new Soviet juggernaut, had been reduced to virtual zombies. Yet these same men managed to hold off the new, massive Soviet assault on the isthmus. Still, with a well-coordinated land and air armada now numbering 460,000 men, divided into two massive armies—the 7th Army, led by Meretskov, on the left, and the 13th Army, led by the Finnish-born Soviet general Vladimir A. Grendahl (formerly Wladimir Grundahl), on the right—and backed up by 3,350 artillery pieces, 3,000 tanks, and 1,300 aircraft (just the portion of the total force allocated to the isthmus), it was only a matter of time before the Russians broke through.[38]

To be sure, there was still good news for Fennophiles if they knew where to look for it, especially north of Lake Ladoga, where in late February the Finnish 23rd Division, using the by now tried and true *motti* tactics, completed the destruction of another Soviet division, the 18th. However, on the main Karelian front, where, after intense fighting, the Russians forced the first breach in the Finns' defenses in the Lahde district and were continuing to pour through, time was fast running out. On February 17, by which time the break in the Finnish defense line had been expanded to eight kilometers, Mannerheim, having sized up the situation himself after a rare visit to the front line, authorized a general retreat of the Second Finnish Corps, led by General Harald Ohqvist, to the intermediate Finnish line running from Vuoksi to Kamara. Meanwhile, on the eastern side of the isthmus their comrades stubbornly continued to resist the assaults of Grendahl's force.[39]

Four days later the hard-driving Russians broke into that as well, and Ohqvist's men were forced to withdraw to their final line, running from the Vuoksi, in the middle of the isthmus, through Viipuri itself. Pausing only briefly, Timoshenko now sought to reduce the city once known as "the Paris of Finland," now a smoking shadow of its former self, with a double envelopment, as one Soviet force moved by land from the east while another came up from the south, via the ice-bound Bay of Viipuri. There, in another one of the war's forgotten battles, the new Red juggernaut sought to gain the western shore, while the sparse Finnish artillery pounded holes in the ice and Finnish fighters strafed them from the air.[40]

Once again, as in December, readers and listeners around the world—for radio was now present, too—were stirred by new tales of Finnish heroism. However, despite the Finns' tenacious defense, it was clear that the Winter War was in its final act. Even Finland's staunchest friends, including her friends in the press, following events as best they could from Helsinki, could see that now; correspondents were no longer allowed to go near the isthmus by paranoid Finnish press censors. Thus, on February 27, a sad but clear-eyed Virginia Cowles wrote in her dispatch for the *Sunday Times*: "It is impossible for journalists to make predictions. One can only draw the obvious conclusion that a small force of approximately 300,000 men cannot hold out indefinitely against an army with an unlimited supply of manpower and which can afford to fight a war of attrition.

Unless Russia is diverted in another direction or several hundred thousand troops arrive in Finland the country is bound to be conquered in the end."[41]

Russia was not diverted in another direction. Indeed, it was precisely Stalin's fear that he would be diverted by the half-baked Allied rescue mission, which he seems to have taken quite seriously, and would have to fight the British and French in Scandinavia, perhaps alongside his German allies—a prospect that he understandably dreaded—that led him to drive Timoshenko to push his men on. Indeed, somewhat paradoxically, even though it was never actually launched, the now forgotten Operation Avon Head wound up playing a significant role in the Winter War. The very threat of the Allies landing in Sweden and making their way to Finland—even though the paltry subforce was assigned to the secondary objective of assisting the Finns, rather than Avon Head's original Churchillian objective of seizing Sweden's iron ore deposits—was sufficient to make Stalin anxious. Doubtless it was also a factor, if not the main factor, in making Stalin decide to bring the war to a halt before Finland could actually be conquered. First, however, the prestige of the Red Army had to be restored.

A brief aside, if I may: I daresay that the story of the Winter War, the complete story, with its cat's cradle of interwoven political, diplomatic, military, and intellectual strands, is far more complex than meets the eye. On the one hand, one cannot understand the military dimension of the war without taking into account the political-diplomatic context in which it took place; on the other hand, it is folly to write about the political and diplomatic dimension if one takes one's eye off what was actually taking place on the battlefield. I try to do both in my account of this still dimly understood war, which really was an extended fifteen-week-long battle—hence the Finnish title of the book, *Taistelu Suomesta* (*The Battle of Finland*)—while alternating between its constantly shifting planes. At the same time I devote the preponderance of my attention to the battlefront, which was still the main driver of the war. It was, of course, because of how well the Finns had done on the battlefield during the first month of the war—as well as how well and dramatically the Finns' initial military successes and corresponding Soviet debacle were conveyed by the Western media—that convinced Stalin and Molotov to change their minds and negotiate with the true democratically-elected Finnish government, and not the ersatz Democratic Republic of Finland, in late January, while the world was still agog at the graphic photos of the horrific aftermath of the decimation of the Soviet 44th Division at Raate Road.

The off-stage political and diplomatic developments and shenanigans also have their place in the saga. If Timoshenko and the highly motivated cadres of the second Soviet wave had had their way, they would have indeed been pleased to make a belated birthday gift of Helsinki to Stalin, as now seemed increasingly feasible. That, Stalin—the palpably incompetent Voroshilov having been discreetly removed from the scene—decided, with his eye nervously cocked towards Narvik, where the first boatloads of the putative Finnish rescue force were supposed to land, would be nice but no longer necessary. He would treat with the Finns again. Also, doubtless, the extraordinary fight the Finns had put up, as well as their remarkable show of unity—had persuaded him that even if he was able to conquer Finland, he would have at least as much difficulty governing the Finns as had the tsars. Yes, Stalin decided—the entreaties of Madame Kollontai also quite likely played a role here—he would talk to the Finns again. But first the prestige of the great Red Army would be restored.

Now, to paraphrase Molotov, it was the soldiers' turn to speak, and they were speaking well. The Soviet pincers were indeed closing fast. On March 5, the 123rd Soviet Division entered the suburbs of Viipuri, while its sister unit, the Soviet 28th Corps, continued with its remarkable island-hopping campaign, ruthlessly overcoming the garrison at Tuppura fortress (which plays a supporting role in the narrative), as well as those on the surrounding islands of the Viipuri archipelago. Sensing that the gulf was the most sensitive and vulnerable point of the Finnish rear line, and cognizant that they only had a limited time before the ice began to break up, the Russians now shifted the greatest weight of their entire offensive effort in that direction, sending wave after wave of men and machines out over the frozen-over bay, while Finnish planes and artillery blasted holes in the ice, causing many to fall in. No matter: there was no stopping the Soviets now.[42]

Desperate for the Finns to hold on, Eduoard Daladier, the French prime minister, who had tied his own political fortune to the success of the "Finnish wild goose enterprise," recklessly offered to send several more times the relatively paltry force of 15,000 men assigned to Avon Head. However, the Finns, after some hesitation, correctly perceived the desperation of Daladier's gambit, which achieved nothing except to get several thousand more Finns and Russians killed, and refused to issue the official public appeal for help that the Allies insisted on in order to legitimize the seaborne assault: such niceties were still important at this relatively civilized point of World War II.[43]

On March 5, the same day that Timoshenko's men assaulted Viipuri, his forces to the southwest stormed ashore and established their first beachhead at the village of Vilianiemi, on the now blood-soaked western shoreline of Viipuri Bay. The gates to Helsinki were indeed open now. That same day a Finnish peace delegation led by Prime Minister Risto Ryti secretly set off for Moscow via Stockholm to begin negotiations with Stalin. Two days later the Finns finally reached Moscow, where they learned that the Kremlin's new terms were harsher than they had imagined. In addition to ceding all of Karelia, Molotov—Stalin himself did not participate, preferring to leave the affair to his chief political henchman—now also demanded the entire Ryabachi peninsula in the far north of Finland and a band of territory in the Salla district in Lapland. Ominously, the Finns were also now required to build a railroad connecting the Murmansk Railroad with the strategic port of Tornio on the Gulf of Bothnia, signaling the Soviets' possible intention to annex Finland after all, as per its original plan. Naturally, Helsinki also had to sign the obligatory treaty of mutual assistance. And, of course, the Kremlin still wanted a long-term lease to the strategic port of Hanko.[44]

The Finns had arrived hoping to bargain with the Soviets, as they had done—or at least had tried to do—the previous November. However, there would be no bargaining this time. The bullet-headed Soviet foreign commissar made that very clear. The flustered Ryti tried to get Molotov to soften the terms. Nothing doing. The best Molotov would do, however, was to leave out the treaty of mutual assistance. Molotov gave the Finns two choices: sign or keep fighting.

While back in Helsinki, the dismayed Finnish cabinet deliberated on whether to accept, the Finnish Army, still in the dark, kept on fighting. And so did their no less blinkered Soviet counterparts, as they continued to batter their way into Viipuri.[45]

At his headquarters, General Ohqvist, who had been ordered to hold Finland's second city at all costs, and who was still unaware of the Moscow negotiations, recorded in his diary: "This is an awful gamble we are taking. It is possible that we can keep Viipuri in our hands until tomorrow night. If we are ordered to continue resistance beyond that it means that either the city or the troops will be doomed."[46]

That same day, March 9, after a final pessimistic situation report from Mannerheim and much wringing of hands, the cabinet reluctantly cabled Ryti and his fellow delegates instructing them to sign the dreaded treaty. There was no choice, really: the Finnish Army was losing a thousand men a day at that point. It was no longer possible to speak of a Finnish "line" on the gulf coast: from the Baltic shore to the farthest Russian advance, now just six kilometers from the edge of Viipuri, the entire shoreline was a chaotic series of savage delaying actions. Still, the men of the Finnish Coastal Group, stationed along the western shoreline of the bay, and the Second Corps, fighting in Viipuri city, refused to succumb. Try as they might, the Soviets were never able to close the last few kilometers that stood between them and final victory. On the day that the armistice was announced to the shocked Finnish nation, the Finnish flag still flew over Viipuri Castle.[47]

One of the things that sustained the defenders of Viipuri, one must point out again, was the prospect of Allied, including American, support, as unrealistic as that was. Finns were unwilling to believe that America, their best friend in the free world, as well as the country they admired and identified with the most, could allow them to be annihilated. Naively, they had mistaken all the brave and bellicose words from the United States—including a spontaneous and impolitic anti-Soviet jeremiad that Roosevelt had delivered from the White House in February to a group of pro-Communist American college students—all gleefully conveyed by the equally naive Finnish press, for a desire to actually go to war for their hard-pressed Nordic democratic cousins.[48]

This was indeed a tremendous letdown, as Carl Mydans, the famed *Life* writer-photographer who covered the Winter War, discovered up close during the days following the Finnish surrender, when he found himself on a train with a group of embittered Finnish soldiers. Before the armistice, his American accent might have been greeted with a smile and a nod and a thumbs up. Not anymore. Now it was a liability. "Your country was going to help!" a Finnish officer angrily exclaimed to him, grabbing Mydans by the shoulders. "A half-dozen God-damned Brewster fighters with no spare parts is all we got from you! And the British sent us guns from the last war that wouldn't even work!" Then he collapsed in tears.[49]

That was an exaggeration, of course. In point of fact, America sent a dozen Brewster fighters; however, they were outmoded. And the British sent quite a few guns and planes as well, and not all of them were from the last war, either.[50] The main point is that, alongside their unshakeable love of country and formidable fighting skills, the Finns had also been sustained by the prospect of receiving significant material assistance and manpower from the Allies, over and above what they had already provided—in addition to the 12,000 volunteers from around the world, including the United States, France, and Britain. This is why in order to fully understand the war it is vital to understand the entire military-politico and intellectual map on which it was conducted, not merely the relatively small square of Europe in which it was actually fought, as well as the outsized role the cheerleading Western media played.

In point of fact, the notion that America—or anyone—could really have saved the Finns once Stalin woke from his narcoma and put his best military foot forward was probably a delusion. It really was only a matter of time before the Soviets remedied their initial faux blitzkrieg strategy and overcame the recalcitrant Finns.

Indeed, once one peels away the layers of myth and examines what actually happened, as I tried to do during the three years I researched this book, both in Finland and in Russia, what is most striking about the war is how long and how well the Finns were able to resist. The truth is, even when one removes the distorting effect of the Western media, as well as that of the rigid Finnish press censorship, there is a core of truth to the *legenda* of the Winter War, which perhaps explains why it still has such abiding force in Finland. As such, the *Talvisota* clearly ranks among the great defensive sagas of military history, alongside Thermopylae, Masada, the Alamo, and the Battle of Britain.

Beyond that, I have tried here to do justice to the bravery and prowess displayed by both sides of this extraordinary conflict while also giving the reader some idea of why for 105 days in late 1939 and early 1940 the Winter War captured the imagination of the world, as well as why it continues to fascinate scholars and practitioners of the military arts up to the present day.

Gordon F. Sander

June 2012

Ithaca, New York

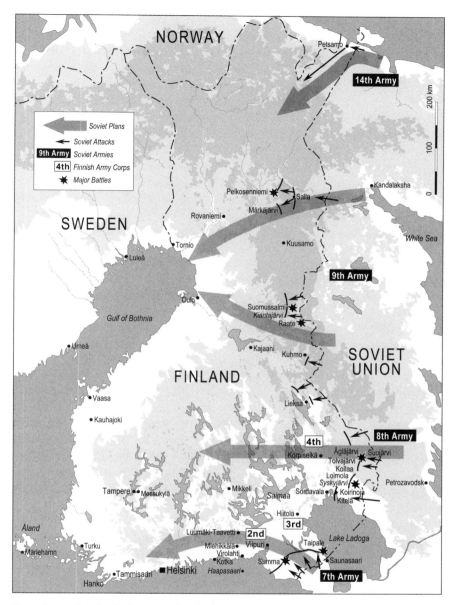

Map 1. Soviet plan for the invasion of Finland.

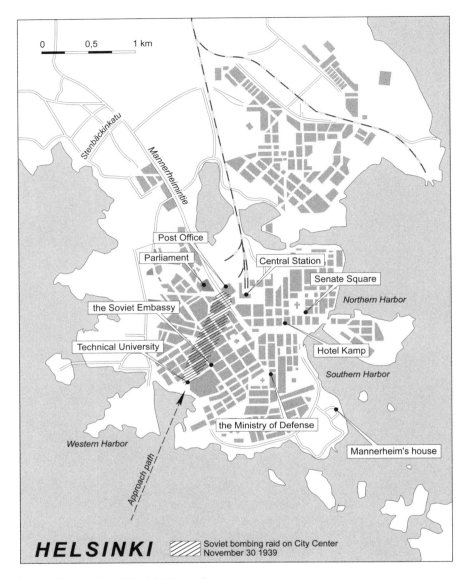

Map 2. The bombing of Helsinki, November 30, 1939.

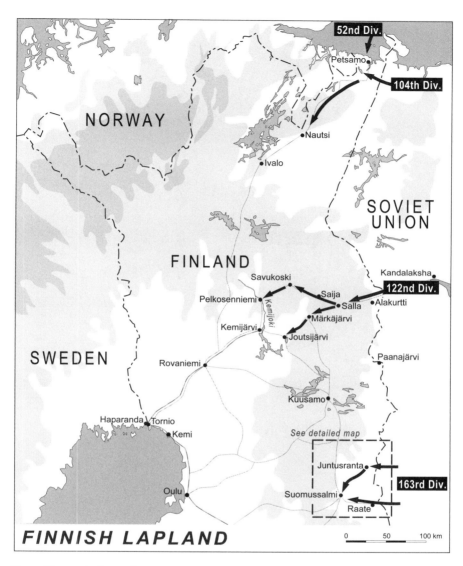

Map 3. The war in the north.

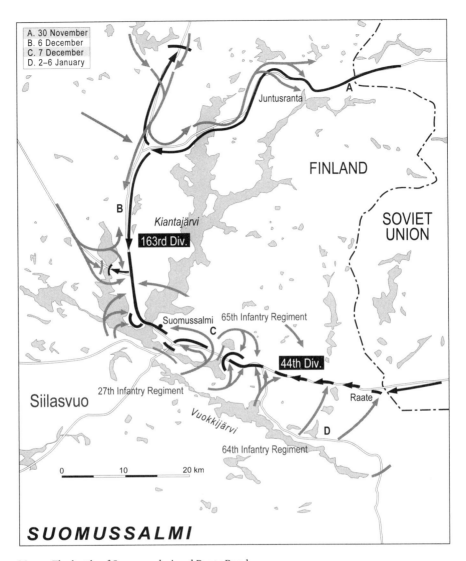

A. 30 November
B. 6 December
C. 7 December
D. 2–6 January

Juntusranta

FINLAND

SOVIET
UNION

B

Kiantajärvi

163rd Div.

Suomussalmi   65th Infantry Regiment

C

44th Div.

27th Infantry Regiment

Raate

Siilasvuo

Vuokkijärvi

D

64th Infantry Regiment

0   10   20 km

SUOMUSSALMI

Map 4. The battle of Suomussalmi and Raate Road.

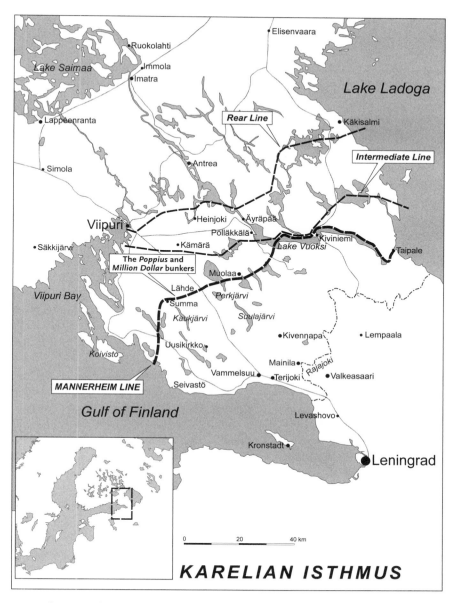

Map 5. The Mannerheim Line.

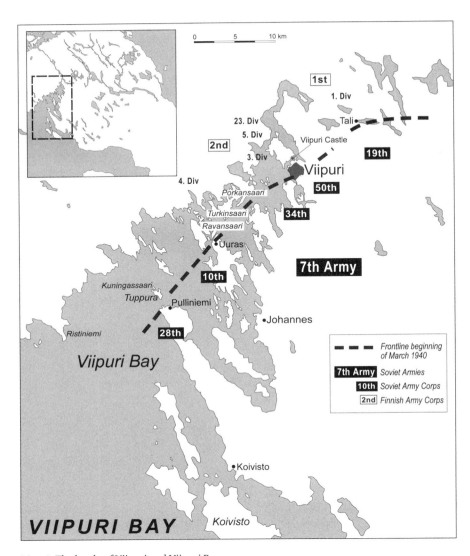

Map 6. The battle of Viipuri and Viipuri Bay.

A Thermopylae Every Day

November 30–December 25, 1939

1

"A Wild Day"

November 30, 1939

RUSSIANS START THEIR INVASION OF FINLAND
PLANES DROP BOMBS ON AIRFIELD AT HELSINKI
WAR STARTS AS U.S. MOVE FOR PEACE IS MADE
  —*New York Times,* November 30, 1939

I remember everything quite clearly. My memories are so clear they still torture
me sometimes. When it's cold and snowy, I can picture myself in those trenches
like it was yesterday.
  —Dr. Eric Malm, who served as a platoon
  leader with the 10th Finnish Regiment on the
  Mannerheim Line

What do I remember the most from the war? It was the incompetence of our
army, as it could not deal with a handful of Finns in a proper manner and in
good time. They [the Finns] showed us how to fight a war.
  —Georgi V. Prusakov, Soviet medic who
  fought the war with the 100th Independent
  Volunteer Ski Battalion

Invading armies rarely signal their intentions with music, but something like that occurred on the afternoon of November 29, 1939, at the border village of Alakurtti, in eastern Lapland. The Finnish frontier guards stationed there that day were astonished to see a Soviet military band, in full regalia, suddenly appear out of the gloaming on the forest road leading to the Russian and Finnish customs barriers. Marching right up to the gate, the khaki-adorned orchestra suddenly stood fast.

Then at a signal from the bandmaster, the musicians proceeded to play "The Internationale." Uncertain how to respond, one of the perplexed Finnish frontier guards called up the commander of the area, Colonel Vila Villamo, a genial warrior who had been commander of the area since the Finnish Civil War twenty years before, and held the receiver out of the window so the former could hear the uninvited Red serenaders.

Upon hearing the old Communist call to arms, the alarmed officer ordered the head guard of the normally sleepy outposts to issue ammunition and stand ready for anything. And so the tense guards did, as the musical berserkers proceeded to play an entire program of Soviet military tunes for the wary guards, as well as the trees, before disappearing into the twilight once again.

Villamo's instincts proved sound: the very next morning, the Finns suffered some of their first dead at Alakurtti. By then, the entire country was under attack.

*

The longest day in the history of modern Helsinki began quietly enough. Christian Ilmoni, a student at Helsinki University, was walking down Stenbackinkatu, a quiet residential street in the center of town, when he saw the first Soviet Tupolev SB-2 bombers plummet out of the low clouds covering the dark morning sky. The time was 9 A.M. The raid, the first of three conducted that day by the Red Air Force, marked the first time that Finns, no less than anyone in that part of the world, had seen a hostile aircraft at least since the Finnish Civil War twenty years before, let alone an entire squadron of bombing planes (as they were then quaintly called) flying in unison.

It was also the first inkling to Helsinkians that Finland was actually, irrevocably at war with the Union of Soviet Socialist Republics, something that— despite the rapidly increasing tensions between the two countries over the past few days, including an obviously trumped-up border incident by the Soviets four days before—many of those like Ilmoni who were caught out by the surprise attack could not take in.

Ilmoni, who was on his way to class that morning, happened to be walking past the home of Juho Kusti Paasikivi, the Finnish minister to Sweden, former prime minister, and future president, when he spotted the first Red bomber flying parallel to the street. Seven weeks before, on October 7, the twenty-one-year-old university student had been amongst the large throng of anxious Helsinkians who had accompanied Paasikivi and his fellow negotiators, Colonel Aladar Paasonen and Minister Counsellor Johan Nykopp, to the main Helsinki railway station, as they prepared to board the night train to Moscow, where Joseph Stalin and Vyacheslav Molotov had "invited" them in order to discuss "concrete political questions." To prove to the Russians that they weren't in a mood to do what the Soviets wanted, the stubborn Finns had decided to take the slow, fifteen-hour train to Moscow rather than fly, as their cowed counterparts from the other independent Baltic nations of Estonia, Latvia, and Lithuania had recently done in response to their respective summonses from the Kremlin.[1]

Nineteen years before, Paasikivi had participated in the negotiations with the three-year-old Soviet Russian entity, then weary and impoverished after six continuous years of war and revolution, at the historic southern Estonian city of Tartu. The subsequent treaty—one of two the Bolsheviks grudgingly signed there, one with the triumphant Finns, the other with the no less ebullient Estonians, who had just won their own hard-fought war of independence from Moscow —confirmed the new 1,600-kilometer-long Soviet-Fenno border, which, as the

Finns insisted, mirrored the one they had shared with Russia during bygone Grand Duchy days.

Additionally, in line with Helsinki's wishes, the treaty they signed, known as the Peace of Tartu, granted *Suomi* the valuable, ice-free Arctic port of Petsamo in exchange for a slice of the Karelian Isthmus, the 150-by-100-kilometer neck of land joining southeastern Finland with northwestern Russia, just as the benevolent Tsar Alexander II had promised his Finnish subjects back in 1860. The steamer carrying Paasikivi and the other exultant Finnish delegates back to Helsinki following that successful conclave, which effectively sealed Finland's century-long quest for independence from Russia, returned to resounding dockside cheers.

That was in 1920. Now, nearly two decades later, the ruddy-faced, sixty-nine-year-old Paasikivi—summoned back from what he had assumed would be his last posting in Stockholm, little thinking that he still had an entire political career ahead of him—prepared to leave to meet with Joseph Stalin, now the all-powerful head of a resurgent Soviet Union intent on reestablishing Russian influence in the Baltic basin. Now, in the second month of what would ultimately erupt into the five-year cataclysm known as the Second World War, it was, once again, the turn of the Communist heirs of Peter the Great and Alexander I to redraw the Baltic map in their favor. Now, as Paasikivi and his anxious four million countrymen knew, as he and his colleagues solemnly boarded the train for Moscow, they held nothing less than the fate of the Finnish nation in their hands.

And yet, anxious though they were, the Finns who flocked to the great train station were not of a mood to appease the Kremlin. Then, as the fateful train pulled out and the avuncular Paasikivi doffed his homburg in farewell, the crowd spontaneously began to sing Luther's hymn, "A Mighty Fortress Is Our God."

As Max Jakobson, who witnessed the scene as a sixteen-year-old youth, would later write, the serenaders who came to see Paasikivi off, as well as those who met his train down the line as it chugged across Karelia, "showed an astonishing, almost unnatural lack of alarm, as if through an undirected, spontaneous, almost organic effort of self-discipline, [they] were silently bracing themselves to face some force of nature. . . . They did not sing patriotic songs on behalf of a policy of appeasement." As Paasikivi told Stalin, "They won't sing for us if we tell them that we have given away Hanko," referring to the historic, strategically located Finnish fort-cum-spa situated on the southernmost tip of Finland that the Kremlin adamantly insisted on having back for itself.[2]

Seven weeks of on-and-off negotiations—which had ultimately foundered over the pivotal issue of Hanko—were helped along by a fabricated incident at the border town of Mainila. There, the Russians, stealing a page from the Germans (who had used a similar pretext for their invasion of Poland), arranged for several of their own soldiers to be killed by what they insisted was Finnish artillery fire. Christian Ilmoni thought he saw Paasikivi look out the window at his house, as the covey of bombers flew by. "I wonder what the Old Man must be thinking now?" he wondered, as he recounted that traumatic day, still crystal clear in retrospect, sixty-five years later.[3]

At first, the unusually low altitude of the Soviet planes—which had flown undetected across the Gulf of Finland from one of the Soviets' new, forcibly acquired Estonian air bases—caused some unsuspecting pedestrians to mistake foe for friend. "The planes were flying absurdly low, less than a thousand feet," Ilmoni recounted. "Some of the people walking nearby actually thought they were our own." "Our own?!" he shouted. *"Can't you see the Red star on the wing?"*[4]

Moments later came several massive explosions, followed by the sound of strafing, mixed with the slow tom-tom of the 40 mm Bofors anti-aircraft guns that had recently been placed at strategic points around the city, belatedly coming into action to meet the surprise attack. Now, instantly, Helsinkians knew the terrible truth. Once again, as had occurred innumerable times over the centuries, through the Swedish-Novgorodian wars of the 1300s, 1400s, and 1500s, through the Lesser and Great Wraths of the eighteenth century, through the Finland War of 1808 by which Finland was severed from Sweden and became a Russian grand duchy, *Suomi* was under attack from the enemy from the East. Once again, the city's ululating air raid sirens confirmed, the Russian "tyrant" had come—except that this time he had come from the air.

Mai-Lis Toivenen née Paavola, a veteran member of *Lotta Svard*, the Finnish women's auxiliary based in her hometown of Koivisto at the head of Viipuri Bay, who served in the organization along with 130,000 other Finnish women during the Winter War, also remembered that epochal morning. The seventeen-year-old Mai-Lis, like so many of her countrywomen, had joined the *Lotta Svard* in the upsurge of patriotism that swept the nation the previous summer, and had worked in a canteen during the autumn. Now she was attending her first class of the day in Viipuri (then Finland's second largest city, located a mere fifty kilometers from the border on the Karelian Isthmus) when the town's alarm began ringing, signaling the start of the Soviet attack.

Unlike her Helsinki kinsmen, Mai-Lis had no difficulty identifying the Red bombers. She had already seen plenty of Stalin's "falcons" (or "eagles") over the past summer as they engaged in arrant—and unchallenged—overflights of Finnish airspace. "I remember seeing how the Russian planes were flying so arrogantly over our skies. They flew so low one could see the faces of the pilots and the Red stars on their wings. It was very odd. Nevertheless we carried on with our lives as best we could."[5]

War tensions and Soviet bombers aside, Mai-Lis remembers the summer of 1939, the summer *avant le deluge,* as a good one. "It was very hot that summer," said Toivenen. "I remember swimming a lot."[6]

The following day, as war clouds continued to gather over northern Europe and the mobilization continued, Mai-Lis donned the curiously sexless smock of the *Lotta Svärd* and returned to her canteen work at the Koivisto Civil Guards house. Still, despite the proximity of war, including those "arrogant" Red fighters, the attractive teenager, like so many Finns of her sheltered generation who had been fortunate enough to grow up during the peaceful and prosperous 1930s, couldn't quite believe that war would actually come.

Then came the morning of November 30, the clanging school alarm and those droning Red airplanes. Moreover, *these* Red intruders were dropping bombs.

Moments later, as Viipuri was enshrouded in geysers of smoke and debris thrown up by the Russian bombs, her frightened teacher led Mai-Lis and her schoolmates to a stone house across the street for protection.

✱

Twenty-four kilometers and a windswept world away, in the middle of the Gulf of Finland, Mai-Lis's fellow auxiliary worker, Anna-Liisa Veijalainen, a member of the Society for the Care of Coastal Soldiers (RSHY), a women's organization which provided food and entertainment for the thousands of Finnish troops manning the dozens of fortresses along Finland's southern coast, was asleep in the upstairs room of the canteen hall of Tuppura, a small fortified island at the mouth of the Viipuri archipelago, on the morning of the Russian invasion.

A year before, Anna-Liisa, then a twenty-one-year-old "domestic science" (as home economics was then called) student in Viipuri, had bravely if somewhat reluctantly accepted an invitation from the SCCS—whose 5,000 volunteer workers labored in the shadows of the far better known *lottas*—to be hostess of Tuppura canteen. Evidently the prior holder of the post, a flighty type, had fled in a panic after the Czechoslovak crisis of 1938 prompted the increasingly nervous Helsinki government to augment its garrisons on many of its island outposts.

Although the job took some getting used to, Anna-Liisa found that she enjoyed her duties, which entailed making large quantities of coffee and doughnuts for the soldiers and coastguardsmen assigned to Tuppura, as well as otherwise making them comfortable. "Work at the canteen started to feel meaningful," she wrote in her moving 2007 memoir, *A Woman at the Front: 1938–45.* "We tried as best as we could to create some coziness for the boys, who at that time rarely got leaves, so the 'war nest' was the only place they could spend their free time."[7]

Anna-Liisa also grew fond of the relatively large "war nest" itself, a converted officer's club, which featured a spacious kitchen, parquet floors, a recreation room with a working gramophone and a relatively *au courant* pile of records, a quiet room where "her boys" could write letters home before flopping on the couch, and floor-to-ceiling windows that looked out on the restive green-blue sea.

She also fell in love with Tuppura itself, with its yellow expanse of stonecrop, chives pushing up from every crack, and wild pansies. "And no place," she adds, "had bigger lilies of the valley than that island. We carried huge bouquets of them and pansies to the tables of our canteen for the boys to admire."[8]

The main island was connected to Kuningassaari—King Island—so called because Gustavus III, the absolutist (and ultimately assassinated) eighteenth-century Swedish sovereign had once alighted there to survey his stormy domain. On the rocky tip of the islet there was a lighthouse that guided the large cruise ships that called on Viipuri, Finland's second largest port, as they navigated the treacherous reefs off the surrounding archipelago. To her delight, Anna-Liisa discovered that the adjoining islet also housed a small, elm-enclosed tennis court where she could relax in solitude for a while before crossing the little white bridge that connected Kuningassaari with the main island to return to the cozy canteen and her appreciative charges.

Like her junior land-based colleague Mai-Lis, Anna-Liisa remembers the summer of 1939 as hot and hectic. By this time she had been serving doughnuts and coffee to the men of Tuppura for nearly a year, while Finland prepared for a possible war with its increasingly bellicose neighbor.

All was relatively quiet until the morning of November 30, when the storm cloud of Red fighters arrived at Tuppura. It was, she later recalled, her co-worker Hertta Turunen's turn to go downstairs to heat the stove and boil the coffee for "the boys" that morning. "She barely had time to get downstairs before the kitchen telephone rang," Anna-Liisa wrote, "when simultaneously several airplanes roared above the fortress almost at rooftop altitude."[9]

Even under the hair-raising circumstances, however, her co-worker was careful of her manners: "As a girl of good upbringing Hertta took the time to knock on the door before shouting in shock: 'The aide-de-camp called, we are at war, and Major von Behr [the commander of Tuppura] ordered us to get to the pier in less than an hour and to leave the island.'"

Quickly throwing on her clothes, the formidable auxiliary worker promptly called the major back. "I explained to [him] that I simply could not depart in an hour without leaving the entire stock of canteen possessions unguarded. I was responsible for them!"[10]

Shortly afterward, after throwing the canteen cashbox into a suitcase and otherwise doing her best to secure the premises as the furious officer stormed down the pier, Anna-Liisa and her two co-workers were physically shoved into a small tugboat for the ride back to Uuraa, the largest of the islands in Viipuri Bay, where the Finns had greater forces and the women would presumably be better protected. Just in case, the self-serious major had told the skipper to make evasive maneuvers if and when the Russian planes returned, "although we found it difficult to see how a small tugboat could manage to evade airplanes on the open sea." Somehow they did.[11]

*

Eeva Kilpi, the noted Finnish writer, was then eleven years of age and living with her family in the hamlet of Hiitola, 200 kilometers north of Viipuri in Karelia. "Our house was on the shore of a small lake," she recalled, "and if I close my eyes I can imagine it is still summer. In Karelia it was always warm and sunny, it seems."[12]

Like many of her fellow Karelian schoolchildren, Kilpi had heard about the possibility of war and worried about it. "I used to pray to God to prevent the war. And I remember that I carried the fear of the war inside my child's heart. We didn't quite believe it would come, that it would come to Hiitola."[13]

"But then, when we were eating lunch [that day], suddenly we saw planes coming straight toward our house and father shouted that we should go immediately back to the cellar. And then the bombs started dropping."[14]

✳

Martha Gellhorn, the well-known American war correspondent, had just arrived in Helsinki the previous day to report on the growing tension between Finland and Russia, little suspecting that those tensions were about to explode into full-fledged war. Gellhorn was getting ready for breakfast in her room on the second floor of the venerable Hotel Kamp, where the foreign press was headquartered, when she heard the first bombs.

The glamorous thirty-six-year-old journalist had already gained international repute for her dispatches for *Collier's* from the Spanish Civil War, where she had met her current paramour, the novelist Ernest Hemingway, with whom she was then living in Cuba. In November, with Germany and Russia's joint annexation of Poland a *fait accompli,* Gellhorn, desirous of reestablishing her journalistic bona fides, wired her editor, Charles Colebaugh, in New York for a frontline assignment.

To the idealistic Bryn Mawr graduate, whose vivid dispatches about the American depression for the Federal Relief Emergency Administration had brought her to the attention of First Lady Eleanor Roosevelt, the stakes were even higher than they had been in Spain, now that as a result of the Nazi-Soviet nonaggression pact the world's two greatest totalitarian states were on the same antidemocratic side. "This was the war to save our skins," Gellhorn wrote. "Now one could only ally one's mind and heart with the innocents—the various unknown peoples who would be paying for [it] with all they had to love and lose."[15]

But where were these new innocents? Poland, divvied up between the Germans and the Russians after its valiant but futile five-week fight, was lost. The Western front was tense but quiet, as the French Army hunkered down in comfort behind the purportedly impregnable Maginot Line. Except for the war at sea, which was beginning to heat up, culminating in the dramatic Battle of the River Plate—the only story that would, briefly, take the world's attention away from the Soviet-Fenno confrontation that winter—and the occasional aerial skirmish between the Royal Air Force and the Luftwaffe over the English Channel, there was no war. There didn't seem to be a war, just a Phony War, as people called it.

Colebaugh advised Gellhorn to go to Finland. "He thought something might happen there." Like most Americans, Gellhorn knew as little about Finland as she did about Poland. She didn't even know where Finland was until she looked it up on a map. Apparently she hadn't even heard of Paavo Nurmi, the Finnish track runner and multiple Olympics hero of the 1920s, then the most famous Finn in the world except perhaps for Jean Sibelius, the great composer. Gellhorn did some more research. She liked what she found. In addition to being hardworking and fiscally responsible and fleet on their feet (and skis), the Finns, she read, were highly literate and talented beyond their numbers, "a good democracy"—a democracy worth saving.[16]

And so on November 10, armed with her Underwood typewriter and a signed letter of introduction from Eleanor Roosevelt, Gellhorn boarded a Belgium-bound Dutch freighter. Pausing a few days in still-neutral Belgium, Gellhorn crossed the North Sea again, this time by plane, bound for Stockholm, where she stopped for a day before finally flying on to Helsinki, arriving on the afternoon of November 29.

It was not yet three o'clock when Gellhorn's cab rumbled to a stop in front of the venerable seventy-year-old hotel, a legacy from Finland's Grand Duchy days. As Helsinki is wont at that time of year, the capital was already cold and dark. There was no time to take a tour of the city or get an update from her fellow correspondents, a motley crew of Americans, Britons, and sundry Scandinavians who had been covering the off-again, on-again Soviet-Fenno negotiations for the past month, and who, she could see, were massed downstairs desultorily going through the day's press communiqués. The storied old hotel, a longtime center of Finnish society and a watering hole for the Finnish intelligentsia at its palm-bedecked café, had been requisitioned by the government for use as a press center. On the night of November 29, perhaps a dozen or so correspondents were in residence there, reduced to filing "local color" features about Finnish dress and cuisine.

Exhausted from her 4,000-mile journey, Gellhorn trooped up the stately old hotel's well-worn carpeted steps to her blacked-out room. Minutes later she was asleep. Then came the bombs. "I'll be damned," Gellhorn muttered, as she ran to her window overlooking Esplanadi. Colebaugh, it turned out, had been right.[17]

"I saw a huge trimotor [sic] bomber go over at about 1,000 meters," she wrote Hemingway several days later. "Low and slow, just wandering around." But this plane was not dropping bombs but thousands of paper leaflets, which fell on the pavement or caught in the trees of the adjoining pocket park. As the reporter continued to peer outside, dozens of well-dressed Helsinkians, most of whom had been caught by surprise, began making their way to the *vaestosuoja,* the crude, timber-lined air raid shelters which had been constructed in the center of the park. Several stooped to pick up the Soviet leaflets.[18] One read: "SOLDIERS! PUT DOWN YOUR ARMS RETURN HOME AND PROTECT YOURSELF! PREVENT STARVATION! WE HAVE BREAD!" And another: "Finnish Comrades! We come to you not as conquerors, but as liberators of the Finnish people from the oppression of capitalists and landlords. We must not shoot each other. At the behest of the imperialists Cajander [Aimo Cajander, the Finnish prime minister], Mannerheim, etc. have broken off negotiations and transformed Finland into an armed camp, subjecting the Finnish people to terrible suffering."[19]

Those Helsinkians who bothered to read the leaflets were stupefied. The undernourished, downtrodden nation referred to in the crudely written Soviet pamphlets had no relation to the comfortable, well-fed country that they knew. Indeed, the crude agit-prop falling from the skies would have been laughable, if it weren't for those deadly serious bombs exploding nearby.

"Molotov's breadbaskets," an unknown wag had dubbed the explosives. The name stuck.

While the astonished newspaperwoman was observing the surreal scene outside her window at the Kamp, Herbert Berridge Elliston, the British-born correspondent for the Boston-based *Christian Science Monitor,* ran to his. The previous day, the forty-four-year-old Elliston, a veteran of the First World War who had fought in the Royal Horse Artillery, had trooped up to his room, just across from Gellhorn's, after investigating the contrived frontier incident at Mainila. "I scrambled from bed and looked out," Elliston wrote.[20] "It was a perfect winter morning, with the sun coming out of a blue sky, unflecked save for one cotton wooly ball cloud. Inside that cloud were Russian planes. Through the trailing steamer of the cloud a couple of planes could be seen in nebulous outline. With its destructive freight, the solitary cloud moved across the heavens like a Spanish galleon in full sail."[21]

After the two-month lull in the West following the fall of Poland, something was finally happening, and Elliston and his excited fellow reporters were right there for the action. "You got the illusion, indeed," Elliston gushed, "that the clouds must have borne the machines all the way across the Gulf of Finland. Presently the cloud arrived overhead a little to my right. All this time noise continued without cease—the dull detonation of exploding bombs breaking through a continual screech of air raid alarms and the rat-tat-tat of machine guns."[22]

At least the newsman was under no illusions about the objective of the raid. "This was a Blitzkrieg designed to overcome and conquer the Finns from the air. I watched intently," Elliston continued, "because victory or defeat in this type of diplomacy-war [sic] depends upon the behavior of the people." Evidently the raid was not having its intended effect. "There was no panic. The people in the park below stayed at the entrance of the bomb shelters and gazed skyward at the Soviet apparition."[23]

In the Kamp press room, Elliston began making calls, trying to find more about the surprise Soviet attack. His first impulse was to ring Risto Ryti, the long-time chairman of the Bank of Finland. Elliston had already met Ryti two years before, during a prewar fact-finding mission to northern Europe in his capacity as financial editor and columnist for the *Monitor*. He had been told beforehand that the central banker—who ran unsuccessfully for president that year against the grandfatherly Kyosti Kallio—was one of the best informed men in Europe.

Not that Ryti was of much help. When the reporter reached "Finland's Alexander Hamilton," as he admiringly described him, he was just as stumped as anyone by the Soviet attack. The perplexed financier told his journalistic acquaintance that he had heard a rumor that Norway had been given an ultimatum by Moscow to hand over the Arctic port of Narvik.[24] Had he heard anything about this? Ryti asked the equally puzzled reporter, as bombs crashed and sirens wailed in the background. Well, if he did, asked the polite Ryti—who, unbeknownst to him, would be appointed prime minister the following day to steer Finland through the crisis—would Elliston be so kind as to give him a ring?

"Of course," Elliston said, putting down the phone and shaking his head. "Storm over Europe!" he thought to himself. "What on earth had Stalin started in [this] part of the world? It was the beginning of a wild day."[25]

For his part, fifteen-year-old Harry Matso was too busy shepherding his schoolmates to safety to be afraid. He, too, had been singing his morning prayers—Jewish prayers—when the first Russian raiders dropped their mixed payload of incendiary bombs and propaganda.

As it happened, the school was located 500 meters from Hietaniemi, Helsinki's main cemetery, where the 200 pupils were quickly evacuated under the supervision of a gymnastics teacher. "Harry," the teacher told Matso, who was assisting him, after the orderly procession reached its destination, "pull all the children under the trees and behind the tombstones." The teacher, quite rightly, was concerned that the children's colorful clothing would make them easy targets for the strafing Soviet planes. Then, as a raider whizzed by a few hundred meters overhead, the teacher dove for cover himself as Matso followed.

When Matso carefully got to his feet, after the all-clear sounded a half-hour or so later, the youth saw that a house bordering the cemetery had been bombed to bits. A bereaved looking man emerged, carrying the limp body of a young girl, apparently his daughter, one of the ninety-six Helsinkians who died on that horrific day.[26]

Finnish prime minister Aimo K. Cajander, the same man whom several days before *Pravda* denounced as "a small beast of prey without sharp teeth and strength but having a cunning lust"—actually a mild-mannered sixty-year-old botanist who had headed Finland's Forest and Park Service prior to assuming office in 1937—was preparing to chair an executive session of the Finnish cabinet in its large, mirror-lined room on the second floor of the main government building, when the first flight of Soviet bombers entered Finnish air space at nine o'clock. In fact, the flight had been timed to coincide with the meeting—one of the few things about the Soviet attack plan that went right.[27]

The purpose of the emergency conclave was to discuss the meaning of the Kremlin's sudden and surprising decision to break off diplomatic relations the night before, which had been conveyed in a somewhat confusing note that the long-time Finnish minister to Moscow and former foreign minister Aarno Yrjo-Koskinen had abruptly been handed ten hours before.[28] "The only aim of our nation is to safeguard the security of the Soviet Union," stated the baffling communiqué, signed by Molotov, "and in particular Leningrad with its population of 3,500,000."

To be sure, the issue of Leningrad's vulnerability to the west—the concern that had originally prompted the Soviet "invitation" to discuss the issue with them—was not an unreasonable concern. After all, the Soviet Union's second largest city was located very close to the border between the two nations—and the Finns had had very close relations with Kaiser Wilhelm, who had sent an expedition of troops to Helsinki that secured the German-backed Whites' victory against the Soviet-backed Reds during the civil war, and reasonably good ones with his eventual successor, Adolf Hitler. One could well understand that concern—which would be validated in June 1941 when the Germans used the "Karelian gateway" to invade northwestern Russia. What was confusing, at least to the Finns, was the next part of Molotov's note.[29]

After accusing the Finnish government of bad faith, the blunt-talking *apparatchik*—who had replaced his more emollient predecessor, Maxim Litvinov, in May—continued: "We can no longer tolerate the present situation, for which the Finnish government bears full responsibility. Our government has decided it can no longer maintain normal relations with Finland."[30]

It certainly sounded like a declaration of war. On the other hand, Molotov seemed to leave some hope that the rapidly deteriorating situation between the two countries could still be resolved through negotiation, mysteriously stating that his country remained ready to meet Finland "more than halfway about territorial questions," including the Karelian peninsula, now half-divided between Finland and the USSR. He also thought he would even be ready to consider the question of "uniting the entire Karelian people and Karelia with their brotherly people, the Finns" (an outcome Molotov wound up ultimately achieving following the cession of Finnish Karelia, and the evacuation westward of virtually the entire population, though doubtless not in the way he envisioned).[31] To further confuse matters, the démarche reiterated the Soviet's utmost respect for Finland's sovereignty and independence.

Did Moscow want war or not? It was hard to figure out. The cabinet debate went back and forth. Then came the explosions of the first Soviet bombs. Now the confusion was over. Now Cajander and his fellow politicians knew, as they rushed to the window and saw smoke billowing from the city center, that Finland was at war.

✳

Actually, the cabinet was slightly behind the times. In point of fact, Finland and the Soviet Union had been in a state of belligerency since 6:50 that morning, when a goodly proportion of the nearly 2,000 field guns the Soviets had at the start of the war, which they managed to wheel up to the border without being detected by the laggard Finnish intelligence, unleashed a huge cannonade. The massive barrage, the largest such bombardment since the end of the First World War, was punctuated by the booming reports of the long-range guns of the naval fortress island at Kronstadt, thirty kilometers west of Leningrad, at the head of the Gulf of Finland.

Seconds later, the still snow-laden frontier became a roiling, roaring, white cauldron, as giant birch trees suddenly turned into twigs. Boulders went flying. The scattered farms and buildings within the fire zone, which had already been hastily evacuated by the government, disintegrated in a cloud of snow and dust. Unfortunately, neither Finnish intelligence, then overseen by an incompetent associate of Mannerheim's by the name of Colonel Lars Rafael Melander, nor the equally blind civil authorities, who were still not willing to believe that war would actually come, had done a very careful job of the evacuation, resulting in the capture of over 4,000 Finnish civilians.

Then, as green rockets fired up into the black sky, signaling the start of the assault, thousands of Soviet troops, many of them screaming and singing, plunged into the Rajajoki River (the river separating then Finnish Karelia and Russian Karelia, now called the Sestra) holding their weapons over their heads. They were followed by something that most Finns, or Finnish troops, had never seen before: tanks. Evidently the Kremlin meant business.

✳

As Harry Berner, then a corporal stationed in the medieval border town of Terijoki, recalled: "On November 28th, we had returned to the central barracks in Terijoki from a one week reconnaissance of the area. Then the next morning we were awakened by this gigantic artillery barrage, through which we could hear the big guns at Kronstadt. None of us had ever experienced, or even imagined, anything like it."[32]

Berner's unit, like most of the Finnish units that experienced the brunt of the Soviet attack, recovered from its shock soon enough and went into fighting retreat mode. "We were ordered out into the streets to delay the enemy as much as possible," he says. "I was posted by the general store. Then we saw Russian troops appear on the outskirts of town, as they poured out of the Rajajoki. We exchanged fire. Those were our orders: fight, delay, retreat. Of course, we didn't have much choice."[33]

The attack made for inspiring copy by Nikolai Virta, a well-known Soviet writer who had signed on with *Pravda* as a combat correspondent.[34] Except in tone, Virta's breathless account essentially squares with Berner's:

> On the stroke of 8 A.M. the signal was flashed and from the south the air was suddenly filled with the whistle of shells, the echo of their detonation, the deeper boom of howitzers and the muffled roar of the heavies. From Kronstadt one heard the distant echo of the great fortress guns. Thirty seconds later the horizon became a sheet of flame. The whole Finnish frontier was ablaze. Then began the rattle of machine guns, answered by those of the Finns. The cannonade continued for thirty minutes along the front of 140 kilometers, eighteen kilometers deep.
>
> Then green rockets shot up, signaling the Red infantry to attack and the troops charged, cheering, toward the frontier. Plunging into the icy waters of [Rajajoki] river, they started work on pontoon bridges. At 9:15 the section's first battalion crossed the frontier on bridges and entered Finnish territory. The forests, so silent an hour ago before the attack, suddenly filled with the roaring of the motors of tanks, the clank of caterpillar links and the sirens of the machines along the snow-covered roads.[35]

Interestingly, Virta was sporting enough to give Berner and his fellow defenders credit: "The enemy resists with determination." The tone of his reportage would become more vituperative and less charitable toward the Finnish enemy as the Soviet advance bogged down, and would continue thus as scores of mines and booby traps that Finnish sappers had left behind in Terijoki began blowing up his comrades, but for the moment Virta was all gung-ho.[36]

While Harry Berner and his colleagues were retreating before the onrushing Red hordes on the Rajajoki, 200 kilometers to the northeast, a mortarman by the name of Reino Oksanen was busy trying to stay warm. Like most of the men of his battalion, Oksanen hailed from the town of Messukyla near the southern central industrial city of Tampere. One of the strengths of the Finnish Army was that most of its men were drawn from the same area. "It was a good thing as we knew each other well when the fighting began. We knew each other's qualities."[37]

Oksanen completed his compulsory military training in 1935. It was then that he received instruction in the use of the light 81 mm mortar, one of nine such weapons assigned to each company. Not that he expected to put that training to use anytime soon. After all, Finland and Russia were at peace, or supposed to be. That all had changed in the fall of 1939. "Trouble had been brewing for a long time. But when they [the Army] started handing out calls for special training in

October, we knew that this was serious. We were told to bring winter clothing. And guns. We were supposed to have submachine guns, but in reality they were quite rare. I was given a standard Pystykorva rifle, as were we all."[38]

Oksanen and his fellow soldiers from Messukyla were first assembled in a Tampere linen factory along with the rest of the 16th Regiment, which was led by Lt. Aaro Pajari, who would later distinguish himself in the pivotal battle of Tolvajarvi. Oksanen slept side by side with his comrades on the floor of the factory. The next day, November 15, they were dispatched by train to the Luumaki-Taavetti area of Ladoga-Karelia, the area north of Finland's Lake Ladoga, where the entire division dug in.

Still, like the great majority of Finns, the men from Messukyla were skeptical that war would actually come: "Even then we debated amongst ourselves whether Finland would have to go to war." Still, the general mood was very defiant. "We took turns in bragging how we would annihilate the 'Russkies'—or at least some of us did," Oksanen said. "There was this one man from Tampere who was full of enthusiasm when the negotiations were underway. He said he would be disappointed if peace endured. He was eager, he said, for Russky blood. Of course, when the fighting began in earnest he amounted to nothing."[39]

Marshal Carl Gustaf Emil Mannerheim was having breakfast with his niece's husband, Bjorn Weckmann, at his mansion in Kaivopuisto, Helsinki's fashionable diplomatic district, when they were startled by the sound of bombs.

It was a sound, one suspects, that the venerable Finnish general, who at seventy-two retained the ramrod posture of the imperial chevalier he had once been, at once dreaded and welcomed. Dreaded because it signaled the start of a costly war which he knew, as chairman of Finland's defense council, a post he had repeatedly resigned in frustration, Finland was not properly prepared to fight and couldn't possibly win.

Once again, as it had twenty years before, the country of his birth needed him. First, in 1918, following Finland's declaration of independence from Bolshevik Russia, the Finnish government had turned to Mannerheim, asking him to take command of the disparate White counterrevolutionary forces and quash the nascent Red rebellion that Lenin had engineered. Additionally, he had to disarm the Russian troops still stationed in Finland. Few generals have ever been handed a more difficult set of tasks. But Mannerheim, who had spent the greater part of his adult life in Russia and was a member of Finland's Swedish-speaking minority and hitherto a virtual unknown in his own country, succeeded in bringing the brutal civil war, which cost an estimated 37,000 lives and included atrocities on both sides, to an end, securing the republic's independence.[40]

Following that, Mannerheim, who later that year left Finland out of disgust with its increasingly pro-German inclinations, was asked by the Finnish cabinet to turn around and help batten down Finnish sovereignty, by obtaining recognition from the skeptical Allies. Assenting, the versatile soldier-diplomat proceeded to wow both London and Paris with his dashing looks and courtly manners, as well as his manifest love and passion for his native land. "From capital to capital he went, pleading the cause for Finland," wrote Herbert Elliston. "He not only won recognition for Finland; he won friends for her."[41]

Befriending or even understanding the enigmatic former imperial officer was a different matter. No man could be curter, as Henry Bell, Great Britain's first consul to Helsinki, discovered when he came to call on Mannerheim one day at the London residence of the aloof former Russian general. Mannerheim had generally been genial to him, Bell wrote.

"One day, however," Bell continued, "Mannerheim was more brusque. He addressed me in Swedish instead of the usual English. He hardly acknowledged my formal greeting, and he would not listen to what I had come to say. Sitting behind his great table, with a map of Finland and another of Russia in front of him, he said severely, 'Herr Consul, do you bring me good news today?'"[42]

"I blushed and stammered: 'I regret, Your Excellency . . .'"[43]

"'Herr Consul,' Mannerheim interjected, 'if you do not soon bring me good news that Britain has recognized the independence of Finland, your visits will no longer be welcome. Good day.'"[44]

In the event, the inscrutable Mannerheim succeeded so well at his diplomatic mission that in December 1918, he was summoned back to Helsinki and named Regent. There was talk of making him king; certainly he had the ingredients of one. However, like George Washington, a figure to whom he was frequently compared, Mannerheim refused.

Instead, he preferred to run for president. However, Mannerheim, still bearing the bloody stigma of the excesses of the White forces during the recent civil war, in which scores of Finnish Communists had been summarily executed (and for which he seems to have been at least indirectly responsible), lost to the more homely, down-to-earth Kaarlo Juho Stahlberg. For most Finns, the distant, haughty, outspokenly anti-Communist general was, in the final analysis, too charged, too complicated a figure for them to entrust the peacetime destiny of their fragile young republic.[45]

And so "The Liberator," as he was now called, at the relatively young age of fifty-one, rode off into the Finnish sunset. The finicky Mannerheim now gladly turned away from the untidy maelstrom of Finnish politics and devoted himself to humanitarian pursuits, becoming a major supporter of the Finnish Red Cross and helping to found Finland's first child welfare organization. As Douglas MacArthur, the great American general who was in many ways Mannerheim's spiritual kinsman, once famously put it, old generals never die, they just fade away.[46]

Except that, like many early retired generals, Mannerheim wasn't very happy about just fading away. Photos of Mannerheim from the interwar period, during which he also served as chairman of the board of the commercial Bank of Helsinki, show him looking tense and distracted. At heart he was still a soldier. These were Mannerheim's wilderness years. Reputedly, at one point during the late 1920s, the old soldier was so bored with civilian life that he inquired about joining the Foreign Legion.[47]

In any event, if Mannerheim wished to fade away, he made sure that he did it within general viewing distance, renting a large manor house in the Kaivopuisto diplomatic district (the same one that today houses the Mannerheim Museum), filling it with all manner of trophies and military mementos from his far-flung life, including the year he spent reconnoitering China on horseback for the Russian intelligence service, and quietly waiting to see if his services were needed again.[48]

✱

They were. In 1931, as a resurgent Russia began to flex its military muscles, the newly elected president, Pehr Evin Svinhufvud, asked Mannerheim to assume the chairmanship of Finland's Defense Council, an advisory board charged with overseeing the build-up of Finland's armed forces and border defenses. Particularly important was the part man-made, part natural Karelian defensive line running from the Gulf of Finland through Summa to the Vuoksi River and ending at Taipale, which separated Finland from the Soviet Union and which Mannerheim himself initiated in 1918. Perhaps inevitably, it eventually took his name—even though he himself had very little to do with the ultimate design of the line itself.[49]

More recently, as the crisis with Russia reached a head, he also oversaw the partial mobilization of Finland's armed forces. This was Mannerheim's least happy posting. Angered at the refusal of the government, which had continued to remain complacent about the Soviet armed threat, to allocate adequate monies for defense, including for the as yet incomplete Karelian defensive line, he resigned the position several times, including, most recently, in June 1939. Informed of the negotiations between the government and Moscow before the talks broke down, Mannerheim had urged the cabinet to try to find some way of satisfying the Kremlin without forcing a fight. "We must absolutely come to an agreement," he urged.[50]

"Mannerheim knew how to be afraid," as Finnish historian Veijo Meri put it, "a good quality in a soldier." Also, to a surprising degree for a man who was on record as refusing to shake the hand of a Communist, he understood and even empathized with the Kremlin's legitimate strategic concerns, however clumsily expressed, about protecting the approaches to Leningrad in a future conflict.[51]

"The White General, whom Communist propagandists liked to call the 'butcher of the working class,' was probably the last person the Russians expected to see their point of view," Max Jakobson notes. "Yet Mannerheim stood then as later for moderation and flexibility in foreign policy, and as a former tsarist officer could appreciate the problems of Russia's defense planners."[52]

After all, as Stalin had pointed out in the Moscow talks, the British had used Koivisto as an anchorage to launch a successful motorboat raid on the Soviet base at Kronstadt in 1919 as part of their "unofficial" but decisive aid to newly independent Estonia, then battling its own Red insurgency (as Finland had also successfully done, with German help, the year before). The Russians had sound reason to be fearful, too. As Stalin told the skeptical Finnish delegates who questioned his concern about another Great Power using Finnish territory to attack Russia at some future date, "Everything can change in this world" (true indeed, as Stalin would again learn in June 1941, when his putative Nazi ally turned against the USSR).[53]

During the months leading up to the Moscow talks, Mannerheim continued to advise the Cajander government to cede the Russians as much as possible without destroying the country's power to put up a good defensive fight, proposing that it grant the Soviets several of the larger islands in the Gulf of Finland, as well as moving the Soviet-Fenno border westward and giving up some territory in Karelia. When the cabinet told him that it could not survive the public outcry that would follow even a suggestion of such sacrifices, Mannerheim went further, proposing to risk his own prestige and vouch for the necessity of such concessions. (The government did not take him up on the offer.)[54]

Moreover, he said, "The army cannot fight." Of course, this was an exaggeration. What Mannerheim meant, of course, was that the Finns did not have enough to fight with, which was perfectly true. By the fall of 1939, after a strenuous rearmament that he had instigated, the Finnish Army could place 265,000 men in the field, an extraordinary number for a nation of only 3.7 million. But what sort of equipment did they have with which to fight? The army possessed a total of ten battle-ready ancient Vickers-type tanks (half of which would be destroyed in a catastrophic engagement in February 1940). Some of the army's rifles dated to the 1890s.[55]

The then much-vaunted Mannerheim Line, often and wrongly compared to France's far more complex, far more sophisticated Maginot Line, in fact had only two "showcase bunkers," the so-called Poppius and Million Dollar bunkers that were anything like the Maginot's interconnected bastions; the other 110-odd strongpoints were fairly rudimentary. Moreover, as historian Carl Frederik-Geust points out, unlike the Maginot, the Mannerheim Line was meant to delay an invader, not repel him, although it did a pretty fair job of the latter when the test ultimately came. The Soviet writer and war correspondent Leonid Sobolev, who later accompanied the Russian marines who ultimately overcame those three forts and their less heavily armored interlocking defenses, was certainly impressed:[56]

This powerful position of two armored bunkers, or, more accurately, forts, was built over several years. . . . The art and skill of the best European engineers were invested into this ensemble of fortifications, which even the first-class European defence sector would envy. All forts, bunkers, trenches and snipers' nests protect each other. Then the best trained Finnish Home Guards were brought here, they were shown this concrete and steel, anti-tank rocks, underground galleries and mines, camouflaged anti-tank gun positions, sniper nests in trees, ten rows of barbed wire and full ammunition storages. . . . One could, indeed, hold out here as long as one had to. The splinters of our heaviest shells, which exploded next to the bunker, did no harm. Even a direct hit from a heavy round could only shake this monstrous shell; bite off a chunk of concrete, but not more. A direct hit from artillery at long range is a matter of pure luck, one chance in a thousand.

Of course, the army would still fight. And so would Mannerheim. Although there was no explicit agreement about this, it came to be understood that, if worse came to worst and war broke out, Mannerheim himself would become commander-in-chief.

Now, on that fateful morning of awakening, as Russian bombers darkened the skies over Helsinki, Mannerheim knew that his moment had come. Now, once again, his country needed him, and that was all that mattered. In the end, he wasn't so complicated after all. Mannerheim was going to do what he was born and bred to do, and the opportunity reinvigorated him.

Inside Mannerheim's trophy-festooned manse was a painting by his old friend and comrade-in-arms Akseli Gallen-Kallela, showing a group of imaginary Finnish ski soldiers swathed in white, apparently advancing through a forest clearing to strike at the historic Russian foe. The artist had executed it forty years before, in 1899, to protest Tsar Nicholas II's notorious ukase suspending Finnish autonomy. Gallen-Kallela, who died in 1931, evidently had considered the painting too provocative to display publicly and had kept it as part of his private collection. After the civil war, in which the passionate nationalist served as Mannerheim's aide-de-camp, the artist, also known as "Finland's painter," had given his old commander the painting as a gift.[57]

Mannerheim had hung the canvas on a prominent place of the wall of his study. Did he steal a look at it on this day, November 30, 1939, as that martial fantasy was about to become a reality and he suited up for his new command? Or perhaps he thought about Gallen-Kallela's son Jorma, then serving as an officer on the front line in Karelia, on whom he also doted.[58]

As smoke from the first Russian bombs rose in the distance, Mannerheim, in full regalia, strode to the Ministry of Defense on Korkeavuorenkatu, just a few minutes away from his Kaivo home. This was a different Mannerheim from the careworn elder of weeks before. Gone were the depression and weariness of old age. "I hereby give notice that I am assuming the post of commander-in-chief of which so much has been said," Mannerheim peremptorily declared.[59]

The minister informed his top commander about the situation. The situation was not good. The Soviets, who evidently had been building up their forces for weeks, had invaded Finland at nine points along the winding, 1,600-kilometer border separating the two countries, including a main thrust across the isthmus. Niukkanen estimated the invading force would be at least two million men, backed up by at least five thousand pieces of heavy artillery and several hundred tanks, plus a thousand planes.[60] (Niukkanen's figures were somewhat off: the initial striking force comprised 400,000 men, 2,000 tanks, 2,000 field guns, and 2,000 planes, all of which would be doubled or more by the end of the war). In addition to Helsinki, the minister reported, numerous other Finnish towns and cities, including Viipuri and Lahti, were reporting air raids.[61]

There was more. The Soviet navy had also been in action, attacking several islands and coastal fortresses with heavy gunfire. If Mannerheim was daunted by the magnitude of the attack, or by the leviathan task that now awaited him, he did not show it. Taking his leave of Niukkanen, Mannerheim next visited President Kallio, where he withdrew his most recent resignation and formally assumed the post of commander-in-chief, before returning to his house.[62]

Word of Mannerheim's reappointment quickly spread. For most Finns, that was all they needed to know. That night, as the skyline of Helsinki was wreathed in flames, Herbert Elliston took note of the electric effect of Mannerheim's return on the populace: "As I walked among the ruins of Helsinki's bombed streets, I saw bill posters [of Mannerheim's appointment] being put up," he wrote. "I can vouch for the fact that no proclamation ever geared a nation into fighting mood more successfully than the proclamation making Mannerheim commander-in-chief."[63]

The second raid, a shorter but more lethal one involving even more bombers, began at 2:55 P.M., just as Helsinki was beginning to recover from the first one. This time, however, the Soviet planes only carried bombs and incendiaries.

Once again, as during the first raid, which evidently had been aimed at Malmi Airport, the city's recently inaugurated international airport, the raiders' aim was abysmal. Targeting the main railroad station, whence Paasikivi had embarked on his successive, frustrating sorties, the bombers instead battered the large square in front of it, including a commuter bus that had just taken on its passengers, instantly incinerating it; a photo of the bus with the mangled remains of several Finnish civilians, one of the indelible images of the terror attack, splayed across the front pages of the world's press the next day.[64]

Several fire bombs were also dropped on Helsinki's prestigious Technical University on Bulevardi, one of the capital's most elegant avenues, all but obliterating it and killing a number of staff and students; the Russians also managed to break most of the windows of the large, nearby Soviet legation to the considerable satisfaction of the population.

After unleashing their bombs, the planes from the second raid swooped down to machine gun targets of opportunity, mostly fleeing civilians, wounding or killing dozens more before returning to their bases in Estonia, while further eastward, their fellow Soviet airmen returned to their bases in Leningrad after wreaking havoc on Viipuri.[65]

The Soviet planes were at brazen, treetop level, recalled Olavi Eronen, then a message runner from Viipuri stationed with his regiment at Kuolemajarvi, a small village located on the western side of the Mannerheim Line. Like many if not most of his fellow soldiers, Eronen was taken completely by surprise by the outbreak of hostilities.

"We did not believe a war would come," he later recalled. "We had this non-aggression pact with the Russians, so people stayed in their homes until the last moment. The night before I was at home and went to the sauna. At seven in the morning I left for my regiment. When I walked down the steps, my father opened the window and shouted that the war had started. The station master at Terijoki had called and said the big guns at Kronstadt had opened up."[66]

As the cannonade continued, Eronen hastened to the small town of Seivasto, near the fire zone, to evacuate the stunned residents. Looking up, he saw a fleet of Soviet bombers bound for Viipuri and other points west. "The sky was full of planes." Several hours later, the raiders came back, but at much lower altitude. "For some reason, they had been told to fly really low, just above the treeline. Apparently they had a doctrine that this was the safest way to return. Anyway, as I was escorting the villagers, I turned around after I heard a strange noise and realized that one of the Red planes was flying directly towards me. He was so low I felt that I could almost touch him with my hand."[67]

"I fired several shots at it with my rifle, but apparently I did not hit anything vital," noted Eronen. Soon he thought better of such foolishness. "Only later did it occur to me that those planes had many gunners on them and that I was an easy target standing in the open." For its part, the Soviet Air Force, which would lose numerous bombers to ground fire during the successive raids of the next three days as Finnish anti-aircraft crews sprang into action, would later revise its policy. "Later in the war they did not fly so low," Eronen wryly observed.[68]

Martha Gellhorn was having a hasty, belated repast at the Kamp when the second Russian raid began. "I never felt such explosions. The whole place rocked. Must have been like March in Barcelona," she wrote to Hemingway, referring to the Fascist Italian forces' attack on the republican Catalonian capital and its outskirts in March 1938; the two had developed a shorthand based on their experiences in Spain. "I went out and there was a huge curtain of smoke rolling down the street and people were saying: Gas-Gas. That was pretty awful, I may tell you. I left my mask in New York and I really thought: okay we are lost."[69]

Fortunately, it was a false alarm, one of the many noxious rumors that wafted about the shell-shocked capital during those first terror-filled days. There was no gas used in battle, one of the few horrors of the First World War that had not carried over into the Second, at least as yet. Another rumor, which also proved false—or exaggerated—was that the Russians were going to drop parachute troops on the capital. In fact, the Russians, who were probably the most advanced country in terms of paratroop tactics in the world and had made parachuting something of a national sport, did drop small groups of reconnaissance troops, including a number of Finnish-speaking spies, in several parts of the country, including the Karelian Isthmus and the Petsamo region in the far north, to disastrous effect: the vast majority were captured and shot on the spot, or picked off while still airborne. If they did manage to land safely, the paratroopers had difficulty assembling in the thick Finnish trees. Nevertheless, the very use of these troops—the first time this novel form of warfare was employed on a modern battlefield—was sufficient to send a wave of terror that reached Helsinki.[70]

But no, there was no gas. And no parachutists—at least as yet. Relieved, the intrepid American reporter plunged outside, following the smoke, soon coming across "3 colossal fires, four apartment houses—just plain people's homes—burning like tissue paper. One house, by a gas station," Gellhorn continued, "had a vast hole blown in its side and a man shapeless and dead the way our little man on the corner of Florida [was]," invoking her and Hemingway's shared memories of the Fascist bombing of Barcelona three years before.[71]

Accompanying Gellhorn were two Italian journalists who had also just arrived in the Finnish capital in time to see the first Soviet bombs fall. Enraged by the memory of the Spanish war, which Francisco Franco, the rebel leader and current (and future) dictator had won with the aid of his fellow German and Italian advisors against their Republican foes and Soviet advisors, the American spitfire couldn't resist the opportunity to goad the Italians. "Now you see what it's like to be on the other side, gentlemen, don't you?" she asked. Later, Gellhorn would be surprised to find that those same Italian Fascist journalists she lambasted that afternoon were actually—along with their enraged leader, Benito Mussolini—on the right side, the Finnish side, the democratic side this time, at least for the moment.[72]

In the event, Il Duce had had little sympathy or understanding for the non-aggression pact his ally, Nazi Germany, had signed with the Soviet Union. To him, as well as to many of his Fascist subjects, the Russian invasion of Finland was simply Communist aggression, and he had no qualms about saying so, even writing Adolf Hitler a pointed note to this effect. Over the next few days, Rome, like many world capitals, was the scene of violent anti-Soviet protests as well as effusive demonstrations of sympathy for Finland. Hundreds of enraged Italians deluged the Finnish embassy offering to take up arms for Helsinki.[73]

Indeed, Mussolini, for his part, was so put out about the Russian action that Hitler dispatched his foreign minister, Joachim Ribbentrop, to Rome to get him to calm down and not say or do anything that might offend the Kremlin.

Not that Hitler was particularly happy with the Russian invasion himself. Although the pact he had signed with Stalin had theoretically given the Kremlin a free hand to operate in the Baltic, he had at least expected to be warned of such a drastic move. He had not. Moreover, Hitler, like many Germans, felt a natural bond with and sympathy for Finland, with which Germany had long enjoyed a special political and cultural relationship dating back to the nineteenth century. When Finnish high school students studied a second language—or, rather, a third one, after Swedish, the language of their prior mother country—it was German. It was an expedition of German troops in 1918, during the civil war, which had helped decide the matter in favor of the Whites, under Mannerheim's command, thus securing Finnish independence.

In many ways, Finland, which had suppressed its own abortive Fascist putsch in 1932, but still had many officers or former officers of a right-wing bent— including one, Kurt Wallenius, who would rise to fame during the Winter War— was a natural partner for the Third Reich (as it would become during the ensuing Continuation War, when the two countries were co-belligerents). The Finnish and German armed forces, including the Finnish and German intelligence services, also enjoyed extensive cooperation during the 1930s.

However, for the moment, Hitler needed the Russians more than he needed the Finns, as much as he admired them and their commander-in-chief, so the Fuhrer, who was capable of compromise (at least at that stage of the war), said nothing (at least publicly), and told his unhappy Italian ally to do the same.[74] Joseph Goebbels, the Nazi propaganda chief, also hewed to the party line, publicly reprimanding the Finns for their obstinacy and ties with Nazi Germany's principal declared enemy, England, although for several days he allowed the first upbeat Finnish military communiqués to run side by side with the equally roseate (and misleading) Soviet ones, before he reluctantly suppressed them.

No, those Italian journalists who were the butt of Martha Gellhorn's barbed remarks were actually on Finland's side, too. The unexpected Russo-Fenno conflict, which most observers assumed would be a quick walkover, blurred a lot of ideological lines—at least at first.

Indeed, it would take some days before Gellhorn and a lot of other people could comprehend the surprise Russian attack and all of its political implications. All she knew for the moment was that she had unwittingly stumbled onto the biggest story in the world, and she went with it, turning in some of the finest prose of her career. "War started at nine o'clock promptly," began "Bombs from a Low Sky," her first lengthy dispatch from Helsinki for *Collier's*.

The people of Helsinki stood in the streets and listened to the painful rising and falling and always louder wail of the siren. For the first time in history they heard the sound of bombs falling on their city. This is the modern way of declaring war. The people moved unhurriedly to bomb shelters or took cover in doorways and waited.

That morning Helsinki was a frozen city inhabited by sleepwalkers. The war had come too fast and all the faces and all the eyes looked stunned and unbelieving. . . . There were five great explosions and afterward the stillness itself was dreadful. Then a rumor flew through the quiet, broken streets: poison gas. Anything was believed now.

We shuffled through broken glass in the streets. The gray afternoon was darker with smoke. The bombed houses on this block were so shrouded in flames that you could not see through into the ruins. Turning left, we ran toward the light of another fire. The Technical School, a vast granite square of buildings, had been hit. The houses around it and on the next street were gutted clean, with flames leaping out of all the empty windows. Firemen worked fast and silently but there was nothing much to do except try to put out the fire. Later they could dig for the bodies.[75]

Clearly, despite the weeks of preparations and drills, the city authorities—who until recently had been more concerned with the preparations for the eagerly anticipated 1940 Helsinki Summer Olympic Games and had only established a civil defense office for the capital but two months before—were badly caught off guard by the aerial firestorm. Witness the helter-skelter nature of the evacuation of the capital that began immediately after the first raid, which particularly shocked Gellhorn:

At a street corner, in the early oncoming night, a woman flagged a bus and put her child on it. She did not have time to kiss the child good-bye and no one said anything. The woman turned and walked back into the bombed street. The bus was collecting children to take them away, anywhere, no one knew but out of the city. A curious migration started that afternoon and went on all night. Lost children, whose parents were gone in the burning buildings or were separated in the confusion of the sudden attack, straggled out alone or in twos and threes, taking any road that led away from what they had seen. Days later the state radio was still calling their names, trying to find their families for them.[76]

Just as she had in her partisan but essentially reliable reporting from Spain, Gellhorn allowed her anger at the aggressor to seep through: "I thought it would be fine if the ones who order the bombing would walk on the ground some time and see what it is like."[77]

Back at the Kamp, Gellhorn's colleagues were jubilant. Now, after all the weeks of waiting, finally there was something to write about. One Canadian journalist had just come back from the Western front, where all was still quiet, far too quiet. "Only [a few] casualties over there and we've been hanging over there for weeks," he exclaimed. Obviously this new dustup between Finland and the Soviet Union was going to be a better show. One Danish journalist, who had witnessed the bomb attack on the train station and the attendant carnage, was perversely delighted. "I have an idea that this is going to be the best story of my career," the pleased scribe declared to no one in particular. "I've just been plain lucky. Everything has gone so well for me. Bus burning and everything."⁷⁸

Pekka Tiilikainen, a younger reporter for YLE, Finnish state radio, whose dispatches from around the battlefront would make him a star, interviewed some of the troops who bore the brunt of the first fighting: "We then came to Oravakyto," Tiilikainen wrote in his memoir, *Radioselostajana tulilinjoilla* (Radio reporter at the front), "where we met the first troops who had been in the fighting. This was an infantry unit. In a darkened house we learned what war feels like."⁷⁹

Amongst the soldiers Tiilikainen interviewed was a lieutenant by the name of Viskari and a sergeant named Reponen. "I asked them only one thing: 'How did it look and feel?' Usually in radio reporting, these questions are too bland to elicit a response, but not this time. [The boys] told of being right on the border when a few guards on a bridge met their deaths from a hail of bullets from an enemy machine gun. And then the action started."⁸⁰

According to the Finns Tiilikainen interviewed, they had gotten the better of the invaders: "The Russians tried to attack, but were bloodily beaten back. Some of the enemy were able to advance in the gloom right up to a machine gun emplacement, but a merciless hail of bullets beat the Ivans back. The first attack was repulsed," wrote Tiilikainen in Manichean terms popular at the time, "and the cradle of Karelia drank up the blood of the enemy. The snowdrifts were painted red."⁸¹

For his part, Geoffrey Cox, the veteran correspondent for the *Daily Express* who arrived in Helsinki on the evening of the thirtieth to find the city wreathed in flames, couldn't comprehend the reasoning behind the raid.

"Why did the Soviet carry out the raid?" wondered Cox, a native New Zealander who also had covered the Czechoslovak crisis and the Spanish Civil War for the British daily. "Was it a deliberate attempt to stun civilian morale? The answer [was] known only to the commanders of the Red Army." Cox concluded—and examination of Russian documents bears him out on this point—that the raid was intended for military objectives, but had been carried out "clumsily."[82]

And yet the Kremlin must have known that even if the raid had been more accurate, it still would have caused civilian casualties. "What I believe to be nearest to the truth," Cox decided, "is that the Russians made the attack for the same reason that they were to begin their invasion with inferior troops—because they thought the social structure of Finland was so rotten [that] one push would dislodge the present rulers [and] bring home the fact that the Russians meant business."[83]

If so, as subsequent events would prove, the Russian rulers were badly misguided: "The Finns were more socially united than at any period since 1918. This sudden blow from the sky cemented cracks that still remained in that unity. Men of the Left who would have resented the return of Mannerheim were so infuriated by the brutality of this raid that they supported the war wholeheartedly."[84]

"Indeed," Cox continues, "the raid and the photographs it provided were used throughout Finland in the first month of the war as the main weapon of home propaganda. On every front I was to visit later man after man spoke angrily of this afternoon of November the 30th. I saw newspapers with photographs of the burning streets of Helsinki in peasants' homes and workers' flats all over the country. Not a little of the steel strength of Finnish morale in [the war] was due to the raid on Helsinki."[85]

Eleven hundred kilometers away, CBS Radio Berlin bureau chief William Shirer, then on holiday in Switzerland, angrily listened to the first reports of the Soviet sneak attack from the capital of their erstwhile German allies. Constrained by the dictates of the Soviet-friendly German censorship, Shirer later reported the attack in equal tones.[86]

Privately, the noted American broadcaster could hardly contain himself. "The Soviet Union has invaded Finland!" he confided to his journal, which would later become the famous *Berlin Diary.* "The great champion of the working class, the mighty preacher against 'Fascist aggression,' the righteous stander-up for the 'scrupulous and punctilious observance of treaties,' (to quote Molotov of a month ago), has fallen upon the most decent and workable little democracy in Europe in violation of half a dozen 'solemn' treaties. I have raged for thirty hours," the livid radioman wrote, "[and] could not sleep."[87]

Across the Atlantic that evening, in Washington, D.C., a train bearing President Franklin D. Roosevelt back to the capital from a short trip to his vacation home in Warm Springs, Georgia, was just pulling into Union Station when a special delegation from the State Department, comprising Secretary of State Cordell Hull and Undersecretary Sumner Welles, drove to the terminal to personally inform the president of the news of the Russian offensive. Special late editions with banner headlines about the attack were already on sale at the great terminal where the somber group went to meet Roosevelt's train.

Roosevelt, who six years previously had taken the politically unpopular move of recognizing the Soviet regime, was nonplussed by the news. Several hours earlier the cable informing the State Department of the Soviet invasion had triggered an internal debate there about the proper response, which would continue to roil Washington for weeks to come. The normally even-keeled Welles, in a rare temper, advocated breaking relations with the Kremlin. Hull, his ever-cautious superior, was doubtful. Such a decision might be exceedingly popular, he noted, but gradually the tide of indignation would recede and the State Department would be left "holding the bag."[88]

Twenty-five years before, President Woodrow Wilson had been equally shocked by Germany's invasion of neutral Belgium—the "rape of Belgium," it was called; the invasion, along with the well-publicized atrocities against Belgian civilians, was the first of a series of steps which helped break down American isolationism, and which led, two years later, to America joining the war.

Now Roosevelt used similar terminology to describe Russia's invasion of Finland. "This dreadful rape of Finland," the president described it in a letter to his friend, Thomas McVeagh. "People are asking why one should have anything to do with the present Soviet leaders because their idea of civilization and human happiness is so totally different from ours. The whole of the United States is not only horrified but thoroughly angry."[89]

At the same time, the interventionist-minded president was legally bound to follow a policy of strict neutrality. It was a policy FDR had been working to whittle down via a series of neutrality acts, a process that had begun in 1937 with his "Quarantine the Aggressor" speech in Chicago—a process that would culminate, two years later, with the United States becoming a virtual co-belligerent of Great Britain before the December 1941 Japanese attack on Pearl Harbor vitiated American neutrality. Unquestionably, the Russian invasion of Finland was one stop on that journey. As Assistant Secretary of State Adolf Berle recorded in his diary several days after the Russian invasion, "U.S. neutrality is not as safe as it was a week ago."[90]

However, as much as FDR and millions of Americans sympathized with Finland, the fact remained that large segments of the American body politic, particularly business and labor, were still firmly isolationist (and would continue to be right up until Pearl Harbor). Evidently all options were discussed at State, up to and including going to war.[91]

While Roosevelt pondered the matter, he agreed to meet with the Finnish minister, Hjalmar Procope. Procope, who had become a familiar person in the U.S. business world in the 1930s owing to his position as head of the Finnish Paper Association, had agreed to head the small, three-man Finnish legation in 1938 as tensions with the Soviet increased, with a view toward enlisting American diplomatic support to intercede with the Kremlin.

Tall, suave, and well-spoken, Procope was already a fixture on the Washington cocktail party circuit. Now that Finland had suddenly become the *cause célèbre* of the Christmas season, he would become even more sought after, never failing to seize an opportunity to use his considerable charm to plead Finland's case. Meeting with the president, Procope urged Roosevelt to break off relations with the Kremlin. FDR agreed to consider it. At the same time, he hoped to be able to help broker a peace between the Finns and the Soviets, and he wondered if sundering relations with Moscow would prove counterproductive in that regard. (Ultimately, on the advice of Hull, he decided against it.)[92]

Still, U.S. prestige, as well as popular opinion, demanded that the chief executive make a strong statement on the matter. Roosevelt's first move was so cautious as to be virtually meaningless: to issue a strong but generalized statement deploring the bombing of civilians that had occurred that day in Helsinki and urging both sides in the as yet undeclared war to forswear more such bombing. As one writer aptly put it, "The United States was now on record as being against evil."

At the same time, the pigskin-loving president, former assistant naval secretary and diehard Navy football fan who was a fixture at the annual Army-Navy game in Philadelphia, had intimated that because of the Soviet invasion he was considering not attending the game; after seven years in office, the social schedule of the savior of America was followed with the same interest as that of a king. Not attending a football game: now *that* would be a statement.

By the following day Roosevelt had considerably ratcheted up his rhetoric. He also made it perfectly clear who the bad guys were: "The Soviet naval and military bombings within Finnish territory has come as a profound shock to the government and people of the United States. Despite efforts made to solve the dispute by peaceful methods . . . one power has chosen to resort to force of arms."

Strong words. And the president still hadn't decided yet whether he was going to attend the Army-Navy game.[93]

However, 350 Finnish Americans—in its excitement, the *Helsingin Sanomat*, the leading Finnish daily, reported 3,000—had already decided what they were going to do: they were going to fight! A week later, the men, who called themselves the Finnish American Legion, would sail for Helsinki to join the 12,000 other volunteers from around the world who voyaged to Finland to join the fight.[94]

✻

On the other side of the Bothnian Sea, the government of the other neutral country most affected by the war, Sweden, was also having an internal debate about how to react to the invasion. Some cabinet members, led by the activist foreign minister Rickard Sandler, advised all aid short of war, including setting up a joint defense with Finland to defend the Aland Islands, the semi-autonomous,

Swedish-speaking, Finnish-controlled archipelago lying between the two countries. Other ministers demurred. Unlike the distant United States, which was in no immediate danger itself no matter what action it took, Sweden had to watch out: the wrong move could immediately bring down Russian—or German—bombers on its head.[95]

Publicly, the government, led by Per Albin Hansson, the devoutly neutralist Social Democratic prime minister, maintained a strict silence. There was no doubt, however, how the Swedish public felt about the matter. "It is difficult to express the feeling of horror and anger that has swept the entire population of Sweden, Norway, and Denmark as the result of Russia's attack on Finland," wrote the Nordic correspondent for the *New York Times* on December 2. That same day 2,000 Swedish students descended on the Finnish embassy in Stockholm, crying, "We are for Finland!" and other pro-Finnish slogans, much as their kinsmen in Rome, Paris, and other cities had done.[96]

Back in the Karelian combat zone, Olavi Eronen was busy shepherding the benumbed villagers of Seivasto westward to safety behind the Mannerheim Line.

"I left at nightfall and gathered the people of the village together. Of course all the able-bodied men were in the service, so only women, children, and the elderly were left. Never have I seen such silent people. Nobody said anything. Each one had their valuables wrapped up in a sheet. That was all that they could take with them. Of course every one left willingly. No one wanted to be overrun by the Russians. I drove them behind the lines, then another truck took them from there."[97]

Amongst those who were evacuated from Karelia were Eeva Kilpi and her family. "We were very much afraid of being taken to Siberia," she said. "Every child knew, rightly or wrongly, that they could be taken to Siberia. And that was a terrible feeling. We also knew that it was a total fight, that if we're not safe here, we're not safe anywhere."[98]

To be sure, the first Russian troops to penetrate into what had formerly been Finnish Karelia found the going surprisingly easy, as Dmitri Krutshih, then in command of a small Soviet patrol unit, later remembered. Krutshih had been told that there was a large wooden fence at the border.

"So at 6 A.M. on November 30th we arrived at the border, I asked the border guards, where is the Big Fence? There was no fence, just a path, that was it. So we captured the first village. Then we moved forward. We captured the second village. Then we entered the third village. . . . We surrounded Finnish forces and blew them to pieces."[99]

Seven hundred and twenty kilometers to the north, along the densely wooded, lightly defended Soviet-Fenno border near the central Finnish parish of Suomussalmi, advance elements of the Soviet 163rd Division, a scratch division that the Leningrad Military District had cobbled together for the operation, was also making excellent time. Its mission was to cut Finland off at its waist.

The thousand or so people living in that remote area, mostly farmers and their families, most of whom were only vaguely aware of the recent tensions between the two countries, were, if anything, even more surprised by the Russian invasion than their countrymen in the south, as one young resident of the nearby village of Saarikyla recalled.[100]

E. (who the author interviewed, but who prefers to remain anonymous), was a sixteen-year-old daughter of a farmer, calmly going about her normal chores on the afternoon of the November 30 when her father went out for a walk. "When he returned," said E., "father said that there was a big fire in the direction of Juntusranta [another village]. He was wondering what was burning there."[101]

In the event, they soon learned, the smoke was coming from the main school building in Juntusranta, which the few panic-stricken Finnish civil guardsmen in the area had put to the torch in order to impede the rapidly advancing Soviet forces.

The family soon discovered just how rapidly the Russians were advancing several hours later when E.'s father left the house to further investigate and ran smack into a number of Russians soldiers on horseback. Soon other mounted Russians appeared in the window of the farmhouse itself, to E. and her mother's consternation.

"My mother said that I must not go out, he will kill us," said E. "But I decided to go out to show them that there were only children inside. As I left, I ran into one of the soldiers and we looked each other in the eyes. 'Finski soldat?'" Were there any Finnish soldiers, the Russian asked in broken Swedish? "I said no, and with my hand I tried to show that we were only children," E. recalled in an emotional interview sixty-nine years later. "The soldier showed me his gun and asked me if I was afraid. But I was brave and said no. He laughed."[102]

All in all, the commanders of the four armies and twenty-six Soviet divisions participating in the initial, border-long assault could report to Kliment Voroshilov, the clueless defense commissar who was nominally in charge of the operation, that all was going according to plan.

What was the plan? Actually, there were two plans: the original plan, emphasizing one main thrust through the Karelian Isthmus, drawn up by Boris Shaposhnikov—previously the head of the Leningrad Military District, now head of the Soviet general staff—reflecting a clear-eyed assessment of Finnish capabilities, which Stalin had angrily discarded; and a subsequent, much flashier one, clearly influenced by the recent German blitzkrieg of Poland, and which the widely dispersed Soviet forces were now executing.[103]

The first plan, which Shaposhnikov had developed during the summer of 1939 when the possible necessity of a "retaliatory strike" against Finland first arose, before the outbreak of the Second World War, had—wisely—assumed "a harsh and difficult war lasting months, at least."[104]

Shaposhnikov, one of the few tsarist holdovers who had managed to reach high rank in the Red Army, as well as survive the purges of the 1930s, knew of which he spoke. He had visited Finland several times during his long career, including during his posting as commander of the Leningrad Military District— the same entity that had been entrusted with the new strike against Finland— between 1935 and 1937, before he had been promoted to chief of staff. He also—presciently—emphasized that any war against Finland had to be carried out quickly, or she would receive significant help from outside.[105]

Stalin, however, who generally valued the fifty-seven-year-old general's advice, scoffed at the latter's conservatism. "You are asking for such immense strength and resources to defeat a country like Finland," he declared.[106]

Instead, Stalin ordered Kirill Meretskov, who had succeeded Shaposhnikov as head of the Leningrad Military District, to draw up a new plan that would accomplish the desired result in a much shorter time. Meretskov later recalled the extraordinary scene when he met The Boss (as he called him). Also present was "an important Comintern official and well-known activist of the world Communist movement" by the name of Otto Ville Kuusinen. "I was told of the concern caused to our leadership by the anti-Soviet line of the Finnish government."[107]

"Finland," Stalin said, "could easily become a bridgehead for anti-Soviet action by either of the two main imperialist groupings—the German or the Anglo-French. If Finland should strike, various counteractions were made open to us. I was made responsible for drawing up a plan to protect the frontier from aggression, and to plan a counterattack against the Finnish armed forces."[108]

"An amazing scene!" wrote the Russian historian Edward Radzinsky. "Not one of those present, of course, seriously thought that little Finland would attack the immense [Soviet] empire. Nobody seriously believed that Hitler, with whom they were just concluding successful negotiations, or England or France, to whom they were also talking, would launch an 'action against the Soviet Union' from Finland." Meretskov, Stalin, and Kuusinen "all knew they were really talking about preparations for the annexation of Finland."[109]

The negotiations with the Finns over territory had been a ruse, after all, or at least partly so. At some point during the fall, the Russian dictator, evidently encouraged by the Soviet embassy's fanciful reports that the "oppressed" Finns were ripe for "liberation," as well as the urgings of Andrei Zhdanov, the Communist boss of Leningrad, who had long been making aggressive noises about Finland, had revised his plans. Now he no longer merely wanted Finnish territory; he wanted Finland.

Not the type to ask questions, Meretskov, one of the few middle-level Soviet generals of any ability who had survived the purges, hastily proceeded to devise a "defensive" plan to counter the Finns' contemplated "aggression" in two or three weeks by means of a co-ordinated westward advance by four different armies at eight different points along the entire length of the Soviet-Fenno border.[110]

Under that plan, one army, the 7th, comprising twelve to fourteen divisions, would attack Finnish defenses along the Mannerheim Line on the isthmus. A second army, the 8th, composed of six rifle divisions and two tank brigades, would turn the northern flank of the isthmus defense by circling around Lake Ladoga's north shore, breaking through the relatively thin Finnish lines there, and striking south to take the fortifications from the rear. A third army, the 9th, consisting of five rifle divisions and a number of attached armored units, was to thrust westward across Finland's waist at Suomussalmi toward the Bothnian Sea, cutting the country in half. Finally, a fourth army, the 14th, consisting of three divisions with attached armor, would sweep down from the north, capturing the arctic port of Petsamo, and eventually the Lappish capital of Rovaniemi.[111]

In truth, Meretskov's revised plan had a number of things going for it. The meteorological timing was right: Finland's rivers and lakes had begun to freeze, allowing Soviet forces to move rapidly, particularly in the isthmus, while the snows of deep winter that the Finns thrived in had yet to arrive. Also, the new plan had the element of surprise: as Mannerheim readily admitted, he was not prepared for the number of troops the Russians used north of Ladoga. It even might have worked—indeed, at one point during the first week of the war, came close to working—had the demoralized, poorly led and coordinated Red Army of 1939 with which it had been entrusted been the better led, pre-purge Red Army of 1937. Nevertheless, as would soon become clear, Meretskov's plan was far too ambitious. It dispersed forces amongst too many salients and was also based on both an insufficient understanding of Finnish topography and, perhaps most important, a gross underestimate of the intelligence and character of the Finnish soldier and the resilience of the Finnish nation.[112]

Not that Stalin himself was concerned. So confident was the Soviet generalissimo of the success of his armies and the flashy, nine-prong invasion plan "that he didn't even bother to take a meeting [of the Politburo]," future Soviet premier Nikita Khrushchev recalled. "He thought all he had to do was fire a few artillery shots and the Finns would capitulate."[113]

✱

Shortly past midnight on December 1, as a train evacuating the *eduskunta* made its way to the secret location in the town of Kauhajoki in Ostrobothnia (as southwestern Finland is called) and Helsinki continued to blaze, Gustaf Mannerheim's first order of the day was broadcast over national radio.[114]

His stirring message was directed as much to the Finnish people as to the hard-pressed Finnish army, now struggling to contain the Soviet intruder. It was difficult for some Finns to understand Mannerheim, a member of the country's Swedish-speaking minority whose command of Finnish, the country's main language and that of 90 percent of his troops, was rusty. Few Finns minded.

"*Brave Finland soldiers,*" he declared. "*I undertake this task at an hour when our hereditary enemy once again attacks our country. Confidence in its chief is the first condition of success. You know me and I know you, and I know the whole country is ready to fulfill its duty unto the death.*"[115]

Now the Kremlin, and the world, had its answer: Finland would fight. But for how long? And with what?

2

"They Shall Not Get Us as a Present"

December 1–11, 1939

FINNS' CABINET RESIGNS AS SOVIET BOMBS CITIES
NEW GOVERNMENT EXPECTED TO SEEK A TRUCE
RUSSIA SEIZES PORT AND ISLANDS; 200 ARE KILLED
   —*New York Times,* December 1, 1939

If the first day of the new Soviet-Fenno war was "wild," as Herbert Elliston wrote, the next few days were even wilder, for everyone involved. Elliston and his colleagues at the Kamp did their best to sort out the concatenating developments on the political and diplomatic front, including back-to-back announcements of two different Finnish governments, one newly appointed and the other imposed by the Soviets, while trying to discern what was taking place on the multiple battlefronts. The flood of dispatches and photos emanating from the hotel—particularly the graphic ones of the bombed bus and its unfortunate passengers near the railway station—helped fan the rising international horror and indignation.

All well and good. But could that horror and indignation be translated into concrete aid for the beset country? Finland's friends wondered. More to the point: could the Finns hold out long enough against the mighty Red military machine for it to matter? The revised Soviet war plan called for a campaign of two or three weeks at most. The Russian military attaché in Berlin told CBS newsman William Shirer that he expected the operation to take "three days at the most."[1]

The initial expectations of many Western observers were similarly pessimistic. Thus, on December 2, the normally astute English parliamentarian Harold Nicholson recorded in his journal that "the Finns are putting up a good fight." "However," he confidently predicted, "they will collapse in a few days." In a similar vein, an analyst for the *New York Times* breezily speculated about how much autonomy the Kremlin would grant Finland once Helsinki capitulated.[2]

Apparently, these observers knew as much, or as little, about the Finnish character as Stalin did. However, it would take another Soviet-administered shock, on December 1, to make Finns fully comprehend the mortal nature of the storm that now faced them as a united nation.

First Finland experienced a quick political makeover. Thus, on midnight of November 30, not long after Mannerheim's limousine had left the president's palace after he had withdrawn his resignation as commander-in-chief, another vehicle bearing the deposed prime minister, Cajander, left for another meeting with the weary president so that the latter could tender *his* resignation. Seated alongside the crestfallen prime minister was the man who had just deposed him, Vaino Tanner.

The bombs that had fallen on Helsinki on November 30 had convinced Tanner that Finland needed a new government to deal with the Kremlin, one more amenable to Stalin and Molotov, one without the objectionable Cajander and the discredited (in Moscow's eyes) foreign minister, Eljas Erkko, one that could make peace. As it turned out, this was wishful thinking on the Social Democratic leader's part, but he didn't know it at the time.[3]

Thus, after that morning's bomb-truncated cabinet meeting, Tanner had stayed behind with President Kallio to inform him of his plan to save the country. Moving quickly, he next persuaded the other Social Democratic ministers to agree to the audacious plan. Then he met with the party's parliamentary group at the *eduskuntatalo,* the imposing parliament house, just before the legislators were due to meet to take their last action at that site, a vote of confidence in the government, before being bussed out of town to the site of the *eduskunta*'s new location in Kauhajoki, some 400 kilometers away on the western side of Finland—at that time, still considered safe from the Soviet bombers.[4]

"We must ask for an armistice," Tanner told the solemn conclave, as flames from a bombed office building opposite flickered in the window. Earlier, the government could not have made greater concessions; Finnish public opinion would not have allowed it. Now, he continued, a new government must be set up that could resume negotiations, unaware that the Kremlin's ambitions had considerably expanded since the initial negotiations: the Soviets would no longer be mollified by any territorial concessions by any legally appointed cabinet, and certainly any cabinet that included Tanner himself, whom Stalin and Molotov privately loathed.[5] How could they not after the manner in which he had introduced himself to Stalin during the abortive Moscow negotiations six weeks before? "I am a Menshevik," Tanner joked at one point to Stalin. Stalin, not known for his sense of irony, was not amused. But Tanner, who envisioned himself as foreign minister in the new emergency government, didn't know this yet. The meeting adjourned. Parliament duly voted its confidence in the Cajander government. The appreciative prime minister, who had already experienced one of the worst days of his life, murmured his thanks.[6]

Then Tanner made his move. Taking the flustered Cajander aside, Tanner explained that the vote was only pro forma. It absolved the cabinet for responsibility for the war but nothing more. Now it was time for the prime minister to gracefully bow out. Cajander had no choice, of course: as head of the strongest party in the cabinet, Tanner held the reins of power. The prime minister reluctantly agreed. So far so good, Tanner thought as he piled into a car with the subdued Cajander around midnight, to inform the new coalition cabinet of the sudden shake-up: President Kallio, who had since been moved to a safe house on tiny Kuusisaari Island to the west of the capital, along with Defense Minister Niukkanen and Ernst von Born, the former Finnish minister without portfolio, representing the Agrarian Party and the Swedish People's Party, respectively.[7]

It seemed a logical enough move at the time, as Geoffrey Cox noted: "They [Tanner and his allies] knew that the Moscow press and radio were thundering that it was impossible to deal any longer with the present Finnish Government. If Cajander and Erkko resigned perhaps the Russians might come back to the conference table. At least that change might stop Helsinki from being bombed again the next morning."[8]

In the meantime, rumors of the virtual coup d'état wafted back to the smoke-filled press room of the Kamp. Inevitably, as often occurs during such events, some of the reports got it wrong. Thus, the United Press published a 3 A.M. flash that Tanner himself would be the new Finnish premier; also, that he wanted to give in to all the Kremlin's demands, which wasn't true either. He just wanted to talk. And he wanted those bombs to stop.[9]

Tanner also definitely wasn't interested in being prime minister. The self-chosen cabinet-maker had another man in mind for the job: Risto Ryti, a man known for being cool under pressure, albeit under peacetime conditions. President Kallio approved of the choice. Although most of Ryti's recent experience had been in the banking field, Ryti had had considerable experience with defense matters as well. Moreover, the veteran financier "enjoyed a good reputation in all circles, including those of industrialists and businessmen to whose loyal collaboration we should now have to appeal." Also, Ryti had had no prior dealings with the Kremlin.[10]

Naturally, the commander-in-chief also had to be consulted. Mannerheim, who wasn't particularly taken with Ryti—a judgment he would revise—demurred at first before giving his approval. Now all the well-meaning Tanner had to do was to persuade "Finland's fiscal fix-it man" to take the job.

And so promptly the following morning, December 1, as soon as the Bank of Finland opened its doors, Tanner called on Ryti to put the idea to him. Shortly afterward, President Kallio, who had once been a director of the bank himself, stopped by to see if he could help close the deal.

Predictably, Ryti at first refused. His most recent flirtation with politics, in 1938, when he ran unsuccessfully for president against Kallio, had not been a happy one. Anyway, he preferred managing Finland, as it were, from the familiar vantage point of his desk. Tanner and Kallio persisted. The Fatherland needed him. Still, Ryti hesitated. Then, according to Tanner, "I made what was probably, from my own point of view, the most imprudent promise of my life by saying that if he, Ryti, would consent to become Prime Minister, I would undertake to serve as foreign minister in an interim capacity." It was a promise which Tanner—who would, in 1946 along with Ryti, wind up spending several years in jail after a Soviet-instigated postwar kangaroo court found the two men guilty of "war crimes"—would indeed live to rue. (As Tanner put it in his memoir, "When he [Ryti] resisted his own induction into the government, he was entirely in the right.")[11]

Apparently, Tanner's offer was the clincher. Ryti acceded. Having so decided, the prime minister–designate calmly went about forming his government. Joining Ryti in the new cabinet was Juho Paasikivi, who now exchanged his post as ambassador to Sweden with Erkko and became minister without portfolio. Together with Tanner, these three—along with Mannerheim—would henceforth control Finnish foreign policy for the remainder of the war.

The new cabinet, an amalgam consisting of the Agrarian Party, Ryti's party (five seats), Tanner's Social Democrats (four), the Coalition Party (three), and the Swedish People's Party (three), was, other than the switch in the two topmost positions, not radically different from its predecessor. As Tanner put it, "This was very likely the quickest change of government in Finland's history."[12]

*

At quarter past one, the by now familiar wail of air raid sirens announcing the appearance of another covey of Stalin's "eagles" in the skies over Helsinki sent the city's haggard residents scurrying once again to the nearest bomb shelters, while other Soviet bombers ranged the entire southern part of the country, bombing Viipuri, Kouvola, and ten other Finnish localities.

For his part, Geoffrey Cox—who, like Martha Gellhorn and many of the correspondents at the Kamp, had already experienced his share of bombing raids during the Spanish Civil War—preferred to catch up on his sleep. But not for long, as he recalls:

> At that moment there was a great pounding on the door. I jumped out, grabbed my dressing gown and opened the door to find standing there a tall angular woman in [her] late thirties, wearing a very British coat and skirt and a thin greyish fur that looked right out of a country drawing room. She was hammering on the door with a woman's shoe and shouting in English in a very country voice, "Come on, come on. I'm a fully trained air warden. Downstairs!"
>
> Moments later, the same creature appeared, shouting orders at the pedestrians who had gathered in the hotel foyer to escape the raid. "Now then, all against the wall. All against the wall," she shouted in English. The patient Finnish women who had rushed in from the street stood in

amazement. This, their expressions seemed to say, is clearly part of modern war. Strange women shout out in strange tongues.[13]

The results of the raid, the second of three that day, were less amusing: fifty killed and a score injured. However, the psychological damage was far worse on the city, which had yet to grow inured to the idea, no less the reality, of being bombed from the air.[14]

The *Daily Express* reporter saw evidence of the city's frayed nervous system everywhere that day: in the haggard faces of bank and shop customers, on trams, where there were quarrels about places and luggage; at the Kamp, where the once jolly porters had grown tired and irritable.

Could Helsinki take it? It wasn't clear yet.

Fortunately, for the Finns, the accuracy of the anti-aircraft batteries stationed around the city was beginning to improve. Seven of the low-flying SB-2s were shot out of the sky that day, one of them by a former Finnish world champion level trap-shooter by the name of Dr. Ake af Forselles, who had won second place in the 1937 world trap shooting championship. His machine gun crew was stationed atop the observation tower of the imposing new stadium that had been built to accommodate the 1940 Summer Olympics, hardly the purpose the excited city fathers had in mind for it when they ordered the state-of-the-art facility's construction for the quadrennial event. On December 3, to the surprise of no one, the offices of the organizing committee for the Olympiad were closed. The games themselves would remain in limbo for another five months until they were officially canceled in April 1940. The stadium remained an anti-aircraft post, and the reliable Dr. af Forselles remained in uniform, shooting away at SB-2s instead of clay pigeons.[15]

At one point during that crazed second day of the war, Cox managed to visit the grisly scene of one of the downed raiders:

> The tangled smashed pieces were on fire. The tail, with the letters 'S. B.' and a huge dull red Soviet star, lay against a tree. Nearby was a bloody, tangled mess that had been the pilot's head and his khaki-clad torso. His hands were tightly clenched. . . . The bodies of the two other members of the crew had already been carried away. Finnish guards came up with a piece of planking, dragging the smashed torso on to it and carried it away, too.

Viewing the carnage, Cox couldn't help but wonder what motivated the vanquished airman:

What had he been, this pilot, I wondered, whose life had finished like this? Young, eager to fight for Socialism, to build a better world? After adventure, or just a better job? It no longer mattered to him. His life was finished on this grey afternoon as he flew above the buildings of Helsinki. . . .

What had he thought when he received his orders to bring his plane and its cargo of bombs over this city? My mind went back to the air battles I had watched over Madrid when the snub-nosed Soviet chasers had meant salvation and freedom from the [Fascist] bombers. Crowds had cheered them as deliverers—crowds very like these quiet faced Finns who stared at this wreckage as they had stared towards the sky a few moments before.[16]

Some of the Finns who came across crew members who survived the wreckage after their bombers were shot down were reportedly not so passive. According to *Time,* two downed Soviet pilots who extricated themselves from the wreckage of their plane were set upon by enraged citizens and killed. While plausible in light of the citizenry's anger, the validity of this incident has never been confirmed.[17]

All this madness would stop, Tanner was convinced, once Moscow was informed of the new, more peaceable Ryti-led government.

The United States had already offered its services to mediate between Helsinki and Moscow. Would it agree to do so again? Word was relayed to the American embassy, which got back to the State Department, which got back to the president, who readily agreed. Roosevelt called his ambassador to Moscow, Laurence Steinhardt, and instructed him to arrange a meeting with Molotov as soon as possible. Molotov assented; the meeting was arranged.[18]

And so at 10 P.M. Moscow time on the evening of December 1, as cleaning crews in Helsinki and the other bombed localities cleared the rubble from the latest raids, Steinhardt, acting as emissary for both the United States and the hopeful new Finnish government, met the Russian foreign minister in his offices at the Kremlin. One can picture the tense scene as the former colonel, who had already made it clear that he was no friend of Moscow, sat down opposite Stalin's new right-hand man.[19]

Perhaps Winston Churchill, who did business with Molotov on numerous occasions both before and during the Second World War, described him best:

[Molotov was] a man of outstanding ability and cold-blooded ruthlessness. He had survived the fearful hazards and ordeals to which all Bolshevik leaders had been subjected in the years of triumphant revolution. . . . His cannonball head, black moustache, and comprehending eyes, his slab face, his verbal adroitness and imperturbable demeanour, were appropriate manifestations of his qualities and skill. He was above all men fitted to be the agent and instrument of the policy of an incalculable machine. . . . I have never seen a human being who more perfectly represented the modern conception of a robot.[20]

One of America's leading Sovietologists, the late George Kennan, draws a similar portrait in his 1960 memoir. Kennan, who briefly served as American ambassador to the Kremlin himself, remembered Molotov as "a man with the physique of the old-time barroom bouncer, with iron nerves and poker face, imperturbable, stubborn, immovable in argument, and withal a master chess player who never missed a move, who let nothing escape him."[21]

Such was the nature of the man who, as much if not more than Stalin, shaped Soviet policy toward Finland, and who now faced Ambassador Steinhardt.

Steinhardt's mission was twofold. First, he officially conveyed President Roosevelt's rather bland and self-obvious statement of the previous day condemning the bombing of cities and civilian centers, and asking the Kremlin to forswear the same. For the appearance of even-handedness, Washington had also asked Helsinki to accept the same stricture, which of course the latter readily agreed to do—as if the relatively minuscule Finnish Air Force had had either the inclination, wherewithal, or opportunity to terrorize Soviet cities on its own. Now, Steinhardt continued, would Moscow, which clearly *had* bombed Finnish cities, agree to the same eminently reasonable caveat, at least until the hostilities between the two nations were resolved?[22]

Molotov replied with a bold-faced lie. President Roosevelt must have been misinformed, he told the disbelieving ambassador, who doubtless had seen the grisly photos of the Helsinki bombing; the president's suggestion was completely wrong-headed. The Soviet Union had not bombed towns and would not have done so because "it considered the interests of the Finnish population no less than the people under any government." It only had bombed airdromes (as airfields were then called) and would continue to do so.[23]

Anyway, Molotov continued witheringly, since the United States was "5,000 miles away it might fail to see this." But "facts were facts." Consequently, he continued, deadpan, the president's undertaking was "pointless."[24]

The American envoy gamely moved on to the next, more portentous item, the new Finnish government. He had been instructed to inform the Soviets that Finland had a new cabinet headed by Vaino Tanner, which was very interested in resuming negotiations. In the confusion surrounding the overnight changeover, the ambassador had also gotten his information wrong. It didn't really matter. Steinhardt could have told Molotov that the new Finnish premier was Santa Claus and it wouldn't have changed matters.[25]

In the event, Molotov seized on this (mistaken) information to launch into a mini-tirade against Tanner. *Tanner?* Tanner was "unsuitable," Molotov said. Worse, he was the "evil genius" behind the breakdown of the November negotiations. Now, if the talks had been led by Paasikivi, whom the Russians knew and trusted, things might have turned out differently.[26] For this reason, he continued, the Soviet government had no reason to expect any good to come of the new government.[27]

Now came Molotov's coup de grace. Besides, he continued, the Kremlin was no longer interested in doing business with the present Helsinki government. Instead, it had a new negotiating partner: the "Finnish People's Republic," led by Otto Ville Kuusinen. Surely the ambassador would agree that the formation of the Kuusinen government was "a new and important factor" in the situation.[28]

To be sure, several hours before, Moscow Radio had broadcast a dispatch from Tass, the official Soviet news agency, that a "People's Government of the Democratic Republic of Finland" had been established in Terijoki by Finnish leftists and "rebel soldiers." The report had been immediately dismissed by Finnish officials as so much propaganda. Steinhardt, who had been in transit that evening, apparently hadn't caught it. That was most unfortunate, Molotov said, because that was with whom the Kremlin was now doing business.[29]

End of interview. On the face of it, the *New York Times* reported the next day, "it would appear to be a very sharp rebuff to Roosevelt's offer—a rebuff made particularly cynical by the reference to the 'government' of Kuusinen."[30]

*

If Ambassador Steinhardt's meeting with the Soviet foreign minister was a startling rebuke to the American government and its attempt to bring an end to the new Soviet-Fenno hostilities, it was infinitely more so to the new Finnish government, and particularly to the man who had put it together, Tanner. Twenty-four hours before, he had been convinced that he could steer the beset Finnish nation to safer waters. Now, he was chagrined to learn, the whole thing had really been his fault, no less that he had been the "evil genius" behind the breakdown of the November negotiations! And what sort of bad joke was this so-called Finnish Democratic People's Republic to which Molotov had referred?

*

To be sure, on the face of it there was much to laugh at about the Finnish Democratic Republic, or the People's Democratic Republic of Finland (PDRF), as Molotov had called it: there seemed to be some doubt about what exactly to call the new creature during its first days.

The Finnish Democratic Republic wasn't the Kremlin's first puppet regime. During the Polish-Soviet war of 1920 the Kremlin had tried to rationalize its military offensive against the democratic government of Warsaw by concluding an agreement with Julian Marchlewski's so-called Provisional Revolutionary Soviet of Poland. Then there were the "bilateral agreements" between Moscow and Estonia, Latvia, and Lithuania by which the intimidated governments of those still (barely) independent countries had "agreed" to accept Russian forces onto their soil. Still, this new creation of Moscow's was quite a piece of work, starting from the top and the PDRF's prime minister and foreign minister, Otto Ville Kuusinen.[31]

Not that Kuusinen, who had been a leader of the January 1918 revolution that created the short-lived Soviet-backed Finnish "republic," was entirely without ability. Indeed, from a theoretical point of view, he was the perfect man to head the puppet regime. After all, twenty years before he had been one of the leaders of the Red government that had fought Gustaf Mannerheim and the Whites. Later, Kuusinen had fled to the Soviet Union, where he had shown some promise as a dialectician, penning a long and incisive analysis of the civil war in which he declared that the greater error of the Finnish Social Democratic Party was that it had not been outspokenly Communist enough. Finnish workers, he said, wanted to fight for more than their leaders were prepared to accept.[32]

Perhaps Kuusinen had a point, but that was twenty years ago. Since then, Kuusinen, one of the few former Finnish Reds to escape the Great Purge of the 1930s, when many of the latter were "severely judged"—executed, in Stalinist parlance—for being unreliable, had distinguished himself primarily as a survivor and a Communist factotum. He had played a modest bureaucratic role in the Comintern until Stalin and Molotov suddenly thrust him into the glare of the spotlight as their man in Terijoki and soon, they hoped, in Helsinki as well.

Kuusinen certainly doesn't look comfortable in the first portrait of him in his official capacity that *Pravda* published on December 3, which shows him dressed in an ill-fitting suit standing behind a table alongside the smug countenances of Stalin, Voroshilov, and Zhdanov as Molotov signed a new Mutual Assistance and Friendship Pact between the USSR and the PDRF. Indeed, in that classic photo of Soviet stage-management, Kuusinen looks very much like the second choice that he was. (Moscow's first choice for the post was said to be another Finnish Communist by the name of Arvo Tuominen.) No matter: according to *Pravda,* the news of the new Finnish government was not only received with "jubilant enthusiasm by the people of Leningrad"—but, already on the first day of its formation—"the *kolkhozniks* [collective workers] of Tatarstan [a Soviet republic in the lower Volga region of Russia] 'heartily welcomed'" the puppet entity.[33]

Then why the glum look on Kuusinen's face? Certainly "Premier Kuusinen" could not have been but overjoyed with the generous terms Comrades Stalin and Molotov had offered his government in return for its assistance and friendship. Alongside the *Pravda* photo was a map of the new Fenno-Soviet frontier that had been "agreed upon": apart from a lease by Russia of Hanko, only a small area of Finnish territory northwest of Leningrad—less than halfway toward Viipuri—and some islands in the Baltic sea and part of the Rybachi Peninsula in the far north were to be ceded to the Soviet Union. In return, the PDRF received large stretches of Karelia, including the entire Olonets area, east of Lake Ladoga.[34]

G.E.R. Gedye, the Moscow correspondent of the *New York Times,* reported the announcement of the Terijoki regime's spontaneous generation and its pact with its Russian kinsmen in withering terms:

The conclusion of a "treaty of mutual assistance and friendship" between the "democratic republic of Finland" [apparently Gedye was also confused as to what to call the regime]—a band of Finnish émigrés, who, under the wing of the Red Army, nominated themselves as a government yesterday was announced over the radio today. . . . Despite the fact that the whole Finnish frontier was ablaze between the warring armies, Otto Kuusinen was able, according to the text [of the pact] to sign the treaty in Moscow.[35]

"By a nice touch," Gedye drily continued, "the treaty concludes by providing for the exchange of instruments of ratification in Helsinki as soon as possible. Apparently it is recognized in Moscow that the 'government' set up as the co-signatory of this interesting document has yet to acquire a capital as well as a country." Evidently the author of this "interesting document" expected these rites to take place very soon—perhaps within a matter of days.[36]

To help accomplish his "historic emancipative mission," Kuusinen had even been given his own army, the Finnish People's Army. This motley force, which ultimately numbered over 22,000 but saw little to no combat, was mostly composed of Finnish-speaking Ingrians who had been hastily impressed for the occasion.[37]

One of the bewildered youths who were drafted into the FPA was an eighteen-year-old physics student at Leningrad University by the name of Edward Hynninen. Recalling his service in the "liberation army" sixty years later, Hynninen still sounded confused about the experience. "The story is like this," Hynninen, who ultimately became a commercial artist, remembered in a 2008 interview:

I was drafted into the Red Army on November 17, 1939, two weeks before the war broke out. I started my army service in Petrozavodsk. The official version of the events was that we had to relocate the border from Leningrad and that the Finns did not agree and had provoked our troops at Mainila. So the Soviet Union had to move the border away from Leningrad by force. I was given training as a phone operator.[38]

That is how the matter was presented to us. I can't say I believed it but I must say that it all felt very strange. I believed the whole state of affairs was not normal. More strange things happened later. [To wit:] About one week later our battalion was suddenly sent to Leningrad and we were issued new uniforms! Now we know that those uniforms were captured by the Red Army in Poland. So we were lined up and our battalion commander and the political officer announced that we were part of the Finnish People's Army. "What is this?" I thought. One had to be an idiot not to understand the trick.

As for the ethnic composition of his fighting comrades, Hynninen noted, "First there were only Ingrians and Karelians, but evidently they ran out of Ingrians and Karelians and had to take other ethnic groups—Belorussians, Russians, Ukrainians, even Georgians, in order to fill the ranks. They were also issued the same Polish uniforms. It was all very strange."[39]

✳

Then there was the PDRF's program, with its promises to reduce the Finnish working day to eight hours—even though the eight-hour day had been the law in Finland for years. Doubtless many Finns had a laugh reading that.

However, the establishment of the Russian regime wasn't very amusing to the legitimate Finnish government. For, if Moscow denied its very existence, how could it continue negotiations? Now, the government realized, as did the Finnish people, they were no longer engaged in a conflict over a question of military lines or frontiers. Now Finns knew they were fighting for their very existence as an independent nation. That is what that impromptu concert at the border crossing at Alakurtti three days before had been about. Stalin and Molotov were no longer merely interested in Hanko: now they wanted Finland entire.

Ryti, the new prime minister, was defiant when a reporter from the *New York Times* reached him at his bank desk on the morning of December 2. The cabinet had met through the night to discuss the dismaying upshot of Ambassador Steinhardt's bizarre tête-à-tête with Molotov and the latter's de facto recognition of the "Kuusinen government." Dawn, along with the prospect of further Soviet air raids, was breaking when the shaken Finnish executive spoke to the American reporter.

The normally soft-spoken financier told the reporter that he still hoped to resume negotiations with Moscow, "but, if settlement cannot be reached," he vowed, "*we will fight on.*" Regarding the so-called "Kuusinen government," Ryti was openly contemptuous. "This man Kuusinen," he continued, "should not be called a Finn. He is an expatriate. He fled our country long ago."[40]

The prime minister–designate was livid about the prior day's destruction. "Yesterday's raids were terrible," he seethed. "They killed our women and children." Asked about the military situation, Ryti maintained that it was "not unfavorable." "Fighting is going on most fronts. We shot down seventeen Russian planes and destroyed fourteen tanks on Friday [the previous day]." "Our troops," he insisted, "are giving a good account of themselves."[41]

✳

The small Finnish Air Force was also beginning to give a good account of itself. Four of the downed Russian planes, the Finnish public was pleased to learn, were shot down in aerial combat. Senior Sergeant Toivo Uuttu of *Lentolaivue* (Flying Squadron 26), based at Immola, forty-five kilometers north of Mikkeli, recorded the first confirmed air kill. Flying one of the FAF's antiquated, single-seat Bristol Bulldog biplane fighters, Uuttu succeeded in getting a top-of-the-line Soviet I-16 fighter in the sights of his Vickers machine gun shortly before noon and dispatched the intruder. Later that day, Uuttu's rickety aircraft was also hit, forcing him to crash-land on the ice of tiny Lake Muolaanjarvi, in the center of the isthmus.[42]

That same day, the country's coastal troops were giving as good as they got in a number of classic ship-to-shore shootouts with the Soviet Navy, including one at Hanko involving the Russian cruiser *Kirov* and a flotilla of destroyers. That engagement began when the *Kirov,* hoping for surprise, appeared out of the early morning haze with its escorts. However, the rusty gun crews of the Russian man o' war had difficulty getting the range of the contested fort's batteries.[43]

But the Hanko men were ready for the *Kirov.* Soon the Russian cruiser was straddled with water spouts from the powerful batteries at Russaro, a small island south of the town that the Finns had originally offered to Moscow during the abortive November negotiations (and that also would briefly figure in the later talks to end the war). Minutes later, the charging ship reportedly took two well-placed hits in its stern, killing seventeen Soviet sailors and injuring a score more. Retiring into the fog, the damaged vessel immediately lost power, spinning about in the strong current.[44]

In their jubilation, the artillerymen reported the cruiser sunk. It wasn't. Ultimately, the damaged boat was ignominiously towed to the newly acquired Soviet naval station at Liepaja, in Latvia, for repairs before returning to Leningrad (where the *Kirov* provided gunfire support during the Finnish-supported siege of that city during the subsequent German invasion of Russia). But it had been a stirring victory for the Finns nevertheless and the news of the engagement, which was trumpeted on the front page of that morning's *Helsingin Sanomat,* galvanized the country.[45]

At the same time, Ryti's interview with the American newsman left no doubt that he was the right man for the job. Here, at this early hour, sitting at his familiar bank desk, as the capital braced itself for another day of bombing raids and other Soviet mayhem, Ryti showed that he had the stuff to lead his country.

On the telephone with the *Times* reporter, Ryti said, "Tell the American people we will not surrender. The Finnish people will fight to the last. We admire America and also expect to give you more cause to admire us. We are prepared to fight to the last man. *To the last man,*" he repeated. And he hung up and got back to work.[46]

The scales had also dropped from Vaino Tanner's eyes. The new foreign minister told a reporter that he still hoped to get an agreement with Russia if possible, "but our aim is to defend our independence and safety. All other questions are put aside. That is the only program this government has before it." The government, he insisted, still intended to remain in Helsinki as long as possible. "We don't think they can occupy Helsinki," he continued. "The only danger," he said, looking up, "is from the skies."[47]

The effect of the back-to-back shocks on the Finnish people—of the terror raids and the announcement of the Kuusinen regime—was essentially the same.

Now, all of a sudden, Finns knew what they were fighting for—their property, their dignity, their independence, as well as their lives. Instead of causing the walls of the "White Guardist" capitalist regime to crumble and fall, as Stalin had deluded himself, the invasion of Finland had accomplished the opposite.

"Indeed a revolution *did* take place in Finland, but not of the kind Kuusinen had hoped for," Max Jakobson writes. "It was a revolution of national unity. And at last the 'popular front' came into being, though not in the Marxist sense of the term: it was the Eastern front." If anything, the Finnish people were ahead of their leaders. As Jakobson notes: "Popular reaction to the Soviet invasion was less shocked or alarmed than the official one. Somehow the public had instinctively made a sounder judgment of Russian intentions than had its political leaders who had refused to face up to the possibility of war and failed to prepare the country for it."[48]

Or, as a young boy taking shelter in a Helsinki doorway during that day's raids told Martha Gellhorn, as another group of Soviet bombers flew overhead, "Little by little I am getting angrier and angrier."[49]

At last, two days after the first bombs dropped on Finland, the tangled political and diplomatic outlines of this strange new conflict which had suddenly burst upon the world were becoming clearer. Matters were further clarified the afternoon of December 2, when the cabinet held another meeting to discuss the government's program for dealing with the crisis. Also present, in addition to the weary ministers, were Kyosti Kallio and Gustaf Mannerheim. This would be the last cabinet meeting that Mannerheim, who was then based at the aged Hotel Helsinki, would hold for some time: the next day, December 3, the commander-in-chief would move his headquarters to the small Western Savo city of Mikkeli, which had also been his headquarters during the civil war.[50]

Taking the helm, Tanner outlined a two-point program. First order of business: to ask Sweden to help with garrisoning the Aland Islands, that quixotic, strategically significant Baltic island group lying betwixt Finland and Sweden and that the League of Nations, in its most notable success, had twenty years before awarded to Finland. Of course, if Sweden agreed to help defend the islands she would thus effectively become a co-belligerent of Finland. Which, of course, was the point. Tanner's second objective: to reestablish contact with the Kremlin with a view toward resuming negotiations.[51]

Tanner decided to deal with the first point right then and there by phoning his fellow Social Democrat Per Albin Hansson, the Swedish prime minister. Hansson's answer was not long in coming. Sorry, he told his old social democratic colleague from across the Bothnian Sea, Sweden was very sympathetic to Finland's plight; she would be happy to provide Finland with arms and materiel; however, she would definitely not help Finland defend the Aland archipelago. That was the position of the Swedish government.[52]

In point of fact—to complicate matters a little further—the Swedish foreign minister, Rickard Sandler, the most pro-Finnish member of the cabinet, had advocated garrisoning the Alands. But Sandler was out. He had been forced to resign that day in order to appease Russia's erstwhile ally, Nazi Germany, which had criticized the activist Social Democrat foreign minister for supposedly encouraging Finland to provoke Russia, as well as advocating a pro-British foreign policy, one of several moves the conflict-averse Swedes took to appease Berlin. With Sandler gone, the position of the Swedish government was crystal clear, Hansson told Tanner: no garrisoning of the Alands. And so it would remain.[53]

According to one account, President Kallio, not in the best of health anyway, collapsed upon hearing this and excoriated Sweden for letting Finland down. Tanner, more stoic, simply responded by saying, "Since we have to drop point one, let us get on with point two." At which point Juho Niukkanen, the defense minister, came up with what was surely the craziest idea of the day. "Why don't we offer Germany the Aland Islands in exchange for military aid?" The idea was so ridiculous it wasn't even discussed.[54]

Instead the discussion turned back to the question of negotiations. What did the commander-in-chief think about this? Despite his fiery words on November 30, Mannerheim was still in favor of resuming contact with Moscow, if possible. His reason: the still-vexing problem of ammunition. Supplies were critically low, he pointed out. The infantry only had sufficient ammunition for two months of fighting, provided, miracle of miracles, it could hold out that long. Additionally, there was light artillery support for three weeks and heavy artillery supplies for a mere nineteen days.[55]

Mannerheim feared, under the circumstances, that Sweden might refuse transit of ammunition through her territory in order to preserve her neutrality, in which case no credible defense could be mounted. It was an old refrain of the general's, but under the circumstances it now took on more urgency. The army would fight—was fighting, and fighting well—but it could not mount an effective defense if Sweden and its increasingly cautious government changed its mind and decided to bar ammunition supplies for her neighbor. In fact, although Sweden ultimately allowed a limited amount of ammunition to be transported across its border, the question of ammunition continued to haunt Mannerheim and the Finns for the rest of the war.[56]

Therefore, the commander-in-chief endorsed Tanner's second point: to resume talks as soon as possible, if possible. At which point the general excused himself to return to his improvised headquarters in order to supervise operations on the fast-changing battlefront, as well as his pending move to Mikkeli, where the Army's main headquarters was located (for the moment), so as to be nearer the main front.

So it was agreed. Moscow was to be contacted. The government would reach out to the invader. It would not capitulate; however, it had "new positive proposals to make." Washington had already struck out, so once again Tanner phoned Hansson in Stockholm. Would Hansson's minister in Moscow, Vilhelm Assarsson (who would later play a supporting role in the final peace negotiations), contact Molotov and tell him that Finland, the elected government of Finland, was still willing to talk? Hansson, who certainly had no interest in having the Finnish People's Republic—as the Terijoki entity now officially called itself—as his neighbor, agreed. The message was sent.[57]

Several hours later came the inevitable news. Molotov had replied to Assarsson's inquiry with a curt note to the effect that the Soviet Union only recognized the Finnish People's Republic (as it was now officially called) as the legitimate government of Finland. The time for parleying was past. It was war. Now, as Stalin had put it at the end of the failed November negotiations, it was time to let the soldiers have their say.[58]

*

We have already discussed the Russian strategy. What was Finland's strategy?

First, we must consider again the man who was charged with executing it, Gustaf Mannerheim, and the incredible situation that presented itself before him. He was seventy-two and had last been on active duty more than twenty years before, when many of the men upon whom he would now have to rely were either toddlers or even unborn. Mannerheim's authority was absolute. On the other hand, his health was uncertain; the strain of the past few months, when he had watched a deteriorating situation without being able to check it, had been extremely severe. Henceforth he would have to depend, in the last resort, on his own military judgment.

Well and good. But how sound was that judgment? This remained to be seen. After all, despite his impeccable military pedigree, Mannerheim hadn't actually fought in a war for over twenty years and the vastly superior, well-equipped Russian foe he now faced was quite different than the indigenous, Kremlin-backed Reds he had faced during the civil war. So, correspondingly, was the excruciating challenge he faced, for now he was head of an army in a war that, despite its ability and commitment, he knew it could not win. He embraced the army nevertheless, and his staff and his generals in the field, all of whom he had chosen to retain, obeyed him faithfully.

So much for Mannerheim the man. What of his strategy? How did he plan on meeting the Red armies that were at this moment pouring over the Soviet-Finnish border, and in some cases already making alarming headway, particularly in the center and far north of the country?

Mannerheim's strategy, devised years before, was predicated on some pretty harsh realities. Obviously Russia was the only likely opponent, and it was delusory to think that Finland could successfully defend herself against the Red Army for an indefinite period of time. In the long run, Finland's only guarantee of survival was the conscience of Western civilization. Finland, it was hoped, would be regarded as a vital outpost of everything the Western powers stood for, and as such would not be allowed to vanish from the map.

Thus was born a strategy designed to enable Finland to hang on long enough for outside aid to reach it. If that hope proved chimerical—as it ultimately did—the only thing left to do was to resist so fiercely that the Russians would opt for a negotiated settlement rather than total conquest.[59]

If, however, Stalin did seek total subjugation, as he, Molotov, Zhdanov, and the other members of his circle now evidently intended, the Finnish Army would, as Risto Ryti declared to that *New York Times* reporter, fight to the last man. In short, Mannerheim's plans were not based on the absurd hope of outright victory, but, as veteran correspondent John Langdon-Davies put it, on "the most honorable annihilation, with the faint hope that the conscience of mankind would find an alternative solution as a reward for bravery and singleness of purpose."[60]

An honorable annihilation. That, essentially, was the basis of the Finnish strategy, in the eventuality of a Russian invasion. Those were the extraordinary realities and assumptions upon which Finnish war strategy had been based. Put another way, the Mannerheim strategy was based, to a large degree, on faith in his own judgment and military leadership, faith in his army, and faith in the conscience of the free world. That faith would largely be validated in the trying weeks to come, except in the latter category.

Mannerheim's strategy also had been based on certain geographical and material assumptions, most notably that given the size of the Finnish army, his force of nine divisions could not defend every part of its 1,600-kilometer border with the USSR, and also that it would not have to.

Only on the Karelian Isthmus, it had been assumed, could a large modern army be sustained in prolonged campaigning. In planning for a possible war, the only place where Mannerheim and his staff were truly concerned was Ladoga-Karelia, the region of Karelia north of Lake Ladoga. There, in a corridor 130–160 kilometers wide, were two good roads that led from the border to the interior. One started at Petrozavodsk, the largest city in Russian Karelia. The other ran from the Murmansk railroad along the rocky coast of Lake Ladoga; the two lines converged near the tiny village of Kitela. Just a day's march beyond Kitela was a crucial section of Finland's railroad network, along with good roads leading north and south.[61]

This was, in effect, the "back door" to the isthmus. The road net would support the movement of large formations, including armor, and it seemed logical for the Russians to make an attempt to break through here, wheel south, and take the Mannerheim Line from the rear—as the 8th Army was indeed just then attempting to do.

Anticipating such a Soviet thrust, the Finnish High Command had held war exercises in Ladoga-Karelia several times during the 1930s and had devised what it felt was a sound plan for dealing with the threat. The Finns would let the

Russians come in and advance along the converging roads until they reached a strong line of prepared defenses that ran Lake Ladoga–Kitela–Lake Syskyjarvi. Mannerheim and his planners had reasoned as follows: once the Russians were pinned down, with their long supply lines stretched out behind them, a strong Finnish counterattack would fall on their right flank from the supposedly impassable wilderness below Loimola and Kollaa, cut off the head of their main force, and methodically destroy it. That was the plan.[62]

Mannerheim and his staff had allocated what seemed an adequate force for this task: two infantry divisions and three battalions of border troops, all of them about as well equipped as any units in the Finnish Army (which wasn't saying much), organized into the 4th Corps, under the command of Major General Juho Heiskanen.

However, the Russian 8th Army, commanded by I. H. Habarov (and later Grigory Shtern), had some unpleasant surprises in store for Heiskanen. During the fall, a new railroad line had been extended from 8th Army's supply base in Petrozavodsk up to the border, just opposite the small Finnish town of Suojarvi. This unforeseen preparation nearly doubled the Russians' supply capability on this front.

Thus, when the war broke out on November 30, the Russians had attacked not with three divisions, the maximum number Mannerheim believed they could sustain, but with nine, totalling nearly 120,000 men, together with four brigades of armor. This was probably the cleverest aspect of the Soviet plan.[63]

Most alarming of all, noted Mannerheim as he and his staff tensely pored over their maps by the light of their gooseneck lamps at Mikkeli at the start of the war, was the attack of two entire divisions up in the direction of Suojarvi, where they had expected nothing stronger than reconnaissance patrols. In those first few days of the conflict there was virtually nothing to stop these Soviet units from outflanking the entire 4th Corps line from the northeast, or from rolling through Tolvajarvi, north of Ladoga, in a westerly thrust and running amok in the interior of Finland, as they very nearly did.

The marshal spent many difficult hours during those hectic initial days deciding how best to employ his scant reserves to counter the far-flung threats. Originally intending to retain all available reserves for the main front in the isthmus, he was compelled instead to disperse them piecemeal toward the town of Suomussalmi, in the eastern central part of the country, as well as the area around Tolvajarvi Lake to meet the unexpectedly strong Soviet pincers there. Mannerheim was also shocked to learn that Suomussalmi had already fallen on the first day to the Soviet 163rd Division.[64]

With those hasty troop dispositions, the stage was set for some of the most dramatic battles in modern history. Although the odds were staggering, Mannerheim correctly discerned in the fast-moving situation the opportunity for daring countermoves. Each of the enemy's thrusts through the northern wilds was a serious threat in itself; however, as yet none of the motorized elements of the ersatz Soviet blitzkrieg could cooperate with those on their flanks because they were separated by tracts of roadless, trackless, unforgiving woods. Here was a critical weakness of the Soviet plan. It was one that Mannerheim and his generals could and would capitalize on.

As is the norm at the start of a war, Mannerheim was concerned with personnel issues, particularly regarding his top officers, who often failed to measure up to his demanding standards.

Mannerheim was less concerned with his rank-and-file troops, who were giving a good account of themselves, despite several novel and disturbing sights, such as tanks. The sight of Russian T-26 tanks rumbling across a field directly toward them, en masse or singly, was sufficient to put some panic-stricken Finns to flight.

No less disconcerting for the Finns was the sight of massed Soviet troops charging at them, directly into the line of fire. One of the frontline troops who had to contend with these suicidal attacks was Eric Malm, then a corporal in the 10th Regiment. "Their attacks were based on numbers," said Malm. "It was an incredible thing to see—and experience." "Their tactics made no sense. They also weren't dressed properly, to say the least. No skis, long trench coats hindering their movements. You had to wonder at the mentality of the people in charge of this madness. . . . They had no skis so they were easy targets."[65]

The stress of having to mow down these onrushing, buffalo-like hordes was too much for some Finnish troops, particularly machine-gunners, who sometimes had to be relieved because of battle stress (even though that malady was not officially recognized yet).

To be sure, the Finnish commander-in-chief did have some initial qualms about the loyalty of his troops. In particular, he had concerns about those in the Suomussalmi area, which, with its contingent of bitter-enders from the civil war and their like-minded kinsmen, was reputed to be "red"—a concern heightened with the appearance of a number of fifth-columnists behind Finnish lines, including several in Finnish uniform and a number of Finnish exiles whom the Soviets had parachuted in. During the first weeks of the war, there also were some scattered cases of espionage and sabotage elsewhere around the country. Those traitors who were caught were dealt with quickly and harshly. Thus, on December 13, the *New York Times* reported that a spy ring that included a Finnish captain and lieutenant had been rounded up, given summary courts-martial, and summarily executed.[66]

In the meantime, Finnish casualties continued to mount. Mannerheim insisted on having the names of the fallen officers read to him individually. The general would nod simply as each hero's name was read to him by one of his adjutants. One of the early fallen was Jorma Gallen-Kallela, the son of his old friend and aide-de-camp Aleksi, the victim of the crew of a downed Russian bomber.

On the afternoon of December 1, two Russian air crewmen had been seen parachuting from a stricken SB-2 in Lempiala, near Viipuri and the start of the isthmus. The crew were believed to have taken shelter in an abandoned farm nearby. Lt. Gallen-Kallela and Captain Adolf Ehrnrooth approached the farm. Apparently Jorma was walking point. The diehard Russian crewmen, convinced that surrender was tantamount to suicide, were determined to resist. Shots rang out. Gallen-Kallela fell, mortally wounded. Ehrnrooth reacted swiftly, killing one aviator with his rifle and seriously wounding the other. When Ehrnrooth looked to his comrade, he was dead.

*

No, there was little doubt in Mannerheim's mind that his troops were equal to the crisis. Indeed, as he had declared in his first Order of the Day, he knew them and they knew him, and during the arduous days and weeks to come, they would more than validate his confidence and vice versa.

How well the distant if beloved commander and his men got to know each other was another matter. What mattered was that they knew him, or at least they felt they did. The personal touch wasn't necessary. They needed an icon, and the great general, looking down on them from the photos of him tacked to the walls of their regimental headquarters and dugouts, provided one.

At the same time, Mannerheim wasn't so sure about all his generals, most notably his predecessor, General Hugo Osterman, who, following his own succession to the army's top post, had been given command of Finnish troops on the all-important isthmus. The exacting commander-in-chief was not at all happy with accounts of the way in which the light advance forces guarding the gateway to Finland had been deployed.[67] It was Mannerheim's decided opinion that too much ground had been sacrificed to the invader. Partly this was the result of poor intelligence, never the Finnish army's strong suit, thanks in considerable part to the weak man Mannerheim had appointed for the job, Lars Melander.

Most important, Mannerheim felt that Osterman had simply been too passive. On the afternoon of December 3, having barely had time to change his uniform after hurrying from Helsinki to his relocated headquarters at Mikkeli, the new Finnish generalissimo motored 230 kilometers to Imatra to deliver the message to Osterman personally—though not before peremptorily firing his first general, Juho Heiskanen. Heiskanen was the commander of the 4th Corps, in Ladoga-Karelia, one of whose divisions (the 3rd Finnish Division) had retreated; he was replaced with another major general, Woldemar Hagglund.

In his memoirs, Mannerheim is frank about his disappointment with Osterman. It is easy, as one reads his unforgiving lines, to envision him imperiously dressing Osterman down at that tempestuous meeting—which resulted in both generals offering their resignations:

The frontier zone was intimately known to our troops and for twenty years active delaying actions on the Karelian Isthmus had become almost a dogma in their training. . . .

In spite of my emphatic orders, the fighting was taken up by altogether insufficient forces that made long delaying actions impossible. An excellent opportunity was lost. This was the more regrettable, since the enemy, as expected, advanced in massed formations and avoided the forests, which had been mined in many places.

The showdown seems to have worked. As a result, Osterman's forces offered palpably stronger resistance during the remainder of the first week of the war, including launching several night raids on Russian lines. Still, by this time, most of the frontier zone had been irretrievably lost.[68]

Thus, by December 6, after a week of intense fighting at the nine different incursion points—as best as could be comprehended after collating the conflicting and confused reports from the long battlefront—the most that could be said from the Finnish point of view was that, as their prime minister had hopefully put it, the situation continued not to be unfavorable.

On the other hand, it wasn't exactly favorable either. Indeed, as the marshal recalls, there were grounds for outright alarm. Thus, on December 6, Finnish Independence Day, Mannerheim writes,

> Bad news arrived from all fronts. On the Karelian Isthmus, the enemy on December 6th opened up the expected offensive on the Taipale sector, where there were practically no reserves. In the direction of Suomussalmi, two enemy columns had succeeded in joining forces in the village. In the Ladoga sector, too, the enemy's two southernmost columns had made contact in the neighborhood of Koirinoja. The situation was most alarming in the direction [of] Suojarvi.[69]

At the same time, Mannerheim had also begun to lay the tactical and strategic groundwork for the "battles of annihilation" that would shock the Soviets and thrill the world. Thus, several days before, while Mannerheim was taking stock of the bad news pouring in from the various fronts, the commander-in-chief had taken a pivotal meeting at his headquarters with a tough forty-two-year-old colonel and former battalion commander during the civil war by the name of Paavo Talvela, who, after serving with the 27th Prussian Jaeger Regiment during World War I, had written his War College thesis on theoretical battles that might occur in a future war in the Tolvajarvi sector.[70]

It was 4 A.M. when Talvela, who was one of the few officers who could say that he knew the remote commander-in-chief well, arrived at Mannerheim's new headquarters in Mikkeli. Despite the early hour, the latter was in full dress uniform when the younger man arrived. After a quick exchange of salutes, the two men turned to the Tolvajarvi sector of the battle map and began their deliberations.[71]

✳

For its part, the Soviet High Command wasn't exactly thrilled with the state of affairs at that point, either. Indeed, while Molotov and Stalin were happily embracing Otto Kuusinen as the chosen emancipator of the Finnish people at the headquarters for the People's Commissariat for Defense and General Staff in Leningrad, Kliment Voroshilov, the defense commissar, who was still nominally in charge of the operation, and Boris Shaposhnikov, the Soviet chief of staff, were beginning to evince genuine concern regarding the slowness of Kirill Meretskov's would-be blitzkrieg.

Of the four Russian armies, only the 14th, in the far north, which had quickly taken its first objective, the port of Petsamo, seemed to be making satisfactory progress, as well as possibly the 9th, with its initial deceptive victory at Suomussalmi. Elsewhere, however, the other invading Russian armies were making little or no progress toward their objectives.[72]

As Finnish military historian Ohto Manninen writes: "The attack did not go at all according to the preconceptions of the Soviet military and political leadership. The course of events was in every respect different from what had been presumed." Shaposhnikov's original, clear-eyed view of the character and quality of the Finnish fighting forces, as well as the difficulties presented by the Finnish terrain, was fast becoming realized. Finnish resistance was much greater than expected.

"Once the attack has commenced," the Soviet battle orders had read, "the action of the troops must be determined, they cannot be tied down to frontline battles where the enemy's fortified positions are." But that is exactly what had been happening, as Manninen notes. "The battle became prolonged, and every kilometer of the advance had to be accomplished with great difficulty. After crossing the border quickly, the attack stopped completely."[73]

Thus, on December 3, the same day that Mannerheim hastened to Imatra to galvanize Osterman, Meretskov was similarly exhorting his own subalterns. "We cannot slouch down in Finland for a long time," he stated in a directive addressed to his four army commanders.[74]

✳

Another indication that the Soviet offensive was proving more difficult than anticipated was the increasingly anti-Finnish tone of the Soviet reportage of the war, or what passed as such, particularly the latest dispatches from the Mannerheim Line by Nikolai Virta, whose initial admiration for the Finns had given way to indignation.

The playwright-cum-war correspondent was particularly put out by the myriad mines that the Finns had left for the invader in Terijoki before evacuating the former coastal resort and future seat of the Finnish People's Democratic Republic. "What cads," Virta quoted a Russian soldier with the 7th Army in a dispatch of December 4. "They can't fight and break their heads running from us, but how well they make such nastiness. Hardly had the first Red fighter set foot on Finnish soil when an explosion rent the air—a mine! Mines are everywhere."[75]

Undoubtedly Finns were capable of doing devilish things with mines, as Harold Denny, the correspondent of the *New York Times,* averred in a description of the explosive handiwork they left behind at Petsamo for the Russians to find. "The Finnish soldier's sense of humor on the battlefield sometimes can take very grim turns indeed," Denny wrote, once he was clear of the cloying Finnish censors.

> When the Russians were advancing in the Petsamo region almost unopposed in the early days of the war the Finnish patrol destroyed every building in Petsamo's main settlement except the Finnish bath and prepared with fiendish ingenuity to receive the Russians.
>
> The first Russian soldiers arriving took refuge from the cold in the bath. In one corner was a well. A Russian soldier seized the rope and began hauling up a bucket of water. It was a booby trap. The well exploded, killing several Russian soldiers. But it was bitterly cold and after the excitement from this disaster had died down, a Russian pulled out the damper of the stove preparatory to lighting a fire. That set off another explosion which killed more Russians. The remainder rushed out and threw themselves into a near-by depression. That also was mined and all but two or three were killed. The survivors rushed blindly toward the bordering forest and as they reached it struck Finn wire which set off another mine and killed them.

According to Denny, the Finns who had set this fiendish series of traps watched the fruition of their grim practical joke from the safety of the nearby woods before skiing off to tell their comrades the story. "It was long a big laugh in Arctic circles."[76]

In the same vein, the Soviet military press also began complaining about the tactics employed by Finnish ski troops while paying inadvertent homage to them. "The enemy does not engage in open battle," complained the anonymous correspondent of *Red Karelia,* but rather resorts to "bandit tactics in sudden attacks on our columns. Hidden under white robes and thus skillfully camouflaged, they suddenly dart from the woods to shoot at our advancing units," the half-irate, half-admiring Soviet correspondent wrote. "Then in all haste they run, frequently taking off their boots to ski only in their stockings."

Mannerheim himself would have found little to quibble about with this description of Finnish ski tactics. Indeed, the Soviet themselves would soon, unsuccessfully, attempt to emulate them by bringing in a special detachment of their own ski troops (in addition to the handful they used at the beginning of the conflict) to counter the *belaya smert,* or "white death," as some Soviet troops referred to the ghostly Finnish troops.[77]

On the other hand, much of what the Russian press reported about the Finns was sheer fiction, particularly the increasing number of atrocity stories it relayed to its gullible readers. For example, I. Shominen, writing in the army paper *Red Star,* relayed the story of the supposed torture of a Soviet scout by invading Finnish troops near a Russian village outside Petrozavodsk, where Red soldiers had supposedly found the carbonized body of the murdered soldier lying on glowing coals bound with wires. An aged woman, apparently the only survivor of the unnamed village, sat beside the body, and told Shominen the story of what had supposedly happened when the Finns arrived at the mythical village.

"White Guardists beat the soldier wearing the red star with steel rods and prodded him with bayonets" in order to make him speak, the putative bystander claimed. Of course the soldier refused. "Finally they stabbed him in the stomach, put out his eyes and threw him into the flames."[78]

Previously, the Kremlin had only sought to demonize Tanner and Mannerheim. Now, as the Finnish troops proved more difficult to subdue, as well as deaf to Radio Moscow's exhortations to welcome their "liberators," it had become necessary to tar them as well—although the only effect of these calumnies was to make the Soviet infantrymen frightened to death of being taken prisoner by the alleged "butchers."

"Their propaganda was very strong," asserts Eric Malm. "I know, for instance, that two of our officers crept out to Russian lines to take prisoners. They encountered two soldiers, one of whom detonated a hand grenade under his stomach so he couldn't be taken prisoner. Their own propaganda had told them that if they were captured by the Finns, their fate would be worse than death."[79]

*

"We have to finish the matter quickly with a determined offensive by our troops," Meretskov ordered on December 3.

Who, then, were these "troops"? And who were their leaders?[80]

The Russians had numbers, they had machines—in some cases very good machines—but clearly most of them were lacking in the subtler aspects of the martial art. Leadership proved grossly inadequate; some of the units deployed were equipped with undoubtedly good and modern weapons, but more often than not these were unsuitable to the unfamiliar Finnish terrain. Thus, the Soviet's heavy flat-trajectory guns and tanks were virtually useless in the dense Finnish woodlands. So, by and large, were their otherwise capable 45 mm anti-tank guns, as not one Finnish tank came to oppose them—at least at first. Instead the Finns decided to employ their handful of antiquated Renault tanks and vintage Vickers-type tanks either for training purposes or stationary gun emplacements.[81]

As Catherine Merridale writes in *Ivan's War,* her study of the Russian Army during World War II:

> Thirteen of the forty rifle divisions that the Red Army fielded in Finland had been formed for less than a year by the winter of 1939–40. The others tended, as was the policy at the time, to have been brought up to strength—peopled with strangers—in the last weeks before their mobilization for the front. In place of long-established trust, the *politruks* [the Soviet political officers assigned each unit] nurtured these people's party spirit, or worse a fabricated 'friendliness.' 'Friendliness' was no substitute for professionalism, let alone mutual trust. These men had not trained together.
>
> Party spirit [could not] help when the men were afraid. . . . Without a basic understanding of their role, soldiers found battles incomprehensible and terrifying. Some were frightened of their own shadows. An infantryman in the Seventh Army caused havoc one morning when he shrieked so loudly that his whole battalion took fright.[82]

A reporter from Associated Press, one of the first journalists allowed to interview the hundreds of frightened, miserable Russian prisoners who were captured during the initial phase of the war, provided this snapshot of a typical Soviet infantryman: "A Russian prisoner interviewed said he had been drafted in Smolensk Province in September and sent to the front with very little training. He said he surrendered to the Finns because Russian officers kept machine guns at [their backs]. The man, a peasant who said his age was 25, reported that he had been told he was drafted to help defend Leningrad."[83]

How could such an army, frightened of the enemy—frightened of itself—be expected to carry out a "determined offensive"? It was simple: it could not.

And yet, even with such "inferior material," it must also be recorded, the Russians did come close to making a major breakthrough during that first wild week. On the evening of December 6, the seventh day of the war, the 50th Rifle Corps, commanded by General Vladimir Grendahl—a former Finnish Red of Swedo-Finnish extraction who had joined the Soviet Army after fighting in the Finnish Civil War—having routed Finnish covering troops on the isthmus, succeeded in reaching the southern shore of the Vuoksen-virta and Suvanto-jarvi waterways, comprising the eastern edge of the Mannerheim Line. One of the Russian vanguard units, the 18th Rifle Regiment, had even managed to pursue the retreating Finns across the Taipale River, forming a small but potentially potent bridgehead at Koukunniemi.[84]

Electrified by the news, V. E. Yakovlev, the commander of the 7th Army, immediately telephoned Grendahl, ordering him to concentrate his forces and attack the northern shore. However, the gods of war were not smiling on the

Finnish-born army commander. Lacking sufficient artillery support and pontoons to make the crossing, Grendahl decided to postpone the attack until the following day.

Another reason for Grendahl's hesitation was that the opposite shore was controlled by the elaborate system of fire points that comprised that end of the Mannerheim Line. Could he have succeeded? If he had, and he had managed to expand the bridgehead at Koukunniemi, there is no telling what would have happened. Certainly it had been a very near thing.[85]

In any event, by the following day, when the break in the line was reinforced, it was too late. As Carl Van Dyke writes, "The 7th Army had missed its one and only chance to bring its offensive to a rapid and offensive conclusion."

In the meantime, another attempted crossing on the Eastern Isthmus at a particularly turbulent juncture of the Vuoksi River at Kiviniemi (now known as Losevo) was about to meet even greater failure, as Bair Irincheev describes in his book *War of the White Death*. As Irincheev, who has visited the site himself, notes, the notion of trying to ford the river at that point, which is today a popular spot for white-water rafting, was daft. Along with the rough water, the misbegotten operation was further handicapped by the fact that Kombrig Zaitsev, commander of the 90th Division, was relying on hopelessly dated intelligence about what his troops faced on the other, northern side.

Nevertheless, on December 7, the assault was made. The result was an even greater debacle:

> As soon as the pontoons and tanks reached the middle of the river's northern bank, a current of overwhelming power drove [the Soviet troops] towards the rapids and blown bridges. At the same moment the Finns illuminated the rapids with searchlights and opened devastating machine gun fire at the pontoons and the crossing point on the southern bank. Finnish mortars and artillery joined the barrage as well.

V. V. Tkachev, a Soviet sergeant-major who participated in the amphibious attack, further described the hellish crossing under fire:

> It was like this. We were crossing the river in the middle, the two other crossings were dummy [feints]. There was an open field in front of the river, some kilometer-and-a-half wide. There was a freshly dug trench across the field to the crossing. The assault began. Our men ran into the field towards the river, and the Finnish artillery immediately hit them with shrapnel. Everyone was pinned down. I was next to the trench at the moment. We rushed to the river along the trench.
>
> We reached the bank and saw the bodies of our dead sappers lying in heaps, and there was no crossing ready! The bank was steep, so we dived down to the river. There were several rowboats below. "Move fellows,

move!" We jumped into the boats and rowed like crazy, although what could we do on the other bank? Each one of us had fifteen rifle rounds and one F-1 hand grenade. Not much of a soldier! Thirty-two of us made it to the other bank. There were piles of logs there. I ordered: 'Disperse!' We took cover behind the logs, and the Finns hit them hard with artillery! An artillery round went through three rows and the rest flew into the river. I thought that the whole mass of logs would crash into the river and take us down too.

Thus, by the end of the first week of fighting, both sides had cause for self-reproach. Essentially the two adversaries had fought each other to a draw. But a draw was still a moral victory for the Finns. They certainly hadn't "collapsed," as Harold Nicholson, the British politician, had believed, and as had so many others, including Stalin and the more deluded members of his coterie. Indeed, the entire Soviet operation was beginning to look more and more like a fiasco.[86]

"FIRST WEEK A SOVIET FAILURE," trumpeted a front-page headline in the *New York Times* on December 7. "Soviet Russia's plan for a lightning war in Finland with the obvious aim of causing a subsequent collapse of the Finnish government must be considered hopelessly stranded," the paper's Danish stringer observed. "Finland is not yet another Poland. Despite the use of enormous forces employing tanks, armored cars and planes, the attempt to break through the Finns' Mannerheim Line has been unsuccessful up to the time of the latest reports today."[87]

One thing was certainly clear: the USSR had already lost on the front of world opinion. Everywhere the tide of horror and indignation at the Russian invasion continued to mount, giving rise to furious anti-Soviet and anti-Communist demonstrations and protests of various forms, as well as swelling the number of volunteers from various nations who wished to enlist in "brave little Finland's gallant fight."

That same day, December 7, in downtown Budapest, over 2,000 jeering, whistling right-wing Hungarian students staged a mass anti-Russian, pro-Finnish protest before marching to the Finnish embassy, where their self-appointed leader, Josef Ambruss, personally delivered a message of support to the Finnish minister, Onni Talas. "All Hungarians are following the heroic battles of the Finnish people," Ambruss declared before mustering his followers and marching on to the Italian Legation, where they cheered Mussolini, whose criticism of the invasion had been widely reported, and hurled imprecations at Russia. "Police made no attempt to interfere," according to the United Press.[88]

Presumably, some of Ambruss's followers were amongst the extraordinary number of Hungarians, estimated at 25,000, who applied to fight for their linguistic cousins. Eventually 350 of these were selected, after rigorous examination, and sent to Finland as a battalion under the command of Captain Imre Kemery Nagy, a right-wing activist.[89]

"It is beginning to look as if another 'International Brigade' [is] in the process of forming," wrote Herbert Matthews, the Rome correspondent of the *New York Times,* referring to the increasing numbers of private citizens from Sweden, Hungary, the United States, and other countries from around the world who were coming forward, with or without their government's encouragement, to fight for Finland. This one would be to fight Communism, whereas in Spain it was to fight Fascism.[90]

The wave of anger at the Soviets even made itself felt at sea. When the invasion was announced to the passengers and crew of the Swedish American liner *Gripsholm,* bound from Copenhagen to New York, some of the crew "threatened to throw the four or five Russian passengers aboard overboard."[91]

The British government, which had been so slow to condemn Russia, was also coming around. Prime Minister Neville Chamberlain's initial reaction to the invasion, as well as the accompanying public uproar, had been churlish. "The situation is complicated by Stalin's latest performance," the British prime minister recorded in his diary on December 3. "[It] seems to have provoked far more indignation than Hitler's attack on Poland, though it was no worse morally," he wrote before adding, somewhat mysteriously, "and in its development is likely to be much less brutal." Apparently Chamberlain, though hardly a friend of the Soviets, still had faith in Stalin's ultimate decency.[92]

"I suppose," noted Chamberlain, "the world was not so sure that the Poles were free from fault as the Finns." As far as His Majesty's Government was concerned, Stalin's latest "adventure" was little more than an annoyance and a distraction from the main act—to defeat the Nazis.[93]

By December 5, however, Chamberlain's foreign minister, Lord Halifax, was excoriating the Kremlin in the House of Lords for its "inexcusable act of aggression." In response to the increasing and outspoken opposition of the British public to the invasion, Chamberlain announced that Finland could acquire planes from Britain, and soon a deal for twenty Gloster Gladiator pursuit fighters was made, the first of the nearly ninety aircraft of various kinds the British would give or sell to Finland.[94]

Although it never actually reached riotous proportions, nowhere, with the possible exception of Sweden, was the general public's anger at the Kremlin greater than in the United States.

Witness the tear-stained article syndicated columnist Anne O'Hare McCormick posted on December 2, entitled "Finland Fights Alone but on the Side of Angels."[95]

"Perhaps it was because of Finland that one noticed the angels in the shop windows this morning," McCormick's paean to *Suomi* began.

The mind's eye was on other windows—the clean, bright glass of Helsinki, with its glazed-brick and steel office buildings, its up-to-date housing, its famous railway station. The Finns were as proud as Punch of their capital, which by stubborn industry they had transformed into a strikingly modern city in twenty years. . . .

The Finns would not have built so many glass walls if they had dreamed that their powerful neighbor would visit them with bombs. They would not have started out to work and school and market Thursday morning if they had imagined they were at war.[96]

Apparently, like many at that early juncture of the conflict, the American journalist considered the Finns' cause to be hopeless.

It has been a thin year for the side of the angels. It has been a black year for the weak. The invasion of Finland puts an end to whatever illusions remained that in a predatory world, governed by no law but force, small nations can survive by their own power or by the moral support of powerful friends. The Finns at this writing are continuing their brave resistance against a wholly unprovoked attack, but the battle they are fighting was hopeless from the moment the Soviet government decided to attack in force.[97]

In anticipation of possible protests, the Kremlin already decided that day to withdraw its exhibit from the 1939–40 New York World's Fair. The aggressively chauvinistic pavilion, whose main feature consisted of a mammoth, seventy-nine-foot stainless steel statue of a worker holding aloft a red star, had already been a subject of stormy controversy. If anyone desired proof of the Soviets' expansionist worldview, here it was: the exhibit completely dominated the exposition's foreign area. Now, as anger at the Soviet invasion continued to rise, Russian officials wisely decided to demolish the exhibit and withdraw from the World's Fair altogether.[98]

It was none too soon, the New York Times opined on its editorial page. "After the events of the last few weeks the Government of Russia would be an unwanted and unwelcome visitor [to] an exposition undertaken in a spirit of mutual confidence and good will," the paper thundered.[99]

Soviet officials were presumably more put out by a statement released at this time by Alexander Kerensky—the one-time revolutionary who became Russian prime minister following the October Revolution, whom Lenin and the Bolsheviks subsequently pushed aside and was now living in bitter exile in the United States—appealing to the American public not to confuse Stalin's action with "the real wishes of the Russian people." "All Russian democrats and true Russian patriots protest against the shameful and dishonorable action of Stalin in Finland."[100]

What were the real wishes of the Russian people? It wasn't easy to ascertain, although there were increasing indications that they were not exactly enamored with Stalin's latest adventure, either. The Russian press, for its part, continued to be filled with vituperation for the Finns, with bloodcurdling reports of alleged Finnish atrocities along with vague, unsubstantiated reports of putative Soviet victories against the black-hearted "White Guardists." "Naturally," G.E.R. Gedye, noted, "every reference to the widespread [international] indignation [is] suppressed, as [is] any mention of [the] constant bombings of cities and towns."[101]

And yet, restricted though Gedye's movements were, the observant reporter had picked up signs of unease with what was happening to the north: "Deprived of all knowledge as they are, Soviet citizens, including even members of the Communist party, are bewildered and uneasy as to what is happening [in Finland]."[102]

To be sure, outwardly there were no signs in the Russian capital that the USSR was engaged in a major war. "It would seem," Gedye wrote, "that the government has made no preparations as yet for the possibility of a major conflict developing over Finland." Thus, on December 5, the third anniversary of the adoption of the Stalinist Constitution, while Soviet troops were hurling themselves at Finnish machine guns on the Mannerheim Line, a festive mood obtained in Moscow. Red banners flew and military bands played, while a massive bank of searchlights shone their beams on serried banks of revolving crystal globes.[103]

Not so in Leningrad, where the hospitals were beginning to fill with casualties from the war and a citywide blackout had been imposed; however, since he was forbidden to go there Gedye couldn't see that.

By contrast, the picture the Finnish capital presented was a grim one. By day, workers boarded up windows with wooden planks or placed sandbags around buildings. At night pedestrians groped their way through the blacked-out streets.

As it happened, there were no further Russian bombing attacks on either December 2 or 3. The respite was generally ascribed to a combination of the poor weather and the arrival, on the second, of the *Donau,* a large German merchant ship Berlin had dispatched in order to evacuate its 700 nationals in the city, along with those of its totalitarian allies. The presence of the large ship, which was due to sail early on the morning of December 4 with its jittery complement of Russians, Germans, Italians, and Estonians, was considered a temporary guarantee of safety for the beleaguered city.[104]

Once it sailed, it was believed, the dread bombing would resume. Propelling this belief, according to the *New York Times,* was "a rumor credited to well-intentioned circles" that Russian bombers intended to attack Helsinki with gas, along with a horde of gas-mask wearing paratroops, if Finland refused to capitulate. The British vice consul, Nigel Allan, found the rumor sufficiently credible to round up the remaining British nationals in the city and put them in cars, with the aid of a number of deputies. In the event, the rumor proved unfounded; however, for weeks to follow many Helsinkians—and journalists—kept their gas masks at hand.[105]

*

Another journalist and member of the original Kamp press corps who was still in Helsinki at this time was Herbert Elliston. After a week of covering the Finnish story, his paper, *The Christian Science Monitor*, was sending another reporter to relieve him. Elliston was torn. On the one hand, he was reluctant to leave the scene of his big scoop. On the other hand, Elliston, who was also a correspondent for the American Broadcasting Corporation, had had difficulty getting airtime from Finnish radio to transmit his reports. Meanwhile, Curt Bloch of the *New York Times* had had his own problems getting photos to Stockholm for transmission to New York. When Bloch invited Elliston to fly there with him, after taking the train from Helsinki to Turku, his colleague hedged.

"When the novelty of this thing wears off," the blunt-talking Bloch assured Elliston, "they'll forget all about you and Helsinki. And this thing is bound to get so hard that there'll probably be a dictatorship which will clamp down on talks anyway. When the bloody Germans get out, the Bolshies will knock hell out of this place, and then where will you be? Ryti will disappear, and the military will be in charge."[106]

"Besides," Bloch persisted, referring to the overbearing Finnish press censorship, "how do you know that even now we are getting the right dope?" Still, Elliston hesitated, so Bloch took another tack. "And you say you're interested in the Finns," he needled. "Why not see a few instead of hanging around the Hotel Kamp?"[107]

That did it. So, after settling his bill at the hotel, as well as paying for another room several days in advance in case he wanted to come back, there Elliston was, an hour later, at a cafe in the Helsinki railway station, ticket in hand for Turku, the westernmost Finnish city where Bloch had booked a plane to fly to Stockholm four days hence. Hearing that Elliston spoke English, a neatly dressed, English-speaking Finn at the next table turned to him and spontaneously spoke his mind.

"We are just plain mad, mad, mad, through and through," the Finn told Elliston. "We're just thinking mad, not talking mad," he explained.[108]

"First the bombs, then the leaflets telling us how happier we'd be when the Russians took Helsinki, and finally the machine-gunning. Do they mean *us* in all this junk about conditions in Finland? Are they crazy? You should have seen the faces of the boys in the forts [near Helsinki] when those Russians tried to blot them out. They were white with rage." And he said what I heard many Finns say before: "You know we are Westerners and those Russians are Easterners."[109]

A few minutes later, the two American pressmen found themselves wedged into the passageway of their packed second-class coach, sitting on their bags, patiently waiting with the hundreds of other passengers aboard for the westward-bound train to pull out.

Observing his fellow refugees, Elliston was struck, above all, by how unearthly quiet they were. If fear was present it was a very quiet, subdued, *Finnish* fear. "I could now vaguely discern the people sitting in their seats and all down the aisle. What struck me was the quietness of everybody. In any other country, it seemed to me there would have been pandemonium. . . . Except for the occasional wailing of an infant you could hear scarcely a sound beyond the shuffling involved in getting settled down."[110]

Now, with light streaming into the car, Elliston noticed something else unusual: all the baggage racks were bare.

We looked around in the light that came streaming in. The first thing to do was to make ourselves as comfortable as we could. After all, in one train or another we were going to be traveling all day. We began to attend to our baggage. I looked up at the racks. Empty! What on earth were these people fleeing with then?

Bloch saw me look at the empty racks and then at the people. "Just look at their backs," he advised. That was the explanation. They were all sitting bolt upright, with their possessions on their knees, and their bags behind their backs. Waiting! "They're ready to quit this train as soon as the Russians start machine-gunning or bombing."[111]

There had already been at least one widely reported incident of Russian planes machine-gunning a train out of Imatra, whereupon the engineer had responded by halting the train. Then the passengers ran for cover in the woods, a scene that would be repeated hundreds of times over the next fourteen weeks. Now, on day three of the war, these same, stolid, clear-minded Finns had already collectively adopted the most sensible train-evacuation form.

"Extraordinary people," Elliston said admiringly as the train rumbled westward. Bloch agreed.[112]

*

All may have been well and calm aboard the Helsinki-to-Turku express; however, in Helsinki, wild with rumors of a possible gas-cum-paratroop attack, fear still reigned.

Back in Helsinki, things were finally beginning to settle down. By December 6, Independence Day, the capital was in working order again. Telephone, telegraph, mail, and railroads were operating normally, the *New York Times* reported. "Large bus lines are maintaining traffic quite as in peacetime and there are not even noteworthy delays in communications."[113]

The Finns' secret weapon, their strategic reserve of *sisu,* had begun to kick in. "Steadily, the Finns fought [their] sense of shock," Cox wrote. "They fought it in a typically Finnish way, by concentrating on the job at hand."[114]

*

Some Helsinkians, like young Harry Matso, who had gallantly led his classmates to safety on the afternoon of November 30, took pride in not joining the initial panic and staying put. At fifteen, he may have been too young to fight, but he wasn't too young to understand that he was part of a bigger effort.

"I *wanted* to stay [in Helsinki]," he declared. "I wanted to be part of the war." And so he would: several days later, Matso was given a position as a guard in an air shelter. Matso's father also granted him one special dispensation because of the war. "After the first day," he says, "my father gave me permission to smoke."[115]

*

Then, on December 7, just as things were returning to normal, the Finnish High Command did a very stupid thing. In one of its most irresponsible acts it reported, without proper investigation, that the Russians had used poison gas on the Ladoga front. It seems that Helsinki was equally anxious to demonize the other side. The frightening announcement was immediately and vehemently denied by Moscow. But who could believe Moscow, after its blithe insistence that it only bombed airfields? Perhaps the Russians had; perhaps they hadn't.[116]

In the meantime, Helsinkians continued to scan the leaden skies for Russian parachutes. The fact that the few paratroops the Russians had reportedly used had been immediately overcome didn't matter, as the *Times* noted on December 7: "Even if the Russians have been somewhat unsuccessful in the past with troops of this type, who have been immediately disarmed, it is realized that this type of warfare is only in its experimental stage. However, every square mile of the city is studded with machine gun nests able to open a withering fire on parachute troops."[117]

There would not be another Soviet raid on Helsinki for several weeks. But no one knew that then. Indubitably, those nerve-wracking first days left a lasting impact on Helsinkians, as well as on the reporters whose job it was to relate their ordeal to the world. "When I watched families trudging out at night to sleep in the frozen woods and when I saw the strain on face after face," wrote Geoffrey Cox, "I felt that this suffering, whatever the cause of it, was itself definitely evil. After those days in Helsinki I could always understand why Finns fought as they did and why they remained solidly behind men like Mannerheim and Ryti, whom many of them had regarded all their lives as their chief enemies. No pamphlets or propaganda broadcast could undo the effect of those days."[118]

✳

It was at about this time that Alpo Reinikainen, an infantryman assigned to the Mannerheim Line, was meditating upon the motives and fates of four Russian reconnaissance parachutists who had been dropped near his regiment's position. These Russians were no dolts: one of them had made it to the door of Reinikainen's headquarters, only to be dispatched by the alert sentry after the intruder couldn't come up with the unit's correct password.[119]

Although many of his comrades were filled with hatred for the enemy, Reinikainen himself could only feel a combination of pity and awe as he contemplated the bullet-ridden corpses, as he confided to his diary:

> Yesterday I saw the enemy for the first time. Four men, reconnaissance parachutists, their bloody heads bare. Young men hardly in their twenties, each head pierced by at least one bullet. The footprints they had made in the ice as they ran and crawled were marked by blood for a long way. They had fought to their last breath. I unwittingly felt respect for the enemy, youths lying there at my feet and sorrow at their fate.
>
> They were certainly enemies, Russkies. But I couldn't help pitying them, [while] respect[ing] their bravery and mental strength but [it still] seems incomprehensible. They surely believed they were sacrificing their lives for a good cause. But *what* cause? We are fighting for our freedom. They had come to free the Finnish people from the capitalist yoke.

And yet the more Reinikainen thought about those lifeless Russians, the less their deaths made sense to him. "What purpose gives the enemy this bravery and spirit of self-sacrifice? *What?*"[120]

✳

It was in this charged atmosphere that the Finnish government, represented by Prime Minister Ryti, Foreign Minister Tanner, and several of their fellow ministers, welcomed the Helsinki diplomatic corps to a high-spirited, if somewhat surreal, reception to celebrate the twenty-second anniversary of Finland's independence at the Hotel Kamp on the evening of December 6.[121]

Finnish embassies abroad commemorated the holiday, occurring as it did at the very moment of the nation's greatest peril, as best they saw fit or not at all.

For his part, Hjalmar Procope, the Finnish ambassador to the United States, who had been spending most of the past week running around Washington trying to raise American aid, deemed the occasion too serious to celebrate with the usual embassy reception. "Wednesday marks the twenty-second anniversary of Finland's independence," he declared. "There is no time for celebrating. Every effort and every penny goes now to fight the Russian aggressor."[122]

At the same time, he used the occasion to draw attention to the close ties between Finland and the United States. "It was on December 6, 1917, that our people declared their freedom from the Russian Bolsheviki and created probably the closest counterpart to the American Republic that exists today in the world."[123]

Back in Helsinki, the occasion was also deemed too serious for the usual annual reception at the president's palace, which was canceled. However, the Foreign Ministry decided that it had to do something to demonstrate to the world that it was functioning, so instead it organized a similar reception at the Kamp.

It was a somewhat unusual affair. Because of the impromptu nature of the event, messengers delivered the invitations orally. Also, because of the wartime conditions, the usual black tie was disposed of and both Finnish officials and guests were told to come as they wished. Still, Vaino Tanner was somewhat nonplussed when the otherwise conservative education minister, Uuno Hannula, turned up in a red cardigan and rubber boots. The minister's dishabille was forgiven.

Still, under the circumstances, basically all went well, as the various guests—which included the German minister, Wipert von Bluecher, and the American minister, Arnold Schoenfeld—dutifully pretended to enjoy themselves as best they could, partaking of the plentiful hors d'oeuvres while making sure their gas masks were within reach. The resident press corps, happy for the diversion and liquid refreshments, was also invited to the in-house fete.

Along with Ryti and Tanner was the new minister without portfolio, Juho Paasikivi. A rumor—again false—had it that Paasikivi had left for Moscow to resume negotiations. Paasikivi's presence at the soiree threw water on that notion. Indeed, it would be some time before Paasikivi would return to Moscow.[124]

Despite the difficult conditions under which the reception was held, the government officials who managed to attend the reception were upbeat. Their spirits were particularly buoyed by the congratulatory message that President Roosevelt had sent to President Kallio earlier in honor of the anniversary. In it the American leader expressed the hope that "these tragic days may not be long in giving way to a happier era." Roosevelt's telegram, which was considered unusually effusive for the occasion, was taken—wrongly, as it would turn out—as a promissory note of substantive American aid to come. Its contents were also read over the radio as part of the traditional president's day broadcast, following a recording of "The Star Spangled Banner."[125]

Then the president spoke. Kallio minced no words in denouncing the Russian aggressor. "Our peaceful towns have been bombed," the Finnish leader asserted in his melodramatic address, "women and children killed, not to speak of those victims claimed by the defense of our borders. It looks as though that mighty power wants to rob us of the independence which that nation itself recognized."[126]

Kallio also included a plaintive appeal to the outside world for help, the first of several such appeals the Finnish government would issue in coming weeks. "The Finnish people," he declared, "awaits expectantly to see whether other nations will tolerate the destruction aimed against us." In the meantime, he assured the many anxious Finns listening on their radio sets around the country, "we can absolutely trust in the fact that our soldiers on land, sea, and in the air, under the honored supreme commander, are fulfilling their heroic duty."[127]

This was followed by a stirring taped rendition of "Finlandia," the national anthem. After the reception at the Kamp ended, Ryti and Tanner thanked their guests for attending. Then all present grabbed their coats and gas masks and made their way out into the night, feeling their way through the silent, blacked-out city.

Exiting later, Tanner pronounced himself satisfied with the unusual soiree. Perhaps the relatively sparse refreshments, which he had personally procured with the aid of Elanto, the Social Democratic cooperative, left something to be desired, as did the atmosphere. But at least the government had accomplished its mission: to prove to the world that, Radio Moscow to the contrary, the legitimate Finnish government was still alive and well.

"A complete blackout was in effect," Tanner wrote later, "and the overcast sky did not permit the feeblest glow to light the march of the homeward bound. But the evening had served its purpose: that the world press [would] never again carry the legend about the government which had 'fled to an unknown destination'" —as some pressmen had wrongly inferred from Parliament's relocation to its new "secret" location in Ostrobothnia.[128]

While his colleagues at the Kamp were clinking glasses with the cabinet and writing their stories at the bar, Elliston was ambling around Turku with Curt Bloch, collecting more local color while they waited to take the plane to Stockholm. By now, the two Americans had acquired an interpreter, an earnest young Finnish woman by the name of Aili Peltonen.

Once again Elliston was impressed with the stoicism of the Finns he met, as well as that of the city itself, which struck him as preternaturally quiet, even as it battened down in preparation for the aerial storm to come. "There was no full-throated defy of Stalin or of the Russians; just the boarding up of the shops methodically."

"You hear the nails being driven in, but it's not as loud as I would have expected," he remarked to his cicerone. The Englishman was struck by his guide's solemn response: "Very seriously she responded, in language that was Biblical in style and cadence: 'Now you see they will cast down bombs upon us, and destroy our homes, so that we must be quiet.'"[129]

All was indeed silent, with the exception of the frequent air raid sirens, two of which interrupted a dinner he was enjoying with Peltonen at the Hamburger Bors (Hamburger Exchange), then one of the city's few passable restaurants, forcing the journalist and his companion to duck into the cellar air raid shelter.

To be sure, there was little question, in this Turku cellar, how the average Finn felt about their former overlords, as the newspaperman related a disparaging story he overheard about the 1904 Russo-Japanese war, which had ended disastrously for Moscow.

> One of our fellow cave dwellers was telling a story. In 1904, he said the Japanese sunk the flagship of the Russian fleet in Far Eastern waters, and the news was put up on a bulletin board in the streets of Helsinki. The notice was in Finnish. A Russian officer kept trying to make out what was printed, but finally gave it up and, turning to a Finnish boy standing next to him, demanded: "What does it mean?" The Finnish boy, quick as a flash, responded: "Japonski: boom, boom, boom! Russky: boolie, boolie, boolie!"

"Even I could understand such language," Elliston remarked, "and I laughed even before Aili interpreted the story. How the Finns despised the Russians! Tsarist and Bolshevik equally."

Then the all-clear sounded, and the subterraneans returned to their meals.[130] "We can get used to anything," a waitress told Elliston as he exited into the Turku night, "even Russians dropping things on us."[131]

Elliston and Bloch had stumbled on that crucial adjunct of *sisu* that helped Finns get through the Winter War: their droll—sometimes darkly droll—sense of humor. Then, of course, there were always plenty of Russian jokes to go around. Perhaps the most famous of these, which may or may not have been based on an actual incident, had a panic-stricken Russian soldier surrendering, or trying to surrender, to Finnish authorities.

"Don't shoot," the man exclaimed with his hands raised. "I am a Russian capitalist!"[132]

To be sure, Turku's sense of humor would be sorely tested over the next thirteen weeks, as the Red Air Force, flying over from their bases in Estonia, would, in the course of the sixty-one air raids they launched against the city—over seven times as many as Helsinki suffered—drop many more of "Molotov's breadbaskets."[133]

While he was in town, Elliston dropped by the local YLE studio to listen to the news, where he was surprised to hear the words of a Russian prisoner. Evidently a microphone had been placed in the interrogation room, allowing the captive soldier's words to be broadcast around Finland, while Elliston listened with the aid of another Russian-speaking Finn:

One of the listeners [in the studio] knew Russian. The Russian said he was surprised the Finns didn't kill their wounded. He'd heard that that was the Finnish custom. He went on to say that he was surprised to get any food at all, because he had been told that Finland was starving, and awaited Russian deliverance from its oppressors. He asked about his comrades' machine-gunning of Finnish civilians. The woebegone prisoner apologized, [and] said it must have been done by war-crazy Russians.[134]

The unwitting Russian radio celebrity was clearly pleased with the way he had been treated. When the interrogator asked him what advice he had for his fellow "emancipators," he replied: "To be taken prisoner by the Finns." Next, as an audial chaser, the expressionless studio manager switched to Radio Moscow, "where [we] heard the usual threats that within so many hours Helsinki would be in ruins."

In keeping with their kinsmen around the country, the 80,000 inhabitants of Turku celebrated Independence Day quietly; no speech-making or flag-waving here. There was, however, one parade down the main street, a simple affair consisting of a line of marching soldiers, singing. "Hear dear Finland, our Holy Oath," they sang out, as the citizenry silently watched on.

Never shall violent hands be put on Thee;
We will defend Thee, we will give our blood for Thee.
Be sure your sons are always on their guard.[135]

*

To the west of Turku, in the freezing waters between the Aland archipelago and Sweden, a group of Finnish servicemen spent December 6 in a submerged state. They were the twenty-seven crew members of the Finnish submarine *Iku-Turso.*

At the outbreak of the war, Finland boasted a squadron of five submersibles —the *Vetehinen, Vesihiisi, Iku-Turso, Vesikko,* and the *Saukko.* Not that this was very many in comparison with her Nordic neighbors: Sweden had twenty, Norway nine. The aging subs, which carried between thirteen and twenty-seven crewmen, dated from the early 1930s, when submarines were all the rage amongst Europe's navies.[136]

In retrospect, the monies would probably have been better spent purchasing planes or anti-tank guns. By 1939, the subs were obsolescent, and the torpedoes they carried were defective; the boats were also ill equipped to dive in the extremely harsh, icy conditions that often prevailed in the surrounding Baltic waters, making their use highly problematic. Still, the 150 men who served aboard the elderly submersibles, which were initially based in Helsinki, considered themselves the Navy's elite, as Antti Okko, a veteran torpedoman on the *Iku-Turso,* recalled: "We kind of thought that we were better than the rest of the guys in the Navy."[137]

Then the war came, and the *Iku-Turso,* along with her sister ship, the *Vetehinen,* were detached and sent to Saaristomeri near Turku in order to patrol the waters of the Bothnian Sea as a flotilla. "I remember, on Independence Day, we were monitoring the traffic between Aland and Sweden," Okko remembered. The *Iku-Turso* had been told to be on the lookout for a Russian merchant ship, the *Ivan Papanen,* while the *Vetehinen* trained its periscopes for *Jermak,* an icebreaker. All day and all night Okko and his mates remained in readiness.[138]

"We were stalking that boat for a week," the ex-torpedoman recalled, his voice still tinged with disappointment seventy years later. "But I was ready." (The *Ivan Papanen* escaped detection, apparently disguised as a Latvian vessel; the *Vetehinen* later made contact with the *Jermak* but lost her in a squall.)[139]

And so they would remain for another three weeks, until the fast coagulating waters of the Gulf of Finland froze over, effectively ending Otto's and his fellow submariners' fighting days (as such), as well as any naval actions either side might contemplate. In the event, the Finnish subs were stripped of their 76 mm Bofors guns, which were added to Turku's aircraft defenses.[140]

Unfortunately for Finland, because of the exceptionally cold winter, the gulf would remain frozen for an unusually long time, well into March, enabling the Russians to contemplate attacking the Finnish coast over the ice, but that is something which neither belligerent could have foreseen, or even imagined, at the time.

The *Iku-Torso* and *Vetehinen* were not the only submarines patrolling the waters of the Baltic Sea. On December 9, in a significant escalation of the war, the Kremlin, hoping to repeat the Allies' successful blockade of Imperial Germany during the First World War, imposed a similar ban on sea traffic to and from Finland, threatening to sink any and every ship that approached within twenty nautical miles of the Finnish coast.[141]

Enforcement of the blockade was assigned to the Soviets' large Baltic fleet of thirty submarines. However, the blockade, like the initial land invasion, wound up being a bust. Merchant ships traveling to and from Finland were effectively assembled into convoys. The only reported Soviet submarine attack, on January 13, 1940, before the eastern Baltic became entirely unnavigable, was a misfire: a faulty depth charge exploded prematurely and sunk the Finnish escort vessel *Aura II,* along with its crew of twenty-six. The Soviets also lost at least one submarine to Finnish mines, the *S-2,* which divers discovered in June 2009 in the Aland Islands. By comparison, the minuscule Finnish navy came off rather well.[142]

Besides Elliston and Bloch, another journalist conspicuously absent at the Independence Day fete at the Kamp was Martha Gellhorn. Perhaps the Finnish people could trust in the fact that their soldiers were doing their duty, but the intrepid writer had to see for herself.

Wielding the letter of introduction she had from Eleanor Roosevelt, Gellhorn managed to wangle a personal tour of the Mannerheim Line. And so, on the evening of December 6, the heavily swathed reporter was in a camouflaged Finnish staff car, slipping and sliding her way en route to meet General Osterman, the commander of the Army of the Isthmus at his sumptuous headquarters at Sortala Manor, outside Viipuri.

It seems that the Russians were not the only ones worried about mines. "The road was just wide enough for the car and here it narrowed to a bridge," Gellhorn wrote in *Collier's,* then one of America's most popular weekly magazines.

> The blued lamps of the car only dimly lit the frozen snow four feet ahead. "Be careful," the soldier said to our driver. We had been driving in low and barely seemed to move. Suddenly the tail light showed a red-painted pole to the left. The bridge felt different from the road, smoother and even more slippery. When we were across, the soldier let out his breath. "That's pretty dangerous," he explained. "Those mined bridges—if you skid, I mean. One of our men hit such a mine and we couldn't even find him. There's another to cross now." [143]

Gellhorn's car cleared the bridge by a meter. Soon, after crossing another frosted field, the transfixed correspondent could see the light of battle—flashes from Finnish artillery—reminiscent of an approaching thunderstorm, followed by a company of infantry moving silently through the fastness.

> This night war in snow and ice with unending forest hiding the armies was too fantastic to be true. . . . Gun flashes from the Finnish batteries burned like summer lightning against the sky and the noise of the outgoing shells was very loud and blurred, and, like an echo, we would hear the explosions as they landed. For an hour I had been waiting to hear the Russian batteries reply and still they were silent. . . . The line of soldiers stretched far forward into the darkness. I thought it was probably a company of 150 men but couldn't be sure; most of them, wearing white overalls, seemed part of the snow. [144]

Eventually Gellhorn reached General Osterman's lavish headquarters.

> We were led into a small, equally elegant salon where scale maps were pinned on the wall, and a long, business-like table was the only furnishings. The general [Osterman] a gray, slender, shy man, came in presently from a trip to the front. The talk was friendly and formal and unrevealing, as it always is with army officers, and at last I asked for permission to go to the front. The general said presently that it would be impossible—I would have to walk eight kilometers through these forests where every inch of ground seemed to either be taken up by a tree or a granite boulder, and between

rocks and trees the snow drifts [were] as high as your neck. I said, in French to Finnish via the aide-de-camp that I was prepared to walk through anything.[145]

Sorry: nothing doing. However, Gellhorn was allowed to interview—and awaken—a group of soldiers resting nearby, who proceeded to relay their amazement at the seemingly mindless tactics the Russians had used in their assault on the Mannerheim Line. The soldiers, the writer found, were not without pity for their foe: "Here, as everywhere else, I heard soldiers and officers express regret that other men should have to die stupidly and wastefully like slaughtered animals."[146]

The *Collier's* reporter was also evidently the first correspondent allowed to visit a number of Russian prisoners at Viipuri prison, a forlorn group that included pilots who had participated in the earlier raids:

> The chief warden of this prison was a spare gray man with pince-nez and a stammer and the gentle manner of a professor. He was talking in Russian with a Soviet flier. The flier was a man of thirty-two with a sad, tired face and two days' growth of beard, and he stood as straight as his fatigue would let him and answered questions in a soft, humble voice. He did not move and his voice did not change, but standing so, tears rolled down his face, and the warden and the jailers turned away because they did not want to look.
>
> We walked down stone steps into the cellar and two Russian soldiers were let out of barred cells. They also stood in this tight, rigid manner, and I thought probably they expected to be shot. One was a tall man of thirty-seven and the other a boy of twenty-three. . . . They were very thin and their clothing was of the crudest sort. They repeated what all the others said: they were told Finland was attacking them, and so they were fighting to save Russia.[147]

Another captured Soviet aviator told Gellhorn that "they had been told the Finns have neither anti-aircraft nor pursuit planes." (Did this help explain the Soviets' mad low-flying tactics?)[148]

The climax of the gallivanting reporter's sortie was a high-spirited visit with the pilots of *Lentolaivue 24* (Flying Squadron 24) and their charismatic commander, Captain Gustav Erik Magnusson:

> I was taken to the great airfield of this sector, where fighter planes were stationed. Not much can be written about it. Even when you were on the field you could see nothing. The planes were hidden in the woods and in their own dugouts. All the vastly complicated organization work was carried on in dugouts which looked like snowdrifts. We stepped over sweet-smelling

pine boughs that camouflaged a dugout where a crack pursuit squadron has its quarters.[149]

A memorable photo of Gellhorn's visit to *Lentolaivue 24* survives, and it would become her most cherished souvenir of her Finnish sojourn. It shows a smiling Jorma Sarvanto, who would soon become Finland's first ace, holding a guitar and standing next to his glamorous, fur-adorned visitor, along with several of his beaming, fellow aviators, the very picture of Fenno-American harmony.[150] Moreover, Gellhorn came away from her visit to the front with renewed hope and admiration for the supposed Finnish underdogs:

> One cannot know what will happen in a war from one day to the next, and certainly guessing is even more hazardous in a war between such unequal forces, but it is safe to say that the Finns have a trained army, helped by knowledge of the terrain; the soldiers are well equipped and wonderfully fed. The army has that sound and comforting gaiety of good troops. It has confidence in its leaders. And it has the determination of those who fight on their own soil. One Finnish pilot spoke for them all when he said, "They will not get us as a present."[151]

Gellhorn qualified her upbeat report of how the Finns were faring by saying that she could only speak of conditions on the Karelian front. "I don't know what is going on in the north, where it is no more than 125 miles [200 kilometers] from the Russian border to the Finnish coast of the Bothnian Gulf and the vital railway line that connects Finland and Sweden. . . . Nor does anyone know what the Russian army has in store [there]."[152]

Martha Gellhorn might have further qualified her eyewitness report from the Mannerheim Line if she had known that the infantry attack she had witnessed wound up being a failure.

One of those troops who participated in the abortive counteroffensive, which was beaten back after intense fighting the following morning, was Corporal Harry Berner. "On the sixth we were ordered to counterattack," he said. "We did this on skis. The attack failed completely. Our physical condition was just too poor."[153]

Still, Gellhorn's reading of Finnish morale was on the mark, as a correspondent for the Associated Press who was permitted to visit the Mannerheim Line several days later confirmed in his dispatch of December 9; it was headed "with the Finnish Army on the Karelian Front." "The Russian Army, with artillery and tanks, pounded unsuccessfully today at this strongly held sector of the Finnish front," began the report, foreshadowing the much larger assault on the line that was to come a week later. "Working feverishly to strengthen their already elaborate defense system, the Finns expressed confidence in their ability to hold indefinitely along this line, still well in advance of their main Mannerheim Line. New and larger thrusts were expected, but the Finns believed they could be thrown back, too."[154]

The AP writer marveled, as did so many foreign observers, at the Finns' ability to keep themselves—and their horses—warm: "Despite zero and subzero temperatures the Finns are comfortable in their warm tents with wood stoves and straw floors. Their horses, accustomed to the extreme cold, are quartered in camouflaged stables in the woods and herds of cows are kept near the front to provide plenty of butter and milk."[155]

All in all, a pretty nice set-up. And then, of course, there were the *saunas*. "The Finns are so sure of themselves they have built saunas in the woods!" the reporter marveled. "The Russians, on the other hand, the Finns say, must be uncomfortable, since they have no tents and must depend on open fires to keep warm at night."[156]

*

What *was* happening in the far north? It was difficult to tell. The press communiqués issued by the hidebound Finnish Press Bureau were only minimally more helpful than the Soviet ones. Indeed, in some cases, such as the report about the Soviet's alleged use of gas, they were even less truthful. Here, as in so many other conflicts, truth was the first casualty of war.

Thus, too, the confusion about the fate of Petsamo. According to the Finns, who were as loath to admit to any defeat as the Russians, they had retaken the Arctic port after a bitter fight while capturing 1,500 Russian prisoners, as the gullible Western press had reported the week before. The Russians—correctly— insisted otherwise.

Not that the Russians had much to boast about. In fact, Petsamo, Finland's northernmost port, was captured by the Red Army on December 2 in an amphibious operation when two Russian divisions overwhelmed the relatively minuscule Finnish detachment of three companies, at a cost of 1,200 dead and 2,900 wounded—and only then after the Finns put up a Thermopylae-like fight before retreating.

However, only 72 Soviet soldiers were made prisoner, not the 1,500 the Finns claimed. The Finnish position there, an ad hoc formation comprising three companies led by Captain Antti Pennanen, also known as Detachment Pennanen, was virtually decimated, suffering 89 dead and 135 wounded, while 16 Finns were captured.[157]

*

Not only was it difficult to get the news. With the covey of zealous, green-shaded Finnish press censors stationed at the Kamp redacting much of the correspondents' copy, it was becoming increasingly difficult to get the news out.

By contrast, ironically enough, correspondents stationed in Moscow didn't have to worry about censors. As a gesture of good will toward the Western press, Molotov had abolished press censorship when he replaced Maxim Litvinov. Of course, correspondents' movements were still restricted, and they were tailed by the NKVD, the Soviet secret police, everywhere they went. But, astonishingly, they were free to file their copy without submitting it for approval. That situation would soon change, as the war progressed and the Kremlin's embarrassment grew, but in this respect the Moscow press corps was actually freer than its Finnish counterpart.[158]

In his frustration with the Finnish press censors Cox and another reporter friend, Barbro Alving, the well-known and well-regarded correspondent of the Swedish newspaper *Dagens Nyheter* and a fellow veteran of the Spanish Civil War, decided to take their own unguided tour of the northern battlefront—provided they could find it.

They found it. Thus a day and a long freezing train ride later the surprised Englishman and his colleague found themselves interviewing a group of Finnish soldiers recovering from wounds suffered during the first mass Russian attack on Lake Kiantajärvi, at Suomussalmi, at a military hospital near the central city of Kajaani, prior to the initial Soviet victory there. All told Cox and Alving the same story. "When they [the Russian soldiers] came out on to the ice of Lake Kianta, one soldier told Cox, 'they were like a dense black crowd. . . . We waited until they were only 200 meters off, and fired right into them with machine guns and rifles. When they broke their dead were heaped on the ice.'"[159]

Like the soldiers Gellhorn had interviewed, these Finns had little respect for their opponents:

> Their shooting was bad—they shot chiefly from the hip with little or no covering fire from support sections. But all had echoed one statement: "There are so many of them, so many." Their eyes seemed to darken as they spoke. You could see rising up in these men's minds the vision of great masses pouring down these snow-covered roads and of the gigantic forces ranged behind them over there in the Soviet Union.[160]

Shortly afterward, Cox found himself being ushered past a sentry in a goatskin coat and fixed bayonet into the office of General Wiljo Tuompo, the commander of the North Finland Group, in the general's villa outside Kajaani. Soon afterward, Mannerheim would divide Tuompo's vast command, encompassing the entire northern host of the country, into two, giving the northernmost sector, encompassing most of Finnish Lapland, to the flamboyant general Kurt Wallenius, who had been allowed to return to the ranks after a period of self-exile; however, for the moment Tuompo was sole commander of the 20,000 or so Finnish troops tasked with stopping the two Russian armies then making their way through the woodlands of eastern-central and northern Finland.

Far from the burly, aggressive figure Cox expected, the reporter found the general a "quiet figure of medium height who looked like a schoolmaster." Tuompo, a farmer's son who had become an authority on national defense policy, was wearing the regulation Finnish general's kit: horn-rimmed spectacles, brown boots, gray stockings pulled up to the knees of his breeches, a double row of medal ribbons on his chest. The obligatory photograph of President Kallio hung on the wall; none of Mannerheim (at least not yet).[161]

Next to the photograph was a map on which Tuompo had sketched out what was happening in the three sectors of his immediate front—Kuhmo, fifty kilometers directly to the east; Lieksa, 150 kilometers away, in Ladoga-Karelia, to the far southeast; and Suomussalmi, fifty kilometers away, to the immediate northeast. Kuhmo, the area commander indicated with his pointer, was the center of a fan-like series of attacks that the Soviets had sent against Finland's waistline and were still fanning out, and where the Finns apparently had suffered heavy casualties.

Unsurprisingly, Tuompo was not entirely forthcoming about the parlous situation, particularly in embattled Suomussalmi. "To the north, two divisions— the 163rd and the 44th—were moving towards Suomussalmi village," he said to Cox. Either Tuompo was being disingenuous or he had bad information, always a possibility given the poor quality of Finnish intelligence. In fact, as noted, the 163rd Division, after routing the defenders, had taken and still held Suomussalmi, although it was having an increasingly difficult time holding its position, which is why the crack Ukrainian 44th Division, then advancing from the south, had been dispatched to assist it.[162]

In any case, Tuompo confided, as he and Cox pored over a map of the central Finnish front, if the Russians managed to hold on and capture Suomussalmi, that would secure their right flank and allow them to move on to Kajaani itself, where a railway ran across Finland to the west, thus making it possible for them to bisect the country, which was obviously their objective.

At the same time, another full Russian division had crossed the border near Lieksa, apparently intending to cut the north-south railway there, before driving north to link up at Nurmes with the other division, the 54th, which the Finns were fighting near Kuhmo. Such was the ostensibly grim situation in northern and central Finland. He had to admit, Tuompo declared, turning away from the map, the Russians had begun their campaign with "a flying start": "They came in at once with full materials, tanks, armored cars, artillery." Nor was the North Group commander as quick to dismiss the Soviet infantry as some of his men. "It is too early to judge the quality of their men," he observed. "They have attacked so far in masses. But after all they have masses of men."[163]

Surprisingly, Tuompo also remarked on the Soviet's ability to infiltrate his own ranks with their indigenous agents. Several of the audacious turncoats had even been clever enough to get close to his headquarters.

The advance guard at Suomussalmi was made up of Finnish-speaking troops from Russian Karelia. We noticed that they fought much better than the ordinary Russian troops. Some we took prisoners. They said that there had been Finnish Communist exiles amongst them. They have sent some Finnish exiles as spies. . . . Two of them, on skis, came through the woods and hailed an army car outside Kajaani. They pretended to be peasants and asked a lot of questions of the officers in the car. One of the officers got suspicious, and asked for their papers. They had none. We have been hitting back with our patrols, [but] last night three men got through the forest and burned two planes on an aerodrome on the lake just on the other side of the border. They got away on their skis without being caught.[164]

Nevertheless, fifth columnists notwithstanding, Tuompo had faith in the quality and skill of his men, and their ability to thwart the invader. "We have had ten days of fighting now," he remarked to Cox, "and in that time our troops have developed the necessary aggressive spirit. We have had losses, of course, but there is a price you have to pay for that essential sense of aggressiveness."[165]

"It seemed rash for a General commanding part of a small army very much on the defensive to talk about 'aggressive spirit,'" Cox thought. But, as he was to discover, "that was the principle of the whole of the Finnish defense—counterattack. They fought a war of movement, of repeated attacks on Russian communications, which necessitated the utmost and aggressive fighting spirit from their men. In Finland attack undoubtedly proved the best defense. There was no Maginot Line mentality in northern Finland."[166]

"I'm sorry I can't tell you much at the moment," Tuompo concluded the interview with a friendly laugh. "Come back in a month's time and I might have something interesting to show you." Cox also laughed, in wonder: "The idea that the Finns would still be fighting in a month, no less than a week, particularly in light of all those heavily equipped Russian troops then surging through the eastern forests, seemed to me pure wishful thinking."[167]

Cox got a glimpse of that aggressive spirit General Tuompo was alluding to a few hours later when he was allowed to visit one of the small units that were then trying to fend off the Soviet 54th Division outside Kuhmo.

Like so many other correspondents, he found himself swept away by the sheer beauty of the martial landscape he beheld. "I looked at my watch and saw with surprise that it was only two-thirty in the afternoon." Despite the early hour,

dusk was already beginning. The cloudy sky had turned a leaden grey; the same shade seemed to creep over the snow-covered pines, their branches still and drooping under the snow, and over the snow road. As the light slackened further all perspective went. Trees, roads, and sky were one flat backdrop, and the trunks and branches were mere pencil lines. This hour of dusk in the Finnish forests came to fascinate me. Now that I saw it for the first time I almost forgot the war.[168]

The war came back with a start once he saw some of the men advancing toward him from around the bend. At first Cox thought the Finns looked comical in their billowing snow capes.

I thought of many things—of penguins, and the Ku Klux Klan, and oversize pyjamas and pantomime dames. One man, in front, with his cape drawn tightly over his bulky uniform, was like the figure in the Michelin tyre [sic] advertisements.

Any thoughts of laughter, however, were dispelled as soon as he saw the fighters' careworn faces, and those of their officers.

Then I saw the faces behind the white cowls. There was nothing comic about them. Brown, set faces, with dark weary eyes and a thin stubble of beard, they had that set, fatalistic look of men who are on their way to or from battle. . . .
A car, painted white as camouflage too, turned the bend in the road and two officers got out. They too had beards and their eyes were bloodshot as they came up to give a message to the man on the field telephone. In the woods ahead, the machine gun started again.[169]

Cox, still getting his bearings in this exotic war, asked one of the officers if he could proceed to the front. The Finnish officer found the question odd.

The front? What front? There isn't one. This is the front, here—or a half a mile ahead, or a half a mile behind—anywhere where the patrols happen to be. We've got a couple of trees across the road just ahead, as a tank barrier, but I wouldn't even call that the front. All we have are our forest patrols, on the move all the time, and ahead of them the Russians. This is a war without fronts.[170]

So it was:

It was a time of ragged engagements between Russian advance guards and Finnish frontier troops. Each side was feeling out its enemy. The Russians, who had the initiative, were carrying out a gigantic infiltration, with divisions moving into Finland seeking out the weakest points. The Finns were striking back at them wherever they came, trying to feel out the enemy's strength before moving any of their precious reserves.[171]

With his veteran's eye, Cox did a quick inventory of the spectral troops, most of whom, he learned, were Swedish-speaking inhabitants of the Turku area. Most wore new boots, indicating that they were reservists. Of course, each man carried a *puukko*, the traditional Finnish knife, swinging from his belt. Aside from that,

> they carried a minimum of equipment—a rifle, bayonet, water bottle, light haversack. They had no entrenching tools. Their ammunition was in pouches slung from the belt. They wore no overcoats, for these would have been too heavy for movement in the forest. . . .
>
> Some had mittens, or gloves with a slit just under the first finger of the right hand to free it for trigger use. Others had gloves of fine wool that did not jam around the trigger. Some wore balaclava caps over their ears—but none had the flaps of their caps down. They wanted to be able to hear the slightest sound. In all my time in Finland I never saw a soldier with ear flaps on his cap down, however bitterly cold it was.[172]

In short, the men were perfectly dressed for the occasion. They also did not lack for food:

> On sledges were piled cases of ammunition; red cardboard boxes which contained crisp, hard Finnish bread; sacks filled with red "Dutch" cheeses. Two sleds carried cans of milk. Each man was allowed a liter of this a day. . . . On a sled under the trees a field kitchen was being tended by two cooks. They lifted the lid off and showed me a great copper of stew—reindeer and veal. Another kitchen nearby was cooking up oatmeal porridge, a standby for every meal.[173]

Later Cox interviewed the officer in charge of the sector, a careworn twenty-seven-year-old regular army captain. "I think I got five hours' sleep in the first three days of the war," he said. "We did not expect them to attack on this road and we had to rush our preparations. They have put in at least one full regiment on this approach alone. This means 3,000 men and about twenty field guns and a great number of mortars and grenade throwing."[174]

Tuompo's men, like their comrades further south, were still experimenting with anti-tank tactics. Apparently the Molotov cocktail, the kerosene-filled bottle that would become the Finns' favorite tank-killer of choice, and which would ultimately be credited with destroying or disabling 2,000 Soviet tanks, was not yet in widespread use.[175]

> When [the Russians] first attacked they used armored cars, at least in the North. But after two had been destroyed by hand grenades they sent back for light tanks. They used the first of [those] yesterday, and we managed to

knock two of them out. We got the first one by tying seven hand grenades together. Then one of our men skied up, rolled it over the tank and flung himself in the snow. The grenades broke the caterpillar right off the side of the tank.[176]

The officer understandably demurred at confiding how many men he had. Cox guessed that the paltry Finnish force consisted of two or three companies at most. The previous night, the captain continued, the Russians had put down fifty shells a minute on the front lines by the road. The Finns, lacking artillery or anti-tank guns, had no means to reply. Fortunately, the Soviet had not sent bombers to the area, at least not as yet. There had been some fighters, he noted, but they had dropped pamphlets, not bombs. The pamphlets had urged the men to drop their arms and join the Red Army. The tired officer grinned when he spoke of these pamphlets. They did not seem to worry him.

The weary frontier commander stopped smiling when he described the fate of his dead. The Russians, he said, stripped all of the dead when they could get to them. He thought that they wanted the warm clothing and boots, though it was also possible that they might want the uniforms for spies or for dropping saboteurs from parachutes. He had himself seen the stripped body of a Finn, whom his men had brought back to camp one night. Even the man's name tag was missing. Nevertheless, the officer did not seem to harbor any particular animus toward the enemy. That was just the way they were, he said matter-of-factly.

The officer also claimed that the Russians shot their wounded when they retreated; he had also seen this with his own eyes. However, even though the notion of shooting one's wounded would have horrified any Finn, he accepted this, too, as one of the grim exigencies of Arctic warfare. "It was sometimes quite essential because you could not leave a man to freeze to death suffering terribly. Morphine would have been more efficient but a [Russian] soldier does not have morphine with him."[177]

What, the reporter asked him, would happen if the Russians managed to push their way into Kuhmo itself, which had already been evacuated?

"If we fall back behind, we will burn the village," the officer said evenly. "It's the only way, for then the Russians will have no shelter when the real cold comes," referring to the double-digit subzero temperatures just around the corner. "It's the old way we've used against them for generations," he said quietly. Nevertheless he felt the situation was in hand.[178]

It was the captain's turn to ask the inquiring Englishman a question. "He asked me when Britain would come to Finland's aid." Cox was at a loss to answer. "The odds were so unfair that it seemed to them that every country in the world must rush to their aid. They were not so much angered as amazed that no one showed any sign of helping them." News from the outside world, including word of the hundreds of young Swedes, Hungarians, Italians, Britons, and other young men from ultimately sixteen nations around the world who were signing up to volunteer to fight for Finland, as excitedly heralded in the Helsinki papers, had not yet reached this frontier outpost. The captain thanked Cox for coming so far to hear his story. And next time, one of his exhausted men added, could he please bring some anti-tank guns with him? Then, as a machine gun sputtered in the distance, one by one, the men slid off.[179]

✳

Later that day Vaino Hakkila, the venerable speaker of the Finnish Parliament, broadcast his own emotional appeal to the world. "To all the peoples of the world," Hakkila declared—

> The Finnish people, who always have tried to work with all other nations, have founded their future on their peaceful work. Today they are the victims of brutal aggression from their eastern neighbor without having given any cause for aggression.
>
> We have no choice. This struggle has been forced upon us. The people of Finland fight for their independence, their freedom and their homes. We are defending our fatherland, our democratic regime, our religion, our homes and all that civilized peoples hold sacred.[180]

As President Kallio had done in his Independence Day broadcast four days before, the sixty-seven-year-old Hakkila, not one generally known for his oratory, couched his appeal in biblical terms. Nothing less than the fate of Christian civilization depended on the outcome of the unequal struggle being waged between Finland and the barbarian hordes that besieged it. "We have given proof," the bespectacled Social Democrat proclaimed, "that we wanted to do all we could in this struggle, but we believe the civilized world, which had given us testimony of its great sympathy, will not leave us to fight alone against an enemy more numerous than ourselves. Our position as the advance guard of Western civilization gives us the right to expect active help from other civilized nations."

"To all these nations," he closed, "the Finnish Parliament now sends its appeal."[181]

The fact was that Hakkila's appeal was somewhat redundant. Perhaps it was an exaggeration to call it "active aid"; however, a growing torrent of money, war materiel, and volunteers was beginning to flow Finland's way.

Thus, that very same day, December 10, the U.S. government began to put its money where its mouth was by granting Finland a $10 million loan via the Export-Import Bank and the Reconstruction Finance Corporation. Originally, the Roosevelt administration had wanted to make the loan for $4 million. However, FDR himself had intervened and raised the amount to $10 million. There was only one catch, and it was a big one: to Helsinki's dismay, Congress's largesse was limited to the "purchase of agricultural surpluses and other civilian supplies," and could not be used to purchase military goods.[182]

That day, too, the 350 volunteers from the United States, most of them of Finnish descent, set sail to fight for Finland on the *S.S. Gripsholm*—the same vessel that had been thrown into a furor by the news of the Russian invasion a week before. Newsreel cameras captured the American volunteers on the deck of the *Gripsholm* singing "Finlandia" with their fists raised. To be sure, they were only 350, not the 3,000 the *Helsingin Sanomat* had originally said were coming. Still, it was something. (The American contingent would also soon be augmented by a group of volunteer ambulance drivers, as well as half a dozen pilots.)[183]

Some of those sorely needed anti-tank guns that the plaintive soldier at Kuhmo had asked Geoffrey Cox for would also be forthcoming, not from Britain but from Sweden, which would wind up donating 85 Bofors anti-aircraft guns to Finland, along with 18 anti-tank cannons, 89 artillery pieces, and 77,000 rifles.[184]

In the meantime, several thousand Swedes had descended on recruiting stations around the nominally neutral country to offer their services to their beset neighbor. Indeed, that very same day, the Swedish major general Ernst Linder, an old comrade of Mannerheim who had commanded the Swedish volunteers who fought during the Finnish Civil War, announced that he was confident that he would be able to raise two divisions of volunteers to fight for Finland once more.

Orvar Nilsson, an eighteen-year-old Swede from the southwestern Swedish town of Halmstad, then in his last year in lyceum, was one of the first to heed the call. On the afternoon of November 30, he and his horrified schoolmates had listened to the first reports of the Russian invasion over the radio. Two days later the duly outraged teenager was the first from his school to report to the local recruiting station for volunteers for Finland.

"We felt that Finland's fight was our fight, as well," he said. "And a week later there I was aboard a train bound for Finland, cleaning my rifle." It would be another two months before Nilsson and his fellow Swedes also passed muster, received additional training with the Finnish Army, and actually saw combat. And yet the fact remained, just as the men of the International Brigades had done during the Spanish Civil War, young men from around the world were also streaming to Finland, often as not at their own expense, to risk their lives for Finland.[185]

(A more accurate precedent for the foreign volunteer effort during the Winter War than the Spanish Civil War probably occurred during the Greek War of Independence, when a motley crew of men from around the world, led by that great romantic Lord Byron, sailed to Turkey's embattled Greek province, not to fight for any particular ideology or as proxies for the Communist or Fascist powers, as occurred in Spain, but simply to fight for Greece's freedom. Indeed, as we have seen, the fight for Finland crossed ideological lines, uniting leftists disillusioned by Soviet aggression with, in some cases, outright Fascists, like the handful of Italian volunteers who managed to get to Finland and others who simply came to fight for Finland's freedom. That is why, in *The Diplomacy of the Winter War,* Max Jakobson calls the Finnish volunteer force "a Byron brigade"— even though their total numbers, 12,000 by the time all had finally arrived— were closer to that of a division.)

✳

Hakkila made another speech on the afternoon of December 10, this one directed to the Finnish nation, exhorting it to stubborn resistance, reminding it of the "courage and military efficiency" its fighting sons were demonstrating, and thanking the latter for the same. "We as representatives of the Finnish people," he declared, "thank our defense forces and trust everyone will do his duty."[186]

At the very hour Hakkila was broadcasting those fighting words in Yleisradio studios in downtown Helsinki, the 3,000 men of the 16th Regiment under the command of Lt. Colonel Aaro Pajari were illustrating that same spirit in a strange, wild, hand-to-hand engagement with elements of the 139th Russian Division in the frosted woodlands east of Lake Tolvajarvi in Finland's near north.

The bizarre engagement, which became known as "The Sausage War" (for reasons soon apparent), took place when a battalion of the division, one of the more competently led Russian units during the first phase of the war, somehow eluded Finnish sentries, emerged suddenly from the forest, and attacked Pajari's supply line. It also occurred at a key juncture of the Battle of Tolvajarvi, at the very moment when Pajari, along with his commander, Colonel Talvela, were about to unleash their carefully planned counterattack against the intruder.

Several days before, Pajari, a savvy guerrilla fighter who would go on to become a major general, had personally led the men of the regiment's Second Battalion—on a bold, expertly planned and executed early morning ambush against two battalions from the Soviet 139th Division, encamped at Aglavari on the eastern shore of Lake Tolvajarvi. Pajari's raid, as it became known, achieved complete surprise, killing an estimated 200 Russians. Indeed, it was so successful that by the time he and his men extracted themselves from the ambush site the remnants of the two Soviet battalions were engaged in a firefight with each other. After the nerve-racking raid, the exhausted colonel—who, unbeknownst to his men, suffered from a heart condition—collapsed and had to be transported back to his lines in an improvised litter.[187]

News of the raid's success, the first Finnish victory anywhere on the front, spread quickly. The Russians, it showed, could not only be beaten; they could be made fools of. Indeed, the Reds were hurt so badly that they attempted no large-scale actions for the next two days, December 9 and 10. In the meantime, thus emboldened and the latter now recovered, Talvela and Pajari went ahead with their plans to counterattack.

Now, on the evening of December 11, the Russian brigade commander, Beljajev, preempted the Finns by launching his own attack on Finnish supply and artillery troops at Varolampi and on the Korpisalka-Tolvajarvi road, taking the Finns instead by surprise. Then something odd happened. In the event, the first target overrun by the raiders from the 718th Rifle Regiment was a field kitchen with large vats of Finnish sausage soup. After scattering the handful of panic-stricken cooks who stood in their way, the attackers, exhausted and famished after a five-day march in subzero temperatures and without hot food, caught a whiff of the soup, paused, and thirstily began to sup it. The momentum of the original attack vanished, and the startled Finns received a priceless interval of time in which to recover.[188]

As the Finns' luck would have it, Pajari just happened to be returning from a nearby meeting with Talvela when the Russians attacked. Acting swiftly, Pajari put together a scratch force comprising some 100 cooks, medics, supply sergeants, and artillerists and personally led them in a robust counterattack, shouting orders in a fierce parade-ground voice. The ensuing "Sausage War" was close, brutal, and without mercy.

Two of Pajari's men formed an efficient hunter-killer team. One man carried a powerful flashlight, while the other took one of the Finnish Army's prized 4,000 Suomi submachine guns, the durable machine gun that was especially effective in close combat. The team prowled the woods, locating isolated groups of Russians or individual stragglers. When the prey was spotted, the light was switched on, and the Russians invariably froze like deer, whence the gunner cut them down with efficient bursts of 9 mm slugs.[189]

While this hand-to-hand melee was going on, two hastily summoned companies of Finnish frontline troops (the 1st and 4th companies of the 16th Infantry Regiment) arrived and attacked the Russians from the east. During the height of the fighting, the ancient Finnish war cry, "*Hakkaa Paalle!*"—"*No quarter!*"—was heard. By 4 A.M. the Russians were in full retreat, leaving about 100 of their dead strewn about on the forest floor, and by dawn the fighting had died out entirely.

Exact Russian casualties are hard to estimate, as they would be for the numerous subsequent clashes along the snowbound border, for many men died unseen and uncounted in the forest; however, out of the entire battalion only a few dozen men are known to have made it back to Russian lines. Daylight revealed at least 100 frozen corpses strewn around the bullet-ridden soup pots of the field kitchen. Some of the dead still had pieces of sausage stuck to their lips.[190]

The following day, December 12, as planned, the main Finnish counterattack at Tolvajarvi began. It was successful. Eleven days later, after pushing the demoralized remnants of Beljajev's division nearly back to the Russian border, Talvela's men stood on the banks of the Aittojoki River.[191]

One of those who participated in the pivotal battle, along with his durable comrades from Messukyla, was mortarman Reino Oksanen.

Oksanen's first contact with the enemy, an encounter with a Russian tank on December 4 at the start of the see-saw, eleven-day battle, was particularly memorable: "As soon as we had put the mortar into position, a lone Russian tank came straight towards us. There were no troops behind it, just this tank. It didn't shoot at us, however. It just kept on coming. We had to disassemble the mortar in a hurry, as the tank was about to run over it. The tank, obviously on a reconnaissance mission, went past us just a few meters away."[192]

Oksanen and his fellow troopers were less fearful than astonished by the iron beast. "We were very excited, trying to figure out ways to stop the tank. But we had nothing to stop it with. No anti-tank weapons of any kind. Not even Molotov cocktails. They came later. Someone piped up and suggested that a tank could be stopped by thrusting an iron bar into its tracks, but we didn't have those. So the tank went by us and came back a little while later. We couldn't do anything but watch it go."[193]

At first it was slow going, Oksanen said, recalling the key battle. "It was not a very long way from Tolvajarvi to Aittojoki but we were advancing fast, so we had to pack and unpack our mortars constantly." Eventually Oksanen picked up the trick. "Pretty soon we started chasing the Red Army. And we chased them all the way to Aittojoki."[194]

Although Soviet newspapers continued to boast of the Russian army's success, the weary survivors of the initial offensive knew otherwise. A letter written on December 12 by a soldier in the 49th Division, which had been involved in the failed assault at Kiviniemi on the Karelian peninsula, was full of anger and despair. Amongst other things the soldier, from Leningrad, was particularly distressed at the apparent absence of the Soviet Air Force, at least on his front. Elsewhere Red bombers might be busy bombing Finnish cities, but in the skies above Karelia they were nowhere to be seen, at least as yet. The miserable soldier was further demoralized by the rumor that Germany, Russia's putative ally, was aiding the Finns, along with Fascist Italy:

My dear family! The Finns fire shrapnel salvos at us and very few will make it back home. One more thing—it looks like Italy and Germany are helping the Finns. We went into battle at 0800 on 30 November, and have not seen a single Soviet aircraft, just the Finnish ones. We were told that our air force is grounded due to poor visibility, but apparently visibility is good for the Finns. If we continue fighting like this, we will not finish the war against Finland in six months, not to mention the six days as we had planned before. After twelve days of fighting we [cannot] evacuate our dead and wounded from the front line. What's next? I have no idea. We had three regiments in our 49th Rifle Division, after twelve days we have only two regiments left.

*

Herbert Elliston had left Finland by now, having spent two weeks in the country —not very long at all, yet long enough to convert him into an unabashed cheerleader for Finland, as well as to make a raft of native friends. One of them was Riita Parkkali, a young Helsinkian who had been the sole Finn on the *S.S. Drottningholm,* the Swedish ocean liner on which the reporter had originally sailed from New York to Gothenberg en route to Helsinki. Parkkali had worked in the Finnish legation in Washington and had rushed back to be with her fiancé, her family, and her people when war clouds began gathering.

Parkkali's touching letter, to which she thoughtfully appended a photo of herself—and which Elliston included in his book *Finland Fights!* which he whipped together as soon as he returned to the United States—gives as a good a picture as any of the spirit that animated the Finnish nation at this time.

Evidently, Parkkali had had an appointment at the Foreign Ministry in Helsinki to meet Elliston before he left for Turku; however, she had been delayed because she had had to help her sister evacuate her children from the capital, so they had missed each other. "I was terribly sorry about the appointment," she apologized, "but I had to help my sister in getting her children away."

> When I got to the [Foreign Ministry], you had left, and weren't at the hotel. I have had to do so much since then away from Helsinki. Now I am back for my—wedding! My future husband is in the army like everybody. He will get two days' holiday, and then back again to face our dear friends across the frontier. Friends, they call themselves—friends because they want to help the suffering Finnish people!
>
> Well, my bridal bouquet will be a lovely gas mask, and the wedding march will be the splitting sound of bombs. Dear, thoughtful friends across the border! After the wedding I shall go to the Red Cross, and work with my husband, who is a doctor.

"This thing"—the war—"has united our people," the impassioned young woman wrote. "There have been parties and languages but now there are only Finns fighting for Finland."[195]

3

Steamroller Blues

December 12–25, 1939

I like Finns. They give good tips. And besides I feel sorry for them. They're so small, and Russia's so big.
    —Warren Townsend, New York taxicab driver, *New York Times,* December 13, 1939

President Kyosti Kallio appealed to the "whole civilized world" to aid Finland with war materials in the war with Russia. He said he "could not believe" that the rest of the world would be content to express only sympathy and leave Finland alone to repel the invading Red Army. Nevertheless, he added, Finland was determined to fight even if adequate aid was not forthcoming.
    —*New York Times,* December 18, 1939

While the world looked on with increasing astonishment, as Reino Oksanen and his comrades were chasing the Soviet 139th Division all the way back to Aitto-joki, putting paid any thoughts of a Finnish collapse—as well as quashing Otto Kuusinen's dreams of occupying the presidential palace in Helsinki—the Finnish government's last best hope of ending the new war through diplomatic means was playing itself out in the cold halls of the vast, marble-lined Palace of Peace, the headquarters of the League of Nations, in Geneva, Switzerland.

Vaino Tanner's intention in reaching out to the League, which had thus far been little more than a spectator to the war, was twofold: to place Finland's case against Russian aggression before the world, which it did, and to shame the Kremlin back to the peace table, which it did not. Instead, in the end, the only tangible result of the appeal to the League was to expose the bankruptcy of the system of collective security of which it had been designed to be guarantor and bring down the pillars of the Palace of Peace for good.

It was, however, quite a good show while it lasted. Many of the seated delegates who arrived in Geneva on December 9 to attend the surprise General Assembly session to take up Finland's request for help could remember the momentous afternoon in 1934, when the hitherto pariah USSR was admitted into the world organization—and the Soviet foreign commissar, the frumpled, professorial Maxim Litvinov, was formally seated as the Russian delegate. Just the fact that the Soviet Union wished to join the putatively moribund body in the first place was considered significant. Perhaps the rumors of the League's demise were premature, after all.

"We are faced now with the task of preventing war," Litvinov forthrightly announced, as some skeptical delegates, convinced that the avowedly peace-loving commissar in their midst was in fact a wolf in sheep's clothing, rolled their eyes heavenward. "We must also tell ourselves that any war sooner or later will bring distress to all countries, both to the combatants and non-combatant peoples." The Kremlin was now on record. Its decidedly unsuccessful experience fifteen years before with trying to extend its borders, and its ideology, to its neighbors—including Finland, where it had backed the losing Red side during the 1919 civil war, as well as the Baltic republics and Poland, where its forces, or proxy forces, had also been roundly beaten—had for all practical purposes ended its dream of a world Communist revolution. Or at least one achieved by violent means.[1]

The "new," post-revolutionary Soviet Union didn't wish to cause trouble with its neighbors: witness the non-aggression pact with capitalist Finland it had signed in 1932 and reaffirmed in 1934 for ten years. The post-Trotskyite Russia wanted peace and, just as important, was willing to join with the other non-Fascist European powers to ensure it. This had led to Litvinov's recent, enthusiastic, if ultimately frustrating efforts to forge a "Peace Front" led by Russia, France, and Great Britain to stop Nazi Germany, which had since swallowed up Austria and Czechoslovakia, from further extending *its* New Order.[2]

But that was then. This was now. Now, in December 1939, with Moscow and Berlin allies, the new European war in its fourth month, and the Soviet-Fenno "side war" in its second week, the defrocked Litvinov's sole known duty was to mutely attend sessions of the Supreme Soviet and nod his approval with his less pacific, *Lebensraum*-minded successor, Vyacheslav Molotov.

There was considerable excitement when it was learned that Rudolf Holsti, the respected former Finnish foreign minister, now the Finnish delegate to Geneva, had officially asked the League secretary, Joseph Avenol, to call a special session of the body's General Assembly to act on Russia's aggression, as per its original, nearly forgotten covenant. Since the new European war had broken out, the League, which had been founded expressly to prevent such an event, had been, in effect, invisible in plain sight. Now, all of a sudden—as it had after Italy's 1935 invasion of Ethiopia, which the League, including the Soviets, had condemned—it was faced once more with a political issue of an acutely dramatic kind.[3]

The farcical result of Tanner's Geneva gambit was foretold when the member nation whose actions were the subject of the debate, the Union of Soviet Socialist Republics, made it very clear that it would definitely not be participating. There was no need, Molotov wrote the League secretary, Avenol. After all, as the world well knew, Moscow had no issue with the "Finnish Democratic Republic," as Molotov now called it, with which it had concluded a pact of mutual assistance and cooperation. Indeed, according to the Russian foreign commissar's peremptory note, the so-called delegate from Helsinki, Holsti, was an imposter and ought to be ejected.[4]

This was the scene when the League met for its first session, on December 11, to hear Holsti formally present his country's case against the Kremlin. The worldwide sympathy for "brave little Finland," as she was now universally known, was reflected in the warm applause that greeted Holsti when he took the rostrum in the General Assembly's sweeping, mural-lined new hall.

As the hushed General Assembly listened on, Holsti, one of Finland's best-known diplomats, launched into his presentation. There was a bitter irony to Holsti's appearance. It was Holsti who as foreign minister had signed the "Good Neighbor" agreement (as it was called) between Helsinki and Moscow in February 1937. Meanwhile, the Soviet delegate, Jacob Suritz—a Jew who at one time had been Stalin's ambassador to Berlin and was now ambassador to Paris as well as Geneva, and had been a close friend of the deposed foreign commissar, Litvinov— had reportedly taken refuge in a nearby hotel and refused to show his face, leaving several minor Soviet functionaries to take his place (which also conveniently allowed him to conceal his personal embarrassment over the Finnish affair).[5]

"Nothing shows better to what moral depths the Soviet government has fallen," the Finn bitterly exclaimed, "than its attempt to prevent Finland from raising her voice by installing in a little frontier village a false government of traitors who are paid by Russia and then claiming that that is the real government of Finland."

That Finland, Holsti cried,

> in no way represented the real Finland, the Finland that is fighting for her existence against enormous odds . . . the Finland that is fighting not only for life and liberties but for those of other peoples! Gentlemen, the Finnish people are doing their duty toward the whole civilized world. They are paying for it with their lives. They ask only to live in peace and to do their humble part in making a better structure for humanity. They consider that that is their duty.

"Gentlemen," he concluded, "you too must do your duty. *Give us peace.*"[6]

Joseph Avenol next informed the delegates that he had telegraphed Moscow three times but had received a reply to only one of his cables, the one challenging the legitimacy of the sitting Helsinki government. The session then decided to elect a commission to study Holsti's indictment. This proved easier said than done. As both Germany and the Soviets hoped and expected, the European neutrals, including the other three Nordic nations, were reluctant to move. Nevertheless, a committee was appointed.

The angriest delegate in Geneva besides Holsti was from Argentina. He was all for taking concerted action against the aggressor; so was neighboring

Uruguay. As the French journalist Stephane Lauzanne, reporting from Geneva for *Matin* on December 12, noted: "The courage of the neutrals is inversely proportional to their distance from the lair of the beast. The Scandinavians say: 'It is better to help Finland than to judge the Soviet Union.' But the South Americans are angry. They say indignantly: 'We are sick and tired of actions which paralyze justice.'"[7]

The legalistic charades continued. The committee formed to study the Finnish question submitted a resolution to the General Assembly condemning Soviet aggression and urging all member states to give Finland all possible material and humanitarian aid. It also forthrightly stated that the USSR, by its own action, had placed itself outside the League of Nations. The resolution was duly passed by the General Assembly on December 14, but only after President Carl Hambro, who was also speaker of the Norwegian parliament, played an old parliamentary trick: he simply asked all those in favor of the resolution to remain seated. No delegate was brave enough to rise and declare he was actually for the Soviet Union.[8]

The motion then moved on to the League's highest body, the Council. By the time the Swedes, the Latvians, the Greeks, and various other intimidated members had dropped out, after offering their excuses, only seven of the organ's fifteen members remained: Britain, France, Belgium, the Union of South Africa, Egypt, Bolivia, and the Dominican Republic—"not the most impressive collection of nations to act as guardians of the conscience of mankind," as Jakobson wryly notes. The rump Council then duly voted to expel the Soviet Union, while also directing the organization's members to offer Finland "all possible assistance."[9]

With that half-hearted measure this odd session of the League came to an end—and so, effectively, did the League. So much for Tanner's notion of appealing to the world's conscience, at least via Geneva. Everyone realized that, as far as aid to Finland was concerned, little of a practical nature had been achieved.

Holsti, the Finnish delegate—who later became a professor at Stanford University, having had his fill of the diplomatic world—could not be blamed for looking disconsolate as the delegates to what would prove to be the last assembly of the League of Nations filed out of the Palace of Peace onto the graceful Rue de la Paix, perhaps tarrying a bit to do their Christmas shopping in the elegant Swiss city, or to squeeze in a spot of skiing before returning home.

Little wonder that Tass, the official Russian news agency, reported that "authoritative Soviet circles" had received the news of the Council's decision with ironic smiles.[10]

*

Vaino Tanner, too, regarded the League of Nations' decision to expel the Soviets as an empty victory, if that. His efforts to resume contact with the Kremlin having thus failed, in his despair Tanner decided to reach out personally to Molotov, whom he had met in November, broadcasting a speech in Russian beseeching his counterpart to renew negotiations. Tanner reminded the Russian people of Stalin's own words, which he had seen displayed on one of the public buildings when he had last visited Moscow in November: "The Soviet Union covets not one inch of foreign territory but will defend to the last every inch of its own territory."[11]

"Gospodin [Mister] Molotov," Tanner asked somewhat meekly, "how can you reconcile these lofty principles with your shameless attack upon little, peace-loving Finland?"

Do not doubt, Tanner reminded Molotov, that the people of Finland would fight to the last to defend their territory. Nevertheless, he continued, the Finnish government—the authentic Finnish government—was "ready to renew negotiations and even to agree to substantial concessions."[12]

Tanner's message contained an inherent contradiction: if indeed Molotov had acted in bad faith in November—as the elaborate preparations that the Soviets had made for invading and annexing Finland, including exhuming Kuusinen, made clear they had—why should he expect him to negotiate in good faith with the Finnish government now (apart from the fact that the Kremlin no longer even recognized it)?

And with that, the overwrought Finnish foreign minister motored back to Olympic Stadium, where the Foreign Ministry was now based, along with Dr. af Forselles, the sharpshooter-turned-anti-aircraft gunner and his crew, to await word of "Gospodin" Vyacheslav Molotov's reply to his plea.

❋

Ever since the surprise Soviet attack of November 30 and the surprising Finnish response, the eyes of the free world—as well as a good part of the totalitarian one, to judge from the attention the conflict received in the Italian and Japanese press—had been riveted on the eastern Baltic. "From Stockholm to Tokyo, a worldwide audience followed the war as they would a tennis match," wrote Richard Collier in *War cos,* his excellent book about the war correspondents of World War II.[13]

One of the reasons for this interest, to be sure, was the intrinsically dramatic nature of the lopsided contest, as well as the unprecedented conditions in which it was being fought. Another was the number, quality, and involvement of the journalists who covered the conflict; by the end of the war over 300 journalists representing several dozen nations had voyaged to Helsinki to report on the war for their far-flung readers. Although the Winter War may be little remembered today outside of Finland, in December 1939, it was the main event.[14]

Just as significantly, the *Talvisota* occurred square in the middle of the six-month lull in the European war known as the "Phony War," or "The Sitzkrieg," stretching from September 27, when Poland capitulated to Nazi Germany and her new ally, the Soviets, and April 7, 1940, when the Germans invaded Norway and Denmark, followed a month later by the Nazi blitzkrieg against the Low

Countries and France, when all hell finally broke loose on the Western front. Put another way, to use Collier's metaphor, not much was happening on the other "courts," at least of a military nature.

The main Western front itself between France and Germany was quiet again, the dust having settled from the much-ballyhooed visit the week before of King George VI to the 400,000 men of the British Expeditionary Force who had just arrived to take their place alongside their fighting French comrades. The "Tommies" had just "tasted actual warfare," as the *Times* of London enthused on December 11, describing one of the BEF's first clashes with a German night patrol near the Siegfried Line.[15]

"So far there have been no casualties on the British side," the *Times* conceded. However, the paper was quick to point out, the Germans did lose one of their Alsatian watch dogs during the engagement, thus answering the sardonic accusations of German propagandists that England intended France to shoulder the burden of the fighting if and when hostilities became general: "When the first British rifle fired," the *Times* harrumphed, "it flung back the answer of Great Britain and France to the claim diligently spread by German propagandists grimacing into their microphones, that Great Britain is willing to fight to the last Frenchman."[16]

Joseph Goebbels, the Reichsminister for Propaganda and Public Enlightenment, had also tried to sow similar doubts via the air, as Germany's ally, the Russians, had done over Helsinki two weeks before, by having anti-British propaganda leaflets dropped over the French lines; aerial agit-prop was very much in season. However, the German contribution to the *guerre de confettis* (confetti war) was more subtle than the Soviets', consisting of single slips of paper. "In the autumn the leaves fall," the sinister sheets read. "So fall the *poilus* [French infantrymen] fighting for the English." The obverse read: "In the spring the leaves come again. Not so the *poilus*." The British tried the same stratagem with the Germans, dropping cleverly written anti-Nazi propaganda over German lines—truth raids, they were called. *C'est la guerre,* circa December 1939.[17]

Amongst the highlights of King George's whirlwind trip was a bilateral awards ceremony, in which he and General Maurice Gamelin, the French commander-in-chief and the chief author of the passive strategy that would soon doom France, exchanged medals and kisses; a parade of sabre-wielding Algerian *spahi* cavalry; a hearty luncheon of chicken pie and cheese with a group of polite French troops; and an inspiring tour of the subterranean splendors of Gamelin's pride and joy, the Maginot Line, which, with its hundreds of revolving turrets, artillery pieces, fixed casemates, and 100 kilometers of underground chambers, comprised the most formidable (no less the most expensive) defense line the world had ever seen—and one to which the much less redoubtable Mannerheim Line had often been wrongly compared.[18]

Once the excitement surrounding the British royal's visit died down, the nearly half million "Tommies" and "territorials" returned to their patrols manning their sectors of the Maginot Line. Those fortunate enough to be granted leave headed for the City of Light and *Paris et l'amour* to see the likes of Maurice Chevalier and Josephine Baker cavort in *Paris Reste Paris* at the Casino de Paris, revivals of *Cyrano de Bergerac* and *Madame Sans-Gene* at the Comedie Française, and other non-martial divertissements. Once they emerged, however, the British troops were disappointed and confused by the rather cold reception they received from the French citizenry, who were beginning to show distinct signs of defeatism.

For their part, the Britons, including their troops, still had faith in His Majesty, as well as to a slightly lesser extent in His Majesty's Government. Thus the enthusiastic cheers that greeted the king when he alighted on French soil, as well as the somewhat more muted though earnest ones for his prime minister, Neville Chamberlain—who, after finally having seen the futility of appeasing Hitler, seemed earnest enough about prosecuting the war with the Third Reich, even though he hadn't done very much.

Indeed, Chamberlain's smartest move thus far may well have been the appointment of his longtime nemesis and eventual successor, Winston Churchill, as Lord of the Admiralty. Thus far, Churchill, ever toying with ways to get at the Germans, some half-baked, some not, had been kept on a short leash, much to his dismay. That would soon change. According to a poll published that week, 61 percent of the British people backed the way Chamberlain was conducting the war—not exactly a rousing show of support, but good enough. The British people might not be in a warring mood, but they were resolute, after a fashion. Few thought that "World War No. 2," as it was being called in some quarters, would last more than a year; certainly no one had any idea that it would shortly mushroom into the titanic, global conflagration it would become. In fact, aside from the Germans' lightning invasion of Poland, nothing much had happened at all.[19]

Morale also appeared to be high on the other side of the Siegfried Line in Germany, according to the *Times,* although there was unhappiness with the rationing restrictions the Nazi government had imposed, as clarified in a recent broadcast by Goebbels, Hitler's top mouthpiece, who reminded his listeners that this Christmas they would be limited to purchasing only one pair of stockings and two neckties.

Additionally, because of the strain the war had placed on the Reich's postal service, Goebbels—the same man who, four years and millions of lives lost hence, would be shouting himself hoarse exhorting Germans to prepare for *Totalier Krieg* (total war)—asked the German public to please *not* send out Christmas cards. Next Christmas, Christmas 1940, of course, it wouldn't matter. The war, Goebbels assured them, would be over by then and they could go back to their normal business.[20]

*

Unbeknownst to the German public, while it dutifully scrimped and saved and mouthed fealty to Hitler's Third Reich, in newly occupied Poland the groundwork for genocide was already being laid. Already the previous month, Poland's new anti-Semitic rulers had begun herding the Jewish population of the Polish capital into the new Jewish ghetto, while their kinsmen elsewhere in the conquered nation suffered similar or worse indignities.

Thus, on December 9, approximately 200 exhausted and starving Polish Jews, mainly middle-aged men from Hrubieszow and Chelm, crossed the River Bug into Soviet-occupied Poland, after having been force-marched from their homes by their new German overlords. Over the previous week, the astonished Russians learned that over 400 other Jewish marchers had been kicked or clubbed or shot to death by their guards, a preview of the greater horrors to come, both in Poland and the other Nazi-occupied countries. Not wishing to antagonize their German allies, the Russians said nothing about this.[21]

On December 7, 1939, William Shirer, the Berlin correspondent for CBS Radio, who had protested so loudly in his diary about the Russian invasion of Finland eight days before, engaged in an audial tête-à-tête with his London colleague Edward Murrow. Murrow was soon to become famous for his broadcasts from London during the Blitz, the name to be given the following year to the horrific German air offensive against Great Britain, which the Soviets' air war against Finland presaged, uniting that embattled nation.

Picking his words carefully because of German censorship, Shirer replied, "Well, [the German man in the street] has been told, and I think he believes, that this is going to be the decisive year and that the war will be over before next New Year's."[22]

"The average fellow you talk to here [in Berlin], thinks that there's going to be a lot of action early in the spring," Shirer predicted, correctly as it turned out, "probably in the air, probably against England." Next, the two radiomen turned to the topic that was on everyone's mind those days: Finland.[23]

"British sympathy is overwhelmingly with the Finns," Murrow affirmed, speaking freely from Broadcasting House in London. "The papers, radio, newsreels, denounce the Russian invasion in the strongest possible terms and express great admiration for the Finnish resistance. The general attitude seems to be that Britain should assist the Finns in every possible way without handicapping her own effort."

"How does Germany feel regarding all the shooting northward?" Murrow then asked his colleague in Berlin.[24]

"Well, officially Germany's neutral," his Berlin-based colleague carefully replied, mindful of the Nazi censor listening nearby, "and of course the people haven't forgotten that it was German help which enabled Finland to win its independence from Russia in 1918–19.[25] . . . But now things are different. Germany is lined up with Russia, and Berlin is not pleased at the prospect of Britain and

France sending military aid to Finland. The Germans say that they have a feeling that Britain and France are giving aid to Finland more to gain a foothold in Scandinavia against Germany than against Russia."[26] Consequently, Shirer said, there was "very little news of the Finnish war. It's a painful subject in Germany, though the press publishes the war communiqués of both sides."[27]

✱

There certainly was plenty of news of "the Finnish war" on the other side of the English Channel that week, and sensational news at that. On December 11, the same day that King George returned from his visit to France, the *Times* ran a dispatch about the rapidly evolving state of Finnish battlefield tactics with the following headline:

WAR IN ARCTIC DARKNESS
FINNS SHOOTING BY SEARCHLIGHT
WHITE BATS ON SKIS.[28]

Significantly, the article by the weapons-savvy correspondent began with a description of the already legendary Suomi machine pistol:

The troops, who wear white uniforms, are armed with quick-firing pistols which are practically short rifles of the Browning type—a Finnish variety of the Bergmann [a German-designed semi-automatic pistol], with a magazine holding 25 cartridges. Transport of war material is made by sleighs shaped like cradles, which are drawn by six men in front with two pushing in the rear. Heavy guns are transported on skis 65 centimeters wide, drawn by the small Finnish horses, which travel quickly even when sunk deeply into the snow.[29]

"The operations are carried on in the darkness of the northern winter," the writer continued, indulging in a spot of hyperbole, *"and move in the darkness like white bats."*[30] "In every platoon," the author breathlessly continued, somewhat fancifully, "there are two or three searchlight men," who wear a powerful reflector hanging from their necks.

Once in contact with the enemy the searchlight man is left alone and brings the reflector into play, penetrating the darkness for about 500 yards ahead. The other soldiers, hidden among the trees in the shadows which flank the illuminated zone, advance rapidly and unperceived towards the dazzled enemy, firing their pistols effectively at short range. But the "searchlight man" is a doomed man; the first shots are for him, and that is why to be a "searchlight man" is a great honour, reserved as a reward for those who have distinguished themselves for their bravery.[31]

In point of fact, as seen at Tolvajarvi, the Finnish Army did employ search-lights; however, the assertion that there were specific "searchlight men" was something of an exaggeration. But this is the sort of effect that covering the Winter War could have on an imaginative correspondent.

∗

There was one other sector in the new world war besides Finland, which also made for good copy that December: the war at sea. On land as well as in the air, the Allies and the Germans might well have been throwing little more than pam-phlets and paper leaves at each other, punctuated by the occasional rifle shot, but on as well as under the water the two sides definitely meant business. Hit-ler's U-boat arm, which would ultimately come close to strangling Great Britain in the battle over the Atlantic sea lanes, had already notched a number of strik-ing victories. The first was in mid-September, when one of his undersea raiders torpedoed and sank the British aircraft carrier *The Courageous.* The second was even more spectacular: on October 17, another German submersible managed to penetrate the Royal Navy's base at Scapa Flow in the Orkney Islands off Scot-land, sank the battleship *Royal Oak* with the loss of all hands, and then escaped, wounding British pride to the quick and deeply embarrassing Churchill and the Admiralty.

In the meantime, Hitler had unleashed his two principal *Panzerschiff* (battle-ships) as surface raiders: the pocket battleships *Admiral Graf Spee* and *Deutsch-land,* the latter of which had recently been renamed the *Lützow* to avoid negative publicity in the event that a vessel bearing Germany's name should sink. As it turned out, the ship proved a disappointment and was recalled, having captured two freighters as well as the neutral U.S. ship *The City of Flint,* a prize that Hit-ler did not need. However, *Admiral Graf Spee,* led by its gallant, anachronistic captain, Hans Langsdorff, more than made up for her sister ship, sinking nine ships in the South Atlantic and the Indian Ocean by mid-December before be-ing tracked down, engaged, and trapped by His Majesty's South Atlantic Fleet in Montevideo harbor on December 17, whereupon Langsdorff, ignoring Hitler's orders, decided to scuttle his ship, as the newsreel cameras rolled.[32]

Churchill, who had anxiously followed the drama from London, proudly de-clared that the triumph "gave intense joy to the British nation and enhanced our prestige around the world. The spectacle of the three smaller British ships"—the heavy cruiser *Exeter* and the light cruisers *Ajax* and *Achilles,* which com-bined to take on the German man o' war—"unhesitatingly attacking and putting to flight their far more heavily gunned and armored antagonist was admired everywhere."[33]

The naval drama on the other side of the world received only fleeting mention in Finnish papers. Although many, if not most, Finns would have been cheered by the British triumph, most were too busy fighting their own battle to pay much attention to what was happening in the South Atlantic.

By contrast, the *Graf Spee* story received considerable play in the official Soviet press, to the puzzlement of some Russians, who were anxious to hear more about the nebulous war with their Finnish neighbors that *their* men were currently fighting. "We read a lot about the *Graf Spee* and the 'imperialists' war'—the Soviet's alternative expression for the war between the Allies and the Axis—but very little about the Finnish war," one puzzled Russian citizen told the *New York Times.*[34]

∗

There was one other story that week that took up a considerable number of column inches on both sides of the Atlantic: the grand opening in Atlanta of the film *Gone with the Wind.*

The premiere itself—"the cinema event for which the U.S. has palpitated for," as *Time* put it—a three-day extravaganza co-produced by MGM and the city of Atlanta, didn't disappoint either. Thus on December 15—while a forlorn Vaino Tanner waited for Vyacheslav Molotov's reply to his plea to come to the peace table—an estimated 300,000 Atlantans, many of them wearing period hoop skirts and pantalets or tight trousers and sideburns, and waving Confederate flags, lined up for seven miles to cheer and goggle at the procession of open cars ferrying the star-studded cast, which had driven in from the airport. As part of the hoopla, an eleven-year-old girl was given the chance of receiving an early Christmas gift or a kiss from Clark Gable; she opted for the latter. (For the record, Gable kissed her on the cheek.) When Gable chivalrously obliged, the girl chirped, "Does this make me a woman?"[35]

And yet, even amidst the self-involved, sun-kissed climes of Hollywood, consciousness of Finland's ordeal was keen. There are numerous references to Finland in the gossipy journal that Christopher Isherwood, the expatriate British writer who moved to Los Angeles in 1939, kept at this time. Thus, on December 6, Isherwood, best known as the author of *Berlin Stories,* wrote, "The Finns are pushing back the Russians in the far north." On December 23, with Finland all the rage amongst his Hollywood friends, he declared, "Finland is America's Sweetheart Number One!"[36]

∗

Fennomania also raged amidst the secluded groves of academe. America's cosseted collegians might well be preoccupied with cheering on the varsity, as Martha Gellhorn had suggested, but a goodly many of them too were cheering for Finland that fall, as the anonymous historian of the Cornell University Class of 1942 penned in the class yearbook, in fond retrospect:

> Late fall saw increasing tension between Russia and brave, honest little Finland; and finally the Red Army was marching toward Helsinki. How we laughed when the Communists stubbed a toe on the Mannerheim Line; how

we marvelled at the pictures of Russians frozen stiff; how we sympathized with the indomitable spirit of the Finns and detested the bullying Reds![37]

In any case, America certainly did give a damn about Finland and its war with the bullying Reds—albeit from a safe, neutral distance—and would continue to heartily do so for three more months. Such was the temper of the times and of a world, including the free world, which had not quite gotten used to the notion that it was at war but certainly enjoyed the spectacle the Soviets and the Finns were putting on in the freezing moors of distant Karelia.

✳

Helsinkians, for their part, were already getting well used to the idea that they were at war, and probably would be for some time, as the *New York Times* of December 13 noted: "After twelve days of war, normal life is beginning to be revived." Six daily newspapers were being published, and the streetcars and buses were running as well, albeit on restricted schedules.[38]

Although the sheer terror of the previous week had subsided, consciousness of the danger of new Soviet raids was everywhere apparent. All around the relatively young capital the cobblestone streets echoed with the sound of workmen putting up boards.[39] Gas masks were no longer in short supply, thanks to emergency shipments from Britain, Sweden, and Norway; they even came in brightly colored children's models, just as they had in England, for the few tots who had not yet been evacuated to western Finland, Sweden, or (as in a few cases) Denmark.

The writer also was impressed, as were so many other correspondents, with the number of women in uniform and their can-do attitude. "Nearly every woman left in town is in uniform," he observed. "Finland has more women in war work than any of the Western nations. They stand by at twenty first-aid stations, awaiting a resumption of Russian air raids."[40]

✳

Martha Gellhorn wrote about one of those women, a friend of hers who worked in one of the auxiliary services (it is not clear which one) who came to dinner at the Kamp one day in early December, in one of her last dispatches for *Collier's*.

Like many of those who remained in the car-less capital, her dinner companion, a firewoman who was assisting in clearing away the rubble remaining from the initial raids, got around by bicycle. The latter arrived at the Kamp in standard fireman's uniform of slicker and helmet, looking tired and worn from her back-breaking as well as heart-breaking work, which included searching for the bodies of bombing victims from the earlier raids. Although the last raid on Helsinki was on December 3, there were still some missing at that point.

Gellhorn was joined for dinner by a number of her fellow reporters. When her friend, who was evidently of some means, shed her uniform, Gellhorn discovered that she hadn't lost her fashion sense.

A lady came to dine with us at the Kamp. She parked her bicycle against the carved pillars of the lobby and took off her fireman's helmet and her slicker. She was young and pretty and wore smart slacks and two diamond rings and looked tired because her work began at six in the morning and ended at eight at night. She had given her two cars to the government, and her country house would soon be a hospital and she was living alone in Helsinki because her husband and four brothers were at the front.

She was very quiet through dinner, and later, talking to her alone, I learned that they had just found some more children buried under the bombed houses. . . . She had not talked at all and suddenly she talked grimly, and in a low furious voice, mixing English and French and German, to describe one child.[41]

It was a girl she had found and she told me about this child, and as she talked her face was cold and drawn with anger. Then she was suddenly very tired.[42]

Gellhorn's unnamed friend's mood had rebounded by the end of the meal, at which point the other men seated around her in the bustling hotel dining room, concerned about her safety in the deserted city, gallantly offered to escort her home. Not necessary, said the determined young feminist: "The men offered to see her home and she laughed, saying that she rode everywhere at any hour on her bicycle and it was too early in the war to start bad habits like escorting women who were perfectly able to get on by themselves."[43]

Before they parted, Gellhorn asked her friend whether perhaps she would be better off in the country and out of harm's way.

"Of course not," she responded, before redonning her helmet and slicker and pedaling off. "I would like to go to the front and be near my man, but I am more useful here."[44]

For his part, Vaino Tanner was also getting used to the idea that Finland would be at war for a while, as he continued to wait for a reply from Molotov on the evening of December 15.

He need not have bothered. As might have been expected, the Finnish foreign minister's impassioned plea for conciliation did not impress Molotov a whit. As far as he was concerned, Tanner, whom he, like Stalin, despised, was an imposter; the only Finn authorized to discuss foreign relations with the Kremlin was Otto Ville Kuusinen.

In any event, the Russian army artillery had already replied for him. Earlier that morning, December 15, a phalanx of Russian artillery—including several long-range "railroad guns," backed by several hundred Russian bombers and planes—subjected Finnish fortifications on the eastern side of the Karelian Isthmus near Taipale to a terrific bombardment.[45]

The cannonade, which lasted eight hours, sounded the prelude to the 7th Army's second assault on the Mannerheim Line. The move was hardly a surprise. For several days, the Russian lines had resounded with the sound of explosions and test-firing, presaging the new offensive. General Osterman, the hard-pressed commander of the 50,000 Finnish troops manning the line, responded by ordering his men to rework barbed wire fences, reinforce machine gun positions, construct more traps and ditches and lay more mines, while Mannerheim, Lieutenant General Karl Lennart Oesch, his chief of staff, and Major General Aksel Airo, his quartermaster, and chief planner, continued to monitor the fast-moving situation as best they could from the giant headquarters room in Mikkeli.

Hunkered down in their trenches and pillboxes on the far side of the river, the Finns were prepared, or as prepared as they could be, for the new onslaught. "My boys didn't ask questions," Niilo Kenjakka, a platoon leader, one of the units holding the line, later recalled:

> They simply took their positions, some on one knee, some just standing against the bank of the ditch and with almost childish obedience began to look into the darkness towards the enemy. Older men, as they were leaving, whispered advice to the younger boys: "Be ready for the baptism of fire because the enemy knows you are green and will try his damnedest to break through, so you better hold these positions."[46]

The Finns did have one surprise in store for the invaders, care of Oy Alkoholi-liike Ab, the Finnish state liquor authority: large quantities of kerosene bombs. The bombs, which consisted of a bottle containing fuel, a wick, and two large storm matches taped to the side to ignite it, borrowed from a similar device developed by rebel forces for use against tanks and fortifications in the Spanish Civil War. The operating instructions for the Finnish model were the same as for the Spanish: get as close to your target as possible, light the wick, throw, and run like mad from the resulting explosion.

However, the Finns were the first to use the bomb *en masse.* Once the projectile's tank-killing qualities were discovered, the government rushed to get them to its troops on the Mannerheim Line; ultimately over half a million such projectiles were produced for Finnish forces during the war.

Harold Denny, an enthusiastic Finnish partisan, who began covering the war for the *New York Times* in mid-December, explained for his readers how the fiery contraptions worked: "The Finns have a rough, home-made weapon that they find very effective," Denny reported in December.

> It is simply a mineral water bottle half filled with gasoline, with a stick attached like a fuse. The Finns hide in pits, over which the advancing tanks crawl. The moment the tanks pass, the Finns emerge, so close to the tanks that the latter's guns cannot open fire on them. The Finns then light the stick

and hurl it at the tank. The bottle explodes and part of the blazing gasoline goes through openings in the tank, often igniting the monster's gasoline or exploding its munitions.[47]

In point of fact, a "proper" Finnish cocktail consisted of a half-liter alcohol bottle, filled—not half-filled, as Denny wrote—with flammable liquid. The exact ingredients changed over the course of the war, with various combinations of ethanol, tar, gasoline, potassium chlorate, tar, and other components.[48]

Actually, the weapon had its drawbacks. Often—too often—the bombs exploded prematurely, enveloping both the attacker and target. Other times they failed to ignite at all. Nevertheless, the Finns were so fond of the bomb's tank-stopping qualities so much that they decided to give it a name. If Stalin could have a weapon named after him—"Stalin's breadbaskets"—then surely his right honorable premier deserved a similar accolade. Hence the Molotov cocktail. The name stuck. So did the weapon, which became one of the *Talvisota*'s enduring legacies, as well as a perverse living memorial to the man it was named after. Two decades later, when the Hungarians and Poles revolted against their postwar Soviet masters, their weapon of choice was, fittingly, the Molotov cocktail. (Molotov, who served as foreign commissar until 1949, was reappointed just in time for the Hungarian and Polish revolts.)[49]

Kirill Meretskov, for his part, was hampered by the sketchy intelligence he possessed about the size, depth, and strength of the renowned Finnish fortifications. In fact, the Mannerheim Line, which had already taken on Maginot-like proportions in the minds of Russian troops, was hardly a Maginot. Unlike the Maginot, with its interconnected system of electrified, multi-level fortresses, the relatively few, twenty-by-twenty-meter pillboxes that comprised the Mannerheim Line's backbone, as well as the larger, showcase Poppius and Million Dollar Bunker emplacements—named after the lieutenant who commanded it and the amount supposedly spent on its construction—were situated too far apart to be able to give each other mutual fire protection.[50]

There was nothing to prevent determined Red infantry from overtaking isolated strongpoints and turning them on the defenders, or to prevent Russian tanks from simply driving up and parking themselves in front of the embrasures and firing away at point-blank range—as in fact some Russian tanks managed to do at the height of the assault. In fact, the vaunted Finnish rampart barely deserved to be called a line.

Meretskov didn't know this at the time. In effect, he and his men were attacking an unknown; his outdated tsarist-era maps didn't help either. The Soviet Supreme Command, which, after the failure of the first assault had taken back overall command of the various Russian forces from the Leningrad Military District, leaving Meretskov technically in charge on December 9, attempted to demythologize the Mannerheim Line by issuing orders such as these: "If a machine gun is suddenly observed," the headquarters directed, "it should not be regarded as a permanent strongpoint; in general there has been too much talk about such points. It must be explained to the infantry that it is completely wrong in believing that every emplacement is a strongpoint."[51]

It is doubtful, however, whether such orders had any effect on the average Russian grunt, nervously waiting to go up against the Mannerheim Line on the sixteenth day of war. There were other things to be scared of besides Finnish machine guns. Many, having heard or read the false reports of Finnish "atrocities," feared being captured. There were the *politruks*, the Soviet political officers who allegedly had guns trained on their backs to prevent their retreat.

Then, too, there was the cold, which had gotten perceptibly worse over the past few days, with temperatures dropping to twenty to thirty degrees below zero Fahrenheit and for which many if not most of the Russian infantrymen, in their thin underwear and outercoats, were ill prepared: the Finnish soldier's best friend, General Winter, had come to his aid. Compared to this, what were a few Finnish machine guns?

Ivan Chetyrbok, a senior sergeant in the 3rd Battalion of the 85th Rifle Regiment, a unit of the 100th Division, one of the seven divisions assigned to the new offensive, was better dressed than most. Not that it made much of a difference in the frigid weather. "There were some rifle divisions before us," he said:

> They were dressed in old-fashioned style, or in autumn or summer uniforms. They had boots with leg wrappings and Budyonny hats. At least we received winter uniforms. We were dressed like Santa Claus; for the first time in the history of the Russian army, we received *shapka* hats. We also had woollen helmet liners, which protected the entire face, with only the eyes and mouth exposed to the elements. [Still] it was hard to turn around in such gear, not to mention fighting a war. Despite all these clothes, it was still cold.
>
> When we were on the way to the front, a lot of trucks were moving in the other direction—the road was narrow and we spent a lot of time in traffic jams. There were also a lot of frostbitten [men] moving from the front to the hospitals.

"Those who walked from the front told us about the bunkers," he said. "We did not understand what they meant." They would, shortly enough.[52]

To be sure, the attitude amongst Chetyrbok's comrades, to hear him recount it, was almost jolly. The 100th had just come from eastern Poland, where it had helped man the new occupation of the new territory the Soviets had acquired there; however, Chetyrbok's men had not as yet seen any combat, or experienced an artillery barrage at close hand. The first thing they did upon arriving at their positions was to line up to eat at a field kitchen. As it happened, the kitchen was located next to a well-camouflaged 76 mm artillery battery.

"Then the cannon fired a salvo!" Chetyrbok said. "We all fell on each other! I remember that our cook was so scared that he put a pot on his head!" Thankful for the food, and the diversion, the shivering men laughed and returned to their jump-off points to wait for the assault to begin. They wouldn't be jolly for much longer.[53]

✳

The fusillade ceased; so did the bombs. The Russian planes disappeared. On the opposite side of the Taipaleenjoki River, on the eastern side at the Mannerheim Line, Niilo Kenjakka's men shook the dirt off their uniforms, got back on their knees, grabbed their Pystykorva rifles and grenades and kerosene bombs—they had yet to acquire their famous sobriquet—and stared into the freezing dark again. What new tricks had the Russians come up with, they wondered, as the inky, tracer-filled skies lightened.

Not many, it developed. Once again, as the shellfire died down and as Kenjakka and his fellow officers raised their binoculars and gazed in astonishment, the Red myrmidons marched across the ice in parade-ground formation, shouting and singing en masse. Because of the shortage of ammunition for the Finnish guns, as well as their relatively short range, the Finnish plan called for holding fire until the enemy emerged into the open on the ice and then firing them at point-blank range. The enemy complied. Like the thunderstruck Russian artillerists who beheld the charging British cavalrymen of the Light Brigade thundering toward them and certain death at Balaklava Heights during the Crimean War eighty-five years before, Kenjakka's men had difficulty believing the evidence of their own eyes as they watched the brown-coated hordes slowly surge forward onto the ice and come into range—except that there was nothing valorous or inspiring about this mass Russian charge. It was just mad.[54]

Once again, the Russian units robotically marched into battle in squares—or more like oblongs—just as Marshal Kutuzov's suicidal hussars had at Borodino in 1812, except that these Russian berserkers faced Maxim machine guns, not muskets, as well as artillery. When one half-decimated Soviet regiment or brigade completed its agreed-upon "program," it withdrew, leaving heaps of bodies on the ice, to make way for the next lumbering horde. The only thing missing this time were the celebratory green rockets.[55]

There was little to celebrate here. As Lev Z. Mekhlis, the chief political commissar of the Red Army, cynically exclaimed at the time, by way of offering a rationale for such suicidal attacks, "They can't kill us all!" Perhaps not, but Mekhlis—then on an inspection trip to the Soviet front line at Suomussalmi, where the Red Army seemed to be doing well, at least for the moment—and his fellow commissars certainly seemed to be trying. Later on, looking back, there would be time for the Finns to take pity on the Russians, but not now.[56]

Meretskov did have one tactical surprise up his sleeve, the mammoth new thirty-ton SMK heavy assault tank that saw action on the Karelian Isthmus for the first time. With its powerful 76.2 mm cannon, the twenty-ton SMK was better suited to take on the Finns' concrete emplacements than the comparatively unprepossessing nine-and-a-half-ton T-26; too, the SMK's larger size, as well as its two 45 mm cannons and three machine guns, made it ideal for shielding and ferrying troops into battle, as well as obliterating any Finns who happened to get in the way (provided it was able to spot them). Western correspondents outdid themselves in finding metaphors to describe the Soviet's new mechanized behemoth: "rolling fort," "land dreadnought," and so on.[57]

One of these agog witnesses, James Aldridge, a London-based Australian native who worked as a reporter for the North American Newspaper Alliance, one of a group of four newspaper syndicate writers who were allowed by the capricious Finnish Press Bureau to watch the action, described the SMK's impressive battlefield debut: "After [the] barrage had cleared away this morning, four thirty-ton Russian tanks appeared from a timber clump and started advancing across the snowy waste. Crouched behind each tank were about twenty infantrymen using it as a shield. Finnish machine guns picked off a few men behind each tank."[58]

One of the Finns' scant Bofors anti-tank guns promptly went into action. The SMK, it seems, was not impregnable: "Then from an outbuilding near the farmhouse from which I watched the battle came the sharp crack of an anti-tank gun and I saw a burst of snow in front of the right-hand tank. From the tanks came fire from guns placed almost under the tank, where I had never seen a tank gun before."[59]

The Bofors' next round was closer. A moment later, the charging two-turreted SMK burst into flames. Still, the other tanks pressed on. Certainly, no one could say that the Russian tankers, nor the infantrymen they were attempting to shepherd across the Finnish minefields, wanted for courage. What they lacked was skill and, even more so, clear orders from the 7th Army's two-headed military and political command.

Soon enough these defects would make themselves manifest, as some of the "land dreadnoughts" rumbled forward. Here, at Taipale, as the Russians tanks milled aimlessly around the moors while the Russian troops continued to fall to Finnish bullets and their desperate commanders shouted into their radios for clarifying orders, the Soviets' failings were writ large for all the world to see: the rigidity of their tactical thinking; the absurdity of having a divided political and military command; and, perhaps most of all, the legacy of Stalin's purges.

The chaos and ineptitude on display on the ground during the Russian assault was mirrored in the air. The Soviet Supreme Command sent dozens of obsolescent I-15 fighters into action that day, evidently hoping that they would recreate the role played by the screaming, terror-sowing Stuka dive bombers in the German blitzkrieg of Poland. However, as was readily evident, the I-15, with its fixed undercarriage, was no Stuka. Also, Stalin's pilots and their inexperienced commanders were somewhat lacking in the fine art of tactical air support.

To be sure, the Red Air Force was not without ability, including the capacity for coordinating its actions with its comrades on the ground as it had convincingly demonstrated several months before during the brief but violent clash with the Japanese at Khalkhin-Gol in Manchuria. It artfully accompanied a force of over 50,000 Soviet troops on the ground, plus 800 tanks, meticulously bombing and strafing enemy positions just ahead of the first wave of tanks.[60]

Little of that aerodynamism or precision bombing skill was on display that day in the skies over Karelia. Clearly, the Red Air Force's success at Khalkhin-Gol —as well as during the invasion of Poland, to the limited degree to which it was involved there—had gone to the Supreme Command's head. Again, most of the pilots the Russians sent into the air over the isthmus were neophytes, with no experience of supporting ground troops, resulting in most of their bombs missing their targets or falling on their own lines. The veterans of Manchuria had been held back, as had been the faster, better I-16 fighters. Stalin and Voroshilov still didn't consider Finland enough of a challenge to send in their best men or equipment.[61]

The same mindless, rigid tactics were employed at Taipale the next day, December 16. Once again, the Russians advanced in parade ground formation into the mouths of the Finnish guns, leaving piles of Red corpses; the Soviet tanks performed their mad, mechanized ballet; and there was a gross lack of coordination between air and ground units.

This time the result was somewhat better for the Soviets, with the Reds piercing the Finnish line in two places. However, by nightfall the Russians had been thrown back thanks to the efforts of the determined defenders wielding kerosene-filled bottles, as well as the excellent marksmanship of the Finnish artillery, and the line was intact again.

Back in camp, the 7th Army's political officers tried to elevate their men's morale and improve their performance by staging "combat socialist competitions," as Carl Van Dyke records:

> Short declarations of hatred for the enemy were [made] by each soldier, commander, and political worker in the unit followed by a unanimous vote to accept the terms of the competition. The basic terms of the competition were as follows: inflict harm on the enemy, seize the enemy's defensive zone with lightning speed, avoid casualties, show mutual aid in battle, always hit one's target and preserve one's combat equipment.[62]

At the conclusion of these comradely powwows, a draft was drawn up. Every soldier was obliged to read the draft, and then the resolution was signed by all the unit and sub-unit commanders present. If the unit or sub-unit did not perform its duties according to the resolution, it could be held "legally" accountable, i.e., executed.[63]

Thus motivated, the men of the 7th Army went in again the following day, December 17, at Taipale. Again, the same bloody scenario was repeated. In the event, the mass "combat socialist competition" was an abject and complete failure: the enemy's defensive zone was not seized; heavy casualties were incurred; the respective units failed to show each other mutual aid; targets were missed; and large quantities of Soviet equipment were lost.[64]

Meretskov was obviously the man to be held accountable for this debacle. But beyond his lack of intelligence about the target he was attacking, beyond the rigid tactics, beyond the hydra-headed Soviet military-politico command apparatus, beyond even his own incompetence and that of his immediate subordinates, as well as that of his floundering, technical superior Voroshilov, the Soviet commander's greatest and most insuperable obstacles remained the low caliber and morale of the individual Russian soldier and the Supreme Command's perverse, almost unfathomable obliviousness to the basic needs of those troops.[65]

A reporter from the *New York Times* was allowed to interview seven of the bedraggled survivors from the first day's attack, the only ones left of a group of sixty which had tried to cross the Taipale River by boat before they were blown out of the water by one of the "suddenly appearing" Finnish machine guns. This group was even more pathetic than the ones Martha Gellhorn had interviewed two weeks before at Viipuri Prison; clearly the quality of the troops employed in the second assault on the Mannerheim Line was even worse than in the first.[66]

The men, all reservists, were relatively old, between thirty-five and forty. They were woefully underdressed. Only one wore boots, the rest thin leather shoes. All had frozen feet. They wore cotton underwear. All appeared to be suffering from malnutrition; the prisoners claimed they only had one meal a day, rice or barley, with a small portion of bread—starvation rations. "I was working in a factory in Leningrad when I was called into the army," said one of the seven, who spoke for the squalid group. "I was getting 145 rubles a month salary. They told me I would get half that much in the army but I got only ten."[67] "None of us are members of the Communist Party," the miserable man continued. "I do not know what this war is about."

All told, Meretskov hurled two divisions, the 49th and the 150th, plus the 29th cavalry, against the hard-pressed Finnish defenders, comprising the 28th, 30th, and 23rd Jaeger Regiments. Both Russian divisions were cut down and hurled back.[68] A letter written by an officer of the decimated 150th Division tells the now-familiar sad story:

Father! We await death every moment. Three times it was very near: one time a Finnish airplane attacked and two times we were under very heavy artillery fire. Many of my comrades were killed or wounded. Trucks are evacuating the wounded day and night. By now the artillery had been firing for sixteen days, but nothing helps to drive the Finns out of there.

The dazed and embittered officer was particularly impressed by the strength and effectiveness of the cleverly connected Finnish bunkers.

> Their fortifications are of eleven layers of soil, then 3 metres of concrete and then more soil on top. If you end up there, you don't notice anything, until you come under fire. Gun ports open automatically and then they start pouring at our infantry and tanks. When our artillery fires at their fortifications, grenades just bounce back. Many men were killed here, many wounded also by friendly fire. We were ordered to withdraw into a forest and at this moment we are digging in against a possible Finnish air raid.

"The defensive actions at Taipale are amongst the most remarkable of the Winter War," Mannerheim wrote later:

> As our opponent generally attacked over the ice and open country, his losses were disproportionately high. The accuracy of our modest artillery made its superiority felt, despite the shortage of modern equipment and ammunition. As regards the enemy's tactics, it was clear that [he] suffered from an obstinate adherence to the original operational plan without the ability to adapt it to the requirements of time and space.

This obstinacy, he wrote, "was later noticeable in all sectors" during the assault.[69]

In fact, the attack at Taipale was a massive feint, a diversion intended to draw Finnish reserves away from Meretskov's main objective, the so-called Viipuri Gateway, on the other bottom side of the isthmus.

Mannerheim and Osterman were prepared for this, too. As the battles of Taipale raged, they had watched as Meretskov assembled more and more troops—another three divisions altogether—on the southern end of the Mannerheim Line for what they hoped would be the breakthrough that would enable them to bequeath Finland to Stalin for the Soviet leader's sixtieth birthday on December 21, the Red Army's original deadline for concluding the Finnish operation.

The main thrust began on December 17 with an ear-shattering barrage in the early morning darkness, accompanied after daybreak by the crash of bombs from hundreds of overflying SB-2s. The focus of the barrage was an area between Summa, the minuscule, now deserted village of several hundred that would become a household name by war's end, and the isthmus railroad leading to Viipuri. This is where the Russians planned on driving through and on to Helsinki.[70] Ultimately, two months later, after the Finns had exhausted their thin reserves, this would be where another commander, Semyon Timoshenko, employing different tactics and superior troops, would crack the Finnish fortifications. But not on December 17, 1939.

Again the Russians used the same, mindless tactics; again the same lack of coordination between the arms was on display: a full division ineffectively supported by over 100 Soviet planes and over 80 tanks. Again the Finnish troops, emerging from their trenches and camouflaged holes with hand grenades and kerosene bombs in hand, repulsed the Soviets, though not without considerable casualties of their own.[71]

The end result was much the same as at Taipale: chaos, and more blood on the ice.

*

Some idea of the utter confusion that existed at the start of the Russian attack can be gleaned from the following excerpt from the report of an interrogation of one Captain Yanov, a tank battalion commander who was captured by the Finns on December 17 after the initial assault at Summa:

> At 0600 hours 17.12 December the movements began to the jumping off positions in the area of Vuosi [Vuoksi River]. This presented incredible difficulties, since the roads were cluttered with various units. On arrival at the jump-off point I discovered . . . another battalion of tanks had crept into my area as well as a second battalion had also arrived there. All units were intermingled, and it was quite impossible to elucidate, who, how, or in what order units were to carry out their duties. . . .
>
> The regimental and light divisional artillery were at that moment also moving into the area . . . and the second line of infantry were also trying to force their way in. . . . There was incredible chaos. I decided to contact the commander of the 650th Rifle Regiment. He said, "I do not know you."
>
> "The 95th Tank Battalion is cooperating with me" [he added]. I explained that, in accordance with my instructions, I was *also* acting with him, but only with the second wave of attack.[72]

In an attempt to sort things out, the perplexed Russian captain had then gone to the regimental chief of staff, who responded by thrusting at him the battle orders, which neither could make sense of. The assault had been set for 0630—half an hour's time. In the meantime, to add to the bedlam, Yanov discovered his radio was on a different frequency than headquarters'.

At this point, Yanov said to hell with it and charged into battle on his own: "I decided to give it all up, as I could make no sense of it, and to await events, and on instruction to enter the action, to take independent personal decisions depending on the course of the battle."[73]

And so Yanov and his tank crew bravely, madly, went off to charge the Mannerheim Line on their own. A number of his fellow tank commanders evidently decided to do the same. Together they were able to make a slight penetration of the Finns' inner perimeter at a high cost: twenty-five—nearly one out of three—of the tanks employed in the assault were destroyed, and hundreds more dead or maimed Russians lay in the snow beyond the Finnish trenches. By the end of the day, the entire line was in Finnish hands again. So, too, was the forlorn Captain Yanov.[74]

Tairo Aholo, a corporal in the Finnish 15th Regiment, one of the units that bore the brunt of the Soviet assault, later recalled the hellish scene.

Our anti-tank teams managed to neutralize several tanks in no-man's-land; one tank hit a mine, but there were still plenty of them coming. The bravest crews drove over our trenches and into our rear. Other tanks started driving back and forth, levelling our barbed wire fence, and a third group of tanks stopped in order to clear passages through anti-tank obstacles. The tanks that drove into our rear were in a vulnerable position—they immediately came under attack from our tank busters. A tank has rather poor visibility and a brave man in a trench with a satchel charge or a petrol bomb is a dangerous opponent for a tank.

About fifty tanks were driving at us on a front of 500 metres; the largest tanks were 8 metres long, 3 metres wide, and 3 metres tall. They quickly drove over open terrain and fired their main guns and machine-guns non-stop, although their fire was inaccurate. A huge mass of infantry advanced behind the tanks in several waves. Although the ground was covered with snow, the Russians did not yet have snow-camouflage suits. This was a clear advantage for us, as we could see our targets.

As before, the result was appalling.

The fire of our automatic weapons stopped the infantry assault, which lasted for several hours. Small dark hillocks—the bodies of our opponents—littered the wide battlefield. There was a terrible number of casualties in front of us. As darkness fell, we could hear the screaming of the wounded, and among other cries we could clearly hear: "Comrade medic!" Two or three enemy tanks that had broken into our rear made it back to their lines.

Undaunted by their losses, the Russians renewed their attack the following day. This time the opening barrage lasted five hours before the mass of poorly coordinated tanks and infantry surged forward. Over seventy tanks were used in this assault; however, a well-timed salvo from the Finnish artillery caught them while they were still a mile from the front, taking the wind out of the attack. Shorn of their tank escort, a number of Russian units nevertheless pushed ahead into the withering storm of fire thrown up by the 4,000 Finnish defenders.[75]

Amongst them were Ivan Chetyrbok and his unlucky comrades from the 85th Regiment. The reluctant berserkers, like the naive German World War I troops in Erich Remarque's celebrated anti-war novel *All Quiet on the Western Front*, found that they had stepped into the very vestibule of hell.

Moreover, their rifles didn't work: "The next morning [December 18] the assault was launched, with three battalions of our regiment. My battalion, the third, was in the middle, the 2nd Battalion was on the right and the 1st was on the left. Then [we found] our rifles had jammed—jammed with snow. It was impossible to fire them."

Still, Chetyrbok and his men gritted their teeth and kept on charging. "So we assaulted the Finnish bunkers with only bayonets." Not that they had much choice in the matter, what with the *politruks'* machine guns trained at their backs. Better to face Finnish bullets, most evidently decided, than Russian ones.[76]

The Russians did notch one tactical success at this time: their shellfire was so intense it managed to disrupt the Finnish 5th Division's phone communications, effectively isolating the weary defenders and adding to their stress—as well as the strain at headquarters. For several days, as the critical battle continued and the fate of the Finnish nation literally hung in the balance, headquarters had only a blurry idea of what was happening on the battlefield.[77]

Nevertheless, the commander-in-chief didn't break his usual routine, taking lunch with Heinrichs, Airo, and the others at the Mikkeli Seurahuone as he did every day. If Mannerheim was under special pressure, he didn't evince it, savoring his customary postprandial cigar and schnapps while his aides took care to let the marshal light up first before dutifully following suit.

Still, for all of the chief's admirable *sang-froid,* it was a close shave. The Russians were learning fast. Moreover, for every square of Budyonny-hat-adorned infantrymen who were cut down by the 5th Division's guns, there were many more—willing and unwilling—to take their place.

Compounding the confusion on the Finnish side was a simultaneous breakdown of their aging radio sets, disrupting communications on the company and battalion level. The canny frontline signalmen responded by improvising their own language, a picaresque brew of Finnish and Swedish, layered with a generous helping of indigenous obscenities designed to confuse Russian eavesdroppers that doubtless would have made their conservative chief blanch. Perhaps it was just as well, then, that the Old Man was out of earshot.[78]

Earlier that day, December 18, the Russians mounted their best-coordinated attack of the offensive, a combined naval and air assault on Fort Saarenpaa, the key coastal fortress located on Koivisto Island near Mai-Lis Toivenen's now evacuated home, which protected the southern end of the Mannerheim Line. Just after eleven o'clock, some seventy Russian fighters and bombers, mostly I-15s and SB-2s, attacked the heavily fortified installation for several hours, dropping hundreds of bombs and throwing up a dust cloud that enshrouded the entire island and could be seen many kilometers away.[79]

The Russian planes employed in the assault were accompanied by the 23,000-ton Soviet battleship *October Revolution,* which came into view at 2 P.M. escorted by a spotter plane and a protective screen of five destroyers, and then engaged the ten-inch guns of the fortress in a close-range shootout worthy of Dodge City. Major Magnusson, the commander of the *Lentolaivue 24* at Immola, 300 kilometers to the north—the same unit that Martha Gellhorn had assisted—ordered a counterattack on the Soviet task force, but it had to be called off because of poor weather conditions, allowing the Russian vessels to continue to hammer away at the isolated fortress until dark, silencing its guns and causing numerous casualties.[80]

The following day, another Soviet battleship, the *Marat,* also attacked the fortress but had to turn away when it was struck by Saarenpaa's guns. However, when the cloud and dust over Saarenpaa cleared and the light of the Finnish winter dawn belatedly arrived, it was found that the damage to the key coastal installation wasn't as serious as it had appeared, and the elite coastal artillerists shook off their shell shock and began pounding away again in support of their beset comrades inland.

*

While Ivan Chetyrbok and his men were charging the Finnish bunkers with fixed bayonets and frozen rifles at Summa on the afternoon of December 18 at the northern end of the Soviet-Fenno border, an equally savage hand-to-hand fight was taking place between two companies of Finnish and Soviet soldiers in the village of Pelkosenniemi, a small Arctic village on the west bank of the Kemijoki River. The village was deserted, the thousand-odd inhabitants having been evacuated three weeks before, at the start of the war, once it became clear that the Soviets had invaded Lapland in force. Now, the churchyard echoed with the sound of the intense battle, which lasted several hours. Grenades, bayonets, and knives were all used.[81]

Commanding the Finnish forces in the village was Colonel Oiva Villamo. It was Villamo who had sounded the alarm on November 29 when the border guard at Alakurtti had telephoned him about the sudden appearance of that fast-stepping blaring brass Red Army band. The band belonged to the 122nd Soviet Rifle Division, a better-than-average Russian division based in Kandalaksha, at the tip of the White Sea. The 122nd's original orders had been to link up with the 104th Division, the Russian division that had successfully invested Petsamo before moving on to Rovaniemi.[82]

As things turned out, the 104th had been stopped halfway down the Arctic Highway; however, thus far the quick-stepping 122nd had made such good progress that it appeared it might be able to do the job itself. On December 10, the 122nd took the border town of Salla, after a stiff fight with the heavily outnumbered, outgunned Finnish forces there. At that point the division split up into two regiment-sized forces, with the lighter force headed southward toward the empty hamlet of Joutsijarvi and a larger, heavily armored one, comprising the 273rd Regiment with an escort of twenty tanks, headed west toward the equally empty village of Savukoski, northwest of Salla. Four days later, the 273rd entered Savukoski unopposed. Now, on December 18, the 569th met its first serious opposition since Salla, as its lead company battled Villamo's 150 troops in the fast-fading Arctic light in the lee of Pelkosenniemi church.[83]

Nevertheless, the division's commander, P. Shevtshenko, with his heavily motorized force of over 5,000 men, didn't appear to be concerned; nor, evidently, was his corps commander, Valerian Frolov, who headed the 9th and 14th Armies, the two units assigned to conquer northern Finland. Surely the small number of Finns they had just encountered in Pelkosenniemi could be brushed aside if reinforcements were brought up.

They ought to have been concerned. In fact, the Finns their men had encountered, and were now fighting, in Pelkosenniemi were a diversionary force. The fight was a feint: the 273rd had walked into a Finnish trap, a trap that would shortly lead to Finland's first outright victory in the far north.[84]

The trap that Shevtshenko's men blundered into on December 18 was the design of Colonel Villamo's new commander and head of Finnish forces in the North, Major General Kurt Martti Wallenius.

At forty-six Wallenius possessed the most colorful résumé of any Finnish general besides Mannerheim, as well as the most radioactive. An accomplished tactician, he learned the military arts after joining the Jaegers—the legendary Finnish volunteers who trained in Germany as light infantry during World War I before returning home to fight in the Finnish Civil War, where they formed the core of the Mannerheim-led White army.[85] During the conflict, Wallenius ably led White forces in Lapland, beating the Soviet-backed Reds there handily and winning his chief's thanks and admiration. Opting to stay in uniform, Wallenius occupied a number of high army posts in the 1920s, including chief of staff. He was also the military attaché at the Finnish embassy in Berlin, a coveted position at the time, and as an ardent Germanophile he eagerly took notes on the rising Nazi movement, gaining the rank of major general before his own love of trouble and Fascist inclinations led him to become involved in a series of shadowy adventures involving the right-wing Lapua Movement. These included, in 1930, the kidnapping of ex-President Stahlberg and his wife, for which he was arrested and somehow found innocent by a complacent Helsinki court.[86]

Wallenius was discharged from the army and moved to Lapua on the western coast in order to help lead the insurgent movement there until it was finally outlawed after the so-called Mantsala Uprising, an attempted putsch that culminated in the hapless Lapuans holing themselves up in a Civil Guard building. The requisite embers for a native right-wing revolution in Finland, insofar as they had existed, had turned cold. The worst of the Depression's effects had blown over. Prices and businesses were rising again. More important, the Finnish nation, unlike the German one, had grown attached to its democratic forms. A radio speech by ex-President Svinhufvud helped to end whatever support the rebels enjoyed. As punishment for his role in the uprising, Wallenius was imprisoned for a year.[87]

Now, seven years later, as part of their own misfired blitzkrieg, the Russians had invaded northern Finland, Wallenius's old stomping grounds, in force. With the Red Army making simultaneous thrusts at Salla, Suomussalmi, Lieksa, and Kuhmo, Mannerheim decided to divide General Tuompo's command, which actually comprised half the country, into two, making Wallenius his second in command and putting him in charge of the far-flung Finnish forces north of the Arctic, who were now called the Lapland Group.

"Now," as Cox, who interviewed Wallenius at his new wolf's nest at the Hotel Pohjanhovi in Rovaniemi, aptly put it, "he was back, gold lace, clinking high boots and all." And he liked it.

"Is it really *him*?" one imagines Rovaniemians asking each other four days before, when the former *putschist* strode through the streets with the restored lions on his epaulette. After all, not very long before, Wallenius and his Lapuan mob had tried to overthrow the Finnish government; now, in a kind of bent Nordic version of the prodigal-son-returneth tale, he had been called to its colors to defend it.[88]

Cox, unlike some of the many journalists who made the pilgrimage to the Hotel Pohjanhovi to interview Wallenius and who were dazzled by his antics (which included storming around in a bear fur suit with his shirt unbuttoned underneath), didn't care for the new Lapp commander and went to see him "with a frank sense of antagonism."[89]

Unquestionably Wallenius was still a Fascist at heart:

It was no accident that German was the only language he knew. [Wallenius] was deeply pro-German. In fact, he was more; he was deeply pro-Nazi. He was in every way the type of man from whom one section of the early Nazis was recruited—a Finnish Goering, as it were, energetic, an able soldier with a real love of campaigning, who had never been able to find in peacetime any job which gave him the sense of activity and purpose that fighting gave him.

He *liked* war. He loved marching up the hall of the Pohjanhovi hotel with every officer springing to his feet and bowing stiffly: he loved driving off in his goatskin coat towards the front; liked stamping around under shellfire, talking with his officers.[90]

Wallenius also liked killing Russians: "His eyes lit up when he described to us the way the Russians were mown down on the ice night after night. 'They lay there in heaps, great heaps,' he cried." Another time, when Cox visited him with a group of other correspondents, Wallenius proudly brandished a captured Russian officer's grooved, French-type bayonet. "There was something terrible in his smile."[91]

At the same time, while taking due note of Wallenius's defects, Cox discerned that the war—at least *this* war—had enabled him to transcend them, at least for a brief while. Two months later, during the fighting at Viipuri, when the volatile general was forced to leave his Lappish habitat and take up another post less to his liking, the megalomaniac in Wallenius would resurface, leading to his dismissal and final downfall.

But for a moment, after Wallenius took over command of Finnish forces in the far North, Cox observes, "the unequal fight he was engaged in gave him a completely different air, an air of courage (of which he had masses) and dignity. Leading a tiny army he reflected the endurance and sacrifice of the men he led. For a moment the Nazi was lost in the General. And the General was most urgently needed, for the Russians were sweeping towards Rovaniemi now almost as fast as they could move."[92]

*

And so they were. By December 14, when Wallenius strutted through the halls of the Pohjanhovi to assume his new command, the regimental task force that had been spun off from the 122nd Division—comprising the Soviet 273rd Regiment along with a reconnaissance battalion and a company of T-28 tanks under Shevtshenko's command—was already rumbling into Savukoski, thirty-five kilometers to the northeast, the last place before the river crossing at Pelkosenniemi. There, Wallenius hoped to stop the surging Russians with the three partial battalions at the 40th Jaeger Regiment—the 1st, 2nd, and 3rd—he had at his disposal. Beyond Pelkosenniemi the road ran flat to Kemijarvi, and thence to Rovaniemi, the 122nd's ultimate objective.[93]

That is when Wallenius the general and veteran Lappish fighter rose to the fore by making two risky but well-calculated moves. The first, which dictated the pre-deployment of the thousand-plus men he had in position in Pelkosenniemi on December 18—one of the units had arrived but a few hours before—involved guessing which of the two roads leading out of the deserted village Shevtshenko would head for once his forces forded the right bank of the Kemijarvi into town. One road led to the Arctic Highway. The other veered southward to Kemijarvi.[94]

Wallenius and Villamo, with their small force, did not have enough men to cover both roads. Wallenius decided to gamble that the Russian commander would do the expected thing and head for Kemijarvi. Consequently he split his forces into three groups. One partial battalion, the 1st, was put in position in the village to bar the direct road to Kemijarvi. That was the force—actually

Wallenius's smallest unit—which the advance guard of the 273rd tangled with on the afternoon of December 18.[95]

The 2nd Battalion, consisting of approximately 500 men, was sent through the forests to the west to wait close to the crossroad, ready to attack the Russian advance guard in the flank. At the same time, Wallenius dispatched his largest force (800 men) from the 3rd Battalion on a twelve-hour march in a huge three-quarter circle to cross the river north of the Russians, move through the woods, and hit at their supply column—their traditional Achilles' heel—at the right moment. That was the basis of Wallenius's strategy.[96]

How many men did Wallenius leave to guard the Arctic Highway? Cox asked him afterward. Three, the veteran fighter told the astonished newspaperman.

> Three held that road for me. I remembered from my experience . . . that the Russians do not easily break away from a rigidly prepared plan. They were clearly aiming for Kemijarvi. Otherwise why should they [the 122nd] have divided their forces neatly into two halves to come on both [the] north and south [side of the] road? Even if the Arctic road [Arctic Highway] was wide open to them and offered a way right into Rovaniemi, which was practically unprotected, I believe they would not have suddenly dashed towards it.
>
> I knew, too, that they could never discover that that other road was open. Nor did they have effective patrols. It was cloudy, and their aircraft could do little scouting. In any case, all our men were hidden in the woods. The Russians were completely blind. We knew every one of their moves, almost minute by minute, for we had a screen of scouts moving through the forest alongside their columns all the way.

"We convoyed them into the position we wanted," Wallenius boasted to Cox.[97]

And so he did. Wallenius's guess about which way the Russians would head after they crossed the Kemijoki into Pelkosenniemi was correct. As planned, the advance guard then encountered the Finnish company he had in place there, igniting the fight around the courtyard.

This in turn sprung the trap he set as the two other detachments slithered off into the woods to strike at the rest of the mile-long, snake-like Soviet caravan early the next morning, December 19, when the Russians would least be expecting them. Later, the Finns would do much the same thing at the better known "battles of annihilation" at Suomussalmi and Raate Road, but Kemijoki River was the first place in which they used these tactics—or had the opportunity to, and credit for same ought to go to the now virtually forgotten Wallenius. It was, unquestionably, a risky strategy. If the ambushers lost their bearings in the thick pathless pinewoods west of Pelkosenniemi, or if they were late, or if they were detected, the whole plan would collapse.[98]

H-Hour was set for 2 A.M. Cox, in the best battlefield description of his 1940 book, vividly describes what happened next:

> Then at exactly 2 A.M., the two flank forces struck. Just on the Finnish side of the river Russian troops and supply wagons suddenly found themselves hit by machine-gun fire out of the forests that a moment before had seemed dead and empty. They fired back, but their enemy was invisible. Their officers sent back scouts to ask for help. But it was too late, for already the main column was under fire.[99]

The main column consisted of five tanks in the front, followed by several officers' cars, then several dozen supply trucks—the Soviet regiment's jugular. Alongside the column, tied to trees, were over 100 horses. This was not unusual. The Red Army, like the Finnish Army, still relied on horses to a surprising extent at this time.[100] Some of the Russian steeds, which were considerably less hardy than Finnish ones, were employed as cavalry; others, particularly during the battles of central and northern Finland, were employed to tow supply sledges, as they were here at Pelkosenniemi.[101]

As for the Russian troops, they slept in the trucks or in small shelters they built on the roadside. Others slept in weapon pits whose bottoms were covered with straw. "They had learned enough by now," Cox recounts, "to build pits for their fires so that they would not be seen by the Finns."

The Soviets' efforts to conceal themselves nearly worked. The Finnish troops, new to combat themselves, were nearly on top of the column before they realized it. Matters were complicated by the fact that the commander of the attacking Finnish force, a captain, also a novice, had fallen through the ice during the long flanking march. Consequently, his clothing, which he could not change, froze on him like boards. He later died of pneumonia. Fortunately, he was able to give the order to fire.[102]

The surprised Russians gave as good as they got, at least at first, as Cox reports:

> When the first fire order was given, madness swept the Russian column. The horses went down in one shrieking, kicking mass. Men who rushed to get their rifles fell. After a few minutes the Russian infantry settled down to fire back. From their pits they opened fire with heavy machine guns fitted with tracer bullets which lit up the woods, searching for the hidden Finns.
>
> Farther back the reserve body of infantry had time to get into position and open fire in steady order. The battle soon developed into a major fight at two points, one around the supply column, the other against the main infantry position about half a mile behind.[103]

The frenzied, no-quarter battle, fought in temperatures of twenty to thirty degrees below zero Fahrenheit, continued throughout the night of December 18 and into the next morning under the incongruously beautiful, starry Lappish skies. At one point, the Finnish 2nd Battalion, which took on the main Russian infantry column, found itself partially surrounded. Then, around dusk, the 1st Battalion, the one that had swung around from the rear, opened fire, and the tide inexorably turned toward the Finns. "The Russians tried to turn the supply lorries," writes Cox, "but Finnish snipers picked off the drivers. Gradually the Finns closed in. A first rush towards the open road was beaten off, but soon they were at work with grenades amongst the lorries. The Russians retreated down the road to join the reserve infantry."[104]

Here, too, the Russians had little chance: "Unable to see the Finns, who had always the cover of the forest, and who moved with trained swiftness, the Russians had a great disadvantage. They were on the road, visible; the Finns were in the forests, invisible. The Finns had surprise; the Russians were off their balance from the start."[105]

It was all over by noon on December 19. The regiment's vanguard had been driven back after the fight in the streets of Pelkosenniemi, leaving the churchyard strewn with dozens of Russian corpses (as well as not a few Finnish ones). "The other section had retreated across the river, routed. The Commander of the main body [Shevtshenko] could do no more. His advance tanks had been captured near the supply column left. He gave the order to retreat, leaving his guns behind."[106]

The 273rd, or what remained of it, kept on retreating, all the way back to Salla. The Soviets had been checked in the Far North. Wallenius's gamble had been vindicated, as had Mannerheim's gamble on him. Mannerheim gives due credit to Wallenius's tactical victory in his memoirs: "The victory at Pelkosenniemi was of great importance for the defense of Lapland," he writes. "Troops could now be released for the front at Kemijarvi, where two regiments tied down two Russian divisions until the end of the war."[107]

Wallenius himself is not mentioned, for Mannerheim would shortly sour on him again, as would most Finns. The general in Wallenius would give way too soon to the crackpot; nevertheless, he had given Finland a significant victory, one barely remembered today.

While the Finnish troops were exchanging their last shots with the retreating foe at Kemijoki River on the afternoon of December 19, the fighting on the Karelian Isthmus, now in its fifth day, was reaching its pinnacle, too, as the Russians launched their heaviest attacks thus far.

The Russians had clearly learned a few things since the start of the offensive. For one thing, their marksmanship was better, as Mannerheim concedes. "There is no question that Russian artillery had learned to concentrate their fire better," he admits. Perhaps some of those combat socialist competitions were having an effect. More likely, it was the practice.[108]

The improvement in the Russians' performance was also evident to James Aldridge, as he watched a battalion-size force of Russians mount a brisk, well-coordinated attack on a key hill in Taipale: "From the Russian lines in the woods came covering fire and the woods became thick with mortar shells and light artillery bursts. Over on the right, where Finnish machine guns were active, a Russian gun opened fire from the opposite end of the wood clump and I saw the bullets chew the tops of small pines where the Finns were hidden."[109]

In the meantime, an escadrille of heavy Soviet tanks had managed to push forward through the intense Finnish fire, with most of their attacked infantry in tow, and reached said hill, as Aldridge, awestruck, continued to take notes while dodging bullets himself. Never again would reporters be allowed so close to the front line (so far as is known). "The Finnish machine gun from its boulder nest had kept on firing, but now a Russian mortar in a timber clump silenced it in a burst of gushing snow, and then the guns of the Russian tanks roared. The Russians were making progress to the top of the hill."[110]

The determined Russian attack was blunted by the equally resolute Finnish defenders—but only just: "Six Russians attempted to come down on the Finns' side of the hill to establish a machine gun nest amongst the granite boulders. But the Finns' fire was too heavy for them and they retreated, leaving two dead."[111]

At Lahde and Summa, where the Soviet 7th Army once again mounted its strongest attack, throwing two more divisions into the onslaught against the bone-weary defenders of the 5th Division, they made even better progress, as a storm group of 100 tanks rumbled westward. Clearly the Russians were less daunted by the Mannerheim Line, now that they were familiar with its limitations: too small boulders employed as anti-tank obstacles, which the Russian tanks proceeded to blast to bits before moving forward to the blazing bunker line itself. The maddened tankers, seemingly intent on leading the way to Helsinki on their own, found that there was nothing stopping them from driving up to the pillboxes and firing at them at point-blank range.[112]

At Lahde, the formidable Poppius bunker, one of the largest and most heavily protected bunkers with its armor-plated casemate and frontal wall, was so badly damaged by the direct tank fire that its embrasures were welded shut, forcing the trapped garrison to resist the Soviet infantry swarming past and over it like soldier ants with grenades and small arms, while they frantically radioed for help.

At Summa, where a mixed force of light and heavy tanks was able to power through the Finns' inner perimeter into the village itself, all hell broke loose as the tankers charged through the deserted streets, while the equally crazed defenders leaped on them, firing their Suomi submachine guns into observation slits, forcing open hatches and pitching grenades and lit kerosene bombs into them, while Soviet fighters buzzed by overhead strafing anything in sight (including, as often as not, their unfortunate comrades below).[113]

Somehow Ivan Chetyrbok, with his snow-filled rifle, survived his regiment's mad banzai charge at the Finnish bunkers. The rest of what he remembered was unadulterated nightmare: "Tanks assaulted the Mannerheim Line alone. Artillery fired on the Line without breaks day and night; the roar of guns was always in the air. I have no idea how much lead and steel they fired on the line. They were firing both on the bunkers and on the Finnish supply lines in the rear. The Finns destroyed tanks with petrol bombs."[114]

Nightmare indeed. Or, to use a term that would soon become familiar as the European War morphed into the Second World War: total war. Here it was, a mixture of the mindless trench warfare of the First World War, combined with some of the horrific features of the greater conflagration to come, right here in the killing zones of Lahde and Summa. Little wonder that John Langdon-Davies called the Winter War "the first total war."[115]

As if enough weren't happening, on this same day, December 19, another front opened up in the cerulean: the air war. For two solid weeks foul weather had hampered or prevented the Red Air Force from launching the kind of all-out, countrywide air offensive it was capable of. The same inclement weather had also essentially grounded the Finnish Air Force, including *Lentolaivue 24,* which had had to scrub its counterattack in defense of besieged Fort Saarenpaa.

Then, suddenly, as if bidden by the gods of war, the gray skies over Finland cleared in the morning, allowing the klieg-like Nordic sun to pop out, an event the light-deprived Finns normally would have welcomed in peacetime. But this was wartime, and now most Finns, particularly those living in Helsinki, Turku, and the other cities and large towns of the south, cursed (or shrugged), for they knew that the change of weather most likely signaled a resumption of Russian bombing raids.[116]

For their part, the men of the 24th Air Squadron couldn't have been happier. For two weeks they had yearned to get into action. Now, all of a sudden, here was their chance, and they seized it with a vengeance.

The Russians, with the benefit of their numbers, had the luxury of being able to split their air force, simultaneously sending hundreds of bombers winging across southern Finland in new raids over many of the country's major cities and ports, including Helsinki, Viipuri, Turku, Hanko, as well as transport facilities—the train from Helsinki to Turku was strafed twice on December 19, sending its passengers diving into the nearest snow bank—while employing much of the rest of their combat-ready force on sorties in support of the new assault on the Mannerheim Line.[117]

Opposing them was the Finnish Air Force, with its modest armada of but several dozen relatively modern Fokkers and other aging fighter craft. Heretofore the FAF's standard practice was to send one interceptor up for every Soviet bomber sortie. But not today, December 19. Helsinki and its sister cities would have to rely on the marksmanship of their respective anti-aircraft installations to repulse the invader. The bantamweight FAF had only one rational option if it wished to inflict any kind of damage on its outsized aerial opponent: to take on the Russians over the isthmus. Not that that option was particularly sane, in light of the overwhelming numbers the jolly rogers of *Lentolaivue 24* were sure to face on that invitingly clear, crystal blue December day.[118]

Then again, one had to be a little *verruckt* (or crazy, as the Germans would say) to join the Finnish Air Force in the first place, especially in 1939. A certain fine madness was part of the pilots' mental armament, one could say. Hence the toast the men of the 24th would drink to each other in their ready room at Immola, the same one that Martha Gellhorn had visited two weeks before, before they went up in the air to face the Big Red Bear. "Tolkku Pois!" they would quip before downing their hot toddies and heading out into the super-frigid air to do battle with the Red Air Force. *Goodbye to reason!*[119]

And so on the morning of the fifth, climactic day of the second Russian offensive against the Mannerheim Line, when the first wave of about 100 SB-2s and DB-3s appeared over the embattled isthmus, an aerial skirmish line of a dozen Fokkers was waiting to receive them.[120]

*

To be sure, in 1939, if one had one's choice of interceptors to choose from, the Fokker D-21, the principal Finnish fighter, with its old-fashioned fixed undercarriage, would probably not be it. The Dutch fighter, which was originally developed for use by the Royal Netherlands East Indies Army Air Force in 1935 before the Finns imported three dozen models just before the start of the Winter War, had other drawbacks. Its air-cooled engine tended to stall at low temperatures, like the ones the men of the 24th faced today. In combat, it could achieve a top speed of 418 kilometers (260 miles) an hour—only slightly less than the SB-2s and DB-3s it was supposed to intercept. It did not maneuver particularly well. Its armament, consisting of four 7.9 mm machine guns, was relatively modest. The best one could say for the Fokker was that it was sturdy and serviceable: it would do. It would have to—at least until the more modern fighters promised Finland by its friends arrived.[121]

The Finnish pilots themselves compensated for the Fokker's deficiencies with their considerable training and artfully worked out tactics. In fact, their seemingly reckless tactics—which often as not entailed climbing above a group of Soviet bombers, and then diving straight into them, guns blazing—had been developed years before. The Finns, with their limited resources, knew from the moment they began developing a serious air force in the late 1920s and early 1930s that they would never be able to mount the large squadrons and wings of airplanes that the larger powers could, particularly their most likely opponent, the Russians. Small formations would have to do.[122]

But, they realized, this needn't be a handicap in facing the large formations of an invader's air force, particularly if those formations could, through aggressive tactics, be broken up into one-on-one duels or chases. Or, as the contemporary Finnish air general and historian Lt. General Heikki Nikunen put it, "Flying in small formations meant continuous flying against bigger numbers. But this could be compensated for by *always attacking regardless of numbers*."[123]

✳

The 24th's deputy leader, Lt. Per-Erik "Pelle" Sovelius, who, along with his wingman, Sgt. Sakari Ikonen, formed one section of that thin white and blue line of gawky Fokkers protecting the isthmus, described the serial dogfight in their after-action report. The first rays of sunshine were glinting off the icebound surfaces of the lakes of the Karelian Isthmus as the aerial berserkers lined up in scrimmage, with Sovelius and Ikonen giving chase the moment the first wing of SB-2s came into view: "On 19.12 from 0955 to 1105 on air combat patrol I was leading the 3rd pair [of fighters] with Sgt. Ikonen on my wing. We were flying over the Antrea area when the radio informed [us] to head southwest. Somewhere near Kamara I observed a 7 plane SB formation and started the chase. The SBs were flying toward the southwest."[124]

With their comparatively slow Fokkers, Sovelius and Ikonen were unable to catch up with that group of Soviet bombers. Then Sovelius noticed another, smaller group of three planes flying a little behind them and headed in the same direction. Once again, the chase was on.

The Finns had already learned from their previous experience with SBs that the Soviet bombers' most vulnerable spot was their rear fuel tanks. Both Sovelius and Ikonen put this knowledge to good use that day, as the latter notes: "Sgt. Ikonen got well behind the plane on the starboard wing and shot it into flames from a very close range at the altitude of 2,000 meters over Kipinola. I tried to get behind the port wingman, but did not have enough speed."

Soon enough, another covey of SBs sailed into view. Remarkably, these bombers were dropping leaflets: apparently, the Supreme Command still felt that it was possible to influence Finnish hearts and minds at that point.[125]

Now the skies over Karelia were abuzz with Russian bombers. Given his choice of prey, Sovelius decided to let the pamphlet-dropping SB-2s go and instead peeled off to attack another trio, with satisfactory results: "During the chase [of the leaflet-dropping bombers] I observed again three SB planes a little below going southwards. I picked the port wingman as my target and shot first at the rear fuselage, when the [Soviet] gunner quit firing. After this I aimed my fire to the port engine, which began to smoke and finally caught fire. The plane fell to the starboard wing and dove towards the sea close to Seivasto about 10 kilometers from the coast."[126]

Scratch one SB-2. But the Finn wasn't finished: "I fired then at the starboard wingman, when his right engine started to pour smoke, but stayed with the lead plane and kept going on."[127]

Two SBs down, one damaged. Sovelius decided to head home. However, the battle wasn't over. On his way back to his base, two I-16s coming out of the sun surprised him, sending bullets rustling into his craft. Unfazed, the Finn instead turned around and gave combat, as he was trained to do. Unfortunately, the slower Fokker wasn't quite up to the job, as Sovelius concedes: "I pulled instantly towards [the attacking I-16s], but noticed that their planes were more maneuverable than mine. I tried to tighten my turns and got the enemy in my sight and fired one burst. I noticed that I had ammunition left only in one gun. After trying to turn as tight as possible I lost control and slipped into a spin."

Fortunately for the Finns, the Soviet pilots had more ammunition than skill. "Judging by their tracers," Sovelius wrote, "the I-16s seemed to fire all the time even when my plane was clearly out of their sights."[128]

Meanwhile, the other FAF sections were busy with their own separate dogfights, creating a spectacular—if somewhat confusing—air show for a group of spellbound correspondents, amongst them the United Press's veteran correspondent Webb Miller.

"This afternoon I witnessed the most spectacular dogfight I have ever seen in any war," wrote Miller, who had also covered the fighting in Spain and China, "a fantastic sight, it lasted for half an hour. Six Finnish planes engaged eleven Soviet most of them bombers. Like a Hollywood film battle it started in wild melee with seventeen planes diving, zooming, sideslipping, and spluttering machine gun bullets."[129]

Presumably to the delight of the Finnish High Command, the wide-eyed American was so impressed by the aerial extravaganza that he overestimated the speed of the defenders' standard-issue Fokkers: "Witnessing the battle convinced me that the Finns have some extraordinarily fast pursuit planes, with skillful, courageous pilots."[130]

Actually, only the latter was true: the FAF indeed had skillful, courageous pilots, but their planes were comparatively slow. However, it didn't look that way from below. "Several times," the American raved, "I saw Finnish planes gain on the Soviet planes, even zoom up under a Russian plane a few times, gaining on it while climbing." Just as they were trained to do.[131]

Another member of Miller's party, a Swedish press officer, whose testimony to the prowess of the Finnish Air Force—as well as to the beauty of the display it put on that day in the Karelian skies—was just as bedazzled and given prominent play in the *Helsingin Sanomat*:

On Wednesday [December 19] we saw 17 planes battle each other, 11 of them Russian, 6 Finn. The battle in the blue sky produced a brilliant, and at the same time, terrifying vision. The planes encountered each other at 2,000 meters. In the bright sun they shone like fireflies, wandering and floating, and making alternately narrow and wide circles. The cold, bitter, calm air caused the planes' exhausts to thicken into long, grey tails. . . . It didn't look like a battle of life and death. Instead it looked like beautiful figures in the sky.[132]

Of course, it *was* a battle of life and death, as the charred remains of the crews of the Soviet bombers the Finns shot down on December 19 bore witness. All told, *Lentolaivue 24* flew 400 sorties that day, downing a dozen bombers—seven SB-2s and five DB-3s—while damaging a score more, considerably hampering the Soviet air offensive and showing the flag for all the world to see.[133]

If anyone, Finns included, doubted that *Suomi* had an effective air force, here, in the awestruck words of Miller and that entranced Swedish press officer, was the undeniable albeit slightly embellished truth. And if anyone—especially the Soviets—thought that the Finns had faster pursuit planes than they actually did, so much the better.

The steady-nerved Lieutenant Sovelius came out of his spin and made it back to base, shaking off his pursuers with a series of evasive maneuvers, before hitting the deck and sputtering back to Immola in his damaged craft. As he flew over the battlefield, Sovelius writes in his report, he could see cannon fire from the fighting going on below. Had he looked closer, he also would have seen the flaming wreckage of dozens of Soviet tanks, the grim remains of the day's climactic land battle. Eight of the twenty machines that had managed to punch their way into Summa were destroyed; by nightfall, the rest had returned to their lines and the last breach in the Mannerheim Line had been patched up. All told, the Russians lost fifty-eight tanks on December 19, including twenty heavy tanks, bringing the total number lost on the Karelian Isthmus to over 250.[134]

That night Ivan Chetyrbok, still counting his good fortune at having survived the previous day's suicidal charge at the Finnish pillboxes, looked out at the enemy lines and saw flames reaching into the night sky.

"Is that a Finnish village burning?" the shell-shocked Russian soldier asked his no less dazed commander. "No," the latter replied. "There is no village there. It's our tanks burning."[135]

Struggling to get a handle on the situation but unwilling to admit defeat, Kirill Meretskov ordered another attack at Summa with more troops the following day, which achieved even less success; this time the lumbering Soviet juggernaut never made it past the outer Finnish defenses.

Morale amongst the hungry, freezing, despairing Russian troops of the 7th Army, never good to begin with, sank to a new low. A letter found on the frozen carcass of one of the thousands who died during the futile five-day offensive speaks for itself: "We march today without food for two days, black like chimneys. Our health is bad. Many soldiers have pneumonia. . . . They promise that combat will end on Stalin's birthday, the 21st of December," the forlorn soldier ended his crumpled-up missive, "but who will believe it?"[136]

"If they had been afraid before," writes Catherine Merridale of the Russian phalanxes waiting their turn to charge into the murderous Finnish fire, "their mood was closer to sheer despair. The Party's tale of easy victory had turned out to be false."[137]

"We're going to find these bunkers everywhere," wrote another traumatized Russian survivor of the battle. "We cannot even collect our injured and dead. The infantry cannot overcome emplacements like these."[138]

The myth of the Finnish superman had been reinforced, and so, for the moment, had that of the Mannerheim Line, even more so now that it had been proved "impregnable." Much the same had happened with the nascent (and equally helpful) myth surrounding the Finnish Air Force: after their losses of December 19, the Russians were even more loathe to tangle with their opposites, often scattering at the sight of the patrolling Finnish planes.

The massive, combined land, naval, and aerial Russian offensive on the Mannerheim Line, the Big Push that the Soviet Supreme Command and Otto Kuusinen had hoped would carry the Red Army to victory and "liberate" Finland in time for the Great Leader's birthday, was over. For the moment, the gateway to Helsinki was safe. The 80,000 bone-weary men belonging to the half-dozen divisions manning the line at this time—from west to east, the 4th Division (Malm's and Eronen's unit), at Summa; the 5th, 1st, 11th, 8th, and finally the 10th, at Taipale—would remain on guard repelling several other smaller Russian assaults over the next week.[139]

"The enemy's attacks could be compared with a badly conducted orchestra, in which the instruments were played out of time"—this is how Mannerheim later summed up the failed Russian offensive. Regarding his own troops, the marshal offers surprisingly muted praise: "The troops in the principal theater of war had stood up to the greatly superior enemy forces far better than I had dared hope and were in fine fighting form." It would seem that Mannerheim, the pessimist, didn't quite believe in his troops as much as he said he did; in any case, in several places in his memoirs he writes how his men surprised him.[140]

More important, the "White Guardists" had also shocked the Russians. If Stalin, Molotov, Voroshilov, and Zhdanov had underestimated the ability and tenaciousness of the Finnish troops, as they clearly had, it was very difficult to do so after the combined, failed actions of December 19.

✳

Mannerheim misstates the condition of his troops: the battle-weary defenders of the Viipuri Gateway were not in fine fighting form. In fact they were utterly exhausted. Nevertheless, at the urging of General Harald Ohquist, the commander of Finnish II Corps, the marshal agreed to a plan the latter had devised several weeks before, a limited counteroffensive against the Soviets. It was Mannerheim's first serious mistake. The counteroffensive, involving three Finnish divisions, was a failure. Mannerheim later listed most of the reasons why it failed, including, most notably in his opinion, Ohquist's failure of nerve.[141]

However, he leaves out an important one: the state of the troops themselves. After repelling Russians in subzero weather for five days straight, let alone being cannonaded and bombarded by Russian artillery and planes, Ohquist's troops were simply in no shape to mount an offensive.

Perhaps, if Mannerheim had deigned to visit the front line himself, something that he would only do once, much later in the war, the distant commander-in-chief would have been able to see this. Instead, he assumed that his men, eager to further revenge themselves upon the aggressor, were capable of mounting another assault.[142]

That simply wasn't the case, as Olavi Eronen, who participated in the failed attack, recalled. "After the first attack our morale was quite low, as casualties were mounting. The counterattack was disastrous in this sense."

"Of course," he adds, "we didn't know about the successful battles in the north yet."[143]

✳

Nowhere was the cheering for Brave Little Finland—the expression was almost axiomatic now—and her army louder or more passionate than in the United States. By now, after three weeks of stop-press coverage of the war, Fennomania had spread throughout the country: according to a mid-December Gallup Poll, a startling 88 percent of American adults were aware of the war and were rooting for the Finns, with only 1 percent in favor of the USSR.[144]

The chief beneficiary of this floodtide of anger and sympathy was Finnish Relief Fund, Inc., the relief fund enthusiastically headed by former president Herbert Hoover. Americans, still clinging to the psychological safety net of neutrality, were conflicted about how much they wanted their government to become involved in the Soviet-Fenno fray. However, they were more than eager to dig into their own pockets to help the Finns out, especially now that they seemed to be holding their own against the "Russkies." "Americans enthusiastically supported the relief program," writes Travis Jacobs, "especially when it became clear that the Finns would not succumb overnight and that their resistance was more than a heroic gesture. Throughout December Finland's valiant defense against the Russian superiority in man-power, fire-power and air power did more than dramatize the struggle—it encouraged relief efforts."[145]

To be sure, of all the strange political fruit created by the Winter War, none was odder than the sudden resurrection of the thirty-first president of the United States. Blamed—in part justifiably, in part for want of a better scapegoat—for the Great Depression, which by 1932 had junked the American economy and put one out of every four Americans out of work, Hoover—once famed for his humanitarian and famine relief work after World War I—had become "the most hated man in America."[146] Now, thanks to the Kremlin's good offices and Hoover's considerable organizational skills, the former chief executive was back in the spotlight, not as failed president but as humanitarian.

Hoover's affection for and knowledge of Finland was genuine, as was his anger at the Soviet invasion. He had visited the world's northernmost nation on numerous occasions in his role as hunger relief administrator after World War I, as well as more recently, and still commanded a reservoir of goodwill there. President Ryti, perhaps innocent of Hoover's domestic reputation, personally cabled Hoover on December 15, the sixteenth day of the war, to express thanks for his efforts: "[The] people of Finland rejoice very much that you, Mr. President, known by people of Finland as their cordial friend for decades, are again heading a movement for our distressed people. In the uneven struggle against the outrageous attackers for existence and for the holiest and highest human values, the people of Finland need every material and moral assistance that possibly can be given."[147]

Thus armed with Ryti's blessing, Hoover suddenly became America's Fennophile Number One, making press appearances and giving impassioned speeches in the effort to raise money for his adopted cause.

Unsurprisingly, because of Finland's rich musical heritage, particularly the work of Jean Sibelius, probably the best-known Finn in the world at that time besides Paavo Nurmi, many of the country's best-known classical musicians also jumped on the blue and white bandwagon. Thus, on December 11, Werner Janssen, the well-known classical conductor and friend of Sibelius, announced that he would lead an orchestra in an all-Sibelius program for Finnish Relief on December 29, offering to pay the cost of the hall and the orchestra himself so that all receipts could go to the great cause. Three weeks earlier, following the Soviet invasion, Janssen had personally cabled Sibelius and asked him to consider becoming his houseguest for the duration of the war, such was his love for the great composer.[148] Sibelius graciously declined his distant protégé's well-meaning invitation, but he professed to be very happy to hear that his music was being played in the Land of the Free. And he was very gratified at America's extraordinary show of support.

"I have two things uppermost in my mind," declared Sibelius, who spoke English well, to an American reporter who telephoned him at the time. "It won't take many words to express them. I am indeed proud of my people and what they are doing these days. And I am happy to witness again the wonderful way in which the great American nation has rallied to the support of Finland. That is all I can say at the moment." Then he hung up.[149]

*

Perhaps the most notable and certainly the noisiest pro-Finnish event was the massive "Help Finland!" rally at Madison Square Garden on December 21, 1939, which also happened to be Stalin's birthday. Joining Hoover on the white-and-blue draped podium was a small galaxy of political luminaries, including New York mayor Fiorello LaGuardia, U.S. senators Robert Wagner and Burton Wheeler, famed columnist (and wife of Sinclair Lewis) Dorothy Thompson, and Hjalmar Procope, the omnipresent Finnish ambassador.[150]

The packed audience listened intently to Hoover's moving testament to Finland, "a little country, carved from the bleak forests of the Far North, scarcely the size of Montana, with but four millions of people," and decry the "primitive savagery" of the Soviet aggressor.

> Finland is a great nation . . . great by the character of its people . . . great by their industry, their education, their art, music and their courage. For 1,200 years the Finns have lived in their beloved Northland. During this time they have been conquered and dominated time and again, but just as often their eternal courage and their determination for freedom have regained for them their independence.
>
> Now they have been barbarously attacked. Their ships have been driven from the seas. They are making a heroic defense against a horde of appalling savages.[151]

Hoover then spoke of his own experience with the country as famine relief administrator twenty years before during the difficult days of 1918 and 1919, when he traveled to Finland and got to know the newborn country firsthand, and the many ways Finns had expressed their gratitude ever since. During his most recent visit, just a year prior, he noted, a farmer, a former beneficiary of his efforts, came to his Helsinki hotel to give him a special gift: a flour sack embroidered with the American flag. Wild cheering.

Soviet barbarousness notwithstanding, Hoover cautioned the audience in the hall, as well as the nationwide radio audience, that Americans themselves should not go to war for the Finns or anyone else. American neutrality and non-belligerency were inviolate he felt.

"For reasons that reach into the whole future of human liberty," the hardened isolationist explained, "America must not join in this European war." However, by contributing to his relief organization "the American people can give their help to the destitute [and] lighten their road of despair."[152]

No, the Finns didn't want Americans to go fight for them, or anything like that; Hoover insisted their dollars would be sufficient. Nor, one inferred, did he think it proper to give the Finns weapons or to lend them the monies to buy them, a point on which he and his co-belligerent, Hjalmar Procope, differed. Following Hoover on the podium, the combative Finnish ambassador drew a big cheer by quoting the American colonial rebel leader Patrick Henry's famous words, "Give me liberty or give me death!"[153]

"Waves of emotion swept the crowd," according to the *New York Times,* "with many men and women weeping." No less than $50,000 was raised for Finnish relief, an appreciable amount for the time.[154]

And yet the question remained, if the liberty of this showcase for freedom was threatened, wasn't the liberty of all freedom-loving nations? The funds collected by Hoover's organization were of course much appreciated; however, like the recent credit granted by the U.S. Congress, they could only be used for food, agricultural supplies, and other humanitarian purposes.

In truth, despite the war, Finland had sufficient food stores. There was no humanitarian crisis, as yet. What the Finns really needed were the planes, the tanks, the ammunition—above all, the men—to continue to hold off the Russians. The butter could wait; what Finland needed now was bombs. Couldn't—shouldn't—the United States do more, some Americans wondered? They would continue to wonder for the remainder of the war.[155]

To be sure, Americans weren't the only ones who were taking note of the Finns' battlefield successes—or who felt that more should be done to help them. Indeed, on the afternoon of December 19, as the fighting on and above the Mannerheim Line was reaching its climax, the Allies' Supreme War Council, including British prime minister Neville Chamberlain and French prime minister Eduoard Daladier, were meeting with their respective military chiefs in an ancient hall in Paris lined with medieval armor to discuss the fluid Scandinavian situation.[156]

Daladier, emboldened by the recent Finnish successes, eager to create a new front as far away from France as possible, was disposed to take firm action. In this, to some degree, he followed the lead of the French press. As Douglas Clark writes in *Three Days to Catastrophe,* the French, still viewing the current war through the prism of the last one, had reached the wrong conclusion from the successful defense of the Mannerheim Line—that static defense worked. It was one that the French would soon rue: "In the Paris political lobbies the clamour for strong, spectacular action was swelling. The first news of Finnish successes in the field had been coming in. Public opinion, already Maginot-minded, pointed exultantly to the Karelian fighting as a demonstration of the 'power of defense,' and it was widely believed that Soviet military was now a proved fiction which could be challenged without risk."[157]

Over the past week the French press, encouraged by the latest dispatches from Finland, had been openly debating the question of whether the Allies should declare war on Russia. Perhaps good use for the *Chasseurs Alpins,* the French mountain troops who had been chastised for taking the offensive on the Western front and were still chomping at the bit, could now be found in the north, helping *la Finlande.*

Meanwhile, sentiment for Finland on the streets of Paris was reaching fever pitch. Jacob Suritz, the Soviet ambassador to Paris, last seen ducking out of the League of Nations in Geneva while it debated his country's invasion of Finland, now found himself confronted with the fury of crowds of Fennophile Frenchmen shouting "Viva Finlande!" when he emerged from his embassy.[158]

Chamberlain, for his part still anxious to avoid breaking relations with Russia, wasn't so sure he wanted to join the fray. He sympathized with the Finns, as did just about everyone in the West by now, but he was hesitant—justifiably so—about getting into a war for them. One enemy at a time would do nicely. But, Daladier insisted, there was a connection: the Swedish ore fields. None other than Fritz Thyssen, the prominent German industrialist who had bankrolled Hitler before the war (before fleeing to Switzerland upon its outbreak), had pointed out that without Sweden's iron fields Germany was bound to lose any war with the Allies. Clearly, the Allies needed to get there first.[159]

Moreover, if the Allies did get there first they would also be in an excellent position to help the Finns. As it happened, Daladier's line of thinking dovetailed, at least somewhat, with that of Winston Churchill, Britain's impetuous naval head and future prime minister, who had reached the same conclusion and had come up with his own rationale for seizing the Swedish ore fields. Seize the fields, help the Finns—that was the basic idea. Two ducks with one stone. Of course, helping the Finns would only be the pretext for such an operation—but they would be helped. Moreover, the Allies had legal justification for such a move in the form of the League of Nations' directive to render the beset Finns "all possible assistance."[160]

Now Chamberlain began to see it, dimly. By the time the four-hour conclave had dispersed, the British delegation had agreed on "the importance of rendering all possible assistance to Finland." Of course, first the Swedes and the Norwegians had to be talked into going along, but that ought not to be an insuperable problem, Chamberlain and Daladier thought. And thus the basis of the daft plan to send British and French troops to Finland was born.[161]

As Clark writes: "After December 19th, nothing could be the same again; and three days later the French Premier felt able to tell the Chamber of Deputies, amid cheers, that France intended to help the Finns 'in no half-hearted manner.'" Of course, in order for such a circuitous plan (if it could be called that) to work, the gallant Finns had to continue to hold out for a while. However, according to the latest reports from the Mannerheim Line, that didn't appear to be a problem. Even one of the Finns' most successful and loud-mouthed generals, Wallenius, the victor of Pelkosenniemi, was openly predicting that the war would last a year.[162]

✻

If the French and the British were following the latest developments from Finland, so, albeit more discreetly—but with no less pleasure—were Russia's allies, the Germans. "German officials are known not to conceal their satisfaction over the Red Army reverses," G.E.R. Gedye reported in the New York Times, also noting "the slighting manner in which German military personnel in Moscow speak of the Red Army." Gedye maintained that the Soviet leaders well knew this, along with the Germans' "barely hidden sympathy for Finland."[163]

The German military's contempt for the Red Army and its performance in Finland was confirmed in a withering staff report issued in late December lambasting the Red Army for its "poor communications," "uneven troops," and "lack of fighting quality," concluding that it was "no match for an army with modern equipment and superior leadership."

Amongst those whose desk the report presumably crossed was Adolf Hitler, who was already forming the same—mistaken—conclusion about the Soviet Army's real worth and making plans for future conquest based upon it. For the moment, Hitler kept mum about the woeful Russian performance and dutifully assisted his ally, even agreeing to allow the Russian ships participating in the not very effective blockade of Finland to dock in German ports. He even managed to overlook the fact that the Russian submarine service, which seemed to be as clumsy as its comrades on land, had mistakenly torpedoed several German steamships. What, after all, were a few steamships amongst friends?[164]

✻

Other neutral nations like the Dutch, lulled into complacency by a century of neutrality and the Grebbe Line—the formidable dike system with which they thought they would be able to hold off the neighboring Germans, if the latter ever made the mistake of invading—were taking heart from the Finnish example. Thus, a reporter for the New Yorker on a visit to Amsterdam that winter wrote: "Rotund Dutchmen solemnly thump their tables in the Astoria Restaurant while waiting for the waiter to clean up the shells of a dozen Zeeland oysters, or the remains of a brace of brown roasted pullets, and declare with conviction that Holland will soon do to Germany what Finland is doing to Russia."[165]

It was not a good comparison. The Dutch had many good qualities; however, after a century and a quarter of peace, their army was hardly in fighting form. Also the Grebbe Line, the forward Dutch riverine defense line, turned out to be about as useful to the Netherlands when the Germans finally invaded—by air—five months later as the Maginot was to the French when their turn shortly came. The New Yorker's correspondent guessed as much: "There are British military experts who think the Dutch Army would hold up to a German advance for just about five minutes." (He wasn't far off: the Dutch capitulated five days later, on May 15, 1940—but only after the *Luftwaffe* obliterated Rotterdam in the worst terror bombing of the European war until then.)[166]

✳

Indeed, the only nation that didn't appear to be taking note of the most recent developments in the war, at least officially, as Stalin's birthday approached was the USSR itself. Not that *Pravda* et al. had published much "news" about the war with Finland in the first place. But now, in mid-December, the topic virtually ceased to exist. In this sense Stalin's Big Day provided convenient cover, giving the Soviet propaganda press an excuse not to talk about Finland and instead to devote its pages to publishing laudatory articles about the Soviet leader by Molotov ("Stalin Continues the Work of Lenin!"), Soviet heavy industry chief Lazar Kaganovich ("Stalin is Lenin Today!"), and Stalin's other top cronies, including, of course, Kliment Voroshilov.[167]

"Our armed forces will defeat any opponent for we have with us our Stalin," the People's Commissar for Defense proclaimed in *Pravda* on December 15, just as the latest wave of bad news for Voroshilov and Stalin reached Moscow about the difficulties Meretskov's troops were encountering, particularly at Tolvajarvi and Suomussalmi. Privately, Stalin and his defense commissar had already had a bitter falling out over the deepening fiasco. This last development was on display at a dinner at this time at the Soviet generalissimo's *dacha*, startling future Soviet premier Nikita Khrushchev, then party head for the Ukraine, which was about to dispatch one of its best home-grown divisions, the 44th, to its destruction at Raate Road in eastern Finland.[168] Stalin, brooding over the debacle, the worst setback to Soviet arms since the Battle of Warsaw twenty years before, suddenly "jumped up in a white hot rage and began to berate Voroshilov," wrote Khrushchev, still amazed at the memory of the incident a quarter of a century later.[169]

If Voroshilov was grateful to his chief patron for sparing his life during the recently concluded purges, which the former had enthusiastically endorsed, his gratitude had escaped him. "You're the one who annihilated the Old Guard of the Army!" he screamed at Stalin according to Khrushchev, as he and the others present, convinced that the normally obsequious Voroshilov had just signed his death warrant, shrank into their chairs. "You had our best generals killed."[170]

"Stalin rebuffed him," Khrushchev continues, and at that, Voroshilov, still in high dudgeon (and perhaps slightly under the influence), picked up a silver platter with a roast suckling pig and smashed it against the table. "It was the only time in my life I witnessed such an incident," Khrushchev wrote. Remarkably, the *contretemps* didn't cause Stalin to lose his soft spot for his overstuffed defense commissar, although it doubtless caused him to wonder whether he was the right person to be in charge of the Finnish campaign. Voroshilov would be brushed aside soon enough.[171]

Meanwhile, the festivities, including opening a stream of birthday messages and cables from Stalin's well-wishers, continued. *Pravda* published a selection of the most fervent hosannas the following day. Place of honor was given to Hitler's telegraphed birthday salutation, which read in part: "Please accept my most sincere congratulations. I send at the same time my very best wishes for your personal good health and for a happy future for the peoples of a friendly Soviet Union."[172]

Even more effusive was the German foreign minister, Joachim Ribbentrop, who had presided over the Berlin-Moscow non-aggression pact, which had set the wheels of conflagration in motion four months before: "Remembering the historic hours at the Kremlin which marked the beginning of a decisive change in the relations of our countries and which thus laid the foundations for long years of friendship between our two peoples, please accept my most cordial congratulations on your 60th birthday."[173]

Third on the list of well-wishers, and apparently still one of Stalin's favorite people, was Otto Ville Kuusinen, whose greetings were printed along with those of all 5,775 members of the First Corps of the Finnish People's Army, who, though they had yet to see combat, were only too happy to send "flaming battle greetings" to Stalin.[174]

Amongst the signatories was Edward Hynninen, still polishing his telegraphic skills in Terijoki with his comrades in the People's Army's signal corps (or what passed as such). Hynninen didn't remember signing his name to Stalin's birthday card seventy years later, but he said it was possible. "Of course they didn't have to ask me."[175]

Conspicuous by its absence from the list of well-wishers that *Pravda* published was the name of Andrei Zhdanov, the Leningrad party chief. Could this have been a coincidence? G.E.R. Gedye, perhaps the most astute amateur Kremlinologist writing from Moscow at that time (unlike his colleague, Walter Duranty, whose reporting from Russia, as well as the Pulitzer Prize he received for the same, were later disowned by the *New York Times*), didn't think so. Zhdanov, Gedye pointed out, "has been throughout the moving spirit in demanding an aggressive policy toward Finland. He is believed to have succeeded in the face of considerable opposition within the Communist Political Bureau in affecting the adoption of such a policy, instead of the waiting tactics and cautious methods for which Mr. Stalin is renowned."[176]

Possibly, too, Zhdanov had been too busy tending to Leningrad business to write. And, in the wake of the Finnish war there was a lot of business to tend to. Three weeks before, Leningraders—for whom the Red Army had supposedly undertaken its "mission"—had been told that the Finnish incursion would be little more than a walkover, at worst. Now the city's hospitals were filling up with casualties from the recent battles. Also, crime in the city was up, as Zhdanov's biographer notes:

> In mid-December the lack of military progress sparked a kind of war scare among the Leningraders. Towards the end of the month, the Leningrad *gorkim* [municipal council] met to discuss a report by [Leningrad] NKVD chief [Sergo] Goglidze on the rise of crime in 1939. The report noted that disorder had especially increased since the beginning of the war with Finland. The city's authorities decided on tougher measures to use against arrested offenders. They also decided to stage show trials against hooligans, introduce a curfew for children, augment parental liability and add more patrols at railroad-stops.[177]

Zhdanov himself had received letters from some of the soldiers he had sent to Finland in which the soldiers themselves complained of the army's lack of battle readiness, their woeful equipment, and the incompetence of their commanders.[178]

In any event, salutations notwithstanding, Joseph Stalin could not have been very happy once his sixtieth birthday finally arrived. Nevertheless, in true Nero form, he and his cronies partied until dawn and past. "An unforgettable night!' Georgi Dmitroff, secretary of the Communist International, wrote in his diary. "I didn't leave until 8 A.M.!"[179]

It is not clear whether the pig-wielding Voroshilov attended the bizarre bash. In any case, he had time to dash off an angry letter to Stalin and Molotov dated that same day about Kirill Meretskov, the now displaced and presumably doomed Soviet commander, and the grievous mistakes he had made thus far. Needless to say, the People's Commissar himself didn't accept any responsibility for the fiasco.

The marshal's proposed remedy: that Meretskov be threatened with court-martial and that a purge be conducted of his 7th Army command if the situation did not improve immediately. "I consider it necessary to conduct a radical purge of corps, divisional and regimental commands," he wrote. "[We] need to replace these cowards and laggards (there are also swine) with loyal and efficient people."[180]

To be sure, that is probably exactly what Meretskov expected to happen to him on December 22, the day after Stalin's marathon birthday party, when he was summoned to the Kremlin for a meeting with The Boss. To be sure, The Boss was not very happy, as Meretskov later wrote, taking his top field commander to task for the army's abysmal performance thus far—while conveniently overlooking his own responsibility for the Finnish debacle. According to Meretskov, Stalin was particularly concerned about the negative effect the botched campaign had had "on our foreign policy, because these days the entire world is looking at us."[181]

However, Joseph Vissarionich Stalin was in a magnanimous mood this day. He decided to give Meretskov a second chance. At the same time he demoted the general: he removed him as military head of the Leningrad Military District and head commander of the four Russian armies assigned to Finland, while letting him remain in charge of the most vital unit, the 7th, the one charged with breaking the Mannerheim Line. Meretskov would have a chance to make good again.[182]

And with that, the duly chastised and relieved Meretskov returned to Leningrad, while the Soviet Supreme Command worked on a new, more sensible plan of action for finishing the decidedly unpleasant Finnish business. Not surprisingly, the Soviet planners wound up coming up with the same plan, for a single, well-prepared thrust through the isthmus that Shaposhnikov, the clear-eyed chief of staff, had presented to Stalin to begin with, and which the latter had rejected as being premised on an overestimate of Finland's ability, and willingness, to resist.[183]

Stalin had already brought in one of his favorite generals, Grigory Shtern, a Jew, to head the 8th Army, which had been assigned to Ladoga-Karelia and had conspicuously failed there as well, a week before. Not yet forty, Shtern, a veteran of the recent border wars with Japan, was one of the few bona fide "stars" of the Red Army.[184]

The scales were finally beginning to fall from Stalin's eyes. Now, after a month that had seen the prestige of the Red Army plunge to an all-time nadir, he was ready to act. Soon there would be other changes, including the selection of a new head commander for the—hopefully—final Soviet push on the isthmus. In the meantime, Stalin decided to take a more hands-on approach to the operation. After the war, Stalin, who was as responsible for the debacle as anyone, demoted Voroshilov to deputy defense commissar.[185]

The Red Air Force, for its part, commemorated its leader's birthday by launching a new series of bombing raids. Amongst the targets was Turku, a city that would become a favorite target for Soviet bombers—where fifteen raiders penetrated the city's anti-aircraft screen, setting many houses in the workers' quarter on fire and killing a dozen people. Helsinki was also bombed again that day, as the raiders once again set fire around the beleaguered city. Amongst the casualties of the December 21 raid was Helsinki's main hospital. The train between Turku and Helsinki, the same one that Herbert Elliston and Curt Bloch had recently taken, was also machine-gunned twice.[186]

*

Meanwhile, the Soviet propaganda machine was putting the best possible spin on the troubled "liberation action." It was not an easy job. After all, the Kremlin had all but assured the world—as well as its own troops—that combat would be over by now.

According to the December 23 issue of *Red Star,* the Red Army had in fact scored "important successes." For example, in the Viipuri area its men had actually advanced an average of 3.2 (2 miles) kilometers a day. This was actually good progress, the defensive-sounding communiqué asserted:

> The foreign press, especially the French and British, regards this rate as too slow, attempting to explain this by the "low fighting capacity" of the Red Army. Some military observers go even farther, asserting that the offensive of the Soviet troops "failed" since there was no "lightning blow" and the Soviet troops failed to do away with the Finnish troops in one week.
>
> Undoubtedly such vilification of the Red Army can be explained by overt and crude slander against the Red Army or by the ignorance of its authors in military affairs.[187]

The propaganda sheet went on to tendentiously compare the relative strengths of the Mannerheim Line, against which the Red Army had made, however intermittently, some progress, and Germany's Siegfried Line, against which the Allies had made no discernible progress whatsoever, thus reinforcing the myth of the Mannerheim Line (which, of course, was fine with the Finns).

> In its defense power this system of artificial fortifications, as for instance, on the Karelian Isthmus, reinforced by natural conditions, is in no way inferior to the defense power of the fortified Siegfried Line against which Anglo-French troops have been rumbling already for four months without making the slightest progress. . . . The Red Army knew of these difficulties in Finland and therefore never expected to annihilate the Finnish troops by one lightning blow.

In short, the Red Army was doing as well as could be expected.[188]

On the more truthful side, the communiqué *did* admit that the Red Army had suffered some casualties, specifically 1,823 killed and 7,000 wounded—perhaps one or two percent of the estimated casualties Moscow had actually suffered thus far. Of course, the communiqué claimed, the Finns had suffered more, with 2,200 killed—considerably less than the true number of 4,000.[189]

Meanwhile, the relatives of some of the woebegone veterans of these "successes" were learning the whole distressing truth from their sons and brothers. "My wife Nastya," a soldier in the 222nd Rifle Regiment wrote home, "the enemy is well camouflaged and delivers sure blows on us. Don't believe the newspapers—they lie. See the truth. We only advanced 3 kilometres in seven days."

*

The equally well-concealed truth was that Finland was suffering an increasing number of casualties. At Tolvajarvi, its first outright victory, the Finnish Army suffered over 30 percent losses. At that rate, the High Command began to wonder how much longer it could afford such victories. After all, its numbers were finite; the USSR's weren't. Every Finnish soldier lost was a soldier lost; a Russian soldier lost was one who could be replaced. At some point—soon—the math would start working against the Finns, regardless of their superior skill and tenacity or the friendly terrain. No one told the Finnish people this either.

*

In the meantime, a group of reporters, including Aldridge, Cox, and Carl Mydans, a writer-photographer from *Life,* got their first blood-freezing look—along with their millions of readers in America and England—at the frozen, bloody, horrific aftermath of the battle of Kemijoki River and the vestiges of the destroyed Soviet 273rd Regiment.

It was the first time that the foreign press was allowed to visit—or photograph—such a scene. There would be other dioramas of death to visit soon, at Suomussalmi and Raate Road. But, at least for these reporters, the aftermath of Kemijoki River had a more indelible impact, partly because it was the first such scene they encountered, but also for another salient fact: that the Finnish dead had not yet been removed, as they would be after Suomussalmi. Future battlefields would be "dressed up" for the press. Not so at Kemijoki River.

For his part, Aldridge had sped up from the Mannerheim Line, managing to traverse the thousand-odd kilometers from Taipale to Pelkosenniemi in three days, no mean feat given all the red tape he had had to endure. The Australian began his memorable account by reminding American readers of the insensate cold in which this strange war was being fought. Never before had reporters had to work in such frigid conditions: "The cold numbs the brain in this Arctic hell, snow sweeps over the darkened wastes, the winds howl and the temperature is 30 below zero. Here the Russians and Finns are battling in blinding snowstorms for possession of ice-covered forests."[190] Then Aldridge describes the killing zone itself:

> It was the most horrible sight I had ever seen. . . . As if the men had been suddenly turned to wax, there were two or three thousand Russians and a few Finns, all frozen in fighting attitudes. Some were locked together, their bayonets within each other's bodies; some were frozen in half-standing positions; some were crouching with their arms crooked, holding the hand grenades they were throwing; some were lying with their rifles shouldered, their legs apart.

Some were frozen kneeling with their hands covering their faces, and others were grotesquely frozen in the positions they assumed when they were shot down while running. Each little group told a story. For example, the place where the Russian cavalry had been wiped out was revealed by a group of horses piled up in the snow around the trees where they had been tethered.[191]

These were the horses that had gone down in that one shrieking mass when Wallenius's men had suddenly emerged from the woods. And there was more:

There was a frozen group of twenty Russians and a few Finns where it was obvious the Finns had surprised some Russian machine gunners while assembling their guns because the Russians' hands still held the parts with which they were working when they looked up and saw the Finns advancing.[192]

If Aldridge was horrified, Cox, while also thunderstruck, had a more detached reaction to the unreal scene confronting him, while also using the same waxen metaphor:

The ruins of the column [of Russian vehicles] lay three quarters of a mile farther on. . . . Still gripping the wheel of the staff car was the driver, his forehead smashed by a bullet—the first of the dead were strewn everywhere. How strange were these bodies, on this road where it was already so cold that if I took my glove off to write I could keep my hand in the air for only a minute. The cold had frozen them into the positions in which they fell. It had, too, slightly shrunken their bodies and features, giving them an artificial, waxen appearance. . . . The whole road was some huge waxwork representation of a battle scene, carefully staged.[193]

There were dead Finns here, too:

The Finns were easy to distinguish. They all had white snow clothes over their grey uniforms, and their boots were of new, yellow leather. Every man's face had been covered by his comrades with a piece of cloth or a fir branch. I drew away the branch from the face of one man, huge in his grey uniform. It was a typical Finnish peasant's face, rounded, with strong curving sweep of jaw. In his death he looked very young—just in the twenties. I had seen enough of this uniform now, in my three weeks in Finland, to realize what this death was going to mean when word of it got back to some red-painted peasant shack in the forests of the south.[194]

Henceforth, as a result of an edict from Mannerheim, reporters were no longer allowed to visit a battlefield until after the Finnish dead had been removed.[195]

And, indeed, word of the fast-mounting number of Finnish dead was getting back to the affected families around the country, including, for example, Anna-Liisa Veijalainen's "family" of young soldiers at her tidy canteen on Tuppura Island, in Viipuri Bay. "When the first casualty report reached our 'family' on December 2nd," she recalled, "all of us needed all of our willpower not to burst into tears. Young Mauri was again the first one to warn us not to talk about the casualties at the dinner table, because the young cadet brother of our brother Aki (second lieutenant) had died at Vammelsuu in the first day of the war. We all tried to act perhaps even a little too merrily."[196]

"Nobody had much appetite, however, and it was heartbreaking to see Aki's eyes." By the end of December thousands of Finnish households—and canteens, too—had experienced the same heartbreak, as the casualties continued to mount. As Veijalainen put it, "Soon we started to receive casualty reports every day," but "one gets used to everything."[197]

*

Then Christmas arrived. All Finns and foreigners who were there remembered it as being a merry one—or as merry as could be under the circumstances.

On Tuppura, "we tried to celebrate Christmas as cozily as possible," remarked Anna-Liisa. Emma Teikari, her fellow auxiliary, prepared a fine Christmas dinner for the entire Tuppura "family." Everyone, believers and non-believers—and in those days most Finns believed—sang the Christmas hymn. "There was no peace on earth, but that Christmas the people were close to each other and wished each other well."[198]

The mood was also upbeat in Helsinki. The panic of the first days of the war was largely gone. On December 24, Christmas Eve, Moscow Radio warned that "if Finland has not given up the fight by 1 P.M. today we will bomb Helsinki, destroying the city, Christmas morning. The town will be levelled to the ground."[199]

And yet most Helsinkians, veterans now, appeared unperturbed. Nothing—not even the threat of Russian bombs—could stop them or their foreign guests from enjoying Christmas. Perhaps it wasn't the brightest Christmas the roughly 60,000 residents remaining in the city had experienced, especially in light of the blackout restrictions, but for Helsinkians, who several weeks before had wondered whether they would be celebrating at all, it was perhaps the most meaningful. On Christmas Eve, United Press reported a sleigh going down Helsinki's main street, Heikinkatu (the present-day Mannerheimintie), with bells ringing: "It was a cheering sight in view of the fact that the entire city is expecting today to bring more bombing raids."[200]

"The morale of both the army and people is wonderful," said G. Tollet, a Helsinki native who also worked for the *New York Times,* in a long-distance telephone interview with his paper. "But we could do better if we had more guns and ammunition. You lend us, and we'll defend us. The American people can be assured that anything they do to help us will not be thrown away."[201]

✳

For Eric Malm and his fellow soldiers of the 10th Regiment, who had been manning the parapets of the Mannerheim Line for three weeks straight, Christmas meant being relieved for the first time—and pure heaven. "On Christmas Day 1939, there had been some fighting for a few days," he said. "Then another regiment took our place on the front line and we got to rest behind the lines. We spent Christmas there and got our presents from home. It was 500 meters from the front, but it felt like another world."[202]

✳

The Finnish press office, anxious for ways to promote the Christmas angle, invited another group of reporters, including Webb Miller, Lynn Heinzerling of the Associated Press, William L. White of CBS, and Harold Denny of the *New York Times,* to see how some of Malm's less fortunate comrades were observing the holiday by inviting them to attend one of the dozens of muted but heartfelt celebrations being held that evening in the snug Finnish *korsus* (dugouts) along the front line.

The result was a series of moving verbal and audial postcards from the battlefront. First, an excerpt from Denny's dispatch:

> We were conducted many miles by automobile—camouflaged white— then, when very close to the front line, we parked our cars under fir trees and went two miles further on foot. The scene at the war front was like a Christmas card. Nothing could have appeared more peaceful. Above was the full moon, which cast such a silvery light over the earth that we wondered why the Red bombers did not come.
>
> There were so many bright stars in the cloudless sky that we were reminded of the star of Bethlehem. Little cottages dotted the landscape, but no light came from their windows, for their owners had fled and the troops that occupied them showed no lights.[203]

Next the group turned off the trail, then fell on their knees to enter the *korsu,* which also served as a battalion headquarters of the unnamed battalion.

> Lying about on blankets over straw were members of the battalion staff. In the center was a little Christmas tree cut from the wood outside, with bells and candles like any proper Christmas tree.
>
> Sitting on a box in front of a field telephone was the captain, commander of the battalion, a fiery eyed-little man, unshaven and showing the need of sleep. As he chatted with us about his men and the Soviet troops confronting

his force, the telephone intermittently tinkled with messages from outposts and regimental headquarters in the rear.[204]

Segue to William White's famous broadcast about the same visit, which purportedly "moved America to tears." The son of William A. White, the influential Kansas-based American editor, White called it "The Last Christmas Tree."

> The [Finnish] officer explained that the fighting had been very hard because the enemy outnumbered them, so when there was no fighting there was time for little sleep.
>   We asked him what the men would have for Christmas dinner and he told us their mess kits would be filled with thick warm, pea soup, rich with pieces of mutton and pork, with plenty of bread spread thick with butter, and for dessert porridge with sugar. And then, because it was Christmas, the army had sent up four Christmas hams, which would be sliced and eaten with the bread.[205]

The officer told the reporters that several sledges had come laden with Christmas presents for the men, including warm sweaters and socks, or Christmas cookies and tarts baked for them, and that there would be something for each man. The reporters asked when the men directly on the front line would receive their gifts. Not until the next day, the captain responded, adhering to the moving Yuletide script, "but they would not mind, because each man knew why he must be there, and what must be done and not one would wish himself in any other place, and because the people of this country love Christmas so much, each one could carry it with him in his heart."[206]

Then the visitors asked the captain if he wouldn't mind if they crawled up on their own to give the troops forward some of the tobacco and sweets they had brought along with them. The officer shook his head. He couldn't take the chance: the Russians were so close that they might hear their boots scrunching in the snow and alert their artillery. Nevertheless, he assured the concerned scribes, the men would receive their presents tomorrow and yes, they would also get to see the Christmas tree. White went on to describe the spare, ceremonial tree:

> The tiny tree was standing near the stove. Little red and white wax candles had been tied by men's clumsy fingers to its branches. The officer said the candles could not be lit, because this might be seen by bombers through the dugout's canvas roof. Also tied to the green spruce twigs were a few gumdrops—the kind you buy twisted in colored wax papers. At the top was tied not a sparkling glass star but a cheap cardboard image of Santa Claus, and this was all. No strips of tinsels, no shining balls, no winking electric lights.[207]

White, who recorded his broadcast later in Helsinki, told his faraway American listeners, "You can be very glad that the Christmas tree in your home tonight is so much finer."

> We asked the officer who sent these ornaments and he smiled kindly and said that they came from a very small girl whose father was out on the last line tonight, and with them a note from her mother explaining that the child was very young and could not understand why he could not come back to them even on Christmas, and had cried bitterly until they let her send him these little things so that at least he could have his own Christmas tree. So the tree would be kept as it is in the dugout until he came back from his outpost tomorrow.[208]

Finally White, nearly overcome himself, signed off:

> *So when you take your last look at your own fine tree tonight before turning out its lights, I think you will like it even better since you know about the last sad little Christmas tree of all, which could not even have its poor candles lit because it faces the land where there is no Christmas.*[209]

One of those listening to "The Last Christmas Tree" that night in his New York City apartment was Robert Sherwood, the acclaimed playwright and former pacifist. Switching off the radio, Sherwood decided what he would do to help Brave Little Finland as well as to help America shake off what he felt was its selfish and suicidal isolationism: he would write a play.

There Shall Be No Night, Sherwood decided to call his piece of theatrical agit-prop. With its pedigree, as well as the topicality of the subject, *There Shall Be No Night* seemed assured of success. But would it see the light of day before the actual conflict that inspired it ended?

Day of infamy. Soviet SB-2 pilots brief themselves before the surprise attack on Helsinki, November 30, 1939. Note the political officer on the right. (Courtesy Carl Fredrik-Geust)

Stunned pedestrian, central Helsinki. Casualties and damage were light, but the shock of the first aerial assault on the Finnish assault was enormous. (Finnish Army Archives)

The Marshal. Gustaf Mannerheim, the revered Finnish commander-in-chief, at a review in Senate Square, 1930s. When the war broke out the veteran soldier was seventy-two. Nevertheless, he answered the nation's summons with alacrity and vision. (Finnish Army Archives)

Prime Minister Risto Ryti, in uniform, consults with staff officers about the fast-moving battlefront situation, December 1939. An emergency appointment, the former banker was more comfortable in a suit but acquitted himself well. (Finnish Army Archives)

The crew of a Soviet T-26 poses for a propaganda photo before undertaking the "liberation of Finland." (Courtesy Carl Fredrik-Geust)

Vaino Tanner, the Finnish foreign minister, broadcasts to the Finnish people. Shortly after the war broke out, Tanner broadcast a personal appeal to the Kremlin for an end to the fighting. It was not answered. (Finnish Army Archives)

The smoking hulks of two Soviet tanks after being destroyed by Molotov cocktail–wielding Finnish ski soldiers. (Courtesy Carl Fredrik-Geust)

Soviet Ilyushin bomber cleared for takeoff, somewhere in northern Russia. (Courtesy Carl Fredrik-Geust)

Finnish officers examine the remains of a shot down SB-2 bomber. Over 700 Red planes were shot down either in combat or by anti-aircraft batteries during the war. (Finnish Army Archives)

Glamorous U.S. correspondent Martha Gellhorn was the first reporter to visit the front line. Here she hams it up with Finnish pilots. (Courtesy Carl Fredrik-Geust)

General Ohqvist, commander of the Army of the Isthmus, briefs some of the dozens of reporters who descended on Helsinki to report on "Brave Little Finland's" struggle. (Finnish Army Archives)

Censorship was tight during the war. Here a Finnish military censor looks over the shoulder of a reporter in the press room at the Hotel Kamp as he files his report. (Finnish Army Archives)

Mannerheim boasted that Finnish troops were fighting "a Thermopylae" every day. Here one of them fires a captured Soviet DB machine gun. (Finnish Army Archives)

The crew of a Finnish Maxim gun awaits the next wave of Red troops. (Finnish Army Archives)

International brigade. Over 12,000 soldiers from two dozen nations, including 8,000 Swedes, like these jaunty ones, came to Finland to fight for *Suomi*. Welcome though they were, few actually saw combat. (Finnish Army Archives)

Kurt Wallenius (left), head of Finnish forces in Lapland and mastermind of the battle of Pelkosenniemi, meets with General Ernest Linder, the top Swedish commander in Rovaniemi. An early hero of the war, the veteran forest fighter would later be cashiered by Mannerheim. (Finnish Army Archives)

Despite fears—and rumors—that they would, the Soviets did not use gas. (Finnish Army Archives)

A company of the "white death," as Soviet troops called Finnish ski troops, executes a *motti* ambush, somewhere in Lapland. (Finnish Army Archives)

Massacre in the north. The grisly aftermath of the destruction of the Soviet 44th Division at Raate Road. (Finnish Army Archives)

Some of the forlorn survivors of the two Red divisions destroyed at Suomussalmi and Raate Road. "We have never seen such soldiers," a Finnish officer declared of the unprepared, ill-equipped troops. Later the Kremlin would send better ones. (Finnish Army Archives)

Once Soviet prisoners realized that they wouldn't be shot, as they had been told, they were extremely cooperative. Here a group of contented prisoners sing the praises of their captors for Finnish radio. (Finnish Army Archives)

War booty. A proud Finnish soldier stands by a captured Soviet T-28 tank. (Finnish Army Archives)

Finnish pilot Jorma Sarvanto was the war's first ace, shooting down a brace of Soviet bombers in less than five minutes. Such widely publicized heroics gave the world—as well as the Finns themselves—a skewed view of Finnish fortunes, which would soon turn. (Courtesy Carl Fredrik-Geust)

A Finnish officer meets the press in his comfortable dugout after the Suomussalmi rout. (Finnish Army Archives)

Finnish morale was high during the deceptive "January interregnum," as the Soviets prepared their second assault. It always helped to have a pretty *lotta* around. (Finnish Army Archives)

The scene at a funeral for four Finnish soldiers. On the home front, the war was already taking its toll. Altogether nearly 25,000 Finns died during the war, including 1,000 civilians. (Finnish Army Archives)

Finnish military cars were painted white in order to protect them from Red marauders. (Finnish Army Archives)

Creative logistics. Where cars couldn't go, reindeer could. (Courtesy Carl Fredrik-Geust)

The leadership of Mannerheim, the towering figure of the war, had a galvanic effect on the nation. Later he would use his enormous prestige to bring the unequal conflict to a halt. (Finnish Army Archives)

One of the forgotten men of the war, the prim and pugnacious Aksel Airo, the Army quartermaster and chief strategist, was Mannerheim's right-hand man. (Finnish Army Archives)

Women at war. Swedish volunteer nurses (in fur hats) mingle with their Finnish sister nurses on the steps of a military hospital. (Finnish Army Archives)

A Finnish air watch *lotta* at her post somewhere in Finland. (Finnish Army Archives)

A clerical *lotta* at her post, pecking away. Altogether over 110,000 Finnish *Lotta Svard* served in various capacities during the war. (Finnish Army Archives)

The Red Army's second coming. The artillery barrage with which the Soviets began their final assault was massive and carefully planned. At one point, over 300,000 shells were fired during a twenty-four-hour period, the most since the Second Battle of the Somme. (Courtesy Bair Irincheev)

Forward Soviet artillery outpost, late February 1940. This time the Soviets wore white. (Courtesy Bair Irincheev)

Dazed from the constant artillery barrages and lack of sleep, the hard-pressed Finns did their best to hold off the concentrated Soviet assault. (Finnish Army Archives)

End in sight. Finns flee burning town. (Finnish Army Archives)

Total war. A Soviet T-26 tank outfitted with a flamethrower spews death near the Mannerheim Line, February 1940. (Courtesy Carl Fredrik-Geust)

The remains of the vaunted Million Dollar Bunker after the assault. (Courtesy Carl Fredrik-Geust)

Apocalypse then. Karelian scene after the assault. (Courtesy Carl Fredrik-Geust)

Finnish troops strike a defiant pose after the shock armistice. Many wanted to continue fighting. (Finnish Army Archives)

Some of the 5,000 Soviet prisoners captured by the Finns prepare to be repatriated, not looking very pleased at the prospect. Many were later shot. (Finnish Army Archives)

As part of the draconian peace terms, Finland had to cede 10 percent of its territory, including the entire Karelian peninsula. Almost all the population in the ceded areas, including these Karelians, chose to leave rather than live under Soviet occupation. (Finnish Army Archives)

Helsinki in mourning. The
scene outside the Hotel
Kamp, March 13, 1940.
(Finnish Army Archives)

Three-quarters of a century later, the example of Finland's remarkable and inspiring
resistance during the Winter War continues to serve, in Winston Churchill's immortal
words, to show "what free men can do." (Finnish Army Archives)

II

Interregnum

December 26, 1939–February 5, 1940

4

The Suomussalmi Factor

December 26, 1939–January 7, 1940

The first phase of the Russo-Finnish war is now at an end, with the repulse of all the Russian attacks between the Arctic Ocean and Lake Ladoga. Finland is thus temporarily freed from any further anxiety in the North, and the Russians appear likely for the present to confine their attention to attempts to break through in the South by sheer weight of numbers.
   —Major George Fielding Eliot, *Life Magazine,* December 26, 1939

The nation stood as one man behind their armed forces in the calm and determined knowledge that the struggle must go on. But on the threshold of the new year, an objective observer could not help feeling gloomy presentiments. The prestige of the Soviet Union demanded that we be defeated, and we would have to count on increased pressure.
   —Gustaf Mannerheim, *Memoirs*

But if justice and a rightful cause cannot withstand against the weighted odds of might and brute force, we shall perish. Yet if we perish from lack of guns and ammunition, which is now our imperative need, we hope and believe that our fight will have been an inspiration to the civilized world.
   —Georg Gripenberg, Finnish minister to London, December 26, 1939

Perhaps it was the beauty of the morning that made the terrible Russian debacle all the more ghastly. The rising sun had drenched the snow-covered forest, and the trees like lace Valentines, with a strange pink light that seemed to glow for miles. The landscape was only marred by the charred framework of a house. . . . Then we turned a bend in the road and came upon the full horror of the scene. For four miles [six kilometers] the roads and forests were strewn with the bodies of men and horses.
   —Virginia Cowles, on the aftermath of the second part of the battle of Suomussalmi, the destruction of the 44th Division at Raate Road, *Sunday Times* (London), February 4, 1940

No, Stalin wouldn't get Finland as a present, as that Finnish pilot from the 24th squadron had told Martha Gellhorn when she visited its base at Immola on December 6, when the war was still young. That much was clear now. If the Russians wished to impose Communist rule on Finland on behalf of their erstwhile protégé, Otto Ville Kuusinen, they would have to change their troops, their tactics, and their commanders; after the resounding Russian defeats at Tolva-jarvi and Kemijoki River, as well as the failure of their second massed assault on the Mannerheim Line, things would have to change.

They would. New, better-trained troops, including ski troops from Siberia, were on their way. Tactics were being revised. Already on December 28, a new directive was issued to cover future operations in Finland. Henceforth, front commanders were ordered not to rush blindly ahead into the withering Finnish fire, but to wait until the artillery had properly "softened up" the target. The suicidal—and futile—mass attacks of the first three weeks of the war were nixed. If the pillboxes of the forward line of defense were not obliterated, then the troops should not be committed to an attack. Sending newly arrived divisions or reinforcements straight into action was forbidden. Staff officers would henceforth concern themselves with the condition of their troops and their weapons.

Much of this was elemental; some of it was new. All of it had to be processed. That would take time. Also, Stalin, after demoting Meretskov and pushing aside Voroshilov, had not yet settled on a new overall commander for the operation. In the meantime, a new factor—the prospective Allied expeditionary force to succor Finland that the British and the French had tentatively agreed on at their meeting in Paris—had entered into the equation. Would the farfetched sounding operation actually take place? Would the Swedes and Norwegians, thus far adamantly neutral and over whose territory such an expedition would have to pass en route to Finland, enable it to happen?

Hanson Baldwin, the incisive military analyst for the *New York Times,* summed up the matter thusly: "A study of the first three weeks of the war, and a review of the Russian tactical system based upon the slow-moving, ponderous, crushing mass definitely indicate that the Finns can 'hold the fort,'" he wrote on December 24. "How long they can hold it without such aid is problematical; much depends upon the weather; much on the number of troops the Soviet hurls into the campaign."[1]

That is pretty much where things stood insofar as Finland was concerned as 1939 came to an end—as well as how most Finns saw the situation. Then, following the New Year, a new factor entered into the ever-complex Finnish equation, following the Finnish army's serial victories at Suomussalmi and Raate Road, an extraordinarily drawn-out affair spanning the last week of December and the first week of January that culminated in the destruction of two entire Soviet divisions.

Now the constitutionally skeptical Finns began believing their own press. Some deluded themselves into thinking that if they could do that to the "Russkies," maybe they didn't need so much help after all!

In any event, Martha Gellhorn, for one, wouldn't be around to see how things played out, having left Helsinki on Christmas Day on board a plane bound for

Stockholm, thence for Paris, thence via ship for home. A month of covering the war had been sufficient for her, she decided; a month in the cold and dark of Finland, a month of negotiating the blacked-out corridors and boozed-up male scribes of the Hotel Kamp would do. Actually, Gellhorn hadn't planned on leaving Finland just yet. However, when Frank Haynes, the assistant American military attaché, ran into the forlorn-looking woman several days before Christmas and told her that there was an empty seat on a plane he was taking to Stockholm and would she like it, she quickly assented.[2]

Gellhorn loved Finland, believed in it; that certainly was clear in the three long, heartfelt features she wrote for *Collier's*. Gellhorn also wanted the free world—and America—to do more for Finland. She made that point when she met her friend, Eleanor Roosevelt, in Washington, on the way home to Cuba and Hemingway's sun-kissed hacienda. Would she please try to get the president to do more for Finland? The First Lady agreed while bemoaning what a terrible thing war was and hoping that the United States would continue to stay well out of it. In any event, Gellhorn would not see the curtain fall. But a fellow reporter and friend of hers by the name of Virginia Cowles would.[3]

*

Like Gellhorn, Cowles was smart, beautiful, and fearless. A former model who had made the unlikely transition to war correspondent, she went on to cover both the Italian invasion of Ethiopia and the Spanish Civil War, where she met Gellhorn. In Spain, she covered both sides of the civil war, enjoying the unique honor of being alternately arrested by both the republicans and the loyalists —and living to write about the tale. The title of her 1941 memoir, *Looking for Trouble,* says it all. Cowles also met Gellhorn in Spain. Unsurprisingly, the two became fast friends. They even did some reporting together in London, where both were based for a while in the late 1930s. Gellhorn, who had also met Hemingway in Spain, decided to return to Cuba to be with her rumbustious paramour. Cowles, preferring London, decided to remain there and soon was writing for both British and American newspapers. Later during the war, after Gellhorn had redonned her war correspondent's patch, following her divorce from Hemingway, the two friends' paths would again cross many times on the battlefield.

Like Gellhorn, Cowles was extremely well connected. If Gellhorn knew everyone in New York and Washington, Cowles knew everybody in London. If Gellhorn had access to the White House via her close acquaintance with Eleanor Roosevelt, Cowles had access to No. 10 Downing Street via her friendship with Lord of the Admiralty Winston Churchill, soon to become prime minister.[4]

It was at a New Year's Eve party in London where Churchill was a guest that the peripatetic Cowles decided that her next assignment would be to cover the war in Finland. Like most of those present on that fateful evening, as the "phony war" in the West continued to drone on, Churchill had a presentiment that things would soon change, both for him and the world: "The house was overflowing with people and an accordion-player went around the room playing all the popular tunes. I remember Mr. Churchill singing 'Run, Rabbit, Run' with great verve."[5]

"Run Rabbit Run," a song written by Noel Gay and Ralph Butler for Gay's show *The Little Dog Laughed,* was one of the best-known London ditties of the day. Its lyrics went:

> *On the farm, every Friday*
> *On the farm, it's rabbit pie every day*
> *So every Friday that ever comes along*
> *I get up early and sing this song*
> *Run rabbit-run-Run! Run! Run!*
> *Run-rabbit-run-Run! Run! Run!*[6]

It became even more popular after the lyrics were changed to poke fun at the Germans:

> *Run Adolf Run Adolf—Run! Run! Run!*

One can well imagine the Lord of the Admiralty leading his fellow partiers in the chorus as they sang out

> *Run Adolf Run Adolf—Run! Run! Run!*[7]

Amidst the high spirits, there was a portent of the more difficult days soon to come, once "The Phony War" in the winter of 1940 came to an end:

> But when the clock struck twelve a solemnity fell over the group. Mr. Churchill took Freda Casa Maury [Marquesa de Casa Maury, an English socialite best known for being the mistress of the Prince of Wales] and me on either side of him; we all joined hands in a circle and sang Auld Lang Syne. In everybody's mind was the question of what 1940 would bring. When Mr. Churchill sang out the old year, he seemed deeply moved, as though he had a premonition that a few months later he would be asked to guide the British Empire through the most critical days it had ever faced.[8]

For her part, Cowles decided that her compass pointed eastward, to Finland. Like Gellhorn, she had a soft spot for underdogs, and from the look of the headlines, the Finnish underdogs seemed to be doing pretty well. Like Harold Nicholson, like virtually everyone in England (not to mention the Russians themselves), Cowles too had expected the Finns to collapse within a day or two. But now, a month later, the Finns, against all odds, were still holding on. "That night had a special significance for me," she wrote. "When the headlines [had] announced that Helsinki had been bombed I thought it would be another Poland—that the country would be obliterated so quickly there would be little chance of getting there before it was over. Then the papers began recording the amazing feats of the Finns; incredible though it seemed, the Russian 'steam-roller' was being held in check."[9]

In the event, Cowles had already traveled to the Soviet Union, had covered the hideous 1937 Moscow purge trials, and had reported on the Red Army, including one of its crack divisions, the 44th (whose paths she would soon cross again, in the most horrific way, in northern Finland). The story was a natural for her. So on that first morning of 1940, Cowles decided: next stop, Helsinki.

On the other side of the Atlantic, Hjalmar Procope, the Finnish minister to Washington, issued his own portentous New Year's prediction. If Finland "can hold the bridge," the indefatigable Finnish diplomat solemnly opined, "as I am convinced we will do—then 1940 may go down in history as the year in which the great black march back into the dark ages was stopped."[10]

Could Finland continue to hold out? And for how long? Those were the main questions on Virginia Cowles's mind as she encased herself in a sheepskin coat and a half-dozen sweaters and boarded her plane at an airfield in northern England, bound for Finland and her next *Dangerous Assignment*.[11]

Looking back, Cowles recalled how strange it was to fly to what in effect had become a war within a war: "When you took off from the aerodrome 'somewhere in England' and flew over the North Sea in a plane with the windows frosted over so you couldn't see out, it was very much World War No. 2. It was still World War No. 2 at Amsterdam and Copenhagen; but at Malmo the issue began to get shaky. When you asked for the latest war news, the answer was: 'Which?' . . . By the time you reached Stockholm there was no longer any doubt: 'the war' meant Molotov cocktails and Soviet bombers."[12]

✳

There was no question, Cowles discovered during a twenty-four-hour stopover in Stockholm, where Sweden stood on the Finnish war: Sweden was wholeheartedly for Finland, even if her government was artfully straddling the fence: "Stockholm was in a state of tension. The papers carried advertisements calling for volunteers, the restaurants were filled with women canvassing for funds, and the hotels decorated with posters saying: 'Defend Sweden by Helping Finland Now.'"

On December 28, the Swedish papers proudly announced that the first contingent of Swedish volunteers, amongst them Orvar Nilsson of Halmstad, the southwestern Swedish city, had arrived in northern Finland to begin their training. It would be some time—nearly two months—before Nilsson and his colleagues would see any real action. First the Finns had to train them. Meanwhile, a group of Swedish aviators who had also enthusiastically signed up had been allowed to go straight to the aerial front line along with their obsolescent but very welcome dozen Gloster Gladiator single seater biplanes and four Hawker Hart bombers.[13]

There were enough Swedes to form a separate squadron: *Lentorykentti F 19*. Based in Kemi, the Swedish volunteers were already put to work on January 12 —six weeks before their comrades on the ground saw any combat—by the Finnish Air Force, taking charge of the aerial defense of northern Finland and allowing the FAF to use its remaining air power on the Karelian front.[14]

∗

Professional soldiers weren't the only ones who were enlisting to fight for Finland. Some of Sweden's best-known athletes also signed up to do battle with the Russians, including marathon runner Thore Enochsson, former heavyweight boxing champion Bertil Molander, decathlon champion Lennart Dahl, and champion skier Sven Utterstrom.

Although the Swedish government itself under the helm of Prime Minister Per Albin Hansson remained studiously neutral in its statements, the passionately Fennophile Swedish Army itself felt no such constraints. Officers and enlisted men were told straight out that they could go to Finland if they wished. In some barracks commanders even called their men on parade and asked if they wished to volunteer.

At the same time, Sweden being cautious Sweden, the flow of volunteers was being rigidly controlled by the Swedish general staff, which, concerned about the country's own defense—understandably so in light of the trouble in the neighborhood—insisted that the number of men allowed to leave for Finland be limited to one-tenth of the regular mobilized force of the Swedish army, which at that moment meant 7,000. Ultimately, a little more than that—8,600 out of the 12,600 who volunteered, a not inconsiderable number—were allowed to go. Eager for as much help as possible, Finland would ultimately ask for more.[15]

Some Swedish officers wanted to do even more. "We should intervene with all our forces," one officer told Geoffrey Cox as he traveled with a group of Swedish volunteers on the train to Haparanda, the closest rail station to Finland, and the most common transit point for Swedes going to fight there. "If Finland goes, Sweden goes too. Four hundred thousand Swedes," the overly optimistic officer said, referring to the total number of reserves and standing troops Sweden could theoretically throw into the fight, "and three hundred thousand Finns make seven hundred thousand men. It is a simple sum of arithmetic. Their experience and our resources would make an unbeatable army. Believe me, there is not an officer of importance in the Swedish army who does not believe we should be there with all our might."[16]

There didn't seem any prospect of that happening soon. Nevertheless, Sweden cared, cared deeply about its former Finnish province, and the considerable and growing number and amount of both materiel and volunteers it was sending to Finland proved it.

Cox was impressed. At the same time, like most of the Western correspondents who had done time in Finland, the sojourning reporter could not help but be struck by the dissimilitude between the complacent, slightly guilt-ridden atmosphere of "fat Sweden," as he called it, and the "Spartan, almost religious atmosphere of struggle" in its former province. The stark disparity between the two countries hit him on Christmas Eve, as he took a walking tour of Stockholm's brightly lit harbor and the venerable quays of Gamla Stan, the city's cobblestone-paved Old Town. He was en route to the Cafe Royal, the famed dance hall of the Grand Hotel, the city's most luxe hotel, which would soon play a role in the negotiations leading to the end of the war. There he would meet his colleague, Walter Duranty, the special Moscow correspondent (and sometime Soviet apologist) of the *New York Times*.[17]

The city was truly another world, as the impressed newspaperman writes:

> Stockholm on Christmas Eve was sheer beauty. From every window Christmas trees, bright with lights, showed in the blocks of flats and houses of the suburbs. The yellow buildings round the quays had their coating of white snow. At night the modern buildings beyond the royal palace were jewelled masses of brightly lit windows. In the incredible Moorish decor of the Cafe Royal, I sat with Walter Duranty while a jazz band played for a tea dance.
>
> The dining-room tables at the back were being loaded with Christmas *smorgasbord;* the men and women were well-dressed. It was the richest city I have seen.

"Then," Cox recounted, "I thought of men lying in snow dugouts for days on end. I thought of the patrols working through the woods in temperatures of twenty to thirty below zero; and this wealth seemed a little disgusting."[18]

Compounding Cox's disgust was the knowledge that a large fraction of Sweden's wealth derived from its formidable armaments industry, including Bofors. "For much of this prosperity I knew was based on war, or other people's wars," he commented. "Kiruna iron ore, Bofors guns and other armaments not only had brought Sweden wealth now, but had done so during the last war," Cox continued, alluding to World War I, when the country was neutral (as it had been since the Napoleonic Wars).[19]

Amongst Europe's major powers, only the Netherlands—which, with its extensive colonies, was still considered one of Europe's powers, and which also had been neutral during World War I and had a significant armaments industry—had enjoyed as long a peaceful hiatus, one from which it also profited.[20]

"I knew that other countries lived just as much from armaments," Cox conceded. "And that the Swedes could point to the fact that they had not misspent their gains. Their clean cities, healthy people, magnificent blocks of flats, showed that. But the impression [of ill-gotten gain] remained."[21]

To be sure, the Finnish High Command, which had been extremely glad to take receipt of a considerable number of quick-firing Bofors anti-aircraft guns and anti-tank guns, and was extremely keen for more, did not have the luxury of making such fine moral distinctions.

Stockholm was indeed rich and beautiful, as Stockholm has always been. It also wasn't Helsinki, where the action was. One night, though, while Cox was visiting the posh Stockholm flat of his colleague and sometime traveling companion Barbro Alving, the *Dagens Nyheter* correspondent who also was taking a welcome break from the front, Cox was reminded of the proximity of the war—the one with Molotov cocktails and Soviet bombers. Alving's cozy flat was full of the good things about Swedish life: "Her modern sitting room was full of the atmosphere of the creativeness of peace—newly designed modern furniture, books, magazines, modern lighting. Her baby played round the Christmas tree, which was lit and standing by the window. Outside the voices of children tobogganing in the woods in the dusk came up shrilly. Headlights of cars taking people to concerts, theatres, restaurants, showed on the snow below."[22]

Then suddenly, high above this peaceful, prosperous tableau shot three searchlights that proceeded to slowly sweep the skies, searching for airborne intruders, an unsettling reminder of the proximity of the Finnish War.

Sweden might not be in the full shadow of the war's eclipse, like Finland, but it was still in its penumbra.

*

Anxious to get into the fray herself, the first thing that Virginia Cowles did, once she shook off the snow and dropped her bags at the Kamp, was to set off on a trip to Hanko, the strategic port town that the Russians had wanted so badly before the war—and now, in their dudgeon, apparently wished to firebomb out of existence. She sped off along with two other Swedish journalists in a white camouflaged press car for what turned out to be a bumpy ride indeed. Their chauffeur was a tall, silent Finnish police officer in a huge reindeer cap with two revolvers strapped to his belt.

The widespread physical damage wrought by weeks of the indiscriminate Soviet bombing was immediately manifest. All along the winding southern coast Cowles passed through villages and towns that had been bombed and machine-gunned. The cold was intense: every few minutes their mute driver had to stop the car so that he could pour glycerine over the windshield to melt the ice. They also had to make frequent stops for coffee to warm themselves up. Nevertheless Cowles was happy: she was back in her element.

Then, at Tammisaari, the last town before Hanko, two sentries suddenly jumped into the middle of the road to warn the travelers of imminent danger from above:

> They shouted that the Russian planes were coming, and told us to run for shelter. When we got out we heard the whine of engines, and straining our eyes against the sky, counted nearly twenty silver specks. We ran across a field and into the cellar of a farmhouse; there were already a dozen people there, several women, the rest farm laborers. The brick ceiling was so low, most of them were sitting on the floor between sacks of potatoes, jars of preserved fruit, and huge pails of milk.[23]

Cowles was surprised at the Finns' nonchalant attitude:

> There was no trace of alarm, only a quiet weariness. An elderly farmer, evidently the head of the household, told us that the day before they had spent six hours in the shelter; more than 200 planes had flown over the village and dropped nearly 150 bombs. Most of the bombs had landed in the fields and lakes and only three houses had been hit. He spoke dispassionately as though the ordeal had been an act of nature, as unavoidable as an earthquake.[24]

No sooner had the travelers gotten back on the road than they heard the nauseating drone of bomber engines again and had to repeat the procedure, scrambling for the protection of a field while nine Red marauders passed by overhead.

Once they finally arrived in the historic seaside town—which, prior to Finnish independence, had been a popular resort for Russian nobility—the visitors found that twenty buildings had been hit. Ten were still afire:

> Great billows of smoke were still rising in the air. The roads were littered with mattresses, chairs, and household articles, which the soldiers had salvaged from the fire. The charred framework of the houses stood out blackly against the snow, but there were no curious pedestrians to inspect the damage, for icy winds from the sea swept through the streets. I have never felt such cold.[25]

Half-frozen, the press contingent, along with a young army lieutenant who had been detailed to show them the sights of bombed-but-unbowed Hanko, stumbled into a corner cafe to warm up. The amiable proprietor brought them hot sandwiches and coffee. Then, as they were greedily chowing down, he confided something: "He informed us cheerfully [that] the top floor of the house was on fire. It had been struck by an incendiary bomb two hours before. His sons were fighting it, and he was confident everything would soon be under control."[26]

"Somehow," Cowles wrote, "it was an odd experience to be sipping coffee in a burning building." That is what it was like to take a day trip to Hanko in January 1940. All told, the Red Air Force bombed Hanko seventy-two times during the *Talvisota*—the most of any locality.[27]

✳

On the return trip to Helsinki that night, once it was dark and the danger of being immolated by a Soviet incendiary had passed, the foreigners stopped again at the coastal town of Tammisaari to take supper at the local inn. The recently strafed porch of the inn still had bullet holes in it; nevertheless the atmosphere inside was jovial.

At one point a soldier got up to play the gramophone, but a waitress told him sternly that it was forbidden—doing so would make it impossible to hear the air raid sirens. Reluctantly, the music-starved soldier complied.[28]

The police driver then informed Cowles and her companions that it was impossible to leave for Helsinki before midnight. Instead, the group spent the evening eating and tippling with the town mayor and other local officials while toasting the portrait of the Marshal. The strain of the last few days of bombing had been so great, the mayor of Tammisaari told Cowles, "that now they only wanted to laugh, and the conversation was subsequently maintained at a high pitch of hilarity. Members of the party took turns in relating amusing incidents that had occurred during the raids. Someone passed a bag of sugar around the table, and everyone laughed very much because the shop printed on the cover had been blown up that very morning."[29]

The deranged day trip wasn't over. Later, en route to Helsinki, the wayfarers' car crashed. With only dim blue headlights, and ice forming almost instantaneously on the windshield, the driver had trouble distinguishing the snow-covered road from the surrounding field and ran smack into a truck on one side of the road, wrecking the vehicle. Fortunately, none of the travelers was hurt. All the same, they now had no car.

It was 4 A.M. The stranded, benumbed scribes saw a glow in the distance; it turned out to be a large barn. They pushed the door open to find lights blazing and over a hundred cows being assiduously milked by a group of female farmhands. "One of the milkmaids led us up to the big house and ran to awaken her mistress. A few minutes later the lady of the house appeared, a middle-aged woman, immaculately groomed, with a string of pearls around her neck, and apparently unperturbed by the fact that it was four in the morning."[30]

In the event, the mistress of the house spoke fluent English, something not very common in the Finnish countryside in those days. Sympathizing with the voyagers' plight, the helpful woman brought them blankets and tea and led them to her fireplace, where she quietly put a log on. Soon, all was well again.

As the fire crackled, their generous hostess made conversation about the weather, remarking that it had not been so cold for years, but that it was a good thing for the Finnish Army. "She said [that] it had been the same in the terrible winter campaign in the days of Charles XII of Sweden, when the Finns had succeeded in repelling the Russian onslaught."[31]

Several hours later, another government car arrived to take Cowles and her Swedish colleagues back to Helsinki. Their kind host wished them good luck. "I believe God will not let us perish beneath so terrible a foe and that in the end all will be well," she said softly as they departed.[32]

✳

Later, after Cowles had experienced and seen the effects of dozens more of such raids—which would ultimately kill nearly a thousand Finnish civilians and displace thousands more from their shattered homes—she would write about her reaction to the Soviet bombing campaign.

> It is difficult to describe indiscriminate aerial warfare against a civilian population in a country with a temperature thirty degrees Fahrenheit below zero. But if you can visualize farm girls stumbling through snow for the uncertain safety of their cellars; bombs falling on frozen villages unprotected by a single anti-aircraft gun; men standing helplessly in front of blazing buildings with no apparatus to fight the fires, and others desperately trying to salvage their belongings from burning wreckage—if you can visualize these things and picture even the children in remote hamlets wearing white covers over their coats as camouflage against low-flying Russian machine gunners—you can get some idea of what this war was like.[33]

✳

The Helsinki that Virginia Cowles found when she arrived in town the fifth week of the war was considerably different from the one Martha Gellhorn had known. The city was a veteran now, with the scars to show for it. The Technical University and other surrounding buildings that had been destroyed on that first day still lay in ruins, as did dozens of other structures that had been bombed during the more recent raids. Eerily, the curtains of the shuttered Soviet legation, which had been damaged during that first unforgettable raid, blew in the wind, like wraiths.[34]

Close to 6,000 Finns had died thus far during the first month of the war, including 600 civilians. Every day their obituaries ran in the papers. Died December 18. *Pro Patria.* Died December 23. *Pro Patria.* Died December 27. *Pro Patria.*

Most poignant were the ones for the children, like this one, from *Hufvudstadsbladet,* the leading daily for Finland's Swedish-speaking population, of a ten-year-old killed during the first raid, from his mother:

"My dear little George, born June 3, 1928, killed in the air raid on November 30, 1939. Maja Eriksson, nee Blom."[35]

Or this one, which refers to the raid as an "accident," as if it had been the will of God:

"Our only child, Tor Jorgen Segersven, killed in an accident November 30, 1939. At the age of 15 he departed, leaving us in great sorrow. Mourned by his mother, father and grandfather."[36]

Still, life went on.

Sixteen-year-old Harry Matso was continuing to do his part by working as a guard at an air raid shelter. "I had very little time off," he said. "If I had any free time, I would spend it with my friends. We didn't have any time to go to the movies or for normal recreation. But that was okay. Because, I felt, I was doing my part."[37]

Some things—most things, actually—about Helsinki had changed since those terrifying first few days. For one, the once bustling metropolis of 300,000, now reduced to a fifth of its prewar population, was virtually deserted. The Russian bombers, when they came, flew higher now, the better to avoid the sharpshooting Dr. af Forselles and his machine gun crew at Olympic Stadium and their comrades stationed around the city.

One thing about Helsinki that hadn't changed was the Kamp. Still the nerve center of the capital, Cowles found the venerable hotel abuzz with excitement as journalists, photographers, Finnish press officials, and military men pushed into the lobby. It seemed that every day another phalanx of eager, shivering journalists would arrive to cover the Soviet-Fenno "tennis match." Those who couldn't fit into the Kamp were accommodated at the nearby Hotel Seurahuone: that's where the government press room was. And that's where the best people-watching was, too, as Cowles found.

Amidst all this hullabaloo, Cowles recognized another journalist comrade, Webb Miller of the United Press. Miller had just returned from reporting on the fighting on and above the Mannerheim Line. Like most of his colleagues, Miller was a confirmed Fennophile by now. "They're the damnedest fighters I've ever seen," the exuberant reporter declared to Cowles over lunch.[38]

"They're not afraid of anything!" he exclaimed between bites. "And talk about improvisation—they invent their weapons as they go along." As an example, Miller cited a new tank-busting tactic the crafty Finns had just come up with that entailed tying a land mine to a string and waiting for a Russian tank to rumble by before detonating it at just the right moment. The enthusiastic American said that the Finns had taken out a number of heavy tanks in this manner.[39]

There were two wars going on in Finland at this time, the UP man excitedly explained. The first was the positional war on the Mannerheim Line, the one he had just come back from, which was being waged with "Western front methods," though with indigenous variations, like the aforementioned mines and the newly minted Molotov cocktail. That war remained in a state of stasis.

The second war, Miller explained, was the "guerrilla war," in the north. Initially thrown into confusion by the Soviets' unexpected drive there, the Finns were doing even better there, thanks to their tenacity and ingenuity, as well as their intimate knowledge of the densely forested terrains—along with an astonishing amount of Russian incompetence. In fact, Miller told Cowles, those "damn" Finns had just wiped out two entire divisions up there in a tiny, hard-to-pronounce place near the central eastern border called Suomussalmi.[40]

*

Suomussalmi. Siilasvuo. Raate Road.

Three-quarters of a century later, those names still carry mythological weight in Finland, and with good reason. Unquestionably, the destruction of the 163rd Division at Suomussalmi, and the subsequent decimation of the highly regarded 44th Division at Raate Road by the outnumbered, out-equipped Finnish forces led by Colonel Hjalmar Siilasvuo, ranks as one of modern Finland's proudest moments, as well as a classic military double victory with few if any precedents in the history of modern warfare.

However, like the Winter War myth itself, the Suomussalmi myth obscures a number of less tidy actualities. For one, the battles at Suomussalmi and Raate Road, however successfully they turned out, were the direct result of a failure by perhaps the Finnish Army's weakest arm, its intelligence division. An incompetent colonel by the name of Lars Melander, an old crony of Mannerheim's, ran the intelligence division, which basically explains why he was given the position as well as why he was able to hold on to it, long after his incompetence had been proven.[41]

The fact is, General Headquarters should not have been as surprised as it was by the initial Russian thrust across the border at Suomussalmi. Although Stalin's decision to invade Finland at nine different points, including the expected thrust on the isthmus, was clearly somewhat daft, some of those northerly infiltrations actually made strategic sense. One of these was the thrust at Suojarvi, north of Lake Ladoga, which was ultimately repelled and beaten back at Tolvajarvi.[42]

Another was the attack on Suomussalmi. If one were looking to bisect Finland, Suomussalmi, which lay astride Finland's waist, was as good a place as any to make one's jumping-off point. With roads leading in different directions, the small Kainuu region village fifty kilometers west of the border crossing at Raate was an obvious target; having seized it, the Russians would be able to move north, west, or south. At least one cadet in the Soviet military academy in the 1930s wrote his dissertation about the advantages of attacking in this area in a future war with Finland and how to go about it; Suomussalmi was prominently mentioned. U. A. Kakonen, the Finnish assistant military attaché in Moscow before the war, got wind of this and passed the information on to Melander's staff. Nothing was done.[43]

Put another way, Suomussalmi ought never to have happened. The Soviets, obviously contemplating an attack on the strategically located village, had been able to construct over the past half-year a new road wide enough to convey tanks right up to the Soviet-Fenno border, a major factor in the success of their surprise attack at that point. An aerial reconnaissance flight of the area would have detected the new highway. Inexplicably, none was ordered; none was sent.

Consequently, when the first two regiments of the Soviet 163rd Division, the 662nd Infantry Regiment and the 81st Mountain Infantry Regiment, stormed over the border at the Karttimo gate on the morning of November 30, 4,500 strong, the Finnish army only had a handful of men in place. The first army officer to encounter the invader, an unfortunate reserve second lieutenant by the name of Martti Elo, met with outright disbelief when he phoned in his report; shortly afterward, the overcome man shot himself.

If the Finnish Army had had a competent intelligence section, the 163rd—not one of Russia's best divisions—would have been stopped at the border.

No less egregious, as already noted, was the failure of the civil authorities in the Suomussalmi region, like their incompetent colleagues in the Suojarvi area in the south, to warn the local civilian population in time to evacuate. That failure led to a real human tragedy: the capture by the Soviets of 263 men, women, and children from Juntusranta and the surrounding area, 14 of whom were killed by the NKVD. Ten more of the "hostages" later died at the converted logging camp at Kintismaki on the Soviet side of the border to which they were transported.[44]

✳

Essentially, the story of Suomussalmi is the story of Kemijoki River multiplied. Like Kemijoki River, credit for the historic victory there was the result of three factors: the boldness, cunning, and decisiveness of the commander, Siilasvuo; the ability of Mannerheim and his staff to properly assess the situation, once it became clear that the enemy had invaded in force, and to get Siilasvuo the reinforcements he needed on time; and the courage, skill, and resourcefulness of the men of the 9th Division.

Additionally, the battle introduced a new concept into the world's military lexicon: *motti,* the Finnish word for cordwood, as in reducing a unit to *motti* and "chopping it up" until it disintegrates or disappears—the woodland version of divide and conquer. Siilasvuo took the concept to a spectacular level, so to speak, annihilating two entire divisions, one right after another. Not since the battle of Tannenberg, the German *coup de main* at the beginning of World War I, when General Ludendorff, with a force of just over 165,000 men, was able to smash a Russian force nearly three times as large, had the world witnessed such a masterfully executed and decisive feat of arms on the field of battle between two such disparate-sized forces. And Tannenberg had not been fought at a temperature of forty degrees below zero.[45]

Essentially, the historic five-week battle can be broken down into three parts. The action in the first part, which lasted until December 11, was dictated by the Soviets, as they enveloped Suomussalmi in a pincer movement with two different forces from disparate directions. The first, larger force, consisting of the 662nd and 81st Regiments—the elements of the 163rd Division that had initially poured across the border on November 30—moved southward, parallel to the spider-like Lake Kianta, en route to the division's intermediate objective, Suomussalmi, where they arrived at the end of the first week of December, after overwhelming the sparse Finnish forces in the area. It will be recalled that Geoffrey Cox interviewed some of the dazed casualties from the initial clash there when he visited the field hospital at Kajaani.[46]

Ultimately, the 163rd's objective was Oulu, the Finnish port city a mere 150 kilometers to the west on the other side of Finland's waist, whence the troops were expected to push on to the Swedish border, thus successfully cutting the country in half—quite a responsibility for what was, at best, a mediocre fighting unit. Nevertheless, the Leningrad Military District, which was still technically in charge of the invasion, was so confident that the 163rd and its commander, Andrei Zelentsov, would be able to do this that his troops were ordered to make sure that they stopped exactly at the Swedish border and respected any Swedish or Norwegian troops they encountered.

In the meantime, while the 163rd's two Oulu-bound regiments moved toward Suomussalmi, a second smaller force comprising the 305th Regiment of the crack Ukrainian 44th Division followed the 163rd Division's tracks along Raate Road, the unpaved but critical thoroughfare linking Suomussalmi with the border hamlet of Raate directly east.

With only sixty men in place in the Lake Kianta area, and a battalion stationed along Raate Road, the surprised Finns were at first able to do little more than fight delaying actions, and the two Soviet pincers successfully met in Suomussalmi on December 7. Just before they arrived, Finnish forces reluctantly put the village to the torch. Afterward the 500 Finnish troops retreated to positions across a narrow lake, grimly watching on as the Soviet attackers swarmed into the destroyed village and dug in.[47]

The Russians would not be comfortable for long. Quickly conferring by phone on how best to confront the new salient, Mannerheim and the commander responsible for the area, General Tuompo—who was then, as we have seen, also desperately trying to stem the simultaneous Red thrusts further south at Kuhmo and Lieksa with his sparse forces—decided to put Siilasvuo, commander of the Oulu-based 9th Division, in charge of all forces in the Suomussalmi sector, in the belief that the tough Swedo-Finn would be the right man for the job.[48]

On December 9, after a brief delay because of a collision on the Oulu-Kajaani rail line—there was no direct rail line to Suomussalmi, the closest stop to the isolated town being Kontiomaki, some sixty kilometers away (still true today)—Siilasvuo arrived on the scene with the first of his regiments, the 27th. With no time to lose, the colonel quickly took stock of the situation, reconnoitering and noting the Russian positions, and quickly designed his counterattack.

Taking his first gamble, Siilasvuo stationed a company of machine gunners to mask the frozen waterway south of Suomussalmi and waited for reinforcements. Two days later, on December 11, he and his men, now numbering over 1,500, were ready to strike. The second phase of the battle, which would span the next two weeks and eventuate in the destruction of the 163rd Division, had begun. Siilasvuo controlled the action from now on, with a generous assist from the weather, which was getting colder by the day.[49]

Siilasvuo's first move was to launch a surprise attack on the road connecting Suomussalmi with Raate, severing the Soviet force in the village from their supply. He then ordered the main body of attackers to move toward the village, leaving only two companies to cover the way to the east on an isthmus between two lakes—another gamble. Simultaneously, smaller detachments cut the Russians' communications with the north.[50]

The Soviet 25th Regiment, which was part of the 44th, obligingly withdrew toward the Soviet frontier to a point eight kilometers along Raate Road and began to dig in behind a line of barbed wire. Meanwhile, the 163rd, harried day and night by the speeding, wraith-like Finnish troops, split up into two forces with one remaining in the village, while the other withdrew across the ice at the lower end of Lake Kianta. Now the Finns had two separate forces to attack instead of one large one, much like Kurt Wallenius did with the 122nd at Pelkosenniemi. Now, too, the Russians were introduced to the *motti* tactic, albeit on a larger scale. Being unfamiliar with such unconventional tactics, they were naturally unprepared to cope with them.[51]

Just as Wallenius had done with the doomed 273rd Regiment in the earlier battle, Siilasvuo expertly "convoyed" the 163rd into position for the kill. Here, again, the Soviets were crippled by their lack of reconnaissance. At no time were any Russian patrols found by the Finns more than three kilometers away from the roadway.[52]

But the 163rd was a larger force than the 273rd. It would take longer to crack. By December 15, after five days of battling the Soviets, Siilasvuo's men were exhausted. Also, the Russians were proving a formidable foe; despite bitter fighting, the Finns were not able to destroy the *motti* they had carved off. Once again, the Finns were lacking in ordnance. That would be forthcoming. On December 16, Siilasvuo received his first battery of artillery from Mannerheim, two days later another, and, on the twentieth, two desperately needed anti-tank guns to parry the 163rd's substantive tank force. They weren't enough, but they would do.[53]

In the interim, alarming reports also reached the Finnish commander from the direction of Raate village, just inside the border crossing to the east. The 305th, the regiment that had moved up the road after the initial Finnish counterattack, was headed back in the direction of Suomussalmi to close the gap. At once, Siilasvuo made another bold move, ordering the two companies guarding the road to move up through the forest and make a feint attack at the head of the Russian column before it was able to get under way.

The scheme worked. Suomis blazing, *puukkos* unsheathed, Siilasvuo's soldiers now assaulted the head of the 25th Regiment at night, mowing down several dozen men along with several hundred wailing, mortally wounded horses. Rearing and panicking, the surviving animals threw the rest of the Russian column into confusion. Fearing that this was the first move in a major attack, Zelentsov ordered his men to dig in again, while he radioed back to corps headquarters for instructions.[54]

As Siilasvuo had hoped, V. Dukhanov, the overall corps commander in charge of both the 9th and 14th Armies, ordered Zelentsov to wait while the remainder of the 44th Division came up the road to join him. They had already massed on the border and would be there in three days. "But," Mannerheim writes in his own analysis of the battle, "how could such a weak force hold up a whole division for any length of time?" If it did, Siilasvuo, facing the reunited and redoubled Soviet force, would have had little choice but to withdraw from the village and let the besieged 163rd go.[55]

Then, just as the Finnish commander had planned and hoped, the 44th and its long wagon train got piled up on Raate Road. Siilasvuo would have time to finish off the 163rd; and by now, with the additional men and equipment that Mannerheim, closely following the situation from Mikkeli, had peeled off from his minuscule reserves and sped to him, he would be able to do the job.[56]

The end game for the Soviet 163rd Division began on December 27. Detachment Wolf, a special unit commanded by Lt. Col. Paavo Susitaival—a former member of parliament from the right-wing party, IKL, who had participated in the Lapua Movement along with Kurt Wallenius—signalled the opening of the final act of the battle when his fleet, ski-borne troops cut off the Russians' escape route to the north.[57]

Instantly, Siilasvuo launched his main offensive, attacking the trapped division at Suomussalmi and across Lake Kianta at half a dozen points, sending his men on a multiple "buttonhook" around the various trapped Soviet *mottis* and moving in for the kill. The main attack, coming from the woods, was directed at the division's supply train. Here Russian troops sleeping by the road were suddenly enfiladed from fifty points. Now, as Geoffrey Cox writes, "It was the same story as at Kemijoki River. The Finns, invisible, were sheltered by trees; the Russians were on the open road. Other Finnish patrols had moved across the lake [Kianta] and were hitting the Russians in the rear. Everything that moved on the road was attacked. Lorries could not get through to the troops. Field kitchens could not work."[58]

The panicked, disoriented Russian troops fired into the woods, but there were no Finns there. Like phantoms, they were here, there, everywhere. Here were the "white bats" that the imaginative *Times* of London correspondent had described earlier. But they were no joke to the transmogrified Russians.

The following day, December 28, Siilasvuo's men made a decisive penetration of the *motti* at Hulkonniemi, on the side of the lake opposite Suomussalmi, dispersing it and causing the large knot of Russians there to flee in a panic back across the expanse of ice. Another fright set in amongst the remaining men at the village, and soon all but a third of the division was fleeing eastward, whence they came.[59]

Zelentsov's retreat was well implemented—probably the only reason he wasn't immediately executed following the Red debacle. Slowly, carefully, he formed up his surviving force of approximately 2,000 into a column on either side of which he placed his remaining twenty tanks. Slowly, carefully, up the center of Lake Kianta, the haggard column proceeded, helped along by its gun-toting *politruks*. The Finns, who were also working along the lakeshore, fired at the retreating Russians with their machine guns, but they were too far away for them to do much damage.[60]

The Finnish Air Force was also in on the kill: three twin-engine, Browning gun–mounted Bristol Blenheim bombers—which made up about a quarter of the force's extremely modest bomber wing—flew over the retreating infantry, firing at the remnants of the annihilated division.[61]

And then the Russians were gone, leaving the exhausted but elated Finns to count the dead, rope up the half-crazed, half-frozen survivors, and collect the considerable booty the routed invader had left behind. The Finns immediately buried 1,500 men; thousands more lay in the woods, their frozen corpses not to be discovered until the spring, if at all. All told, an estimated 13,000 to 27,000 Russians died in the course of the seesaw month-long battle, as against 1,000 Finns. Twenty-one hundred Russian prisoners were captured. Many were found stumbling around the woods, delirious, or shivering in holes, as well as frozen stiff.[62]

Niilo Haikola, then a seventeen-year-old military policeman from Suomussalmi, was one of those assigned to round up the Russian stragglers. "The assignment we received was to clear the area," he recalled. "We did this with dogs." At one point Haikola came across twenty soldiers hiding in a series of shallow dugouts. "They were happy to surrender, especially once they discovered that they would not be killed right away. They were tired, cold and hungry," he recalled. "We gave them cigarettes. And when we found any food amongst the stuff the Soviets left behind, we gave that to them too."[63]

✻

The Soviets left quite a lot of stuff behind: 27 guns, 11 tanks, 150 trucks, 250 horses, and a large quantity of infantry weapons and ammunition. The impressive cache made a welcome contribution to the Finnish war effort. More significantly, they left behind the battered prestige of the Red Army.[64]

On New Year's Eve, Finnish headquarters officially announced the recapture of Suomussalmi and the destruction of the 163rd Division. The joyous news was received like kismet in Helsinki. On its front page the *Helsingin Sanomat* roared:

GREAT VICTORY IN SUOMUSSALMI!

before printing a detailed listing of the captured materiel. At New Year's Eve parties in the capital some proprietors broke open a new bottle of their wine for their guests. Exulting Finns had two new toasts. "Suomussalmi!" and "Siilasvuo!"[65]

But the tale wasn't over yet for Siilasvuo and the men of the 9th Division. Alexey Vinogradov's 44th Division, now bivouacked along Raate Road, still had to be dealt with. After weeks of fighting, Siilasvuo's men had reached the limits of their endurance, but they were to be given no rest. And so off they trudged in the direction of Raate, skis, poles, and rifles slung over their shoulders; they trudged off to dispose of the next set of Red *mottis*.[66]

Technically speaking, the process of cutting up an enemy column into *motti*, also known as *motitus*, entails three stages: (1) reconnaissance and blocking, (2) attack and isolation, and (3) annihilation. The long motorized column of the 44th, comprising 18,000 men now stretched along the length of Raate Road, had already undergone the first stage. Vinogradov's column had been "measured" by Siilasvuo's patrols, operating in the dark; the line was already cut by primitive *abattoirs*. Now it was time to proceed to the next two stages of the operation.[67]

Amidst the vast mechanized flotsam left behind in the snows of Suomussalmi, the Finns found reams of the multiple, futile orders issued by Vinogradov and his frantic staff. Hjalmar Siilasvuo was considerably more economical with his words. He later told an American reporter that he issued a total of two written orders during the battle of Suomussalmi: one during the first battle, at Suomussalmi, on the eve of the final attack, the other at Raate Road.[68]

While the 9,000 men of the reinforced 9th Division trudged off to complete the *motitus* of the 44th Division, E. and her family, along with the other 266 residents of the Juntusranta area who were caught up by the initial Soviet invasion in their parish, were on their way to a primitive, converted Soviet logging camp near Kintismaki, forty kilometers on the other side of the border, to spend the duration of the war.

"The trip took about three or four days," E., then sixteen years old, recalled. "I remember being tired and hungry. And of course we froze. When we left

Juntusranta I only had a woollen cardigan and stockings which I had knitted myself. I also had a blouse and skirt in my backpack."[69]

Before the "hostages," or internees, departed, they formed a "committee" of five or six to liaise with their captors. "You have to remember that this whole thing began because the Russians wanted to secure our safety," E. said in a 2009 interview. According to her, the group communicated with the Russians with the aid of an American Finn—apparently one of the hundreds of American Communists who emigrated to Russia during the interwar period to help build the worker's paradise—by the name of Roine.[70]

At some point early in the trip, according to researchers, the group was apparently met by a number of NKVD agents who interviewed or examined the villagers to see who might pose a security threat after they were taken across the border. Verifiable details about this aspect of this forgotten (nay, ignored) episode of Finnish history are sketchy. The only thing that is known is that by the time the group crossed the border, fourteen of their number had been killed.

E., perhaps understandably, has no memory of the murders of her former neighbors. She also has relatively nice things to say about Stalin. "At that time Stalin's orders were that civilians must not be disturbed and their property must be respected," she said. A psychologist might say that E. is a victim of a retroactive form of Stockholm syndrome—identifying with her captors.[71] Then again, one must also bear in mind that she was one of the five hostages or detainees (whatever one wishes to call them) who elected to remain in the Soviet Union after she and the surviving members of the Juntusranta group were allowed to leave the camp in June 1940, a decision for which she would later be ostracized by her fellow citizens.[72]

Still, her testimony bears powerful witness to an important, and forgotten, side of the story of Suomussalmi. Whether or not E. is a victim of Stockholm syndrome, one thing is clear: she was a victim, as were the 265 other members of this tragic group—a victim of war.[73]

"On the road from Juntusranta to Kintismaki," she continued, "we were under the 'protection' of the Red Army. Then after we came to Lonka [the first town on the other side of the border] we were asked whether we preferred to be under the control of the army or whether we would prefer to have civilian authorities above us. The committee said that they would prefer to be under civilian control, so from that point the militia escorted them to the border."[74]

"Mostly I remember being tired and hungry," E. said. At one point the group stopped at a schoolhouse. The teenager was so exhausted she immediately fell asleep on the floor. When she woke up there was a knot of quizzical people standing over her.[75]

"Who is she?" said one. "She does not wake up." So she got up. "But I was scared because I didn't know anyone." But she did: amongst the crowd was a cousin of hers. The two embraced and joined up with the others. They reached their destination, the former Soviet logging camp at Kintismaki that had been hastily converted into an internment camp sometime around January 5. Years later, E. would draw a diagram of the camp, which included two stores, a cafeteria, and a smoke sauna, making sure that each building had a chimney with smoke coming out of it (except the sauna). The cold, unhygienic, fenced-in reality of it was, by all reports, considerably less pleasant.[76]

"We didn't feel like prisoners or hostages," she said. But of course they were: the internees were under guard. The map also indicates a large militia barracks. "One has to remember that the Russians took us in order to guarantee our safety because we were in the middle of the fighting," E. pointed out.[77]

This they did, in a manner of speaking. Unfortunately, the group's putative Russian saviors couldn't guarantee the safety of the drinking water: over thirteen of the group died, reportedly from quaffing the contaminated water. The camp did include a rudimentary clinic, but it didn't have a doctor or advanced equipment. "There were some old people who died because of heart failure," E. sadly recorded. "But most of those who died did so because of the infected water."[78]

"The nurse at the clinic [apparently the only staff] did her best to help, she even tried to get some of the patients transferred across the border back to Finland." The food the Russians served their involuntary guests was passable. Unfortunately, there wasn't enough of it. "The food at the camp was mostly cabbage soup with potatoes and bits of meat. Sometimes we had corn cakes."[79]

However, some of the internees went hungry because they refused to eat the food, E. claims. "Some people 'starved' because they did not want to eat food which they were not used to. They said, 'We do not eat this at home, so we will not eat it here, either.'"[80]

Inevitably, there were arguments amongst the group. "Those people who at home were quiet-spoken or conservative remained so at the camp," the former internee remembered. "Those who were 'big mouths' at home, were 'big mouths' at the camp. Sometimes they caused trouble. Sometimes, too, people talked about other people to the militia." The nightmare would continue for six months.[81]

Back in Finland, the number of Russian prisoners of war was increasing, as K. J. Eskelund, another member of the crack team of reporters covering the Finnish story for the *New York Times,* noted in his dispatch of December 28. "Hundreds of Russian prisoners now have been transported from the fronts into Central Finland," he wrote.[82]

By almost all accounts—including their own—the Russians, thrilled to be alive, received excellent treatment from the Finns, but sometimes they were not treated so well by their own, Eskelund reported. "A railway official told me today that they [the prisoners] were brought to the camps in large cattle trucks and when one day the prison train was machine-gunned by Russian fliers, the Russian prisoners were mad with fear."[83]

Captured Soviet *politruks* in particular had to watch their back: "In a truck arriving yesterday at the prison camp, Russian soldiers strangled one of their officers who had been put in with them. 'Now we are quits with him,' they explained. At the front officers sometimes fired upon us from behind when we were going to attack."[84]

Originally, it appears, Finnish military press censors were reluctant to allow the press to photograph their prisoners, perhaps for fear of provoking the already thoroughly embarrassed Kremlin and the possible repercussions that might have for their own prisoners; but now pictures of Russian POWs were allowed, even encouraged. The images of the bedraggled Russian survivors of the battles of Kemijoki River and Suomussalmi in their shabby, threadbare uniforms, wearing lost expressions, along with the no less shocking ones of their mummified comrades left on the field who, as often as not, had died from the intense cold as from Finnish bullets, stunned the world while adding to Soviet chagrin.[85]

Instead of anger, the predominant attitude toward the prisoners on the part of their captors seems to have been sympathy, with a strong layer of contempt, not so much for the men themselves but for the barbarous system that produced them, and which they were putatively defending.

At one point, after the massacre at Suomussalmi, Carl Mydans, from *Life,* came across a group of Finns having sport with a Russian prisoner. His story is revealing: "Circling around the man, snarling menacingly, they jeered at him and threatened him with their knives. They feinted kicks at him with their boots, and clicked the mechanisms of their weapons at him. The prisoner was on the verge of hysteria."[86]

At that point a Finnish officer, a major, walked into the room, admonishing the men and reestablishing order. Gently he calmed the prisoner before continuing with his own interrogation.

The wretched man said he was a dairy worker from Leningrad, that he had a wife and four children. He said he had been told by his own officers that he would soon be marching to Helsinki—at which point the other soldiers in the room began laughing and hooting. The major quieted them and proceeded with his interrogation. When it was over, he gently reached over and handed the man a cigarette.

He [the prisoner] hesitated, then looked full into the eyes of the Finn. Suddenly tears welled down his dirt-caked face and rolled off his encrusted padded uniform. The room went silent. Gently, the major placed the cigarette on the corner of the table and turned away as if to study the papers before him. For a long moment he sat withdrawn in silence while the Russian continued to tremble, his face now smeared where he had rubbed the tears with his padded cuff.[87]

Mydans, his photojournalistic instincts working overtime, asked the major if he could take a picture. The major agreed. The *Life* photographer took out his camera and flash gun. The Russian, never having seen a flash camera before, cowered before it and started crying again. After trying to assure his uncomprehending subject of his benign intentions, Mydans went ahead and took the shot, firing his flash gun, setting the man off again: "The Russian wheeled around screaming. He sagged to his knees and grabbed the table, weeping, stuttering in Russian."[88]

Again, the kind Finnish major came to the man's rescue, while the enlisted men skulked away in shame. "The major jumped up and gently raised the sobbing prisoner, 'You're not hurt,' he repeated soothingly, 'we're only taking your picture.' He reached for my camera and held it to the Russian's wet face. 'Look through the window,' he spoke as one would speak to a child."[89]

Slowly, the Russian responded. "The [Russian's] furtive eyes flickered about the room. One eye caught the finder and two hands reached up slowly and took hold of my camera. For a minute he peered through it at me and into the little group of Finns who waited, quiet and embarrassed."[90]

Now he got it: "Suddenly there was a flicker of a smile, then a laugh, then as the major held him he shook with screams of laughter."[91]

Relieved, his former tormentors joined in the laughter. One of them put the blanket back over the man's head and he was escorted out of the room to great merriment. The officer had the last word. "As the major passed me on the way back," Mydans wrote, "he stopped, hesitated before me, started on again. Over his shoulder, he said harshly in English: 'The Russians are pigs!'"[92]

There is, it should be noted, one other troubling story regarding the Finnish treatment of prisoners of war. On December 18, the *New York Times* published an unconfirmed report that in order to discourage the Soviets from bombing civilian centers, a number of Russians were being held in hospitals and important public buildings, a charge that was later repeated by *Time* magazine. However, this was never proven.

In any event, even if this troubling charge had been true, it doesn't seem to have deterred the Kremlin, which continued with their indiscriminate bombing regardless and even intensified it over the next few weeks, including bombing the main prison camp at Kajaani where most of the prisoners captured at Suomussalmi were held. The truth is, the Kremlin didn't seem to care about whether its prisoners returned alive or not. This was confirmed following the armistice, when an estimated 500 of the more than 5,000 Russians whom the Finns took prisoner were repatriated and then summarily shot, while most of the rest vanished.[93]

One of the many horror stories to come out of Suomussalmi was that of a female nurse the Finns captured.

Later, Virginia Cowles interviewed the inconsolable woman, as best as she could in between hysterical sobs:

> The most amazing story of all was from the Russian nurse. This twenty-three-year-old girl, the only woman prisoner in Finland, was captured when the Finns routed the 163rd Division. She was a girl of medium size, with broad Slavic features and eyes which were filled with sadness. She wore a wool press provided for her by the Finns; her only other clothes were the men's army uniform she had been wearing when captured.[94]

Eventually, with difficulty, Cowles got her story. Several months before, the woman explained, she had been living with her husband and child in Leningrad. "Then she [the nurse] received a mobilization order. Thinking it was only for autumn maneuvers, she was not particularly worried. In November, however, she was attached to the 163rd Division and a month later forced to cross into Finland. Although miserable and frightened, she was sent with two other nurses to a front-line first-aid post."[95]

The other nurses were wounded in the intense fighting and removed to a field hospital behind the line, leaving the Leningrad woman the only staff member, along with a doctor. When the 163rd's commander, Zelentsov, finally ordered his retreat on December 30, the Russian nurse and doctor were unable to get back to base and wound up, like the others, wandering around the woods before they were picked up by a Finnish patrol.[96]

Later, the bodies of the two other nurses were found in the field hospital, an old farmhouse. Ebbe Munck, a noted Danish explorer and journalist who was covering the war for the Copenhagen press, had the misfortune of being amongst the first ones to discover the blood-curdling sight. Hospital is probably too generous a word for what Munck found there, as he described it to Cowles:

> One room had been fitted as an operation theatre. On the table lay a corpse, his stomach frozen, his stomach hastily sewn up with string. Blood had oozed out all over the table, so that it looked like a butcher's shop. One wounded man, his arm hacked off as if with a chopper, had been left to die in the corner. Besides the table was a bag of surgical instruments all first class and still packed. There was a big jar of frozen human blood with which the Soviets had been experimenting with transfusions.[97]

In the schoolyard were a number of wooden shelters where local children used to leave their bicycles and ponies. They were filled instead with wounded who had frozen in their beds after the Russians had evacuated, "stacked high with naked bodies, white, like planks of wood," Munck recounted.[98]

The grisly story never appeared in the press, quite likely because Mannerheim killed it. As much as he despised the foe, publishing atrocity stories—including ones about outrages committed by the Russians against their own troops—apparently went against his aristocratic code.

While Munck and others were confronting the macabre vestiges of the decimated 163rd Division, the blocked and stranded 44th Division was undergoing its own death agony at Raate Road, as Hjalmar Siilasvuo's men methodically went about their bloody work.

The desperate struggle of the division is carefully recorded in its combat diary, complete with testimony to the Suomi machine guns that the Finnish stealth attackers used as they fell upon it. Excerpts:

> *January 1, 1940.*
> The 3rd battalion of the 122nd artillery regiment is in firing position. The 1st battalion of the 179th howitzer artillery regiment is about to arrive. . . . Enemy started offensive against the 2nd battalion of the 146th regiment. . . . The first assault was repelled; the enemy repeated the assault but was beaten back. After failing in its first two assaults, the enemy started outflanking the battalion. . . . [99]

> *January 2, 1940.*
> The enemy opened artillery fire against the 1st battalion. . . . One battery of the 122nd artillery regimental HQ at 2340 went over to the offensive against the Finnish regiment during the night, making a barricade on the 21st kilometer. Bypassing the 146th regiment simultaneously from two sides, the enemy surrounded the regiment and inflicted heavy losses on it with fire from submachine-guns. Two batteries from the 122nd artillery regiment lost all its horses and most of its men to the enemy's fire. [100]

And so it went.

The Finnish public, already excited by the outcome of the first battle of Suomussalmi, knew nothing as yet about the sequel then taking place along Raate Road. One shattered Russian division was good enough for the moment.

In the interim, there were other promising tidings of varying kinds for Finland and her friends during the first week of January 1940. For one, foreign volunteers from all directions were en route to Finland. Thus, on January 4, the *New York Times* reported that the first contingent of 200 fighting Fennophiles from Hungary had left Budapest. That same day came a dispatch from Oslo about the pending departure of the first group of 150 Norwegian volunteers. "All are extraordinarily well-equipped, with new uniforms and special Winter outfits," the paper declared. [101]

Again, on that same day—the *Times* was devoting several pages to its coverage of the war by now—it was reported that three Russian reconnaissance parachutists had been captured. In the same article, the *Times,* indulging in a bit of black humor, related the painful fate of the last Russian paratrooper to be captured: "More than a week ago a stubborn parachutist refused to surrender even when surrounded by Finns. Every time they approached he machine-gunned them. The Finns, not wishing to kill the lonely Russian, procured a load of buckshot and fired at him. He surrendered, but the Finns had to pay dearly for their good nature, as they had to pick out all the shot."[102]

The next day, there was the grotesque report via Stockholm of a Finnish patrol on the Salla front in eastern Lapland, which had suddenly come across a detachment of 150 Russian troops. The Finns made ready to engage the soldiers —until they realized they were all frozen.[103]

Also on January 4 the *Times* published a long column by Harold Denny about a Finnish pamphlet raid on Leningrad. Not content to best them on the battlefield, the Finns were also going toe to toe with the Soviets on the propaganda front. Most of the Finnish pamphlets were fairly predictable, showing captured Russian soldiers, their names suppressed, remarking about how well they were treated and how Russia had misled them, and so forth.[104]

A customized leaflet designed with Soviet pilots in mind was also produced and dropped on Russian lines at this time. The leaflet, which borders on the surreal, contains, on the left side, a guarantee in Russian of $10,000 and a free trip to any country of a defecting pilot's choice—although the country the brochure's creators clearly had in mind was the United States, California in particular. On the right side, by way of illustrating the putative paradise that awaits the lucky airman on the far side of the Rajajoki River, there is a photo of a villa in California with a palm tree; beneath it is a picture of Henry Fonda, the American movie star, from one of his films showing him lying in bed (evidently a hospital bed of some kind) while being tended to by a nurse with a very good bedside manner. Or perhaps it's his girlfriend. It's not clear. At any rate, the supposed pilot-cum-defector looks very happy.[105]

It is not known how successful these pamphlets were; however, the fact that the Finns had the time to concoct such wistful *confetti de la guerre,* no less the gumption to drop them on the Russians (if in fact they did), is remarkable.

Meanwhile, along the icy hell of Raate Road, the envelopment of the 44th Division was well under way. The resulting bedlam—including a friendly fire incident—is chillingly portrayed in the pages of the matter-of-fact Soviet combat diarist.

January 5, 1940
    The 2nd battalion, 146th regiment left their defenses on the southeastern shore of Hataiola lake without permission and came to the positions of the

3rd battalion, 305th regiment, where it formed a defensive line facing south. . . . We have no news from the 9th company, 146th regiment. [Apparently] the company is still surrounded.

A scout[ing] party of two platoons that went to make contact with the 7th and 9th companies during the night could not reach them. They came under fire and are now fighting the enemy. . . .

An airplane with red stars flew over the road and fired at our troops.[106]

At five o'clock, Vinogradov, the 44th's barely functional commander, sent the following message to corps headquarters: "The situation of the division is hard, especially with food, men exhausted and starved, we have about 400 wounded. Horses are dying, no petrol, we are almost out of ammunition. The enemy is attacking us from the front. Morale is low, some commanders are deserting."[107]

"I am in urgent need of help," Vinogradov cabled, requesting permission to retreat. Headquarters told him to wait; his request would first have to be approved by Mekhlis, the commissar-in-chief of the corps and field representative of Stalin.

January 6, 1940.
The division is fighting encirclement. . . . The 25th regiment is now encircled. Radio message from 46th regiment: "Give us help, they are finishing us off, give us help (repeated several times). We are under heavy artillery fire . . . "[108]

✳

The next day came the news that Finland had its first ace: Jorma Sarvanto, of *Lentolaivue 24,* the same dashing airman who had wistfully serenaded Martha Gellhorn the month before, had managed to shoot down six Ilyushin DB-3 long-range bombers in the course of several minutes.

On the morning of January 6, Sarvanto had been on combat air patrol in his Fokker D-21, waiting for Russian aircraft to appear, when a horde of seven of the gawky tri-engine Ilyushin bombers dutifully poked over the horizon, flying in box formation. Immediately, Sarvanto climbed at full throttle and attacked out of the sun, diving straight into the middle of the Soviet formation, closing rapidly with the rearmost group of Red bombers. As the enemy gunners spotted him, smoky trails zipped past Sarvanto's cockpit. At thirty yards Sarvanto got off his first, hammering burst. Suddenly the starboard wing of one of the DB-3s burst into a ball of flame.[109]

Next, Sarvanto shifted his attention to the fallen plane's neighbor. Calmly the Finn watched as his bullets ate up the bomber's starboard engine cowling. A moment later the Russian plane combusted. That made two victims. Next Sarvanto turned his sights on the third member of the group, aiming a seam of bullets at the hulking craft's vulnerable blue belly. The stricken Ilyushin faltered for a moment; then its wing dropped off.[110]

Now Sarvanto whirled around and took on the second formation of bombers. Steadily closing in, he fired again, shooting off the rudder of one of the ungainly, relatively slow bombers. That made four down. Seconds later, Sarvanto sent another stream of lead into the cockpit of another DB-3, killing its crew instantly. The next victim wasn't as cooperative. The pilot of this DB-3 was no novice, trying every trick in the book to get away from the Finn doggedly at his tail. It was no use. Controls shot away, the stricken craft plummeted to earth, crashing in a plume of snow and smoke.[111]

That left one more intruder to deal with. Again, Sarvanto caught up with his intended target, which was high-tailing it back to Russian lines. He pressed the gun button. This time nothing happened: no more ammo, the Finnish lament. Cursing, the frustrated fighter pilot peeled off and made for home. By now he was practically out of fuel. After a rough landing, Sarvanto turned around to inspect his plane: it was completely shot up. Then he looked at his watch: the entire fight, he later estimated, had taken five minutes.

A short while later, Sarvanto was recounting the details of the engagement to several admiring FAF mechanics when two Fokkers slid to a halt on the frozen lake. Lieutenant Sovelius and Sergeant Ikonen, the same pilots who had taken part in the December 19 aerial bushwhack, emerged from their planes with big grins on their faces: they had seen the fight from a distance, flown over, and finished off the surviving DB-3 themselves. That made seven.[112]

Europe had its first ace, and Finland had a new hero. Everything, it seemed, was going *Suomi*'s way. Then two days later, on January 9, came the most astounding news of all: the destruction of the Soviet 44th Division at Raate Road.

A Russian major captured at Raate Road, a former tsarist officer, later recounted his ill-fated division's final hours. According to the major, the 44th, from the Ukraine, well deserved its top reputation (in contrast to the cobbled-together 163rd). His men were well trained, he insisted. However, they weren't prepared for combat in the frigid conditions they encountered at Suomussalmi and Raate Road; nor, obviously, were they prepared for Siilasvuo's mass *motti* tactics. Also, he concluded, it didn't help that the division's commander, Vinogradov, was an utter incompetent.[113]

At one point early in the debacle, while the Finns were still executing the second stage of the division's *motitus,* the prisoner claimed, he and several other officers urged Vinogradov to give the order to retreat.

> He refused. Instead he sent, the next day [January 4], two companies of the 146th regiment—the only two in that regiment still in any shape to fight—and one battalion of the 25th to force a way to the frontier and let the supplies come through [the 44th's supply train had been held up further

down the road]. But they were held up by Finnish fire from the woods and could not do the job.

We sent them more men to force open the stranglehold of our communications, and kept on doing this for three days. Each time we lost heavily. All this time our men were suffering heavily from cold and hunger. By January 6, the men were panicky and so weak they were unable to move.[114]

Finally, on the evening of January 6, Vinogradov received permission from V. I. Chuikov, the new commander of the 9th Army, to retreat.[115] "At 9 P.M. Vinogradov told me to take over command of the remnants of the 146th and fight a rear-guard action," the major said. "He then got into a tank and drove off in a column with seven tanks and drove off. At 9:30, with three officers and two hundred men, all that was left of the regiment, we began to march back." Eighteen kilometers from the frontier, he stumbled off the road and fell asleep. The next morning the Russians were found asleep and taken prisoner.[116]

The 44th Division was no more. Only a small fraction of the unit—even smaller than what remained of the 163rd Division after Suomussalmi—managed to escape Siilasvuo's trap and break through to the border. The haul of captured equipment was correspondingly greater: 70 guns, 43 tanks, 270 trucks, 300 machine guns, 6,000 rifles, 32 field kitchens, and 1,170 horses. The number of prisoners taken this time—1,300—was also greater, as were the estimated Russian casualties—approximately 6,000; it was difficult to say for certain because snow drifts covered the area immediately afterward. (Final estimates of the number of Russian soldiers killed at Raate Road range from 6,000 to as many as 17,500. Most likely, the true number was somewhere in between.)[117]

The Russians seemed to be more put out by the loss of the equipment than that of their men: Moscow Radio announced that if the Finns didn't return the Soviet equipment they recovered at Suomussalmi and Raate, the Kremlin would declare war on Finland![118]

Vinogradov himself made it back across the border, only to be immediately executed, along with his chief of staff O. I. Volkov, and his divisional commissar, I. T. Pakhomenko, in front of a formation of their surviving troops.[119]

The impact on the Finnish public of this second, even more complete victory, coming so soon after the electrifying news of the victory at Suomussalmi, was tremendous. In Helsinki strangers embraced. Church bells rang, just as they would in London in 1942 after Britain's first great land victory over the Germans, at El Alamein, when Winston Churchill declared: "No, this is not the end, nor is it the beginning of the end. Perhaps it is the end of the beginning." That, too, is how it seemed to many Finns after Suomussalmi and Raate Road.[120]

The celebration extended as far as the Mannerheim Line. The news of the double victory had an immediate and palpable effect on the morale of the troops there, Olavi Eronen recalled.

"The news of the two victories at Suomussalmi enormously elevated our spirits," he said. "We hadn't heard very much about the other victories, but we certainly heard about Suomussalmi. Finally, we thought, we had a chance." Evidently Finnish G.H.Q. did too: "The winter war in the north is ours," it roundly declared in the communiqué that apparently gave the war its name.[121]

Predictably, the world press had another field day with the news. As Allen Chew writes in *The White Death,* "The concentrated carnage along the Raate Road—especially in the western section where thousands of Russians had been isolated for five days before their agony ended—was the most dramatic evidence of a Soviet military fiasco that the war produced."[122]

The Finns were wiping out whole divisions now. What many people, including the Finns, seemed to forget, at least for the moment, was that the Russians still had quite a few more divisions to bring up.

*

Virginia Cowles, arriving at the frozen Raate Road killing ground several weeks after the fact, was also impressed. And infinitely depressed:

> Perhaps it was the beauty of the morning that the terrible Russian debacle seemed all the more ghastly when we came upon it. The rising sun had drenched the snow-colored forest, and the trees, like lace Valentines, with a strange pink light that seemed to glow for miles. The landscape was marred only by the charred framework of a house; then an overturned truck and two battered trucks.[123] . . . Then, we turned a bend in the road and came upon the full horror of the scene. For miles the road and forests were strewn with the bodies of men and horses; with wrecked tanks, field kitchens, trucks, gun carriages, maps, books and articles of clothing. The corpses were frozen as hard as petrified wood. All were frozen in the positions in which they were huddled. What these troops suffered in the cold is not difficult to imagine.[124]

The killing also took its toll on the killers, as Geoffrey Cox, one of the first reporters on the scene, saw when he encountered some of Siilasvuo's depleted men returning from the battlefield. "It was the sight I remember most vividly in the Finnish war," he writes. "Coming towards me in one long stream were the men who had fought the battle, returning to rest; moving up were the fresh troops. The men from the front came on skis, on foot, piled four or five on sledges pulled by ponies. 'Molotov,' they called, pointing to them, and laughing. Others rode on lorries. Their snow capes were stained yellow, grimy. Their rifles were slung on their backs."[125]

"Their faces," Cox writes, "were the faces of men who had seen terrible things and looked on death for many days. Many had cheeks and foreheads blackened with fire of machine guns. Almost all had dark, staring, exhausted eyes. They were unshaven, bronzed. Some had the lined look of old men. Others stared fixedly ahead, or plodded on their skis, their faces set."[126]

✳

Mannerheim was unstinting in his praise of Siilasvuo, whom he immediately promoted to major general, as well as his stalwart men: "The victory of Suomussalmi was again the result of a battlefield command exercised in a bold and purposeful manner, the tough endurance of the troops, and clever use of country and conditions. The commander, Colonel Siilasvuo, well deserved [his] general's epaulettes."[127]

The combination of the victories at Kemijoki River and Suomussalmi effectively disabused the Soviet High Command of any desire to attempt to invade northern Finland again.

However, the "battle of annihilation" at Suomussalmi, though clearly deserving of the name, was not quite the watershed it seemed. Indeed, the most concrete result of the Finnish victory at that tiny hitherto unknown Finnish village was to stiffen the Kremlin's determination to regain its vanished military prestige. As Chew notes, "The very magnitude of their victory was a liability to the Finns. After such a severe blow to the Red Army's prestige, its commanders were not anxious to see the war end before they could achieve compensating victories."[128]

At the time, it seems, many of Finland's friends abroad—as well as not a few Finns themselves—were giving the serial victories at Suomussalmi and Raate Road *too* much weight, as the *Times* of London noted. "To the impressive list of Finnish victories has now been added one even more brilliant," observed the paper's (anonymous) military correspondent in a prescient essay that could have been entitled, "Beware the Suomussalmi Factor."

> Yet even this exploit of the Finns gives no warrant for the excessive optimism which has exceeded the first acute apprehension in the minds of their friends in this country. Many people believe that the Russians will make no further effort on a great scale before the spring, by which time "something may have turned up" and in any event Finland will have received the supplies and warlike stores from outside.
>
> This Micawber-like attitude may not, however, prove adequate. In the first place it is not certain that the Russians will not continue the offensive, because although they may be unable to maintain a greater number of troops than at present, they can always replace exhausted and depleted formations by fresh [ones]. Secondly, even if Finland should receive the most lavish support by the spring, that might well be too late. After the snows have disappeared the conditions will be such as to deprive the Finns of some of the great advantages which they now possess.[129]

*

In fact, Stalin had decided that the Russians would continue their offensive, after the requisite period of retraining and reorganization. The Soviet dictator had no choice, really, if he wished to retain the esteem of the Red Army, which he was rapidly losing, no less than of his own people, who were beginning to wonder why the "liberation" of Finland was taking so long, and who, though effectively shielded from the Western media, were bound to hear of the debacle in the north, however belatedly, at some point.

Stalin had also decided who would lead the new drive: a hard-nosed former machine-gunner and World War I veteran and First Army Commander (as top Russian generals were then known) by the name of Semyon Timoshenko. After fighting for the Imperial Russian Army on the German front, Timoshenko had joined the Red Army in 1918 and never looked back—though, like all of Stalin's generals, he periodically had to look over his shoulder.[130]

Moving to the cavalry, Timoshenko served as a commander in the First Cavalry Army during the civil war, as well as during the Soviet-Polish war of 1920, in which the tenacious Poles defeated the Russians at the Battle of Warsaw, the one major Communist defeat prior to the Finnish morass. Slowly rising through the Red ranks during the interwar years, he was appointed deputy head at the Belorussia Military District, before transferring to a similar post in the Kiev Special Military District two years later.[131]

Above all, Timoshenko was a survivor. Winning Stalin's favor in the 1930s, he managed to survive the great purge of the Red Army, becoming head of the Kiev Military District in 1938; however, he was no stooge. By the time of the Winter War, Timoshenko was known as a capable military leader who was well versed in tactical and operational concepts. A traditionalist, he favored the frontal strike concept rather than "war of maneuver" advocated by the murdered Mikhail Tukachevsky, which made Timoshenko the ideal candidate to command the armies being massed for the single thrust offensive on the Mannerheim Line, as called for in Shaposhnikov's original strategic plan, which Stalin had decided to revive. The question was: Did he want the job?[132]

At a meeting several days after the Red disaster at Suomussalmi, at which representatives of the various Russian military districts were present, and before the even direr news came in from Raate Road, where one of Timoshenko's best divisions, the 44th, from Kiev, was in the process of being cut up, Stalin asked which men present would like the thankless job of replacing Meretskov and leading the revamped operation.[133]

Timoshenko volunteered that he would take the position on the condition that he received the additional, massive manpower and firepower he needed. Stalin, now finally alive to the actual situation and anxious to remove the blot on the once revered Red Army's escutcheon, agreed to give him what he needed.[134]

On January 7, just as the hapless Vinogradov was in the process of retreating across the border to Russia with the remainder of his butchered unit and Finland was toasting anew the health of the men of the 9th Division, the Supreme Soviet High Command Moscow officially informed the Leningrad Military District that management of "the battle against the Finnish White Guardists" was now in the charge of Semyon Timoshenko and his newly reorganized Northwestern Front.[135]

The new, no-nonsense, bullet-headed Russian commander immediately took charge. Suspending offensive operations, he launched an intense, nationwide search by telephone, by proxy, as well as in person for the best troops he could find for the final drive—including and especially ski troops who actually knew how to ski. At the same time, via a combination of probing attacks and aerial reconnaissance, a methodical inventory of the Mannerheim Line was conducted.[136]

Taking a page from his eighteenth-century predecessor, Alexander Suvorov, who constructed an elaborate model of the Turkish defenses at Izmail before his successful siege of the redoubtable fort there in 1791, Timoshenko used the intelligence his men brought back to build mock-ups of the main Finnish fortifications. In contrast to the two prior frontal assaults on the Finnish bastion, next time, he was determined, his army would know exactly what it was doing as well as what it was attacking.[137]

At about this time, several thousand dejected and benumbed Russian survivors of the battles of Suomussalmi and Raate Road returned, unheralded, to their homes.

One of them was the father of Russian journalist Yevgeny Davidov, then seven years old and living in Petrozavodsk. Before the war, Davidov recalled visiting his father, then a conscript in the 163rd Division boot camp at Novgorod. He seemed resigned to his fate then, but he was not unhappy. After all, he was fighting for a glorious cause: the emancipation of Finland.

Then came Suomussalmi. "I still remember my mother crying on New Year's Day, 1940," he said. "But I couldn't understand why." His traumatized father wasn't of much help, either, once he finally came home, refusing to speak about his experiences in Finland, as did many if not most of the Russian survivors of the Winter War. He never spoke about them again—until 2004, when Davidov became involved in a new Russian-Fenno project to create a Winter War memorial on the site of the Raate Road massacre.[138]

Then, only then, after his half-century silence, did he break his silence. "Oh Suomussalmi!" he exclaimed to his son, still pained at the memory. "We had a hard time there!"[139]

5

"Nothing of Importance on the Front"

January 8–20, 1940

In a heroic stand that has captured the imagination of the world in little more than a month of fighting, tiny Finland is beating off the armies of a country fifty times her size along make-shift battle lines where the white of the Arctic snow is crimson with the red of Russian blood.
     —Associated Press, January 15, 1940, quoted in Oliver
     Gramling, *Free Men Are Fighting*

On the Karelian Isthmus the war is mainly a matter of digging in and skirmishing, more like the Western Front than any other part in Finland.
     —*The Times* (London), January 19, 1940

"Nothing of importance on the front." Throughout December's fighting, as the two armies were locked in struggle on the Mannerheim Line and points north, and the Red "steamroller" gradually shuddered to a halt, the anonymous author of the daily Soviet military communiqué would robotically repeat those same words:
     Nothing of importance on the front.
     After Tolvajarvi: "Nothing of importance on the front." After Summa: "Nothing of importance on the front." After Suomussalmi: "Nothing of importance on the front."
     That is not to say that the oft-exaggerated pronunciamentos issued by the Finnish High Command were necessarily models of truthfulness. But at least the daily Finnish military bulletin bore some relation to reality (even though that reality was also highly censored).
     Now, in mid-January, as fighting on the isthmus wound down, the communiqués issued by the two sides began to coincide. Thus, on January 9, the Finnish Army issued its shortest news summary to date. To wit:

     Land—Except for patrol and artillery activity on both sides, January 8 passed quietly everywhere.
     Sea—No operations.
     Air—On the air front nothing worth mentioning.[1]

     Thus began the interregnum between the war's two principal acts, also known as "the January lull." All told, it was to last a little less than four weeks.

If it is possible to say that there was a "happy time" or a "good time" during the Winter War—at least from the Finnish point of view—this was it, while the victory bells of Suomussalmi and Raate Road still chimed in the nation's ears.

✳

While the fighting on the isthmus had petered out, for the most part—except for Russian probing attacks, as Timoshenko began laying the groundwork for the next offensive—the media spotlight shifted to the far north again. There, Kurt Wallenius continued to give the Russians major problems, pushing back the remainder of the Soviet salient at Salla while also sending some of his men on daring long-distance penetration raids into Russian territory itself, including sabotage attacks against the vulnerable Murmansk-Leningrad railroad line. Wallenius was an international media star by now, and reveling in it. "A Finn completely in his element is Kurt Wallenius," declared *Life* in a lavish photo essay about the war during the second week of January. The magazine noted Wallenius's problematic resume: "He is the same Wallenius whose Fascist friends helped push through the anti-Communist laws in 1930 and whose success so went to his head that in 1932 he led a revolt against the democratic government in Finland."[2] However, the American weekly affirmed, he "has since learned his lesson, been taken back in the Army and is leading the Finns in the north with boundless gusto and genuine ability." The prodigal general returneth was depicted by a photo of Wallenius smiling broadly while decked out in his trademark open bearskin coat, with pistol and flashlight dangling from his exposed belt.

The *New York Times* likewise praised Wallenius and his swashbuckling, lead-from-the-front style: "He is said to spend much time in the front lines, exposing himself to danger with a contempt for death that has amazed his men, and his example is looked upon as an important factor in the Finns' ardent fighting spirit."[3]

Colonel (soon to be Major General) Hjalmar Siilasvuo, architect of the recent "annihilation victories" of Suomussalmi and Raate Road, was not mentioned. The hell-raising Wallenius made better copy. With Wallenius riding high and not much else ostensibly happening in the war, large numbers of the international press now made the long overnight train trip from Helsinki, descending on the celebrated general's headquarters at the Hotel Pohjanhovi in Rovaniemi. After weeks of being cooped up in the stuffy, poorly heated Kamp, many if not most of the journalists who checked into the Pohjanhovi were happy for the change in venue.

For one, the Pohjanhovi, one of the new wave of modern Finnish hotels built to accommodate the rising, prewar Lappish tourist trade, was more than adequately heated, with central heating and fireplaces on every floor, as well as a state-of-the-art elevator, which management was fond of calling "the most northernly lift in the world." Too, the Pohjanhovi had Wallenius, who could be seen storming in or out of the hotel every few hours, furry coat flapping in the Arctic wind, surrounded by saluting aides. Most important, the Pohjanhovi had Rovaniemi, and Rovaniemi was definitely not Helsinki.[4]

Geoffrey Cox, now back from his sortie to Stockholm, wound up spending five weeks in Rovaniemi in late December and January. He was very happy about that, as he wrote in *The Red Army Moves* after he returned to London in 1941. It was in the Lappish capital, Cox asserts, that he really came to know Finland, and where he experienced the true grit of the Finnish people as they confronted the mortal storm, witnessing the life of the nation in a way he hadn't been able to do in Helsinki.

Every morning at the Pohjanhovi would begin in the same raucous, time-honored fashion, with the by now obligatory Russian air raid. The Red Air Force was paying much more attention to the north now. When the air raid siren would go off, the motley, chattering, laughing crowd of hotel guests, staff, military and hospital personnel (half of the hotel had been converted to a hospital), Rovaniemians who happened to be skiing by, and perhaps an errant reindeer herdsman, sans reindeer, noisily convened in the large shelter trench next to the hotel. The Pohjanhovi "shelter party" was considerably more high-spirited than the grim Helsinki *vaestosuoja* affairs, as Cox fondly notes: "Lottas, nurses, correspondents, soldiers talked and joked. A seventeen year old boy kept watch by the entrance. Gradually away from beyond the low hills, we heard the hum of planes. They came closer and closer, clearly flying very high."[5]

Sometimes the swarm of SB-2s and DB-3s would bomb the town itself, where they invariably would try to hit a bridge across the Kemijoki River, which also happened to be located only a few hundred meters or so away from the Pohjanhovi, in which case the bomb shelter bonhomie would cease for a moment. The town's lone Bofors anti-aircraft gun would bark. Bombs would drop, sometimes jarringly close to the shelter and the hotel. One of the enemy aircraft might be seen to be trailing smoke overhead before disappearing over the orange, midwinter horizon.

In the event, the Soviet bombardiers assigned to the north were just as inept as the ones bombing the south, because the bridge was never hit. (In fact, Cox says that in all his time in Finland, not once did he ever see a bridge destroyed or even damaged by Soviet bombs.)[6]

Or sometimes, the Red planes would head further west to deliver their flaming greetings (as the Soviets put it) to Kemi and Oulu. Then the all-clear would sound, and the resilient little city—"large village" would be more accurate (the 1939 population of Rovaniemi was approximately 1,000)—would return to its wartime rhythm, and the shelter occupants would return to the hotel to warm themselves before one of the fireplaces, tend to their patients, file their copy, or return to their war maps. The traffic in front of the hotel—one part civilian, one part military, one part reindeer—would resume, and the business of Rovaniemi, sans tourists, would continue.

Sometimes, when Cox wasn't covering battlefield matters, he would pop in to visit the village barber, who was definitely not your typical 1939 Finnish barber (if there was such a thing). For one, she was a woman, and an extremely attractive one at that. Cox, who seems to have had a crush on her, describes her as "dark-haired, chic, sophisticated." She also was enterprising, with two shops, one for men, another for women, "both fitted up as smartly and modernly as anything you [would] see in the biggest British cities."[7]

Or the venturesome newspaperman would go for a sauna in one of the town's old-fashioned public baths, as he amusingly records: "You took off your clothes in a cubicle in a dressing-room, then took your towel and walked past groups of curious Rovaniemians and soldiers back on leave, till you got to the steam room. Here an ancient hag [sic] steamed down till she was nothing but a skeleton with a covering of skin, hurled a beaker of water on to the stones."[8] Cox would lie there until the sweat drenched him, along with perhaps one of his journalistic comrades, before running out and rolling around in the snow.

As best as Cox could tell, northern Finns were eating as well as their southern countrymen, with most of the major staples—butter, milk, sausage, reindeer meat, even herring—readily available. Indeed, he writes, he never ate or felt better than he did during his beguiling, and inspiring, interlude in Rovaniemi. "Until the very end," he writes, "there was never any lack of foodstuffs in Finland. It must be one of the rare cases of a country which finished its war without one person suffering any degree of malnutrition."[9] (It should be noted that the Finnish authorities were sufficiently concerned about the consumption of sandwiches—evidently an offshoot of shelter life—to issue a warning about the "danger" of eating too many of them, although this "unhealthy" habit seems to have been confined to Helsinki.)

Cox also found Rovaniemi culturally well endowed, with several bookshops offering tomes in French, English, and German. There was even a British circle for the study of English and English literature. In its own picaresque way, Rovaniemi had it all. Withal, Cox found life in mid-*Talvisota* Rovaniemi little affected by the war. "It was only as the fighting wore on, and you passed again and again a coffin being dragged through the streets on a sled and noticed how more and more women were wearing mourning—their black was like a blow against the white snow—that you could feel the price of it."[10]

Above all, Cox was deeply and forever impressed by Rovaniemi's steadfastness and unity of spirit. For him the spirit of the Winter War was no myth, but something quite real and palpable and never more so than in Rovaniemi. "Never once in all the five weeks in Rovaniemi did I come across any sign of antagonism to the war, or of feeling that Soviet Russia, and not a Mannerheim-led Finland, was the true spiritual home of these peasants and workers," Cox declares. "I felt here always a solid communal spirit of resistance right till the end; even the war weariness that ultimately came, never showed itself in any manifestations, personal or public, against the war policy of the Government."[11]

Cox was particularly struck by Rovaniemi's solidarity of spirit on Saturday night, when much of the town gathered in the restaurant of the Pohjanhovi to talk and listen to the war bulletins on the radio. In prewar times, the towns-people would gather here to dance. Not now. All dancing—or almost all—had been stopped during the war.[12] "For the Finns," Cox observes, "war [was] almost a religious act, to be taken with the requisite grimness. It was a terrible tribute to the blood-letting that their previous wars had brought."[13]

Then, the next night, Sunday, the Lappish capital would return to normal as the town youth would hang out, bitter temperatures notwithstanding, and "one would see the same strolling pairs of girls, the same loitering groups of boys on the street corners that can be seen on the streets of any small town of the world."[14]

*

Where Geoffrey Cox went, Virginia Cowles was sure to follow. Sure enough, in late January, the intrepid correspondent for the *Sunday Times* also checked into the Pohjanhovi—but not before another hair-raising foray, to the war's north-ernmost front, along the upper reaches of the 500-kilometer Arctic Highway, where the 104th Division, after overrunning Petsamo—the Russians' only bona fide success thus far—had been stymied from advancing further southward by Wallenius's far-ranging "white bats."

Traveling this time with two other journalists, Harold Denny and Desmond Tighe of the *New York Times* and the *Times* of London, respectively, Cowles's lat-est expedition turned out to be something of a reprise of her white-knuckle ex-pedition to Hanko—except that the temperatures were even colder now, with the thermometer registering thirty-two degrees below zero Fahrenheit when she and her party set out from Rovaniemi in another chauffeured white press car. This time, however, Cowles, in a get-up that included ski suit, sheepskin coat, eight sweaters, four pairs of socks, three mufflers, and two pairs of gloves (amongst other items), was fully prepared.[15]

The trip, the first undertaken by any journalists along the Arctic Highway, included a stop for dinner in Ivalo, along with a stomach-churning postprandial Soviet air raid; the Russians, with more experienced pilots, were also flying at night now.

*

In any event, the distaff American correspondent was ready for some rest and recreation by the time her car deposited her back at the Pohjanhovi.

The hotel had been seriously damaged during the interim, thanks to the intense Soviet bombing, seriously enough to jar the nerves of the proprietor, who refused to allow anyone to remain in the building during daylight hours. All guests were now pushed out, forcibly if necessary, promptly at 8:30 and in-structed not to return until 3:00. This was war, after all.[16]

That left recreation, which, this being Rovaniemi, meant skiing, in which Cowles took her turn at the town's famous ski run. An amateur, the transplanted New Yorker managed to fall on her face every few hundred meters. Fortunately, someone had contrived to have a kindly Finnish lieutenant follow the comely former society girl down the run to help her up when she fell. "There, there," said the officer given this difficult duty, gently lifting her to her feet. "I'm sure you'll do better next time."[17]

Of course, she never did. Still, Cowles maintained, in between spills, it was fun to go "down the run with the sky above you a warm thick blue and the sun sparkling on the snow." It would have even been possible to forget about the war altogether, if not for the necessity of dodging the machine gun emplacements sticking up through the snow here and there.[18]

Cowles also had time to help organize and participate in a multinational shooting competition amongst the resident journalists at the Rovaniemi shooting range. Unfortunately, she wasn't much better at that sport, either: "As we represented a half dozen different nationalities, we paired off in teams and made it a small Olympic games: England, France, Finland, Sweden, America, Germany. The Finns won, and I am ashamed to say that I let Walter Kerr [of the *New York Herald Tribune*] down so badly America got the booby prize."[19]

After the competition, Herbert Uxhull, a Baltic German who worked for the United Press, turned to Eddie Ward, a correspondent for the BBC. Cowles recorded this amusing exchange:

"I suppose you and I ought to be really shooting at each other."

"Good God, why?"

"The war."

"The war. Oh, you mean the *other* war! Come to think of it, I suppose we should. Extraordinary how one forgets."

"Extraordinary, I thought, what a mad world it is," Cowles wrote later; "that was the only time I heard the 'other war' mentioned."[20]

Cox, still enamored of Rovaniemi, also headed south eventually, reluctantly leaving at the beginning of February to return to Helsinki, just before the now-expected final Russian offensive on the isthmus began.

Several days before he did, Cox visited perhaps the municipality's most famous site, as well as its most scenic, the towering ski jump, located on the outskirts of town. Normally a sports site, the sixty-meter tower was now utilized as a lookout for aircraft. At its base was a small hut, where two *lottas* assigned to the air watch were making coffee before ascending to take their hoary two-hour turns as lookouts.

The by now confirmed Fennophile found this the most inspiring spot in town, not to mention the chilliest. Not that he seemed to mind, particularly after he met the amiable pair on top, a young *lotta* from Viipuri and her equally buoyant, fourteen-year-old, rifle-toting male guard: "I climbed the 200 feet [320 meters] up the swaying, whistling wooden stairs. On top the wind was icy cold and felt as if a fully-grown man was pulling at your sleeve. On the upper platform, where the skiers began their run, a seventeen year old girl, her cheeks flushed with the wind, her fair hair thrust under a grey fur cap, stood wrapped in a great goat-skin, Robinson Crusoe coat."[21]

The fair-haired *lotta* hailed from Viipuri. It turned out that she had been visiting her sister, living in Rovaniemi, when the war broke out, and had volunteered to be a lookout. Three days a week, for eight hours a day, two hours on, two hours off, she watched from the tower, ready to phone down to the hut below the moment that enemy aircraft came into view, now virtually a daily occurrence. Her vigilant young guard was there to protect her from Soviet machine guns.

*

Having by now seen the thousands of *lottas* in action, the international press was just as impressed with them as they were with the Finnish frontline troops they supported. Witness the following encomium from the syndicated American journalist Leland Stowe, who began covering the war in mid-December:

"The Finnish women were a unique factor and most surprising of all," wrote Stowe, whose unabashedly pro-Finnish dispatches from the war appeared in the *Chicago Daily News* and hundreds of other American newspapers. "Their Lotta organization had been founded with the Republic," he explained, "and for twenty years girls from the age of ten and women up to sixty had been trained for a wide variety of wartime services."

> There were Lotta nurses, Lotta supply units, Lotta fire wardens, Lotta canteen workers, and Lottas of a dozen varieties. Some of them had served as cooks at the regular army maneuvers for years and we found them performing the army's kitchen duties, quietly and smilingly, close to every front. Many other young Lottas, some in their late teens, served as air wardens on top of water towers and buildings and spent hours at a time watching for Russian planes while exposed to paralyzing temperatures of twenty five or thirty five degrees below.
>
> Everywhere we went these magnificent Finnish women gave examples of the greatest fortitude and devotion. Without thought of praise and with the naturalness of pioneer wives and daughters the Finnish women took over men's jobs, thereby releasing tens of thousands of men for active fighting.[22]

"I am quite certain," Stowe later wrote, "that no war—certainly no modern war—has ever been fought in which women have contributed so widely and effectively to a nation's defense as in Finland. In this sense I can think of no other people who have fought so completely as a people. Hitler's Nazis—even they—have never organized German women on such an efficient basis; but the Finns did this democratically and of their own volition. Women the world over must look to Finnish women for the supreme lesson in practical patriotism."[23]

*

Inevitably, too, some of those valiant women would make the ultimate sacrifice —air wardens too benumbed to climb down safely from their high towers after hours of remaining at their post, who then toppled over to their deaths; or others who died from Russian machine guns and bombs, or other causes.

"Three members of the *Lotta Svard* forces have carried out their duties to the end," read Gustaf Mannerheim's order of the day of December 26, 1939. "They remained faithfully at their dangerous posts and are the first Lottas to be killed in action."[24]

*

There would be more such deaths, including, in one horrific case, the mother and sister of a luckless second lieutenant by the name of Hukari who was one of Anna-Liisa Veijalainen's young charges on Tuppura. The previous summer the nineteen-year-old Viipuri native had lost his father. Then, in late December, Hukari's home was destroyed by a salvo from one of the Russians' huge, 350 mm long-range railway guns (or "ghost cannon," as the Finns called them), forcing his mother, sister, and two young brothers to evacuate to Kuopio in the Finnish lake country, where Hukari's mother and sister became *lottas*.[25]

Then, one day at the end of the "quiet phase" of the war, as Anna-Liisa calls it, came word that both Hukari's mother and sister had died during a bombing attack on Kuopio. As Anna-Liisa recounts,

> When those tidings arrived, we were all devastated. We felt it was simply too much for one family. As that tall, pale boy, struck steadily in the heart, walked unsteadily to the canteen and his upstairs room, I felt like screaming to God: "Where are you, if you let this kind of thing happen?"
>
> After a while, I followed him to his room. He sat at the table leaning his head on his hands, and I tried to stutter some words of consolation. "I am now the only supporter of two little brothers, and I don't even have a single photograph of my home and family members!"[26]

In the meantime, Veijalainen, already an experienced death counselor, carefully moved Hukari's pistol, lying on a nearby table, out of arm's reach "just in case." All told, sixty-four *lottas,* including the tragic Hukari women, would perish before the end of the *Talvisota.*

*

Mai-Lis Toivenen, now serving in the air watch near her native Koivisto, also had her close calls. On January 14, the day before she moved to her new post,

Toivenen was combing her hair in front of the mirror when suddenly she heard the sound of fighter planes approaching, causing her to dive to the floor. Then came the sound of machine gun bullets, followed by the sickening crump of bombs falling nearby. When she got up later there was a bullet in the mirror opposite the spot where she had been standing.

Then, in mid-January, after Mai-Lis turned eighteen, she was "promoted" to the local air watch. As she recalled:

> The watch tower was built on top of three pine trees. The platform was thin, with only a few planks of timber to support it. We worked in pairs, in two-hour shifts. We had binoculars and a phone. We were never taught how to spot which planes were enemy or friendly. We just sort of learned as we went all along. When we saw a Russian plane, we called in the information to a bunker nearby.[27]

The enemy planes came in great numbers, she recalled. First came the fighters, strafing everything in sight, followed by droves of bombers. Nevertheless, the position of air warden was not without its amusing moments—such as the time when Mai-Lis's fellow *lotta* sentry showed up with curlers in her hair. "It didn't matter that we were at war. She just wanted to look good."[28]

Sometimes, when she was off duty, the young air warden would write letters to her mother with thoughts about her exciting new life, like the following, which she penned in January:

> *Mother—*
>   I am in the air watch now. Yesterday I was alone here for the first time. It's very cold. I am wearing trousers, two fur coats and all the woollen clothing I own. Russian fighters have been flying above me all day. It is a very bright day. The fighters are shooting all the time. . . .
>   *This is exciting. It is so beautiful. The trees are covered with snow. Bombs are dropping all the time. It is war and we all hope it is going to end very soon.*[29]

"Of course, we wanted the war to end," the veteran *lotta* said, years later. "But we were prepared to fight indefinitely. Our morale couldn't have been better."[30]

While Mai-Lis kept a steady lookout for Russian aerial intruders, the majority of *lottas,* stationed behind the lines, went about their cooking, sewing, and other vital chores. Amongst those watching, at the canteen near her Karelian home, was young Eeva Kilpi. "The women knitted all kinds of woolen things for the soldiers," she remembered. "For example, they made face masks, so only the eyes and mouth could be seen. And they also made these horrible gloves, where there was a hole in place of the first finger. It was for the rifle, of course."[31]

Occasionally, the future writer recalled, she would make her own modest literary contribution. "I wrote some poems. They would go, like 'God, help us.' Or 'God protect us.' And then I tried to make them rhyme. And then I would put them in with the boxes of food."[32]

Sometimes the *lottas'* duties were even more trying, as another future writer, Inkeri Kilpinen,[33] who was thirteen at the time of the war, remembered. "Then there is something which has never been done in any other country or war," she said.

> The lottas would take care of the dead. And the young lottas washed them [the deceased soldiers] and because it was winter, the bodies were often frozen. And so their bodies had to be melted, and then they were washed, and they put them in nice and beautiful clothing. And then the men put them into coffins, because the bodies were heavy and then they were sent, all of them, each one, to their home. And the young lottas did this.[34]

In the meantime, the international media continued to sing the praises of the Finnish frontline soldiers themselves. "Whatever may be the ultimate outcome of Russia's war on Finland," wrote Harold Denny in his analysis for the *New York Times,* "the Finnish soldier already has won a place in the world's respect by his bravery, fortitude and resourcefulness. His performance has hardly been excelled in history, if indeed has ever been equalled."[35]

Although the new stalemate that had settled in on the Mannerheim Line had obviously frayed the nerves of the frontline troops, the morale of the men hunkered down in their trenches and dugouts along the isthmus remained strong, wrote Denny. "Picturing the Finnish troops in their trenches and dugouts and in their rare periods of rest behind the lines," he continued, "one is apt to see them as grim and nerve-racked heroes, weary and worn by weeks of hard fighting, holding out desperately against overwhelming odds."[36]

"But," the American declared after his most recent visit to the frontline Finnish fortifications, "that is not the impression they give when one mingles with them. Tired they are, and they are fighting with steady determination, but there is nothing grim about them and they wear no air of desperation. On the contrary, the Finnish soldiers are the most smiling and cheerful I have seen anywhere."[37]

Olavi Eronen and Eric Malm, whose regiments, the 10th and the 11th, respectively, were stationed on the line for the entire war, don't recall things being quite as upbeat as Denny pictured, but they agree that the morale of the frontline troops was generally good, even if life near the wire did have its harder moments, particularly toward the end.

"The most important thing, of course, was food," said Eric Malm. "It was always good, because you were always hungry. It was taken to Marjapellonmaki"—the town closest to where he was stationed—"by horse and sled from some kilometers behind the lines. But we ate, and we ate well."[38]

The most difficult thing, both men agreed, was being able to hear as well as see the Russians as they scurried about preparing for their next offensive, and not being able to do anything about it. "We could hear them almost daily during that period," he said, referring to the long January lull. "They were living on the other side of the brook, in fact. We could hear them and see them. But we couldn't do anything about it because of our lack of ammunition."[39]

"The worst thing during the winter war," Eronen agreed, "was the lack of artillery shells. We could hear the Russkies preparing for attack, so we could have made a pre-emptive attack, but we didn't have enough shells so we couldn't. We had to wait for the actual attack, when it came, to shoot, and not before. That was frustrating."[40]

The lack of ammunition and other materiel was a major theme in a mid-January report about the situation in Finland by Wayne C. Taylor, a representative of the American Red Cross who visited Finland at this time. "The Finns, while driving back the Russians again and again, have had to count every cartridge and shell for their supply is limited. Unless Finland gets real help she cannot continue [her] brilliant defense," the American declared, according to a dispatch published in the *New York Times* on January 20.[41]

The men on the front line did their best to conserve the ammunition they had—and their wits to boot. Sometimes, especially while on guard duty for long periods of time, one's imagination could run away, as happened to Malm one night when he was staring into the obsidian night near Marjapellonmaki. "One lonely night in January I heard steps in front of me," he said. "I took my rifle and aimed. I thought it was a Russian."[42]

"But no, it was a silver fox," he said. The Finnish infantryman's first inclination was to shoot, but then he thought better of it: "I was a keen hunter before the war, but I felt that there had been enough shooting as it was, so I let it go." In between the long spells of sentinel duty, the troops would retire to their dugouts. "We played cards and talked with our buddies and tried to keep warm," said Eronen.[43]

The men of Tuppura Fortress, in Viipuri Bay, had a greater variety of recreational options, including, on several special occasions, live entertainment "imported" from the mainland, said Anna-Liisa Veijalainen. "During the January 'quiet phase' we hosted, in addition to our own [amateur] entertainers, a theater group from the capital." The group included such "names" as Teppo Elonpera, Aku Korhonen, Joel Rinne, and the singer Sointu Kouvo, who sang the hit song "Tuulia, tuulia tuu."

"The boys found it [the song] hard to get out of their heads," the hostess of Tuppura observed. Rounding out the company was the famed Helsinki xylophonist Eino Katajavuori, who ended the memorable evening on a tuneful note. The war indeed seemed very far away that night as Katajavuori's nimble hands coaxed a melody from his exotic instrument and as the waves crashed on the beach fifty meters away.[44]

*

Twenty kilometers to the east, on the other side of the Mannerheim Line, Nikolai Bavin was also doing his best to keep warm. Bavin was a Russian marine assigned to guard duty at the Soviet Ladoga Flotilla base at Saunasaari, a small bay on the western coast of Lake Ladoga, some fifteen kilometers south of Taipale.

The cold is what Bavin, a native of Naro-Fominsk, a town in the Moscow region, remembered most about the Winter War when the former Red Navy veteran spoke about it nearly seventy years later in his flat on the outskirts of St. Petersburg. "The winter was cold, so guard duty was one half-hour at the maximum," said Bavin, who also was boxing champion of the Baltic Fleet. In contrast to his woebegone comrades in the Red Army, Bavin was properly dressed for the occasion. "We were very well dressed for guard duty," he said. "I took care of it myself. But it was cold!"[45]

In all, there were about 140 Soviet sailors and marines assigned to the Saunasaari marina, which the Russians took over in December after they invaded and converted it into a dock for their own gunboats; the vessels' cannon were used as artillery to shell the Finnish lines at Taipale after the vast lake—at 17,700 square kilometers, Europe's largest—froze over in late December. Bavin's unit's task was to guard the iced-in Russian boats from the long-distance penetration raids the Finns at Taipale would occasionally launch.[46]

This proved easier said than done, Bavin concedes. "Those Finns were smart fighters," he said. "They would appear out of nowhere, fire at us and disappear into the woods, usually too quickly for us to react." Mostly, though, it was quiet—and cold. "There was one skirmish [in] early December, when we lost three men. After that it was more peaceful. It wasn't bad duty, really. It was just cold."[47]

Bavin accepted the premise for the war—at least the stated premise, to protect Leningrad, if not some of the Soviet folderol used to justify it. He readily admits that the Mainila border incident was a fabrication. "The Finnish government can be blamed for the Winter War," Bavin said, "but the first shots were fired by us, of course."[48]

As far as the Finns themselves were concerned, Bavin stated, he basically had good feelings toward them, as did most of his fellow marines. Occasionally, he was asked to take charge of the handful of Finnish prisoners of war, captured in the area, part of the estimated 1,000 Finnish military POWs seized during the conflict. "I always treated them well," he said. According to Bavin, the Finns were just as afraid of the Russians, as vice versa. "The first thing I had to do generally was to calm them [the Finnish prisoners] down. They always asked if they were to be executed! I have no idea why they were afraid. I just told them that it was OK."[49]

As in the army, there was a *politruk* assigned to the Saunasaari marina, but he seems to have been an easy-going sort compared to the more belligerent kind found in the Red Army. "In every platoon there were men who looked after our 'political loyalty.' We had good relations with them. There were no tensions."[50]

All in all, life at the Saunasaari base sounds a bit like a Soviet version of *Mr. Roberts,* the famous 1956 movie starring Henry Fonda, based on a play of the same name about life aboard a U.S. cargo ship somewhere in the backwaters of the South Pacific during World War II on its regular run between "apathy and tedium and back."

Not that Saunasaari, only a few kilometers behind the Russian front lines, was exactly a backwater. But sometimes, as Bavin paced the dock of the relatively isolated bay, with only the wind for company, it certainly felt like it. Nearly every day, Russian bombers would fly overhead on their way to Finland. "Of course we saw the Red Air Force, but they just passed over us. They certainly flew a lot of sorties."[51]

Paradise it was not; nevertheless, Bavin's lot was certainly better than that of the tatterdemalion Red Army soldiers hunkered down on the wrong side of the Mannerheim Line, no less Bavin's luckless comrades who were then fighting and freezing to death in the unforgiving fells of the north. "We did hear about the failures," he said, "but only through word of mouth, nothing official. Of course we were surprised. On the other hand, we knew that the Finns were tough warriors, and extremely skillful on skis. Anyway, there was nothing that we could do about it. We were there to guard the boats, and that's what we did."[52]

Unlike their comrades up north, the relatively isolated men of the Soviet Ladoga Flotilla didn't have to worry about their field kitchens being captured or destroyed. "We ate well," Bavin said. "They [the base cooks] would bring us food in thermoses. That was good."

The real opponent was the biting cold. "They gave us geese fat to cover our hands and faces and protect us from the frostbite," said Bavin. "But it was still cold. That is what I remember most. The cold. We had a dugout there where we set a barrel and installed a chimney to burn wood. That helped somewhat. The stove produced heat, but also a lot of smoke and smut. We all looked like chimney cleaners." In a word, morale at the Soviet gunboat base at Saunasaari was passable.[53]

Entertainment was not a high priority for the Baltic Fleet at this time. There certainly weren't any visiting theatrical troupes or xylophonists, as there were on the Finnish side. There were, however, occasional boxing demonstrations, courtesy of the brawny Bavin (indoors, of course).[54]

"Of course I did some boxing there at Saunasaari, although I didn't have much competition there," Bavin boasted. "Rarely would an opponent last past the third round. That was good. But the thing I remember most was the cold. And the waiting."[55]

The boxing Russian marine did recall one jarring incident from this time involving the Finnish Air Force. Sometime "in late January or early February," he remembered, "our anti-aircraft guns shot down a Finnish plane. There were two Finnish pilots in it. It was a wooden plane. There were two Finnish pilots in it." A check of the records confirms that on January 29, 1940, the Finnish Air Force conducted a raid on the Saunasaari base in which one Fokker fighter was shot down "by extremely sharp and accurate anti-aircraft fire. We buried the pilots. Of course—we had to," said Bavin. "Other than that day we never saw the Finnish Air Force again."[56]

"And how are things in Helsinki?"

That was one of the questions that reporters put to passengers disembarking from the *Drottningholm,* a Swedish American line vessel that had docked in New York in January. The press was particularly interested in talking to the considerable number of passengers aboard who had come from the war-torn capital; such was the extraordinary level of interest amongst American readers in the exotic Arctic war.

The answer depended on whom one spoke to. According to Georg von Essen, a Finnish journalist based in Sweden who had spent the second week of January in Helsinki, things were remarkably calm, Soviet bombs notwithstanding. Von Essen told the *New York Times* that on his first day in town he had had lunch with a Finnish friend: "While they were eating he counted the sound of at least fifty bombs. The other diners in the restaurant ignored them and kept on eating. His friend laughed at the bombing. The outskirts of Helsinki have been ravaged by the aerial bombardment, Mr. Von Essen said, but the main part of the city had not been damaged."[57]

A Finnish widow who had sailed to New York to marry an American she had met the year before, however, remembered things differently. "It was terrible," she exclaimed to the *Times* reporter. "For six weeks you never took your clothes off. You didn't dare to go across the street. Some houses were burning, others were in ruins." The Finnish woman decided to leave the capital as soon as her sister sent her a ticket for the *Drottningholm.*[58]

Another passenger whose trip had originated in Finland, one Ernest Hjertberg, a former Swedish Olympic track and field coach, attributed the Finns' "splendid resistance" to their sports-mindedness. "The Finns, the Scandinavians and the Germans," he said smugly, were "the only really fit people."[59]

And how do surviving Helsinkians remember life in the capital during the *Talvisota?* Somewhere in between the aforementioned versions. "Things were not so bad," said Harry Matso. "Of course, there was no dancing allowed. But there were some concerts with military bands. We cheered the good news—while also taking our news communiqués with a large grain of salt, particularly the part when they came to our casualties. We knew that the Russians were losing a lot of people, but we also knew that we were losing too many. Basically, we hoped for the best."[60]

*

On January 19, Webb Miller, who used the January interregnum to file light features about life on the Finnish home front, reported that *Suomi* was in the midst of that perennial wartime phenomenon: a marriage boom. Soldiers who were headed for the front (or the few lucky ones who had been granted brief home leave) were in such a rush to get hitched to their paramours that the government had decided to abolish the normal regulation requiring an official announcement of pending nuptials in a newspaper three weeks before the happy occasion.

Interestingly, that same day, by way of underlining the government's renewed confidence in its own survivability, the Finnish Minister of Social Affairs (and future prime minister), Karl-August Fagerholm, announced that Finland would soon offer guaranteed war-risk insurance to all Finnish citizens to protect them from losses incurred during the conflict, the first country ever to do so.[61]

Fagerholm took the occasion of the announcement to enlighten an American reporter on the fundaments of the Finnish *folkhemmet* (welfare state) versus Soviet totalitarianism. "The theory behind this is that organized society, as embodied in the State, must bear the burden of war damages rather than let this be borne by individuals," he explained, "because war is an emergency affecting the whole State, not just individuals in the State. This is based on the realization that this is a totalitarian war and every organized group must bear its responsibilities."[62]

Collaborating with insurance companies, the government had worked out a system to do away with the exemption in life insurance policies for payment for death caused by war. Too, fire insurance had also been arranged for homeowners.

"Finland, in her twenty-one years of independence," the admiring reporter noted, quoting Fagerholm, had worked out "an advanced system of labor and social welfare laws and Mr. Fagerholm said that thus far, even in war conditions, the country [had] been able to keep them in force. It was the government's intention, he said, to retain them unchanged even in the emergency with which the country finds itself confronted."[63]

The minister also proudly noted that the eight-hour work law was still in force, while in industries vital to the war effort, when necessary, time and a half and double-time would also be paid. Several days later, on January 23, as further proof of the nation's unity, Fagerholm announced that Finnish industrial and trade union officials had agreed to submit to arbitration any and all major disputes and questions that arose between them during the war. "This agreement is beneficial not only to the workers and employers, but to the whole nation," he stated.[64]

The next day, the multitasking minister traveled to Stockholm to investigate the condition of the approximately 20,000 Finnish children who had been evacuated there, which he found to be good. Then Fagerholm flew on to Oslo to appeal to Norway to send regular troops and fighter aircraft to Finland (an appeal that fell on deaf ears; the Norwegians did, however, agree to allow some of their aircraft mechanics to travel to Finland to assist the FAF). A Finnish social affairs minister had to wear many hats in January 1940.[65]

During the interim, Finns' spirits had been considerably strengthened by a fighting speech Winston Churchill delivered over the BBC the next day in which Finland played a prominent role. The speech, in which the ever-aggressive British naval head made an appeal to the neutral nations of Europe to join with Britain and France in making common cause against the forces of "aggression and wrong," clearly sought, amongst other things, to goad Finland's two cautious Nordic neighbors into overcoming their hesitation about allowing the proposed Allied expeditionary force to succor Finland to transit their territory.

Neutrality, Churchill seemed to be saying, was a delusion; witness Nazi Germany's lack of respect for neutral ships: "Neutral ships are sunk without law or mercy, not only by the blind and wanton mine but by the cold, considered, deliberately aimed torpedo. The Dutch, the Belgians, the Danes, the Swedes, and above all the Norwegians have their ships destroyed whenever they can be caught upon the seas. It is only in the British and French convoys that safety is to be found."[66]

After devoting the first part of his speech to the "main" European war, between the Allies and Germany, and how mistaken the aforementioned neutrals were in thinking that they could avoid becoming embroiled in that conflict, Churchill turned his attention to the other war being waged by Germany's ally, Russia, against Finland. "All Scandinavia," Churchill noted, "dwells brooding under Nazi and Bolshevik threats."

"If it is courage that is preventing you from joining in the fray," said Churchill, speaking in words intended at once to shame and inspire, then he urged his listeners to look to Finland: "Only Finland, superb, nay sublime, in the jaws of peril," he somberly declared, raising his voice a notch.

Finland shows what free men can do. The service rendered by Finland to mankind is magnificent.[67] There, exposed for all the world to see, is the military incapacity of the Red Army and of the Red Air Force. Many illusions about Soviet Russia have been dispelled in these few and fierce weeks of fighting in the Arctic Circle. Everyone can see how communism robs the soul of a nation, how it makes it abject and hungry in peace and proves it base and abominable in war.[68]

Who would think that Churchill was referring to the same Soviet Russia with which, eighteen months hence following Hitler's invasion of the USSR, Great Britain would hasten to ally herself? But for the moment, Russia was still evil incarnate, and the cause of Finland was the cause of mankind.

"We cannot tell what the fate of Finland may be," Churchill declared, "but no more mournful spectacle could be presented to what is left of civilized mankind than that this splendid northern race should be at last worn down and reduced to servitude worse than death by the dull brutish force of overwhelming numbers."[69]

"If the light of freedom which still burns so brightly in the frozen North should be finally quenched," His Majesty's Lord of the Admiralty ominously continued, as invisible cymbals clashed in the background, "it might well herald a return to the Dark Ages when every vestige of human progress during 2,000 years would be engulfed."[70]

"But what would happen," Churchill declared, invoking the now all-but-forgotten directive of the League of Nations to offer Finland every possible form of aid and assistance, "if all these neutral nations I have mentioned were with one spontaneous impulse to do their duty in accordance with the covenant of the League and were to stand together with the British and French empires against aggression and wrong?"[71]

Finns, hearing Churchill's speech over the BBC or reading excerpts in their newspapers, took heart from the Briton's fighting words. Surely, surely, if Winston Churchill felt so strongly about their country's fate, then perhaps there really was something to all this talk about sending an expeditionary force to help them fight the "Russkies." The *New York Times* interpreted it that way:

> If Churchill feels so strongly about Finland, is it likely that the British will allow her to be overrun and enslaved without making a serious effort to save her? Mr. Churchill is a power in the British war cabinet, and he would hardly have spoken as he did, to such a vast audience at home and abroad, if the cabinet as a whole were not inclined to give military help on an effective scale.[72]

However, Harold Nicholson—the same Harold Nicholson who, six weeks before, felt sure that Finland would collapse after a few days—had a different reaction listening to his friend's fiery speech over the radio. The British public, he predicted, even though their country was supposed to be in a state of war, was not yet ready for Churchill's oratorical tattoo, or the Manichean picture of the world he outlined. The "phony war" was not quite over—at least yet.

We listen to Winston Churchill on the wireless after dinner. He is a little too rhetorical, and I do not think that his speech will really have gone down with the masses. He is too belligerent for this pacifist age, and although once anger comes to steel our sloppiness, his voice will be welcome to them, at the moment it reminds them of heroism which they do not really feel.[73]

As it happened, in this case Nicholson was right and the *New York Times* was wrong. Churchill, who, characteristically, had not cleared his bellicose speech with his cabinet, was indeed ahead of himself. He certainly was ahead of the neutrals to whom his combative words had been aimed, for whom the maintenance of peace at all costs was still paramount. If Churchill wanted to make Adolf run, run, run, in the words of his beloved ditty, he was privileged to do so. However, the governments of all the neutral nations Churchill had listed in his speech—the Dutch, the Belgians, the Swedes, the Norwegians, the Danes, all—all fired back that it was not for Churchill to instruct them how to shape their foreign policy or ask them to forsake their cherished neutral status.

As the Danish paper *Politiken* put it, "The small neutral states will feel no gratitude to Churchill because he is dragging them in." Moreover, it sounded to many of the non-aligned states as though the British and the French felt that the best way to defeat Germany was by fighting her elsewhere than in France—in the East, in the North, anywhere but France—which, of course, was true, at least as far as the French were concerned. One of the reasons, probably the main reason, why Edouard Daladier was anxious to get involved with Finland was not so much because the Finns were holding the line for Western civilization, as he claimed, but because Finland was not France.[74]

And, of course, Churchill, too, had had a pretext: one of the reasons why he wanted to help the Finns by sending an Allied expeditionary force to succor them via northern Norway and Sweden was because he wished to get at the Swedish iron ore fields that the Germans needed for their war effort.

It didn't matter. The Foreign Office was so taken aback by the violent reaction to Churchill's speech that it immediately disavowed it. Not only was the fighting lord's call to arms too provocative for the neutrals; it was too inflammatory for his own government, as well as the masses of the democratic nations on both sides of the Atlantic who were still, as Nicholson noted, pacifist at heart. The British bulldog's voice was not welcome—yet.[75]

In the end, Churchill's speech had only been rhetoric. But what rhetoric. No one could deny the basic truth of Churchill's message: the fact was that the Finns, in their fight with the Soviets, were indeed showing what free men could do, and the thrilling example of the Finnish nation, "superb, nay, sublime in the face of tyranny," who had thus far successfully beaten that threat, was sufficiently inspiring for some 12,000 men from nearly two dozen nations around the world to risk their lives to fight for her.

Unfortunately for Finland, Churchill's message wasn't sufficiently persuasive to cause the governments of Sweden or Norway—or the United States, for that matter—to forsake their coveted and, as events would all too soon prove, delusory neutrality and completely cast their lot with the "sublime" Finns.

∗

While Churchill was broadcasting his paean to the Finns via the BBC, Semyon Timoshenko was methodically preparing for his imminent push on the Karelian Isthmus, touring the front, familiarizing himself with the terrain, studying Finnish defenses, bringing up new, first-line troops from around Russia, and putting his revived million-man assault force through an intensive program in winter warfare.

Timoshenko was a great believer in Suvorov's maxim, "The harder you study, the easier the battle." And so he studied, and he prepared, and so did his men. No more cannon fodder or mass suicidal attacks for him. His troops, the new Russian commander made clear to his underlings, would be the best in the Soviet Union. His troops would advance in coherent echelons, not shapeless squares. His army and air force would go in forward, in tight formation, in constant communication with each other as well as headquarters, according to Timoshenko's revised tactical doctrine, which he had adapted after studying the artillery tactics of the First World War.[76] Thus, the final assault on the Finnish fortifications would begin with a massive, systematic preparatory artillery barrage. While the cannonade was taking place, the combined armed units would assemble at their jumping-off points thirty minutes before the attack.

"Then," as Carl Van Dyke explains, "when the regimental commander received the order from divisional headquarters to begin the attack he [would be] instructed to order the artillery commanders to switch from artillery preparation to creeping barrage in order to pave the way for the assault by combined arms units."[77] According to Timoshenko's carefully calibrated system, forty-eight pieces of artillery were to be concentrated in every kilometer in the area of the actual assault, just as they were in the successful Brusilov Offensive of 1917, one of the imperial Russian army's few successes during the First World War. "Strict battle control was required because combined arms units were following in the wake of the creeping barrage. Battle control fell to the regimental commander who was responsible for maintaining continuous communication with his artillery commanders via radio, telephone and courier. Advancing 200 meters behind the creeping barrage [would be] the first echelon infantry and tanks, clearing [the] way through the defensive obstacles up to the fortified fire points."

Timoshenko had a special name for the tactical doctrine he developed to reduce the Mannerheim Line: "The wall of fire."[78]

∗

Walter Duranty of the *New York Times* laid out the stakes very clearly in his dispatch of January 20, 1940. According to Duranty, Stalin and his advisors had been originally divided about whether to agree to an armistice, "which would be tantamount to an admission of failure to conquer that small and stubborn nation" or to launch a new, possibly costly, offensive.[79]

Apparently the double disgrace of Suomussalmi and Raate Road had decided that issue, according to Duranty: "It is now proved that the Russians have decided that the prestige of the Red Army must be regained and that [it was possible] to do so with a massive coup de force. The Russians are now concentrating more of their forces and supplies on the southern and eastern borders of Finland. Their aim is to crush the Finns before military supplies being sent to Finland from foreign countries can arrive in volume." There was no doubt now: Semyon Timoshenko would have his Wall of Fire.[80]

6

Grand Hotel

January 21–February 5, 1940

The soldiers of Finland, in six weeks of war, have made a brave beginning on the most glorious page in Finland's history. If they can fight off the Russian juggernaut for a few months more, they will have made Finland's name forever.
　　—Life Magazine, January 21, 1940

During the very intense air raids directed against the civil population of Finland yesterday, several hundred Soviet aeroplanes dropped about 3,000 bombs in various districts, including Tampere, Turku, Pori, Raumo, Lahti and Kouvola. There were also many machine gun attacks from the air, but thanks to efficient organization of civilian defense, as far as is known only three civilians were killed and 35 wounded.
　　—The Times (London), January 21, 1940

I am a Communist party member, but for the moment I am puzzled and admit it. I was not surprised when we were called on to occupy Finland. We had been told that the people of Finland, like those in Poland, needed us to help them. I believed it and I think our leaders believed it, but we found a different story. We found every Finn was against us, and we were out-maneuvered and out-fought. And then I began to wonder.
　　—Captain Alexsei Klimstoff, captured Russian aviator,
　　New York Times, January 25, 1940

While the new Russian commander, Semyon Timoshenko, meticulously went about preparing for the next Soviet offensive, and Eric Malm and Olavi Eronen tried to keep warm on their side of the Mannerheim Line, and Nikolai Bavin kept a sharp lookout and tried to keep warm on his, an interesting and momentous development was taking place on the diplomatic front. It occurred not in Finland, or in Russia for that matter, but in Sweden; not in a chancery, embassy, or government building, but in a hotel; and not just any hotel, but the grandest in northern Europe—Stockholm's Grand Hotel. It was here, in a "secret" room above the tinkling glasses and shimmying dancers of the Cafe Royal, that two old friends, as well as two of the era's most extraordinary women, a playwright and an ambassador, respectively, participated in one of the most unusual, long-running *kaffee klatsches* in history, as well as one that had a direct impact on the war.

The playwright's name was Hella Wuolijoki; her friend was Alexandra Kollontai, the Russian ambassador. Both women had colorful vitae, to say the least. A native of Estonia, Wuolijoki married Salo Wuolijoki, a friend of Lenin, and a member of the Finnish parliament in 1918, taking Finnish nationality. Divorcing him in 1924, the Estonian-born firebrand decided to become a playwright, writing dramas that combined her left-wing views with her emerging feminism. Wuolijoki also was a businesswoman, working as a director of a Karelian timber company, as well as chairwoman of the board of an oil company, Suomen Nafta. She also hosted a salon for like-minded souls at her apartment and her estate at Marleback, in southern Finland, near Kouvola. A formidable woman indeed, as well as a dangerous one in the eyes of many conservative Finns.[1]

Likewise Alexandra Kollontai. One of the legendary figures of the Russian Revolution, Kollontai's father was a tsarist general. Her mother was the daughter of a wealthy Finnish timber merchant; hence her interest in Finland. Educated in Switzerland and elsewhere by private tutors, Kollontai returned to her native land in 1899, where she joined the Russian Social Democratic Party and witnessed the popular 1905 uprising and bloody crackdown by tsarist authorities known as Bloody Sunday. She also began writing, making Finland one of her main themes; one of her published works was called "Finland and Socialism."[2]

Returning to Russia in 1917 to participate in the Revolution, Kollontai became People's Commissar for Social Welfare, in which capacity she was an outspoken advocate of women's equality. At the same time, somewhat to the dismay of her old comrade, Lenin, she also became known for her theory of non-possessive love, asserting that the sexual act must be seen as something "as natural as having a glass of water." Such views, as well as other diversionist inclinations, could well have caused Kollontai to lose her life in Moscow's treacherous waters.[3]

Instead, the Party deemed that Kollontai's talents could be put to more useful (and less troublesome) purposes as a diplomat. So, in 1923, she began a long period of exile under diplomatic guise, serving as Soviet ambassador to Norway and Mexico—reputedly becoming the world's first female ambassador—before alighting in Stockholm in 1937. It was probably just as well for the natural-born rebel that she wasn't around during the purges of the 1930s; by the time her boat docked in the Stockholm archipelago, she was one of the few "old Bolsheviks" left around to tell the tale. Evidently, it humored Stalin to keep Kollontai there. Quite likely, Molotov and he expected Kollontai, then in her late sixties, to also expire there. They certainly didn't expect their envoy to get mixed up in foreign policy matters.[4]

*

It all began with a letter that Wuolijoki, who was distressed about the war, wrote to Vaino Tanner in early January, in which she offered to use her connections with the Soviet regime to get the talks between the two belligerents in the yet undeclared war going again. This was precisely what the distressed Finnish foreign minister had been trying to do for weeks. Specifically, Wuolijoki proposed that she go to Stockholm to talk to her old salon friend and kindred spirit Alexandra Kollontai.

Unsurprisingly, Tanner was caught off-guard by Wuolijoki's unorthodox offer, as Max Jakobson writes:

> It was, on the face of it, a bizarre idea. One of Finland's most prominent fellow-travellers, Mme. Wuolijoki was known as an eccentric lady whose political reliability and discretion were far from impeccable. Her plays dealt with strong-willed "progressive" women who outwit their masculine opponents in politics, and it must have seemed to Tanner that her proposition was more like an outline for the plot of another Wuolijoki drama than a realistic diplomatic move.[5]

Nevertheless, surprised though he was, Tanner, who had tried virtually everything else to get the Kremlin to talk to him—including his bathetic radio appeal of December 15, while putting out additional diplomatic feelers via other intermediaries, all for naught—decided "that Finland could not afford to leave any chance, however remote, of re-establishing contact with the Soviet government untried." In the meantime, Kollontai, who was as anxious as Wuolijoki to end the war that was devastating her beloved Karelia, had indicated that she would be pleased to receive her old friend.[6]

After conferring with Ryti and Paasikivi—apparently Tanner thought the idea was too absurd to run it past Mannerheim—Wuolijoki, "the most extraordinary ambassador Finland has ever had," was permitted to travel to Stockholm to meet with Kollontai and see what she could do. Thus credentialed, the special envoy, traveling incognito, left for Stockholm, arriving on January 10. From then on, for virtually every day for the next three weeks, Wuolijoki would enter the hotel's famed revolving doors and make her way to an upper-floor room, where she would meet her old friend, Madame Kollontai. Doubtless Tanner had little if any hope of anything serious developing from this strange gambit. Instead, his decision to deputize Wuolijoki may well have been the smartest move that he made during the *Talvisota*.[7]

It didn't work out quite the way he expected, but it worked: "Their [Wuolijoki's and Kollontai's] way of conducting business was, by standards of professional diplomacy, horrifyingly unconventional and haphazard," writes Jakobson. "They kept no proper records; they freely spiced their reports with personal comments; they drew upon their vivid imaginations to embellish, and improve upon, their official instructions; in short, they acted like two matchmakers determined to lead, or if need be, mislead, a reluctant and suspicious couple into matrimony."[8]

"But in the end," as the historian observes, "they got Finnish-Soviet peace negotiations started." Indeed, the back channel to the Kremlin that Wuolijoki set up at the Grand Hotel worked so well that on February 5 Tanner himself came knocking on Madame Kollontai's hotel room.[9]

By then, the new Russian offensive on the Karelian Isthmus had begun. But nothing would have stopped that. Stalin had decreed: the stain on the escutcheon of the Red Army had to be removed, *would* be removed, irrespective of the human cost. Timoshenko had his orders; they were irrevocable, irrespective of any talks, unorthodox or otherwise. Suomussalmi and Raate Road would be avenged. Nothing less than the honor of the Soviet Union demanded it.

At the same time, Stalin and Molotov, increasingly apprehensive about the possibility of getting tangled up with the English and French—something they very much didn't want—simultaneously decided that they would start talking to Helsinki again so that they could end the war as soon as Russia's tarnished military prestige had been restored. Of course, no one bothered to tell Otto Ville Kuusinen about this, much less Edward Hynninen and his comrades in the Finnish People's Army, as they continued to drill for their prospective triumphal parade into Helsinki.

*

While Madame Wuolijoki and Madame Kollontai continued with their tête-à-tête at the Grand Hotel, several hundred kilometers to the east at Finnish General Headquarters in Mikkeli, Gustaf Mannerheim continued with his usual routine. He rose early to receive his first situation report before proceeding to the map tables to check the latest dispositions, as his chief operations aide, Aksel Airo, also known as "the quiet general," hovered nearby, nodding and taking notes, while occasionally giving his own advice.

Like Charles de Gaulle of France, the contemporary military figure he most resembles, Mannerheim was not one who easily accepted criticism from his subordinates, as his earlier set-to with General Osterman made clear (although he seems to have listened to Airo). Nor was he given to small talk or self-doubt. Mannerheim knew what he was doing, and the extraordinary results he and his men had achieved since November 30 had largely borne him out.

De Gaulle, whose rendezvous with destiny waited down the road, felt that he was France incarnate and acted accordingly. Did his fellow elitist, Mannerheim, believe the same of himself and Finland? Not quite, but close. If the Swedish-speaking Finn didn't feel himself to be the living embodiment of *Suomi*—a little difficult to do given his rusty Finnish—he certainly felt that it was his destiny to save it, as de Gaulle felt with France. So far, to be sure, he had done a pretty good job of it. Certainly he had made very few mistakes.

Mannerheim's arrogance—unlike that of de Gaulle, who really hadn't accomplished anything as yet—was earned. That said, his ramrod posture and robust mien notwithstanding, there was no getting around the fact that he was seventy-two years old. At an age when most of his peers were frolicking with their grandchildren or poring over their stamp collections, Mannerheim was actively commanding, on an hour-to-hour basis, the armed forces of a nation battling for its life against a vastly superior foe—a titanic responsibility that would have crushed a younger man. It invigorated him, but it also drained him. By the end of the day after twelve or fourteen hours on duty, he would look very much like the aged man he was.

Never did Mannerheim look more careworn than when Airo brought him the daily casualty list, reminding him that despite the relative lack of activity on the main front, in Karelia, the army was still incurring serious losses. Thus, for example, on January 25, the 7th Division at Taipale announced that its overall losses since the beginning of the war numbered over 800 men killed in action and more than 2,000 wounded. Although total casualties in January were down from December—3,300, as opposed to 5,400—that was certainly nothing to cheer about.[10]

Mannerheim would take the morbid sheet from Airo and look out the window at some unknown point in the distance. The victories at Suomussalmi and Raate Road had not significantly affected his thinking (even though he now seemed to think that his men could hold off the Russians until spring). Finland might appear to be winning the war, but this was not a war that Finland could win, not at least without active, significant, and immediate help, and, despite the promising noises emanating from the British and French, the prospect of that occurring seemed to be diminishing by the day.[11]

Not that the cautious Mannerheim put much store in the prospects of Allied intervention, as his biographer Jagerskiold notes:

> From the start Mannerheim was distrustful of intervention by the Western powers. He had not supported the activity of Finnish diplomats in Paris and London, because of his fear that intervention in the north would force Germany to the Soviet side without, of itself, having any decisive significance for the war being waged by Finland. He did not believe that the Western powers had sufficient resources for such a large undertaking, and he knew the difficult character of the terrain in the far north on the shores of the Arctic Ocean.[12]

Too, Mannerheim remembered the messy and embarrassing debacle that resulted the last time the Allies tried to insert themselves into the northern latitudes, in 1919, when they sent an expeditionary force to northern Russia to help put down the Bolshevik revolution and wound up being put down and kicked out themselves.

The Russians remembered 1919 as well. They encouraged other countries that were thinking of intervening in the Soviet's unfinished Finnish business to do the same, as Alexander Scherbakoff, secretary of the Moscow Communist party, declared at a memorial mass at the Bolshoi commemorating the sixteenth anniversary of Lenin's death. The Soviet Union, said Scherbakoff in a fiery speech in the presence of Stalin, Molotov, and Voroshilov, was as prepared as it was in 1919 to "crush" any foreign meddling and determined to "free the Finnish workers from their oppression."[13]

On the other hand, if the Allies could get him and his men some artillery and airplanes quickly, that might make a difference. Perhaps he and his men might be able to hold off the Soviet until the spring. And then, who knew? As it was, Mannerheim was heartened and gratified by the slowly increasing amount of men and munitions that were arriving from abroad, especially from Sweden.

On January 19, following the apparent deaths of three Swedish aviators after two of their planes crashed and another was shot down—actually only one Swede, Anders Zachau, was killed, while the other two were taken prisoner and later tortured by the Russians—Mannerheim felt it significant enough to make their deaths the subject of his order of the day.

Otherwise, the news was generally good. Witness the upbeat Finnish communiqué issued on January 22, 1940:

Land—On the Karelian Isthmus there was chiefly harassing artillery fire on January 21st. Our artillery silenced a few enemy batteries. In the late afternoon, the enemy began concentrating for a new attack on Taipale. The attack was quenched in its infancy. In the course of the day our troops destroyed two tanks.

After yesterday's fighting about 120 dead have been counted in our foremost positions, and on the ground in front of our lines are the bodies of several hundred others.[14]

The confident-sounding communiqué went on to describe in mocking terms the Soviet's clumsy attempt at psychological warfare: "The enemy tried to give effect to his attacks by loudspeakers mounted in his positions, which exhorted our men to surrender, declaring that [Viipuri] would be taken within 48 hours and that the Germans were coming to help him and will kill all Finns."[15]

One wonders what Adolf Hitler would have said to that. Not interfering with the Russians while they attempted to "emancipate" Finland was one thing, but invoking the Wehrmacht's name in vain was quite another. (Apparently, this sort of thing stopped very quickly after that; whether or not this was the result of a protest from the German government is not clear.)

Next, the bulletin referred to the newest front on the war, north of Lake Ladoga, where the Supreme Command, evidently ignoring the lessons of Kemijoki River and Suomussalmi, would let another division, the 54th, be "chopped up" in the frozen morass of the Finnish wilderness. Hjalmar Siilasvuo, the hero of Suomussalmi, and the battle-hardened men of the 9th Division, now re-equipped with the booty they had captured at Raate Road, were in the process of seeing to that:

Northeast of Lake Ladoga our troops are fighting successfully and repelling the enemy's repeated attacks.

In the direction of Kitela, the enemy lost three officers and about 120 men and five enemy tanks and armored cars were destroyed.

In the direction of Loimola the enemy attacked our positions at Kollaanjoki. The attack was repulsed, the enemy losing about 450 men killed and five tanks, which our men destroyed.[16]

And so on. Indeed, if one were to judge from the Finnish military communiqués issued throughout January and well into February, all was well after the final Russian offensive commenced.

Of course, Mannerheim, ever the realist, knew otherwise, but he tried not to let his pessimism show. After all, part of Mannerheim's job—one could argue the most important part—was to project supreme confidence in himself, his men, and his mission, even if that mission was inherently doomed.

No general ever played the part better—even during the occasional Russian bombing raid. In the event, Mikkeli was one of the most heavily bombed Finnish cities during the *Talvisota*, doubtless in part because Mannerheim's headquarters was located there. All told, the Russian Air Force raided the headquarters' city three dozen times during the war, killing over fifty of its citizens and, at one point, nearly obliterating the city center.[17]

In early January, Mannerheim was having his usual lunch at the Mikkeli Seurahuone with his staff when the sirens signaling yet another visit from the Red Air Force sounded. True to form, despite the pleadings of his companions, the redoubtable commander-in-chief refused to interrupt his meal and repair with them to the nearest air raid shelter. "If Finland needs me I shall live," he is alleged to have said. "If not, why go to a shelter?" The next moment a bomb exploded just outside, shaking the building, breaking several windows, and sending the panic-stricken *lottas*, who had hitherto refused to leave the marshal's side, running out into the street—with the exception of the one who had been serving Mannerheim. When the raid was over and the danger past, Mannerheim is said to have called the iron-willed *lotta* over to him and pinned a medal for bravery on her uniform. Then he calmly continued with his lunch.[18]

After the raid, Finnish Army headquarters was moved to Otava, twelve kilometers away, just to be safe, and then yet again in early March to Inkila Manor, another thirty-five kilometers away, after the former was bombed as well. In this sense, Mannerheim was a moving target. He may not have visited the front very often, but because of the incessant Russian raids—which would grow in intensity after January—he was certainly in constant danger.

In addition to his normal duties, Mannerheim also received an increasing number of foreign guests and dignitaries at this time. One of the most prominent of these was the British trade unionist Sir Walter Citrine, who led a fact-finding delegation that visited Finland between January 21 and February 4. One of Britain's most powerful and influential labor figures, Citrine was general secretary of the country's Trade Union Confederation, a post he had held since 1926 (and would continue in until 1945).

Biting cold notwithstanding, Citrine and his bundled-up associates were favorably impressed by what they found during their much-publicized two-week sojourn in Finland, during which they divided their time between inspecting the Finnish home front, visiting schools, factories, other workplaces, and the various battlefronts, and interviewing soldiers and officers as well as captured Russian prisoners.[19]

They found that the Communist propaganda machine's picture of an oppressed, downtrodden Finland, which apparently still carried considerable weight in left-wing English circles, could not have been further from the truth. If anything, as Citrine noted in *My Finnish Diary*, the widely read Penguin paperback he wrote about the trip, living and working conditions in Finland were as good if not better than in Britain: "A legal eight hour day was in existence, wages were comparatively high, twelve days' holiday were normally in operation and proper overtime rates were paid. Food was excellent and cheaper than in the United Kingdom, but clothing, housing and manufacturing articles seemed dearer."[20]

Less surprisingly, Citrine also found that most of the positive things he had heard and read about the Finnish troops *were* true. Like other Western observers, he was particularly taken with the way the Finns managed to keep warm and clean in the subzero temperatures at the front.

> We visited the fighting units, and saw vast masses of captured tanks, mobile artillery, and guns. It seemed as though the Russians must have lost most of their weapons, but in reality it could only have been a small part. The Finns were very ingenious. They had devised strongly constructed underground quarters for the troops, heated against the intense cold, and also stables where the horses were carefully looked after. The soldiers were clean and spruce, and regularly used the steam bath, the *sauna,* so popular in Finland.[21]

Next to his initiation to sauna, Citrine was perhaps most impressed by Mannerheim himself, of whom he had already read and heard much. Although Mannerheim, with his manifold responsibilities, was not keen about visitors in general, he was pleased to make time for those whom he thought might be able to produce concrete assistance to his underequipped men, particularly those from England.

If anything, Citrine's expectations of the marshal were surpassed when they met: "Seventy two years old, he stood well over six feet, and spoke English with a noticeable accent. He had a strong face, with great powers of concentration visible on his brows and a determined square jaw. He wore no ribbons, a single large white cross with gold borders being his only decoration."[22]

After the usual salutations, Mannerheim got right to the point. He told Sir Walter that his men were outgunned and outranged. The thing they needed most was heavy guns, particularly howitzers. Would Citrine please see what he could do to obtain these, Mannerheim asked with emotion? "Your army is the best equipped in the world, Sir Walter," Mannerheim continued, before he returned to his small, well-organized office to review the latest situation reports. "It doesn't matter where I have met them. I have always admired their equipment. That is why I hope that Great Britain can now spare some for little Finland."[23]

Citrine vowed that he would do his best to help, a promise he repeated in a later interview with the Finnish press. "If the Finns had not made so brave a stand Britain would only have shrugged and said 'sorry.' But now little Finland deserved our admiration and this admiration is resulting in material aid. We understand that the Finns will be in a far more difficult position in the spring and we will do our best to get all the help they deserve before that time."[24]

Sir Walter was good to his word. When he returned to London, he told reporters that the Finns desperately needed at least two divisions of men of good quality, able to withstand the rigors of the Finnish climate. In the meantime, their most vital requirement was for heavy planes.[25]

On the other side of the Atlantic, America continued to go wild for Finland. Although the U.S. Congress might well be dragging its feet in passing a new $20 million loan for the fighting Finns, the American people made up for their government's timorousness by engaging in a veritable orgy of parties, dances, auctions, and benefits to raise money for the blue and white.

Thus, for example, on January 21, an exhibit of paintings by 146 American artists, including such noted painters as Edward Hopper, went up for display at the prestigious Grand Central gallery at the Waldorf Astoria, proceeds from same to be donated to Finnish relief.[26]

Broadway also did its part, with virtually every play on the Great White Way holding special benefit performances for Finland, including one for *Skylark*, a new play starring the well-known Gertrude Lawrence; the now familiar dynamic duo of Herbert Hoover and Hjalmar Procope were in attendance. (The only dissenter on Broadway was left-wing producer Herbert Shumlin, who refused to allow a benefit performance of his current production of *Tobacco Road*, a decision that was seconded by his friend and favorite playwright, Lillian Hellman, who also refused to allow the cast of her long-running play *The Little Foxes* to do the same. Like that of its brethren chapters around the world, the American Communist Party line, depicting the Finns as the aggressors, died hard.)[27]

Meanwhile, Robert Sherwood, a member of the Algonquin Hotel's famous

Round Table, was holed up feverishly revising his pro-Finnish, anti-isolationist play. *There Shall Be No Night*, he decided to call it, after the well-known passage in the Book of Revelation: *There shall be no night there: They need no lamp nor light of the sun, for the Lord God gives them light. . . .*

✱

Not every friend of Finland sought the limelight. Thus the anonymous big-hearted Washington, D.C., donor who bought out the entire second night's showing of *Gone with the Wind* resold the seats for $3 to $10 apiece and turned over the $13,000 in proceeds to the Hoover fund.

High society was also getting into the act. Well-heeled New Yorkers were literally jumping for Finland—or at least their horses were—thanks to the Metropolitan Equestrian Club, which announced a special high-jumping contest, followed by a supper dance cabaret at the Waldorf Astoria, where, according to the festive announcement, "several well-known orchestras will play for continuous dancing in the grand ballroom, where there will be a profusion of balloons in the pale blue and white of Finland, and red, white and blue of the United States. The patriotic motif will be repeated on the tables surrounding the dance floor and in the adjoining rooms."[28]

Sports associations, particularly those representing winter sports, were also eager to assist the cause. Thus, on January 20, the National Ski Association announced, somewhat grumpily, that it too would jump on the Finnish bandwagon, even though it hadn't been asked yet: "Golf, tennis, hockey, boxing, baseball and polo are asked to do something for the Finns. Skiing does not have to be asked: the Finns are our friends and we have every reason to admire them more than the followers of any other sport."[29]

Then, on January 20, the Hoover fund announced the ultimate fund-raising coup: the world's most famous runner, Paavo Nurmi, along with his countryman and fellow track specialist Taisto Maki, had agreed to come to the United States to give a special series of exhibitions to raise money for Finnish relief. At forty-three, Nurmi, the great Olympics star of the 1920s, was too old to fight, yet Finnish forty-two-year-olds had just been called to service. Maki, twenty-nine, who had broken several of his friend's records before going into the army, had been wounded by a shell splinter during the initial Russian offensive in Karelia, from which he had recently recovered.

Following their tour of the United States, an elated Hoover told reporters, the two celebrated runners would be feted with their own ticker-tape parade up Broadway. Of course, all this ballyhoo was played up in the Finnish papers.[30]

✱

Meanwhile, back in Stockholm, activity on the back-door diplomatic channel that Madame Wuolijoki and Madame Kollontai had contrived was beginning to pick up.

Unsurprisingly, Vyacheslav Molotov's first reaction upon learning about the Wuolijoki-Kollontai dialogue was as skeptical as Tanner's; however, he didn't brush it aside. Instead, he dispatched Boris Yartsev, the one-time second secretary to the Soviet embassy in Helsinki and undercover spy who had first sounded out the Finnish government about the possibility of territorial concessions back in 1938, to check it out. In the meantime, the Swedish foreign minister, Christian Gunther, had also learned of the odd doings taking place above the Cafe Royal. Consequently, on January 25, he decided once again to offer his good offices to the indirect but rapidly cohering "peace channel" that Wuolijoki and Kollontai had set up.[31]

Apparently, Yartsev reported favorably back to Molotov, because four days later, on January 29, the latter sent Kollontai a message for Gunther for transmission to Tanner. The first sentence of the message could not have been more dramatic: "The Government of the Soviet Union is not opposed in principle to negotiating an agreement with the Ryti-Tanner Government."[32]

"With these words," Jakobson writes, "the Kuusinen government, the chief obstacle to peace, was dispatched to the limbo of lost Communist causes and was never heard from again."[33]

There was steel in the gloved hand Molotov extended, however; in the same message in which he asked what concessions Helsinki was now prepared to make, the determined Soviet commissar also strongly implied that there wasn't much time for the Finnish government to decide.

Risto Ryti, Vaino Tanner, and Juho Paasikivi, the triumvirate running the Finnish government, were divided. As he had been during the original Moscow talks, Paasikivi was in favor of giving the Russians a base on the Gulf of Finland—if not at Hanko, as they originally demanded, then somewhere else. Ryti and Tanner were not. Nor was Mannerheim, at the time.[34]

Instead, after conferring, the trio decided to offer a compromise: the Finnish government was willing to make some territorial concessions to the Kremlin on the isthmus; it also proposed that the Gulf of Finland be neutralized. However, it was silent regarding the main Soviet demand, for Hanko. "Finland must also consider her own security," read the note the government drafted for Ryti to take to Kollontai. "The importance of this has been shown by recent events."[35]

Ryti, in a hopeful mood, then flew to Stockholm to deliver the note to the Russian envoy for her to transmit to Moscow. He would not be optimistic for long.[36]

*

Once again, the Kremlin replied with artillery and bombs. On the morning of February 1, while the Finnish prime minister was still in Stockholm, and before he had had a chance to deliver his note to Madame Kollontai, the crashing overture of the long anticipated Russian offensive began, with its main point at Summa. Even Mannerheim was surprised by its vehemence, as he writes: "The barrage exceeded anything our troops had hitherto experienced. That was also true of the attacks from the air, with not less than 500 aircraft. At noon, the tanks rolled up, followed by infantry protected by smokescreens. The battle raged the whole day."

The attack was beaten back everywhere. "But," as Mannerheim notes, "we were soon to learn that this was only a beginning."[37]

The following day, by way of reinforcing the point, the Russian Air Force, which had been increasingly active over the last week, launched another great air offensive against Finland, as another armada of bombers and fighters hit numerous Finnish localities. In the most devastating raid, on the western port city of Pori, Russian bombers hit a bomb shelter killing fourteen people, while leveling much of the town. Sortavala in northern Karelia was also severely hit.[38]

The following day, Vaino Tanner himself, desperate to keep the flame of peace flickering, arrived at the Grand Hotel, as Jakobson relates: "The meeting was arranged in a conspiratorial manner. The place chosen was Madame Wuolijoki's room at the Grand Hotel. The Soviet diplomat went there first. Then at 11 A.M. Tanner slipped into the hotel through a back door and, avoiding the elevators in the crowded lobby, walked up the service stairs without meeting anybody before reaching the room. As soon as he had arrived, Madame Wuolijoki withdrew, leaving the Finnish foreign minister and the Soviet envoy alone for an hour to see what they would achieve."[39]

But Semyon Timoshenko's guns spoke first. The January "lull" was effectively over. The final act of the war had begun.

The Reckoning

February 6–March 13, 1940

7

The Red Army's Second Turn

February 6–23, 1940

*The barrage exceeded anything our troops had hitherto experienced.
That the Russians had now learned to "orchestrate" the different arms was
apparent from the way artillery fire was cleverly adapted to the movements
of the infantry.*
    —Gustaf Mannerheim, *Memoirs*

*In talking and fumbling we had lost three weeks, which cost us dearly,
since the battles at the front [had] taken an unfavourable turn.*
    —Vaino Tanner, *The Winter War*

*Forward, Samoilovskaia Company!
The overwhelmed enemy runs
And on the concrete reinforced fort
The Red Flag is already unfurled.
Thus the Division rolled
Like lava on the enemy,
Yesterday's flicker is today's flame.*
    —Poem by Alexsandr Tvardovsky dedicated to the men of
    the 123rd Division who broke through the Mannerheim
    Line on February 11, 1940

*The series of battles here may be called something like the "Summa miracle,"
comparable to the Somme and Verdun . . . .*
    —Finnish High Command, February 13, 1940

Vaino Tanner, the well-meaning if somewhat out-of-his-depth Finnish foreign minister, was bewildered. Tanner was often bewildered, but today, February 6, 1940, the sixty-ninth day of the as yet undeclared war between Finland and the Soviet Union, he was more bewildered than usual. Several minutes before, he had entered Alexandra Kollontai's room at the Grand Hotel in Stockholm full of hope. The Soviet ambassador, who, along with her friend the playwright Hella Wuolijoki, had finally managed to get peace talks going between Moscow and Helsinki, was holding a cable in her hands. Four days before, Tanner, Ryti, and Paasikivi, elated over Molotov's and Stalin's decision to reestablish communications with their government—the legitimate elected government of Finland, as opposed to the Terijoki one led by Otto Ville Kuusinen—had sent Moscow their opening terms for the new talks. Or, rather, for the prospective talks.[1]

On that day, February 2, Helsinki's negotiating position was still strong. Although the new, long-anticipated third Russian offensive on the Mannerheim Line had begun the day before with the biggest artillery barrage since the First World War, coupled with a no less stupendous aerial bombardment, Finnish morale was still high, buoyed by the great defensive victories at Suomussalmi and Raate Road—and further inspirited by what appeared to be the imminent destruction by Hjalmar Siilasvuo and the redeployed 9th Division of another Russian division north of Lake Ladoga—as well as the prospect of significant aid from abroad, not to mention the increasing number of foreign volunteers who were arriving. No ground had been lost—yet. No strongpoints had been lost—yet (at least none that had been reported). Pulverized though they were, sleep deprived though they were, the morale of the 100,000 Finnish soldiers who manned the undulating, 110-kilometer-long frontline fortifications protecting Finland proper remained strong, as did that of the Finnish public.[2]

The Finnish government's opening terms for the proposed peace negotiations —neutralization of the Gulf of Finland, the offer of some territory along the isthmus in return for an equal amount of territory from the Soviets—reflected that confidence. Helsinki—or at least the Tanner-Ryti-Paasikivi cabal that was now in effect running it—wanted peace, but a fair peace, as well as a peace that they could sell to the rest of the cabinet and the country as a whole. After nine weeks of war that had already killed over 9,000 Finnish soldiers and civilians and had left a considerable portion of the country in ruins from Soviet bombs, the Finnish government was prepared to bring the war to a close—particularly now that the Kremlin was no longer trying to replace it with a puppet regime of its own.[3]

However, it would not abase itself. And it was not prepared to hand over Hanko, as Molotov now again demanded. That demand stood, Molotov reiterated via Madame Kollontai three days later. Whereupon Tanner, desperate to keep the peace ball going, had stuck his neck out and offered an unnamed island in the Gulf of Finland on his own. That is where matters stood when Vaino Tanner walked into Madame Kollontai's room.

Vaino Tanner didn't need to read Molotov's telegram. The "tragic look" on the Soviet envoy's face said it all. "WE REGRET," the cable read, "THAT THE PROPOSAL" (for Tanner's proffered, as yet unnamed island) "DOES NOT OFFER SUFFICIENT BASIS FOR NEGOTIATIONS." So there it was, once again: the mailed Soviet fist in the velvet glove.[4]

Kollontai, seeing the stricken look on her guest's face, tried to soften the bad news by pointing out Molotov's "encouraging" tone. Perhaps, she said hopefully, if he could tell her which island he had in mind? Now Tanner balked. He felt that he had gone far out enough on his own. And with that, the Finnish foreign minister prepared to return to Helsinki to confer with the other members of the "peace faction" of the cabinet and try to figure out what to do next. And thus began three weeks of what Tanner later described as "talking and fumbling."[5]

If Vaino Tanner was perplexed when he left Madame Kollontai's room at the Grand Hotel, he was even more so when he returned to his underground office at Olympic Stadium in Helsinki and reviewed the most recent developments on the various diplomatic and military fronts.

There, amongst the large pile, was a cable from Harry Holma, the Finnish envoy to Paris, enthusiastically informing his chief of the decision taken by the Allies' Supreme Council, two days before, in which the British and French governments had definitely committed themselves to sending an Allied expeditionary force to relieve Finland. Operation Avon Head, the nebulous operation was called.[6]

Tanner himself was less thrilled about Operation Avon Head. For one, the details of the expedition, which called for transporting an unspecified number of British and French troops to Narvik, then having some of them veer off to Finland via Swedish territory, were vague. How did the Allies expect to secure the cooperation of the Norwegian and Swedish governments, both of which had voiced their opposition in strong terms to such a plan? Holma's upbeat message said little about this.

Tanner also wasn't happy about Holma's role in the strange affair. "I was astonished at Holma's actions in Paris," Tanner wrote. "Without special authority or instructions from Helsinki, he and Colonel Paasonen"—the same Paasonen who had accompanied him and Paasikivi to Moscow the previous November, now the Finnish military attaché in Paris—"had zealously tried to secure the assistance of the Western powers, and the fact that matters had reached this stage was clearly, in part, the result of their actions. With this information," Tanner said, "the situation had become more complicated."[7]

The meeting of British and French governments that took place in Paris on February 5, 1940, the fifth meeting of the Allied War Council, was one of the best attended such parleys of the war thus far. The British delegation, led by Prime Minister Neville Chamberlain, included no fewer than four members of his cabinet, three generals, including the British chief of staff, General Edmund Ironside, one admiral, and a squadron of other diplomats. The French, led by President Edouard Daladier and the French chief of staff, General Gamelin, were also well represented.

Unlike some of the other prior fractious meetings between the two prickly Allies, comity and goodwill were present in quantity. The only quality that was eminently lacking was common sense. "The whole meeting," as Douglas Clark writes, "as one looks back at it, seems suffused with fantasy and wishful thinking."[8]

Somehow, thanks in part to the ministrations of politicians and military writers on both sides of the channel, as well as a lot of wooly thinking on the parts of the respective British and military staffs, especially that of General Edmund Ironside, Great Britain's storied, if somewhat befogged, chief of staff—who had held command of one sort or another since the Boer War and had only recently been made chief of staff (a position he would not hold for long)—the Allies' vague commitment of December to assist Finland had cohered into a plan, or something of a plan.

Some idea of the character of the cloudy—and cynical—thinking that went into that plan can be gleaned from Ironside's diary. Thus, on Christmas Day 1939, following the last council, where the outlines of the grandiose feint-cum-expedition first took form, the British chief of staff confided: "I believe we have stumbled on a means of upsetting the [Germans]. One can only call it 'stumbling,' for we have given it no steady thought."[9]

Now six weeks later, here the Allies were attentively listening to the British explain the still hazy, bifurcated scheme—one which called for, in effect, shifting the main locus of the European war from the stalemated Western front to the Nordic region. Which, of course, was the real reason it appealed to Daladier and the French staff. If French blood was to be shed, let it be shed far away from France. Daladier and General Gamelin, who had just finished overseeing the completion of the "impregnable" Maginot Line, were even willing to commit their elite Alpine unit, the legendary *Chasseurs Alpins,* to the project; besides, the Grenoble-based French mountain troops would be more in their snowy element in the northern latitudes.[10]

Most important, Chamberlain and Daladier, neither of whom was known for decisiveness, would be seen by their respective publics, restive after months of "phony war," to be doing *something* to hurt the Germans, as well as something active to succor the heroic Finns, over and above the not inconsiderable material aid they had already committed.

The French, for their part, had already donated:

145 planes, including 30 fighters
496 artillery pieces of various caliber
5,000 machine guns
400,000 rifles
200,000 hand grenades[11]

The British had been no less generous, allocating the following for shipment to Finland:

120 fighters
24 Bristol Blenheim bombers
10,000 anti-tank mines
50,000 hand grenades
25 howitzers
100 machine guns[12]

Because of the difficulties involved in shipping—or flying—the aforementioned equipment to Finland, most of which had to be transshipped via Norway, only a fraction had yet arrived in Helsinki, or would do so before the end of the war. Nor was all of the equipment for free. Still, no one could deny that the Allies had put their materiel where their mouths were.[13]

But now, according to the agreed-upon Anglo-Franco plan, His Majesty's Government and the Third Republic were committing themselves to sending their own regular troops to the cause.

According to the plan, as outlined for the assembled emissaries, the operation called for some three British and French divisions to embark for Narvik and three other northern Norwegian ports on or about March 20, with the first detachment of 15,000 setting off for Finland via neutral Norway and Sweden, and the remaining 10,000 entraining for Gallivare, in Sweden, to secure the iron ore that Germany needed for its own war effort.[14]

That, Chamberlain told the assembled politicians and brass hats, was the gist of the thing. To be sure, Chamberlain reminded the Council, as did Ironside, the Allies had to remember that their principal enemy was Germany.

> At the same time, they could not allow Finland to be crushed in the war with the Soviet Union since this would be a major defeat for the West. The correct Allied strategy for Scandinavia was, therefore, to combine aid to the Finns with a thrust at Germany's war-making resources. . . . A drive from the Norwegian cast to the Finnish frontier by way of the precious ironfields [at Gallivare] would achieve the double purpose.[15]

It was really a splendid plan, Chamberlain insisted. Here was the means, indeed, "to kill two birds with one stone." He and his military staff had considered every possible contingency, he insisted, including the likelihood that Hitler would be provoked to oppose the initial Allied landing. That, after all, was the point of the thing—or one of the points of the project.[16]

"No doubt Hitler would move," Douglas Clark writes, in his reconstruction of the cloudy thinking behind the strange, inchoate scheme, "so the Allied expeditionary force must be sufficiently big and well organized to sustain Norway and Sweden against the counterblow." Nor would volunteers do, much appreciated as they were. Regular Allied divisions were essential. Three or four at the least.[17]

The impressive expedition had been carefully thought through, the British prime minister declared, obviously pleased with himself. But then someone had the clarity and courage to ask the prime minister: Really? Would not the arrival of regular troops in the war zone serve to provoke the Soviets?[18]

Absolutely not, Chamberlain replied, evenly. "They could go in the guise of 'volunteers,' like the regular Italian soldiers Rome had sent to Spain during the Civil War."[19]

And what about the Norwegians and Swedes, who had continued to reject the notion of Allied aid all along, while emphasizing their intention to maintain their neutral status? How—and why—could they be induced to go along with Operation Avon Head, especially since it virtually guaranteed that their countries would be swept into the war? Of course, Chamberlain had thought about this. His response: have the Finns themselves call on their fellow League of Nations members and Nordic brothers to open their borders, and railroads to the Helsinki-bound AEF, as per the League's original directive.[20]

Or, as Clark puts it: "At an appropriate moment the Finnish Government should appeal publicly for Western military support and request Oslo and Stockholm to allow the Allied expeditionary force passage under the Geneva pledge. The West would then promise the neutrals all necessary armed backing to meet a German attack and all would be well."

But would it, Daladier meekly wondered? "What if the Norwegians and Swedes still refused to cooperate? Chamberlain shrugged off the objection. They might talk about their neutral rights and lodge formal protests; but that they would try to stop the expedition by force he regarded as utterly improbable." And so what Geoffrey Cox would call "surely the maddest of all the strategic ideas which were to emerge in World War II" was officially under way.[21]

As Clark acidly notes, there were so many holes in the Allies' supposedly foolproof plan it was hard to know where to begin: "The risks of goading the Soviet Union into open war with the Allies were brushed aside. The power and competence of the German war machine were under-valued. Troops and resources of priceless value to the Western Front were to be transplanted from one war to another. The determination of Norway and Sweden to maintain their neutrality was misjudged, and, by Chamberlain at least, virtually disregarded."[22]

And on top of all these miscalculations, the whole thing depended on the Finns pulling the trigger: "Worst of all, the decision to hinge the dispatch of Western forces to Scandinavia on an appeal by Finland was almost incredibly irresponsible. Helsinki might make the appeal. It might not. In effect, the Western powers were submitting themselves, their war policy, their future strategy—perhaps their very survival—to the will of this little State."[23]

Of course, no one bothered to inform the Helsinki government about this. It would find out in good time, as the Cabinet would, several days later, via the plan's chief cheerleader, the longtime (since 1927) Finnish ambassador to Paris Harri Holma. Just like his Washington counterpart, Hjalmar Procope, Holma had become a major figure in the French capitol since the invasion. Apparently he didn't mind being left out of the Council meeting. Two months before, Tanner had instructed Holma to get the French to do something. Now, thanks in no small part to his ministrations, the Daladier and Chamberlain governments *were* actually doing something—even though that vague something made no coherent sense.[24]

"By comparison with the contemporary, typically meticulous German plans, these Allied preparations [were] vague, irresolute and amateurish," as one historian puts it. "The pretext of going to help Finland [was] most unconvincing since [the plan's] obvious intention [was] to devote more effort to stopping the Swedish iron ore reaching Germany."[25]

The communiqué the Allies issued after their powwow could not have been less clear. Finland was not even mentioned: "The Supreme War Council examined from all angles the diverse elements in the present situation with regard to the general conduct of the war in the spirit of close cooperation which inspires the action of the two governments. Complete agreement was reached on all points considered."[26]

Little wonder that Tanner was perplexed, as well as annoyed, when he read Holma's enthusiastic cable: the very party whom this inspired plan was supposed to help had not even been entrusted with the details of her salvation! Little wonder, too, that one month later, when the hard-pressed Finns, their backs now veritably against the wall, and the boats with their would-be rescuers set to embark—skis, snowshoes, Finnish-English dictionaries and all—that Helsinki balked and chose to come to terms with Moscow instead.

And yet, the "Finnish wild goose enterprise"—as the formidable General Alan Brooke, who would succeed the stumbling Ironside as British chief of staff, called Operation Avon Head—by raising the possibility of Allied involvement in the Soviet-Fenno conflict (something Stalin and Molotov definitely did not want at all) wound up becoming a factor in bringing the war to a close.[27]

✳

To the Hotel Kamp press corps, still affected by the afterglow of the great—if deceptive—Finnish defensive victories of December and January, as well as not having much else to go on besides the increasingly opaque Finnish military communiqués the Finnish General Staff issued every day, the picture was quite clear: the Finns were still winning the war.

Thus, on February 5, the day when Vaino Tanner arrived in Stockholm on his first peace-making journey, as well as the same day that the Allies met in Paris, the *New York Times,* taking note of the latest attack on the Summa sector of the Mannerheim Line, ran a front-page article headlined "MANNERHEIM DRIVE WANES. "The Soviet offensive against the Mannerheim Line in the Summa sector ebbed away yesterday," it reported. The dispatch, by K. J. Eskelund, was strangely reminiscent of the ones the paper had published in December during the previous Russian offensive:

Early this morning, before sunrise, a Russian detachment advanced at
Summa. When it reached a point where Soviet losses had been heaviest,
the Finns opened fire and the Russians retreated. A short distance back, the
Soviet officers stopped the retreat and ordered the men to dig new lines.
This was an immensely perilous venture, for the Russians were clearly
visible. Soon, the Finnish artillery corrected its range and shells began to
explode amongst the Russians. The retreat was resumed and the Soviet
retired to its original trenches.

Over 4,000 bodies were left behind, scattered in the snow.[28]

In the event, the *New York Times* was misinformed. The "failed" assault Eskel-
und described was actually one of a series of overlapping probing and diversionary attacks intended at once to exhaust the already weary Finnish defenders and
find the best spot in the Mannerheim Line to spearhead the actual breakthrough
drive, while confusing the Finns.[29]

In fact, even though the Summa sector had been under virtually continuous artillery attack for a week, the main drive against the Finnish fortifications
was not scheduled to take place until February 11, in another five days. Most
important, the *New York Times* notwithstanding, this million-man Russian army
was most assuredly not the lumbering, flat-footed giant that had lurched helter-
skelter over the Finnish border ten weeks before, but something different altogether: a mean, monstrous, well-oiled, highly efficient machine.

That much was clear from the start. It certainly was clear to the hundred or
so benumbed Finns who had the misfortune of having their two pillboxes—the
Finnish strongpoints officially known as Sk1 and Sk2 in the Summa sector—
selected as the target of the first demonstration operation by the men of the
355th Rifle Regiment of the 100th Soviet Division on February 1, 1940, the first
night of the carefully staggered "rolling" Soviet offensive.[30]

The 100th, one recalls, was Ivan Chetyrbok's division—the same unfortunate
unit that the Finns had routed and partly destroyed during the botched offensive
of December 19, 1939. Now, remanned, retrained, and re-equipped, it had been
assigned to the first echelon of Timoshenko's new offensive, one of the fourteen
Soviet rifle divisions thus designated, along with the concomitant honor and responsibility of helping to restore both its and the Red Army's tattered prestige.[31]

During the previous Russian offensive, in December, the two reinforced Finnish strongpoints, two of a cluster of a dozen strongpoints in the Summa sector,
had been in the thick of the fighting, as their Maxim guns cut down the blindly
charging Russian infantrymen while the equally directionless Soviet tanks
milled around the open field in front of the bunkers' gunports. But that was before the Russians knew what they were doing. That was then. This was now.
This Russian Army knew what it was doing. The roles had been reversed. Now it
was the Finns' turn to be fazed.[32]

*

Captain M. Korovin, a military engineer and commander of the 90th Independent Sapper Battalion, certainly wasn't fazed. It was the morning of February 2.
The time: 6:40 A.M. The place: the entrance to the battered, but still intact battle
bunker, Sk2.[33]

For the past eighteen hours the three dozen men assigned to the fort—one of
the more formidable of the Mannerheim Line pillboxes, with its three machine
nests and swiveling cupola—along with the garrison of its less formidable neighbor, the casemate known as Sk1, had been locked in a death struggle with the
approximately 300 men of the Soviet "storm group" from the Soviet 355th Rifle
Regiment who had been assigned to the reduction of the two Finnish pillboxes.[34]

The well-concealed operation was preceded by a reconnaissance-in-force followed by some furtive trench-digging, as Korovin's commander, who had equal
rank, Captain M. Sipovich, described in a 1941 interview.

> What lay in front of my battalion? To the right there was bunker No. 45
> [Sk2] with its many gun ports and embrasures—to the left, bunker No.
> 44 [Sk1] with its two gun ports. The trench between them, equipped with
> armor shields with rifle ports, had exits to the forest behind. This is where
> the enemy's field units and artillery and mortar were located. Dragon teeth
> and barbed wire fences lay between my battalion and the bunkers.[35]

Next, a squad of Russian engineers surreptitiously dug a number of trenches
close to the concrete dragon's teeth which, along with barbed wire, comprised
the Finns' outer perimeter. In this way, Sipovich's men had cleared two jumping-
off areas for the actual assault.

"Before the assault," Sipovich continues, "we worked out a detailed plan for
capturing the bunker [Sk2], double checked our coordination with our attached
and supporting units." Next the storm group, which consisted of a platoon of
sappers as well as a platoon of T-28 tanks, along with a detachment of field artillery, was briefed on the details of the mission, including the simultaneous massive "creeping" scheduled for the afternoon of February 1. "They also were told
that when closing with the enemy, they should be as close to the barrage as possible, and that they should not stay in the same spot for a long time."[36]

Every angle of the operation, including and especially the importance of
communications between the participating arms, one of the many weak points
of the prior drive, had been carefully considered, anticipated, and addressed.
Thus, the commander of the 4th Company, a lieutenant named Grishin, was designated to lead the actual assault. Grishin had been given a direct phone line to
the staff of the 2nd Battalion, the Russian unit assigned to provide artillery support, so that he could properly call in support from its artillery and correct the
accompanying sub-cannonade.[37]

*

The day of the massive, main cannonade arrived, along with the 100th's special demonstration exercise against the unsuspecting garrisons of Sk1 and Sk2. Anxiously following the operation from divisional headquarters several kilometers away was its commander, A. N. Yermakov, along with his no less anxious commander, the demoted and reassigned Kirill Meretskov, now the head of the 7th Army, whose career—and perhaps his life—depended on its success.[38]

At first, the "demonstration operation," one of a number of such exercises conducted under the cover of the titanic opening barrage, essentially went according to plan. "At 12:15 on February 1st, our artillery opened fire. Using the barrage for cover, the 4th Company occupied the trenches that we had prepared in advance. The 1st Battalion of our regiment was on the company's right flank. The 4th Company left the trenches and started its advance. The 1st Battalion also moved ahead."[39]

The Russian veteran gives due credit to the tenacity of the Finnish defenders, as well as the accuracy and stopping power of the outnumbered Finnish artillery. As always, the unforgiving weather was also a problem. "The enemy showered [us] with hurricane fire. The battalion was stopped by his heavy artillery. The two tank platoons were stopped by the deep snow."[40] Nevertheless, the 4th Company, under the resolute young Soviet lieutenant's leadership, continued its advance to the target line, making sure to stay out of the frontal fire pouring out of the two bunkers. Then the attackers ran into another snafu: while traversing the Finnish obstacle field, their explosives-laden armored sled, an innovation Russian engineers had conjured up for the new drive, blew up.[41]

Meanwhile, the surviving members of the 4th Company, which had also suffered serious casualties, continued to advance under a hailstorm of bullets and mortar fire from the grove behind the two Finnish strongpoints, while the five tanks of the accompanying tank platoon slowly blasted their way through the protective dragon's teeth. The battle raged on, as Sipovich, watching through his binoculars, looked on. The Finnish gunners, alert to the danger to their showcase fort, responded accordingly.[42]

> By this time the 4th Company was already on top of bunker [Sk2]. It was supposed to advance further, to the forest [behind the bunker], having left the 3rd Platoon as a blocking party at the pillbox. However it suffered heavy losses, while the enemy's artillery and mortar fire froze it in place. Despite this, the company firmly held on [to the top of] the bunker. From the unbelievable intensity of fire one could deduce how important this particular fortification was to the Finns.[43]

The pitched battle was approaching its climax. By now 4th Company had been winnowed down to a mere twenty-eight men. Several of the Russian assaulters now climbed down the sides of the bunker and attempted unsuccessfully to blow up one of Sk2's gun ports with the small amount of explosives they carried with them. Unsurprisingly, they failed: it was a lesson to be learned and disseminated for future such operations by the Section for the Study of Combat Experience, a laboratory the scientific-minded Soviets had established to analyze their battlefield experiences.[44]

Instead, to the dismay of the men inside, Sipovich's troops were able to cover up the pillbox's ports by furiously covering them with stones, snow, and dirt. "They could hear threatening shouts from inside the pillbox." The besieged Finnish garrison tried to escape by running out the back door; however, another group of soldiers, led by the company's *politruk,* named Formichev, "was there with hand grenades at the ready" and stopped them.[45]

In the meantime, members of the garrison of the smaller adjoining emplacement, Sk1, had also joined in the battle, running through the trench connecting the two forts. They, too, were stopped by the Russians. During the melee Grishin's men were ably supported by tanks and artillery fire made possible by the direct telephone lines that now linked them with the regimental artillery, as Timoshenko had decreed—telephone lines manned by personnel who knew what they were doing.[46]

The furious engagement continued throughout the day and night of February 1. Now came the moment of truth: "It grew dark. The engineers brought in the supplies necessary for the explosion. We came to a decision to explode the bunker from the roof. The roof of the pillbox had been cleared from dirt and stones by our artillery during [the numerous bombardments]."[47]

Now it was the turn of 4th Company's sappers, led by their commander, Korovin. Taking charge of his platoon, Korovin led the men through the obstacle field to the doomed Finnish bunker. This time the Russian sappers brought a full 600 kilograms of explosives with them. However, they were only able to destroy three of the bunker's gun ports, leaving eight untouched. The determined Korovin now ordered his sappers to bring another 1,600 kilograms of TNT to finish the job.[48]

Now, at 6:40 A.M. on the morning of February 2, standing at the entrance to the battered bunker, his clothes and gas mask riddled with bullet holes, shivering from the subzero cold, the Russian officer had his turn to show what he was made of. While his amazed comrades, who had retreated at his command to a safe distance, looked on, Korovin pushed the plunger.[49]

When the dust cloud cleared, the redoubtable Russian sapper was still standing, Sk2 had been destroyed, the remainder of the Finnish crew had been killed, and the Red Army had two new heroes. Sometime later the Russians would release a photo of a clutch of cheering Russian soldiers carrying Korovin and Sipovich on their shoulders. It does not appear to be staged.[50]

Back at the 100th Division's headquarters, Kirill Meretskov, the beleaguered 7th Army commander, was also pleased at the result. Meretskov now ordered Yermakov, the division's commander, to order another storm group, comprised of the 5th Company of his 355th Regiment, along with two T-26 tanks, to employ the same methods successfully demonstrated by Captains Sipovich and Korovin to attack Sk2's smaller, though still imposing neighbor, the smaller Sk1. This time, Yermakov made sure that the tank-infantry assault team brought adequate explosives with them to finish the job in one blow.[51]

During the evening of February 2 and into the next day, the regiment's 2nd and 3rd Battalions continued to hold the shattered pillboxes, successfully withstanding several fierce Finnish counterassaults. The Red Army, not wishing to telegraph its move, did not include the reduction of the two Finnish fortresses in its daily military communiqué. Even if it had, it probably would not have been believed.[52]

Needless to say, Finnish General Headquarters didn't mention the Soviet feat of arms at its next press briefing. Nevertheless, as was clear to the stunned occupants of the other fortresses in the sector, this was not the same Red Army they had faced two months before.[53]

*

There were other signs over the next few days, as Timoshenko ratcheted up his "crescendo offensive," of the remarkably swift transformation the Red Army had undergone under his rigorous, demanding tutelage. For example, there was the fire control balloon hovering over the Mannerheim Line, at Taipale, expertly directing the Red artillery; that was new. Too, there was the Russian map that the Finns stumbled upon with the exact coordinates for their command post: Timoshenko clearly had up-to-date intelligence, as well (something that the Finnish Army too often lacked).[54]

One of the first—and few—outside observers to discern the change was the anonymous military correspondent of the *Times* of London. "It is evident," he wrote, in his prescient analysis published on February 3, the third day of the offensive,

> that the recent pause in the Russian attacks on the Mannerheim Line
> has been due to preparation for a fresh operation with fresh methods.
> Reports of the fighting have often given the impression that the attacks
> were not scientifically supported by artillery fire, and against a strongly
> prepared position the tank is a comparably feeble weapon without the
> fullest cooperation of other arms, especially when the element of surprise is
> lacking, as it must be on the Karelian Isthmus.[55]
>   . . . The tactics of the latest Russian assault against the centre of the Line
> certainly do not lack ingenuity.

First the Russian artillery carried out a really heavy artillery preliminary bombardment with the object of destroying defense works, putting machine guns out of action, and demoralizing the garrison. Then, in order to carry the assaulting troops to close quarters, what are best described as armored sledges were pushed forward by heavy tanks, while their approach was concealed by smoke-screens, emitted by light tanks on the flanks.

. . . On approaching the Finnish outposts, the detachments on the sledges sprang off, carrying their light machine guns and automatic rifles, and dashed for cover.[56]

There was no need for the friends of Finland amongst the paper's readers to panic just yet: "So far it does not appear that the attackers have achieved any deep penetration by these methods, though they may have established themselves within the outpost zone." Of course, what the savvy *Times* reporter didn't know was that the reason the Russians had not achieved deep penetration of the Mannerheim Line yet was because it was not the Red command's intent to do so—yet. The operations of the first three days, essentially an extended reconnaissance-in-force, were but a curtain raiser for the onslaught to come.[57]

However, virtually alone amongst the so-called experts writing about the war, the paper's writer had correctly discerned what would turn out to be one of the great shocks of the war, alongside the haplessness of the Red Army's initial performance—namely how quickly and how completely it had managed to transform itself. As Carl Van Dyke notes, "Most foreign military commentators continued to dismiss the Red Army's ability to conduct modern warfare. Others, who had the patience to follow the development of Red Army operations on the Karelian Isthmus, later acknowledged the Red Army's surprising degree of organizational adaptability."[58]

Another writer who noticed the dramatic improvement in the Red Army's *modus operandi* (at least in retrospect) was Geoffrey Cox. "On the Isthmus the change-over in the tank formations, bringing the heavier tanks to the fore on the German model, and the use of armored sledges showed adaptability and improvisation," he wrote in his postwar analysis. Cox was particularly impressed with Timoshenko's flair for logistics, traditionally a Russian weakness. "They [the Soviets] had only five roads and two lines of railway on which to bring up their supplies to the Isthmus and mass their troops for the attack. These were moved into position and changed over repeatedly without a hitch. . . . The Red Army made mistakes in Finland, but it had something which not all armies have—a willingness to learn from its errors."[59]

Impressed though he was with the Russians' new élan, as well as its "scientific" methods and improved equipment, the *Times'* commentator made it clear in his summary of the ramped-up bomber offensive that Stalin had ordered that he himself was no fan of the Soviets. "Merciless bombing of towns and villages continues," he wrote. "But the Russians are not attacking the central part of

Helsinki. Whatever be their reason for this," he drily concluded, alluding to the Soviet's already established disregard for human life, "it is not humanity, as the other activities of the Red Air Force prove."[60]

✳

Needless to say, Semyon Timoshenko was also impressed, and relieved, by the 4th Company's signal success, as Van Dyke writes: "He was aware that an army normally required years of strenuous training and combat experience before its command corps was proficient in directive control and its troops capable of combined arms tactics. He was not confident that the Red Army's tactical deficiencies would be ironed out by one week of untested techniques."[61]

Clearly there was much that still needed to be worked out. The new top Russian commander—and future Soviet defense chief—was decidedly not happy to learn that in one of the demonstration operations his tanks had fired on their own supporting troops and had prematurely abandoned the fight: shades of December 19.[62]

Nonetheless, after correlating his information with N. Korneev, the head of the Russians' "scientific" Section for the Study of Combat Experience, Timoshenko was sufficiently confident to order Meretskov, now his subordinate, to continue the rehearsal exercises up until February 5 "in order to gradually introduce more Red Army troops to the heat of battle and confuse the enemy about the time and duration of the new [general] offensive."[63]

Next, Timoshenko ordered Meretskov, the 100th and the 123rd Divisions were to begin a breakthrough operation against the other forts in the Summa sector. He also ordered Meretskov's colleague, Vladimir Grendahl, the Finnish-born commander of the newly formed 13th Army on the eastern side of the isthmus at Taipale, to begin an assault with his first echelon divisions at his end of the Mannerheim Line, preparatory to the main offensive, tentatively scheduled for February 11. That was when Timoshenko intended to unleash his Wall of Fire and break the Mannerheim Line for good.[64]

✳

Adding to the rising sense of terror and confusion on the Finnish side at this time was the Russian decision to drop additional parachutists around the country. Thus, on February 7, United Press reported that a group of fifty Soviet parachutists, dressed in Finnish uniforms, had been killed by Finnish patrols near Rovaniemi "as they were about to blow up a bridge. . . . The parachutists, it was believed, were Karelian Russians who speak Finnish and look like Finns, or Finnish Communists who lived for a few years in Russia and were sent back to engage in propaganda and sabotage work."

Apparently not all the intruders were found. Thus, two days later, the news agency reported that Finnish troops and police in Lapland were still engaged in a major manhunt for the remaining sky troopers.[65]

The specially trained troops were also employed on the isthmus, a tactic that was particularly frightening to the women of the auxiliary services who were stationed there, as Mai-Lis Toivenen attests:

There was a lot of machine gun fire around my post, because the enemy knew our location. Of course I had heard about the parachutists before—everyone had—but didn't know whether it was true.[66] . . . Then [in early February] just before the new offensive two Russian paratroopers were shot and killed just two kilometers from my tower. I also saw the footsteps of a paratrooper near the tower. Whether it was one of the ones that were caught, I don't know. Anyway, after that they put two guards in front of my tower. As you can imagine we were quite terrified.[67]

Over on Tuppura Island, Anna-Liisa Veijalainen had a similar scare at about this time, as she recalls:

One evening a patrol went out to hunt for reconnaissance parachutists. They had been dropped somewhere nearby from an airplane. . . . That night I went timidly and without undressing to my room [in the canteen] to sleep. It was so cold I had to wrap several blankets around me. Suddenly at three or four in the morning I heard someone running hard along the corridor, someone wearing heavy boots. The parachutists, I thought.

Suddenly her door swung open and someone shone a flashlight in her face. Screaming, Anna-Liisa jumped out of bed and shut the door closed. Then, strangely, nothing happened.[68] Recovering her composure, Veijalainen put her ear to the door and listened closely, whereupon she heard someone speaking Finnish, which put her at ease: evidently she hadn't heard that the latest batch of Russian paratroopers included Finnish speakers.[69]

I calmed down enough to ask who was behind the door. [Fortunately] it was only our own Second Lieutenant Kunnas, who had caught the flu and lost his voice. He could hardly do more than whisper. Now I had the courage to step outside. I saw two freezing, shivering men. They were still frightened themselves because of my screaming! They had thought that all the women of the house had left the island.

Once they regained their voices, Kunnas and his companion, another officer, said that they had been transporting "several horse loads of freezing civil guard boys across Viipuri Bay and away from the war."[70]

The incident ended peaceably enough, as Anna-Liisa and her assistant tried to make the travelers comfortable before they set out on their perilous journey.

We got the boys in and lit a fire in the stove to make some hot juice for them. We put our last buns and biscuits on the table, and there probably weren't enough for the officers and the boys. Soon they had to continue if they wanted to cross the frozen bay before dawn. There were some 7–8 kilometers of open ice and it was not safe to move in daylight.[71]

"I felt like crying," she remembered, "because I could not help the young travelers anymore."

And she thought they had been parachutists! Shaking her head, the young woman wrapped herself in her three blankets and went back to bed.[72]

✳

Perhaps the most confused party at this time was the press. The fact was, everywhere but the isthmus, the war was going well for the Finns. "It was an extraordinary situation," said Virginia Cowles:

> On all the other fronts the Russian advances had been halted by some of the most spectacular fighting in history. On the waistline front, Russian attempts to drive through to the Gulf of Bothnia, cutting Finland in two, had met with smashing defeats and the loss of nearly 85,000 [sic] lives; on the Arctic front the Russian sweep down the Great Arctic Highway to the center of Finland had been stopped after a penetration of only seventy miles [112 kilometers].[73]

Meanwhile, north of Lake Ladoga, the Red thrust designed to outflank the Mannerheim Line had been broken, and the attacking troops had been broken up into *mottis,* the 168th Division forming what was called the Great Motti, while the 18th Division was isolated and effectively destroyed. "But on the Isthmus the story was a different one. Although the Finns had succeeded in out-maneuvering and outfighting the Russians on every occasion where strategy and tactics had come into play, on the Isthmus front—the only sector in Finland where actual trench warfare was taking place—only two things counted: men and guns."[74]

Unfortunately for the Finns, the war on the isthmus was the only one that really counted now.

Moreover, as the men of the Soviet 7th Army had already shown, the Russians had already learned a thing or two about strategy and tactics. All the assumptions about the isthmus war—that the Russians would wait at least one more month to launch another full-out offensive, that if and when they did, it would be as ineffectual as the first two, and, finally, that when the Russians finally did launch their drive the Finns would be assisted by their one true ally, General Weather—were about to be blown sky-high.[75]

It would take some time before the international press, as well as the rest of the world, would, or could, come to grips with that ineluctable reality. It would take three more weeks for the Finnish government, as an entire entity, to come to grips with it and respond accordingly—and then only after Gustaf Mannerheim almost literally knocked their heads together.

The Finnish public, thanks in large part to the intense censorship in the domestic media, would not fully understand it until the very day the war ended.

On February 6, the same day the *New York Times* mistakenly reported that the new drive on the Mannerheim Line had waned, the Russian attack became general all along the front with the main thrust still aimed at Summa.

For the next five days the already well pummeled men of the Finnish 3rd Division took everything the Russians had: "Bombed from the air, bombarded by artillery day and night, and under continuous attack by the infantry during the day, the Finns held their positions with grim determination. During one twenty four hour period the Russians fired as many as 300,000 shells on Finnish lines."[76]

Still, the men of the 3rd Division took it. And gave a lot of it back, too. Ivan Chetyrbok, who had managed to survive the last drive against Summa, in December, and who was one of the estimated 50,000 men the Russians sent against the Finnish strongpoint, describes what it was like to participate in this one:

Early in the morning [of the 6th] we were ready to assault from the forward trench.

I thought this was it, it was so bad. The end. The Finnish fire was so strong. We were on other slope of a hill in a small forest. I thought this was it. I could not lift my hand. That's how heavy the fire was. I lifted a tree branch. It was shot out of my hand.

Then they brought a howitzer. I had never seen a heavy howitzer so close to the front line. It fired on the [Finnish] bunker all day long. When our artillery fired a salvo, the explosives were like one wall of earth. A solid wall. The earth stood up![77]

And so it went, day after day. Every day for seven hours the Russian guns poured shells on the macerated Finnish defenses. Then at daybreak a mass of Soviet planes as thick as locusts flew high over their lines and dropped their high explosive loads. Then the tanks would come, sometimes accompanied by smokescreens, towing sleds of infantry. Then they would stop at the dragon's teeth and the infantry in the sleds would charge.[78]

In Moscow, Stalin was impatiently waiting to see whether his "engines," as he liked to refer to his troops, had settled matters. "Our air force has been called into action," he told Nikita Khrushchev, referring to the accelerated bomber offensive he had ordered at this time. "The Finns only have their skis left," the Russian leader said, disparagingly, "and their supply of skis never runs out."[79]

Stalin was mistaken. As the men of Summa had proved, and were proving at that very moment, the Finns still had their *sisu*. What they lacked, desperately, as John Langdon-Davies wrote, was the one thing that no one could supply: sleep. "Officers have described to me how their machine gun crews continued to fight and obey orders crying like children, too tired to keep their eyes open. It was an army of sleepwalkers, of automata, fighting in a tortured dream. . . . The Summa sector, its material defenses fallen to pieces, was no longer held by rational creatures but by men in delirium."[80]

＊

Vaino Tanner was feeling better. It was February 8, and the Finnish foreign minister was holding a cable from his predecessor Eljas Erkko, now the Finnish minister to Stockholm. Two days prior, after receiving Molotov's flat rejection of his unnamed Baltic island-for-peace offer, he had left Sweden in a funk. Then had come the bewildering—and annoying—news of the Allies' decision to send an expeditionary force to Finland, "a proposition so vague that no one knew what might come of it."[81]

Neville Chamberlain's grandiloquent report to the House of Commons that afternoon about the Supreme War Council's meeting did not make Tanner feel any more confident about the Allies' new Nordic venture. He noted that the results achieved in the Grand Council meeting were more valuable than those achieved by any other meeting. He also said that help is coming to Finland:

> The Finnish nation continues its brave battle against the enemy, who is using his aircraft to break the psychological resistance of the Finnish people by burning homes, bombing hospitals of wounded people and strafing inhabitants with machine guns. The success of the Finnish arms has awakened the admiration of the whole world. We are joyful that the help we have given to Finland has been valuable to her.[82]

"And I am glad to say," the British prime minister airily concluded, "that more help is coming."[83]

＊

Now, on February 8—which also happened to be the eighth day of the Russian offensive on the Mannerheim Line—had come word from Madame Kollontai that Molotov had inquired via third parties as to which island Finland was thinking of offering the Soviets. Tanner brightened; this was good news. Evidently the Allies' decision to insert themselves, however artlessly, into the Soviet-Fenno conflict was having an effect: the rabid editorial in that day's *Pravda,* warning the Allies that any attempt to use Finland "as a base for military intervention" would be "crushed by Red Army blows," seemed to indicate as much.[84]

Or perhaps Molotov was throwing him a curve; certainly the calculating—if sometimes slow on the uptake—Soviet foreign commissar had shown that he was capable of that. In any case, the elusive dove of peace was aloft again. If only Tanner could catch it. Of course, Tanner knew which island he would like to offer Molotov—Jussaro, the same small island off Hanko the Finns had initially offered Moscow during the abortive November negotiations.[85]

But Finland was not the Soviet Union, and Tanner was foreign minister, not foreign commissar. There was only so much he could do on his own. As it was, Tanner had considerably stuck his neck out by suggesting such a deal in the first place during his still secret liaison with Kollontai at the Grand Hotel. A great deal of talking and briefing and consulting had to be done before he could proceed further.

At that foggy juncture of the war, only two other members of the cabinet—Ryti and Paasikivi—were aware of the exotic doings that had taken place in Stockholm, or that Tanner had been in touch with Moscow in the first place. President Kallio didn't know; he would have to be briefed. Marshal Mannerheim, the commander-in-chief, was also mostly in the dark; he and the other generals would have to be consulted. It also would be good to get their opinion of what was happening.[86]

Tanner had been too busy handling matters on the diplomatic front to keep abreast of the military situation—certainly from the sound of the upbeat updates emanating from Finnish general headquarters all was well, or nearly well. "The pressure of the enemy continued in the Isthmus yesterday," the Finnish Army's bulletin for February 8 confidently announced, "but all attacks were repulsed."[87]

At the same time, headquarters had issued a compilation of the formidable Russians' losses in destroyed or captured war material since the start of the war. Amongst other quantities the impressive, meticulously kept list included the following:

546 tanks
308 airplanes
203 artillery pieces
294 machine guns
552 trucks and autos
1,560 horses
20 tractors
50 automatic rifles
63 field kitchens
12 observation balloons
135 automatic revolvers[88]

There was even talk about mounting an exhibit of some of the captured Soviet booty in Helsinki. Doubtless Tanner had also heard about the setback to Russian arms north at Ladoga.

On the home front, all seemed to be reasonably well. Most likely, too, the foreign minister was aware of the latest extension of the advanced Finnish social welfare system, a new presidential decree overhauling the armed forces' payment system, such that each soldier, regardless of rank, received a set monthly salary. According to the new system, the family of every Finnish soldier would henceforth receive a salary, ranging from 500 markka for a private to 2,500 markka for a general. The basic salary was to be further supplemented by 150 markka for a soldier's first child and an additional 100 markka for each subsequent child.[89]

Clearly, these were anything but the manifestations of a nation on the verge of defeat. That very day, Mannerheim's new friend, Sir Walter Citrine, the British labor leader, had proclaimed that "the Finns were a race of supermen!"[90]

Meanwhile, on the eastern isthmus, Vladimir Grendahl, the Finnish-born commander of the 13th Army formerly known as Wladimir Grondahl, was ordered to use his first echelon forces on a simultaneous assault on the Finnish positions at Taipale.[91] At the same time, in another preview of things to come, another infantry column was to mount a long curving march across the thick ice and outflank the Finns there.[92]

However, the main show was still on the other side of the isthmus, around Lake Summajarvi. After the 100th Division, commanded by Yermakov, and its sister division the 123rd, led by Filip Fedorovich Aliabushev, broke through the Finnish defenses in sectors of Summa and Lahde, the second echelon troops, comprised of the 7th Rifle Division and the 20th Tank Brigade, were to follow and enlarge the breach. That was the basic plan, and the Russian commander, Timoshenko, was confident that he had both men and equipment in order to realize it.[93]

To be sure, Timoshenko had an advantage in manpower in the target sector, but what was more important was that, in contrast to the exhausted men of the Finnish 3rd Division whom the men of the first Soviet echelon faced, his troops were thoroughly rested. They also enjoyed a strong, if not necessarily overpowering, threefold advantage in guns—77 per kilometer along the front line compared to the Finns' 20—and 36 tanks per kilometer compared to the Finns' 12 anti-tank guns.[94]

The Russians also enjoyed total air superiority. Although the fearless pilots of *Lentolaivue 24* continued to shoot down Russian planes with regularity, the days of ambushing flights of Soviet bombers were over. As part of the armed forces reorganization, Timoshenko had made sure that the pilots assigned to the new offensive were top of the line. The Russians had also learned something about Finnish air tactics by now. Soon, too, the Red Air Force would even be doing some ambushing of their own. Perhaps most important, and most remarkable, the Russians retained the element of surprise.

To be sure, there was one thing that Timoshenko most definitely lacked: junior officers. As Van Dyke notes, on the eve of the final offensive, the Soviet 50th Rifle Corps, the striking force assigned to break through the Mannerheim Line, still lacked over a thousand officers in its middle ranks, a legacy of Stalin's purges. There was little that Timoshenko could do about this but hope that the intensive training with which he had inculcated his men, including the need for accurate and continuous battlefield intelligence, which had been so glaringly lacking in the prior two offensives, would make up for this deficiency.[95]

Thus, both the 100th and 123rd Divisions were connected to 50th Rifle Corps headquarters, as well as to each other, by every means possible, including telegraph, telephone, radio, cavalry, and dog messengers. If nothing else, this Russian Army was connected.[96]

In any event, Timoshenko certainly wasn't relying on "friendliness" to accomplish his mission. He also was no fan of the commissar system; if anything, the former cavalryman preferred the discipline of the old tsarist army. In any event, although each division still had its *politruks,* this time, he made sure, they would be aiming their guns at Finns, not at Russians.[97]

In the meantime, the devastating hurricane of Russian artillery fire continued to rain down on the Finns.

The following day, February 10, another new member of the Kamp press corps, Thomas Hawkins, visited the Finnish front line. Hawkins was a reporter for the Associated Press, and he and another American correspondent—apparently the only two reporters allowed to do so—along with a watchful Finnish escort officer —traveled by sled and foot under the near-continuous Russian "softening up" barrage in order to ascertain the status of the defenses in the pivotal Summa sector.

The experience, as Hawkins describes it, was surreal: "Eight inch shells fell within fifty yards [80 meters], breaking and snapping snow-laden branches and falling into the woods on either side of the narrow path. After a half dozen had whined overhead our party took refuge in a Finnish dug out. For thirty minutes shells dropped around our dug out [which] shook from the explosions before the Russian artillery shifted its range to another sector."[98]

"Four times," according to the impressed reporter, "we watched as telephone reports told of frontal attacks by Soviet tank units, which [according to the Finnish escort officer] time after time were thrown back. Artillery shells of three to twelve inches [eight to thirty centimeters] in caliber fell at the rate of twenty per minute amidst the sputter and zip of occasional howitzer and trench mortar firing." At one point during the unremitting fusillade, Hawkins counted 106 bursts per minute—nearly two a second.[99]

The escort officer, for his part, made light of the barrage, telling the skeptical newsmen that it was lighter than it had been on numerous occasions over the past few weeks. Nevertheless, he conceded that perhaps it was too dangerous to venture outside at least for the moment. At the same time, he took the occasion to show Hawkins and his (unnamed) companion a bit of Finnish hospitality. As he wrote: "While hoping for the firing to diminish so we could go on, our officer served us tea with bread and liver paste. The dugout was warm and rug-lined with strips of red carpet on the walls and a well-laid wooden floor. Bookshelves also hung on the walls."[100]

Pausing occasionally in between calls on the old-style French wind-up telephone, the Finn gave his guests his own somewhat roseate view of the battle raging outside. To be sure, he admitted, the enemy had introduced some new equipment into this offensive; however, in every other respect, his suicidal tactics and modus operandi were the same. So had been the result of the battle. "It was like the slaughter of cattle," he remarked, with grim satisfaction. "Our men killed thousands."[101]

Of course this was true. What he neglected to say was that the Russians had many more thousands to spare. "We are holding our positions and will continue to hold them," he confidently declared, as the *korsu* reverberated from the deafening barrage.[102]

*

A somewhat more realistic picture of actual conditions in the trenches, as well as what it was actually like to experience the new Soviet onslaught, may be derived from a letter written by another soldier from his dugout front, which Virginia Cowles had obtained from Frank Haynes, the helpful American military attaché whom she had also befriended. He in turn had obtained it from his chauffeur. The soldier, named Lasse, was Haynes's chauffeur's brother. It is dated February 10, 1940, at 6:35 A.M.

"Dear Brother," the moving letter, which Cowles reprinted in full in her memoir, begins, "Now I know what an artillery barrage is like. . . . If there had not been that frightful, tearing artillery fire with its rending explosions one would have felt pity for the grey Russian masses who in their long overcoats waded up to their thighs in soft snow against the death-spitting mouths of our machine guns."[103]

Again, the rampaging Russians sound much like the ones the Finns had faced several months before: "Obediently and silently, they came, trying to make use of armored shields, but in vain. Everything was futile. Murderous fire swept the field time after time leaving only twisted heaps of bodies, which soon became immobile. The tanks advancing ahead of the infantry were destroyed by our anti-tank weapons and by skillfully thrown bundles of hand grenades tied together."[104]

In short, according to Lasse, everything was pretty much a repeat of the previous failed Soviet offensive—except for that "frightful, tearing artillery fire," whose effect on him and his men he describes in blood-freezing details. "Artillery sickness," he calls it.

I am not ashamed to confess that artillery fire to me, as well as to most of the others, is simply revolting. I have not yet suffered from "artillery sickness," although I feel like pressing my hands against my ears and crying out in pain. The explosions of six-inch shells on an average of every fourth second over the course of nine consecutive hours, the incessant detonations, screaming splinters and blinding bursts of flame create in our bodies unspeakable terror, which can only be overcome by exercising one's entire psychic courage.

As the traumatized Finn recounts, it is one thing to experience such a relentless cannonade. It was, however, "killing to try to be an example to one's men," he wrote his brother, "to joke, suck calmly on one's pipe, feeling at the same time that every nerve is taut as a violin string."[105] Clearly, some of Lasse's men had begun to lose their minds as a result of the relentless pounding:

To know that if one should for one second give up one's self control the hands would begin to shake, the head to nod and the eyes to flinch, which has happened to several of my men. It is terrible to try to make such a man carry on his duty by encouragement and threats, but so far I have succeeded and every time prompt action has been required the men have been ready.[106]

Despite the drumfire barrage, and the rising number of psychological casualties (even if they were not recognized as such), the men of Lasse's unit had not as yet sustained serious physical casualties; the following day, as the final Russian "sequence" (a word which Timoshenko was fond of) unfolded, that situation would change.

In any case, to judge from the steadfast soldier's letter, there was no question of his and his men's resolve:

Up to now I have been afraid that we either stand or fall, but now there is no longer an alternative—we will stand. The whole battalion has only one man dead (he died in a field hospital) and we have had on the average one wounded man every second day. Usually the wounds have not been dangerous. I have not lost any of my men, although our quarters are far from being safe.[107]

Withal, the picture this stalwart if shaken Finnish officer paints of life in his rattling *korsu,* with its complement of walking wounded, is tragic—and inspiring.

Again and again the diarist returns to the Finns' greatest woe: the lack of sleep. "A couple of men have gone off their heads," the Finn, who seems to be going out of his skull a little himself, admits, "and a couple of others are on the way, but it is because of our heavy guard and patrol duty and the consequent lack of sleep, not because of anxiety." As if there was a difference.[108]

The hard-pressed officer continues in a plaintive tone:

We are tired and we need men who would at least do manual labor and stand guard duty so that we could get some rest once in a while. I know that we are going to be replaced soon and taken to the rear to rest, and then I hope to get a few days leave.

But at the same time my mind is burdened with anxiety for those who remain here. Not because of any fear of defeat, but, because, while the Russians change their men four times, we can change ours but once, and we always have fresh forces against us.[109]

It was just as Semyon Timoshenko had planned. "Gnawing through" is the way the systematic Russian commander described the rationale behind his offensive strategy. First, he would exhaust the outnumbered Finns by wearing down their psychological defenses; then his echelons would break down their physical ones.[110]

As William Trotter avers,

Factored into Timoshenko's equation was a simple but savage truth. Russian units could be rotated when casualties, exhaustion, or depleted supplies lessened their performance. Finnish units could not. The cumulative strain on the defenders was designed to grind them down not only physically but psychologically, by depriving them of sleep, warmth, hope itself. Eventually, as they shuffled the same increasingly burned-out units to meet threat after threat, even Finns would reach their breaking point.

By the evidence of Lasse's letter, Timoshenko's calculations were working.[111]

The Finnish High Command, for its part, was clearly unprepared for both the fury and magnitude of the blazing Russian cannonade—which (as the *New York Times* earlier noted) saw the Red artillery expend as many as 300,000 shells in a twenty-four-hour period—as well as the psychological effect it would have on its troops. With little or no previous experience of modern positional warfare, a concept like "shell shock"—or what today would be called post-traumatic stress disorder—didn't register with the general staff. The assumption was that their troops could tough out anything the Russians could throw at them. After all, they were Finns. In this respect, as John Langdon-Davies notes, Mannerheim and his staff made a fundamental, if understandable, mistake:

It was not that they [the Finnish High Command] had made any errors in their estimate of the difficulties which the Russians would encounter in the nature of the terrain; nor had the army formations been destroyed, although the loss of officers was beginning to be extremely serious. It was the psychological effect that had been underestimated. Casualties are not only a matter of killed, wounded, and prisoners; to these categories must be added that of "lost through nervous exhaustion."[112]

To be sure, in hindsight, the Finnish High Command would have been better off withdrawing its men altogether from the Mannerheim Line, rather than subject them to the punishment they now endured, which only played into Timoshenko's cold-blooded but effective strategy: "Had they known before the gigantic nature of this artillery bombardment they would have done better to have abandoned the war of positions at the outset and trust to guerilla [warfare] on the Isthmus."[113]

Perhaps. At any rate, it was too late now. The time for realizing Gallen-Kallela's *February Fantasy*, the painting that hung in Mannerheim's mansion opposite his cot, with its vision of fleet-footed Finns raising havoc with the hereditary enemy, was over. Now it was time for the unveiling of Semyon Timoshenko's very different steel-tipped nightmare.

✳

Lasse ends his poignant missive by wondering, as many of his men did at this time, what Finland's friends were doing for her:

> My dear brother, what is Sweden doing for us? And will America help? Write soon and tell me. I am starved for news.
> Yours,
> *Lasse*[114]

✳

What *were* Sweden and America doing to help Finland at this time, many Finns wondered.

Well, for one, both countries were mounting stirring ice shows on *Suomi*'s behalf. After weeks of noisemaking, America's efforts for Finland were indeed attaining nearly surreal heights of silliness: witness the star-studded "ice carnival" for Finnish Relief held at the picturesque, sunken ice skating rink at New York City's Rockefeller Center two nights before, February 8. If nothing else, America's stars were certainly turning out for Brave Little Finland. Thus on February 6, a "Help Finland Cabaret" at the Waldorf Astoria attracted a horde of celebrities, including actors John Barrymore and Edward G. Robinson.

Guest of honor at the affair, needless to say, was the omnipresent face of Finnish relief, Herbert Hoover.[115] Two days later the hardy septuagenarian was present at the Rockefeller Center ice rink to preside over an affair that epitomized the fatuousness of America's infatuation with Finland: a glittery if slightly moronic skating exhibition-cum-fashion show with fifteen beaming models, sitting in specially sculpted "ice chairs," displaying a collection of spring tweeds, sports, and evening clothes for Finland's benefit while "several hundred sympathizers of Finland, including members of society and stars of the stage crowded around the rink."[116]

Amongst those presiding over this bizarre fund-raising event was Finland's omnipresent minister, Hjalmar Procope, who had once again taken the train up from the capital to join his co-belligerent, Hoover, for The Cause. If one looked closely at this perfect picture of Fennophile bonhomie, however, one could see that the debonair minister's smile was somewhat forced. Appreciative though he was of America's manifest goodwill, Procope's patience was running out.

For two months Procope had begged, pleaded, and button-holed every one he could in Washington in order to expedite a desperately needed unrestricted loan for his country that could be used to purchase the tanks and bombers she needed to survive the Russian onslaught, only to see the measure revised—with the cautious White House's tacit blessing—into a loan for non-military credits. Still, even that watered-down measure had yet to be passed by Congress.[117]

No doubt if President Roosevelt, who had made his personal support for Finland clear on numerous occasions, had his druthers, the American government would have done more for Finland by now; however, FDR, mindful of America's strong isolationist sentiment, as well as the ever-cautious voice of his determinedly non-interventionist secretary of state, Cordell Hull, had decided not to push things. And so, to Procope and his staff's immense frustration, things had not been pushed.[118]

Two days later, on February 10, while the Senate continued to debate the weakened bill, Roosevelt, apparently frustrated that he couldn't do more for the Finns—or as much as he would like—underlined his personal sympathy for the Finns when he spoke to a rowdy crowd of 5,000 members of the left-wing student organization the American Youth Congress on the south lawn of the White House.

"That American sympathies are 98% with the Finns in their effort to stave off invasion of their own soil is axiomatic," Roosevelt told the hostile collegians, who, ironically, felt that his administration was doing too much for Finland, thereby raising the prospect of a possible war with the USSR. They wound up booing him, to the discomfiture of his nervous Secret Service guard looking on. "That America wants to help them by lending them money is axiomatic," FDR declared with a broad grin, seemingly taking heart from the jeering crowd (apparently the only time the chief executive of the United States has been booed by a group of invited guests in his own backyard).[119]

Brave words, even though Roosevelt's own official action, or inaction, didn't match them. The president's sentiments were duly reported in the next day's *Helsingin Sanomat,* encouraging many Finns. They meant little.[120]

While the New York City Council president and his lithe partner were performing their exhibition ice trot for *Suomi* at Rockefeller Center, in neutral Sweden, sympathy for Finland was also reaching an icy apogee. Thus, the stirring show the Swedes put on for their Finnish brothers as part of an exhibition hockey game between the two national teams took place on the afternoon of February 11 in Stockholm. In the game, attended by 10,000 screaming fans, Sweden defeated Finland 2 to 1. However, the score seemed beside the point to the roaring spectators, who rushed onto the ice afterward and carried the Finnish team on their shoulders around the arena, whence (according to the United Press), "the Swedish National Ice Queen and Princesses skated hand in hand with the Finnish team members, carrying the blue and white Finnish colors."[121]

At the same time, unbeknownst to the cheering spectators, the final "sequence" of the meticulous Russian assault on the Mannerheim Line had begun.

∗

As it happened, the men of the Finnish 3rd Division in the hard-pressed Summa sector of the Mannerheim Line caught a break on February 11. Timoshenko had ordered a carpet bombing of Finnish positions to coincide with that day's final sledgehammer thrust. To the Russians' annoyance, a thick fog covered the isthmus that morning, forcing the Red Air Force to scrub the operation.[122]

Feodor Gorolenko, the head of the 50th Army Corps, gave the signal to his artillerists to proceed with the meticulously worked out cannonade at 8:40 A.M. Once again, as they had for the past two weeks, the men of Summa gritted their teeth, shut their eyes, and wished that they were somewhere else—perhaps in the archipelago with their wives and children, if they had families, or with their sweethearts, enjoying a long ago white summer night. The imagination can work wonders in situations such as these. Or perhaps the bombarded Finns tried reading, if their shaking hands were capable of reading a book. Or gazed at the photos of Finnish film stars tacked to the log walls. Anything to blot out the downpour of steel that came hurling down on them.[123]

But, the stupefied defenders soon noticed, there was something distinctly different about that day's initial serving of Russian ordnance: this bombardment included direct as well as hanging fire. "Unlike earlier artillery fire," historian John Erickson notes, "this attack was accurate and overwhelming, and the high number of direct hits stunned the Finnish defenders."[124]

There was also something else about the fusillade of February 11, the Finns observed, once they stuck their heads over the snow-fringed parapets or looked through their ice-obscured gun ports at the enemy. Actually there were several things. For one, there were the oncoming troops themselves. In stark contrast to their easy-to-shoot brown-clad predecessors, these attackers were properly camouflaged in white, as well as protected from the Finnish fire by the Russians' new-fangled armored sledges. Some of the troops even had skis. Even more remarkably, they appeared to know how to use them.[125]

The Finns looked on, duly amazed, as the Soviet tanks, in serried rows, methodically made their way through the holes in the obstacle zones the Russian sapper-engineer teams had carefully prepared. Sometimes a tank would burst into flame from a well-aimed Finnish artillery burst, or from a Molotov cocktail thrown by a hidden Finn. However, they didn't break ranks. Altogether, the Russians lost seventy-two medium and heavy tanks on February 11. It didn't matter. They had hundreds more in reserve.[126]

Soon, once again, the Finnish machine guns began chattering, toppling thousands of the onrushing infantry. It didn't matter, either. There were three more committed, well-trained, well-disciplined echelons of troops behind them.[127]

For Semyon Timoshenko, this was also the moment of truth. One may well surmise the Russian's own perfervid thoughts. The outcome of the war—perhaps even the fate of the USSR itself, if one were to believe some commentators—depended upon the rapid success of the new Russian offensive. Meanwhile, to the outside world, Timoshenko was largely unknown and would remain so for some time. Remarkably, even the press didn't know the name of the new Russian commander.[128]

At one point that afternoon, according to Van Dyke, the anxious Soviet commandant visited a battery of his artillery "to supervise the work of the artillery and watch the progress of the battle." What Timoshenko saw there apparently pleased him: "Timoshenko was impressed with the speed and accuracy of the gunners working the guns so furiously that their half-nude bodies glistened with sweat despite the subzero temperatures." The scene reminded the Red general of the clockwork production of a well-run factory.[129]

Vaino Tanner was having another bad day. A very bad day.

It was now February 12. The past four days—ever since he had put his *bête noire,* Molotov, on hold—had been intensely busy ones for the Finnish foreign minister. It hadn't been easy for Tanner to do, but basically all the concerned parties had gotten with the program, so to speak—the peace program. First, Tanner had spoken with the president, Kallio.[130]

Unsurprisingly, the aging Finnish president, who was only just recovering from the experience of having the olive branch he had personally extended to the Kremlin publicly and contemptuously flung aside (as Tanner's offering had previously been), was, in Tanner's understated words, "not at all enthusiastic about" passing the peace pipe to the Kremlin again.

Nonetheless, despite his aversion to giving up the island of Jussaro to the Russians, Kallio had reluctantly approved Tanner's proposed offer.[131]

Two days later, Tanner and Ryti, who also were on the same wavelength (for the moment), had traveled by train to Otava, the small town ten kilometers west of Mikkeli, whence Army headquarters had once again been moved, to meet with Marshal Mannerheim and the other Finnish generals who composed the Defense Council in order to bring them up to date, and vice versa.[132]

"Finland has three alternatives," Tanner patiently explained to the down-cast council, listing them in order of preference: peace, aid from Sweden, or aid from Western powers. To Tanner's relief the Defense Council agreed to yield Jussaro and sue for peace with Moscow. Ryti and Tanner's sortie to Otava had been successful.[133]

✱

Then things began to get murky again.

Unfortunately, peace was definitely not at hand. Upon his return to the capi-tal on February 14, Tanner discovered that rumors about the possible peace talks with Moscow had begun to spread. To refute these, he issued a deliberately dis-ingenuous public statement denying that he had been in touch with Moscow. As might have been expected, Tanner's ill-considered statement (which he neglects to mention in his book) only served to further stoke rumors, while annoying his fellow peacemongers, Ryti and Paasikivi, to boot.[134]

Still, the determined peacemaker had persevered. Now if he could only get the rest of the cabinet with the program, all would be fine. Now matters began to get even murkier. Once again, as he had with Mannerheim and the Defense Council, Tanner, in his meeting with the cabinet's Foreign Affairs Committee, laid out the three possible options at that point: peace in exchange for Jussaro, aid from Sweden, or help from the Allies.[135]

The upshot was further chaos and confusion, as Jakobson writes: "Tanner received wholehearted support from Ryti and Paasikivi, and a more hesitant endorsement from the President. The two members of the Agrarian Party, Ni-ukkanen (Defense) and Hannula (Education), firmly opposed making peace on Tanner's terms, and Soderhjelm (Justice) held it was impossible for Finland to part with Jussaro. The differences between the two groups proved irreconcil-able, and the chief policy making body of the Cabinet remained split."[136]

The result was that "at the most critical point of the war Finland was left without united and single-minded political leadership." For the sake of national unity, the schism was covered up. All were agreed that this was hardly the right time for a public display of dissent. Nevertheless the divide, which would con-tinue to hinder the helter-skelter peace-making process for the remaining four weeks of the war, was real.[137]

✱

Army Commander First Class Semyon Timoshenko was pleased—or at least as pleased as the self-contained Russian general normally allowed himself to be. At long last, the goal that had eluded the Soviets for two months, the piercing of the Mannerheim Line, had been accomplished. Not that he had not had some anxious moments over the past forty-eight hours.

In the event, the Finnish forts located in the Summa sector, which had been assigned to the Soviet 100th Division, had proved more difficult to crack than expected: "The frontal assault was caught immediately in deadly cross-fire between two [Finnish forts]. Subsequent reinforcements failed to gain any ground, and late that evening [Brigade Commander] Yermakov ordered his regiments back to their jumping-off positions."[138]

The story was different on the other side of Summajarvi Lake, in the Lahde sector assigned to Aliabushev's division, the 123rd. That unit's assignment was to assault the three hills dominating the area and take out the handful of reinforced firepoints located there, as pinpointed by the also markedly improved Russian intelligence and confirmed during the various preliminary attacks; then punch through to the Finnish support line at the rear of the sector. Once the division reached that line it would be within striking distance of several key road junctions.[139]

The Russians gave particular thought to the manner in which they used their artillery in this sector. No fewer than 100 batteries of heavy artillery were used in the initial "softening up" phase. They were extremely effective, as Mannerheim himself attests in his memoirs: "As the Summa position had shown itself too difficult to crack, the weight of the attack [was] transferred towards the East of the Lahde sector. The attack was preceded by a violent barrage from about a hundred batteries concentrated against a small sector where trenches and nests collapsed together."[140]

That was just the beginning.

At the same time, Aliabushev ordered the men working his flat trajectory cannon to conduct ten-to-fifteen-minute "fire raids" against the two principal targets in the sector, the heavily armored Poppius (Sk4) and Million Dollar (Sk5) strongpoints, which had also been the scene of intense fighting during the December assault, as well as other targets "followed by false transfer of fire to targets in the enemy rear in order to confuse the Finns and catch them exposed in their trenches by the next raid."[141]

The doomed occupants of the two "showcase bunkers" as well as the handful of others scattered around the perimeter found themselves on the receiving end of the most sophisticated artillery barrage in the history of modern warfare, a precisely targeted, interlocking blitz of steel, and a harbinger of the equally lethal and effective bombardments the Soviets would conduct later during the Second World War at Stalingrad, and during the final drive on Berlin with their whizzing *katyusha* rocket batteries.[142]

A devoted student of Timoshenko's tactical doctrine, with its emphasis on the value and importance of "real time," rather than anecdotal battle reconnaissance, Aliabushev had dutifully spent a great deal of time on improving communications between artillery and infantry, to the point where his earpiece-adorned forward artillery observers could follow and correct the cannonade from as close as 75 to 100 meters away.[143]

Whatever Timoshenko did, it worked, the Finnish commander-in-chief concedes, not without a trace of grudging admiration: "The defenders suffered heavy losses, and were unable to prevent tanks and infantry from pouring into their positions. The first wave continued right up to the rear line of the defensive position, while the following waves began to roll it up from the sides."[144]

The Soviet 255th Regiment's assault on the hill the Russians somewhat mysteriously called "No. 65.5," where the multi-chamber Poppius bunker was located, was the most immediately successful. Within minutes of reaching their jumping-off positions, the Soviet storm troops were pouring over the already crumbling pillbox, while the heavy tanks accompanying them nonchalantly wheeled up to the surrounded fortress and fired point-blank at its dozen embrasures, as machine gun fire whined and panged harmlessly off their sides.[145]

This was not a new tactic. The Russian tanks had done this, or tried to do this, during their December offensive, but then the Finns would come out and paste them with grenades and their homemade kerosene bombs. This was not possible now. The savvy Russians had studied and improved their tactics to the point where each vehicle was covered by enfilade fire from other vehicles. Within minutes of the initial attack the panicked men of Poppius began to pour out of the doomed emplacement: the Mannerheim Line had begun to crack.[146]

At 1 P.M. on that fateful day of February 11, 1940, less than an hour after the start of the attack, a red banner was seen waving over the abandoned fort. Moving quickly, the spirited Russian assaulters surrounded and captured the other Lahde redoubts and fire points. Frantically, Finnish troops in the rear of the sector manhandled their Bofors 37 mm anti-tank guns into place to try to stem the Red tide; however, there were, as usual, too few of the weapons. Moreover, Finnish troops were tired.[147]

Extremely tired, a point that cannot be overemphasized, as Cox wrote. "The breakthrough [at Lahde]," he observes, "had not been caused by the destruction of the Finnish forts. It came because the Finns were exhausted. They were shell drunk, automata moving into position. Had they reserves, the positions might still have been held. But they had none available, so all they could do was drop back, towards a rear which was almost as dangerous as the front."[148]

Inevitably, "one position after another was lost," Mannerheim sadly notes, "until the enemy had made a breakthrough nearly a mile [two kilometers] in depth."[149]

The fight over the Million Dollar Bunker, in particular, was just as frantic as it had been during the prior Russian assault, in December: "Several times the strong point was submerged beneath waves of Red infantry, and each time it was cleared off with grenades and Suomi fire. Individual Russians tried to wriggle in through the firing ports, and there were a number of hand-to-hand encounters."[150]

The struggle, which continued through the night, ended much the same way the initial "demonstration operation" fight had over the smaller Finnish strongpoint, Sk2, led by the men of the 90th Sapper Battalion. Several times the Russians called out for the crew of the besieged fortress to surrender. The Finns replied by shouting obscenities.[151]

This time, however, the Russians, learning from experience, had brought along enough TNT: "Then at 5 in the morning of the 12th, enemy sappers placed a [227 kg] block of TNT on top of a shellfire crack on the roof of the main chamber. The resulting blast killed every man inside and left a thirty foot [fifty meter] hole in the roof of the fortress."[152]

Even then, Finnish troops stationed nearby continued to resist, before they were forced to retire to the rear of the area. However, the strain on the frontline troops was beginning to take its toll. The 3rd Division, which had been in the Line for a month, was so exhausted that its men could hardly keep their eyes open, even in the face of oncoming tanks.[153]

The situation continued to deteriorate, as Mannerheim ruefully records.

In order to restore the balance at the Lahde sector through a counterattack, I placed the 5th Division at the disposal of the Commander of the Army [Osterman], but the very same day [the 12th] it had to be used for the relief of the 3rd Division in the Summa sector. The counterattack was therefore carried out by only one regiment, whose commander, Colonel [Vaino] Polttila, was mortally wounded. Part of the lost ground was recaptured, but lost again after a furious Russian counter-attack.[154]

Timoshenko's echelons continued to pour in, enlarging the breach in the Line. At his headquarters, the hard-pressed Finnish commander, Osterman, feverishly working the phones, was able to close some of the breach; however, he had no more reserves available and the gains were lost again by that night.[155]

By the end of February 13, with strong artillery support, the hard-driving men of the Soviet 123rd Division had forced themselves into the terrain around the Lahde intersection. Now, having punched a hole a few kilometers wide in the Finnish lines, the tanks circled to form a wagon train and dug in. The gate to Viipuri—or Vyborg, as the Western press, preferring the city's Swedish name, called it—and beyond that Helsinki, was open. The myth of the "impregnable" Mannerheim Line was no more.[156]

Now, thrilled with the news of the 123rd's breakthrough, Timoshenko telephoned Meretskov with orders for the follow-up attack. Timoshenko was reportedly pleased with Aliabushev's use of his second echelon, which had been "thrown into the battle at the psychologically decisive moment."[157]

Not that the exacting Russian commander was entirely happy with the new assault. While he was heaping praise on Aliabushev, Timoshenko also criticized the commanders of the 10th and 34th Corps, which he had assigned to the assault on the western end of the Line, "for their slackness and warned that in the future he would make sure that everyone would have to answer for his actions."

Still, on the whole, the demanding conductor of the Russian symphony of fire was pleased. So was the Soviet High Command. So was Stalin, who was closely following developments. So, too, was Vyacheslav Molotov. The time had come, the People's Commissar for Foreign Affairs decided, after apprising himself of the breakthrough, to up the ante for the Finns.[158]

✱

Vaino Tanner was having an extremely bad day. It was the morning of Tuesday, February 13. The peripatetic Finnish foreign minister was in Stockholm now, conferring with the Swedish prime minister, Per Albin Hansson, and his foreign minister, Christian Gunther, in Hansson's plush office at the Swedish Chancellery. In the distance, the lights of the "Venice of the North" flickered and glowed—in stark contrast to the blacked-out ones in *Helsingfors,* as the Swedes called Helsinki. The talks were not going well. Nothing was going well, in fact.[159]

The creeping barrage of bad news had already begun that morning, when Tanner was in Turku waiting for his flight to Sweden. Before he boarded, a courier had handed him a letter from Eljas Erkko, his envoy to Stockholm, informing him of the Soviet's new peace terms.

Tanner's heart sank when he read Erkko's letter. Molotov had changed his mind. Molotov was no longer interested in a mere island. Now he wanted more, much more. Now Finland had to give up Hanko, the isthmus, *and* the eastern shore of Lake Ladoga.[160]

To put it mildly, Tanner writes: "The positions of the two nations were very far apart. Instead of further discussing the cession of a small island, the Soviet Union was demanding the inclusion of whole provinces on its side of the line."[161]

"The letter made me very pessimistic." Little wonder.

Now, as he had two months before over the telephone after the initial Russian attack, Tanner asked his old friend and socialist colleague, Swedish prime minister Hansson, this time face to face, whether *Sverige* would finally consent to send regular troops to her besieged neighbor's aid with Finland on the ropes.[162]

The Finnish foreign minister, clearly under duress, did his best to sway the stone-faced Hansson and the equally silent Gunther: "I set forth my case. Finland sought peace. But the steps in that direction had not led to anything. For this reason we must go on with the war for the time being. Finland could not fight on its own resources and therefore must procure aid. We would prefer to limit ourselves to aid from Scandinavia."[163]

Tanner expressed his gratitude for the not inconsiderable number of Swedish volunteers who had entrained for Finland thus far. But the volunteer route was too slow. The great majority of the Swedes who had crossed the border to fight were still in training; only the small group of aviators comprising the Swedish Voluntary Flying Corps was in action.[164]

It was time for the Swedish government to get more actively involved, Tanner insisted. "Sweden ought to send volunteers as trained units, in the same fashion as the German Kondor forces had functioned in the Spanish Civil War. If Sweden should do this, it would certainly help negotiations toward peace."[165] If Sweden would not do this for her embattled Nordic neighbor, the anxious Finnish foreign minister continued, Finland "would have to rely on Western aid. This, however, could have weighty consequences. Finland would become a participant in the major [European] war, and possibly Sweden and Norway as well."

The Swedish officials patiently waited for Tanner to finish. "With all this in mind, the Finnish government wanted to know the attitude of the Swedish government toward the procurement of increased aid."[166]

The clock ticked. The Swedish public, Hansson evenly explained to his crestfallen visitor, "would not back an intervention in Finland, not even with units of volunteers. How could such units be raised, he asked. The government could not order anyone to volunteer."[167]

Then, of course, there were the Germans to think about. "Hansson was convinced that if Sweden joined the Finnish war, the Western powers would sever their relations with the Soviet Union, and then Germany was bound to take action against Scandinavia."

Tanner protested: he had different information. Finnish representatives had been assured by German diplomats that the Reich would not interfere.[168] Sorry, the now exasperated Swedish prime minister countered. The answer was still *Nej*.[169]

And what if the prospective Allied expeditionary force came off? Would Sweden allow British and French troops to travel across its territory (as Chamberlain had blithely assumed)? The answer was the same. All the Swedish ministers could offer their beset Finnish visitor was the advice that the best thing to do was to sue for peace.[170]

Of course, Tanner hardly needed that advice. "He had thought about nothing [else] but peace since the first bombs fell. But he had hoped that Sweden, by promising troops, might help him to obtain peace on easier terms." It was no use. The door to Swedish aid had—almost literally—been slammed in Tanner's face. Gathering himself, the chastened Finnish foreign minister excused himself and prepared to return to Helsinki to deliver the bad news to his colleagues.[171]

A difficult day indeed. Worse was to come. Now it was nearly midnight. Tanner was home in Helsinki, after the long, lonely flight from Stockholm via Torku. The careworn diplomat was about to turn in when the phone rang. Ryti was on the line with catastrophic news: the Russians had broken through at Lahde. "The breach is not large," Ryti told the shocked Tanner, "but it was dangerous. An attempt was being made to close it." Unsurprisingly, Vaino Tanner got very little sleep that night.[172]

"A day of adversities" is how Tanner describes it. First the letter from Erkko informing him of Molotov's new demands, then the rebuff from the Swedes; now the news of the Russian breakthrough. "The end of the war was in sight." The question now was: how would the war end?[173]

∗

The foreign press, for its part, continued to be largely in the dark. The Finnish government's capricious, high-handed attitude didn't help.

"With a curious amateur approach to the Press the Finnish press officers tried to give people scoops," observes Cox. "They would take one man on an exclusive story," for example the aforementioned Thomas Hawkins, "irritating every other correspondent."[174]

The basic problem, Cox contends, was that "they disliked most of us. We were nuisances. They were running their own war and they did not want propaganda except along their own lines. We tried to argue with them that the truth was the best propaganda, but only a few ever realized that. Many officers realized our point of view and did everything they could to get the Finnish Command to give us facilities. But they were men without influence."[175]

Virginia Cowles was another journalist who chafed at the Finnish government's paranoid and uneven policy attitude toward the media, while at the same time acknowledging that it might have at least some basis in reason.

> For news we had to rely on the laconic official communiqué which was handed out in Helsinki every evening; on land operations it usually averaged no more than a hundred and fifty words. The reason the Finns observed these restrictions was that success depended on the secrecy of their movements, the surprise of their outflanking attacks, and the cunning of their strategy.
>
> They couldn't take the chance of correspondents, with first-hand knowledge of their tactics, leaving the country, and inadvertently giving information to the enemy. It was also forbidden to criticize the Russian tactics for fear the enemy might profit by his mistakes and correct them.[176]

"Needless to say," she added, "the number of Finnish troop concentrations and casualties were never revealed. The result was that the press could only work on conjecture."[177]

The truth, of course, was that Finnish losses, while only a fraction of those suffered by the Russians, were mounting daily, as in the battered 3rd Division, which had borne the brunt of the Russian assault; for example, some battalions were down to 250 men. At Summa alone the Finns had already lost an estimated 700 men, a massive number.[178]

All this was concealed. When reporters tried to sneak into their copy the number of Finnish casualties, or even rough estimates, the unseen censors with green eyeshades at the Kamp who reviewed all copy before it was allowed to go out redacted the reports. The bereaved joined the conspiracy of silence: the widows of the fallen were discouraged from wearing black. Still, evidence of the increasing death toll was not hard to find. All one had to do was to look at the obituaries section of the *Helsingin Sanomat* or *Hufvudstadsbladet*, and count the crosses. Finland was hurting.

Journalists could feel it in the heaviness of the atmosphere of the few local restaurants that were still open when they ventured beyond the Kamp. Occasionally, they could hear it, too, as when Ilta Helsingus, the young press officer who worked at the hotel, button-holed Leland Stowe and pleaded, "Please can't you write something to get help quickly? It is getting very bad now." The difficulty with obtaining fresh fruits and vegetables, most of which had to be shipped in from the Continent, hitherto not a problem, had also begun to evince itself now that the waters around Finland had frozen over.[179]

"Like everyone in Helsinki, worn down by the complete lack of fruits and salads and by the unbroken strain of eighteen hour days and by the terrific brunt of this coldest Finnish winter in sixty years, her face was drawn and colorless now," Stowe recalled. "Now for the first time [she] was depressed and anxious."[180]

Stonewalled by the government, the members of the Kamp corps wound up interviewing each other, leading to wild, unfounded rumors. Cowles draws a memorable picture of the manic scene in the Kamp press room at this time: "The press room of the Hotel Kamp overflowed with correspondents from a dozen different capitals, arguing, doubting, grumbling, questioning. The telephone rang continuously. From one end of the hotel to the other you could hear journalists shouting their stories across Europe—to Stockholm, Copenhagen, Amsterdam, Paris and London, and even across the Atlantic to New York."[181]

Most of those press people had only the vaguest notion of what they were shouting about—which of course suited the Finnish Press Bureau just fine.

It also suited Gustaf Mannerheim. To most newspapermen the Finnish commander was as remote as a "war god," says Cox, whose only contact with the aloof Finnish commander had been that one accidental, dramatic sighting early in the war, at the Hotel Seurahuone, on December 3, before Mannerheim left Helsinki for Mikkeli.[182]

The only other times the regal Finnish commander-in-chief deigned to meet the general media was once at Christmas, when a small group of baffled reporters (not including Cox) were summoned to his headquarters in Mikkeli to hear the marshal read a curt declaration before being dismissed, and an interview Mannerheim gave to the correspondent of *Match,* the prominent French weekly magazine, because it was owned by a friend. Aside from that, Mannerheim was the Invisible General to the press while retaining a very strong and palpable presence. After all, as every reporter knew, it was Mannerheim, not the competent, self-effacing Ryti, nor the well-meaning but overwhelmed Tanner, and certainly not Niukkanen, the low-profile defense minister, who was really running the war.[183]

According to Cox, Mannerheim viewed the press as "annoying people who had spent a great deal of their time criticizing him and who interfered with wars which were the business of soldiers, and soldiers only." The government's attitude toward the press derived from the top down: Mannerheim despised the press. Therefore the government despised the press. It was as simple as that. The brief official communiqué issued on February 13, 1940, with its casual, almost off-hand, twenty-word reference to the Russian breakthrough two days before, did little to dispel the media's confusion. "In the area east of Summa," it noted, "the enemy [has] succeeded in capturing a few of our most advanced gun positions."[184]

Nor did the equally opaque, purplish, hyperbolic bulletin that the High Command released the following day, February 14, do very much to clear things up. "The fighting on the isthmus surpasses in intensity even the most strenuous battles of the [First] World War," the announcement declared. "An enormous amount of material, planes, infantry and artillery has been used. The enemy tries to use every weapon at his disposal. The expenditure of shells is no less than 300,000 in one day.[185] This has been going on for several days."[186]

"The Russians," the High Command conceded, "have used very good troops. For instance, last night [February 13] there was intensive fighting in which the Finns preferred to use their knives." Nevertheless, "despite this," as well as the aforementioned loss of "a few forts," the military spokesman blithely insisted, "Finnish resistance remains unbroken."[187]

Meanwhile, he continued, the Russians were reported to have suffered enormous losses of men and equipment at Summa—at least 30,000 to 50,000, as well as 200 tanks. "There are enormous heaps"—the Finns were fond of that word—"of dead Russians before our lines." There was no mention of Finnish losses.[188]

✱

The following day, February 14, James Aldridge, who had been covering the war now since December, filed his latest dispatch from Helsinki. One of those journalists who enjoyed most favored status by the fickle authorities, Aldridge had just returned from the aftermath of the fighting at Summa, where the tangled mounds of dead Russians he had been shown reminded him of the waxen tableaux he had seen the prior month after the battle of Suomussalmi. The Australian native had no doubt that the new Soviet drive on the Mannerheim Line, the graphic evidence of which he had personally seen, was now the central event of the Winter War.[189]

The gravity of the military situation, if not its actual dimensions, were underscored at an extraordinary press conference for foreign correspondents convened by President Kallio at his mansion overlooking Helsinki Harbor that day, at which the government assured the assembled press that the Mannerheim Line had not been broken. Aldridge, whose skepticism of the government line was becoming increasingly clear, was not so sure.[190]

Vaino Tanner, who by now had received his own briefing on the situation on the front, was more candid in a private talk he had with the skeptical newspaperman. "The position of the war in the Summa is a day-to-day matter," the foreign minister confessed. "It is no doubt the biggest and most important battle of the war."[191]

However, Tanner was confident, the situation was not lost. "We have given up some admittedly important positions," he conceded, "but then all positions, big and small, are important. Yes, from the information I have received, the Russians are in Summa, but you know what their losses have been."[192]

Gustaf Mannerheim was also keen to know what was going on. It was February 14, and Mannerheim and his top strategist, Aksel Airo, were en route to Viipuri in the Finnish commander's limousine, with its familiar plate number, SA1. Sometimes, Airo later noted, his boss also slept in his car during his rare forays from headquarters.[193]

One suspects that the Finnish commander didn't sleep in his car on that particular day, as he sped to Viipuri. He had a lot on his mind—namely how to deal with the salient the Russians had punched into the line at Lahde, and with what. The simple fact was that Finland was running out of men. That same day a desperate headquarters had issued the order for the call-up of men ages forty-two and forty-three to the colors. There was even talk of issuing amnesties to convicts serving sentences of less than a year. (Ultimately, men of up to forty-six were conscripted.)[194]

To be sure, no sooner than Mannerheim's limousine pulled into Viipuri than the sirens started wailing, signaling the start of another Soviet air raid. Mannerheim and Airo were in the courtyard of the ancient castle there when bombs began to fall. In the event, both men escaped injury. Still, it wasn't a very good omen. Once the all-clear sounded, Mannerheim and Airo drove on to Saarela Manor, the headquarters of the Second Corps, to meet with General Osterman, the commander of Finnish forces in the isthmus, and General Harald Ohquist, the Second Corps commander.[195]

The situation for the Finns, particularly the prospect of obtaining reinforcements and obtaining them in good time, was not promising. Timoshenko, the Soviet commander, with his endless reserves, had the luxury of moving divisions around, whereas the best his hard-strapped Finnish counterpart could do, as he put it, was to "manipulate battalions," and even those weren't arriving on time.[196]

Two relief battalions from the 62nd Infantry in the Kotka sector, on the southern coast near Helsinki, which Mannerheim had sent to the front and which had been expected to arrive that day, February 14, were delayed in transit after a heavy Soviet air raid had succeeded in cutting the rail line. Another battalion, the 3rd, Ohquist's staff confirmed, was on its way to Leipasuo in open cars at a temperature of −30 C., could at best not be expected before midday, and then without baggage. The two battalions from the Kotka sector could not be brought up before the following day [February 15]. [Ohquist] had managed to scrape together a battalion of Defense Corps in Viipuri, which was being transported to Summa by means of cars.[197]

"Scrape" is the word: said corps included boys in their teens.[198]

That morning the Russians had overrun the main Finnish support line at Lahde; however, they had not advanced further. It is not clear whether this was because of confused communications or lack of initiative on the part of Timoshenko's field commanders. Nevertheless, there was little question that Timoshenko would try to expand the bulge his men had blasted out the next day.[199]

The Finnish troops had to be drawn back, but how far? There were two options: pull back several kilometers behind the first, now sundered Finnish defense line, to the intermediate line running between Leipasuo and Rajamaki, which only had a few fortified points; or withdraw even further back to the much stronger rear line then anchored at Viipuri. At the latter, according to Geoffrey Cox, a new line of forts was being built with the aid of General Badoux, the Belgian officer who had been one of the foreign experts who had helped build the original fortifications back in 1925. These hastily constructed strongpoints were being strengthened with concrete "aprons" to prevent them being levered out again.[200]

The meeting between Generals Mannerheim, Osterman, and Ohquist, predictably, was a tense one, as the men went back and forth about how far to draw back their men. "Osterman favored pulling back all the way to the Rear Line, anchored on Viipuri, and using the half-finished Intermediate Line. Ohquist, prodded by Mannerheim, came out in favor of making a determined stand along the Intermediate line," according to William Trotter.[201]

The latent hostility between Mannerheim and Osterman, which had been building again since their heated confrontation after the initial Russian assault back in December when the two men had clashed over a similar issue, now came out into the open, as Trotter writes: "Mannerheim pointedly snubbed Osterman and talked tactics directly with Ohquist, who was, after all, Osterman's subordinate. This violation of the chain of command was only the latest symptom of the friction between Mannerheim and his Isthmus commander for some weeks."[202]

There was, of course, a third, much more drastic option open to Mannerheim, as Swedish officers later pointed out to Cox: the guerilla option. To wit: "Swedish officers, with whom I spoke in Stockholm, early in March, were of the opinion that the best thing that the Finns could do would be to draw back and let the Russians advance into Central and Southern Finland, as they had allowed them to advance in the north. Then, on the roads, they could ambush them and try to cut their communications."[203]

No doubt this contingency had occurred to the participants of the key conclave at Saarela Manor. But what did it entail? "It meant that the Finns must decide to give up, if necessary, Helsinki and the thickly populated southern areas of the country. It meant great suffering for a huge mass of civilians and mass immigration behind the central lake system. It meant that the Finns north of Ladoga would be outflanked, and that the whole area in which the army had been fighting, with considerable success, would have to be given up."[204]

But this was too painful to think about, much less speak about. Moreover, by this time Mannerheim had reluctantly but inevitably come to identify with the Line that had been named after him. "The Line was his Line," Cox asserts. "He was convinced that the war would be won or lost there." Too, there was the political dimension to be taken into consideration. Withdrawing to the stronger rear line, although the more defensible option from a strictly military viewpoint, would, Mannerheim feared, undercut Finland's negotiating position with the Soviets.[205]

To be sure, Mannerheim was playing his cards very close to his chest: none of his top battlefield generals were aware that there had even been any contact with Moscow. Doubtless it would have demoralized them to know that the government was parleying with the same enemy whom they were battling at that very moment. Of course, Mannerheim knew that any decision to withdraw was bound to cause a storm with the Finnish public.[206]

As Airo later explained: "The fact that we had been able to stop the Russians before on the Isthmus, and the successful defensive battles we had fought, had engendered the unfounded belief that Finland could cope with anything. The public didn't understand what kind of massive efforts and consumption of material these achievements had cost and how they had strained our resources to the utmost."[207]

The ultimate decision was Mannerheim's, and his alone, to make. This was the excruciating position he was in. The fraught meeting broke up. Before he left, Mannerheim made a mental note to deal with the obstreperous Osterman. First he had a decision to make.[208]

By the time his limousine had returned to Otava, from what turned out to be Mannerheim's only visit to the front during the war, Mannerheim had decided. Assuming the situation at the front remained as is, and the salient created by the Russian breakthrough could not be eliminated, Finnish troops were to withdraw to the intermediate line, he ordered. Shortly afterward, the humiliated Osterman tendered his resignation as commander of the Army of the Karelian Isthmus. He was quickly replaced by the more pliable General Erik Heinrichs, formerly head of the 3rd Corps.[209]

The situation for the Finnish Army now quickly deteriorated. The next day, February 15, the Soviets resumed their attack at Lahde. The swirling, well-organized Russians quickly overran the spent defenders and moved north. Later that day another breach was made in the lines on the road to Kamara. It was evident that a full-scale retreat from the coast to Lake Muolaanjärvi was necessary. Summa would have to be abandoned. At 3:45 that afternoon, the formal order to withdraw to the Intermediate Line was issued.[210]

In an article published on February 16, Hanson Baldwin, the military analyst of the *New York Times,* reacting to the yet unconfirmed report that Summa had fallen, downplayed its significance.

"There is no doubt that the Russians have made some gains on the Karelian Isthmus, particularly in the Summa sector," the respected columnist opined. "Probably a number of machine gun nests, outposts and some concrete and steel pillboxes that form part of the Mannerheim system have been captured, but there is no evidence that the Soviets have entered the main line."[211]

Baldwin clearly sympathized with the embattled Finns, but he hedged his bets. If, he postulated, the Russians were able to take Summa, along with the coastal guns at Koivisto that protected the Mannerheim Line's right flank, then things might begin to get difficult for the Finns. However, the commentator didn't think that would happen. The normally savvy Baldwin was behind the times (so to speak). In fact, Summa had already been captured, and the Finns had already withdrawn to their intermediate line. Within a week, the overwhelmed Finns would be forced to retire yet again to their rear line, and the key installation at Koivisto would fall.[212]

For his part, Kliment Voroshilov didn't think that the fall of Summa was insignificant.

As N. N. Voronov, the chief Soviet artillerist who had helped orchestrate the fiendishly effective barrage that preceded the successful offensive, recalls, the Soviet defense minister was so stunned when an ecstatic Kirill Meretskov phoned him with the news of Summa's fall that he refused to believe it. "On February 15th the hurricane of our bombs and shells descended on Summa," Voronov proudly wrote. "After the artillery had shifted its fire to the required depth, infantry and tanks simultaneously attacked and began to advance successfully. This time the enemy did not hold out. His flanks were in danger of encirclement, and he began to retreat. The strongpoint fell before my eyes."[213]

Voronov is embellishing. In fact, Summa had already been abandoned. The rest of his account rings true, however: "Upon returning to the command post of the 7th Army, I witnessed a telephone conversation between Meretskov and the People's Commissar of Defense. No one in Moscow would believe that our troops had captured Summa. Upon seeing me, Meretskov spoke into the telephone:[214] 'Comrade People's Commissar,' Meretskov assured the People's Commissar of Defense, asking him to hold the line. 'Voronov has just come in. He saw everything with his own eyes.'"

Taking the receiver, the chief of Soviet artillery had happily confirmed Meretskov's report. "I gave a detailed report of the course of the battle to the People's Commissar. Nonetheless, he asked me three times if the report that the strongpoint had been taken was true."

It was true, Voronov told the disbelieving commissar back in Leningrad. "Finally his irritated tone became warm and friendly. The People's Commissar wished the troops a successful completion of this offensive."[215]

Now it was the Red Army's turn to crow. For days, the Soviets had insisted, in their time-honored fashion, that "nothing of importance" was occurring on the isthmus.

Not anymore. On February 14 the normally disinformative Soviet communiqué fairly sang out the news: "Feb 14—Intense activity of infantry units and artillery continued in a number of sectors. On the Karelian Isthmus successful actions of Soviet troops continuing. Enemy unable to withstand onslaughts of Soviet troops and falls back, suffering heavy losses. As a result of [their] successful actions, Soviet troops occupied sixteen of the enemy's defensive fortifications, including eight iron and concrete forts."[216]

And the strangest thing about this was that it was all true.

Although the battered and bruised Finnish Army of the Isthmus, now under the command of General Heinrichs, was able to withdraw to the intermediate line in fairly good order, things were beginning to look very unfavorable indeed. On February 16, the newly arrived, green Finnish 62nd Infantry Regiment, unable to withstand Voronov's "hurricane of fire," broke up in panic and abandoned its position.

The truth was in the seeing. Witness the terse report filed by a Finnish aviator who had the audacity to fly his rickety Gloster Gladiator over the Red juggernaut on that day: "Plane GL-272, height 200 meters. Observations: main force heading from Kamara station westwards, first troops are at the bend of Suurjoki River consisting of 10 tanks and 15 vehicles of motorized troops. Three tanks and 5 vehicles. Three tanks towards Kamara village, two kilometers away. Lehtola-Kamara road full of tanks and motorized troops, firing at aircraft."[217]

*

Meanwhile, several kilometers and a world away in Helsinki, hundreds of Finns, blithely unaware of the Red Army's breakthrough, were making a beeline for the Helsinki Fair Hall—the building the Finns had intended to be used for the indoor games of the now canceled 1940 Olympiad—to see the brand new exhibit of captured Russian war booty that opened to the public that same day. Amongst other things, the bizarre show included the remains of two SB-2 bombers shot down, as well as various examples of Soviet ordnance, including the Kremlin's principal calling card, the hated "Molotov breadbaskets" with their sixty individual small incendiary bombs, which had wreaked so much havoc around the country; parachute mines of the sort the Russians had lately been dropping in the Gulf of Finland; and the recently arrived so-called "electron" incendiary bombs, which were capable of generating heat of 2,000 degrees centigrade.[218]

Standing alongside one of the bombers, in all his captive glory, was the *pièce de résistance,* a mannequin dressed in a Soviet pilot's fur overall, complete with gas mask. Additionally, the popular show, which attracted 13,000 wide-eyed visitors during its first week, included two intact Soviet light tanks, their turrets clearly showing the anti-tank gun hits that had put them out of commission, as well as several Russian field and mountain guns.[219]

Near the planes, just in case visitors missed the point, was a poster proclaiming the impressive number of Soviet warplanes that Finnish anti-aircraft crews, with the aid of their capable *Lotta Svard* spotters, had managed to shoot down thus far, 387. As far as the average Helsinkian could see, Finland was still winning the war, and the outlandish display further encouraged that willful delusion.[220]

*

While the duly impressed citizenry gawked at shot down Soviet aircraft at Helsinki Fair Hall, the remaining close to 4,000 airworthy ones, including the new and additional craft that had been sped to the Northwestern Front, especially the latest, faster I-16 fighters, were still unpleasantly active, as Anna-Liisa Veijalainen discovered on the afternoon of February 17, when a pair of Soviet fighters surprised her in the *sauna.*

The officer on duty that day shook his head in wonderment when he saw the formidable canteen hostess stride through the snow en route to *sauna* for her daily ablutions, seemingly without a care in the world. Although Finnish troops had succeeded in withdrawing to the intermediate defense line following the breakthrough at Lahde in fairly good order, there was no telling how long they would be able to check the Red forces.[221]

The gravity of the general situation was underscored by that day's proclamation by Mannerheim of an extraordinary order to his troops urging them to stand fast. "Soldiers," the message began, ". . . the moment has come when by stern and vigorous measures the enemy's attacks must be stopped at the new defensive line, to whose support I have dispatched from my reserve new forces and artillery. You can rest assured the enemy will never be able to break my defensive system. From a formation in depth we are raising new fortified positions to wear down unto the end his offensive power."[222]

In addition, over the last few days, as part of the ramped up Soviet air offensive, the Viipuri archipelago and coastal area had been subjected to increasing aerial attacks. No matter: nothing was going to stop Anna-Liisa from *sauna*.[223] Hence the young woman's surprise when, upon entering the hut and doffing her clothes, the wooden structure began to rattle.

> I had made it happily to the sauna benches, cast some water on the stones and was enjoying the sweet warmth when two fighter planes attacked the fortress with their machine guns. The roof of the sauna rattled and it felt as if the fighters would dive straight inside.
>
> I jumped from the benches and crouched as low as I could between the sauna wall and the water tank. From there I watched the birch tree outside the sauna get hit by rounds of machine gun fire, as its icy branches hit the ground. The firing did not last long, but to me it seemed like an eternity— especially because I had no clothes on![224]
>
> The low-flying fighters did a thorough job of shooting up the island.
>
> It was a miracle that no one died or even was wounded, although the bullets shattered many of the windows in the barracks, and one round missed our telephone operator by only inches.

Shortly afterward, another group of low-flying Russian bombers zoomed by, heading for nearby Uuraansaari Island. "They flew low, like a flock of birds, just above [the port of] Uuraa, and we could see smoke and columns of dust clearly from the island. It looked as if no one could survive such a bombing, but when the mail horse returned in the evening, we learned to our relief that fortunately there had been few casualties there, as well."[225]

The following evening, February 18, a captain named Waren, whose men had been building new machine gun emplacements on Tuppura, informed the doughty canteen worker that soon the remaining laborers would be conveyed back westward across the bay to the mainland. The engineer advised her to join them. Otherwise she might have to flee the island on skis. There was no ignoring the swelling Red tide now.[226]

And so, with a heavy heart, Anna-Liisa once again made ready to evacuate the windswept world within a world she had come to love, and leave her beloved "boys." On the morning of February 20, the stricken auxiliary, her trusty canteen box by her side, boarded the horse-drawn sleigh that was supposed to take her to safety.

I stared at the moonlit sea, listened to the rumble of the artillery and the buzzing of the airplanes and took one last walk nearby. Uuraa and Johannes [a town on the eastern side of the bay] were on fire—the whole sky above the coast seemed to be in flames. Nobody wanted to go on the open ice before the moon set—it shone brightly past midnight and the fires also added to the light.

We departed in the wee hours around three or four A.M. The driver did not have much cargo so I managed to fit my rucksack as well as my skis in the sleigh. Then I tried to balance on top of the cargo, squeezing close to the canteen cash box.

Veijalainen was joined by the harried evacuees from the village of Vatnuori on Pulliniemi peninsula, on the western side of the bay, and their respective conveyances. Soon the sad caravan made its way across the frozen bay. Needless to say, she was in shock. "I stared numbly at the island that had become so dear to me, and to which I believed I would return."[227]

Her reverie was not to last for long. Sure enough, before the evacuees made it to the other side of the bay, they were attacked by Soviet fighters. "We had just made it safely past Kuningassaari [the small islet adjoining the main island] when the first fighter plane detected our group. Tracer bullets whistled in our ears as we dove into the snow and lay as low as possible. The drivers had their hands full trying to hold the terrified horses," she writes. Was Anna-Liisa worried about losing her life? No, she was worried about losing the cash box. "Later I realized how silly I had been. Why not use the metal box to protect my head, instead?"[228]

✳

Later that same day, February 20, having received the proper clearance from higher-ups, Virginia Cowles was on a train from Helsinki bound for Sortavala, where she and a number of fellow journalists had been invited to view the scene of the Finnish Army's latest triumph over the encircled Soviet 18th Division, north of Lake Ladoga.[229]

The morale of the soldiers, who were bound on the crowded train for the fighting on the isthmus—the front the government did not wish her to see—was good. By now, like many if not most of her colleagues, Cowles too had come to identify with the soldiers packed around her. "The soldiers had been home on leave and were now returning to the front. They were husky, broad-shouldered men in high spirits. A few of them slept, a few of them stared silently out of the window, but most of them sat laughing and talking, every now and then breaking loudly into marching songs."[230]

The Finns were friendly, offering Cowles and the other members of her party dried apricots, bread, and sausages. These were not the troops of a defeated nation, she felt, as she smiled back. The idea of defeat couldn't be further from their minds.

During normal times, the journey from Helsinki to Sortavala took six hours. Now, because of the incessant Russian air attacks and the attendant delays, it took nearly two days. Cowles didn't seem to mind.

> Some of the time we read and some of the time just stared out of the window. The great sweep of snow was not monotonous. There was an awesome grandeur about it, and every now and then you caught a picture which stamped itself vividly on your memory.
>
> I remember the hospital trains moving slowly across the white panorama, the blinds pulled down and the red crosses painted on the sides frozen over with ice, the freight trains panting into the stations, some with cars riddled with machine gun bullets or smashed where bombs had hit them.[231]

Another time, Cowles espied a cavalry train, hurtling by, heading south, in the direction of the main Karelian front, as she looked over her frosted-over window. "The doors of the box cars were open and we caught a glimpse of the soldiers and horses. Some of them stood in the opening—huge men with brilliant red cheeks, dressed in fur caps and ankle-length coats, a race of giants going to war."[232]

Occasionally the train would stop at a town along the line, whereupon she and the other passengers, troops and correspondents all, would pour off to escape the foul air and grab some refreshments at the station café—assuming it was still in operation. One such strafed trackside facility had all its windows shattered. Inside the grim place was but one dim bulb, the only one still working. However, that was no hindrance to the assiduous staff. In the semidarkness half a dozen canteen *lottas* stood behind a counter pouring out hot coffee for the freezing passengers, managing to serve the whole lot in twenty minutes.[233]

Soon the well-swathed correspondent reboarded the train, along with her shouting, back-slapping passengers, and was lost in thought. She found it hard to reconcile the Finns' contagious bonhomie with the grave reality of the situation. The end, she knew, was in sight, even if they didn't. How long would it take? How would the cataclysm end? How much more would Finland have to endure before it did end? "I looked at the faces around me and wondered how many would return."[234]

✳

One suspects that Gustaf Mannerheim had similar thoughts as he entered headquarters that same morning of February 20 and prepared to meet his two scheduled visitors, General Christopher George Ling, the British military envoy, and his French counterpart, Colonel Jean Ganeval. The past week had been amongst the most trying of the storied marshal's life. The Russian breakthrough at Lahde; the hurried, bomb-interrupted trip to Viipuri; the difficult decision to withdraw to the intermediate line; the emotional appeal to his troops to stand fast.[235] All these concatenating shocks had taken a palpable toll on the seventy-two-year-old Finnish commander-in-chief.

Over the past forty-eight hours the battlefield situation had only gotten worse. After a brief respite, the Soviet juggernaut had already broken through the intermediate line at two points. Casualties were mounting daily. Two days before, for example, nearly 300 Finnish troops had died at Kirvesmaki, on the eastern end of the line, near Taipale, which had also come under Russian pressure.[236]

The Swedish government's refusal to get further involved in the conflict—at least officially—and particularly the humiliating way that refusal had been conveyed, had also come as a devastating blow. Mannerheim later wrote scathingly of the hypocritical attitude of the Swedish government.

> [Swedish] Prime Minister Hansson, in a speech in the summer of 1940, defended Sweden's policy with the argument that Sweden's attitude during the Second World War had been decided beforehand and followed the lines practiced for decades. After everything that has taken place since 1939, it is plain how hazardous it is to adhere to a standpoint which deprives the leadership of its freedom of action and makes its intentions clear to the adversary. . . .
>
> Neutrality is in our days no magic formula which can prevent Great Powers from utilizing the weakness of small States for their own ends. Sweden because of the weakness of small States, became a pawn in the game of the Great Powers, and her nearest neighbors became victims.[237]

On February 16, following a leak, the Swedish press had then published an article containing the purported substance of the painful conversation that Prime Minister Hansson, the stalwart upholder of Swedish neutrality, had had three days prior with Vaino Tanner, in which he had rebuffed the Finn's request both for more active aid, as well as refusing once again to grant Allied rescuers transit rights. Hansson then publicly acknowledged the veracity of the article—to the anger and dismay of many Swedes, who had been hoping that the government would do more, not less, for their hard-pressed Finnish brothers.[238]

"It is Finland that is Europe's advanced guard against Asia," cried the *Goteborgs Handels och Sjofartstidning* on February 18, as the controversy grew. "We are content to spend money and to allow a number of volunteers to cross our border." But that had not been enough for the paper, which already referred to the conflict taking place across the Bothnian Sea in the past tense. "Sweden failed. She failed democracy's cause. She failed a brother in the hour of distress. She failed her historic obligations and failed her own future. Those who now make these decisions are carrying a frightful responsibility. They have the responsibility for our people's existence. This is a matter of our life, a matter of everything that is of consequence."[239]

Mannerheim, who was following the brouhaha across the water closely, couldn't have agreed more.

Then, the next day, February 19, King Gustav—who was also commander-in-chief of the Swedish Armed Forces, the last Swedish royal to hold that post, as well as the last sovereign to hold any real power—made an extraordinary move, one of the most extraordinary acts of his reign. Against the wishes of his cabinet (as well as his pro-Finnish son), the king joined the fray, issuing a public statement repeating what his prime minister, Hansson, had so clumsily said a few days before, if somewhat more tactfully. The king began by reiterating his moral support for Finland.

> For the entire time I have been following with great admiration our brother country, Finland, in a heroic fight against superior forces. Sweden has from the beginning through volunteers and other help tried to assist Finland.
>
> But from the first day I stated clearly to Finland that their country could not expect military intervention by Sweden.
>
> With sorrow in my heart I am, after the closest consideration, of the opinion that we in the present situation must hold fast to this decision [not to send Finland regular Swedish troops] because it is my absolute opinion that if Sweden now should intervene in Finland it would cause the direct risk that we should not only be drawn into the war with Russia, but also the war between the great powers and I have not been able to take the responsibility to face such a risk.[240]

"The King's words as if by magic quieted the storm that Hansson's statement had caused," writes Max Jakobson. "It changed nothing, but it did satisfy people's emotions." That was it: if Hansson had effectively shut the door to Swedish aid, the widely revered King Gustav had locked it. And, to Mannerheim's bitter and everlasting disappointment—it would remain shut.[241]

Two years later, upon the commencement of Operation Barbarossa, the German invasion of the Soviet Union, Gustav, who was known to privately harbor Fascist sympathies, would commend Hitler for helping rid the world of the "Bolshevik menace." Meantime, the Hansson government signed an agreement with Berlin allowing two weekly sealed trains packed with *Wehrmacht* soldiers and carrying Swedish guards to cross its territory to Oslo to relieve German troops there, and vice-versa. This so-called *Permitentraffik* (permitted traffic) between Germany and Sweden was allowed to continue until August of that year, when Stockholm realized that Germany would probably lose the war.[242]

The cumulative effect of these military and diplomatic blows had left Mannerheim reeling. "The final Soviet successes," his biographer writes, "came as a shock made all the worse because hopes of increased Swedish help had been publicly shattered." It was against this distressing setting that Mannerheim prepared to meet his British and French guests. The last time General Ling had visited, several weeks before, the Finnish commander-in-chief, perhaps slightly affected by the Suomussalmi factor himself, had told Ling that he was confident that Finnish troops could hold out until May.[243]

✱

The tense conclave between Mannerheim and his would-be rescuers on February 20 was decidedly less friendly than their last one, as both parties played their cards close to their chests, as Clark records: "Ling was reticent about the timing and strength of the coming Anglo-French expedition. Nor could he say whether it was likely to get a friendly reception from the neutrals. But on one matter he was quite clear: the first Western soldiers to reach Scandinavian soil would be fully occupied with the counter-action which Hitler would certainly launch against Norway and Sweden. The reinforcing of the Finnish armies would have to take second place."[244]

If Ling was reticent with Mannerheim, so was Mannerheim with Ling, opting not to tell the latter about the peace feelers Helsinki had tried to put out to Moscow.

On one level, Mannerheim seemed to be vexed with Ling's sad tidings. Or was he? "It is hard to believe that Mannerheim was surprised by Ling's news, or that it greatly vexed him. As a military strategist he must have seen it coming. As a politician he now had a lever for extricating Finland from the war on the best terms that in her desperate situation she could hope for."

"The warning that Allied reinforcements would take time to arrive offered him the chance to knock some sense into the heads of the politicians in Helsinki and encourage them to press more vigorously for a speedy peace," Clark concludes. Which is exactly what Mannerheim proceeded to do.[245]

✱

Several days later in Washington, Hjalmar Procope was the guest of honor at a melancholy fund-raiser at the home of a well-heeled Washingtonian. Two short months before, the Finnish envoy had been one of the most sought after figures in the capital. Now, however, after eight weeks of pleading the Finnish case with the U.S. government and with little more to show for his troubles than a credit restricted to non-military supplies, the Finnish envoy had become an object of pity.

Drew Pearson, the noted Washington columnist, wrote up the sad little affair the next day. The headline for his column said it all: *Desperate Finns Bite Nails While High-Hat Parties Proceed Futile.* As he witheringly put it,

Most popular but most pathetic pastime of Washington society these days is raising money for Finland.

Distinguished and well-meaning ladies hold afternoon tea and dinner parties in which the problem of Finnish relief is discussed and dissected fore and afterwards.

Meanwhile Hjalmar Procope, distraught Minister of Finland, sits and listens. He is polite, but it is easy to see that while this conversation rages, he is thinking of anti-aircraft guns and airplanes and how many weeks more his country can last.[246]

At last, the overcome ambassador gets up to speak.

His voice breaks, the tears stream down his face, the meeting adjourns. The ladies have had their emotional spree, but little has been accomplished for Finland.[247]

Pearson's barbed piece ends with a confidential "flash" from the well-connected columnist's private intelligence network: "Note—Confidential dispatches report that Finland's condition becomes daily worse. Troops are exhausted. There are almost no replacements. It may be a matter of weeks."[248]

On February 21, the Finns caught one more break from their erstwhile ally, General Weather—their last, as it turned out—when a violent snowstorm descended on the country, forcing a halt to both Russian ground and air operations. That morning, at 8 A.M., earlier than ever before, and while it was still dark, air raid sirens sounded again in Helsinki, routing the hardy but haggard 60,000 or so remaining residents of the capital out of their beds and into their shelters again. Earlier during the war the encroaching bombers would have waited an hour more for the late Finnish daybreak to attack. Now, however, the dark was no obstacle to the Red Air Force and its newly arrived crop of nocturnally adept pilots. Then, mercifully, came the sheltering snow, shielding Helsinki from further attack. Helsinkians, looking out their windows at the white tempest, hoped it would never stop.[249]

8

The Gates of Viipuri

February 24–March 12, 1940

*We have been left alone. Western aid cannot save us: it would only turn
Finland into a battleground between the Great Powers.*
     —Vaino Tanner, speaking to the Finnish cabinet, February 28,
     1940, quoted in Jakobson, *Diplomacy of the Winter War*

*FINNS REPULSE ATTACKS ON GULF ICE; 100 DIE AS RUSSIANS BOMB
HOSPITAL*
     Drive for Mainland from Island Bases Halted by Coast Guns and Planes—
     25 Women Victims in Fierce Raid on Town
     —*New York Times,* March 5, 1940

*By last week, a U.S. citizen who had neither danced, knitted, orated, played
bridge, bingo, banqueted, or just shelled out for Finland was simply nowhere
socially. The U.S. mood had changed: isolationism had been thrown away
with last year's calendar. On its March engagement pad, the U.S. marked
"Save Finland."*
     —*Time,* March 11, 1940

The date: February 28, 1940. The place: Vyacheslav Molotov's office overlooking
Red Square. The Soviet commissar was on the telephone with Alexandra Kollontai, his ambassador to Sweden. Molotov was not happy. A week before he had
sent to Christian Gunther, the Swedish foreign minister—who, along with Kollontai, had been acting as his go-betweens with the Helsinki government—his
latest set of "military minimum demands" for preconditions for peace talks with
the harried Finns.[1]
     The demands, reflecting the success of the Red Army's new offensive on the
Mannerheim Line, were steep. As the price of peace, Molotov now wanted not
only a long lease to Hanko, but the cession of the entire southeastern corner of
Finland, including most of Finnish Karelia. This would roughly correspond to
the line Peter the Great had drawn at the peace of Uusikaupunki in 1721 following his pivotal victory with his Danish and Polish coalition partners over Sweden
in the Great Northern War—the war that made Russia a Baltic power for the first
time.
     There was more. Moscow now demanded the Ryabachi peninsula in the
north, as well as a slice of the Salla sector of eastern Lapland. Additionally,
Finland had to join the USSR and Estonia in a mutual assistance pact for the
defense of the Gulf of Finland. As a minor—and disingenuous—concession,

Molotov omitted the earlier Soviet claim on areas in the far north; that could be tacked on later. This, as Molotov put it, was "the logic of war."[2]

Shocked by the new Soviet demands (though it ought not to have been), the already divided Finnish cabinet had remained mum. Those crack troops Chamberlain and Daladier were promising (or was it threatening?) to send the beset Finns suddenly looked more promising. On February 24, the newly appointed British minister to Helsinki, Gordon Vereker, had assured Vaino Tanner that a 20,000-man Allied expeditionary force would sail by March 15, arriving in Finland no later than April 15.[3]

Still, Tanner had his doubts, as Jakobson notes:

> This was, on the face of it, a heartening message. But how would the troops get through Norway and Sweden? On this point the Allied diplomats in Helsinki could give only vague answers. They talked of exerting "moral pressure" on Sweden and Norway, but were unable to say what might be done if the pressure failed. They could not say because their governments had not made up their minds. They were still confident that a final desperate appeal from Finland could not fail to move her western neighbors.

The Finns, of course, still had to set the bizarre caravan in motion: "There was not much time to lose: the Finnish government was told the appeal had to be issued at the latest on March 5, if the troop ships were to sail five days later."[4]

In short, the government found itself confronted with two choices, neither of them appealing: accept Molotov's new demands, lose Karelia, and make peace with the Kremlin; or the hardly more attractive one of issuing the formal appeal that would initiate the quixotic Allied rescue effort and most likely turn Finland, as well as the rest of Scandinavia, into a new theater of war between the Great Powers. Faced with these unappetizing options, the cabinet once again, foolhardily, decided to keep Molotov waiting for an answer.[5]

While the cabinet was thus temporizing on February 26, following an unsuccessful counterattack against the fast-moving Soviet forces, Heinrichs's drained troops retreated to their positions on the rear line that ran through Viipuri. In the counterattack at Honkaniemi, the Finns had hoped to catch the Russians off guard by deploying its small contingent of thirteen outdated, poorly maintained Vickers tanks for the first time against the invader. The attack was a fiasco. Only six of the obsolescent vehicles were able to make it to the battle line, and these soon got stuck, providing easy target practice for the mass of Soviet tanks facing them. Only one of the contraptions survived the debacle, the first and last Finnish tank attack of the war.[6]

The disaster was made complete by one of the worst friendly-fire incidents of the *Talvisota,* when the preliminary artillery barrage that was supposed to pave the way for the assault instead came down on the accompanying troops. Now it was the Finns who were having difficulty synchronizing their arms. Spreading out through the besieged city and its suburbs, the tired, demoralized troops passed out their last bullets and shells and waited for the next Soviet assault.[7]

Scanning the deserted, blackened city through their binoculars, their eyes alighted upon one cheering sight: the huge flag of Finland, floating unconcernedly from the top of ancient Viipuri Castle, the same citadel that Tyrgils Knuttson, the battling Swedish crusader, had built back in 1293. It had been fought over countless times by succeeding legions of Swedes, Russians, and Finns, and had yet survived as a symbol of Finnish resistance. For how long, the Finns wondered, would that flag continue to fly?[8]

In the meantime, Viipuri itself, once considered one of Finland's liveliest and most sophisticated cities, had become a shadow of its former self, its buildings shelled and destroyed, its once lively parks pitted by bomb craters, its formerly bustling streets inhabited now only by the pigeons and a few sentries, "a dead city awaiting its doom," as a haunted Webb Miller termed it in his United Press dispatch that he filed after a visit with a colleague from *Newsweek* on February 26:

> What was once Finland's gayest city, a center for lake country tourists, contained no living thing except some sentries, a few other soldiers and some pigeons. There was almost complete silence. During our stay there was only one heavy explosion, somewhere on the southern edge of town.
>
> We inspected the town on foot, since the streets were piled high with snow, abandoned furniture and the debris of houses that had fallen on the roadway. Bombs and shells have made the city the worst picture of devastation in Finland.
>
> There is neither water nor electric light. Street car wires lie useless in the snow beside the tracks. Huge trees in the central park are torn and lie in shell holes.[9]

Except for the historic castle, most of the city's structures, including its once magnificent Lutheran Church, built in 1849, had been destroyed, Miller noted. The hotel where he and his fellow correspondents had last stayed several weeks before was still on fire from the prior day's air raid, smoke bellowing from a dozen windows.[10]

There was one slightly encouraging sign for Finnish sympathizers: three British Blenheim bombers, perhaps part of the most recent batch the British had sent—and that had actually arrived in time—swooped over the smashed city, not that they were much of a counter to the immense Soviet air fleet which dominated the leaden skies.

Taking it all in with a sigh and a shrug, the dog-tired defenders of Viipuri and Viipuri Bay, numbering perhaps 20,000 in all, facing a Soviet assault force at least ten times as large, hunkered down and waited stoically to make their last stand.

They would not have to wait long.

By February 27, Timoshenko's forces, emboldened by the fall of Koivisto, including the fortress at Saarenpaa, had destroyed or captured the remaining key fortified Finnish positions on the east shore of Viipuri Bay and were ready to continue the offensive. Taking another page from Peter the Great, Molotov's equally impatient colleagues at the Main Military Soviet (as the Soviet Supreme Command was also called) had given Semyon Timoshenko his final marching orders: to destroy the Finnish army in a double encirclement of Viipuri like the one Peter the Great had successfully executed two centuries before, before continuing on to Helsinki—unless, of course, Helsinki capitulated first, as Molotov, who himself was becoming increasingly nervous about the prospect of engaging with the British and French, very much hoped.[11]

For the Soviets the time had come for a bold move, and Timoshenko, who was just as keen to finish the job as quickly and as decisively as possible—for it is well to keep in mind that he was fighting as much to restore the prestige of the Red Army as to defeat the Finns—was prepared to act boldly. As Van Dyke wrote:

> To accomplish [this], Timoshenko subordinated the Baltic Fleet command to his Northwestern Front headquarters and ordered it to organize diversionary strikes against the Finnish coast from Kotka to [the] Ristiniemi Peninsula, while Pavlov's 28th Rifle Corps attacked the north-west shore of Vyborg Bay. Timoshenko entrusted the other pincer of the double encirclement to Gorolenko's 50th Rifle Corps which was to converge on the Saimaa Canal from the East, while the 10th and 34th Rifle Corps hammered at the Finnish defenses on the southern approaches to Vyborg, and Grendahl's 13th Army tied down Finnish forces along the Vuoksi lake system and at Taipale.[12]

In manpower terms, twelve Soviet divisions along with five Soviet tank brigades—approximately a quarter of a million men—were about to hurl themselves in the Viipuri area against two understrength, ammunition-poor, bone-tired Finnish divisions of less than twenty thousand.

Already that day, February 28, some of Timoshenko's units had made contact with the Finnish rear line before being stopped—ironically enough by artillery fire from cannon the Finns had captured from the Russians at Suomussalmi.[13]

The stage was set for the final act of the war.

✳

Finally, on February 28, Molotov, not one known for his patience, blew his cool. Grabbing the phone, the agitated foreign commissar phoned Stockholm and ordered Madame Kollontai to tell the Swedes to tell the Finns (this was a very roundabout "postal route," one must recall) that he had to have an answer within forty-eight hours. *Or else.*[14]

The fractious Finnish cabinet agreed: it had to make up its mind—the first time it had agreed on anything in some time. Clearly, both the military as well as the diplomatic walls were closing in. Koivisto, abandoned; the withdrawal from the intermediate line; alliance with Sweden refused; Viipuri surrounded and in ruins. Despite the ministers' large capacity for denial, these things could no longer be ignored.[15]

Even the *New York Times,* its blue-and-white-tinted glasses finally shattered, was finally getting it right: witness the dispatch from its newest (and evidently most objective) man in Helsinki, George Axellson, following the Finnish military's (belated) admission about the loss of the crucial fortifications at Koivisto.

"The Finns today admitted that they have abandoned their Koivisto fort," the article, headlined "VYBORG 'KEY FORT' TAKEN," read:

> This is the most depressing news received here since the war began. Even if it does not necessarily mean that Vyborg's fate is sealed, it places that city in a situation more serious than ever before. The forts of Koivisto have been called the key to the bay, and the island was one of the strong points the Russians wanted in their October demands. Curiously enough, it was at Koivisto that the former Kaiser and the late tsar in 1905 signed a military pact that just turned out to be another scrap of paper.[16]

Would a peace treaty with the tsars' Communist successors also turn out to be a scrap of paper? Would Moscow respect the sovereignty of the Finnish state it had just defeated—the same state it had tried to supplant with Otto Ville Kuusinen? This horrific—but plausible—prospect also had to be taken into account before the cabinet could give the Politburo a reply.

First—quite sensibly—the ministers wanted to know what their military chief, Mannerheim, thought about the situation. And so the following day, February 29, a delegation led by Prime Minister Ryti, sans the disconsolate Tanner, dutifully took the train to Otava to hear what Mannerheim and his generals had to say.[17]

*

Given the chance to pound some sense into the politicians' heads, the no-nonsense Finnish commander-in-chief seized it, giving the ministers a realistic—and decidedly pessimistic—briefing on the situation.

The facts were quite simple. However, if the cabinet needed them spelled out, Mannerheim was happy to do so. The Finnish Army, down to its last reserves, was spent, the marshal explained. The troops were doing their best, but it was only a matter of time before the Russians were in Viipuri itself. The latest bulletins from the front had only underscored the gravity of the situation. The previous night the commander of the Finnish 2nd Division, which had withdrawn to the eastern side of the Vuoksi River and was now defending the Sintolanniemi-Vuosalmi line from the sledgehammer Russian attacks, issued this bleak assessment: "Today we are okay. Tomorrow we'll be really struggling and the day after tomorrow the 2nd Division will no longer exist as a fighting unit unless we get full assistance from III Army Corps."[18]

Would there be a "tomorrow"? That was a valid question: at the very moment Mannerheim was rendering his grim situation report, Timoshenko had launched his final offensive.

God certainly didn't seem to be smiling on Finland at the moment, despite the Pope's fervent prayers: the previous day, in a widely publicized move, Pope Pius XII had donated a sealed prayer on behalf of Finland to a Pro Finlandia auction organized by Bukowski's auction house of Stockholm.[19]

Witness the uncongenial weather. By this time of year, as all knew, the spring thaw would have begun, making the mud-filled tank traps that the Finns had laboriously built difficult for the Russian tanks to negotiate. Instead, in the continued extremely cold weather, they had frozen over, making it easy for Stalin's tanks to drive over them. Worse, according to the latest reports, Viipuri Bay remained frozen solid. Normally, by late February, that body of water would be a jagged, impassable mass. Now, to the dismay of the retreating Finns it was as smooth as a skating rink and thick enough to bear heavy vehicles. Once Finland's greatest ally, General Winter had finally betrayed her for good. No, the situation did not look good at all. In fact, it looked downright unfavorable.[20]

Mannerheim continued his downbeat *tour d' horizon*. The door to Sweden was closed; the proposed Allied relief expedition too small in scope. That same day France's ambassador to Helsinki, Charles Magny, aware of Helsinki's dilemma, had urged the government to issue the formal League of Nations–endorsed appeal for assistance that would, theoretically, persuade the Swedes and Norwegians to come to their senses, retire all this folderol about neutrality, and allow the Allies to come to Finland's aid. However, even in the unlikely event that the Swedes and Norwegians changed their minds and allowed the expeditionary force to cross their territory, the commander-in-chief pointed out as the ministers listened unsmilingly, what good would 10,000 or even 15,000 troops do Finland in April?[21]

Finland had no choice, Mannerheim forthrightly stated. Terrible as the terms were, they had to be accepted; either that or face annihilation, and even the iron-willed Finnish generalissimo could not do that now.

The war, it seemed, had finally gotten to Mannerheim, too. He had listened to too many casualty reports by now; he could not bear anymore. How many more lives could Finland spare? For example, the latest report was that the 7th Division, then fighting in Taipale, was losing 100 men a day. And that was on the "strong," eastern side of the Mannerheim Line.[22]

Sentiment had its place; now it was time to think about survival. As Veijo Meri, the Finnish historian, wrote, Mannerheim knew how to be afraid, and now he was afraid, very afraid, for Finland. In public, Mannerheim was still very much the defiant chieftain. Just several weeks before, when the new assault had begun, he had proclaimed: "We shall fight to the last old man and child. We shall burn our forests and houses, destroy our cities and industries, and what we yield will be cursed by the scourge of God!"

But now he knew it was time for Finland to strike her colors—if there was to be a Finland at all.[23]

He then asked his fellow generals to give their individual situation reports, presuming that they would agree with his grim assessment.

Whereupon, as Mannerheim records, the incredible happened: his generals, in effect, staged a mutiny: they wanted to fight on. "I requested the generals present to give the Ministers their opinion of the situation. When they had done so, I found, somewhat to my astonishment, that with one exception their opinion was that we should hold on and that the battle could and must continue."[24]

The way Mannerheim saw it, the glass was half empty; but to his generals, it was half full. Yes, the situation on the isthmus was grave, his subordinates conceded. Yes, the men had now retreated to the rear line, but they were standing fast and they would continue to do so. Moreover, there was such good news from north of the Ladoga, where after the elimination of the *motti* at Lemetti the destruction of the rest of the Soviet 18th Division seemed certain.[25]

The generals had taken their chief's fighting words to heart, perhaps too much so. The most difficult thing for a fighting general to do—and all of Mannerheim's generals were fighting generals—is to sheath his sword, and these generals simply could not stomach doing so. At least not yet. They wanted to fight to the last man.

However, their leader was no longer willing to endorse or countenance such a prospect. His only objective now was to save Finland and what remained of its army so that it might live to fight again. If the fighting and dying lasted much longer, with entire companies of men now being killed every day, soon that would no longer be possible. Taking his generals aside, he in effect ordered them to revise their situation report. "While the Ministers went aside to confer, I seized the opportunity to give the generals my reasons for the opinion which had grown to conviction. I told them that I did not think we should allow bitterness over the hard conditions to blind our judgment."

"The Army," the marshal reminded his dejected generals, "was not defeated." This was the key thing. Soon it would be, "and our chance would be lost." The generals reluctantly grasped Mannerheim's point. Then they followed their leader back into the room.[26]

"After a short discussion, I could inform the government delegation that there was no divergence of view among the military commanders concerning the necessity for concluding peace without delay." It was agreed, then. The cabinet, having heard the marshal out, was finally of one mind—or close to one, as Jakobson writes: "Now everyone was ready to submit except [Minister of Education] Hannula, who opposed peace without reservations, while [Minister of Defense]

Niukkanen would agree to it only on conditions that the new border run south of Viipuri. The President, too, was persuaded, and the Foreign Affairs Committee of Parliament approved the majority decision with only one dissenting vote."[27]

Peace, once more, was in sight: with great difficulty, and at great risk to his reputation (not to mention his mental health, one imagines), the redoubtable Finnish military leader had succeeded in injecting some sense in both the politicians' and the generals' heads, forcing them to apprehend and accept the terrible truth. It was, unquestionably, one of Mannerheim's finest hours.

By a majority vote the ministers agreed to send Molotov an affirmative reply.[28]

Not that Finland was willing to go quietly into the night, by any means.

That same day, as if to underline its defiance, Rudolph Holsti, the Finnish delegate to Geneva, hurled another *J'accuse* at the Kremlin, filing a sulphurous 3,000-word letter with the League of Nations, as if that would help matters. In it, Holsti accused Moscow of breaking virtually every rule in civilized warfare, citing in particular the Soviets' continued indiscriminate bombing of civilian targets, as well as their violation of the League-guaranteed neutrality of the Aland Islands with their planes or ships five times. Moscow, no longer a member of the moribund body, did not bother to respond.[29]

The feisty Finnish Air Force—bolstered by the arrival of the most recent batch of British Bristol Blenheims, an especially welcome flight of top-of-the-line Morane fighters from France, and an influx of new volunteer pilots from Sweden, Norway, Denmark, Italy, and the United States, amongst others—was still throwing itself into the fray with abandon, albeit with decidedly mixed results.[30]

Thus that day, February 29, in one of the fiercest dogfights since the beginning of the war, fifteen Finnish fighters engaged a group of thirty-six Russian fighters in the skies above Ruokolahti on the southeast edge of Lake Saimaa in northern Karelia. The engagement ended badly for the Finns. In a battle lasting a little under half an hour, seven Finnish aircraft were shot down and three pilots, including a Danish volunteer, Carl Mogens Kristensen, were killed. It was the saddest day in the history of the Finnish Air Force.[31]

This was the Red Air Force's second turn, too. Moreover, it also had more planes: by the end of the war, Moscow had, astoundingly, committed nearly 4,000 aircraft, including 1,700 bombers and 1,600 fighters, to the redoubled and refocused incursion. The Finnish Air Force, at its peak strength, never had more than 300 aircraft of all kinds, including perhaps 100 fighter planes; also, as much as the volunteers who were streaming into the FAF were appreciated, their quality varied. What had always been a lopsided conflict was now even more so, on every level.[32]

The signs were everywhere: it was time for Finland to throw in the towel while it still could. The text was agreed upon by the cabinet; the cable assenting to the Kremlin's onerous terms was set to go out. And then another cable, not from Moscow or Stockholm but from Paris, changed everything.[33]

✱

Enter the agitated form of Edouard Daladier, the French president, who now, implausibly, briefly—but devastatingly—took center stage in the great northern drama. The frumpy, chain-smoking French politician, who had, albeit with considerable misgivings, presided with his British counterpart, Neville Chamberlain, over the launch of the aspirational Allied expedition, Operation Avon Head, was now utterly committed to it. His very political fate depended on it.[34]

And so early on the morning of March 1, the anguished Frenchman fired off a cable from the Quai d'Orsay to Ryti at his Bank of Finland desk, promising to send to Helsinki's rescue not the 12,000 or 20,000 troops that had been discussed before, but 50,000. Moreover, the French president told the astounded Finns, these troops could and would magically arrive not in April, but at the end of March. As for the vexing question of securing their passage across neutral Norway and Sweden, not to worry: he would personally "guarantee" their passage. As an additional enticement—and here Daladier was really reaching—he also promised to magically send Finland 100 bombers, along with the crews to fly them.[35]

Daladier's move—the diplomatic equivalent of a Hail Mary pass in football—was "insidious," as Jakobson terms it. "It was a gambler's bid, backed by a check without cover. For he must have known perfectly well that he had neither the troops nor the planes nor the transportation to carry it out."[36]

The British, for their part, particularly Churchill and Earl Dowding, Britain's top fighter general, anxious to preserve the Royal Air Force for the struggle with Nazi Germany that they knew would come (as it would, less than a year later), were not willing to go that far. However, in the spirit of things, Chamberlain casually promised that he would send the Finns yet fifty more bombers. The "Finnish wild goose enterprise" had now reached the height of both daftness and mendacity: the French and British were now competing with each other to send troops and weapons that they could neither actually nor rationally spare from their own defense forces.[37]

At the same time, the British prime minister, angered by what he—correctly—perceived as Helsinki's disingenuousness, ominously added that if the Finns treated with the Kremlin, London would sever all military and economic aid forthwith. Thus the Finnish government found itself in an extraordinary and unprecedented situation: "Overnight the Allied promise of aid became a *threat* of aid. Finland was being blackmailed by one of her friends and bribed by the other. It would be hard to find in history another case of a small nation fighting for its life being bullied and cajoled by two Great Powers insisting on helping it against its will."[38]

Unfortunately, Daladier's frantic, eleventh-hour bribe, combined with Chamberlain's corresponding sweetened offer-cum-threat, worked. Impressed by the

Allies' sudden passion, the cabinet decided to withdraw the agreed upon text. Instead of agreeing to his preconditions for talks, a new deliberately dilatory message was sent to Moscow asking Molotov to delineate the proposed post-war border more clearly. Meanwhile, Finland's would-be rescuers, Daladier and Chamberlain, were asked to verify that the putatively enhanced force they were now promising to send Helsinki's way could indeed arrive by the end of March. Once again, the Finnish government had decided to play for time while playing both ends, so to speak, against the middle. It was a decision it would regret.[39]

As if the situation weren't already strange enough as it was, Gunther, the Swedish foreign minister and Finland's designated intermediary with the Kremlin along with Alexandra Kollontai—both of whom were as anxious for the Finns to make peace with the Soviets as Daladier and Chamberlain were for them to continue to make war—conspired to withhold Tanner's bogus reply for fear that it would only serve to further provoke Stalin.[40]

There now followed five days like few others in the annals of modern diplomacy. "March Madness," Clark aptly calls it. If one were to stage it as a light comedy, said play would have the flirtatious Daladier and the badgering Chamberlain off to one side of the proscenium, alternately pleading and threatening the *faux* in-decisive Tanner and Ryti, in the center of the stage, to let them rescue them from the accursed Bolsheviks or else, while off to the other side of the stage Gunther and Kollontai would be urging them to do the right thing and make an appoint-ment to fly to Moscow now—perhaps, as Kollontai had earlier suggested, Stalin might make a "grand gesture" and soften his terms.[41]

Meanwhile, as all this was taking place, Molotov, Stalin's right-hand man, was continuing to pace and fume in his Kremlin office, while waiting for those mis-erable White Guardists to reply. Even the normally level-headed Mannerheim —who had just, with great difficulty, persuaded his generals, as well as his gov-ernment to come to terms with Moscow—seems to have gotten caught up in the frenzy of the moment, endorsing the cabinet's decision to play for time while firing off his own telegram to President Roosevelt asking Washington if it could send him some bombers to help him fend off the Bear.[42]

*

While this diplomatic divertissement was unfolding on the embattled Karelian Isthmus, the curtain was rising for what would turn out to be the final and per-haps strangest battle of the entire war: the battle of Viipuri Bay. One hundred and forty years before, the roughly V-shaped, island-dotted bay—measuring thirty kilometers wide at its base, from Johannes on its eastern shore to Risti-niemi peninsula on the west—was the scene of one of the greatest naval battles of the eighteenth century, between Russian naval forces led by Admiral Vasili Chichagov and the Swedish fleet commanded (not very well) by Gustav III.[43]

Now, as Chichagov's Communist legatees rushed up fresh divisions and supplies from Leningrad and concentrated their forces on the eastern side of the icebound bay, while the Finns fortified their positions on the western one, which also protected the road from Viipuri to Helsinki, the stage was set for another epic battle, except that this one would be mostly fought by foot soldiers and it would be fought on ice, a fittingly strange finale to one of history's strangest wars.[44]

The 10,000 Finnish troops clustered on the western side of the bay also had a new commander: none other than Major General Kurt Wallenius, fresh from his triumphs in the North. Now that the volunteer Swedish/Norwegian ground force, under Mannerheim's old friend and comrade General Ernst Linder, had been assigned to the relatively quiet Salla front while their countrymen guarded the Lappish skies, the hero of Kemijoki River needed a new command.[45]

The High Command had just the thing for him: command of the newly created, all-important Coastal Group, comprising the 4th Division, now strung out along the western shore, as well as the garrisons at Tuppura and the other islands in the bay. On paper, it certainly looked like a good move. In reality, it wasn't. Wallenius, his less heroic qualities rising once more to the fore, wasn't happy about the move. He missed the little eagle's nest he had made for himself at Rovaniemi. He didn't want to go to Viipuri. He wanted to keep on fighting the Russians in the fells, where he was comfortable, not on the rocky islands of Viipuri Bay. Nevertheless, the lion of Lapland went off to assume his new post.[46]

He would not be there for long. Several days later, after reports that the rambunctious head of the newly created Coastal Group had shown up drunk and disorderly for staff meetings, Mannerheim not only unceremoniously relieved Wallenius of his command but forced him out of the army altogether, removing his name from the active list. Finland, he decided, could not afford to entrust its military destiny to fools.[47]

At the same time, in another last-minute move in the sector north of the city, the Finnish High Command ordered the sluices of the Saimaa Canal to be opened, flooding the low-lying, tank-friendly terrain near Tali Station and Repola to a depth of one meter, thereby creating a new, unforeseen obstacle for Timoshenko: the Finns still had some arrows left in their quiver, too.[48]

❋

That same day, March 1, a small number of fortunate Finnish soldiers were given leave. One of them was Eric Malm, whose 10th Regiment had been in the thick of the fighting on the Mannerheim Line since the beginning of the new offensive. "Because the regiment had served so long, some people were finally given leave. The Russians had stopped for a moment, so it was considered ok for a few of us to go."

Ecstatic, though still sad to leave his comrades behind, Malm bid the thirty fellow soldiers of his platoon farewell and headed home for Helsinki for ten days, little suspecting that when he returned most of his confreres would be dead.[49]

✱

Another soldier who gladly took his leave at about this time was Simo Hayha, the unassuming young farmer who had become the Finnish Army's top sniper. As of February 17, Hayha, whose regiment, the 34th, had been involved in the successful fighting north of Lake Ladoga, had been accredited with an astounding 219 kills—the reported number would eventually rise to as high as 505 (542 if one includes unconfirmed deaths)—and his superiors felt that he was also due for a rest. Soon, too, Hayha, who insisted on using the old "iron sight" Pystykorva rifle rather than one with telescopic sights, was also back in the line.[50]

Anna-Liisa Veijalainen, the displaced mistress of Tuppura canteen, also went on leave at this time, having been given her first (albeit enforced) leave since August. Sadly, she boarded the train to Varkaus in the lake country now frozen over before transferring to another one for the short ride northward to her home in Leppavirta.[51]

As the ancient bus skidded into town, Anna-Liisa was perplexed to find the roads jammed with people in their Sunday best, evidently headed for church. But it wasn't Sunday. What was up? After alighting from the bus, she ran into a friend who invited her to come along. Still baffled, she agreed. Finally she figured it out: "It was a soldier's funeral. A big one."[52]

Because the young woman had not had time to change out of her uniform— a "tarnished ski costume"—upon entering the town church, she climbed to the balcony, overlooking the altar.

> To my horror I saw a row of nine coffins in front of the altar. No wonder, actually, as the men of my parish fought in Kollaa throughout the Winter War, and that is where these soldiers had been killed. After surviving the initial shock, I started watching the funeral congregation and got frightened when I saw my mother sitting on the family member bench.
>
> We had not received any mail since early February, and it was March 1st. I now realized that one of the deceased had to be my stepfather.

When the priest began his sermon, Anna-Liisa also realized, with a start, that two of the other coffins belonged to two of her schoolmates.[53] In the event, she was more saddened by the loss of her friends than that of her stepfather:

> Naturally I was shocked, although I found it difficult to mourn for my stepfather. I had never been able to stand him because of his violent nature and alcohol abuse. My mother had bore me out of wedlock and my stepfather never liked me. Even as a young girl, I lived in another house where I worked and gave my mother a part of my small salary.

Finally, the sermon came to an end, breaking the young woman's bittersweet reverie. Sadly, she joined the mourners and walked to the town cemetery, where the war's rising toll was made painfully manifest by the rows of fresh gravestones, 100 in all.[54]

There was one more rude surprise to come, care of the Russian Air Force. "After the sermon was over, the hundreds of mourners streamed towards the heroes' grave, where almost 100 soldiers had been buried in the early Winter War months. As if on cue, the Russians appeared once again to honor their handiwork. A squadron of some twenty bombers was flying above the village but did not drop any bombs there. Obviously they were headed to some more important target."

"The people walked on quite calmly," Anna-Liisa wrote, "but my knees almost failed. I had gotten used to the fact that whenever there were airplanes in sight they would drop something or other."[55]

Also on March 1 came a vivid reminder that Finns were not the only ones shedding blood for the Fatherland: a bulletin from Stockholm announcing that Lt. Col. Magnus Dyrssen, one of the original organizers of the *Svenska Frivilligarden,* the Swedish volunteer corps, and commander of the volunteer battalion *Stridsgruppen SFK* under General Linder, which had just taken over the Salla front from Kurt Wallenius's Lapland group, had been killed in combat.[56]

Bitter though Mannerheim was over the Swedish government's adamant refusal to render more extensive official aid to Finland, no one was more moved by and appreciative of the efforts of those Swedes and Norwegians who had taken the train to Haparanda to fight for their sister democracy, as well as those who, like, Dyrssen, paid the highest price. "Our Swedish and Norwegian brothers carried out the task for which five Finnish battalions had up to then been responsible, evidence that, despite 130 years of peace, Sweden and Norway still produced brave soldiers. We will always gratefully remember this token of Northern solidarity, and our thoughts go out with reverence to our fallen Swedish and Norwegian brothers-in-arms."[57]

As much as these noble sentiments were appreciated, Mannerheim was somewhat mistaken. Although the Swedish contingent suffered casualties— twenty-eight dead along with fifty wounded—there were no casualties amongst the much smaller Norwegian contingent.[58]

That day, by way of underscoring the contribution that Swedes from all walks of life were continuing to make, the United Press announced that 1,500 Swedish workers had left for Finland to work in war industry plants, while the Committee of Swedish Trade Unions declared that another 9,000 factory workers would be ready to entrain for Helsinki within the week. Simultaneously, in a reminder of the not insignificant contribution by Denmark (which Mannerheim, mysteriously, ignores in his memoirs), the United Press reported that 300 Danish metal workers were also leaving for Helsinki that night in order to relieve Finnish workers for service in the army; they were to join the 300 other Danes, including 15 pilots, who had already left to fight alongside their Finnish brothers.[59]

The *New York Times* was no longer in denial of the deteriorating situation in Finland: "RUSSIANS WITHIN MILE OF VYBORG: CITY BURNING, FINNS IN RETREAT," the front page of its late March 1 edition proclaimed.[60]

In the meantime, behind closed doors in Helsinki, Moscow, Stockholm, London, and Paris, the light comic opera otherwise known as March Madness reached *tempo furioso.* Here, in no special order, is some of what transpired on March 2 alone:

> Edouard Daladier, the French premier, sent *demarches* to the Swedish and Norwegian foreign ministries, respectively, informing them of the Allies' intention of sending troops across their territory, effectively presenting with a *fait accompli.*[61]
>
> The British government wrote Oslo and Stockholm informing them of the same.[62]
>
> Along with his peremptory note to the Swedes, Daladier appealed directly to King Gustav, asking him for his support for the proposed Allied expedition.[63]
>
> The Swedish sovereign immediately responded with a brusque counter-appeal of his own to the Allies reasserting the sanctity of Swedish neutrality and asking Daladier and Chamberlain to kindly respect the same.[64]
>
> Gunther, the Swedish foreign minister, who was just as determined to stop the Allied expedition from getting underway, told the Finnish ambassador, Erkko, that his nation would forfeit all Swedish support if, "for the sake of Viipuri and Sortavala"—as he casually dismissed the Finns' desperate desire not to give up those cherished Karelian cities—she turned to her Allied suitors for aid. "If that happened, he said, the Swedish government would have to tell Parliament that Finland had failed to take advantage of an opportunity to make peace. Then Sweden would have to think of herself and retain all the arms earmarked for Finland for her own use."[65]
>
> The Finns, unaware that Gunther, with the connivance of Madame Kollontai, the Russian envoy, had withheld their deliberately dilatory reply of the day before to Molotov's ultimatum, wondered why they hadn't heard from Moscow.[66]
>
> *Ad interim,* in Moscow, Vyacheslav Molotov, ignorant of Gunther's and Kollontai's decision to withhold Helsinki's reply, continued to nervously bide his time, while he waited to hear from the exasperating Finns.

Additionally, on March 2, Semyon Timoshenko, under pressure from his higher-ups to complete the stubborn Finns' military *denouement,* launched the next "sequence" of his offensive. Thousands of Russians waded in slow motion through the chest-high water in the Tali sector to the rear of Viipuri, intent on entering the ghost city from that quarter, and the men of the Finnish 23rd Division tried to hold them off. Meanwhile, four other Russian divisions in front of the city, the 138th, 7th, 24th, and 100th, drove for the line from Käremäenlahti to Tammisuo, just as firmly held by the men of the Finnish 3rd and 5th Divisions, and the white-clad shock troops of Dmitri Pavlov's 28th Rifle Corps simultaneously began their attack from their jumping-off points at Lihaniemi and Pulliniemi, on the eastern shore of Viipuri Bay, pouring onto the ice and making their way for the western shore via the intervening islands, held by Wallenius's Coastal Group.[67]

All three engagements involved ferocious fighting, as well as manifold acts of heroism and bravery on both sides. (According to some of the Finns fighting in the Tali sector, Trotter writes, the Russian soldiers who slogged through the ice-cold waters unleashed on them after they opened the Saimaa Canal "were the most courageous Red soldiers they had ever seen.") However, of the three, the battle of Viipuri Bay was perhaps the most intense, as well as the most arduous,[68] as Mannerheim relates.

The icebound bay was also the arena of the three-prong battle where the Soviets displayed the greatest audacity and ingenuity:

On March 2nd, the enemy established contact with our rear position (at Tali). However it was not there, but at the Gulf of Viipuri that the situation turned out to be the most difficult. The ice was now so strong that it bore heavy tanks, and lanes cut in the ice quickly became frozen hard.

Nor was the cover of snow deep enough to hamper the movement of different arms. The Russians therefore had every chance of developing their whole superiority southwest of Uuras. No fewer than four divisions supported by armor and aircraft went to attack.[69]

As part of the first part of Pavlov's "experimental" island-hopping campaign, the storm troops of the 86th Division doggedly made their way across the iced-over, billiards-smooth gulf, heading for the adjoining islands of Tuppura and Teikari as Finnish artillery shells fell amongst them, making gaping holes in the ice into which both men and machines disappeared, including four T-26 tanks and their crews entire.[70]

Over the next thirty-six hours Anna-Liisa's "boys" on Tuppura did their best to defend the little fortress island before succumbing to the heavily armored Russian force and retreating across the ice to Sakkijarvi on the western mainland, dragging their wounded behind them.

Anna-Liisa, having already returned from her short, sad home leave, and now on

mail duty along with the local priest in Sakkijarvi, learned some of the horrific details of the horrific final hours from the Tuppura garrison's army information officer:

> An attack against our island had been launched from Pulliniemi during the
> night of March 2nd. The boys held their positions the whole night and the
> following day long into the evening. They withdrew only after they had no
> more ammunition and had suffered severe casualties.
>
> The fortress's flare light sergeant, Simo Teikari, had been left on the
> shore of Kuningassaari with both of his legs severed, and he had begged
> Second Lieutenant Aki Serola [who was] skiing by to shoot him. Poor Aki
> had not been able to do it. As the canteen burned down, the Russkies had
> warmed themselves next to the flames while the last of our people managed
> to get off the island in the shelter of darkness, waiting for the opportune
> moment hiding under the boat shed.[71]

It was all a bit much for the young woman to absorb. "I cried and mechani-
cally sorted letters and postcards into slots."[72]

Still, the diplomatic follies continued.
On March 3, Tanner and Ryti, having grown increasingly dubious of the validity, no less the sincerity of the Allies' offer to rescue them, which now included
6,000 more men from Britain and 12,000 from France (at last count), sent a more
conciliatory message to Molotov via Gunther that peace could be made without
delay, as long as the Kremlin did not insist on Sortavala and Viipuri, i.e., Karelia.[73]
Molotov, who was (presumably) following Timoshenko's progress closely,
tellingly did not reply. Now it was the Soviet's turn to be coy.[74]

The second phase of the great battle taking place in and around Viipuri was now
reaching a climax. On the western shore Russian tanks had crashed ashore at a
dozen points. At the same time, as Cox recounts,

> Right out on the ice of the Gulf of Finland, the Soviets carried out an
> audacious strategical narrative which showed that their General Staff was
> now willing to take risks. From Koivisto a column moved thirty-four miles
> [fifty-five kilometers] across the ice and attacked the coast at Virolahti, forty
> miles [sixty-four kilometers] on the Helsinki side of Viipuri.
>
> At the same time, another column moved fifteen miles [twenty-four
> kilometers] from the island of Hogland in the middle of the Gulf, more than
> halfway between Leningrad and Helsinki, and attacked the Finnish position
> at Haapasaari Islands.[75]

The audacious, not to mention suicidal, attack from Hogland was thrown
back by the surprised Finns with the aid of their rapid-firing coastal guns, as

hundreds more Russian dead piled up on the beach along the frozen shore opposite or fell into the gaping holes the artillery shells tore into the ice.

However, even though the bold feint attack failed, it did succeed in forcing Mannerheim's overwhelmed staff to rush other troops from the immediate line around Viipuri to guard the entire length of the Baltic coast, for they could not anticipate where one of the Russian flying columns might hit next.[76]

At the same moment, at the head of Viipuri bay, house-to-house fighting had broken out as the Russians broke into the outskirts of the city itself, while to the north Timoshenko's slogging stormers penetrated the thin Finnish skirmish line southwest of Tali held by Heinrichs's 23rd Division and were running amok around the Finnish rear lines.[77]

For their part, the British and French were beginning to wonder and worry why the clearly beleaguered Finns didn't issue the formal plea for assistance that would allow them to rescue the little nation (as well as get at those Swedish iron ore deposits), which they longed to hear. Still, the Finns hemmed and hawed. In Moscow, an exasperated Molotov was waiting to hear the words of submission he wanted to hear from the Finns.[78]

Finally, on March 5, after receiving the latest encouraging brief about developments on the front, the People's Commissar for Foreign Affairs calculatedly lost his patience for the last time. Sustained by the news from Viipuri, he ended his own two-day silence by sending another message to Tanner informing him in no uncertain terms that if he did not receive an affirmative reply to his earlier ultimatum, including the demands for most of Finnish Karelia, with Sortavala and Viipuri included, stiffer ones would soon be on the way. Additionally, he warned, twisting the knife a little more, he might start doing business with Kuusinen again.[79] Tanner now cabled back, signaling his government's assent and asking the Soviets for an armistice.[80]

The March Madness was nearly over. The farcical quad-national roundelay might have been diverting, if not for the fact, as Jakobson writes, that in effect "several thousand Finns and many more Russians were killed for no other purpose than to help a French prime minister stay in power a little longer." Daladier would ultimately pay for his "insidious" move with his post as prime minister.[81]

At long last, the cabinet had come to its senses. In the event, the pressure from Molotov wasn't necessary. What really forced the minister's hand was the deteriorating military situation.

On that day, March 5, after another round of savage fighting, elements of the Soviet 86th Division, supported by a mass of 100 Soviet tanks along with batteries of heavy guns actually deployed and firing from the ice of the Gulf of Finland, broke the Coastal Group's defensive line. This served to establish a bridgehead at the peninsula around the small town of Vilaniemi on the western side of the bay, while fierce fighting continued on the tiny island redoubts of Ravansaari, Turkinsaari, and Neulasaari that remained nearby.[82]

The Finnish Air Force was now up to 166 combat aircraft, an increase of 44 from just a few weeks before thanks to newly arrived war planes from France, Britain, and Italy. In addition, there were assorted private donations, including three aircraft that the wealthy Swedish airline pilot Count C. G. von Rosen bought from his former employer, KLM, the Dutch airline, and with which von Rosen himself performed a night bombing mission. The newly expanded air force now made numerous aerial attacks against the advancing Soviet forces, strafing troops, blowing up tanks, as well as pounding holes in the ice. (Von Rosen was following a family tradition: his father Eric von Rosen donated the first plane to the fledgling Finnish Air Force in 1918.)[83]

Captain Eino Luukkanen, a pilot with *Lentolaivue 24,* who led a formation of fifteen fighters on one such attack, relates how the biblical-like scene appeared from his cockpit, as he and his men swooped down on the Red troops below and surged across the ice from Tuppura, which they had just captured, to Vilaniemi on the western coast of the bay.

> I am breaking radio silence and order my formation to follow me. Now we are playing the enemy by approaching from their direction. I bank to the left and lead the formation into a dive. There seems to be no lack of targets, because the 4 kilometer distance between Tuppura and Vilaniemi is full of columns, cars, trucks, and tanks.
>
> Above Uuras circles an I-16 squadron and another fighter unit is on the other side of the gulf over Ristiniemi. I continue the shallow dive, the sooner we hit the better for us.[84]

As Luukkanen notes, the Soviet cavalcade was not without protection:

> The range to the nearest targets is only one kilometer, when the air around us fills with explosives and tracers of anti-aircraft fire. Both white and black explosion clouds puff close to us, which attracts the enemy fighters.
>
> My first burst hits an infantry column, next in sight is a line of trucks and finally I manage to fire at two tanks.[85]

One can well imagine the havoc the Finnish ace was creating on the ice below. It didn't matter. Pavlov, the Russian corps commander, had his bridgehead on the western shore and he would keep it.[86]

Now the entire front was in danger of being rolled up. The Finns had deployed all their available reserves and were filling the gaps with schoolboys and men in their late forties. If the Finns were to carry on the fight, a general withdrawal to more defensible lines west of Viipuri had to be executed immediately, Mannerheim told the cabinet after it sought his opinion. On the other hand, if peace talks were initiated, the exhausted troops could be ordered to hold on as long as their declining stores of ammunition held.[87]

Mannerheim's men would surprise him once more. Amazingly, and to their everlasting credit, the haggard defenders of Viipuri and Viipuri Bay would hold on for another week. Their heroic stand would cost Finland dearly. Ultimately, the total losses in the battle of Viipuri Bay alone would amount to some 1,200 dead and 3,500 injured, nearly 10 percent of Finland's total casualties during the *Talvisota*.[88]

✱

The weight of the final battle continued to take its toll on Mannerheim as well. However, he didn't lose his nerve. According to Trotter:

> The strain of circumstances was merciless. Mannerheim was taking the worst gamble of his life and doing it while confined to a chair with a severe case of the flu. Even those who hated him had to admire the iciness of his nerve at this point, knowing that if the Russians did expand their beachhead on the gulf coast, there was nothing between them and Helsinki except a few companies of teenagers with ten days' training.[89]

At this time, too, the Red Air Force was still active all over Finland, carrying out raids against targets around the country, including a particularly heavy bombing raid against Mikkeli, one of the most lethal of the war, in which thirty-three civilians were killed.[90]

The cabinet had no other alternative. On the evening of March 5, after receiving its ailing commander-in-chief's latest situation report, following a heated debate, it voted to accept in principle the Soviet demands as they had been presented. Only one minister, the obdurate Uuno Hannula, voted against it. The reply to Molotov was finally cabled in code, before midnight. The only stipulation the humbled Finns asked for was that Molotov would agree to a ceasefire.[91]

Meanwhile, Helsinki's ardent British and French suitors, Chamberlain and Daladier, who had given the Finns a deadline of March 5 for issuing the public plea for help that was their prerequisite for action, continued to beckon and remonstrate urgently from the wings. Helping to fuel the Allies' ardor were the British and French press, which had come full out for the much-discussed expedition to rescue the Finns to proceed, and let the consequences be damned. The time for sitting on the sidelines was over! Let's help the Finns now! And if that meant war with the Soviets, then so be it.[92]

"It is becoming clearer every day that this war is no side issue," thundered the *Times* of London, on March 5, evoking the specter of the failed Gallipoli military operation of World War I:

> There is no time to waste in debate. As we look back upon the annals of old wars we are constantly struck by the opportunities which have been missed through a policy of false economy, of failure to appreciate the comparative unimportance of risks. The Gallipoli campaign in the last War is an outstanding instance.

Let us not prepare for ourselves once more the melancholy of lost chances—to find perhaps, as we have many a time found in the past, that the will and the means to seize them were really there all the while and that only some misunderstanding prevented us from doing so.

Our interest is clear and there is a moral issue involved as well as the material. The whole sentiment of this country demands that Finland should not be allowed to fall.[93]

It was time to jump once more into the breach, for Finland. A half-century later, Henry Kissinger would marvel at the sheer madness of Operation Avon Head: "For historians the puzzle remains as to what possessed Great Britain and France to come within a hairsbreadth of fighting both the Soviet Union and Nazi Germany simultaneously three months before the collapse of France proved the whole scheme was nothing but a pipedream."[94]

Significantly, Winston Churchill, who had been responsible for the debacle at Gallipoli and who, along with General Ironside, had been responsible for getting Chamberlain to think about getting involved in Scandinavia in the first place, had begun to back away from the operation, now that the possibility of tangling with the Soviets, which he most definitely did not want, loomed as an increasing possibility—although his protégé, Ironside, was all for it. Mixing it up with the Nazis didn't bother him. In fact, that was what Churchill had wanted in the first place. Tangling with both powers was something else. Chamberlain and Daladier, now totally committed to the chimerical operation, however, weren't about to call things off or exit just yet.[95]

Nor, for the moment, as Ryti and the other delegates furtively packed their bags in preparation for flying off to Moscow, did the Finns wish them to. The Allies' offer of aid could still, conceivably, be used as a bargaining chip to help persuade the Russians to modify their terms. And so, the Allies—still blithely unaware that Helsinki had been in contact with Moscow, no less that peace negotiations were about to begin—were asked to extend their deadline until March 12.[96]

Reluctantly, London and Paris agreed. The deadline was extended. The three divisions of troops who had been mustered for Operation Avon Head, and which had been ready to embark, were told to stand down. Daladier, for his part, was getting suspicious. "For several days we have waited for a Finnish appeal that we hasten to their assistance," he pouted, "and it is difficult to understand why its dispatch has again been postponed."[97]

"If it is not received," he warned darkly, "it is impossible for the Western Powers to accept any responsibility for Finland's status after the war."[98]

The following day, March 6, Prime Minister Risto Ryti, still ensconced in his office, received a cable back from Moscow inviting him to send a delegation for peace talks. However, crushingly, Molotov would not agree to an armistice. As the Russian foreign minister himself told Vilhelm Assarsson, the Swedish ambassador, in a request from the latter for a ceasefire on behalf of the Finns, "Why stop the fighting if one cannot rule out the possibility of having to resume it over a difference?" Now that Stockholm had helped to get the Finns to travel to Moscow, the Swedes were also anxious that the meeting between the Russians and the Finns not become another Munich, where two years before Hitler had dismembered Czechoslovakia with Chamberlain's and Daladier's blessing. After all, that wouldn't look good for Sweden, which (in its own way) had pushed Finland to the negotiating table.[99]

Flattering Molotov, Assarsson did his best to change the commissar's mind, pointing out that the Red Army had already accomplished its mission of regaining its prestige by breaking the Mannerheim Line, a striking feat of arms surpassing anything either the Germans or the Allies had accomplished thus far (not that that necessarily meant very much). An armistice for the Finns, the Swedish ambassador argued, would be perceived as a magnanimous gesture.[100]

His listener was unmoved. Hostilities would cease when the peace accord was signed, Molotov flatly declared, not before. Perceptions be damned. The Finns could negotiate under duress.[101]

And so, under duress, that day, the Finnish peace delegation was chosen. Included were Paasikivi, Ryti, Mannerheim's close aide and friend General Rudolph Walden—who, like Paasikivi, had also represented Finland twenty years before in the negotiations with the Russians at Tartu—and Vaino Voionmaa, a former Finnish foreign minister and long-time Social Democratic member of parliament. Tanner, who had worked so hard to achieve the peace, was, to his dismay, left behind for fear of rankling his Soviet opposite, who still loathed him.[102] It was probably just as well. The last days of the war would prove to be Tanner's finest hour.

And so, the following day, March 7, the four somber Finnish delegates drove off to Turku Airport to begin the roundabout journey to Russia, which, to throw off inquiring reporters and other agents, involved a bit of a ruse, flying to Stockholm, then doubling back to Turku and flying to Riga, and then finally flying on to Moscow.[103]

On the surface, Ryti, ever the banker with the pressed suit and careful combover, was his usual unflappable self: the man with ice in his stomach. Still, one can well imagine the perfervid thoughts racing through his mind as he flew to Moscow. Would Stalin make a "grand gesture," as Madame Kollontai had hopefully suggested, and ask for less territory? How much longer could the battered and bruised Finnish Army, now making its last stand at the gates of Viipuri, hold out? How would the Allies react when the truth about the Finns' double-dealing came out?

More important, how would the Finnish public, no less the troops in the field, who also had been kept in the dark about the peace negotiations, react when they discovered that their government was treating with the enemy? Could they accept peace? And what kind of peace could they accept? Certainly not the sort of peace Stalin and Molotov apparently had in mind. If there was any time for Ryti to have ice in his stomach, it was now.

So, too, for Mannerheim. The day before, the Finnish commander-in-chief had received a personal message of thanks from President Kallio, praising him and his men for the great feat of arms they had just achieved north of Lake Ladoga, where the 9th Division, under the direction of Hjalmar Siilasvuo, had finished the job of "chopping up" and immobilizing the Soviet 18th Division. However, Mannerheim's mind was more on the fraught situation at Viipuri, the embattled Viipuri archipelago, and his dwindling reserves. "Now, if ever, our efforts had to be extended to the utmost to give the greatest possible support to our diplomacy. At our training centers were fourteen battalions which constituted our last reserves of manpower. The order was given that these detachments should be assembled in the rear of the chief theater of the war, equipped and armed to the best of our ability."[104]

Any illusions that Ryti and his compatriots might have harbored about Soviet magnanimity were dispelled on the morning of March 8, their second day in Moscow, where, after a fitful night's sleep under virtual quarantine, they were ushered into the room with their Russian opposites for the putative peace negotiations.

For one thing, they were chagrined to find that Stalin wasn't even there. The Russian dictator, evidently unhappy that the Finnish business had gone on as long as it had, had deliberately absented himself. Instead, the Finns found themselves facing the unsmiling visages of Molotov, Andrei Zhdanov, the Leningrad Communist party chief, and Boris Shaposhnikov's deputy chief of staff, Commander (later Marshal) Alexandr Vasilevsky. The Finns' only solace was that their *bête noire,* Otto Ville Kuusinen, hadn't been invited.[105]

Grimly forging ahead, Ryti read the placatory opening statement he had prepared, in which he bid the Russians alter their terms for the sake of future harmonious relations. The People's Commissar for Foreign Affairs wasn't buying it. Instead, Molotov, who was obviously *au courant* with the British and French press, went on the attack. As Trotter writes,

> Molotov was frigid in his reply. Finland had proven itself to be a tool of the British and French imperialists, just as Stalin had [according to Molotov] feared back in November. Molotov pointed out that the London *Times* and *Le Temps* had both openly advocated military action against the Soviet Union.
>
> Ryti protested that his own government could hardly be held accountable for rabble-rousing statements that appeared in the foreign press. True, interjected Zhdanov, but the Finns had never bothered to repudiate these

statements. Molotov then grudgingly conceded that perhaps Finland may not have wished to be a pawn of the Anglo-French strategists, but nevertheless that was how it had worked out and it was from that diplomatic and strategic fact that the current discussions would have to proceed.[106]

Next, as the four Finns listened in dismay, Molotov read out the peace terms. There was to be no grand gesture. Quite the opposite. The Kremlin's demands had not been lessened; rather they had increased. Not only did the Kremlin still want most of Karelia, including Sortavala and Viipuri, as well as a long lease for Hanko. Now, Molotov announced, as he waited for the interpreter to translate his stinging words, Russia also demanded that the Finns cede a strip of territory in both the Salla and Kuusamo districts. Also, ominously, the Kremlin wanted to build a rail line connecting Salla in the east with Tornio in the west, so as to expedite access to Sweden from the Murmansk Railroad.[107]

As a concession, Petsamo would be given back to the Finns; however, Molotov demanded free passage through the Arctic port to Norway. Finally, and no less worryingly, Moscow also wanted the Finns to sign a treaty of mutual assistance and cooperation, like the ones it had wrested from Estonia, Latvia, and Lithuania before it had reabsorbed those independent nations into Mother Russia. Ryti, stunned, opposed the introduction of the new demands, but Molotov blandly replied that if the demands were new to Tanner, it was only because Madame Kollontai must have forgotten to mention them earlier.[108]

As it happened, Molotov had also failed to communicate the new conditions to the Swedes, who were no less taken aback, especially when they learned that the Russians intended to build a railroad across Finland, something that could only be interpreted as a threat to their security—so much so that, as Christian Gunther angrily warned Madame Kollontai, his government might have to revise its attitude about the matter.[109]

However, Molotov had also taken this into consideration. He wasn't concerned about the Swedes. He only was interested in what he wanted from the Finns, and he wasn't going to stop until he got it. "In his dealings with the Finnish delegation," Jakobson writes of Molotov, "he was utterly merciless."

> He refused to discuss the Soviet draft treaty point-by-point: it had to be accepted or rejected as a whole. Yet it was written in such general terms that Ryti could not be sure what he was asked to sign. The new border line, for instance, was defined only by a short list of place names; the map on which it had been drawn was out of date and small in scale, and the line was thick enough to cover a wide zone in nature.[110]

Molotov refused to be more precise. "All that can be settled later," he replied with a straight face. Flabbergasted by the new demands, Ryti and his three shocked colleagues withdrew, protesting that they could not possibly agree to the new terms without consulting Helsinki, and the first "peace" meeting was adjourned. For Ryti, his worst fears were realized. The Finns had walked into a trap, and there was no getting out.[111]

On the other hand, of course, there were still the Allies.

Inevitably, the British and French had gotten wind of what was taking place in Moscow—and were none too happy about it.

"Finland is free to decide her own conduct," an irate French spokesman declared on the evening of March 8, while the Finnish delegates were still reeling from their first bout with the Russians. "If she wants to fight on and appeals to France for help, she is assured of our immediate and firm response." The message from the French was clear: either you invite us in or we will wash our hands of you.[112]

"We know Russia fears you will appeal to the Allies," Daladier warned Helsinki. "Because she fears that an Allied intervention will lead to a Russian catastrophe, *Russia is now ready to negotiate in order to be able to destroy you later* [emphasis added]." It was a valid point.

But who would vouch that Finland would not be destroyed earlier, if it invited Allied help? That was the essential point.[113]

While all this was going on, the Finnish public, which had only a blurred picture of what was taking place on the military front, and absolutely no information about what was transpiring on the diplomatic one, was puzzling over the arcane official communiqué published in the newspapers that day: "According to information in the possession of the Finnish Government the Soviet Union is believed to have planned the presentation of demands to Finland more far-reaching in character than those presented last autumn. Details, however, of these demands are so far lacking."

"The people who read these words assumed at once that there would be no peace," writes Langdon-Davies in his post-mortem. "They did not know of the thousands of Russians advancing across the ice of the Bay of Viipuri and the Gulf of Finland."[114]

The press, however, was beginning to get the idea. The relatively accurate communiqué issued by the Finnish Army on March 8 tells its own story:

> Army. On the Isthmus enemy pressure against the northwest shore of the Bay of Viipuri continued on March 7. Fighting on the capes at the mouth of the bay continued until the evening with our troops still holding their positions. Attacks against our positions on the island [*sic*] were repulsed. Our artillery destroyed several tanks and at least eight guns of the batteries brought by the enemy on to the ice.

Between the Bay of Viipuri and Vuoksi the enemy launched several local attacks which were repelled; seven tanks and two armored cars were destroyed in these attacks. In the direction of Paakkola over 400 enemy dead were left lying in front of our lines after the fighting [of] the previous day. South of Vuosalmi [the] enemy attempt to advance across the Vuoksi River was beaten back. An attempt to attack at Taipale was repelled.[115]

✳

It was against this apocalyptic setting that the Finnish cabinet, now in receipt of Ryti's shocking cable containing the jacked-up Soviet demands, met in two dramatic back-to-back sessions on the afternoon and evening of March 9, 1940, at the Bank of Finland. Shortly before the first session, scheduled for 5 P.M., Tanner was buttonholed by a claque of American and British newspapermen, anxious to confirm the rumors they had heard about the still secret peace negotiations.

Weary from the long days and nights of urgent phone calls and cables and sudden visitors, Tanner did his best to stonewall the scoop-hungry reporters. An excerpt from one of the hurried interviews he gave that afternoon, to the British newspaper *Sunday Express,* is revealing:

Q: Has Finland received peace proposals and if so, how, when and where?
A: All I can tell you is that certain proposals have been made and they are under consideration.
Q: Has Finland replied?
A: I cannot tell you that. The whole world is full of rumors. We would like to answer all questions but just now we cannot tell what is going on, and that is all there is to it.[116]

Pressed further, the clearly distraught foreign minister replied that a decision would probably be reached sometime within the next few days. "If the proposals for settlement are not acceptable," he continued, referring to the situation on the isthmus, "the fighting will continue."[117]

"M. Tanner's voice as he spoke was tired and anxious," the *Express* correspondent noted. "Fighting is still raging on all Finnish fronts," Tanner told him. "The peace negotiations have in no way whatever diminished hostilities."[118]

Tanner was certainly right about the military situation: fighting was indeed raging on all the fronts, including north of Lake Ladoga, where the stalwart men of the 12th Division at Kollaa River, who had been in place since early December, were still, remarkably, holding out against Commander Grigory Shtern's 8th Army. There the fight was essentially going well. But on the most vital front, at Viipuri, it wasn't.[119]

That day the Finnish High Command issued a terse communiqué in which it conceded that the Russians had secured "a restricted foothold on the northwest shore of the bay" and had "captured some islands." "That," as Cox put it, "was the most vital sentence in any communiqué of the war."[120]

The "restricted foothold" the communiqué was referring to was a bridgehead near the Vilaniemi peninsula that the Russians had been able to establish as the 7th Army's left flank converged on the western shore of the blood-spattered bay, cutting the highway from Viipuri to Helsinki. Now the Russians were in a position to cut off the Coastal Group from Second Corps, which continued battling to defend the ancient castle city itself. "As no road network existed in the rear," wrote Mannerheim, "this meant that the whole coastal sector was cut in two and that the enemy would be able to roll up the front unless the headland of Vilaniemi were recaptured."[121]

Despite the Coastal Group's best efforts, the bridgehead that Pavlov's men had captured at such great cost—an estimated 10,000 Russian troops died in the battle for Viipuri Bay alone—remained in Soviet hands. Over the next four days the Russians would expand the salient to a depth of twelve to thirteen kilometers.[122]

That same day, in a last ditch effort to stop the Red tide, the Finnish Air Force launched its largest attack of the war, as a mixed force of Fokkers, Gladiators, Blenheims, and Morane-Saulniers furiously attacked the units of the six massed divisions moving methodically, ineluctably, across the ice. In the dogfight that followed, the Finns shot down three Soviet fighters, while sacrificing three of their own. It was a Pyrrhic victory.[123]

The Russians were now across the bay. That same day, the new commander of the Coastal Group, General Kurt Oesch, the chief of staff, who had hastily replaced the cashiered Wallenius (and who retained Mannerheim's confidence in that position), ordered his men to evacuate all remaining islands in the bay.[124]

From *his* point of view, Timoshenko, the overall Soviet commander, now under intensified pressure from his bosses to finish the job, was actually behind schedule, thanks in part to the havoc caused by the Finns' opening up the sluices of the Saimaa Canal, as Carl Van Dyke points out. "In fact by 9 March, Timoshenko's double encirclement of Vyborg was far behind schedule. In the region north-east of Vyborg [Viipuri], the 7th Army's main problem was overcoming the ever-rising flood waters from the Saimaa Canal: troops who waded across inundated areas had to be immediately pulled from combat in order to dry their uniforms while Red Army artillery had to repel Finnish counterattacks and suppress enemy fire."[125]

Joseph Stalin, increasingly nervous about the prospect of Operation Avon Head going forward, sent Timoshenko a memo urging him to speed it up, specifically mentioning the possibility of "French reinforcements."[126]

From the Finnish point of view, to be sure, Timoshenko was doing well enough. In Viipuri itself, units of the Finnish 3rd and 5th Divisions began preparing for house-to-house fighting. Northeast of Viipuri, near Tali, Russian tanks were running pell-mell, causing one Finnish regiment to panic and flee the field of fire. Military policemen actually had to be brought in to restore discipline. Clearly, the Finnish dikes were breaking.[127]

At his headquarters, General Ohquist, commander of the crumbling Second Corps, still unaware of the new peace negotiations, worryingly recorded in his diary: "This is an awful gamble we are taking! It is possible that we can keep Viipuri in our hands until tomorrow night. If we are ordered to continue resistance beyond that time, it means that either the city or the troops will be doomed."[128]

Meanwhile, back in Helsinki, the political situation remained delicate, as became clear the moment the cabinet convened for its first session at 5 P.M. to discuss the cable from Ryti containing Molotov's latest demands. To say that the assembled ministers were shocked is to understate the case, as Tanner recalls: "The members of the Cabinet were astounded at the harshness of the terms offered. The thought that Finland should be altogether shut off from Lake Ladoga, that two important cities and several important industrial regions should be lost, and that the wholly new demand had been presented for the cession of the Salla area was so novel that at first they all found it difficult to determine their stand." According to Tanner, the discussion was "prolonged and sporadic."[129]

The fissures that Tanner and Ryti had just patched over burst into view again, as several of the outraged ministers, particularly the bellicose ministers of education and defense, Hannula and Niukkanen, respectively called for the government to finally fire the official star shell of distress that would set the Allied rescue caravan in motion so Finland could continue the fight, while Tanner, the chief voice for peace now, along with Ryti in Moscow, wearily reiterated "the ineffectiveness of Western aid and the difficulties of obtaining transit through Sweden."[130]

The turbulent session was interrupted by a call from Mannerheim, who said that he was awaiting word of the situation at the front "and to ask that no final decision be made before we had received [this] data and his own conclusions that same evening, of the 9th." On that discordant note, the still-bickering ministers adjourned.[131]

Two factors ultimately decided the matter.

The first was the assessment of the situation on the isthmus that General Heinrichs, the new commander of the Army of the Isthmus, had prepared at Mannerheim's request, which the increasingly agitated commander-in-chief, in turn, relayed to the cabinet.[132]

"As commander of the Army," began Heinrichs's unrelievedly depressing report, which an ashen Tanner read aloud to the cabinet, "it is my duty to report that the present state of the army is such that continued military operations can lead to nothing but further debilitation and fresh losses of territory."

In support of my view I set forth the loss of personnel which has occurred. The battle strength of battalions is reported now generally to be below 250 men, with the aggregate daily casualties rising into the thousands.

. . . Considerable losses of officers reduce the utility of these diminished units. Through enemy artillery fire our machine gun and antitank weapons have been demolished to such an extent that a noticeable lack is generally apparent on critical fronts.

Since in addition, events on the right wing have made indispensable fresh expenditures of troops on unprepared terrain and at the expense of the present front, the endurance of our defense has been critically weakened.[133]

Heinrichs's well-documented tale of woe, which both Mannerheim and his other lieutenants had endorsed, continued:

Enemy air activity makes the transfer and maintenance of forces decidedly difficult. The commander of the Coastal Group, Lt. Gen. Oesch, has emphasized to me the scanty numbers and moral exhaustion of his forces, and does not . . . believe he can succeed with them. The commander of the Second Army Corps, Lt. Gen. Ohquist, has expressed the opinion that if no surprises take place, his present front may last a week, but no longer, depending upon how the personnel, especially the officer corps, is used. The commander of the Third Army Corps, Major General Talvela, expressed [the] view [that] everything is hanging by a thread.[134]

The cabinet—except for the two holdouts, Hannula and Niukkanen, who wanted to fight on—was duly impressed. Ohquist's prediction that the front could last no longer than a week was particularly telling. Clearly, any help that might arrive from the outside would be too little, too late, to alter the basic situation.[135]

The other factor, besides Heinrichs's report, which finally persuaded the majority of the cabinet that it had no choice but to turn down the Allies and accept the Kremlin's terms, was the disturbing and revealing discrepancy between the French and British offers of aid—100,000 men by March 15 was the latest notional figure the French minister to Helsinki, Charles Magny, had mentioned, while the now more cautious British were reluctant to promise anything like that—as well as the still unresolved problem of obtaining transit rights for the expeditions from Norway and Sweden. How could Finland be expected to entrust its fate to these people?[136]

But beyond that, even if the Allies were able to gain or force passage across Norway and Sweden, and even if the *Chasseurs Alpins* et alia were able to reach Finland in time to make a difference, as Tanner noted above, what would happen then? Did the cabinet really want the responsibility of turning Scandinavia into a staging ground for a clash between the Allies on one side and the Russians and their allies, the Germans, on the other? What sort of extended catastrophe would that portend? And would Finland, which had already suffered so much, necessarily come out any better?[137]

Tanner, in Helsinki, didn't think so; nor did his three colleagues in Moscow.

The harsh but unavoidable decision was made. The Kremlin's new terms would be accepted.[138]

✳

In fact, there are those who think the Kremlin's terms were relatively generous. One of them was historian and Soviet expert George Kennan, who credits the would-be Finnish caper and the prospect it presented of an Anglo-Soviet war on Russia's northwest border with inducing Molotov and Stalin to make peace more quickly than they might have otherwise. After all, the Russians were now winning. The Finnish Army, as Heinrichs's memo made clear, was on the verge of complete collapse.[139]

Army Commander First Class Semyon Timoshenko, for his part, would have liked nothing better, following the imminent fall of Viipuri, to keep on driving to Helsinki. And who knew how much more the Russians might have demanded if and when they reached the capital. But by that time, the British—assuming that the Finns had finally decided to call for their aid—would be on the scene, and Stalin and Molotov didn't want that. "If the British blow was going to be directed towards the North Russian borders," Kennan writes, "that changed everything." He goes on to say that it was probably this consideration that led the Soviets to "end the war with Finland, in March, on terms relatively lenient to the Finns."[140]

But Kennan was not a Finn. To the cabinet, to a man, the revised terms Molotov was now insisting on were both unconscionable and unacceptable. "No one who knows the meaning of and holds regard for justice, fairness and honesty could consider Moscow's peace terms reasonable," as the Fennophile Briton David Hinshaw put it in *Heroic Finland,* expressing what every Finn felt (and what most Finns *still* feel).[141]

But, ultimately, what choice—what reasonable or moral choice—did the Finns have but to accept those terms?

✳

Back in Moscow, Ryti, now virtually a prisoner of the Russians, along with the three other Finnish delegates, Paasikivi, Walden, and Voionmaa, did his best to try to get the Russians to modify their terms. To add to the Finnish prime minister's distress and discomfiture, Moscow state radio denounced him while he was still in the city. The Russians, he cabled the cabinet, would not relent. The only demand from the original list that Molotov dropped—a significant one—was the one about requiring a treaty of mutual assistance and cooperation. However, the triumvirate of Molotov, Zhdanov, and Vasilevsky absolutely refused to budge on their other territorial demands.[142]

The next morning, March 11, President Kallio and the cabinet met for the purpose of authorizing the Finnish delegates in Moscow to sign the treaty. The result of the somber meeting was foreordained. Following Tanner's lead, the cabinet, at last, voted *kylla* (yes) for peace. The two ministerial holdouts, Niukkanen and

Hannula, voted *ei* (no) and immediately tendered their resignations. Finally, ever so reluctantly, Kallio signed the decree granting the delegates the authorization to make peace. As he did so, the stricken president cried out, "This is the most horrible paper I have ever seen! Let the hand wither that is forced to sign such a paper!"[143]And so the terrible but unavoidable deed was done.[144]

✳

On the main battlefront, near once bustling Viipuri, events continued to bear out Mannerheim's and Heinrichs's grim predictions. On the western end of the Viipuri front, Meretskov's men, after finally storming ashore from the islands of Teikari and Tuppura, punched a five-kilometer-wide bulge in the Coastal Group's line, including the villages of Nisalahti and Vilajoki, and was preparing to move further inland. East of the embattled city, on the northeast bank of the Vuoksi where the Finns were holding the line with difficulty, the Russians had thrown another three divisions into the fray. Northeast of Viipuri, on March 9, the Soviet 84th and 123rd Divisions had taken the village of Tali and reached the western side of Lake Leitimojarvi, where the bloodied 23rd Division, now having completely exhausted its reserves, was doing its best to put up a defense.[145]

On March 11 the Russians began another tank attack. By nightfall, they had punched three holes in the Finnish lines west of the lake. Only at Taipale, on the extreme east end of the isthmus, as well as in front of Viipuri itself, were Finnish forces succeeding in keeping the Red assaulters at bay; however, it was only a matter of hours, certainly days, before the Russians also broke through to Viipuri and completed their envisioned double envelopment of the city.[146]

Not that everything was exactly hunky-dory for the Russians. For example, the Soviet 95th Division, which had just arrived to assist with the finishing blow, had lost a third of its strength in three weeks. The Russians were also beginning to suffer serious logistical problems, as the Supreme Command had increasing difficulty moving reinforcements up to the front line over the crowded isthmus roads. At the same time, the fiercely resisting Finns had showed, in a number of remarkable actions, that they could still act aggressively.[147]

✳

Vaino Tanner and the other members of the Finnish cabinet understandably agonized over how the Finnish public would react to the news of the pending acceptance of the Russian terms. The nation's morale was still high. So, on the whole, was that of its army. Some kind of political cover was needed. Consequently, simultaneously with the cable that went out authorizing the Moscow delegates to sign the hated paper, a *demarche* was sent to Stockholm and Oslo formally requesting the Swedish and Norwegian governments to grant transit rights to the Allies for the purpose of assisting the Finnish Army.[148]

This was another feint, but the British and French governments did not know that. They took the Finnish request at face value; here at long last was the signal to set the expeditionary force in motion. Finally, finally, Operation Avon Head was under way. Commanders were briefed; boats were loaded; instructions were given.

The invasion of Scandinavia was to be a semi-peaceable operation—a unique experiment in the history of warfare. The Allied force was not supposed to fight its way through to Finland; yet the commanders were also told not to be deterred by a mere show of resistance or by minor opposition. They were permitted to accept some casualties; yet they were to use force only as an ultimate measure of self-defense should their force be in jeopardy.[149]

What would have happened if the boats carrying those men had actually embarked? Six months later, after the Germans invaded Norway, a similar amphibious operation by the British culminated in disaster in Narvik and helped pave the way for the fall of the Chamberlain government. Would Operation Avon Head also have been a debacle? Most likely, one would think (if not a worse one).[150]

Would the Norwegians and Swedes have offered resistance to the Allied expedition? Perhaps. And what would have happened if those Finnish-bound Allied troops had actually made it to Finland and tangled with the Russians, the prospect that Stalin and Molotov were so anxious to avoid? We shall never know; it remains one of the great "what ifs" of World War II. One thing is certain: it would have made it more difficult for the British and the Soviet Union to come together and fight side by side, as they did a year and a half later when Hitler invaded the USSR.

In the event, at the same time the commanders of the star-crossed Allied expedition were receiving their instructions, President Kallio's authorization to accept Russia's terms was being decoded in Moscow. Shortly after midnight on March 12, as the Russians looked on with satisfaction, one by one the somber-faced Ryti, Paasikivi, Walden, and Voionmaa put their signatures to the Peace of Moscow, as the armistice treaty was called. Firing was to cease at exactly 11 A.M. the following day. There would be no expedition after all, Finland's disappointed (and angry) would-be rescuers were told. The orders to sail were canceled; the Norway-bound boats pitching off the English coast remained there with their troops and supplies unloaded.[151]

Peace had come. It only remained for the Finnish nation to be told the shocking news, as well as the even more shocking terms of that peace.[152]

Tears in Helsinki

March 13, 1940

It was the darkest day in our history, I think.
   —Harry Matso

If the first day of the Winter War was for Finns the longest day of the 105-day conflict, the last day was easily the second longest. If anything, peace, when it came, in the form of Vaino Tanner's radio speech that day, March 13, 1940, announcing the terms of the armistice, was as traumatic if not more so than the incendiary bombs that had suddenly fallen out of the sky the previous November 30.

It had been only two days since the Finnish people, who had been shielded so long from the truth, had first learned that negotiations with the Russians were under way. Still, no one could have imagined that the war, into which the entire nation had thrown itself, in which it had suffered so much and fought so hard, as well as experienced such everlasting glory, would end the way it did.

No journalist who was in Helsinki that dark day would ever forget it. Of all the passages in the droves of books and articles they would write about their experiences during the *Talvisota*, the most affecting are the ones dealing with what they saw and felt as they walked the streets of Helsinki and looked at the faces of the stunned, grief-stricken Finns around then. The experience was all the more vivid—and painful—for the newsmen because, unlike the people around them, they knew what was coming. This was one scoop most would have rather not had.

*

Virginia Cowles, who had been in Stockholm to cover the peace talks along with her colleague, Eddie Ward of the BBC—her second trip to Sweden of the war—was one of the first to get the scoop, thanks to a last-minute question Ward happened to ask Eljas Erkko, the Finnish envoy, during a hurried phone conversation, as she recalls:

> The following day [March 11] there were peace rumors. I ran into a Danish journalist who told me he was positive an agreement had been reached in Moscow, but was unable to get official confirmation of it. Eddie and I had

decided to return to Helsinki that night and rang up Mr. Erkko to arrange for airplane seats. Not expecting a reply, Eddie said to him:

"Is it true that an agreement has been reached in Moscow?"[1]

To Cowles's and Ward's astonishment, Erkko replied in the affirmative. Ward then sent a telegram to the BBC, which was read over the six o'clock news, the first semi-official report that the war was over. Erkko spent the rest of the evening trying to deny the peace rumors. When Cowles arrived at the Stockholm airport shortly afterward, a number of people who had heard the report, including an irate Finnish colonel who refused to believe it, were discussing it.[2]

"Did you hear the report that the BBC is putting out?" the colonel asked the two reporters, unaware that he was speaking to the party—Ward—who was responsible for the BBC report. "That fellow must be crazy," the officer exclaimed. "Peace!" he exclaimed. "We'll make peace when the Russians withdraw every last soldier!" he continued, as the other passengers nodded in agreement. Ward sheepishly agreed and moved away, and waited with Cowles to board their flight.[3]

"When we took off from the aerodrome the lights of Stockholm sparkled like diamonds against the snow," Cowles mused, "and we wondered what price Sweden had paid to keep them blazing." She remained in a pensive mood for the remainder of the flight. "It was a sad trip. Eddie and I were apparently the only passengers who knew what we were returning to, and it somehow seemed to make it worse. . . . I looked at the faces around me, strong, confident faces, and dared not to think what the following day would bring."[4]

Arriving in Turku, Cowles boarded the bus to return to Helsinki. Turku, its quietude long ago sundered, was still very much a city at war: "The Turku morning paper carried headlines of the number of Russian planes shot down the previous day. The only item referring to the negotiations was a small box in the corner of the front page announcing that foreign radio stations were reporting a solution had been reached in Moscow. And this was encircled by a large question mark."[5]

The notice didn't attract the attention of the other passengers, mostly farm girls and road workers wearing white capes over their clothes to camouflage them from the Russian fighters who were still raising havoc around the country.

✳

Back at the Kamp, Cox, like the rest of the resident press corps, had spent the night in a state of suspended animation, waiting for confirmation of the dread news that the peace treaty had been signed.

> That night of the 12th of March I walked around in the black out, past the heaps of snow piled by the footpaths, to the Press Room. Every correspondent knew that tonight we would probably hear something definite.

I looked round the Press Room that night, at the green-covered tables with files of translations from the Finnish Press, the photos of Suomussalmi on the walls, the heavy curtains drawn for the blackout. Here I had heard the first communiqué of the war read out; here I had seen Miss Helsinkis, the pretty Finnish girl who acted as chief secretary, looking every night for the figures of Russian planes brought down.[6]

Cox asked Helsinkis how she felt now. "I live in Viipuri," she responded, sadly. "Last week I saw on a newsreel my flat, smashed to pieces by a bomb. But I don't mind that so much as stopping the fight now when we have suffered so much."[7]

Later that agonizing evening, Cox's fellow scribe, Leland Stowe, was sitting upstairs in the room of Walter Kerr, the popular reporter for the *New York Herald Tribune* (and future celebrated theater critic of the *New York Times*), along with a number of other journalists—including Cox, who had since decided to take out his anxieties on the typewriter: "We tried to cover the heartbreak of it all with feeble jokes. They fell as flat as when poor ashen-faced [Laurin] Zilliacus, commenting on Walter's futile struggles with the telephone, had remarked: 'Probably you forgot to put the nickel in the slot.' We kept writing stories we couldn't file."[8]

Pressed for news, all that the visibly depressed Finnish press officer Laurin Zilliacus could say was that it was possible that peace terms had been signed in Moscow; however, he assumed that the *eduskunta* hadn't voted on them. Otherwise he would have heard.

At least one Finn couldn't wait. "Then the phone rang and a Finnish friend was called. He laid down the receiver and said in a dull voice: 'The first of our friends has just committed suicide.' It was a young woman, a writer by profession."[9]

Shortly afterward, the journalists were summoned again to the press room. Zilliacus was standing mutely in front of the room with a slip in his hand. "Fighting will stop at eleven tomorrow," the dazed man said, forgetting that "tomorrow" was actually that same day. "His voice was that of a man at a funeral. For a moment no one spoke. Then slowly the room emptied, as correspondent after correspondent went to type out his message telling the world that Russia had won."

Foreign minister Tanner, Zilliacus added bleakly, was to speak to the Finnish people at mid-day, detailing the terms of the peace.[10]

Several hundred kilometers to the east, on the bomb-gutted Karelian Isthmus, astonished Finnish officers began receiving word of the imminent ceasefire, which they in turn began to pass on to their equally shocked men. Eric Malm was one of those men. "When our regiment [the 10th]—or what was left of it— went to Miehikkala [a small Finnish town forty kilometers west of Viipuri], on March 13th that morning," he recalled, "an officer from the regiment command post came and said there would be a ceasefire."[11]

"It came out of the blue. When I was on leave, I had heard rumors of some negotiations, but I had no idea that it would be so soon."[12]

Malm's first thought was to get himself to a safe place, especially since Marshal Voronov's hundreds of artillerists, still parked wheel to wheel, seemed intent on shelling Finnish positions until the very last minute—and possibly beyond that as well: "Still the Russian artillery kept shooting, so I made sure I was in the safest place possible, knowing this would stop in just two hours. It would have been too ironic to get killed during the last hours of fighting. Still, the Russian artillery kept pounding us until noon. They had to put in that extra hour."[13]

To be sure, a number of Finnish troops and volunteers were killed after the official ceasefire time of 11 A.M. by the vindictive Soviets. In the north of Finland, just such a tragedy took place near Salla, when the Russians deliberately bombed a group of Swedish and Norwegian volunteers, who had recently taken over the fighting for their Finnish brothers there, causing numerous casualties.[14]

One of those wounded in that horrific incident was Orvar Nillson. Earlier that morning Nillson's men had been told of the ceasefire. "We were disappointed, most of us, I think. We had wanted to do more fighting. After all, that's what we had come for. But we accepted the ceasefire. Then, around noon, an hour after the ceasefire went into effect, two Russian fighters came out of the clouds and dropped several bombs near our encampment."[15]

Nillson was fortunate to survive the incident with a broken arm. Nine of his Swedish comrades—the largest group of volunteers to die at one time—weren't so lucky.[16]

For his part, Nikolai Bavin, the fighting Soviet marine stationed at iced-up Saunasaari, was thrilled that the war was over. "I heard about the armistice over the radio. I was happy that it was over. I had nothing against the Finns."[17]

Eric Malm felt much the same way once the Russian artillery stopped firing. "I was happy that I had survived," said the future doctor, who, like most of his colleagues who survived the Winter War with body and mind intact, also served during the Continuation War, "and sad that so many of my comrades had not."[18]

Perhaps unsurprisingly, there were a lot of Finns who wanted to keep on fighting, too—and did so, as Geoffrey Cox, who would go on to become one of Great Britain's most distinguished news broadcasters after the war, wrote in *The Red Army Moves* the following year:

At Kuhmo one company, warned that they must stop fighting at 11 o'clock Finnish time, had hurled themselves against a Russian position at dawn in their anger, and had fought till almost every man was wiped out. At Viipuri, a Finnish icebreaker, sent in to try and crack the ice of the bay and cut off the Russians on the western shore—a brilliant strategic move—kept moving after eleven o'clock. Russian guns fired on it, killing seventy men.[19]

At Taipale, on the isthmus, where Finnish troops had held their positions since the beginning of the war, and had continued to repulse Timoshenko's men until the bitter end, some of the men actually stood and cheered the news of the ceasefire, thinking that it was the Russians who had succumbed, not them. That was how little they knew what was going on.

It was only later when they realized their mistake that the Finns got angry. By then, of course, it was too late to keep on fighting, but how they wanted to, as Leland Stowe observes: "At eleven o'clock the order to cease firing was given along the entire front. Finnish soldiers who could scarcely stand received it first with astonished disbelief and then with bitter cries of protest. 'To hell with it all! It would be better to go on.' Without munitions, without artillery, without airplanes, the Finns asked nothing except to fight on. In their hearts, they were never defeated."[20]

✳

Now, in Helsinki, and elsewhere, the country was about to experience the supreme shock of Tanner's armistice speech. That morning of March 13, Stowe had tried to brace his Finnish assistant, Clara, for the traumatic news. "I had warned Clara that peace was coming and she had cried 'No, no!' And then fiercely [after he told her what he suspected would be the final terms]: 'But we'll fight if we have nothing but our knives. . . . Hanko? They will take Hanko? I tell you our children and our grandchildren would fight to take Hanko back.'"

"No," Clara had insisted, "they can never do that to us."[21]

✳

But, as Tanner confirmed in the address he bravely made to the country that day, surely one of the most painful addresses any politician has had to make to his own people, "they" had indeed done it. Instinctively, journalists Langdon-Davies, Stowe, and Cox, who had been stationed in Helsinki for most of the *Talvisota,* decided that they did not want to hear Tanner's speech at the Kamp.

"I cast about in my mind for a suitable spot in which to listen to the news," Langdon-Davies recalled. "The last place in the world for such a moment was obviously the press room in the Hotel Kamp. The irrepressible minority of journalists, and especially of cameramen, who had proved themselves incapable of realizing that they were the paid spectators of a national tragedy, would at such a moment be beyond bearing."[22]

Instead, Langdon-Davies made for a nearby canteen operated by Elanto, the Social Democratic–owned restaurant and grocery cooperative—"which I knew to have a wireless, and which would be full, I supposed, of the usual crowd of black-coated workers, shop girls, typists, clerks, soldiers, skilled workmen and the rest. I went there and sat down at a little table. It was early still, and for the next quarter of an hour people came in and took their places at different tables."²³

Stowe had decided to do the same. Cox decided to listen to the speech in the dining hall of the Hotel Seurahuone.

Here are excerpts of what the three heard and saw that memorable, sorrowful afternoon. First Langdon-Davies:

> The wireless had been playing some non-committal light music, the sort of semi-classical frippery which always seems to appear in the morning and mid-day programmes the world over. A woman announcer stated that in a few minutes the Foreign Minister would speak. The wireless orchestra played Martin Luther's hymn.
>
> Luther's hymn came to an end. It had been the same hymn that the otherwise silent crowd had sung spontaneously at Helsinki railway station when last year the negotiators had gone to meet Molotov in Moscow. Without further announcement Foreign Minister Tanner began to speak. He spoke, of course, in Finnish, though the bilingual etiquette of Finland demanded that immediately after there should be a Swedish translation. Scarcely a word had been spoken, and now there was absolute silence. People stared at their plates: the Foreign Minister read out the terms of peace.
>
> Every now and then as the true tragedy unfolded itself my eye was caught by a quick, short movement from one table and then another. It was the movement of a man or a woman suddenly brushing away tears, which could never be allowed to reach their cheeks. Twice there was another movement. Of course, I could not understand anything that was being said, except the proper names. It was the words Viipuri and Hanko that produced this movement. A spasmodic stifled cry, which seemed to come from almost everyone in the room, as if in response to a physical blow from an unseen weapon.
>
> The mother and sister at my own table were now sitting with closed eyes. The girl at the next table was staring at the young man in uniform, as if something incomprehensible had frightened her. Only once there was the slightest interruption. Somewhere down the room, like a pistol shot, a man's voice snapped out, "Never!"²⁴

Cox, at the Seurahuone, watching an equally traumatic tableau, thought about some of the Finns he had met and come to admire and, yes, love, during the three months he had spent covering the war:

> Every name came as a blow. "Viipuri." Gone. I thought of the fair girl on the ski jump in Rovaniemi, who had fought so willingly because she wanted to get back to Viipuri. "You should see the sea there in the evenings in the summer," she had said.

"Sortavala, Kakisalmi [a small city near Viipuri], Hango [*sic*]. . . . On and, on went the names. Suddenly the *Lotta* [seated next to him] burst into tears, her shoulders heaving.[25]

Stowe, for his part, was impressed with Tanner's self-discipline:

Tanner's voice was steady and emotionless, supremely Finnish in its self-control. "We were compelled to accept peace," he said. A dark-haired young woman began to weep silently, hiding her face with her hands.

On all sides of me other faces stared, never registering so much as a twitch of their features. Tanner's voice went steadily on. He was enumerating the Soviet conditions. "My God!" exclaimed an English-speaking girl across the table.

Two more women were crying, but without making a sound. Tanner was explaining how foreign help had failed to come in sufficient strength and in time; how the Scandinavian governments had refused passage for British and French troops.

My eyes were drawn back to the young woman by the window. Now she lay limp in her chair, her face averted toward the drawn curtains. Her shoulders were shaking slowly and ceaselessly.[26]

North of Helsinki in Lahti, Pekka Tiilikainen, the roving YLE reporter, was listening, half-asleep, to a portable radio when Tanner came on. "One program number flowed into another and we were half asleep," he remembered. "Then it came. Out of our radio receiver, softly, came the news of the disaster, wrapped in cotton wool. It came with reasoned, serious phrases. It brought disappointment, bitterness, sorrow. It brought this," he wrote, "even though there were pockets [of soldiers] at the front where this meant salvation from death."[27]

Amongst those sharing Tiilikainen's sorrow and bitterness, along with her thunderstruck family, was Mai-Lis Toivenen, the durable *lotta* and aircraft spotter from Koivisto. Two weeks before, Toivenen, like many of the *lottas* assigned to the areas overrun by the Soviets, had been honorably discharged. She had then joined her mother, Eva, and her three younger brothers, Reijo, Martti, and Eero, at a farmhouse in Korkeakoski, a small town in central Finland whence her family had been evacuated. As it happened, the farm where they were staying didn't have a properly working radio, so the family had to hike down the road to find another place where they could hear the armistice speech.

While they were walking, Mai-Lis later recalled, the five of them had to pass through a clearing in the woods. Looking up through the curtain of the ambient trees, they were greeted by the sight of another curtain, luminously hanging in the night sky: the Northern Lights. A suspicious sort, Eva Paavola took the supernatural sight as a portent. "The war does not end here," she said aloud for her children to hear. "There will be a new war."[28]

Vaino Tanner was completing his speech now. "We must start our lives again," he was saying into the microphone in his small, cell-like studio in downtown Helsinki. "We are going to rise again." But few Finns were listening at that point. The cauterizing speech came to an end. Like an audial bookend, the familiar chords of Luther's hymn *A Mighty Fortress Is Our God* wafted out of the speaker. They seemed hollow now.[29]

In Helsinki, at the Seurahuone, Geoffrey Cox looked on as the last notes of the dirge-like music floated disconsolately around the room. "Men and women stood until the last note died away. Not a soul spoke. Silently they walked out, carrying with them the numb, proud solitude of their grief. The war was over."[30]

Virginia Cowles, who had arrived in town too late to hear Tanner's historic speech, was inconsolable, even though she already knew its tragic gist. Desolate, she sat down in a cafe. A group of Finnish officers came in and took the next table. They had a copy of the morning edition of the *Helsingin Sanomat* containing the peace terms, outlined by a dark black band for mourning.

"They read it silently," wrote Cowles, who herself would go on to become one of the great (if now forgotten) correspondents of World War II, "then one of them crumpled it up angrily and threw it on the floor. No one spoke. They just sat there staring into space." The dejected American correspondent exited the café into the quickly darkening Finnish winter's afternoon and looked up: the flags of *Suomi* were flying at half-mast.[31]

At Inkila Manor, where his headquarters had finally been moved, Gustaf Mannerheim, the Finnish commander-in-chief, was already thinking about the final message to his valiant troops he would deliver the next day. The moving oration was arguably his greatest ever, a continuation of the stirring message he had issued fifteen weeks—a seeming eternity—before, on the first night of the war, as the fires from the first Soviet bombs were still burning. "You did not want war," he began, solemnly.

> You loved peace, work, and progress, but the fight was forced upon you and in it you accomplished great exploits which for centuries to come will shine in the pages of history.
> Soldiers! I have fought on many battlefields but I have never yet seen your equals as warriors. I am proud of you as if you were my own children,

as proud of the man from the northern tundras as of the sons of the broad plains of Ostrobothnia, the forests of Karelia, the smiling tracts of Savo, the rich farms of Hame and Satakunta, the lands of Uusimaa and South West Finland with their whispering birches. I am as proud of the factory worker and the son of the poor cottage as I am of the rich man's contribution of life and limb.

Nevertheless, the audibly exhausted Mannerheim continued,

In spite of all the courage and self-sacrifice the government has been compelled to make peace on harsh terms. Our army was small, and both its reserves and regulars were insufficient. We were not equipped for a war with a great power.[32]

Two hundred kilometers to the east, the defenders of bomb-blackened Viipuri—which had, after all, been the principal objective of the Soviet offensive—received the news of the end of the war, their war, with anger and dismay. And yet if they had had the heart to look up, they would have seen that the flag of Finland was still flying atop Viipuri Castle.

Epilogue

Eva Paavola's grim premonition upon beholding the Northern Lights that night in the forest proved correct. There would be another war with Russia, a longer and even costlier war, as well as a more controversial one. The Continuation War, it was called. It would last three years. But first, the Finnish nation had to execute the terms of the "harsh peace"—as Mannerheim put it—by which the government had agreed to consummate the *Talvisota,* starting with the evacuation of the amputated areas.

There was little time to waste. The withdrawal from all the various amputated areas from Karelia in the south to the Ryabachi Peninsula in the far north, which altogether comprised over 10 percent of Finland's land mass, had to be completed within twelve days. Under the terms of the treaty, the populace of the sundered lands was given the right to decide whether they wished to leave their homes and depart or remain. Virtually all chose to leave. The resultant exodus— "one of the most frenzied migrations in history," John Langdon-Davies calls it— involving over 420,000 people, was a tragedy unto itself.[1]

Virginia Cowles, returning to Hanko for the first time in two months, saw that tragedy, including the anger and misery that would help fuel the subsequent conflict, up close. Accompanying her were Frank Hayne, the U.S. military attaché and his Finnish American chauffeur, the brother of the aforementioned Lasse, who had penned that moving letter from his pulverized *korsu* on the Mannerheim Line back in February, during Timoshenko's final offensive. The chauffeur acted as interpreter.

It made sense that Cowles would wish to return to Hanko. Her Finnish tour, after all, had begun with a day trip to the heavily bombed fortress town. The fifteen-week Soviet-Fenno war was approaching its midpoint then. After the back-to-back victories at Suomussalmi and Raate Road, Finnish morale was high, and so it had been at Hanko. Now, having traveled the length and the breadth of the embattled country, the reporter, whose vivid dispatches from the various battlefronts had brought the war home to millions of newspaper readers on both sides of the Atlantic, had decided to return to the place where her "Finnish affair" had begun.[2]

Cowles's return trip to Hanko, it turned out, was just as eerie as the first one. "When I had last visited Hanko," she recalled, "ten buildings along the main street, hit by incendiary bombs, were burning." Today, however, on the first day following the armistice, there were no fires or air-raid alarms; only the wind sweeping desolately through houses with no window-panes; only shops with caved-in roofs and charred ruins. In the midst of these grim ruins the evacuation was going on. From one house with a bomb crater only ten feet away and a front blackened by the blast, two soldiers were carrying tables and chairs piled high on their backs; from another three small children were bringing kitchen utensils and packing them carefully onto a small sled; from a third, an old man was carrying a mattress stacked with lamps and crockery. The sidewalks in front of the houses were covered with dressers, sewing-machines, bicycles, pictures, and stoves waiting to be put on lorries.[3]

Many of the citizens of the soon-to-be-deserted town were too traumatized to speak. At the Hanko police station, Cowles came across a forlorn woman and her no less miserable daughter who reluctantly agreed to speak to the bundled-up American reporter. The two women, who had run a small *pension* in town, had just registered their names for a truck to take away their belongings. "When it comes," the distraught single mother confessed, "I don't know where we'll go. We've got no relatives and no other prospects of making a living."[4]

Many of the inhabitants of the lost areas, particularly those who had made their living from agriculture, found themselves in the same predicament. Forty thousand farms would have to be found for the displaced, public assistance and shelter for the others. This was rapidly done, though not without difficulty— problems arose, especially when Finnish speakers were relocated to Swedish-speaking areas. But it was done. Finland took care of its own. The woman need not have worried about that.[5]

However, the end of the war had not only deprived the bewildered woman of her livelihood: it had vitiated her reason for living. After three months of constant air raids, she had grown used to the war, including the consciousness that every day that Finland resisted the aggressor, with his incendiary bombs and his anti-personnel bombs, was a day worth living. "Perhaps it's wrong to say it," she remarked, shaking her head sadly, "but it would almost make me happy to hear the sirens again."[6]

Other evacuees were just plain angry, particularly at the government. "Our politicians have betrayed us," one told Cowles. "There is no life this way. Far better to have fought to the end." Some of those politicians shared that anger: when the despised Peace of Moscow came up for a vote in the *eduskunta,* three of the two hundred members voted against ratifying it, nine members abstained, and forty-two angrily walked out. Nevertheless, the treaty was confirmed by a postwar vote of 145–3.[7]

"To a large proportion of the Finnish people, peace came as a painful surprise," conceded Gustaf Mannerheim in his posthumously published autobiography. "It took some time for everyone to realize the circumstances which had induced the government and Parliament to accept the cruel conditions."[8]

Inevitably, Vaino Tanner, as foreign minister, and the politician who was most visibly responsible for the despised treaty, drew considerable ire. Partly to appease the public, partly the Kremlin, Tanner resigned as foreign minister and assumed the lower profile of minister of supply in the postwar government. (The Kremlin, for its part, was not appeased. In June of the following year, it forced Tanner's resignation.)[9]

*

By contrast, Mannerheim himself, the man who deserved just as much blame—or, depending on how one looked at it, credit—for bringing the war to a halt, emerged from the *Talvisota* even more revered than before. After all, it was Mannerheim who had pressured his generals into changing their minds at that pivotal meeting with the members of the cabinet on February 28 about whether the army should continue to fight. It was Mannerheim who had forwarded General Heinrichs's dire situation report to the cabinet during the March 9 meeting at which it reluctantly agreed to accede to Molotov's terms. And it was Mannerheim who had agreed with the "peace faction" within the cabinet not to issue the formal call for help that Neville Chamberlain and Edouard Daladier had anxiously been awaiting in order to get those ships laden with Allied reinforcements under way, a point Mannerheim had conveniently glossed over in his March 14 order of the day: "Unfortunately, the valuable promises of assistance which the Western Powers had given us, could not be realized when our neighbours [Norway and Sweden], concerned for their own security, refused the transit rights for [the promised Allied] troops."[10]

As Douglas Clark rightly points out in *Three Days to Catastrophe,* this was not exactly true. In fact, the British and French had been prepared to force the issue regardless of Swedish and Norwegian opposition. All Helsinki had to do, so to speak, was call. The government had not done this. It was Mannerheim who had—wisely—seen Operation Avon Head for the harebrained scheme it was; who had decided, after all, that it was better for Finland to honorably extricate itself from the war rather than "fight to the end"—but who nevertheless had succeeded in keeping the threat of Allied intervention sufficiently credible to help persuade the Soviets to make peace when they did.[11]

The Finnish public knew nothing of this no less patriotic side of Mannerheim. It only knew Mannerheim the marshal, the man on the white horse, the man who had called his "brave Finland soldiers" to arms December 1, 1939, the general who had overseen the heroic Finnish defensive victories of Tolvajarvi and Suomussalmi, the great *paterfamilias* who in his final speech from the mount (at least for this war) of several nights before had urged his countrymen to accept the "harsh peace" he had also—to his credit—helped engineer. And so they did. No, the people were not angry at Mannerheim; on the contrary, they revered him all the more. They saved their ire for "the politicians," like Tanner.[12]

*

And for the Russians, of course.

Virginia Cowles found that what infuriated the Hanko evacuees most of all was the notion of having to turn over their houses to the enemy, who they were certain would not take proper care of them. The Russians' indiscriminate, seemingly mindless bombing of their town had only enhanced the Finns' hatred and contempt for their age-old enemy.

> One of three nurses standing at the street corner, told us it wouldn't be
> so bad if any other nation were occupying [Hanko], but try as she would,
> it was impossible to think of the Russians as human beings. The second
> one agreed. "At least they won't find anything in my house but four walls
> and a roof. I've even taken the brass taps away." "Yes," said the third. "But
> what a pity it is we have to leave our water tower for them." She pointed
> to the old brick tower, an ancient landmark in the middle of the town.
> "Oh, don't worry about that. After a day or so they're sure to have it out of
> commission."[13]

However, there wasn't much time to talk: there was an evacuation to attend to.

A week later, on March 22, Good Friday, a large Soviet plane with a Red Star on its side landed on iced-over Hanko Bay. A group of Russian soldiers disembarked and made their way into the bombed-out town to meet the lone Finnish officer who had been detailed to escort them, while another detachment was ordered to take up their positions at the new frontier, a barrier of barbed wire across the road to the adjoining town of Tammisaari.

On the Finnish side of the new border the Finns waited, along with a group of photographers. In the distance two figures appeared. Closer and closer they came. They were Russian guards, dressed for the occasion in dress blue uniforms. Marching up to the stoic Finns, in their grey uniforms, they saluted and took up their new position and smiled for the photographers. Hanko was theirs.[14]

*

By then, Cowles and Langdon-Davies and Cox and most of the rest of the Hotel Kamp press corps were gone. Cowles returned to London to reacquaint herself with her friends and wait for something to happen with "World War No. 2," which still seemed to be ambling along rather quietly. She didn't have to wait long. A month later Hitler invaded Denmark and Norway, and a month after that his parachutists and panzers stunned the West by doing an end run around the Maginot Line (as well as the Grebbe Line, the Dutch defense line) and crashing into the Low Countries and France. Cowles was in Paris when the *Wehrmacht* goose-stepped down the Champs Elysees. By then her sub-arctic Finnish tour seemed, in the words of the popular Frank Sinatra tune of the day, very "Long Ago and Far Away." But it would leave an indelible impression: the section of her 1941 memoir, *Looking for Trouble,* devoted to her Finnish adventure is by far the most gripping part of the book.[15]

Geoffrey Cox, Herbert Elliston, and John Langdon-Davies, each of whom also went to cover other battlefronts of World War II, did Cowles one better, devoting entire books to their respective "Finnish affairs." Indeed, it seems that a large proportion of the Kamp corps did so. All for a war that lasted but 105 days.[16]

✳

Ad interim, Finland continued to come to terms with the painful human cost of the war. In his final address Mannerheim had erroneously declared that 15,000 of his "brave soldiers" had died during the conflict. That would have been the accurate figure, more or less, if the war had halted at the end of February. Unfortunately for Finland, it had not. The final total of confirmed deaths of the Finnish Army from all causes actually came to 26,000, along with 44,000 wounded, a staggering number for such a small country. If the United States of 1940 had suffered a similar proportion of casualties, it would have been the equivalent of 2.4 million American casualties.[17]

No less than 4,200 of those deaths had occurred during the last week alone, as the battles for Viipuri and Viipuri Bay had reached their consanguinary climax, an average of 600 a day, an unsustainable number. Mannerheim was in deadly earnest when he had told the cabinet that the army was on the verge of collapse: the war had bled Finland white.[18]

Now, as the corpses of the soldiers who had died during the final days were recovered and shipped to their hometowns, the country came to grips with the actual cost of the war and it reeled once more. Once again, the *lottas* at the dozens of mortuary stations around the country carefully washed and prepared the bodies of the dead for burial. And both Lutheran and Orthodox churches were filled with rows of coffins, as the funerals continued.[19]

Now, with the war over, there was no longer any need to conceal the price of the war for fear of giving comfort to the enemy. Widows were free to mourn openly. And for several weeks the streets of Helsinki and the other Finnish towns and cities were filled with women wearing black.

Nevertheless, although the cost of the war had been high, the Finns did not give way to despair. After several days of mourning, the flags were brought down and stored away. In Helsinki there was a revealing moment when one group of workmen began to pull down the wooden blast barrier in front of one house, while on the opposite side of the street another group of workers continued to nail up an incomplete barrier around one of the many statues that dot the city. Soon all the barriers had come down. It was time to get on with it.[20]

Moreover, although the country was in shock, it was proud. It had, after all, defended and held what was more precious than life, its freedom. Finland, though maimed and a tenth smaller in size, was still Finland, with its sovereignty intact.

*

Meanwhile, that speck in Stalin's eye, the Finnish People's Republic (or whatever one chose to call it), went on record as being one of the world's shortest-lived "republics," while the force that was supposed to install it, along with its designated leader, the estimable Otto Ville Kuusinen, the Finnish People's Army, was suddenly and unceremoniously dissolved.[21]

"It was very strange," recalled Kuusinen's unwilling conscript, Edward Hynninen, who was in training at Terijoki when the armistice was announced. "I was in the midst of my training to be a signals man, and then suddenly the phone rang and we were told to go home. That was it."[22]

Kuusinen himself was rewarded for his loyalty by being made chairman of the presidium of the Karelo-Finnish Soviet Socialist Republic, the Soviet entity comprising former Finnish Karelia, in which post he served until 1956 before being kicked up to the Politburo and being made secretary of the Central Committee of the Communist Party of the USSR. He died in 1964 at the age of eighty-two. Shortly before his death, he submitted a request to the Finnish government via the Soviet embassy that he be allowed to visit Laukaa, the town where he was born, and Jyvaskyla, where he grew up. His request was denied. Kuusinen's ashes are buried in the Kremlin wall.[23]

*

There was mourning, too, in Russia, but of the suppressed kind. In the days following the end of the war the Communist leadership made a show of its "victory over the White Guardists," and the pages of *Pravda* carried a cavalcade of photos of the new Heroes of the Soviet Union that the glorious war had wrought; nevertheless, the Kremlin knew that a victory that had been purchased at such a cost was a moral defeat.[24]

The true attitude of the Russian leadership toward the war was demonstrated by its treatment of the approximately 5,600 Soviet soldiers who had been taken prisoner by the Finns. Upon reaching Soviet territory, the unfortunate men were interviewed by teams of NKVD agents who, after interrogating the men, determined that 500 should be summarily executed for voluntarily surrendering to the enemy, while most of the remaining were sentenced to hard labor.[25]

Unsurprisingly, the Kremlin underestimated the true number of Soviet deaths. The "official" figure for Red casualties, announced by Molotov after the war, was 48,745 dead and 159,000 wounded. No one, including the Russians themselves, believed this at the time. In his memoirs, Nikita Khrushchev, the Cold War Soviet premier, who was Ukrainian Communist party chief during the Winter War, declared that the USSR had lost a million men during the war. (Of course this was an exaggeration, although it is interesting that he would believe this [if he did].) Finnish historians would later revise the figure downward to somewhere between 230,000 and 270,000, with another 200,000 to 300,000 wounded. The most recent estimated range is even lower than that: 80,000 to 126,000 dead, and 187,000 to 264,000 wounded.[26]

However, the Red Army's initial, abysmal performance, along with the Soviet's consequent loss of prestige, could not so easily be shrugged off. Consequently, in April 1940, the Supreme Military Soviet met in conclave in order to examine the lessons of the Finnish campaign and to recommend reforms. Those who attended the meeting agreed that the Soviet army had a number of glaring deficiencies. One was the ineffective way the advanced weapons and equipment had been used by the Soviet defense industry. In contrast to the Finns, who had put their Suomi machine pistols to such effective and devastating use, the Red Army had wrongly dismissed light automatic weapons and submachine guns as "police weapons," thus depriving the infantry of the firepower it needed. This, it was agreed, had to be corrected. Unsurprisingly, it was also agreed that the supply services had failed to provide Russian troops with the proper kind of clothing and stores for the Finnish theater of war.[27]

Intelligence, too, was found to be lacking. Additionally, the Soviet rifle division was seen to be too unwieldy for handling in a major offensive. Cooperation between the infantry and the other arms was poor. All these things were to be amended, and would be, promised Kliment Voroshilov, the Soviet defense commissar, who had helped oversee the original debacle.[28]

Stalin himself summarized the conclusions of the conference when he addressed it on April 17, 1940. In a surprisingly candid statement, the Russian dictator declared that the traditions and experiences of the civil war had hindered the leaders of the army. The cult of the past had to be overcome if the Red Army was to meet the challenge of modern war. What Stalin conveniently left out was that his brutal purge of brilliant officers like Mikhail Tuchachevsky and others who understood the precepts of modern warfare had also eliminated those who could be counted on to put the needed reforms into effect. The result was that those whom he now turned to in order to reorganize the army were products of the same hidebound culture he sought to uproot.[29]

Notwithstanding, a number of significant changes were made. The schizoid military-politico command setup under which military commanders had to have their orders approved by commissars was abolished, and the role of the dreaded *politruks*, the Soviet political officers, was reduced. At the same time, old-fashioned ranks and forms of discipline dating from imperialist times were reinstituted. Clothing, tactics, and equipment for winter operations were revamped, as were tank and aerial tactics.[30]

Many of the needed reforms had not been put into place by the time the *Wehrmacht* invaded the Soviet Union in June 1941; however, it is probably fair to say that the Red Army had reorganized itself just enough to survive the initial German onslaught—if only just. Stalin himself wasn't so sure. Three years later, in a rare moment of candor at the Teheran conference with Churchill and Roosevelt, the Russian generalissimo admitted that his army had shown itself to be very poorly organized during the Winter War, and that even though it had reorganized itself afterward the army that faced Hitler's panzers on the Russian steppes was not a first-class fighting force.[31]

In any event, the Winter War was unquestionably a landmark in the history of the Russian army—although it was not until after the fall of the Soviet Union that Russian historians could acknowledge or write about it with any degree of objectivity, given that the war was the direct result of Russian aggression and began so ignominiously.[32]

The *Talvisota* was also a watershed for Kliment Voroshilov. Old Bolshevik ties notwithstanding, Stalin decided that the Soviet Union could no longer trust its military destiny to someone whose first love was opera. Shortly after the Finnish postmortem, Voroshilov was demoted to deputy commissar and replaced with Semyon Timoshenko.

Voroshilov went on to demonstrate his personal courage, if not military competence, after the German invasion of Russia in June 1941, when, as commander of the short-lived Northwestern Direction, he rallied retreating troops and personally led a counterattack against German tanks armed with only a pistol. In the event, his efforts to stem the German tide were unsuccessful. Replaced by the considerably more able Georgi Zhukov, he nevertheless managed to survive Stalin's wrath again and even have the last laugh, so to speak, ultimately being appointed chairman of the Presidium of the Supreme Head of State in 1953 as part of the triumvirate of Nikita Khrushchev and Georgy Malenkov, which ruled the USSR after his patron's death. In this post he was finally succeeded in 1960 by Leonid Brezhnev. He died in 1969 at the ripe age of eighty-eight. His ashes are buried in the Kremlin Wall necropolis.[33]

The larger political and strategic ramifications of the Winter War were enormous. In France the failure of the government of Edouard Daladier to succor the Finns caused his government to topple eight days after the armistice, on March 21, 1940. Across the Channel, in Great Britain, there was a similar furor, as disappointed Fennophiles lashed out at Neville Chamberlain. Chamberlain survived; however, the vacillation and ineptitude demonstrated during the Finnish fiasco was a key factor in the fall of his cabinet seven weeks later and his replacement with Winston Churchill. (Ironically, Chamberlain fell as a result of pursuing, however incompetently, the Nordic strategy for getting at the Germans that Churchill had initiated.)[34]

Meanwhile, in Berlin, Adolf Hitler had been watching the uneven contest taking place to the north and drawing his own conclusions. The Red Army's initial performance during the *Talvisota* clearly influenced his decision, the following June, to proceed with his ultimately disastrous plan to invade the USSR. As

Churchill writes, "There is no doubt that Hitler and his generals meditated profoundly upon the Finnish exposure, and that it played a potent part in influencing the *Fuhrer*'s thought."[35]

Hitler himself confirmed his own misjudgment on this score in 1942 when he called "the war against Finland . . . a great piece of camouflage, for even then Russia possessed armed forces which placed her amongst the first of the Powers on a par with Germany and Japan." Even then, a year following the Russian invasion, Hitler still believed—perhaps had to believe—that the extraordinary hubris and incompetence displayed by the Kremlin in its botched invasion of its tiny neighbor had been a ruse, a kind of giant feint to fool the West as to its true military capabilities.[36]

Whatever the Kremlin learned or did not learn from the *Talvisota*, it certainly demonstrated that it hadn't learned very much about Finnish pride. The complicated and controversial subject of how Finland decided to join forces—to a degree—with Germany when Hitler launched his blitzkrieg against Russia is not within the province of this book. However, the ham-handedness Moscow displayed in its interference with Finnish affairs in the months immediately following the armistice certainly didn't do very much to enhance Finns' feelings of trust toward its recent opponent. First, the Kremlin nixed a proposal for a Finnish-Swedish alliance on the dubious grounds that the Peace of Moscow forbade Helsinki from entering any coalition that could be directed against the Soviet, even though such a union probably would have guaranteed the opposite. If that wasn't bound to stoke Finnish fears, Moscow's subsequent demand for acquiring the right of transit by land through Finland to and from its newly acquired base at Hanko certainly did.[37]

Even more ominously, Moscow intervened directly in the 1940 Finnish presidential election, declaring its opposition to four of the candidates: Tanner, Mannerheim, former president Pehr Evind Svinhufvud, and the minister to Berlin, Professor Toivo Kivimaki. The only major candidate it didn't object to was Risto Ryti, who was elected.[38]

By then, Finnish tempers were at full boil. And so, in June 1941, when Hitler decided to take on the Soviet behemoth, the Finns, seeing a prime opportunity to recover their lost lands and thus continue the war, which for many had never ceased, Finland went with him, not as a full ally but as a co-belligerent, agreeing to help maintain the siege of Leningrad but refusing to launch its own attack on the city.[39]

Unfortunately, the distinction between co-belligerent and ally was lost on many, if not most, in the West, particularly after the United States, finally shedding its neutrality, simultaneously entered the war in December 1941 against both

Japan and Nazi Germany and threw in its lot with the besieged USSR, along with Great Britain. Suddenly, the same Russia that, only months before, both Churchill and Roosevelt had denounced as tyranny incarnate was their friend and ally. And if Finland was a "near ally" of Germany, then it followed that it was a "near enemy" of the Allies. Great Britain actually declared war on Finland. The United States never did that, but it came close. Hjalmar Procope, once the toast of Washington, wound up being forced to leave Washington as *persona non grata*. Finland, it turned out, had picked the wrong side. Suddenly, tragically, the country that had been seen as a beacon of democracy and bulwark of Western civilization—Brave Little Finland—had become, in the eyes of the West, a pariah state. The honor and glory the Finnish nation and its soldiers had won in the *Talvisota* was blotted out and forgotten. The "last glorious war" became a historical parenthesis, a curiosity of the "early" war, something that had occurred long ago and far away before the real "World War No. 2" began and the final lineup of players was set.[40]

∗

For the generation of Finns who had lived through and fought that war, as well as for their proud descendants, those 105 days, when their hitherto little-known nation stood alone against the Soviet invader and, to paraphrase Churchill, showed what free men and women can do, remain *Suomi*'s finest hour, and well it should.

Seven decades later, one of the rapidly dwindling number of Finnish soldiers who fought in the *Talvisota,* Olavi Eronen, was still in awe of what his countrymen had achieved during those epic fifteen weeks. "Single-mindedness—that was the thing I remember from the war. When the whole nation stands behind an idea, miracles can happen. After the armistice, when I travelled by train to meet my parents somebody in the car started to sing 'The Karelians' Song.' Soon everybody on the train joined in the singing in a triumphant manner."[41]

"*That,*" he said, "was the kind of unity we had then."[42]

Perhaps Gustaf Mannerheim, for whom the Winter War was probably the finest hour of his long military career—which would, incredibly, see him lead Finnish forces again in the even more devastating and bloody (as well as still controversial) three-year Continuation War—best summed up the legacy of the *Talvisota* thus:

"May coming generations not forget the dearly bought lessons of our defensive war. They can with pride look back on the Winter War and find courage and confidence in its glorious history. That an army so inferior in numbers and equipment should have inflicted such serious defeats on an overwhelmingly powerful enemy is something for which it is hard to find a parallel in the history of war. . . . Such a nation has earned the right to live."[43]

Postscript

"There Shall Be No Night"

As Robert Sherwood, the playwright, had anticipated, the Winter War indeed did end while his pro-Finnish play, *There Shall Be No Night,* was still in rehearsal. However, Sherwood's corresponding fear, that the war's conclusion would "render it hopelessly out of date," proved unfounded.[1]

Instead, *There Shall Be No Night* wound up having a long, glamorous, polymorphous run on both sides of the Atlantic that ended, eerily enough, when the theater in which it was playing was literally bombed.

As expected, the play's Providence premiere on March 29, nearly two and a half weeks following the signing of the Peace of Moscow, was a critical success. A month later, on April 29, it opened at Broadway's Alvin Theater to generally rave reviews.[2]

Inevitably, some critics found that the famed playwright had put together his piece of instant agit-prop too hastily. One of them was Brooks Atkinson, theater critic of the *New York Times*. Nevertheless, Atkinson was pleased to give the play, with its standout cast led by the inspired Alfred Lunt and Lynn Fontanne, a shout-out. "If Mr. Sherwood's craftsmanship is often uncertain," Atkinson wrote,

> the Lunts' is unexceptionable. Aroused by the sincerity of their playing, they and their associates are acting it beautifully. Mr. Lunt, who was fooling with Shakespeare a while ago, looks the part of Dr. Valkonen straight in the face and acts it with impersonal sobriety and understanding. . . . As Mrs. Valkonen, Miss Fontanne plays with a light touch in the early scenes and a gallantry in the later ones that round out a completely articulate character. This is one of her finest characterizations.

There Shall Be No Night, Atkinson averred, "honors the theater."[3]

John Mason Brown of the *New York Evening Post* agreed: "No one can complain about the theater being an escapist institution when it conducts a class in current events at once as touching, intelligent and compassionate as *There Shall Be No Night*."

To be sure, by this time the play's currency, as well as its essential message, that those who covet freedom must be willing to fight for it, had been driven home by Hitler's lightning invasion on April 9 of neutral, democratic Denmark and Norway—the same Norway that had been so reluctant to send her troops to Finland (or to grant the Allies transit rights to get there).

The play's relevancy would be even further reinforced but two weeks later when the Nazis, with their panzers and paratroopers (which they employed far more effectively than their Soviet allies had in Finland), skipped over the watery Grebbe Line and conquered the Netherlands, as well as neighboring Belgium and Luxembourg, before detouring around General Gamelin's "impregnable" Maginot Line and vanquishing France in the bargain.

Now Britain stood alone amongst the fighting democracies. Then, in September 1940, came the blitz, placing the stakes involved in the Second World War in even starker silhouette, as Americans listened, horrified, to Edward R. Murrow narrate the Second Burning of London, or watched newsreels of the Nazi terror attacks, just as they had watched the burning of Helsinki, already rapidly fading into memory, the year before.

Meanwhile, theatergoers continued to flock to the Alvin. One of them was Eleanor Roosevelt. Unsurprisingly, the First Lady, whose husband was then inching the country closer to war, loved the play, as she wrote in one of her columns in which she also paid retrospective homage to the Finns' glorious fight:

> Robert Sherwood has written a remarkable play in *There Shall Be No Night*. Of course, Alfred Lunt and Lynn Fontanne give a performance so perfect that I felt I was living in this portrayal on the stage. The rest of the cast is so good that we finished the evening feeling that we had actually been through every experience in that Finnish family's experience, which tragically enough, is now part of the life of so many other people.

She ended with an invocation. "May God grant that if such dark hours fall upon us we may acquit ourselves as well!"[4]

By now, in the fall of 1940, attending *There Shall Be No Night* had become a rite of passage for prominent anti-isolationists, including Charlie Chaplin, just then completing his own anti-Hitler film, *The Great Dictator.*

"Intended to come around afterwards," Chaplin wired the Lunts after he came to Broadway to see the celebrated show, "but we [Chaplin and his wife, Oona, the daughter of Eugene O'Neill] were too deeply moved by the play and your memorable performances. It is a shaft of light shining through the somber skies."[5]

To be sure, not everyone was so moved. The Communist *Daily Worker,* which had loudly supported the Soviet invasion of Finland, called Sherwood "the stooge of the imperialist war mongers," while the right-wing isolationist *Daily Mirror* accused the author of being a militarist.[6]

Sherwood couldn't have been more pleased; this, after all, is why he had written *There Shall Be No Night:* to stir controversy. And so he did.

The author was thrilled when, in November 1940, the Lunts, who had become publicly identified with the play, took it on a rolling 12,000-mile tour of the

United States and Canada, playing to rapt audiences (including the occasional protester), drawn by both its star power—including the Lunts' formidable, long-time co-star Sydney Greenstreet (who would become famous the following year for his role in *The Maltese Falcon*), as well as the Lunts' adoptive son (and rising star) Montgomery Clift—and its blazing relevancy.[7]

It was too late to help the Finns, at least financially, so the Lunts donated their salaries, as well as half of all Canadian profits, to the British, as did Sherwood—their down payment on a Spitfire, as they put it.[8]

Then in June 1941 external events began to overtake the play when the Germans invaded Russia and the Finns joined them as co-belligerents, and a schism opened between Sherwood's stagebound Soviet- and Nazi-hating Finns and the real German-friendly ones people were reading about in the papers. Alfred Lunt was apologetic. "Since the Germans helped them out in 1917, it's natural that they would welcome them again," the actor-producer explained, somewhat nebulously. "They prefer Fascism to Communism." Did they? Most Finns would have disagreed. No matter. The show went on.[9]

Discomfiture became outright embarrassment, however, after Pearl Harbor when the United States declared war on the Axis powers, and vice-versa. With the United States and the USSR now suddenly and quite unexpectedly on the same side, the anti-Russian theme of *There Shall Be No Night* was a definite no-go with Washington. Under pressure from both the White House and the playwrights' guild, the crestfallen author announced that he was withdrawing the play from production. The company gave its last performance on December 18, 1941, in Rochester, Minnesota.[10]

The Lunts, who had planned on touring through February 1942, then reopening the play on Broadway, were crushed. *There Shall Be No Night,* Lunt wrote his friend Theresa Helburn, "has been the greatest privilege and experience of my life in the theater. It can never come about again."[11]

He was wrong.

A year later, on December 15, 1942, *There Shall Be No Night* opened in London at the Aldwych Theater on London's Drury Lane. When the curtain rose to uproarious applause, there were the unbreakable Lunt and Fontanne again, playing the same roles, declaiming the same lines as they had in the original Broadway version.

Now, however, to comport with the changed political landscape, the play was set in Greece during the prior year's German invasion of that since-defeated democracy, while the family's name changed from Valkonen to Vlachos. The now "beloved" Soviet Union had been erased from the script, as had the formerly revered *Suomi.* Now it was the Nazis—who had played a secondary role in the original version—who were the villains. Other than that, it was the same play. Except, of course, that it was now being staged in an actual war zone.[12]

If anything, London audiences, including American servicemen who were preparing to storm the bastions of Nazi-occupied Europe, responded with even greater fervor. London audiences "seemed to weep more than anyone had ever wept at *There Shall Be No Night,*" Lunt wrote. The intense play also gave the normally stiff-upper-lipped British theatergoers, who were, in a sense, already living the play themselves, a chance to vent.[13]

As the Lunts' biographer Margot Peters wrote, "The play had become *theatre vérité,* lines and action from *There Shall Be No Night* reflecting the battle outside the theater doors." In the last act, before Lunt as Vlachos goes off to join the battle against the Soviets-turned-Nazis, he declares, in perhaps the play's most famous line, "Do you hear now—this terrible sound that fills the earth?—it is the death rattle."[14]

"Was he speaking as Karilo Vlachos," writes Peters, "or directly to the audience as Alfred Lunt?" Given the locale, as well as the Lunts' passionate performance, it was hard to tell. In the last scene, when Fontanne picks up a rifle and carefully loads it, "tension would burst into sobs . . . every member of the audience knowing personally the meaning of resistance."[15]

Meanwhile, the Lunts proudly carried on.

They were proud to walk from the Aldwych to the Savoy in the blackout without flashlights. Proud to volunteer as air-raid wardens in the Strand. Proud to greet General Patton backstage. . . . A great crowd gathered at the stage door. When Patton threw open the door he was silhouetted against the light and the roar that burst from the crowd rolled from Shaftesbury Avenue into Piccadilly Circus.[16]

And on they continued, through the end of 1943, on into 1944, until the tension and triumph of D-Day. Meanwhile the Germans had begun bombing London again with their nefarious new V-1 flying bombs.

Then at exactly 2:01 P.M., June 30, 1944, three weeks after D-Day, one of the lethal missiles cut its engine and fell on the Aldwych, killing fifty office workers and pedestrians, including an American soldier waiting to buy a ticket for *There Shall Be No Night,* and demolishing part of the theater.[17]

There Shall Be No Night was no more. With the theater in ruins, the Lunts and the rest of the stalwart cast had little heart for going on. After having given an astounding 1,600 performances, making the play one of the longest-running in transatlantic history, the actors were spent.[18]

And so, strangely, the light of conscience that had been ignited by a Soviet bomb was extinguished by a Nazi one.

Fortunately, as we know, that light was not extinguished and still burns bright over Finland and the rest of the democratic world today.

FINIS

Notes

Introduction

1. Stig Axel Fridolf Jagerskiold, *Mannerheim, Marshal of Finland,* New York, 1988, 111.

2. Nevertheless, the play's story of a small heroic country combatting a big evil power proved adaptable enough for the producers of the London version of the play to keep the plot intact by converting the Finns into Greeks and the Russians into Nazis.

3. Roy Jenkins, *Churchill,* London, 2001, 567.

4. Albert Speer, *Inside the Third Reich,* New York, 1970, 169.

5. "Infantry training was revamped, and the army gave special emphasis to the task of perfecting assault techniques against fixed fortifications, such as those they had overcome in southern Finland. The Red Army became fixated with the lessons of the Winter War, as though these were universal" and ignored "the special conditions of terrain, climate and national characteristics of opposing forces." Roger Reese, *Stalin's Reluctant Soldiers: A Social History of the Red Army, 1925–1941,* Lawrence, Kansas, 1996, 174.

6. Herbert Elliston, *Finland Fights,* Boston, 1940, 135.

7. Ibid.

8. *New York Times,* December 25, 1939.

9. Richard Collier, *The Warcos: The War Correspondents of World War II,* London, 1989, 36.

10. Geoffrey Roberts, *Stalin's Wars: From World War to Cold War, 1939–1953,* New Haven, 2006, 69.

11. Martha Gellhorn, *The Selected Letters of Martha Gellhorn,* New York, 2006, 114.

12. Virginia Cowles, *Looking for Trouble,* New York, 1941, 288–289.

13. Ibid., 289.

14. Ibid., 293–343.

15. Leland Stowe, *No Other Road to Freedom,* New York, 1941, 54.

16. Gellhorn, *Selected Letters,* 55.

17. Geoffrey Cox, *The Red Army Moves,* London, 1941, 75–82.

18. Finns were still bitter about the failure of the Allies to come to their aid in 1977 when I first visited the country. "Why didn't you help us more in 1940?" asked an elderly man who accosted me in the street upon hearing my American accent.

19. Reese, *Stalin's Reluctant Soldiers,* 171–172.

20. Ibid.

21. Veijo Meri, *Beneath the Polar Star: Glimpses of Finnish History,* Helsinki, 1999, 14.

22. Ohto Manninen, *The Soviet Plans for the North Western Theater of Operations in 1939–1944,* Helsinki, 2004, 11–12.

23. Ibid.

24. *Pravda,* December 2, 1939.

25. Nikita Khrushchev, *Khrushchev Remembers,* Boston, 1970, 151.

26. *Time,* December 18, 1939.

27. Ibid.

28. Manninen, *Soviet Plans,* 18.

29. *Time,* December 27, 1939.

30. Manninen, *Soviet Plans,* 21.

31. Douglas Clark, *Three Days to Catastrophe,* London, 1966, 171–172.

32. Travis Beal Jacobs, *America and the Winter War,* New York, 1981, 211.

33. Roberts, *Stalin's Wars,* 48.

34. Ibid., 50.

35. Eloise Engle and Lauri Paananen, *The Winter War: The Russo-Finnish Conflict, 1939–40,* New York, 1973, 122; Manninen, *Soviet Plans,* 42.

36. Manninen, *Soviet Plans,* 44.

37. Cox, *Red Army Moves,* 241.

38. Manninen, *Soviet Plans,* 54–56.

39. Ibid., 47.

40. William Trotter, *A Frozen Hell: The Russo-Finnish War of 1939–40,* Chapel Hill, 1991, 258–260.

41. *Times* (London), February 27, 1940.

42. Manninen, *Soviet Plans,* 55.

43. Ibid., 56.

44. Trotter, *Frozen Hell,* 251.
45. Ibid.
46. Ibid., 260.
47. Ibid.
48. *Helsingin Sanomat,* February 12, 1940.
49. Trotter, *Frozen Hell,* 262.
50. Engle and Paananen, *Winter War,* 155.

Chapter 1. "A Wild Day"

1. Allen Chew, *The White Death: The Epic of the Soviet-Finnish Winter War,* 1971, East Lansing, 3.
2. Max Jakobson, *The Diplomacy of the Winter War,* Cambridge, 1961, 142.
3. Interview with Christian Ilmoni by Tony Ilmoni, March 2006.
4. Ibid.
5. Interview with Mai-Lis Toivenen, March 2009.
6. Ibid.
7. Anna-Liisa Veijalainen, *A Woman at the Front: Memoirs 1938–45,* trans. Pekka Veijalainen, Helsinki, 2007, 15.
8. Ibid., 16.
9. Ibid., 19.
10. Ibid.
11. Ibid.
12. Eeva Kilpi (1928–). Poet, novelist, and memoirist, Kilpi is one of Finland's best-known female writers. Her childhood in former Finnish Karelia is a major theme of her work, as is the pain and dislocation suffered by her family and other Karelians after they were forced to evacuate their homes following the *Talvisota. Fire and Ice* (DVD), dir. Ben Strout, MastersWork Media, 2006.
13. Ibid.
14. Ibid.
15. Martha Gellhorn, *The Face of War,* London, 1986, 55.
16. Caroline Moorehead, *Martha Gellhorn: A Life,* London, 2003, 145.
17. Gellhorn, *Selected Letters,* 114.
18. Ibid.
19. Elliston, *Finland Fights,* Boston, 1940, 135.
20. Ibid., 136.
21. Ibid.
22. Ibid.
23. Ibid., 138.
24. Narvik was the same port that would figure as the port of debarkation for the proposed Allied expeditionary force to relieve Finland. It wound up being occupied by the Nazis after they invaded Norway in April 1940. The Germans also rebuffed an attempt by the British to retake it.
25. Ibid.
26. Interview with Harry Matso, trans. Ilkka Ranta-aho, November 2006.
27. *Pravda,* November 26, 1939.
28. This was a particularly mortifying moment for Yrjo-Koskinen, who as foreign minister had signed the 1932 non-aggression pact between the two countries. Later, after the war broke out, his discomfiture would be increased when the Russians virtually barricaded him and his staff in the Finnish embassy in Moscow, before belatedly putting him and his staff on a train for Riga, the capital of still (barely) independent Latvia, whence they returned to Helsinki.
29. Ibid.
30. Ibid.
31. Ibid. The Karelians, a Baltic-Finnish ethnic group possessing their own language and culture, were then divided between Karelians who lived on the Finnish side of the isthmus and the Russians on theirs, as well as smaller numbers of both nationalities in Ladoga-Karelia.
32. Interview with Harry Berner by Michael Franck, April 2006.
33. Ibid.
34. One of the Soviet Union's most versatile writers, as well as its most favored, Virta (1906–1976) first rose to the fore in 1935 with *Alone,* a novel, which Stalin is known to have liked. He later employed his wartime experiences as a screenwriter, co-writing *The Battle of Stalingrad* (1944).
35. *Pravda,* December 4, 1939.
36. Ibid.
37. Interview with Reino Oksanen by Ilkka Ranta-aho, March 2006.
38. Ibid. The Pystykorva rifle was a Finnish variation of the Mosin-Nagant rifle, the standard, bolt-action military rifle first used by the Russian Imperial Army.
39. Ibid.
40. John H. Wuorinen, *A History of Finland,* New York, 1965, 222.
41. Elliston, *Finland Fights,* 71. Finnish Germanophilia reached its improbable acme in October of that year when the then

pro-monarchist Finnish parliament elected Prince Frederick Charles of Hesse as King of Finland. Frederick's anointment was rendered academic by the abdication of his cousin, Emperor Wilhelm, a month later and the declaration of the German Republic, followed by the armistice ending World War I. In December he formally renounced his throne and Finland adopted a republican constitution.

42. Henry Bell, *Land of Lakes: Memories Keep Me Company,* London, 1950, 173.

43. Ibid.

44. Ibid.

45. Henrik Meinander, *A History of Finland,* trans. Tom Geddes, London, 2011, 130.

46. Jagerskiold, *Mannerheim,* 106–107.

47. Ibid., 82.

48. Elliston, *Finland Fights,* Boston, 1940, 86.

49. Bair Irincheev, *The Mannerheim Line 1920–39: Finnish Fortifications of the Winter War,* Oxford, 2009, 5. In fact, the fortifications were built not at the line which Mannerheim had originally ordered, but along one ordered by the Finnish chief of staff, Maj. General Oscar Enckell, in 1919, while the fortifications themselves were mostly designed by Lt. Col. Johan Fabritius, with the help of a Frenchman, Maj. J. Gros-Coissy.

50. Jagerskiold, *Mannerheim,* 109.

51. Meri, *Beneath the Polar Star,* 14.

52. Jakobson, *Diplomacy of the Winter War,* 129.

53. Engle and Paananen, *Winter War,* 10.

54. Meri, *Beneath the Polar Star,* 14.

55. Ibid.

56. Carl Van Dyke, *The Winter War: The Russo-Finnish War of 1939–40,* London, 1991, 63–64.

57. Martha Noorback, *A Gentleman's Home: The Museum of Gustaf Mannerheim,* Helsinki, 2001.

58. *Talvisodan Historia,* 1, Porvoo (Fin.), 1979.

59. Jagerskiold, *Mannerheim,* 111.

60. Ibid.

61. Manninen, *Soviet Plans,* 17.

62. Jagerskiold, *Mannerheim,* 116.

63. Elliston, *Finland Fights,* 52.

64. Ibid., photo page 7.

65. Trotter, *Frozen Hell,* 50.

66. Interview with Olavi Eronen, trans. Ilkka Ranta-aho, March 2008.

67. Ibid.

68. Ibid.

69. Gellhorn, *Selected Letters,* 114.

70. Ibid.

71. Ibid.

72. Ibid., 116.

73. Trotter, *Frozen Hell,* 196.

74. The German dictator showed how much he admired Mannerheim in May 1942—by which time the Finns and Germans were co-belligerents in the new war with Russia—by flying to Finland to celebrate the marshal's seventy-fifth birthday. As far as Mussolini was concerned, he toed the line on Finland as well, ordering his officials to deny passports to the estimated 5,000 would-be freedom fighters who came forward to fight for Finland. Despite that, 150 Italian volunteers did manage to reach Finland on their own to join the fight. Mussolini did allow an order that the Finnish government had placed for thirty-five top-of-the-line Fiat fighters before the war, in October, to go through, although they were not delivered until February 1940.

75. Gellhorn, *Face of War,* 57.

76. Ibid., 58.

77. Ibid.

78. Elliston, *Finland Fights,* 211.

79. Pekka Tiilikainen, *Radioselostajana tuilinjiola,* Porvoo, 1940, 35.

80. Ibid.

81. Ibid.

82. Cox, *Red Army Moves,* 52.

83. Ibid.

84. Ibid.

85. Ibid.

86. William L. Shirer, *Berlin Diary: The Journal of a Foreign Correspondent 1934–1941,* New York, 1941, 253.

87. Ibid.

88. Travis Beal Jacobs, *America and the Winter War, 1939–1940,* New York, 1981, 91.

89. Ibid., 67.

90. Frank Freidel, *FDR: A Rendezvous with Destiny,* Boston, 1990.

91. Jakobson, *Diplomacy of the Winter War,* 192.

92. Ibid.

93. *New York Times,* December 2, 1939.

94. Trotter, *Frozen Hell,* 199. The

Americans would finally go into action on March 13, 1940, the last day of the war.

95. Wilhelm M. Carlgren, *Swedish Foreign Policy during the Second World War,* trans. Arthur Spencer, London, 1977, 24–27.

96. *New York Times,* December 2, 1939.

97. Eronen interview.

98. Kilpi interview; *Fire and Ice* (DVD).

99. Krutshih interview.

100. Interview with Suomussalmi resident.

101. Interview with "E." by Marketta Raihola, January 2009.

102. Ibid.

103. Trotter, *Frozen Hell,* 34.

104. Manninen, *Soviet 1944,* Helsinki, 2004, 12–13.

105. Ibid.

106. Ibid.

107. Edward Radzinsky, *Stalin,* New York, 1996, 446.

108. Ibid.

109. Ibid.

110. Manninen, *Soviet Plans,* 14–15. According to Zhdanov's biographer, Zhdanov met Molotov and Kuusinen in Stalin's offices on November 15, when plans for turning Finland into a Soviet satellite were discussed. The meeting Meretskov refers to quite likely took place on November 16 or 17.

111. Ibid.

112. Ibid.

113. Nikita Khrushchev, *Khrushchev Remembers,* Boston, 1970, 151.

114. The *eduskunta's* first "secret" session in Kauhajoki was on December 5. It continued to meet there until February 12, 1940, when it was relocated to Helsinki. Amongst the European belligerents, Finland and Great Britain were the only two whose parliaments continued to meet on an uninterrupted basis throughout World War II.

115. *New York Times,* December 3, 1939.

Chapter 2. "They Shall Not Get Us as a Present"

1. Shirer, *Berlin Diary,* 7.

2. Harold Nicholson: *Diaries and Letters 1939–1945,* New York, 1967, 43.

3. Jakobson, *Diplomacy of the Winter War,* 159, 158.

4. Ibid.

5. Ibid., 159.

6. Marvin Rintala, *Four Finns: Political Profiles,* Berkeley, 1969, 62.

7. Jakobson, *Diplomacy of the Winter War,* 159–160.

8. Cox, *Red Army Moves,* 30.

9. *New York Times,* December 1, 1939.

10. Tanner, *Winter War,* 97.

11. Ibid.

12. Ibid., 98.

13. Cox, *Red Army Moves,* 34.

14. Trotter, *Frozen Hell,* 50.

15. Cox, *Red Army Moves,* 113.

16. Ibid., 98.

17. *Time,* December 18, 1939.

18. Jacobs, *America and the Winter War,* 65–66.

19. David J. Dallin, *Soviet Russia's Foreign Policy 1939–1942,* New Haven, 1942, 143.

20. Winston Churchill, *The Second World War, Vol. 1,* Boston, 1948, 333.

21. George Kennan, *Russia and the West under Lenin and Stalin,* Boston, 1960, 335.

22. Dallin, *Soviet Russia's Foreign Policy,* 143.

23. *New York Times,* December 2, 1939.

24. Ibid.

25. Ibid.

26. Paasikivi, who had been on the verge of retiring before the war, later became Finland's president, serving from 1944 to 1956. It was he who laid the groundwork for the country's accommodationist relationship with the Kremlin and, along with his successor, Urho Kekkonen, oversaw relations with the USSR for the next quarter of a century.

27. Ibid.

28. Ibid.

29. Ibid.

30. Ibid.

31. Tanner, *Winter War,* 102–105

32. Trotter, *Frozen Hell,* 58–61.

33. *Pravda,* December 1, 1939.

34. Ibid.

35. *New York Times,* December 1, 1939.

36. Ibid.

37. The Ingrians were another, now also virtually extinct ethnic group (like the Karelians) with their own language and culture dating to medieval times, residing in the Leningrad area.

38. Interview with Edward Hynninen, trans. Bair Irincheev, November 2008.

39. Ibid.

40. *New York Times,* December 3, 1939.

41. Ibid. Ryti's claim regarding the number of Soviet planes destroyed, if not the causes for their demise, corresponds with that noted in Soviet war diaries. According to the latter, seventeen SB-2s were lost on December 1, including seven shot down by Finnish fighters and two by anti-aircraft fire, while five went missing in action—most likely after they were also shot down by fighters—and three were lost to accidents.

42. Kalevi Keskinen and Kari Stenman, *Finnish Air Force 1928–1940*, Volume 2, Espoo, 2006, 47.

43. *Helsingin Sanomat,* December 3, 1939.

44. Ibid.

45. Ibid.

46. Ibid.

47. *New York Times,* December 3, 1939.

48. Jakobson, *Diplomacy of the Winter War,* 171.

49. Gellhorn, *Face of War,* 62.

50. Jakobson, *Diplomacy of the Winter War,* 162; Jagerskiold, *Mannerheim,* 112.

51. Jakobson, *Diplomacy of the Winter War,* 162–163.

52. Ibid.

53. Jakobson, *Diplomacy of the Winter War,* 162. Sandler would continue to be an outspoken critic of Swedish neutrality, as well as an active friend of Finland, at one point traveling to Finland to assist in the humanitarian effort there. Ever the realist, Mannerheim merely shrugged his shoulders.

54. Ibid.

55. Ibid.

56. Ibid.

57. Ibid., 163.

58. Engle and Paananen, *Winter War,* 12.

59. Trotter, *Frozen Hell,* 39–40.

60. John Langdon-Davies, *Finland: The First Total War,* London, 1940, 7.

61. Trotter, *Frozen Hell,* 51.

62. Ibid., 52.

63. Bair Irincheev, *War of the White Death: Finland against the Soviet Union, 1939–40,* London, 2011, 5.

64. Chew, *White Death,* 29.

65. Malm interview.

66. *New York Times,* December 13, 1939. According to Finnish archives, thirty-one turncoats were tried for treason, with most receiving prison sentences of varying lengths. Six Finnish spies who had reinfiltrated from Russia and had been parachuted in were court-martialed and shot.

67. Gustaf Mannerheim, *Memoirs,* London, 1951, 327.

68. Ibid., 326.

69. Ibid., 334.

70. Chew, *White Death,* 31.

71. Ibid., 32.

72. Manninen. *Soviet Plans,* 15.

73. Ibid.

74. Ibid.

75. Quoted in the *New York Times,* December 9, 1939.

76. Ibid.

77. Van Dyke, *Soviet Invasion,* 110. That detachment, called the Dolin Brigade after its commander, was destroyed in combat with Finnish troops at Kuhmo in February.

78. From *Krasnaya Zyeda,* quoted in the *New York Times,* December 18, 1939.

79. Malm interview.

80. Manninen, *Soviet Plans,* 18.

81. Irincheev, *Mannerheim Line,* 21.

82. Catherine Merridale, *Ivan's War: Life and Death in the Red Army, 1939–1945,* New York, 2006, 78.

83. *New York Times,* December 15, 1939.

84. Irincheev, *War of the White Death,* 13.

85. Manninen, *Soviet Plans,* 20.

86. Ibid.

87. *New York Times,* December 7, 1939.

88. *New York Times,* December 8, 1939.

89. Although the government of Count Pal Teleki adopted a publicly neutral stance on the war, it also wound up contributing a significant amount of armaments to the Finnish cause, including 36 anti-aircraft guns, 16 mortars, and 300,000 hand grenades.

90. *New York Times,* December 10, 1939.

91. *New York Times,* December 8, 1939.

92. Neville Chamberlain, *The Neville Chamberlain Diary Letters,* Aldershot, 2000, 501.

93. Ibid.

94. Engle and Paananen, *Winter War,* 155.

95. *New York Times,* December 2, 1939.

96. *New York Daily News,* December 2, 1939.

97. Ibid.

98. *New York Times,* December 7, 1939.

99. *New York Times,* December 3, 1939.

100. *New York Times,* December 4, 1939.

101. *New York Times,* December 6, 1939.
102. Ibid.
103. Ibid.
104. *New York Times,* December 5, 1939.
105. Ibid.
106. Elliston, *Finland Fights,* 308.
107. Ibid., 309.
108. Ibid., 310.
109. Ibid.
110. Ibid.
111. Ibid., 313.
112. Ibid.
113. *New York Times,* December 5, 1939.
114. Cox, *Red Army Moves,* 56.
115. Matso interview.
116. In fact, although the Russians had stores of chemical weapons, as did most of the major belligerents during World War II, they never used them. In January 1940 Lev Z. Mehklis, the chief commissar of the Red Army, asked his superiors for permission to use poison gas against the Finns, but he was turned down by Shaposhnikov, the Soviet chief of staff.
117. *New York Times,* December 7, 1939.
118. Cox, *Red Army Moves,* 57.
119. *Fire and Ice* (DVD).
120. Ibid.
121. Tanner, *Winter War,* 57.
122. *New York Times,* December 7, 1939.
123. Ibid.
124. Ibid.
125. Ibid.
126. Ibid.
127. Ibid.
128. Tanner, *Winter War,* 112.
129. Elliston, *Finland Fights,* 332.
130. Ibid., 336.
131. Ibid.
132. Engle and Paananen, *Winter War,* 23.
133. Van Dyke, *Soviet Invasion,* 93.
134. Elliston, *Finland Fights,* 340.
135. Ibid., 338.
136. Engle and Paananen, *Winter War,* 25.
137. Interview with Antii Okko by Ilpo Murtovaara.
138. Ibid.
139. Ibid.
140. Later in the war, when Finland's reserves were running low, a number of inactive sailors were organized into naval infantry units. One of these, Battalion Haltonen, comprising personnel from Helsinki, fought with distinction in the Battle of Viipuri Bay.
141. Trotter, *Frozen Hell,* 57.

142. *New York Times,* January 13, 1940.
143. Gellhorn, *Selected Letters,* 63.
144. Ibid., 88.
145. Ibid., 66.
146. Ibid.
147. Ibid., 69.
148. Ibid., 70.
149. Ibid.
150. Ibid., 71.
151. Ibid., 72.
152. Ibid.
153. Berner interview.
154. *New York Times,* December 10, 1939.
155. *New York Times,* December 9, 1939.
156. Ibid.
157. Irincheev, *War of the White Death,* 104–105.
158. Cox, *Red Army Moves,* 59.
159. Ibid., 63.
160. Ibid.
161. Ibid., 60.
162. Ibid., 61.
163. Ibid., 62.
164. Ibid.
165. Ibid.
166. Ibid.
167. Ibid., 63.
168. Ibid., 53.
169. Ibid.
170. Ibid., 54.
171. Ibid.
172. Ibid., 55.
173. Ibid.
174. Ibid., 56.
175. Ibid.
176. Ibid.
177. Ibid., 57.
178. The situation *was* in hand. Though threatened, Kuhmo was never taken. The three reinforced Finnish battalions that soon arrived there were able to contain the Soviet 54th Division until the end of the war.
179. Ibid., 58.
180. *New York Times,* December 11, 1939.
181. Ibid. One of the longest-serving parliamentarians in Finnish history, Hakkila (1882–1958) was first elected to the *Eduskunta* in 1918 and served there until 1957, with only a brief interruption in 1948. He was speaker from 1939 to 1945. In 1930 he was kidnapped and beaten by members of the Lapua Movement.
182. *New York Times,* December 12, 1939.
183. Trotter, *Frozen Hell,* 199; *Helsingin Sanomat,* December 4, 1939.

184. Although the British didn't give the Finns any anti-tank cannons, they did contribute 200 1 mm anti-panzer rifles, which were also very effective.

185. Author's interview with Orvar Nilsson, January 2008.

186. *New York Times,* December 11, 1939.

187. Engle and Paananen, *Winter War,* 90.

188. Ibid.

189. Trotter, *Frozen Hell,* 109.

190. Ibid.

191. Ibid.

192. Oksanen interview.

193. Ibid.

194. Ibid.

195. Elliston, *Finland Fights,* 349.

Chapter 3. Steamroller Blues

1. *New York Times,* December 10, 1939.

2. Russian relations with Finland during Litvinov's tenure were not entirely pacific. In 1937 the Soviet violated the Treaty of Tartu by blockading Finnish ships from sailing from Lake Ladoga to the Gulf of Finland.

3. Dallin, *Soviet Russia's Foreign Policy,* 148–149.

4. Ibid.

5. *New York Times,* December 12, 1939.

6. Ibid.

7. Dallin, *Soviet Russia's Foreign Policy,* 150.

8. Ibid.

9. Ibid.

10. Ibid., 151.

11. Ibid., 144.

12. Ibid.

13. Collier, *Warcos,* 19.

14. Ibid.

15. *Times* (London), December 11, 1989.

16. Ibid.

17. William Manchester, *The Last Lion, Winston Spencer Churchill,* Boston, 1983, 568.

18. *Times* (London), December 11, 1939.

19. *Daily Telegraph,* December 7, 1939.

20. *Times* (London), December 20, 1939.

21. http://www.jewishvirtuallibrary.org/source/Holocaust/chronology__1939.html.

22. William L. Shirer, *This Is Berlin: A Narrative History 1938–40,* London, 1999, 153.

23. Ibid.

24. Ibid., 154.

25. Ibid.

26. Ibid.

27. Ibid.

28. *Times* (London), December 11, 1939.

29. Ibid.

30. Ibid. (emphasis in original).

31. Ibid.

32. Three days later the interned Langsdorff wrapped himself in a Swedish naval ensign and committed suicide in Montevideo.

33. Manchester, *Last Lion,* Boston, 1983, 614.

34. *New York Times,* December 12, 1939.

35. *Time,* December 18, 1939.

36. Christopher Isherwood, *Diaries, Volume 1: 1939–1960,* London, 1996, 417.

37. *Cornell University Class of 1942 Yearbook,* Ithaca, New York, 25.

38. *New York Times,* December 13, 1939.

39. Helsinki became the capital of the autonomous grand duchy of Finland in 1827. Before that, it was a small provincial town.

40. Ibid.

41. Gellhorn, *Face of War,* 72.

42. Ibid.

43. Ibid.

44. Ibid.

45. *New York Times,* December 16, 1939.

46. Interview with Niilo Kenjakka, by Marketta Raihala, March 2008.

47. *New York Times,* December 21, 1939.

48. Trotter, *Frozen Hell,* 73.

49. Ibid.

50. Irincheev, *Mannerheim Line,* 21.

51. Van Dyke, *Soviet Invasion.*

52. Interview with Ivan Chetyrbok by Bair Irincheev, 2002.

53. Ibid.

54. Engle and Paananen, *Winter War,* 68.

55. Ibid., 69.

56. Langdon-Davies, *First Total War,* 7.

57. Irincheev, *War of the White Death,* 64.

58. *New York Times,* December 15, 1939.

59. Ibid.

60. Russell Miller, *The Soviet Air Force at War,* Alexandria, Virginia, 1983, 71–73.

61. Ibid.

62. Carl Van Dyke, *The Soviet Invasion of Finland, 1939–1940,* London, 1997, 73.

63. Ibid.

64. Ibid.

65. Merridale, *Ivan's War,* 266–270.

66. *New York Times,* December 18, 1939.

67. Ibid.

68. Irincheev, *War of the White Death,* 24. A typical Russian division at the time consisted of 17,500 men, whereas a Finnish one had but 14,500.

69. Mannerheim, *Memoirs,* 342.
70. Trotter, *Frozen Hell,* 80.
71. Ibid.
72. Van Dyke, *Soviet Invasion,* 74.
73. Ibid., 76.
74. Ibid.
75. Ibid.
76. Chetyrbok interview.
77. Trotter, *Frozen Hell,* 88.
78. Ibid.
79. Ibid., 56–57.
80. Ibid.
81. Chetyrbok interview.
82. Cox, *Red Army Moves,* 76.
83. Ibid.
84. Ibid., 78.
85. The Finnish Army later adopted and kept the Jaeger name, using it to describe its light infantry regiments.
86. Ibid., 70–71.
87. Ibid.
88. Cox, *Red Army Moves,* 71.
89. Ibid., 73.
90. Ibid.
91. Ibid.
92. Ibid., 75.
93. Ibid., 79.
94. Ibid.
95. Ibid.
96. Ibid.
97. Ibid., 79.
98. Ibid.
99. Ibid., 80.
100. The Finnish Army employed over 90,000 horses during the Winter War, of whom 7,200 perished, including 4,000 from enemy fire. The exact number used by the Russians is not known.
101. Ibid.
102. Ibid.
103. Ibid., 81.
104. Ibid.
105. Ibid.
106. Ibid.
107. Mannerheim, *Memoirs,* 341.
108. Ibid., 343.
109. *New York Times,* December 20, 1939.
110. Ibid.
111. Ibid.
112. Trotter, *Frozen Hell,* 82.
113. Ibid., 80.
114. Chetyrbok interview.
115. Langdon-Davies, *First Total War,* 65.

116. *New York Times,* December 21, 1939.
117. Ibid.
118. Ibid.
119. Ibid.
120. Ibid.
121. Ibid.
122. Ibid.
123. Keskinen and Stenman, *Finnish Air Force 1928–40,* Espoo, 2006, 98.
124. Ibid.
125. Ibid.
126. Ibid.
127. Ibid.
128. Ibid.
129. *New York Times,* December 20, 1939.
130. Ibid.
131. Ibid.
132. *Helsingin Sanomat,* December 21, 1939.
133. Ibid.
134. Carl-Fredrik Geust and Antero Uitto, *Mannerheim-linja: Talvisodan legenda,* Jyvaskyla, 2006, 70–71.
135. Chetyrbok interview.
136. Trotter, *Frozen Hell,* 84.
137. Merridale, *Ivan's War,* 79.
138. Ibid.
139. Mannerheim, *Memoirs,* 184.
140. Ibid.
141. Ibid.
142. Ibid.
143. Eronen interview.
144. Jacobs, *America and the Winter War,* 77.
145. Ibid., 110.
146. Mary Beth Norton et al., *A People and a Nation: A History of the United States since 1865,* New York, 2011, 684.
147. *New York Times,* December 16, 1939.
148. *New York Times,* December 30, 1939.
149. *New York Times,* December 6, 1939.
150. *New York Times,* December 21, 1939.
151. Ibid.
152. Ibid.
153. Ibid.
154. Ibid.
155. Jacobs, *America and the Winter War,* 228–235.
156. *New York Times,* December 20, 1939.
157. Clark, *Three Days,* 76.
158. *New York Times,* December 23, 1939.
159. John Erickson, *The Road to Stalingrad: Stalin's War with Nazi Germany,* New Haven, 1999, 121.
160. Ibid.

161. Clark, *Three Days,* 176.

162. Ibid.

163. *New York Times,* December 23, 1939.

164. Trotter, *Frozen Hell,* 57.

165. *New Yorker,* December 21, 1939.

166. Ibid.

167. *New York Times,* December 15, 1939.

168. Ibid.

169. Khrushchev, *Khrushchev Remembers,* 154.

170. Ibid.

171. Ibid.

172. Erickson, *Road to Stalingrad,* 117.

173. Ibid.

174. Ibid.

175. Hynninen interview.

176. *New York Times,* December 22, 1939.

177. Kees Boeterbloem, *The Life and Times of Andrei Zhdanov, 1896–1948,* Montreal, 2004, 201.

178. Ibid.

179. Simon Sebag Montefiore, *In the Court of the Red Star,* New York, 2003, 328.

180. Van Dyke, *Soviet Invasion,* 77.

181. Ibid.

182. Ibid.

183. Ibid.

184. Shtern's star didn't shine for long, particularly after the 8th Army became bogged down in January, when one of his divisions, the 54th, was trapped north of Ladoga. He was one of the generals whom Stalin revenged himself upon after the shock German invasion of Russia in June when he was summarily tried on trumped-up charges and shot.

185. Harold Shukman, *Stalin's Generals,* New York, 1993, 322–323.

186. *New York Times,* December 22, 1939.

187. *New York Times,* December 24, 1939.

188. Ibid.

189. Ibid.

190. *New York Times,* December 24, 1939.

191. Ibid.

192. Ibid.

193. Ibid.

194. Ibid.

195. Cox, *Red Army Moves,* 90. Mydans, who would later call Finnish press censorship "the most destructive I have ever seen," was particularly upset about this.

196. Veijalainen, *Woman at the Front,* 24.

197. Ibid., 25.

198. Ibid.

199. *New York Times,* December 24, 1939.

200. Ibid.

201. *New York Times,* December 25, 1939.

202. Malm interview.

203. *New York Times,* December 27, 1939.

204. Ibid.

205. David Hinshaw, *Heroic Finland,* New York, 1952, 240.

206. Ibid., 241.

207. Ibid.

208. Ibid.

209. Ibid.

Chapter 4. The Suomussalmi Factor

1. *New York Times,* December 24, 1939.

2. Moorehead, *Martha Gellhorn,* 196.

3. Ibid., 199.

4. Cowles, *Looking for Trouble,* 280.

5. Ibid., 286–288.

6. http://www.elyrics.net/read/f/ Flanagan&allen-lyrics/run.rabbit-run-lyrics .html.

7. Ibid.

8. Ibid., 281.

9. Ibid.

10. *New York Times,* January 1, 1940.

11. Cowles, *Looking for Trouble,* 283. *Dangerous Assignment* was a popular U.S. radio serial of the 1930s about the adventures of a hop-scotching foreign correspondent (male, of course).

12. Ibid.

13. Trotter, *Frozen Hell,* 190.

14. Ibid.

15. Cox, *Red Army Moves,* 103–105.

16. Ibid., 108.

17. Cox, *Red Army Moves,* 104.

18. Ibid.

19. Ibid.

20. Dutch neutrality would abruptly end on May 10, 1940, when Holland was invaded by Nazi Germany; the small Dutch Air Force, largely comprised of Fokkers, was knocked out of the sky in one day. Holland would continue to be occupied for the remainder of the war.

21. Ibid.

22. Ibid., 107.

23. Cowles, *Looking for Trouble,* 286.

24. Ibid.

25. Ibid.

26. Ibid., 287.

27. Ibid.

28. Ibid.

29. Ibid., 288.

30. Ibid.

31. Ibid., 289. The hostess's memory was somewhat jumbled. The conflict she was referring to was the Great Northern War (1700–1721), in which a coalition comprising Russia, Denmark-Norway, and Poland-Lithuania contested Swedish supremacy in the eastern Baltic. Although Charles XII, the boisterous Swedish sovereign, indeed used Finnish troops in repelling those of his chief antagonist, Peter the Great of Russia, they were eventually overrun and Finland was occupied. Charles himself was killed by a sniper's bullet in 1718 at Frederiksten in Norway.

32. Ibid.

33. Ibid., 285.

34. Ibid., 299.

35. *New York Times,* December 15, 1939.

36. Ibid.

37. Matso interview.

38. Ibid.

39. Ibid.

40. Cowles, *Looking for Trouble,* 301.

41. Mannerheim finally cashiered Melander in 1944, during the Continuation War.

42. Trotter, *Frozen Hell,* 52–53.

43. Manninen, *Soviet Plans,* 24.

44. Jussi Kamarainen, Einar Ladinen, and Sergei Verigin, *Talvisodan panttivangit,* Helsinki, 2006, 121–135.

45. Richard Holmes, *The Oxford Companion to Military History,* Oxford, 2001, 902–903.

46. Trotter, *Frozen Hell,* 151–152.

47. Ibid., 152.

48. Cox, *Red Army Moves,* 116.

49. Ibid., 117.

50. Trotter, *Frozen Hell,* 155.

51. Cox, *Red Army Moves,* 121.

52. Ibid., 119.

53. Trotter, *Frozen Hell,* 158.

54. Cox, *Red Army Moves,* 118.

55. Mannerheim, *Memoirs,* 339.

56. Chew, *White Death,* 110–114.

57. Jari Leskinen and Antti Juutilainen, eds., *Talvisodan pikkujattilainen,* Helsinki, 1999, 552.

58. Cox, *Red Army Moves,* 119.

59. Richard Condon, *The Winter War*

against Russia, New York, 1972, 72.

60. Cox, *Red Army Moves,* 120.

61. Ibid.

62. Trotter, *Frozen Hell,* 169–70; Chew, *White Death,* 86.

63. Interview with Niilo Haikola by Marketta Raihala, February 2009.

64. Condon, *Winter War,* 92.

65. *Helsingin Sanomat,* December 31, 1939.

66. Condon, *Winter War,* 92.

67. Chew, *White Death,* 69.

68. Ibid.

69. E. interview.

70. Ibid.

71. The Stockholm syndrome took its name following a bank robbery in the Swedish capital in the 1970s in which the robbers took hostages, some of whom ultimately identified with and defended their captors.

72. Kamarainen, Ladinen, and Verigin, *Talvisodan panttivangit,* 96–114.

73. Ibid.

74. Ibid.

75. Ibid.

76. Ibid.

77. Ibid.

78. Ibid.

79. Ibid.

80. Ibid.

81. Ibid.

82. *New York Times,* December 28, 1939.

83. Ibid.

84. Ibid.

85. Trotter, *Frozen Hell,* 183.

86. Ibid.

87. Ibid., 184.

88. Ibid.

89. Ibid., 183.

90. Ibid.

91. Ibid.

92. Ibid. Mydans himself would be captured by the Japanese in 1941 and tortured, an experience that would considerably alter his relative view of captors and captivity before being released as part of a prisoner of war exchange in 1942.

93. Ibid.

94. Cowles, *Looking for Trouble,* 300.

95. Ibid.

96. Ibid.

97. Ibid.

98. Ibid., 301.

99. 44th Division Combat Diary, *Manner-heim Line—Finnish Fortifications of Winter War Period,* http://www.mannerheim-line.com.

100. Ibid.

101. *New York Times,* January 4, 1940. Altogether, 725 Norwegians volunteered to fight for Finland. However, only 150 saw any action, and limited action at that, on the quiet Salla front, where they served along with their Swedish comrades.

102. Ibid.

103. *Times* (London), January 5, 1940.

104. Carl-Fredrik Geust and Gennadiy Petrov, *Red Stars, Volume 5: Baltic Fleet Air Force in the Winter War*, Tampere, 2004, 78.

105. Ibid.

106. 44th Division Combat Diary, *Manner-heim Line—Finnish Fortifications of Winter War Period,* http://www.mannerheim-line.com.

107. Ibid.

108. Ibid.

109. Harold Shukman, *Stalin's Generals,* London, 1993, 239.

110. Carl-Fredrik Geust and Gennadiy Petrov, *Red Stars, Volume 5: Baltic Fleet Air Force in the Winter War*, Tampere, 2004, 112–113.

111. Ibid.

112. Ibid.

113. Cox, *Red Army Moves,* 124.

114. Ibid.

115. The most celebrated Russian general to see duty during the Winter War—and one of the few to survive the second wave of Army purges following the German invasion of Russia in 1941—Chuikov commanded the successful defense of Stalingrad in 1942, eventually rising to the rank of marshal. However, he doesn't seem to have accomplished very much in Finland, except to survive Stalin's wrath.

116. Ibid., 125.

117. Condon, *Winter War,* 93.

118. *New York Times,* January 5, 1940.

119. Trotter, *Frozen Hell,* 170.

120. Winston Churchill, *Never Give In: The Best of Winston Churchill's Speeches,* New York, 2003, 342.

121. Eronen interview; *Time,* January 20, 1940.

122. Chew, *Frozen Hell,* 124.

123. Virginia Cowles, *Sunday Times* (London), February 4, 1940.

124. Ibid.

125. Cox, *Red Army Moves,* 127.

126. Ibid.

127. Mannerheim, *Memoirs,* 340.

128. Chew, *White Death,* 125.

129. *Times* (London), January 10, 1940.

130. Shukman, *Stalin's Generals,* 239.

131. Ibid.

132. Van Dyke, *Soviet Invasion,* 104.

133. Ibid.

134. Ibid.

135. Ibid.

136. Ibid., 105.

137. Trotter, *Frozen Hell,* 208.

138. Author's interview with Yevgeny Davidov, November 2008. The resulting cenotaph, one of the most moving—and imaginative—war memorials ever built, in the author's opinion—not to mention one of the few bilateral projects of its kind—consists of a vast hour glass–shaped field into which thousands of boulders, each supposedly standing for a fallen Finnish or Russian soldier, have been carted. In the middle of the field is a tall metallic sculpture from which depend 105 bells, one for each day of the war, which sound in the wind.

139. Ibid.

Chapter 5. "Nothing of Importance on the Front"

1. *New York Times,* January 10, 1940.

2. *Life,* February 15, 1940.

3. *New York Times,* January 18, 1940.

4. Cox, *Red Army Moves,* 94.

5. Ibid., 93.

6. Ibid.

7. Ibid., 94.

8. Ibid., 95.

9. Ibid., 97.

10. Ibid., 100.

11. Ibid., 98.

12. As far as can be told, the only dancing allowed in the country was at a raffish Helsinki nightclub by the name of the Club de Paris.

13. Ibid., 98.

14. Ibid., 101.

15. Cowles, *Looking for Trouble,* 288.

16. Ibid.

17. Ibid.

18. Ibid.

19. Ibid.

20. Ibid.

21. Cox, *Red Army Moves,* 101.
22. Stowe, *No Other Road,* 190.
23. Ibid.
24. *New York Times,* December 26, 1939.
25. Veijalainen, *Woman at the Front,* 30.
26. Ibid.
27. Toivenen interview.
28. Ibid.
29. Letter from Mai-Lis Toivenen to her mother, February 4, 1940.
30. Toivenen interview.
31. *Fire and Ice* (DVD).
32. Ibid.
33. Inkeri Kilpinen (1926–), a noted playwright, children's author, and novelist.
34. *Fire and Ice* (DVD).
35. Harold Denny, *New York Times Magazine,* February 12, 1940, 12.
36. Ibid.
37. Ibid.
38. Malm interview.
39. Ibid.
40. Eronen interview.
41. *New York Times,* January 20, 1940.
42. Malm interview.
43. Eronen interview.
44. Veijalainen, *Woman at the Front,* 31.
45. Author's interview with Nikolai Bavin, November 2008.
46. Ibid.
47. Ibid.
48. Ibid.
49. Ibid. The Soviets expected to seize far more, preparing several large camps for them.
50. Ibid.
51. Ibid.
52. Ibid.
53. Ibid.
54. Ibid.
55. Ibid.
56. Ibid.
57. *New York Times,* January 32, 1940.
58. Ibid.
59. Ibid.
60. Matso interview.
61. Wayne Wayson, "The Winter War: 105 Days of Finnish Resistance," http:// americanmilitary.academia.edu/Wayne Wayson/Papers/860000/The_Winter _War_105_Days_of_Finnish_Resistance.
62. *New York Times,* January 19, 1940. *Folkhemmet,* a Swedish term that means

"people's home," is one of the founding concepts of Nordic social democracy. Coined by Swedish prime minister Per Albin Hansson, it refers to his desire to replace the traditional class society with a new one based on the principles of equality and understanding, in which most of the people's needs are taken care of by the state. Though less progressive than Sweden, Finland would end up adapting many features of the Swedish *folkhemmet* for its own model.
63. Ibid.
64. Ibid.
65. Tanner, *Winter War,* 161; exhibit at the Norwegian Air Force Museum in Bodo, Norway.
66. *Times* (London), January 20, 1940.
67. Ibid.
68. Ibid.
69. Ibid.
70. Ibid.
71. Ibid.
72. *New York Times,* January 21, 1940.
73. Nicholson, *Diaries and Letters,* 54.
74. *Politiken,* December 20, 1939; Jakobson, *Diplomacy of the Winter War,* 198–199.
75. Jenkins, *Churchill,* 568.
76. Van Dyke, *Soviet Invasion,* 114.
77. Ibid.
78. Ibid.
79. *New York Times,* January 20, 1940.
80. Ibid.

Chapter 6. Grand Hotel

1. Jakobson, *Diplomacy of the Winter War,* 50.
2. Beatrice Farnsworth, "Conversing with Stalin, Surviving the Terror: The Diaries of Aleksandra Kollontai and the Internal Life of Politics," *Slavic Review* 69, no. 4 (2010): 944–964.
3. Ibid.
4. Ibid.
5. Jakobson, *Diplomacy of the Winter War,* 208.
6. Ibid., 209.
7. Ibid. Tanner's gratitude to Wuolijoki was to end, and his original suspicions about the freelance diplomat would be confirmed, during the Continuation War when the latter was found harboring a Soviet parachutist, for which she would be jailed and sentenced to life imprisonment. She was released

following the armistice that ended that war in 1944 and went on to become a member of parliament from the left-wing SKDL faction and a director of YLE radio.

8. Ibid.

9. Ibid.

10. Wayson, "Winter War: 105 Days of Finnish Resistance."

11. Jagerskiold, *Mannerheim,* 118–119.

12. Ibid., 121.

13. *New York Times,* January 23, 1940.

14. *Helsingin Sanomat,* January 22, 1940.

15. Ibid.

16. Ibid.

17. Commemorative issue of *Ilta Sanomat,* February 2010.

18. *New York Times,* January 25, 1940.

19. Walter Citrine, *Two Careers,* London, 1967, 19.

20. Ibid.

21. Ibid.

22. Ibid.

23. Ibid.

24. Ibid.

25. Ibid., 20.

26. *New York Times,* January 22, 1940.

27. Jacobs, *America and the Winter War,* 88.

28. *New York Times,* January 19, 1940.

29. Ibid.

30. Jakobson, *Diplomacy of the Winter War,* 124.

31. Ibid.

32. Ibid., 210.

33. Ibid.

34. Ibid., 211.

35. Ibid.

36. Ibid., 212.

37. Mannerheim, *Memoirs,* 353.

38. Ibid.

39. Jakobson, *Diplomacy of the Winter War,* 213.

Chapter 7. The Red Army's Second Turn

1. Jakobson, *Diplomacy of the Winter War,* 214.

2. Trotter, *Frozen Hell,* 217–218.

3. Jakobson, *Diplomacy of the Winter War,* 214.

4. Ibid.

5. Ibid., 222.

6. Tanner, *Winter War,* 164.

7. Ibid., 149.

8. Clark, *Three Days to Catastrophe,* 118.

9. Ibid.

10. Ibid., 100.

11. Engle and Paananen, *Winter War,* 154.

12. Ibid., 154–155.

13. Trotter, *Frozen Hell,* 198.

14. Clark, *Three Days to Catastrophe,* 122. Two months later, following the German invasion of Norway, Narvik was the site of a pitched sea and land battle between the British and the Germans. The British actually won the sea battle, but botched the land battle and were forced to evacuate, a debacle that led directly to Chamberlain's resignation and his replacement by Winston Churchill.

15. Ibid., 121.

16. Clark, *Three Days to Catastrophe,* 123.

17. Ibid.

18. Ibid.

19. Ibid. During the Spanish Civil War of 1936–38 the Italian government sent an estimated 75,000 such "volunteers" to fight for the Rebel forces headed by Francisco Franco.

20. Ibid.

21. Tanner, *Winter War,* 121; Geoffrey Cox, *Eyewitness: A Memoir of Europe in the 1930s,* Dunedin, New Zealand, 1999.

22. Clark, *Three Days to Catastrophe,* 121.

23. Ibid.

24. Ibid.

25. Ibid.

26. *New York Times,* February 7, 1940.

27. Alan Brooke, *War Diaries, 1939–45,* London, 2003.

28. *New York Times,* February 5, 1940.

29. Ibid.

30. Irincheev, *War of the White Death,* 124.

31. Chetyrbok interview.

32. Cox, *Red Army Moves,* 202.

33. Van Dyke, *Soviet Invasion,* 142.

34. Ibid., 139–142.

35. Internal Soviet interview with Captain M. Sipovich, 1941.

36. Ibid.

37. Van Dyke, *Soviet Invasion,* 142.

38. Ibid., 139–142.

39. Internal Soviet interview with Captain M. Sipovich, 1941.

40. Ibid.

41. Ibid.

42. Ibid.

43. Internal Soviet interview with Captain M. Sipovich, 1941.

44. Ibid.

45. Ibid.

46. Ibid.

47. Ibid.

48. Ibid.

49. Van Dyke, *Soviet Invasion,* 142.

50. Ibid.

51. Ibid., 144–145.

52. Ibid., 144; Irincheev, *War of White Death,* 144–145.

53. *New York Times,* February 3, 1940.

54. Trotter, *Frozen Hell,* 216–217.

55. *Times* (London), February 3, 1940.

56. Ibid.

57. Ibid.

58. Van Dyke, *Soviet Invasion,* 149.

59. Cox, *Red Army Moves,* 241.

60. *Times* (London), February 6, 1940.

61. Van Dyke, *Soviet Invasion,* 139.

62. Ibid.

63. Ibid., 144.

64. Ibid.

65. *New York Times,* February 7, 1940.

66. Toivenen interview.

67. Ibid.

68. Veijalainen, *Woman at the Front,* 33.

69. Although the Red paratroops succeeded in sowing panic amongst the Finnish populace, the Russian experience with airborne troops during the Winter War was, on the whole, so calamitous that the USSR never again used them *en masse* during the Second World War.

70. Ibid.

71. Ibid.

72. Ibid.

73. Cowles, *Looking for Trouble,* 324.

74. Ibid.

75. Trotter, *Frozen Hell,* 218–220.

76. *New York Times,* February 6, 1940.

77. Chetyrbok interview.

78. Langdon-Davies, *First Total War,* 107.

79. Engle and Paananen, *Winter War,* 122.

80. Langdon-Davies, *First Total War,* 108.

81. Tanner, *Winter War,* 149–150.

82. *Times* (London), February 7, 1940.

83. Ibid.

84. *New York Times,* February 9, 1940.

85. Jakobson, *Diplomacy of the Winter War,* 224–225.

86. Ibid.

87. *New York Times,* February 9, 1940.

88. Ibid.

89. Wayson, "Winter War: 105 Days of Finnish Resistance."

90. *Times* (London), February 9, 1940.

91. In an extraordinary coincidence, one of the Finnish troops facing Grendahl's men at Taipale was evidently his own son, Boris, whom the former Finnish Red had left behind for his wife to raise, when he fled to Russia after the civil war and before he joined the Russian Army.

92. Van Dyke, *Soviet Invasion,* 145.

93. Ibid., 145–147.

94. Trotter, *Frozen Hell,* 43–46.

95. Van Dyke, *Soviet Invasion,* 147.

96. Ibid., 148–149.

97. Ibid., 149.

98. *New York Times,* February 11, 1940.

99. Ibid.

100. Ibid.

101. Ibid.

102. Ibid.

103. Ibid., 312.

104. Ibid., 322.

105. Ibid.

106. Ibid.

107. Ibid., 323.

108. Ibid.

109. Ibid.

110. Trotter, *Frozen Hell,* 214.

111. Ibid.

112. Langdon-Davies, *First Total War,* 109.

113. Ibid.

114. Cowles, *Looking for Trouble,* 323.

115. *New York Times,* February 8, 1940.

116. Ibid.

117. Jakobson, *Diplomacy of the Winter War,* 195–196.

118. Jacobs, *America and the Winter War,* 186.

119. *New York Times,* February 11, 1940.

120. *Helsingin Sanomat,* February 11, 1940. It ought to be noted that the Roosevelt administration did authorize the shipment of 44 Buffalo Brewster fighters to Finland, even though only half a dozen arrived before the end of the war. Regarding his surprising speech of February 10, in which FDR blasted those jeering AYC demonstrators, it is clear that Roosevelt was primarily expressing his discomfiture with his delicate political position, caught as he was between pressures

from the interventionist camp, of which he was a not-so-secret member, and the yet stronger isolationist one, than from any special ire at those cantankerous AYC delegates (though it might have seemed otherwise at the time).

121. *New York Times,* February 11, 1940.

122. Trotter, *Frozen Hell,* 227; Manninen, *Soviet Plans,* 43.

123. Engle and Paananen, *Winter War,* 125.

124. Erickson, *Road to Stalingrad,* 119.

125. Ibid.

126. Ibid.

127. Ibid.

128. In the hundreds of articles from the Western press about the war that the author has examined, Timoshenko's name appears but once. Grigory Shtern would wind up being executed, along with a number of other generals who served during the Winter War, during the "mini-purge" Stalin ordered in July 1941 following the German invasion of Russia.

129. Van Dyke, *Soviet Invasion,* 150.

130. Jakobson, *Diplomacy of the Winter War,* 223.

131. Ibid.

132. Ibid.

133. Ibid.

134. Ibid., 231.

135. Ibid., 234.

136. Ibid., 224.

137. Ibid., 225.

138. Van Dyke, *Soviet Invasion,* 150–151.

139. Ibid., 151.

140. Mannerheim, *Memoirs,* 355.

141. Van Dyke, *Soviet Invasion,* 151.

142. Irincheev, *Mannerheim Line,* 38–39.

143. Van Dyke, *Soviet Invasion,* 151–152.

144. Mannerheim, *Memoirs,* 354.

145. Van Dyke, *Soviet Invasion,* 151–152.

146. Trotter, *Frozen Hell,* 228.

147. Ibid.

148. Cox, *Red Army Moves,* 203.

149. Mannerheim, *Memoirs,* 354.

150. Trotter, *Frozen Hell,* 228.

151. Irincheev, *War of the White Death,* 137.

152. Trotter, *Frozen Hell,* 228.

153. Ibid., 229.

154. Mannerheim, *Memoirs,* 354.

155. Ibid.

156. Trotter, *Frozen Hell,* 246–248.

157. Ibid.

158. Ibid.

159. Tanner, *Winter War,* 157.

160. Ibid., 170.

161. Ibid., 156.

162. Ibid., 158.

163. Ibid.

164. Tanner, *Winter War,* 159.

165. Ibid., 159. Nazi Germany, like its Fascist ally, Italy, participated in the Spanish Civil War via a group of 16,000 volunteers taken from its regular armed forces. They were called the Condor Legion.

166. Ibid.

167. Ibid.

168. Ibid.

169. Tanner was probably bluffing here, although it is entirely possible that the pro-Finnish German ambassador, Wipert von Bluecher, had told Tanner something to this effect because that is what he wanted to hear.

170. Jakobson, *Diplomacy of the Winter War,* 229.

171. Clark, *Three Days,* 89.

172. Jakobson, *Diplomacy of the Winter War,* 231.

173. Tanner, *Winter War,* 160.

174. Cox, *Red Army Moves,* 272.

175. Ibid.

176. Cowles, *Looking for Trouble,* 319.

177. Ibid.

178. Trotter, *Frozen Hell,* 232.

179. Stowe, *No Other Road,* 67.

180. Ibid.

181. Cowles, *Looking for Trouble,* 319.

182. Cox, *Red Army Moves,* 143.

183. Ibid.

184. Ibid., 202.

185. How the government was able to come up with that number, which the press duly repeated, is unclear.

186. *New York Times,* February 15, 1940.

187. Ibid.

188. Ibid.

189. *New York Times,* February 14, 1940.

190. Ibid.

191. Ibid.

192. Ibid.

193. Airo, YLE interview.

194. *New York Times,* February 15, 1940.

195. Trotter, *Frozen Hell,* 231.

196. Mannerheim, *Memoirs,* 355.

197. Ibid.

198. Trotter, *Frozen Hell,* 232.

199. Ibid.

200. Cox, *Red Army Moves,* 205.

201. Trotter, *Frozen Hell,* 231.

202. Ibid. Mannerheim, it turns out, was not a great fan of Ohquist either, nor vice versa. In the subsequent Continuation War, when he also commanded Finnish forces, he failed to give Ohquist a meaningful assignment.

203. Cox, *Red Army Moves,* 205.

204. Ibid.

205. Ibid., 206.

206. Ibid.

207. Airo, YLE interview.

208. Chew, *White Death,* 162.

209. Trotter, *Frozen Hell,* 233; Chew, *White Death,* 169.

210. Trotter, *Frozen Hell,* 232–233.

211. *New York Times,* February 16, 1940.

212. Ibid.

213. Engle and Paananen, *Winter War,* 126.

214. Ibid.

215. Ibid.

216. *New York Times,* February 15, 1940.

217. Keskinen and Stenman, *Finnish Air Force,* 114.

218. *Helsingin Sanomat,* February 17, 1940.

219. *Helsingin Sanomat,* February 19, 1940.

220. Ibid.

221. Veijalainen, *Woman at the Front,* 34.

222. *New York Times,* February 19, 1940.

223. Veijalainen, *Woman at the Front,* 34.

224. Ibid.

225. Ibid.

226. Ibid., 35.

227. Ibid.

228. Ibid., 36.

229. Cowles, *Looking for Trouble,* 324.

230. Ibid., 312.

231. Ibid., 313.

232. Ibid.

233. Ibid.

234. Ibid., 325.

235. Mannerheim, *Memoirs,* 391.

236. Ibid.

237. Ibid.

238. Hudson Strode, *Finland Forever,* New York, 1941, 412.

239. Ibid.

240. *New York Times,* February 20, 1940.

241. Jakobson, *Diplomacy of the Winter War,* 233.

242. Carlgren, *Swedish Foreign Policy,* 202–204.

243. Jagerskiold, *Mannerheim,* 123.

244. Clark, *Three Days,* 155.

245. Ibid.

246. Ibid.

247. Ibid.

248. Ibid.

249. Keskinen and Stenman, *Finnish Air Force,* 96; *New York Times,* February 22, 1940.

Chapter 8. The Gates of Viipuri

1. Chew, *White Death,* 196.

2. Van Dyke, *Soviet Invasion,* 175.

3. Jakobson, *Diplomacy of the Winter War,* 235.

4. Ibid.

5. Ibid.

6. Trotter, *Frozen Hell,* 244.

7. Ibid.

8. Ibid., 259.

9. *New York Times,* February 27, 1940.

10. Ibid.

11. Van Dyke, *Soviet Invasion,* 167.

12. Ibid.

13. Trotter, *Frozen Hell,* 257.

14. Jakobson, *Diplomacy of the Winter War,* 238.

15. Ibid.

16. *New York Times,* February 25, 1940.

17. J. E. O. Screen, *Mannerheim: The Years of Preparation,* London, 1970, 151.

18. Condon, *Winter War,* 118.

19. *New York Times,* February 28, 1940.

20. Cox, *Red Army Moves,* 207.

21. Mannerheim, *Memoirs,* 384.

22. Ibid.

23. Ibid.

24. Ibid.

25. Trotter, *Frozen Hell,* 137–140.

26. Mannerheim, *Memoirs,* 384.

27. Ibid.

28. Ibid.

29. *New York Times,* February 29, 1940.

30. Trotter, *Frozen Hell,* 190.

31. Carl-Fredrik Geust, *Red Stars: The Winter War in the Air,* Tampere, 2011, 246–255. Of all the countries that contributed pilots to the Finnish Air Force, Denmark ranked third, after Sweden and Great Britain. Altogether fifteen Danish volunteers flew

with the FAF, of whom no fewer than five were killed in action. Kristensen was the last to perish.

32. Ibid.

33. Jakobson, *Diplomacy of the Winter War,* 239.

34. Ibid., 198.

35. Ibid., 240.

36. Ibid., 241.

37. Clark, *Three Days,* 160–162; Tanner, *Winter War,* 132.

38. Ibid.

39. Ibid.

40. Ibid.

41. Ibid.

42. Jacobs, *America and the Winter War,* 212.

43. Ibid.

44. Trotter, *Frozen Hell,* 257.

45. Ibid.

46. Ibid.

47. Ibid.

48. Ibid., 259.

49. Interview with Eric Malm.

50. Tapio A.M. Saarelainen, *Simo Hayha,* Tampere, 2008. On March 6, 1940, Hayha was shot and seriously injured. While he was recovering, Mannerheim promoted him from corporal to second lieutenant, the fastest such promotion in Finnish Army history.

51. Veijalainen, *Woman at the Front,* 37.

52. Ibid.

53. Ibid.

54. Ibid., 38.

55. Ibid.

56. *New York Times,* March 2, 1940.

57. Mannerheim, *Memoirs,* 360.

58. *Svenska frivilliga I Finland 1939–44,* Stockholm, 143–146.

59. *New York Times,* March 1, 1940. Another country whose contribution to the *Talvisota* Mannerheim evidently forgot was Estonia, which was then suffering a partial Soviet occupation, soon to become a full one, but nevertheless managed to send several hundred volunteers to fight for their Finnish cousins.

60. Ibid.

61. Jakobson, *Diplomacy of the Winter War,* 243–244.

62. Ibid.

63. Ibid.

64. Ibid.

65. Ibid., 246.

66. Ibid.

67. Trotter, *Frozen Hell,* 259.

68. Ibid.

69. Mannerheim, *Memoirs,* 361.

70. Trotter, *Frozen Hell,* 255.

71. Veijalainen, *Woman at the Front,* 40.

72. Ibid., 41.

73. Jakobson, *Diplomacy of the Winter War,* 248.

74. Ibid.

75. Cox, *Red Army Moves,* 208.

76. Trotter, *Frozen Hell,* 257.

77. Ibid.

78. Ibid., 252.

79. Jakobson, *Diplomacy of the Winter War,* 241.

80. Ibid.

81. Ibid.

82. Trotter, *Frozen Hell,* 259.

83. Geust, *Red Stars,* 266–329.

84. Keskinen and Stenman, *Finnish Air Force,* 150–153.

85. Ibid.

86. Irincheev, *War of the White Death,* 193.

87. Jakobson, *Diplomacy of the Winter War,* 248–249; Trotter, *Frozen Hell,* 249.

88. *Talvisodan historia,* IV, 265.

89. Trotter, *Frozen Hell,* 259.

90. Geust, *Red Stars,* 134.

91. Tanner, *Winter War,* 209–214.

92. Clark, *Three Days,* 170, 177.

93. *Times* (London), March 5, 1940.

94. Henry Kissinger, *Diplomacy,* New York, 1994.

95. Clark, *Three Days,* 186.

96. Ibid., 170.

97. Ibid., 171.

98. Ibid.

99. Van Dyke, *Soviet Invasion,* 175.

100. Ibid.

101. Ibid.

102. Tanner, *Winter War,* 217–218.

103. Jakobson, *Diplomacy of the Winter War,* 249.

104. Mannerheim, *Memoirs,* 363.

105. Trotter, *Frozen Hell,* 251.

106. Ibid.

107. Ibid.

108. Jakobson, *Diplomacy of the Winter War,* 250–251.

109. Ibid., 250.

110. Ibid., 251.
111. Ibid.
112. Clark, *Three Days,* 172.
113. Ibid.
114. Langdon-Davies, *Finland,* 113.
115. Cox, *Red Army Moves,* 209.
116. Clark, *Three Days,* 172.
117. Ibid.
118. Ibid.
119. Ibid.
120. Cox, *Red Army Moves,* 209.
121. Mannerheim, *Memoirs,* 362.
122. Trotter, *Frozen Hell,* 259–260.
123. Keskinen and Stenman, 158–160
124. Trotter, *Frozen Hell,* 260.
125. Van Dyke, *Soviet Invasion,* 175.
126. Ibid.
127. Trotter, *Frozen Hell,* 260.
128. Ibid.
129. Tanner, *Winter War,* 226.
130. Ibid.
131. Ibid.
132. Ibid., 227. According to Tanner, Mannerheim repeatedly phoned him during the Moscow negotiations. At one point, Tanner contends, the marshal even suggested offering the Russians a strip of land across northern Finland instead of Karelia, before retracting the suggestion. Unsurprisingly, Mannerheim does not mention this in his autobiography.
133. Ibid.
134. Ibid.
135. Jakobson, *Diplomacy of the Winter War,* 249.
136. Condon, *Winter War,* 145.
137. Ibid.
138. Jakobson, *Diplomacy of the Winter War,* 252.
139. George Kennan, *Russia and the West under Lenin and Stalin,* Boston, 1960, 338.
140. Ibid.
141. Hinshaw, *Heroic Finland,* 118.
142. Chew, *White Death,* 202.
143. Kallio's wish would be granted a few months later when he suffered a stroke that paralyzed his right arm.
144. Jakobson, *Diplomacy of the Winter War,* 252.
145. Manninen, *Soviet Plans,* 55–56.
146. Condon, *Winter War,* 130.
147. Van Dyke, *Soviet Invasion,* 175.
148. Tanner, *Winter War,* 177.

149. Jakobson, *Diplomacy of the Winter War,* 253.
150. Ibid.
151. Clark, *Three Days,* 188, 193; Jakobson, *Diplomacy of the Winter War,* 253.
152. That day there was a sure sign that something significant had happened, or was about to happen: Oy Alkoholiliike Ab, the state alcohol monopoly, closed its doors.

Chapter 9. Tears in Helsinki

1. Cowles, *Looking for Trouble,* 327.
2. Ibid.
3. Ibid.
4. Ibid.
5. Ibid.
6. Cox, *Red Army Moves,* 236.
7. Ibid.
8. Stowe, *No Other Road,* 76.
9. Ibid.
10. Cox, *Red Army Moves,* 227.
11. Malm interview.
12. Ibid.
13. Ibid.
14. Ibid.
15. Nillson interview.
16. *Svenska I Finland 1939–1945,* 143, 146.
17. Bavin interview.
18. Ibid.
19. Cox, *Red Army Moves,* 228.
20. Stowe, *No Other Road,* 72.
21. Ibid.
22. Langdon-Davies, *Finland,* 114.
23. Ibid.
24. Ibid.
25. Cox, *Red Army Moves,* 228. As part of the final terms, the Russians received a thirty-year lease to Hanko.
26. Stowe, *No Other Road,* 72.
27. Pekka Tiilikainen, *Radioselostajana tuilinjoila,* Helsinki, 1940, 203.
28. Toivenen interview.
29. Stowe, *No Other Road,* 76.
30. Cox, *Red Army Moves,* 229.
31. Cowles, *Looking for Trouble,* 329.
32. Langdon-Davies, *Finland,* 118.

Epilogue

1. Chew, *White Death,* 208.
2. Cowles, *Looking for Trouble,* 340–341.
3. Ibid.
4. Ibid., 343.
5. Wuorinen, *History of Finland,* 362.

6. Cowles, *Looking for Trouble,* 342.
7. Ibid.
8. Mannerheim, *Memoirs,* 275.
9. Wuorinen, *History of Finland,* 364.
10. Cowles, *Looking for Trouble,* 342.
11. Clark, *Three Days,* 172; Mannerheim, *Memoirs,* 387.
12. Cox, *Red Army Moves,* 230.
13. Cowles, *Looking for Trouble,* 343.
14. Cox, *Red Army Moves,* 229. But not for long. Soviet troops were forced to evacuate Hanko in December 1941.
15. Cowles, *Looking for Trouble,* 293–343.
16. Engle and Paananen, *Winter War,* 142.
17. Trotter, *Frozen Hell,* 313.
18. Langdon-Davies, *First Total War,* 121.
19. Finnish Jews mourned, too: fifteen members of their small community of 1,700, from the 300 who served, died in combat.
20. Cowles, *Looking for Trouble,* 329.
21. Hynninen interview.
22. Ibid.
23. Ibid.
24. *Pravda,* March 14–20, 1940.
25. Khrushchev, *Khrushchev Remembers,* 153; Roberts, *Stalin's Wars,* 384. Approximately 900 Finns were taken prisoner by the Russians. The treatment of Finnish POWs ranged from fair to extremely harsh, with some prisoners subjected to brainwashing sessions, while a number of others, like the aforementioned Swedish pilots, reported being tortured.
26. A. O. Chubarayan and H. Shukman, eds., *Stalin and the Soviet-Finnish War 1939–40,* London, 2002, 243, 155–169.
27. Ibid.
28. Ibid.
29. Ibid.
30. Hugh Trevor-Roper, ed., *Hitler's Table Talk, 1941–44: His Private Conversations,* London, 1973, 310.
31. Chubarayan and Shukman, *Stalin and the Soviet-Finnish War,* 170–180.
32. An excellent sample of an objective

book about the war by a Russian historian is Bair Irincheev, *War of the White Death.*
33. Harrison Salisbury, *The 900 Days: The Siege of Leningrad,* New York, 1969, 186.
34. Martin Gilbert, *Churchill: A Life,* New York, 1991, 633.
35. Winston Churchill, *The Second World War,* Boston, 1948, 543.
36. Trevor-Roper, *Hitler's Table Talk,* 310.
37. Carlgren, *Swedish Foreign Policy,* 54–55.
38. Anthony Upton, *Finland in Crisis 1940–41,* Ithaca, New York, 192–194.
39. Henrik Meinander, *A History of Finland,* New York, 2011, 153.
40. Jakobson, *Diplomacy of the Winter War,* 257–258.
41. Eronen interview.
42. Ibid.
43. Mannerheim, *Memoirs,* 239.

Postscript. "There Shall Be No Night"

1. Robert Sherwood, *There Shall Be No Night,* New York, 1941, viii.
2. Margot Peters, *Design for Living: Alfred Lunt and Lynn Fontanne,* New York, 2003, 188.
3. *New York Post,* April 30, 1940.
4. Peters, *Design for Living,* 188–189.
5. Ibid.
6. Ibid.
7. Ibid., 192–193.
8. Ibid.
9. Ibid., 197.
10. Ibid.
11. Ibid.
12. Ibid., 206.
13. Ibid., 208.
14. Ibid., 210.
15. Ibid.
16. Ibid., 209.
17. Ibid., 212.
18. Ibid., 213.

Bibliography

Atkinson, Brooks, and Albert Hirschfeld. *The Lively Years 1920–1973*. New York, 1973.

Beevor, Antony. *Stalingrad*. London, 1991.

Beevor, Antony, and Luba Vinogradova. *A Writer at War: Vasily Grossman with the Red Army, 1941–1945*. New York, 2005.

Bell, Henry McGrady. *Land of Lakes: Memories Keep Me Company*. London, 1950.

Boterbloem, Kees. *The Life and Times of Andrei Zhdanov, 1896–1948*. Montreal, 2004.

Brooke, Alan. *War Diaries 1939–1945*. London, 2003.

Brooke, Justin. *The Volunteers: The Full Story of the British Volunteers in Finland, 1939–41*. Upton-upon-Severn, 1990.

Carlgren, Wilhelm M. *Swedish Foreign Policy during the Second World War*. London, 1977.

Chamberlain, Neville. *The Neville Chamberlain Diary Letters*. Aldershot, 2002.

Chew, Allen F. *The White Death: The Epic of the Soviet Finnish War*. East Lansing, 1971.

Chubarayan, A. O., and H. Shukman, eds. *Stalin and the Soviet-Finnish War 1939–40*. London, 2002.

Churchill, Winston. *The Second World War, Volume 1*. Boston, 1948.

Citrine, Walter. *Two Careers*. London, 1967.

Clark, Douglas. *Three Days to Catastrophe*. London, 1966.

Clarkson, Jesse D. *A History of Russia*. New York, 1961.

Collier, Richard. *The Warcos: The War Correspondents of World War Two*. London, 1989.

Connery, Donald S. *The Scandinavians*. New York, 1966.

Cowles, Virginia. *Looking for Trouble*. New York, 1941.

Cox, Geoffrey. *Eyewitness: A Memoir of Europe in the 1930s*. Dunedin (New Zealand), 1999.

———. *The Red Army Moves*. London, 1941.

Dallin, David J. *Soviet Russia's Foreign Policy, 1939–1942*. New Haven, 1942.

Davies, Joseph E. *Mission to Moscow*. Sydney, 1942.

De Ullmann, Stephen. *The Epic of the Finnish Nation*. London, 1940.

Douglas, Roy. *The Advent of War 1939–1940*. London, 1978.

Dziewanowski, M. K. *A History of Soviet Russia*. Englewood Cliffs, 1979.

Elliston, H. B. *Finland Fights*. Boston, 1940.

Engle, Eloise, and Lauri Paananen. *The Winter War*. Harrisburg, 1973.

Erickson, John. *The Road to Stalingrad: Stalin's War with Germany*. New Haven, 1999.

Farnsworth, Beatrice. "Conversing with Stalin, Surviving the Terror: The Diaries of Aleksandra Kollontai and the Internal Life of Politics." *Slavic Review* 69, no. 4 (2010): 944–964.

Fire and Ice. Dir. Ben Strout. MastersWork Media, 2006. DVD.

Firsoff, V. A. *Ski Track on the Battlefield*. London, 1942.

Forslund, Mikael. *Gloster Gladiator and Hawker Hart*. Sweden, 2009.

Gallagher, M. P. *The Soviet History of World War II*. New York, 1963.

Gellhorn, Martha. *The Face of War*. London, 1986.

———. *The Selected Letters of Martha Gellhorn*. New York, 2006.

Geust, Carl-Fredrik. *Red Stars: The Winter War in the Air*. Tampere, 2011.

Geust, Carl-Fredrik, and Antero Uitto. *Hanko in World War II*. Helsinki, 2011.

———. *Mannerheim-linja: Talvisodan legenda*. Jyvaskyla, 2006.

Geust, Carl-Fredrik, and Genadiy Petrov. *Red Stars. Volume 5: Baltic Fleet Air Force in the Winter War*. Tampere, 2004.

Gramling, Oliver. *Free Men Are Fighting: The Story of World War II*. New York, 1942.

Griffiths, Tony. *Scandinavia: At War with Trolls*. New York, 1993.
Harrison, M. *Soviet Planning in Peace and War, 1938–1945*. Cambridge, 1985.
Hinshaw, David. *Heroic Finland*. New York, 1952.
Hitler, Adolf. *Hitler's Table Talk*. London, 1953.
Holmes, Richard. *The Oxford Companion to Military History*. Oxford, 2001.
Innes, Hammond. *Scandinavia*. New York, 1963.
Irincheev, Bair. *The Mannerheim Line, 1920–1939*. London, 2009.
———. *War of the White Death: Finland against the Soviet Union, 1939–40*. London, 2011.
Isherwood, Christopher. *Diaries, Volume 1: 1939–1960*. London, 1996.
Jackson, Robert. *Air Heroes of World War II*. New York, 1978.
Jacobs, Travis Beal. *America and the Winter War*. New York, 1981.
Jagerskiold, Stig Axel Fridolf. *Mannerheim, Marshal of Finland*. New York, 1988.
Jakobson, Max. *The Diplomacy of the Winter War*. Cambridge, 1961.
Jenkins, Roy. *Churchill*. London, 2001.
Jowett, Philip, and Brent Snodgrass. *Finland at War, 1939–45*. Oxford, 2006.
Jutikkala, Eino, with Kauko Pirinen. *A History of Finland*. New York, 1988.
Kamarainen, Jussi, Einar Ladinen, and Sergei Verigin. *Talvisodan panttivangit*. Helsinki, 2006.
Keegan, John. *A History of Warfare*. London, 1993.
———. *The Second World War*. New York, 1990.
Kennan, George F. *Russia and the West under Lenin and Stalin*. Boston, 1960.
Keskinen, Kalevi, and Kari Stenman. *Finnish Air Force 1928–1940, Volume 2*. Espoo, 2006.
———. *Air Fighting School*. Porvoo, 2008.
Khrushchev, Nikita. *Khrushchev Remembers*. Boston, 1970.
Kissinger, Henry. *Diplomacy*. New York, 1994.
Kulju, Mika. *Raatteen Tie: Talvisodan pohjoinen sankaritarina*. Jyväskylä, 2007.
Kuosa, Tauno. *A. F. Airo. Legenda jo Eläessään*. Helsinki, 1979.
Langdon-Davies, John. *Finland: The First Total War*. London, 1940.
Leskinen, Jari, and Antti Juutilainen, eds. *Talvisodan pikkujattilainen*. Helsinki, 1999.
Lewis, Jon E., ed. *The Mammoth Book of Eyewitness World War II*. New York, 2002.
Luce, Henry R., ed. *Time Capsule/1939*. New York, 1968.
———, ed. *Time Capsule/1940*. New York, 1968.
Lukacs, John. *The Duel*. New York, 1991.
———. *June 1941*. New Haven, 2006.
———. *The Last European War, 1939–1941*. New York, 1976.
Lundin, C. Leonard. *Finland in the Second World War*. Bloomington, 1957.
Manchester, William. *The Last Lion*. Boston, 1983.
Mannerheim, Gustaf. *Memoirs*. London, 1951.
Manninen, Ohto. *The Soviet Plans for the North Western Theatre of Operations in 1939–1944*. Helsinki, 2004.
Mason, Herbert Molloy Jr. *The Rise of the Luftwaffe 1918–1940*. New York, 1973.
Meri, Veijo. *Beneath the Polar Star: Glimpses of Finnish History*. Helsinki, 1999.
Merridale, Catherine. *Ivan's War: Life and Death in the Red Army, 1939–1945*. New York, 2006.
Miller, Russell. *The Soviet Air Force at War*. Alexandria, Virginia, 1983.
Montefiore, Simon Sebag. *Stalin: The Court of the Red Tsar*. London, 2003.
Moorehead, Caroline. *Martha Gellhorn: A Life*. London, 2003.
Nicolson, Harold. *Harold Nicolson: Diaries and Letters 1939–1945*. New York, 1967.
Noorback, Martha. *A Gentleman's Home: The Museum of Gustaf Mannerheim*. Helsinki, 2001.
Norton, Mary Beth, Carol Sheriff, David W. Blight, and Howard Chudacoff. *A People and a Nation: A History of the United States since 1865*. New York, 2011.
Nousiainen, Pentti, ed. *Päämajamuseo: Högkvartersmuseet*. Mikkeli, 2002.
Orgill, Douglas. *T34: Russian Armor*. New York, 1971.
Orwell, George. *Orwell: The War Commentaries*. New York, 1985.
Pajari, Risto. *Talvisota Ilmassa*. Porvoo, 2005.

Payne, Robert. *The Rise and Fall of Stalin.* New York, 1965.

Peters, Margot. *Design for Living: Alfred Lunt and Lynn Fontanne: A Biography.* New York, 2003.

Preston, Paul. *We Saw Spain Die: Foreign Correspondents in the Spanish Civil War.* London, 2008.

Radzinsky, Edvard. *Stalin.* New York, 1996.

Reese, Roger. *Stalin's Reluctant Soldiers.* Lawrence, Kansas, 1996.

Rintala, Marvin. *Four Finns.* Berkeley, 1969.

Roberts, Geoffrey. *Stalin's War: From World War to Cold War, 1939–1953.* New Haven, 2006.

Ruutu, Juhani. *Vahva vaikuttaja.* Lahti, 1987.

Saarelainen, Tapio A. M. *Simo Hayha: The Sniper.* Tampere, 2008.

Salisbury, Harrison E. *The 900 Days: The Siege of Leningrad.* New York, 1969.

Salometsä, Erkki. *A. F. Airo. Vaikeneva kenraali.* Hämeenlinna, 1969.

Salovaara, Kalevi. *Paamajakapuunki pommitukessa.* Mikkeli, 1986.

Sander, Gordon. *Off the Map: A Personal History of Finland.* Helsinki, 2011.

———. *The Frank Family That Survived.* London, 2004.

———. "The Kamp Corps: The Joys and Agonies of Covering the Winter War," *Perspectives on the Finnish Winter War*, Winter War-Seminar in Helsinki, March 11, 2010. National Defense University, 2010.

Screen, J. E. O. *Mannerheim: The Years of Preparation.* London, 1970.

Service, Robert. *Stalin: A Biography.* London, 2004.

Sherwood, Robert E. *Roosevelt and Hopkins: An Intimate History.* New York, 1948.

———. *There Shall Be No Night.* New York, 1941.

Shirer, William L. *Berlin Diary: The Journal of a Foreign Correspondent 1934–1941.* New York, 1941.

———. *The Challenge of Scandinavia.* London, 1956.

———. *This is Berlin: A Narrative History 1938–40.* London, 1999.

Shukman, Harold. *Stalin's Generals.* London, 1993.

Stowe, Leland. *No Other Road to Freedom.* New York, 1941.

———. *They Shall Not Sleep.* New York, 1944.

Strode, Hudson. *Finland Forever.* New York, 1941.

Svenska frivilliga I Finland 1939–1944. Stockholm, 1989.

Talvisodan historia, 1–4. Porvoo, 1977–1979.

Tanner, Vaino. *The Winter War.* London 1957.

Thayer, Charles W. *Russia.* New York, 1960.

Tigerstedt, Örnulf, and Richard Winter, eds. *Finland: Landet som kämpade.* Stockholm, 1940.

Tiilikainen, Pekka. *Radioselostajana tuilinjoila.* Helsinki, 1940.

Trevor-Roper, Hugh. *Hitler's Table Talk.* London, 1953.

Trotter, William R. *A Frozen Hell: The Russo-Finnish War of 1939–40.* Chapel Hill, 1991.

Turtola, Martti. *Aksel Fredrik Airo, Taipumaton kenraali.* Keuruu, 1997.

———. *Erik Heinrichs, Mannerheimin ja Paasikiven kenraali.* Keuruu, 1988.

Upton, Anthony F. *Finland 1939–1940.* London, 1974.

———. *Finland in Crisis 1940–1941.* Ithaca, 1965.

Van Dyke, Carl. *The Soviet Invasion of Finland, 1939–1940.* London, 1997.

Veijalainen, Anna-Liisa. *A Woman at the Front: Memoirs 1938–1945.* Lohja, 2007.

Volkogonov, Dmitri. *Stalin: Triumph and Tragedy.* New York, 1991.

Walsh, Warren B., ed. *Readings in Russian History, Volume 2: From Alexander II to the Soviet Period.* Syracuse, 1963.

Ward, E. *Dispatches from Finland, January–April 1940.* London, 1940.

Wayson, Wayne. "The Winter War: 105 Days of Finnish Resistance." http://americanmilitary.academia.edu/WayneWayson/Papers/860000/The_Winter_War_105_Days_of_Finnish_Resistance.

Werth, Alexander. *Russia at War 1941–1945.* New York, 1964.

Wuorinen, John H. *A History of Finland.* New York, 1965.

Index

Page number followed by "m" indicates a map.

unsustainable levels of, 166, 277; at Viipuri and Viipuri Bay, 318, 337

casualties, in Soviet Army, 233, 234, 250, 338–39: of 49th Division, 115; of 163rd Division, 197–98; in assault on Summa, 139; in assault on Taipale, 136; in battle for Petsamo, 104; Leningrad hospitals and, 91, 162–63; from mines and booby traps, 84; official *vs.* actual figures, 165; photographs of, 196; at Raate Road, 203; in Sausage War, 114; in second wave attack, 250, 264, 270

CBS, 169

CBS Radio Berlin, 55, 124

Chamberlain, Neville: and Allied War Council meeting on Finland, 158–59, 245–49; on British military aid, 260; and Czechoslovakia, dismantling of, 313; impact of Finnish loss on, 340; and Operation Avon Head, 294, 301–2, 311; and prosecution of World War II, 123; on Soviet invasion, 89

Chaplin, Charlie, 344

Charles XII (king of Sweden), 185, 356n31

Chetyrbok, Ivan, 132–33, 139–40, 149, 153, 250, 259

Chevalier, Maurice, 123

Chew, Allen, 7–8, 204, 205

Chicago Daily News, 6, 214

Chichagov, Vasili, 302, 303

children; deaths from bombing, 129, 185–86: evacuation of, 53, 128, 223; fear and suffering in war, 58, 121; wartime activities, 186

Christian Science Monitor, 3, 39, 40

Christmas: Finnish celebration of, 168–71; in Sweden, 181–82

Chuikov, V. I., 203, 357n115

Churchill, Winston: and El Alamein, battle of, 203; on Finnish bravery, 15, 223–24; German U-boats and, 126; on Hitler's perspective on Winter War, 340–41; as Lord of Admiralty, 2, 123, 159; on Molotov, 68–69; motives for support of Finland, 225; at New Year's Eve party (1939), 177–78; and Operation Avon Head, 301, 312; as prime minister, 340; as pro-Finnish, 2; speech urging neutral nation involvement, 223–26; and Swedish ore deposits, concerns about, 159

Citrine, Walter, 235–36, 262

City of Flint, The (U.S. merchant ship), 126

civilians, Finnish: and armistice, reactions to, 326, 328–31; and armistice negotiations, concern about reaction of, 313–14, 322; and armistice negotiations, limited knowledge about, 316, 324; casualties, 244; Christmas celebration, 168–69; dancing, wartime taboo regarding, 212, 222, 357n12; and Finn-

ish government communiqués, views on, 222; food shortages, late in war, 278; hatred of Russians, 98, 336; and Mannerheim Line, necessity of defending, 282; morale, 168, 216, 244, 278, 322; and peace negotiations, 282; photographs of, 55, 63; as prisoners, conditions of internment, 9–10, 188; as prisoners, from Suojarvi, 14; as prisoners, from Suomussalmi, 9, 188; as prisoners, treatment of, 188, 193–95; religious faith of, 185, 215, 217; at Suomussalmi, 188; views on war, 16, 55, 74–75, 95, 115, 129, 211–12, 214–15, 342. *See also* women

civilians, Finnish, bombing by Soviets, 50–54, 239, 311: casualties from, 40, 49–50, 55, 67, 185–86, 215, 228, 234, 239, 286, 293, 311; Chamberlain on, 260; civilians' reaction to, 39, 66–67, 75, 91–92, 92–94, 183, 184, 221–22; League of Nations protest against, 300; media on, 255–56; propaganda value of, 55; Ryti on, 73; Soviet denial of, 69

civilians, Finnish, evacuations, 257–58: confusion surrounding, 53; failure to plan for, 12, 53; from Helsinki, 12, 53, 61, 93, 115, 128, 186; before initial attack, 42; of Seivasto, 50, 58; of Suomussalmi, as inadequate, 188; from Tuppura fortress, 286–87

Clark, Douglas, 158, 159, 246, 248, 302, 335

Clift, Montgomery, 345

Coalition Party, cabinet positions, 66

Colebaugh, Charles, 37, 38

Collier, Richard, 4, 121

Collier's magazine, 37, 52–53, 101, 128, 177

Committee of Swedish Trade Unions, 305

communications; Finnish, disruption of, 140; Soviet, 138, 263

Communist government of Finland, Soviet efforts to install, 13

Continuation War, 52, 327, 333, 342, 358–59n7

Cornell University, Class of 1942 yearbook, 127–28

Cowles, Virginia: and armistice, reactions to, 331; career of, 6, 177, 179; on ceded territory, evacuation of, 333–34, 336; Churchill and, 177–78; connections of, 177; decision to go to Finland, 178–79; departure from Finland, 336; on Finnish censorship, 8, 277; on Finnish defeat, approach of, 18–19; and Finnish soldiers, experiences of, 264; flight to Finland, 179; Gellhorn and, 177; at Hotel Kamp, 186; impact of Winter War on, 336–37; *Looking for Trouble*, 6, 8, 177, 337; and northern front, tour of, 212; and Raate Road, battle of, 175, 204; in Rovaniemi, 212–13; and skiing, attempts at, 213; on

Cowles, Virginia (*cont.*)
Soviet bombing, impact of, 185; on Soviet field hospitals, 198; and Soviet prisoners, interview of, 198; on Soviet second wave attack, 258; in Sweden, 179; travel to Hanko, 182–85; on wartime train ride, 287–88; and World War II, 336

Cox, Geoffrey: on air raid wardens, 66–67; on armistice, Finnish reactions to, 327–28, 328–30, 331; on beauty of Finnish landscape, 107–8; departure from Finland, 336; on Finnish calm under pressure, 94; on Finnish censorship, 8; on Finnish change of government, 65; on Finnish unity, 211–12; impact of Winter War on, 337; inspection of downed Soviet bomber, 67–68; and lookout tower, visit to, 213–14; on Mannerheim, 278–79; on Mannerheim Line, breakthrough of, 273, 281–82; on Operation Avon Head, 248; on Pelkosenniemi, battle of, 145, 146, 167; on prosperity of Sweden, 181–82; on Raate Road veterans, exhaustion of, 204–5; in Rovaniemi, 210–12, 213–14; on Soviet adaptations, 17, 255; on Soviet airmen, motivation of, 67–68; on Soviet bombing, 55, 94; on Soviet motives for attack, 54–55; on Suomussalmi, battle of, 191; on Swedish military's desire to intervene, 180; on Viipuri Bay, battle of, 308, 317; visit to front, 105–11, 189; on Wallenius, 143–44

Czechoslovakia, German dismantling of, 313

Dagens Nyheter (Swedish) newspaper, 105, 182
Dahl, Lennart, 180
Daily Express, 67
Daily Mirror, 344
Daily Worker, 344
Daladier, Edouard: and Allied War Council, 245–48; and armistice negotiations, 316; and Czechoslovakia, dismantling of, 313; government, fall of, 340; interest in Winter War, motives for, 158–59, 225, 246; and Operation Avon Head, 20, 246–49, 294, 301–2, 306, 309, 311, 312
Davidov, Yevgeny, 207
Defense Council, Mannerheim on, 46
DeGaulle, Charles, 231
Democratic People's Republic of Finland (DPRF): armed forces of, 72–73; disappearance of, 16, 238, 338; Holsti on, 119; media reports on, 71–72; pact with Soviet Union, 71; political program of, 73; Soviet declaration of, 13, 70–71; Soviet recognition of as sole government, 77, 118–19, 129
Denmark: German invasion of, 336, 343–44;

neutrality, determination to maintain, 225; volunteer fighters from, 300, 362–63n31; volunteer workers from, 305–6
Denny, Harold, 84, 169–70, 200, 212, 217
Deutschland (German battleship), 126
Diplomacy of the Winter War, The (Jakobson), 113
diplomatic relations, Soviet severing of, 41
Dmitroff, Georgi, 163
Dolin Brigade, 351n77
Donau (German merchant ship), 91
Dowding, Earl, 301
DPRF. *See* Democratic People's Republic of Finland
Drottningholm (Swedish liner), 221
Dukhanov, V., 191
Duranty, Walter, 162, 181, 226–27
Dyrssen, Magnus, 305

E. (anonymous source), 59, 193–95
eduskunta (parliament): evacuation to Kauhajoki , 61, 64, 350n114; vote on Peace of Moscow, 334
Ehrnrooth, Adolf, 81
El Alamein, battle of, 203
Eliot, George Fielding, 175
Elliston, Herbert Berridge: assignment to Finland, 6; background of, 39; on bombing of Helsinki, 3–4, 39–40; departure from Finland, 115; *Finland Fights!*, 4, 115; impact of Winter War on, 337; on Mannerheim, 45; reassignment of, 92; on stoicism of Finns, 97–98; travel within Finland, 92–93, 97–99
Elo, Martti, 188
Elonpera, Teppo, 218
Enochsson, Thore, 180
Erickson, John, 269
Erkko, Eljas: and armistice, announcement of, 324–25; and armistice negotiations, 260, 275; and Finnish foreign policy, 66; as foreign minister, 64, 65; and Operation Avon Head, 306; in Ryti cabinet, 66
Eronen, Olavi, 50, 58, 155, 204, 217, 342
Eskelund, K. J., 195, 249
Estonia: independence, 32–33, 47; Soviet air bases in, 34, 98; Soviet annexation of, 10–11, 32, 70; volunteer fighters from, 363n59
Export-Import Bank, 111

Fagerholm, Karl-August, 222–23
Federal Relief Emergency Administration, 37
fifth column in Finland, 16, 80, 106–7, 351n66
Finland: appeals for international aid, 5, 97, 111, 117–20; Fascist element in, 52; *folkhemmet* (welfare state) in, 222, 235, 262, 358n62; and Germany, relationship with, 10, 41, 52,

348–49n41; and Germany, World War II alliance, 2, 341–42, 345; independence, Peace of Tartu and, 32–33; overconfidence of, after early victories, 176; planning for war, inadequacy of, 12; size, *vs.* Soviet Union, 1; Soviet misperception of political climate in, 55, 60; Soviet postwar interference in, 341; state of denial regarding possibility of war, 12, 32, 33, 37, 44, 50, 53, 75; unity in response to Soviet invasion, 16, 55, 74–75, 95, 115, 211–12, 214–15, 342. *See also* cabinet, Finnish; Democratic People's Republic of Finland (DPRF)

Finland, military aid to, 15, 111, 112, 246–47, 353n184: from Allies, European, 1, 15, 22, 124–25; failure to arrive in time, 247; from France, 246, 247, 300, 310; from Great Britain, 21, 89, 128, 246–47, 295, 300, 310, 353n184; from Hungary, 351n89; from Italy, 310, 349n74; from Norway, 128, 223; from Sweden, 112, 128, 181, 182, 233; from U.S., 22. *See also* Operation Avon Head

Finland government: change of, to please Soviets, 64–66, 69–70; continuity of, efforts to demonstrate, 97; reaction to DPRF, 73; Soviet refusal to acknowledge, 77, 118–19, 129

Finland Fights! (Elliston), 4, 115

"Finland Fights Alone but on the Side of Angels" (McCormick), 89–90

Finnish Air Force; aircraft of, 73, 150, 152, 180, 192, 295, 300, 310; casualties, 221, 233; and December 19th Soviet offensive, 149–53; early success of, 15, 73–74; Gellhorn's airfield visit, 10203; image of, 154; in Karelia, 115; *Lentokaivue 24* (Flying quadron 24), 102, 141, 149–53, 201–2, 262, 310; *Lentokaivuwe 26* (Flying Squadron 26), 73–74; *Lentorykmentti* F19, 180; losses, 221, 233, 300, 318; media reports on, 152–53; pilots, 150, 180, 201–2, 300, 305, 362–63n31; reconnaissance by, 284; size of, 300, 310; Soviet losses to, 73, 151–52, 153, 201–2, 351n41; and Soviet second wave attacks, 300, 310, 318; and Suomussalmi, battle of, 192; tactics of, 150–51; and Viipuri, defense of, 310, 318

Finnish American Legion, 57

Finnish Army: 1st Division, 154; 2nd Corps, 18, 21, 318, 319, 320; 2nd Division, 297–98; 3rd Corps, 320; 3rd Division, 259, 269, 273, 277, 307, 318; 4th Corps, 79, 81; 4th Division, 154, 303; 5th Division, 140, 148–49, 154, 274, 307, 318; 7th Division, 232, 298; 8th Division, 154; 9th Division, 188, 233–34; 10th Division, 154; 10th Regiment, 169, 303–4; 12th Division, 317; 15th Regiment,

139; 16th Regiment, 44, 113–14; 23rd Division, 307, 309, 322; 23th Jaeger Regiment, 136; 27th Infantry Regiment, 26m, 28m; 28th Jaeger Regiment, 136; 30th Jaeger Regiment, 136; 40th Jaeger Regiment, 144–47; 62nd Infantry Regiment, 284; 64th Infantry Regiment, 26m, 28m; 65th Infantry Regiment, 28m; 718th Rifle Regiment, 114; adaptability of, 186; advantages of, 14; ammunition and supplies, inadequacy of, 11, 76, 133, 218; anti-tank tactics, 109–10, 130–31, 134, 139, 148–49, 186; Coastal Group, 303, 307, 309, 318, 320, 322; collapse of beneath Soviet advances, 283, 284, 318–19, 319–20; communications, disruption of, 140; counteroffensives of Dec. 6th, 101, 131; counteroffensives of Dec. 19th, 155; counteroffensives on Karelian Isthmus, 15, 27m; counteroffensives Soviet second wave attacks and, 274, 294; counteroffensives as tactic, 107; danger of outflanking, 79; divisions, size of, 353n68; Finnish Coastal Group, tenaciousness of, 21; friendly fire incidents of, 294; funding of, as inadequacy of, 11, 46; horses used by, 146, 354n100; image of, 154; Jaeger units, 142, 354n85; leadership, confidence of soldiers in, 103; Mannerheim's final message to, 331–32; mobilization of, 46; morale of, 9, 15, 55, 103, 203–4, 244, 288, 299, 322; preparations by, 12, 130; reaction to armistice, concern about, 313–14; recruiting and conscription by, 17, 43, 280, 281, 310; reserves and reinforcements, 79, 82, 137, 273, 274, 280, 297, 309, 311, 314, 322; size of, 11, 79; strategy and tactics of, 77–80, 107, 108, 110, 125–26, 219; tanks of, 47, 85, 294; training of, 11, 43–44, 103; weapons, 44, 47, 79, 134, 348n38; weapon shortages, 1, 44, 175, 190, 233. *See also* artillery, Finnish; Finnish soldiers; Finnish Army, military aid to

Finnish Army, casualties, 244, 319, 337: after armistice, 327; Army of the Isthmus, 8–9; in battle for Petsamo, 104; difficulty of hiding number of, 277–78; during January lull, 232; families and friends, reactions to, 168; Finnish removal of, before media tours, 166, 167; Finnish views on, 222; funerals, 304–5, 337; impact on home communities, 211; at Kirvesmaki, 289; *lottas'* washing and preparation of bodies, 217, 337; at Pelkosenniemi, media descriptions of, 166–67; rise in, 80; Soviet estimates of, 165; in Soviet second wave attack, 265, 289; unsustainable levels of, 166, 277; at Viipuri and Viipuri Bay, 318, 337

George VI (king of England), 122, 123
Germany: anti-British propaganda, 122; bombing of Great Britain, 344, 346; and Czechoslovakia, dismantling of, 313; evacuation of nationals from Finland, 91; and Finnish Civil War, intervention in, 10, 41, 52; Finnish relationship with, 10, 41, 52, 348–49n41; and Finnish in World War II alliance, 2, 341–42, 345; invasion of Belgium (WW I), 4, 56, 344; invasion of Denmark, 336, 343–44; invasion of France, 336; invasion of Luxembourg, 344; invasion of Netherlands, 161, 336, 344, 355n20; invasion of Norway, 336, 343–44; invasion of Soviet Union, 2–3, 290; pressure on Sweden from, 76; response to Soviet invasion, 51–52; rumored support of Finland by, 115; ships, 126; Soviet claims of support from, 233; Soviet setbacks in Finland, views on, 160; submarine fleet and, 126–27; views on Allied aid to Finland, 124–25; wartime morale in, 123
Goebbels, Joseph, 52, 122, 123
Goglidze, Sergo, 163
Gone with the Wind premiere, 127
"Good Neighbor" agreement of 1937, 119
Gorolenko, Feodor, 269
Goteborgs Handels och Sjofartstidning (Swedish newspaper), 289
Graf Spee (German battleship), 5, 126, 127
Gramling, Oliver, 208
Grand Hotel (Stockholm): described, 181; peace negotiations at, 16, 228–31, 237–38, 243–45, 260–61, 270–71
Great Britain: and armistice negotiations, 316; attacks on Soviet base at Kronstadt, 47; evacuation of nationals from Finland, 92; Finnish hopes for aid from, 110; impact of Finnish loss on, 340; labor leader inspection of Finnish labor conditions, 235; media, support of Finland, 311–12; meeting with Mannerheim, 288, 291; military aid to Finland, 21, 89, 128, 246–47, 295, 300, 310, 353n184; parliament of, during World War II, 350n114; public opinion on Soviet invasion, 89, 124–25; response to Soviet invasion, 89; support of Estonia, 47; volunteer fighters from, 362n31; in World War II, 123, 341–42, 344, 346. *See also* Allies, European; Operation Avon Head; *entries under* British
Great Depression, 156
Great Northern War, 356n31
Grebbe Line, 160
Greenstreet, Sydney, 345
Grendahl, Vladimir A., 18, 86–87, 256, 262, 296, 360n91

Gripenberg, Georg, 175
Gripsholm (Swedish liner), 89, 112
grit. See *sisu*
Gulf of Finland: freezing over of, 100; in Soviet armistice demands, 293; Soviet crossing of, 308–9, 316
Gunther, Christian, 238, 275–76, 293, 302, 306, 308
Gustav V (king of Sweden), 290, 306
Gustavus III (king of Sweden), 36, 302

Habarov, I. H., 79
Hagglund, Woldemar, 81
Hakkila, Vaino, 111, 113, 352n181
Halifax, Lord, 89
Hambro, Carl, 120
Hanko, 23m: and armistice, negotiation of, 230, 244; bombing of, 149, 183–84; journalists' visit to, 182–85; loss of, in armistice, 329; Soviet demand for lease on, 11, 20, 33, 71, 275, 293; Soviet naval attack on, 74; turnover of, to Soviets, 333–35, 336
Hannula, Uuno, 96, 299, 311, 319, 320, 321–22
Hansson, Per Albin, 58, 75, 77, 180, 275–76, 289, 358n62
Hawkins, Thomas, 263–64, 277
Hayha, Simo, 304, 363n50
Haynes, Frank, 177, 264
Heinrichs, Erik, 130, 140, 282, 284, 294, 309, 319–20
Heinzerling, Lynn, 169
Heiskanen, Juho, 79, 81
Helburn, Theresa, 345
Hellman, Lillian, 236
Helsingin Sanomat newspaper, 57, 74, 112, 152–53, 193, 268
Helsingus, Ilta, 278
Helsinki, 23m: anti-aircraft defenses, 12, 34, 67–68; atmosphere, near war's end, 278; bomb shelters in, 38, 94; as capital, 353n39; Christmas celebration in, 168; evacuation of, 12, 53, 61, 93, 115, 128, 186; exhibition of captured Soviet equipment in, 285; Finnish media in, 128; postwar return to normal life, 337; propaganda leaflets dropped on, 12–13, 38–39
Helsinki, bombing of, 24m, 49–50, 52–53, 149: bodies, recovery of, 128–29; Cabinet meeting interrupted by, 13, 40–42; casualties in, 40, 49–50, 55, 67, 185–86; damage from, 49–50, 51, 52–53, 67, 164, 221; evacuations following, 12, 53, 61, 93, 115, 128, 186; lasting impact of, 94–95; lulls in, 91, 94, 128; officials' confusion about, 39–40; and poison gas, rumors of, 50–51, 53; public reaction to, 39, 66–67, 75, 91–92, 92–94, 221–22;

Helsinki, bombing of (cont.)
recollections of, 3–4, 32, 33–34, 37, 38–39, 39–40, 52–53; reporters' excitement at, 39–40, 54; Soviet motives for, 54–55; strafing runs following, 49–50
Hemingway, Ernest, 37, 50, 51, 177
HMS Achilles (British cruiser), 126
HMS Ajax, 126 (British cruiser), 126
HMS Courageous (British aircraft carrier), 127
HMS Exeter (British cruiser), 126
HMS Royal Oak (British battleship), 126
Hiitola, bombing of, 36–37
histories of Winter War, popularity of, 2
Hitler, Adolf: birthday cable to Stalin, 162; British song mocking, 178; lessons learned from Winter War, 2–3, 17, 160, 340–41; and Mannerheim, admiration for, 349n74; relations with Finland, 41; and Soviet blockade of Finland, 160; and Soviet invasion of Finland, 51–52
Hjertberg, Ernest, 221
Hollywood, interest in Winter War, 127
Holma, Harry, 244, 248–49
Holocaust, in Poland, 123–24
Holsti, Rudolf, 118, 119, 300
Honkaniemi, Finnish counterattack at, 294
Hoover, Herbert, 155–56, 157–58, 236, 237, 267–68
Hopper, Edward, 236
horses, in Winter War, 146, 354n100
Hotel Kamp (Helsinki), 24m: and armistice, announcement of, 325–26, 328; described, 38; Finnish censors at, 277; Finnish independence day celebration at, 95–97; and myth of Finnish invincibility, 15; as press center, 3; press corps life at, 177, 186; Soviet bombing and, 37, 50, 54; and stress of bombing, 67
Hotel Pohjanhovi (Rovaniemi): bombing and, 210, 212; daily routine in, 210, 212; hospital in, 210; press in, 209–14; as Wallenius headquarters, 113, 143, 209–10
Hotel Seurahuone, 186, 278, 329, 331
Hukari family, 215
Hulkonniemi, 192
Hull, Cordell, 55–56, 57, 268
Hungary: military aid to Finland, 351n89; public outrage at Soviet invasion, 88–89; volunteer fighters from, 88–89, 199
Hynninen, Edward, 72–73, 162, 231, 338

Iju-Turso (Finnish submarine), 99–100
Ikonen, Sakari, 151, 202
Ilmoni, Christian, 32, 33–34
Inkila Manor, Finnish Army headquarters at, 234, 331

insurance for war damage, Finland state coverage of individual losses, 222
Irincheev, Bair, 9, 87
Ironside, Edmund, 245, 246, 247, 312
Isherwood, Christopher, 127
Italy: evacuation of nationals from Finland, 91; invasion of Ethiopia, 118; media and Helsinki bombing, 51; media interest in Winter War, 121; military aid to Finland, 310, 349n74; rumored support of Finland by, 115; views on Soviet attack on Finland, 51–52; volunteer fighters from, 51, 300, 349n74
Ivalo, 25m, 212
Ivan Papanen (Finnish merchant ship), 100
Ivan's War (Merridale), 86

Jacobs, Travis, 155
Jaeger units, 142, 354n85
Jagerskjold, S. A. F., 232
Jakobson, Max: on Finnish morale, 9; on Finnish public, on eve of war, 33; on Finnish unity, 75; on Grand Hotel negotiations, 230, 238, 239; on League of Nations, 120; on Mannerheim, 46; on Operation Avon Head, 294, 301; on peace negotiations, 299, 315; on Swedish refusal to help, 290; on volunteer fighters, 113
Janssen, Werner, 156
January lull, 208–9: Finnish ammunition shortages during, 218; Finnish casualties during, 232; Finnish successes during, 233–34; press trips during, 209–13; Soviet Air Force northern focus during, 210
Japan, media interest in Winter War, 121
Jermak (Finnish icebreaker), 100
Jews, Polish, and Holocaust, 123–24
journalists. See media
Joutsijärvi, Soviet attack on, 25m, 142
Juntusranta, Soviet attack on, 25m, 59
Jussaro, offer of to Soviets, 261, 270–71

Kaganovich, Lazar, 161
Kakonen, U. A., 187
Kalevala, 2
Kallio, Kyosti: appeals for help by, 97, 117; and armistice, 321–22, 364n143; and cabinet meeting to discuss invasion, 75, 76; and change of government, 64–66; and defense arrangements, 49; election as president, 40; evacuation from Helsinki, 65; as Finnish independence day celebration, 96–97; and Grand Hotel negotiations, 261, 270; and Mannerheim Line, Soviet breach of, 279; photograph of, in Tuompo headquarters, 106

Mannerheim Line, and bunkers, 137: bunker, Million Dollar, 27m, 47, 131, 272, 273–74; bunker, Poppius, 27m, 47, 131, 148, 272, 273; second-wave demonstration attacks against, 249–53; Soviet tactics against, 148, 176, 253–54, 259, 272–74

Manninen, Otto, 17, 83

Mantsala Uprising, 142–43

Marat (Soviet battleship), 141

Marchlewski, Julian, 70

Märkäjärvi, Soviet attack on, 25m

marriage boom, among departing Finnish soldiers, 222

Matin (French newspaper), 120

Matso, Harry, 40, 94, 186, 222

Matthews, Herbert, 89

McCormick, Anne O'Hare, 89–90

media: accuracy of reports by, 7; and armistice, 324–26; battlefield tours, Finnish removal of dead before, 166, 167; battlefield tours, Pelkosenniemi, 166–67; battlefield tours, Raate Road, 175, 204; battlefield tours, Summa, 279; books on Winter War, 337; British, support of Finland, 311–12; coverage, naïvety of, 3–4; departure from Finland, 336; difficulty getting information out of Finland, 92, 104; on DPRF creation, 71–72; efforts to sort out early developments, 63; fascination with Finnish successes, 3–7, 15, 16; on Finnish Air Force, 152–53; Finnish censorship of, 6, 7, 8–9, 18, 84, 92, 104, 277–78; on Finnish Christmas celebration, 168–71; at Finnish independence day celebration, 96; and Finnish morale, 9; and Finnish potential for success, overestimation of, 249–50; and Finnish soldiers, interviews of, 102, 105, 107–11, 168–71; French, 158–59, 311; front lines visits of, 105–11, 212, 263–64; German censorship of, 55, 124, 125; interviews of Soviet prisoners of war, 98–99, 102, 136, 197–98; Italian, 51, 121; Japanese, interest in Winter War, 121; on *Lotta Svard*, 214–15; Mannerheim's views on, 278–79; number of journalists covering War, 121; press corps in Helsinki, 38, 39; and public perception of War, 13–14; reporters' excitement at bombing of Helsinki, 39–40, 54; as source of historical information, 7–8; and Soviet breach of Mannerheim Line, 279–80; Soviet censorship of, 4, 91, 105; on Soviet second wave attack, 249–50, 258–59; on Soviet SMK tanks, 134; support for Finland, 186, 287; Swedish, on Sweden's refusal to help, 289; technology of, 5; on U.S. aid efforts,

291–92; on Viipuri, destruction of, 295; and Wallenius, fascination with, 143, 209. *See also* photographs from War

media, Finnish: coverage of U.S. support, 237; on Finnish early successes, 54; in Helsinki, 128

media, Soviet: on DPRF government, installation of, 70; on Finnish atrocities, 85, 91, 132; on Finnish government, 65; on Finnish resistance, 43; on Finnish tactics, 83–85; and international outrage, suppression of news about, 91; and Soviet atrocities, suppression of, 91; Soviet successes, claims of, 91, 115; and stalling of invasion, propaganda on, 165; and Winter War, sparse coverage of, 127, 161. *See also* Pravda

Mekhlis, Lev Z., 14, 133, 201, 352n116

Melander, Lars, 81, 187

Memoirs (Mannerheim), 175

Meretskov, Kirill: and December 19th offensive, 153–54; demotion of, 164, 176; and Finnish attack on 50th Corps, 15; invasion planning by, 12, 60–61, 83; on invasion progress, 83, 85; and Mannerheim Line, 131, 135–36, 252, 254, 256, 283–84; summoning to Kremlin, 163–64; and 7th Army command, 14, 18; and Viipuri, assault on, 322; Voroshilov's blaming of, 163

Meri, Veijo, 298

Merridale, Catherine, 86, 154

Mikkeli, bombing of, 234, 311

Miller, Webb, 169, 186–87, 222, 295

mines and booby traps, Finnish: as anti-tank weapon, 139, 186; on bridges, 101; effectiveness of, 43; ships lost to, 100; Soviet media on, 83–84

Molander, Bertil, 180

Molotov, Vyacheslav: and Allied intervention, fear of, 231, 249, 296, 321; appearance of, 68–69; and armistice negotiations, 16, 21, 77, 238, 244, 260–61, 275, 293–94, 296, 302, 306, 308, 309, 313, 314–15, 321; character and personality of, 68–69; decision to negotiate, 231; decision to take all of Finland, 60, 73, 78; and diplomatic relations with Finland, severing of, 41; on Kollontai, 229; and League of Nations hearing on Finland, 118–19; and Mannerheim Line, breakthrough of, 275; meeting with U.S. ambassador, 68–70, 73; on Paasikivi, 55–56; and People's Republic of Finland, establishment of, 13, 71; and Soviet censorship, 105; and Soviet policy toward Finland, 69; and Soviet pre-war demands of Finland, 10–11, 32; and Soviet second wave attack, 296; and

Molotov, Vyacheslav (*cont.*)
  Stalin's birthday, celebration of, 161; and Tanner, dislike of, 55–56, 64, 129, 313; Tanner's efforts to contact, 120–21; on treaties, sanctity of, 55; underestimation of Finnish military, 154–55
Molotov breadbaskets, 39, 285
Molotov cocktail: as Finnish anti-tank weapon, 109–10, 130–31, 148–49; naming of, 131
Moscow, war impact in, 91
motitus, 193. See also *motti* (cordwood) tactics
motti (cordwood) tactics, 8, 15, 18, 188, 190, 193, 202
Munck, Ebbe, 198
Murmansk-Leningrad railroad, Finnish attacks on, 209
Murrow, Edward R., 124, 344
musicians, American, support for Finland, 156
Mussolini, Benito, on Soviet attack on Finland, 51–52, 88, 349n74
Mydans, Carl, 21, 166, 196–97, 356n92
My Finnish Diary (Citrine), 235
mythic accounts of Winter War: and Finnish self-identity, 2; sources of, 1–7; and volunteers from other nations, 1

Nagy, Imre Kemery, 89
Naval war, 15
Nazi-Soviet non-aggression pact (1939), 10, 37, 51, 162
Netherlands: expert views on defenses of, 160–61; fall to Germany, 161, 336, 344, 355n20; lessons learned from Winter War, 160; neutrality of, 181, 225
Neulasaari, 310
neutral nations, Churchill speech urging action by, 223–26
newsreel footage of War, 5
Newsweek magazine, 295
New Year's Eve parties: Finnish, celebration of Suomussalmi victory at, 193; in London (1939), 177–78
New Yorker magazine, 160–61
New York Evening Post, 343
New York Herald Tribune, 326
New York Times: on Churchill speech to neutral nations, 224; difficulties getting information out of Finland, 92; on DPRF, creation of, 71–72; on Finnish ability to hold out, 63, 176, 297, 306; on Finnish ammunition shortages, 218; on Finnish change of government, 63; on Finnish Christmas celebration, 169; on Finnish morale, 168–69; on Finnish soldiers, 217; on Finnish tactics, 84, 130–31; on German pleasure in Soviet setbacks, 160; on

Helsinki, wartime life in, 94, 128, 221; on initiation of war, 31; on Kallio's appeal for help, 117; on Mannerheim Line, breach of, 283; on New York World's Fair, Soviet withdrawal from, 90; on Nordic nations' response to invasion, 58; on poison gas rumors, 91–92; Ryti interview by, 73, 74, 78; on Sherwood's *There Shall Be No Night*, 343; as source of information, 8; on Soviet bombing, 293; on Soviet determination, 226–27; on Soviet invasion, stalling of, 88; on Soviet paratroopers, 8, 199–200; on Soviet prisoners, 136, 195, 197; on Soviet response to U.S. peace efforts, 70; on Soviet second wave attack, 249–50; on Soviet soldiers, views on war, 228; on volunteer fighters, 89, 199; on Wallenius, 209
New York World's Fair, Soviet withdrawal from, 90
Nicholas II (tsar of Russia), 48
Nicholson, Harold, 63, 88, 178–79, 224–25
Nikunen, Heikki, 151
Nilsson, Orvar, 179–80, 327
Niukkanen, Juho, 49–50, 65, 76, 299–300, 319, 320, 321
NKVD. *See* People's Commissariat of Internal Affairs
North American Newspaper Alliance, 134
North American Press Alliance, 6
Northern battlefront: Cox's visit to, 105–11; Finnish successes on, 2, 14, 258, 299, 314, 317; guerrilla war in, Miller on, 187; Soviet attacks near Lake Ladoga, 233; Soviet decision to downplay, 205; Wallenius as commander of, 143, 212. *See also* Pelkosenniemi, battle of; Petsamo
Norway: German invasion of, 336, 343–44; military aid to Finland, 128, 223; neutrality, determination to maintain, 225; and Operation Avon Head, 2, 19, 176, 245, 247, 248, 294, 301, 306, 320, 323, 335; requests for aid from, 223; volunteer fighters from, 199, 300, 305, 357n101
Nurmes, Soviet approach to, 106
Nurmi, Paavo, 38, 156, 237
Nykopp, Johan, 32

October Revolution (Soviet battleship), 15, 141
Oesch, Kurt Lennart, 130, 318, 320
Ohquist, Harald, 18, 21, 155, 280–81, 319, 320, 362n202
Okko, Antti, 100
Oksanen, Reino, 43–44, 114–15
Olympics Games (summer, 1940): cancellation of, 67; Finnish preoccupation with, 53
Olympic stadium: anti-aircraft installations in, 67; Foreign Ministry headquarters at, 121

Operation Avon Head: Allied War Council meetings on, 158–59, 245–49; Allies' last-minute enthusiasm about, 294, 301–2; decision to attempt, 245–47; details of, 247; Finnish awareness of, 245, 248–49; Finnish Cabinet support of, 319; Finnish concerns about, 245, 249, 294, 308, 319, 320, 335; Finnish delays in response to, 309, 311; Finnish official request to Sweden and Norway, 322–23; Finnish rejection of, 19–20, 249, 323; German reaction to, as issue, 247, 291; Mannerheim on, 232, 298, 335; meeting with Finnish on, 291; motives underlying, 159, 225, 246, 247, 249; peace process and, 249, 260, 294, 301–2, 314–15; as poorly planned, 2, 15, 246, 248, 249, 312; possible consequences of implementing, 323; proposal of, 2, 15; Soviet concerns about, 19, 231, 249, 314–15, 318, 321; Soviet reaction to, as issue, 248; Swedish and Norwegian cooperation and, 2, 19, 176, 245, 247, 248, 276, 294, 301, 306, 320, 322–23, 335

Osterman, Hugo: Gellhorn's interview of, 101–2; and Mannerheim Line, breaching of, 274, 280–81; Mannerheim's disciplining of, 81–82, 281; Soviet attack, preparations for, 130; and Viipuri Gateway, defense of, 137

Otava: bombing of, 234; Finnish Army headquarters at, 234, 270–71

Oulu, 25m: Soviet attacks on, 189, 210

Oy Alkoholiliike Ab, 130, 364n152

Paakkola, Soviet attack on, 317

Paasikivi, Juho Kusti: and armistice negotiations, 313, 321; and bombing of Helsinki, 33–34; and Finnish foreign policy, 66; at Finnish independence day celebration, 96; and Grand Hotel negotiations, 230, 243–44, 261, 271; latter career of, 350n26; Molotov on, 55–56; and negotiations, peace terms, views on, 230, 243–44; and Peace of Tartu, 32–33; pre-war negotiations with Soviets, 32–33; in Ryti cabinet, 66

Paasonen, Aladar, 32, 245

Paavola, Eva, 330–31, 333

Paavola, Mai-Lis. See Toivenen, Mai-Lis Paavola

Pajari, Aaro, 44, 113–14

Pakhomenko, I. T., 203

Pal Teleki, Count, 351n89

paratroopers, Soviet, 7–8, 51: capture of, 199–200; Finnish fear of, 51, 91–92, 94, 256–58, 360n69; as first use in modern warfare, 51; killed by Finnish troops, 95; as overall disaster, 360n69; spies as, 256, 351n66

Paris, entertainment in, in late 1930s, 123

parliament of Finland. See eduskunta (parliament)

parliaments, World War II and, 350n114

Pavlov, Dmitri, 307, 310

PDRF (People's Democratic Republic of Finland). See Democratic People's Republic of Finland (DPRF)

Peace of Moscow. See armistice (Peace of Moscow)

Peace of Tartu, 32–33

Pearson, Drew, 291–92

Pelkosenniemi, 23m, 25m

Pelkosenniemi, battle of, 141–47: battlefield, media tours of, 166–67; design of Finnish trap, 144–45; Finnish force, inexperience of, 146; Finnish tactics in, 145; Finnish victory in, 15, 147; initial diversionary Finnish defense, 141–42; as little-studied, 8, 147; Soviet approach to, 25m; as Soviet strategic reverse, 8; and Soviet withdrawal from North, 205; surprise flank attack, 145–47

Peltonen, Aili, 97

Pennanen, Antti, 104

People's Commissariat of Internal Affairs (NKVD): interrogation and murder of Finnish civilian prisoners, 188, 194; interrogation and murder of repatriated Soviet POWs, 338; surveillance of foreign journalists, 105

People's Democratic Republic of Finland (PDRF). See Democratic People's Republic of Finland (DPRF)

Peters, Margot, 346

Peter the Great, 296

Petsamo, 23m, 25m; armistice negotiations and, 315; Finnish acquisition of, 33; Finnish mines and booby traps in, 84; Soviet attack on, 25m; Soviet capture of, 14, 61, 83, 104, 212

photographs from War: of civilian casualties, 55, 63; public interest in, 4; of Soviet casualties, 196; of Soviet prisoners of war, 196

Pius XII (pope), 298

poison gas. See gas attacks

Poland: German invasion of, 10; Holocaust in, 123–24

Polish-Soviet war of 1920, 70

political officers, Soviet. See politruks

Politiken newspaper, 225

politruks (Soviet political attaches): in combat, 253; impact on Soviet Army, 86, 132, 140, 192, 220; role of, postwar reforms in, 3, 339; soldiers' retaliation against, 196; Timoshenko's revised use of, 263

Polttila, Vaino, 274

Pori, bombing of, 239

Ryti, Risto, and armistice negotiations, 21, 73, 302, 308, 312–16, 321: briefing of Finnish officials on, 270–71; Grand Hotel negotiations, 230, 238, 243–44, 261, 271; peace terms, views on, 230, 243–44

Soviet Army (*cont.*)

61, 134, 135, 136, 138, 154, 202; command structure, reforms of, during Winter War, 3, 14, 16, 131, 176, 206, 226; communications, 138, 263; deficiencies of, 10; divisions, size of, 353n68; equipment losses, 192–93, 203, 233, 261, 285; and German invasion of 1941, 3; horses used by, 146, 354n100; junior officers, lack of, 263; leadership, poor quality of, 85; lessons learned from Winter War, 3, 8, 347n5; mass frontal attacks by, 80, 102, 105, 106, 133, 135, 138, 139, 140, 176; medical facilities, 198; planning, rigidity of, 145; postwar review and reforms, 339–40; quality issues faced by, 136; reputation of, 16, 19, 164, 175, 193, 205, 226–27, 231; and roads of Finland, inadequacy of, 132, 138; Section for the Study of Combat Experience, 253, 256; shooting of wounded by, 110; ski units, 84–85, 207, 351n77; sleds, armored, 252, 255, 269; and Stalinist purges, effect of, 61, 134, 161, 263, 339, 361n128; tactics mass, frontal attacks, 80, 102, 105, 106, 133, 135, 138, 139, 140, 176; tactics mass, postwar reforms in, 339; tactics mass, rigidity of, 134, 137; tactics mass, in second wave, 176, 226, 264; tactics mass, tanks and, 135, 138–39; units committed to, in first attack wave, 59; weapons, post-war review of, 339; Winter War performance, review of, 339. *See also* artillery, Soviet; Soviet invasion; Soviet second wave attack; Soviet soldiers; tanks, Soviet

Soviet Army, casualties, 233, 234, 250, 338–39: of 49th Division, 115; of 163rd Division, 197–98; in assault on Summa, 139; in assault on Taipale, 136; in battle for Petsamo, 104; Leningrad hospitals and, 91, 162–63; from mines and booby traps, 84; official *vs.* actual figures, 165; photographs of, 196; at Raate Road, 203; in Sausage War, 114; in second wave attack, 250, 264, 270

Soviet field hospitals, 198

Soviet High Command (*Stavka*): adaptability of, 17; and command of invasion, 14, 207; concerns about invasion progress, 83; decision to revise invasion plan and personnel, 176; and Northern Front, 208

Soviet intelligence: of first wave, poor quality of, 87, 131, 136, 145; postwar review of, 339; of second wave, great improvement in, 254, 272

Soviet invasion: command structure, problems with, 61, 134, 135, 136, 138, 154, 202;

command structure, reforms of, during war, 3, 14, 16, 131, 176, 206, 226; entry points, 49, 61, 79, 143, 187; expectations for quick victory, 10, 11–12, 13, 55, 63; Finnish preparations for, 12, 53; Finnish unity in response to, 16, 55, 74–75, 95, 115, 211–12, 214–15, 342; forces committed to, 49; German response to, 51–52; history of, 34; initial progress of, 58–59, 82, 83, 86–88; Italian response to, 51–52; plans for, 11–12, 23m, 59–61, 83, 164; pretexts for, 7, 12, 33, 38–39, 60, 219, 228, 233; severing of diplomatic relations prior to, 41; shelling prior to, recollections of, 42–44; Soviet media accounts of, 43, 83–85; stalling of, 13, 14, 15, 83, 86–88, 165; as surprise attack, 13, 61; Swedish response to, 57–58; terrain and, 79–80; units involved in, 61; U.S. response to, 55–57; weather and, 61. *See also* Soviet second wave attack

Soviet Navy: attacks by, 49, 74; blockade of Finland, 100, 160; and Fort Saarenpaa, attack on, 140–41; gun crews, poor quality of, 74; poor performance of, 100; ship guns, used as artillery, 219; submarines, 100, 160

Soviet psychological warfare, 233

Soviet second wave attack, 10, 16–17; coastal attacks, 296; communications, emphasis on, 263, 272; coordination of forces in, 251, 256; counterattacks, 274, 294; and Finnish casualties, 265, 289; Finnish collapse beneath pressure of, 283, 284, 318–19, 319–20; Finnish defense against, 17–18; Finnish defense against, alternatives to, 267, 281; Finnish lack of preparation for intensity of, 266–67; full assault, 255, 256, 259, 298; goals of, 226–27, 231; implications of, Finnish delay in grasping, 258–59; initial attacks, 238–39, 249–53; intelligence, great improvement in, 254, 272; logistics of, 255, 322; and Mannerheim Line, breach of, 16, 18, 102, 243, 262, 269–75, 272–75, 276, 279–80, 281, 283; media on, 249–50; plan for, 250, 251, 262, 266; reserves, abundance of, 266, 270, 280; size of force, 18, 296; Soviet adaptations and, 255, 258, 269; Soviet casualties in, 250, 264, 270; Soviet firepower advantage in, 262; Soviet soldiers of, 17, 176, 250, 262, 266, 269, 279; tactics in, 226, 264; units in, as highly-trained, 250; Viipuri, assault on, 18, 19, 20–21, 296, 307–8, 316–17, 322; Soviet soldiers: and armistice, reactions to, 327; capture of, 13–14; fear of capture, 85; fear of Mannerheim

Line, 131–32, 148, 154; Finnish soldiers' views on, 95, 102, 105, 110, 196–97; Finnish stories at expense of, 98; food for, 220; leisure activities of, 220; misinformation given to by Soviet authorities, 99, 102, 228; motivation of, ideological, 95, 102, 228; motivation of, with threats, 86, 132, 135–36, 140, 192, 196; skittishness of, 132–33; sleeping arrangements in field, 146; Soviet abuse of, 198; views on Finnish soldiers, 219; views on Winter War, 219

Soviet soldiers, of first wave: as demoralized and ill-lead, 61, 85–86, 115, 134, 136–37, 154, 163, 165–66, 202–3; improvement with experience, 147–48; poor training and equipment of, 6, 13–14, 16, 55, 80, 85–86, 132, 134, 136, 139, 140, 163, 202; sense of purpose, lack of, 6, 136

Soviet Soldiers, of second wave: highly-trained quality of, 250; revised policies to protect, 176; superior equipment of, 269; superior quality of, 17, 279; as well-rested, 262, 266

Soviet Union: brutality of, exposed in Winter War, 16; expansionism of, 118; and Finnish political climate, misperception of, 55, 60; German invasion of, 2–3, 290, 339–40; and German ties to Finland, as cause of concern, 41; and Holocaust, knowledge of, 124; imprisonment of Finnish government officials, 66; and League of Nations, 5, 117–18, 118–20, 300; postwar interference in Finland, 341; pre-war demands for Finnish territory, 3, 10–11, 32–33, 60; public pronouncements on war, 338; and puppet regimes, history of, 70; relations with Finland, pre-war, 353n2; severing of diplomatic relations prior to attack, 41; treaty of mutual assistance with, as armistice condition, 20, 293, 315, 321; views on war, 338–39; vulnerability to Northern attack, concern about, 11, 41, 60

Soviet veterans, memories of Finnish campaign, 207

Spanish Civil War, 51

Speer, Albert, 2

spies, Soviet, 16, 80, 106–7, 351n66

Stahlberg, Kaarlo J., 142

Stalin, Joseph: and Allied intervention, fear of, 19, 231, 249, 318, 321; and armistice negotiations, 20, 302, 313, 314; birthday, 161–62, 163; birthday, conquest of Finland as present for, 12, 15, 19, 137, 154; decision to negotiate, 15, 16, 19, 231; decision to take all of Finland, 60, 73, 78; expectations for quick victory, 10, 11–12, 13, 60; and Finnish Army, underesti-

mation of, 135; on Finnish resources, 259–60; German invasion and, 355n184; hands-on management of War, decision to adopt, 164; and invasion planning, 12, 60; on Kollontai, 229; and Mannerheim Line, breakthrough of, 274–75; and Meretskov, demotion of, 163–64, 176; and PDRF government, installation of, 13, 71; prestige of, Winter War and, 206; pre-war demands on Finland, 11, 32, 33, 47; purges of, 61, 71, 134, 161, 263, 339, 361n128; and Red Army prestige, determination to restore, 16, 19, 164, 226–27, 231; and Soviet military, post-war review of, 339–40; and Tanner, dislike of, 64; and Timoshenko, support of with adequate troops, 206; underestimation of Finnish military, 154–55; and Voroshilov, 161, 164; and Winter War setbacks, anger at, 161

Stalin's Reluctant Soldiers (Reese), 3, 10

Stalin's Wars (Roberts), 5

State Department, U.S., response to invasion, 55–56

Stavka. See Soviet High Command

Steinhardt, Laurence, 68–70, 73

Stockholm syndrome, 194, 356n71

Stowe, Leland, 6–7, 13–14, 214–15, 278, 326, 328–29, 330

Strahlberg, Kaarlo Juho, 45

Submarines: Finnish, 99–100; German, 126–27; Soviet, 100, 160

Summa, 23m, 27m: Finnish casualties at, 277; Finnish High Command on, 243; media reports on, 249–50; media tours of battlefield, 279; Soviet artillery at, 279; Soviet attacks on, 138–40, 148–49, 153–54, 243, 269–70, 271–72; Soviet casualties at, 279

Sunday Express newspaper, 317

Sunday Times (London), 6, 18, 175

Suojarvi, 23m: capture of, 14; Soviet attack on, 79, 82, 187

Suomussalmi, 23m, 25m, 28m: failure to evacuate, 188; Finnish burning of, 189; Finnish defense of, 79, 188, 189; Finnish troops, loyalty of as issue, 80; Soviet advance guard at, 107; Soviet approach to, 26m, 59, 61, 106, 187–88, 189, 225m; Soviet buildup before attack, 187–88; Soviet capture of, 79, 82, 83, 105, 106, 188, 189; strategic importance of, 106, 187

Suomussalmi, battle of, 25m, 188–93: Finnish casualties, 192; removal of, before media tours, 166, 167; Finnish civilian prisoners in, 10; Finnish intelligence and, 187–88; Finnish tactics in, 8, 15, 145, 188, 190;

Suomussalmi, battle of (cont.)
Finnish victory, factors in, 188; and image of Soviet military, 16; importance of, 205; as legendary Finnish success, 15, 187, 188; main attack, 191–92; Soviet casualties, 187, 192; Soviet equipment captured in, 192–93; Soviet prisoners at, 192; Soviet reactions to loss of, 161, 205, 227, 231; and Soviet reconnaissance, lack of, 190; Soviet veterans of, 207; and Soviet withdrawal from North, 205; weapons shortages and, 190; Western overemphasis on, 205

Supreme Military Soviet, review of Winter War performance, 339

Suritz, Jacob, 119

Susitaival, Paavo, 191

Suvorov, Alexander, 207, 226

Svinhufvud, Pehr Evin, 46, 143, 341

Sweden: appeasement of Germany by, 76; and armistice negotiations, 313, 315; as conduit for ammunition and supplies, 76; Cowles in, 179; evacuation of children to, 223; Finnish requests for help from, 75–76, 275–76, 289; *folkhemmet* (welfare state) in, 358n62; and Grand Hotel negotiations, 238; iron fields, Allied concerns about, 159, 181, 247, 249; military aid to Finland, 112, 128, 181, 182, 233; munitions industry in, 181–82; neutrality, determination to maintain, 225; and Operation Avon Head, 2, 19, 176, 245, 247, 248, 294, 301, 306, 320, 323, 335; postwar alliance with Finland, Soviet rejection of, 341; prosperity of, 181–82; public support for Finland, 179–80, 268–69; response to invasion, 57–58, 179, 180, 289–90; volunteer fighters from, 112, 179–81, 275, 300, 305, 327, 362n31; volunteer workers from, 305

Swedish Army: views on Finnish defense, 281–82; volunteers for Finnish conflict, 180

Swedish People's Party, cabinet positions, 66

Taipale, 23m, 27m: Finnish casualties at, 232, 298; Finnish troops at, armistice and, 328; Soviet artillery at, 254; Soviet attacks at, 129–37, 148, 219, 233, 256, 262, 317, 322

Taipale River, Soviet crossing of, 86–87

Talas, Onni, 88

Talvela, Paavo, 82–83, 113–14, 320

Talvisota. See Winter War

Tammisaari, 23m: civilian response to bombing, 184; Soviet bombing of, 183

tanks, Finnish, 47, 85, 294

tanks, Soviet: and attack on Viipuri, 309; at battle of Tolvajarvi, 115; Finnish anti-tank

tactics, 109–10, 130–31, 134, 139, 148–49, 186; Finnish fear of, 80; as ill-suited for conditions in Finland, 85; inaccuracy of fire by, 139; at Lahde, 273; losses of, 13, 15, 109, 138–39, 153, 233, 234, 261, 270, 279; and Mannerheim Line bunkers, attacks on, 148, 273; poor tactics of, 135, 138–39; in second wave attack, 264, 269–70; SMK heavy assault tank, introduction of, 133–34; snow and, 252; types, 133–34

Tannenberg, battle of, 188

Tanner, Vaino: address to cabinet by, 293; and armistice, 328–31, 335; and cabinet meeting to discuss strategy, 75–77; career after war, 335, 341; on Finnish goals, 74; and Finnish independence day, celebration of, 95–97; as foreign minister, 66; and government of Finland, change of, 64–66; imprisonment by Soviets, 66; and League of Nations, request for help from, 117–18, 120; and Mannerheim Line, Soviet breach of, 276, 279; and Operation Avon Head, 245, 249, 294, 308, 319, 320; Soviet dislike of, 55–56, 64, 129, 313, 335; and Sweden, appeal for help from, 275–76; Wuolijoki and, 358–59n7

Tanner, Vaino, and armistice negotiations: acceptance of Soviet terms, 321–22; briefing of Finnish officials about, 270–71; cost of delays in, 243; efforts to renew, 64, 68, 70, 75–77, 120–21, 129, 229–31, 260–61; Grand Hotel negotiations, 229–31, 238, 239, 243–45, 270–71; inability to participate in, 313; messages to Soviets, 302, 308; military situation and, 319–20; peace terms, views on, 230, 243–45; press interviews on, 317: public denial of, 271; Soviets' increased demands and, 319; turn in war momentum and, 261

Tass, on DPRF government, installation of, 70

Taylor, Wayne C., 218

Technical University (Helsinki), bombing of, 49, 53

Teikari, Emma, 168

Teikari, Simo, 308

Terijoki, 27m; Finnish mines and booby traps in, 83–84; Soviet invasion of, 42

There Shall Be No Night (Sherwood), 2, 171, 236, 343–46

Thompson, Dorothy, 157

Three Days to Catastrophe (Clark), 158, 335

Thyssen, Fritz, 159

Tighe, Desmond, 212

Tiilikainen, Pekka, 54, 330

Time magazine, 13, 15, 197, 293

Times (London): on British force in France,

122; on Finnish military skill, 1; on Finnish tactics, 125; on Karelian Isthmus stalemate, 208; as source of war information, 8, 200; on Soviet bombing, 228, 255–56; on Soviet second wave improvements, 254–55; support of Finland, 311–12

Timoshenko, Semyon K.: background, 206; collection of forces by, 207, 262; as commander of second wave attack, 16, 206–7; as detailed planner, 226; efforts to destroy Finnish Army, 296, 321; front line visits by, 270; and logistical improvements, 255; and Mannerheim Line breakthrough, 274; Mannerheim line reconnaissance, 207; planning of second wave attack, 207, 226, 250, 262, 266; pressure to achieve victory, 19, 307, 318; and retraining of Soviet Army, 254, 256, 263; Stalin's agreement to provide adequate forces to, 206; tactical doctrine, 226; as unknown to outside world, 270, 361n128; and Viipuri, attack on, 18, 20, 137; and Vilaniemi, attack on, 20

Tkachev, V. V., 87–88

Toivenen, Mai-Lis Paavola, 34–35, 215–16, 257, 330

Tollet, G., 168–69

Tolvajarvi, 23m

Tolvajarvi, battle of, 14, 44, 79, 113–15, 166, 187

total war, Winter War as first, 149

Townsend, Warren, 117

trains: Russian strafing of, 93, 288; wartime delays of, 288

Trotter, William, 7–8, 266, 281, 307, 311, 314–15

truth raids, 122

Tukhachevsky, Mikhail, 206, 339

Tuompo, Wiljo, 105–7, 189

Tuppura fortress: canteen hostesses at, 35–36; Christmas celebration on, 168; evacuations from, 286–87; Finnish casualties, reaction to, 168; soldiers' recreation at, 218–19; Soviet air attacks on, 36, 285–86; Soviet capture of, 20; Soviet paratroopers in, 257–58; and Viipuri Bay, defense of, 303, 307–8

Turkinsaari, 310

Turku, 23m: American reporters in, 97–99, 325; bombing of, 98, 149, 164; casualties in, 164; independence day celebration in, 99

Turunen, Hertta, 36

Tvardovsky, Alexsandr, 243

U-boats, German, 126–27

United Press, 65, 88, 168, 256, 269, 295, 305

United States: college student interest in Winter War, 127–28; Finnish hope of support from,

96; Finnish Relief Fund, 155–56; Finnish requests for aid from, 16, 56–57, 302; isolationism, 56, 157, 268, 293; loans to Finland, 111, 236–37, 268; military aid to Finland, 21, 111, 158, 268; peace-making efforts, 68–70; public interest in War, 4, 127–28; 221; public opinion on Soviet invasion, 89–90; public support for Finland, 112, 156, 157–58, 236–37, 267–68, 291–92; response to Soviet invasion, 55–57; support for Finland, 293; volunteer fighters from, 57, 300; in World War II, Finland and, 341–42

Uruguay, at League of Nations, 119–20

Utterstrom, Sven, 180

Ututtu, Toivo, 73

Uuraansaari Island, bombing of, 286

Uxhull, Herbert, 213

Van Dyke, Carl: on Soviet artillery, 226; on Soviet hesitation, 87; on Soviet military, 255, 256, 263; on Soviet motivation, 135; on Soviet second wave attacks, 296, 318; on Timoshenko, front line visit of, 270

Vasilevsky, Alexandr, 314, 321

Vatnuori, evacuations from, 287

Veijalainen, Anna-Liisa: on Christmas celebration, 168; on Finnish casualties, reaction to, 168, 215; on funerals of soldiers, 304–5; on recreational activities at Tuppura, 218–19; at Sakkijarvi, 307–8; and Soviet air attacks, 285–86; on Soviet attack on Tuppura, 36; on Soviet paratroopers, 257–58; as Tuppura canteen hostess, 35–36; visit home on leave, 304–5

Vereker, Gordon, 294

veterans of war, as source of information, 9–10

Viipuri, 23m, 27m: and armistice, 327–28, 329, 315; destruction of, 295; Finnish casualties at, 337; Finnish defense of, 294–95, 298, 303, 311, 316–19, 318, 322; Mannerheim visit to, 280; Soviet attacks on, 18, 20, 21, 28m, 296, 307–8, 316–17, 322; Soviet bombing of, 34–35, 49, 50, 66, 149, 280, 286, 295

Viipuri archipelago, Soviet capture of, 19

Viipuri Bay: battle of, 18, 20, 302–3, 307–11, 317, 318, 337; Soviet beachhead at Vilaniemi and, 20, 309–10, 318

Viipuri Castle, 295, 332

Viipuri Gateway; Soviet efforts to penetrate, 137–41: Soviet penetration of, 137, 274

Vilaniemi, Soviet beachhead at, 20, 309–10, 318

Villamo, Vila, 31–32, 141, 142, 144

Vinogradov, Alexey, 193, 201, 202–3, 207

Virta, Nikolai, 43, 83–84, 348n34
Voionmaa, Vaino, 313, 321, 323
Volkov, O. I., 203
volunteer fighters from other nations, 1: broad
	range of ideologies in, 112–13; casualties
	among, 305, 327; from Denmark, 300,
	362–63n31; from Estonia, 363n59; Finnish
	soldiers' awareness of, 110–11; from Great
	Britain, 362n31; from Hungary, 88–89,
	199; from Italy, 51, 300, 349n74; Manner-
	heim on, 305; from Norway, 199, 300, 305,
	357n101; number of, 21, 112–13; pilots,
	180, 300, 305, 362–63n31; from Sweden,
	112, 179–81, 275, 300, 305, 327, 362n31;
	from United States, 57, 300
volunteer workers from other nations, 305–6
von Behr, Major, 36
von Born, Ernst, 65
von Bluecher, Wipert, 96
von Essen, George, 221
von Rosen, C. G., 310
von Rosen, Eric, 310
Voronov, N. N, 283–84
Voroshilov, Kliment: as commander of invasion,
	59, 136; concerns about invasion progress,
	83; demotion of, 19, 164, 176; and invasion
	planning, 12, 135; and Mannerheim Line,
	breach of, 283–84; and Meretskov, blaming
	of, 163; and PDRF government, installation
	of, 71; postwar career of, 340; quarrel with
	Stalin, 161; and Soviet military, postwar
	review of, 339; and Stalin's birthday, celebra-
	tion of, 161; underestimation of Finnish
	military, 154–55
Vuoksi River, Soviet efforts to cross, 28m, 87–88

Wagner, Robert, 157
Walden, Rudolph, 313, 321, 323
Wallenius, Kurt: appearance, 209; career of,
	142–43, 209; character of, 143–44; command
	of Lapland Group, 143; dismissal of, 143; as
	Fascist, 52, 142, 143, 209; on Finns' ability to
	hold out, 160; Mannerheim's disciplining of,
	303, 318; as media star, 209; and northern
	front, 143, 212; and Pelkosenniemi, battle of,
	143–44, 145, 147; raids into Soviet territory
	ordered by, 209; and Viipuri Bay, defense of,
	303, 307; in Winter War, 105
Warcos (Collier), 4, 121
war cry, ancient Finnish, 114
Ward, Eddie, 213, 324–25
war damage, Finland state coverage of indi-
	vidual losses, 222
War of the White Death (Irincheev), 87

watch towers, *Lotta Svards'* duty on, 213–14,
	215–16
weather: clearing, and resumption of air war,
	149; and timing of Soviet invasion, 61;
	winter as Finnish advantage, 110, 132, 176,
	190, 200, 205, 252, 292; winter and Soviet
	second wave attack, 258, 298
welfare state, Finnish. See *folkhemmet* (welfare
	state) in Finland
Welles, Sumner, 55–56
Wheeler, Burton, 157
White Death, The (Chew), 7–8, 204
White, William A., 170
White, William L., 169, 170–71
wild goose enterprise, Finnish. See Operation
	Avon Head
Wilhelm, Kaiser, 41
Wilson, Woodrow, 56
Winter War: events leading to, 10–11; Finnish
	pride in, 337–38, 342; overview of, 10–22;
	shadow of World War II and, 342
Woman at the Front: 1938–1945, A (Veijalainen),
	35
women: as bombing victims, 293; feminists,
	229; first female ambassador, 229; as inte-
	gral to Finnish war effort, 214–15; in war
	work, 128–29 (*see also Lotta Svard*)
World War II: British views on probable duration
	of, 123; early lull in (Phony War), 3, 5, 37,
	121–22, 177–78; German expansionism, 2–3,
	161, 290, 336, 343–44, 355n20; German
	submarine fleet and, 126–27; limited interest
	in, in Finland, 213; U.S. entry into, 56
writers, accounts of Winter War, 2
Wuolijoki, Hella, 16, 229–31, 237–38, 239, 243,
	358–59n7

Yakovlev, V. E., 86–87
Yanov (Soviet captain), 138–39
Yartsev, Boris, 238
Yermakov, A. N., 252, 254, 262, 272
YLE (Finnish state radio), 54, 98–99
Yrjo-Koskinen, Aarno, 41, 348n28

Zachau, Anders, 221, 233
Zaitsev, Kombrig, 87
Zelentsov, Andrei, 189, 191, 192
Zhdanov, Andrei: and armistice negotiations,
	314–15, 321, 350n110; and DPRF, 71; and
	Soviet decision to take all of Finland, 60, 78;
	as supporter of Soviet invasion, 162; under-
	estimation of Finnish military, 154–55
Zhukov, Georgi, 340
Zilliacus, Laurin, 326